Applied Nonparametric Econometrics

The majority of empirical research in economics ignores the potential benefits of nonparametric methods, while the majority of advances in nonparametric theory ignore the problems faced in applied econometrics. This book helps bridge this gap between applied economists and theoretical nonparametric econometricians. It discusses – in terms that someone with one year of graduate econometrics can understand – basic to advanced nonparametric methods. The analysis starts with density estimation and moves through familiar methods and on to kernel regression, estimation with discrete data, and advanced methods such as estimation with panel data and instrumental variables models. The book addresses issues that arise with programming, computing speed, and application. In each chapter, the methods are applied to actual data, paying attention to presentation of results and potential pitfalls.

Daniel J. Henderson is the J. Weldon and Delores Cole Faculty Fellow at the University of Alabama and a research Fellow at the Institute for the Study of Labor (IZA) in Bonn, Germany and at the Wang Yanan Institute for Studies in Economics, Xiamen University, in Xiamen, China. Formerly an associate and assistant professor of economics at the State University of New York at Binghamton, he has held visiting appointments at the Institute of Statistics, Université Catholique de Louvain, in Louvain-la-Neuve, Belgium, and in the department of economics at Southern Methodist University in Dallas, Texas. He received his PhD in economics from the University of California, Riverside. His work has been published in the *Economic Journal*, the *European Economic Review*, the *International Economic Review*, the *Journal of Applied Econometrics*, the *Journal of Business and Economic Statistics*, the *Journal of Econometrics*, the *Journal of Human Resources*, the *Journal of the Royal Statistical Society*, and *Review of Economics and Statistics*.

Christopher F. Parmeter is an associate professor at the University of Miami. He was formerly an assistant professor in the department of agricultural and applied economics at Virginia Polytechnic Institute and State University and a visiting scholar in Dipartimento di Studi su Politica, Diritto e Societa at the University of Palermo. He received his PhD in economics from the State University of New York at Binghamton. His research focuses on applied econometrics across an array of fields, including economic growth, microfinance, international trade, environmental economics, and health economics. His work has been published in the *Economic Journal*, the *European Economic Review, Health Economics*, the *Journal of Applied Econometrics*, the *Journal of Econometrics*, the *Journal of Environmental Economics and Management*, and *Statistica Sinica*.

Applied Nonparametric Econometrics

DANIEL J. HENDERSON

University of Alabama

CHRISTOPHER F. PARMETER

University of Miami

CAMBRIDGE
UNIVERSITY PRESS

32 Avenue of the Americas, New York, NY 10013-2473, USA

Cambridge University Press is part of the University of Cambridge.

It furthers the University's mission by disseminating knowledge in the pursuit of education, learning, and research at the highest international levels of excellence.

www.cambridge.org
Information on this title: www.cambridge.org/9780521279680

© Daniel J. Henderson and Christopher F. Parmeter 2015

First published 2015

Printed in the United States of America

A catalog record for this publication is available from the British Library.

Library of Congress Cataloging in Publication Data
Henderson, Daniel J.
Applied nonparametric econometrics / Daniel J. Henderson, University of Alabama, Christopher F. Parmeter, University of Miami.
pages cm
ISBN 978-1-107-01025-3 (hardback) – ISBN 978-0-521-27968-0 (pbk.)
1. Econometrics. 2. Nonparametric statistics. I. Parmeter, Christopher F. II. Title.
HB139.H453 2014
330.01'51954–dc23 2014005138

ISBN 978-1-107-01025-3 Hardback
ISBN 978-0-521-27968-0 Paperback

Contents

Contents

1

Introduction

1.1 Overview

The goal of this book is to help bridge the gap between applied economists and theoretical nonparametric econometricians/statisticians. The majority of empirical research in economics ignores the potential benefits of nonparametric methods and many theoretical nonparametric advances ignore the problems faced by practitioners. We do not believe that applied economists dismiss these methods because they do not like them. We believe that they do not employ them because they do not understand how to use them or lack formal training on kernel smoothing. Many theoretical articles and texts that develop nonparametric methods claim that they are useful to empirical researchers, which they often are, but many times the level of mathematics is too high for a typical economist or the detail with which the practical considerations are explained is not adequate except for those well versed in econometrics. At the same time, many of these articles and textbooks skip (or do not have room to include) the nuances of the methods which are necessary for doing solid empirical research.

Although nonparametric kernel methods have been around for nearly six decades, their use in economics journals did not become popular until the twenty-first century (noting that there were influential papers prior to 2000). In our opinion, two major developments have drastically increased the use of nonparametric methods in economics. The first is obvious: computing power. Without computers that can quickly provide estimates (coupled with efficient code), these methods are largely impractical for applied work. Of course, we cannot discount the importance of complementary statistical packages for nonparametric methods, such as the popular np package (Hayfield and Racine, 2008) in the R language (2012). The combination of higher-powered computers and available software has done much to popularize the methods across academic fields.

For economics, the second reason we believe this prevalence has increased of late is the assortment of new estimators which allow researchers to handle discrete data. We know that economic data is generally a combination of continuous and discrete variables. In the past, authors who wanted to use discrete data had to resort to semiparametric methods with little reasoning other than they did not know how to handle discrete data nonparametrically. This required stringent and sometimes unjustified assumptions on the data. For instance, having a dummy variable enter the regression linearly assumes that it is separable from the variables in the nonparametric function and that the only difference between groups is an intercept shift. Neither of these assumptions need hold true for any particular data set. It is not as if authors using these methods necessarily believed this to be true; they simply did not have many options for how to handle this type of data (see Li and Racine, 2007, for a great introduction to nonparametric estimation with discrete data).

Nonparametric methods have advanced to a point where they are of use to applied economists and computers have advanced to a point where using the methods are feasible. In this book we plan to discuss in depth, and in terms that someone with one year of graduate econometrics can understand (say at the level of Greene, 2011), basic to advanced nonparametric methods. Our analysis starts with density estimation in the crudest sense and motivates the procedures through methods that the reader should be familiar with. We then move onto kernel regression, estimation with discrete data, and advanced methods like estimation with panel data and instrumental variables. We spend a lot of time discussing kernel choice and bandwidth selection as well as why one method may be preferable in one setting or another. We also pay close attention to the issues that arise with programming, computing speed, and application. In each chapter we keep derivations to a minimum, but make available on the web the derivations (without skipping steps) of our results. We will give the intuition in the text without the full brunt of the math, but the step-by-step derivation in the online appendix should be a useful learning tool for those who wish to gain additional insight.

Given that we wish to teach nonparametric methods to applied economists, we must include applications. However, as opposed to giving a bunch of simple applications without much insight, we focus on one particular topic that we have researched extensively: economic growth. In each chapter, we apply the methods we discuss to actual data. Given that our focus throughout the book is with respect to economic growth, we take publicly available data and attempt to perform proper applications. We not only show how the methods work in practice, but we also uncover results that have not been studied or that contradict the findings of previous studies. In this respect, we believe that the application sections are of interest by themselves. Also, the data and R code, which can be used to replicate the empirical results in the application section of each chapter (we have done our best to ensure this – e.g., set seeds), can be found on the text's website (http://www.the-smooth-operators.com).

Our hope is that once the readers have finished the first few parts of the book that they will be able to apply these methods to their specific problems, either in the field of economic growth or other areas of economics. We believe that it will be relatively straightforward to apply these methods to most data sets by taking the code available online and making minor modifications as necessary. We hope that this text will help increase the number of applications of nonparametric methods in economics. These powerful tools are widely available in today's applied environment, but we envision that they will be understood by a larger audience. Although statistical packages are essential to the promotion of one's research, this will not result in better research unless users are well-informed about the strengths and limitations of the methods.

1.2 Birth of the text

There was no single defining moment which prompted us to write this text. Most of the reasons came about as we conducted our own research. There were countless times when we were presented with situations that we did not know how to resolve. This was particularly the case in our applied work. Earlier in our careers, a cheap way to get a publication was to read *Econometrica*, the *Journal of the American Statistical Association*, or other high-level statistics/econometrics journals and to code a newly published estimator and apply it to a well-known data set. We would first replicate the results of a Monte Carlo simulation and then we would take that same estimator and run it through a proper data set. We were often confronted with two situations: (1) many times the estimators worked well in simulations (often with a single covariate), but performed poorly with real data (this was often true with less "well-behaved" data); and (2) to analyze the economic results, we were often left without ways to appropriately dissect estimated gradients or it was unclear how to present the results we had. We therefore needed to determine ways to "empiricize" theoretical works. Now, while some of these empirical advances are better than others, we typically noted in our papers that the code was available upon request. We are happy to note that many authors have made use of these offers. The benefit is that this increased citations; the downfall is more referee reports (although these are also beneficial). The combination of these events led us to think that there would be a demand for this type of text. In fact, while writing the text, we also had to figure out ways to "empiricize" estimators that we had not used in the past or required us to think differently about estimators we had used before.

1.3 Who will benefit

In addition to economists, the book may also be useful to researchers in other fields who use typical econometric tools (e.g., regression), such as political science, history, and applied statistics. We feel it will be useful to faculty and graduate students alike. Specifically, the reader should have at least one course in mathematical statistics and one course in linear regression. It would also be helpful, but not necessary, to have had a course in nonlinear regression.

We expect that this book could be part of either a third or fourth semester econometrics course. This text could be used to teach an applied nonparametric econometrics course or as part of a course on applied nonlinear methods. It could be used by itself or paired with a complementary nonparametric book like Li and Racine (2007) or a book covering nonlinear regression methods like Cameron and Trivedi (2005). It is unlikely that this text will be used to teach a more theory-driven econometrics course. There are books in the literature that are more tailored to that approach and we are not pretending to be theoretical econometricians. We are applied econometricians and our expertise is in applying nonparametric methods to data. It is in this realm where our comparative advantage lies. Nevertheless, we make an attempt to explain theoretical concepts in an intuitive way.

1.4 Why this book is relevant

We have noted the problems that most applied economists have with applying nonparametric methods. We have run into many of these problems ourselves in our own work. Here we plan to lay everything out so that you will know how to apply them. We feel that without this text, the cost of learning how to use nonparametric methods with actual data will be too high for many economists. We hope that this text will decrease this cost.

In addition to presenting the material at a different level, we also introduce or further discuss methods that are not in current nonparametric textbooks. This field changes rapidly and hence there appears to be reason to update or write new texts relatively often (note that the book is not meant to be comprehensive, so we will leave out many great papers). For example, our text spends a large amount of time on panel data methods. In particular, we present our panel data estimators for the unbalanced case (noting that the number of journal articles with unbalanced panel in the nonparametric setting is small). Another area which separates us from past textbooks is a chapter on constrained nonparametric estimation. Nonparametric methods relax functional form assumptions, but it is often the case that this leads to violations of economic theory that we assume to hold true. We discuss methods to impose constraints in a nonparametric framework in Chapter 12. In addition, in many of the chapters we provide useful, straightforward tables or derivations that do not exist in the literature and which we believe will be helpful to the practitioner.

Finally, we focus much more on the application of nonparametric methods and what the theory means in terms of the application of such methods. We not only talk about estimation and testing, but we also spend a lot of time on how to present the results. This is often overlooked or results are given for the univariate case (either by considering a single variable or by using counterfactual analysis). While there is nothing inherently wrong with this approach, most economic data sets contain many variables and this often makes presentation difficult. That being said, we do not want our text to be seen as a "cook book." Yes, we discuss how to estimate, test, and present results, but we also try to incorporate intuition from the theoretical underpinnings of these same estimators and tests so that authors can be well informed when they employ these methods.

1.5 Examples

To give a sense of what is to come, and to show how the methods can be applied in many fields, in this section we consider three simple examples. The first is with respect to density estimation and the latter two are via nonparametric regression. These are each univariate examples and so they allow us to show the results in two-dimensional figures. We clearly are ignoring many other factors in each case, but hope that they give you an idea of how powerful the estimators are and what they may be able to accomplish.

1.5.1 *CO$_2$ emissions*

Our first example is in the area of environmental economics. Specifically, we have data (Boden, Marland, and Andres, 2011) on per-capita CO_2 emissions from 152 countries in 1960 and 2005 (balanced sample). The solid line in Figure 1.1 is the kernel density estimate (smoothed histogram) of per-capita CO_2 emissions across 152 countries in

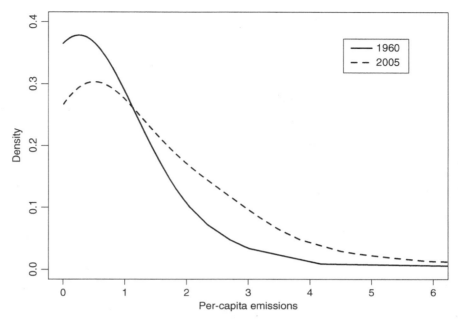

Figure 1.1. Density plots of per-capita CO_2 emissions for 152 countries in the years 1960 and 2005

1960. The dashed line is the kernel density estimate for the same countries in 2005. We see that the 2005 density of per-capita emissions has a shorter mode and is shifted to the right of the 1960 density. Note that each of the densities has a long right-hand-side tail that we cut off to make the figures easier to read. The increase in overall emissions is expected on a national level, but what this shows is that even though population growth has increased dramatically over the 45-year period (from around three billion inhabitants worldwide in 1960 to roughly seven billion in 2005), per capita emissions have still grown. This perhaps shows why there is so much interest in decreasing emissions across the globe.

1.5.2 Age earnings

The first regression example is an application known to many nonparametric econometricians. This example was first presented in Ullah (1985) and it appeared in other papers he has written as well as in his textbook (Pagan and Ullah, 1999, 155). It has also been used as an example in other textbooks (e.g., Ruppert, Wand, and Carroll, 2003, 117), research articles (e.g., Henderson and Parmeter, 2009, 463), and software packages (e.g., the np package in R – Hayfield and Racine, 2008, 11).

In a long line of literature, both econometricians and labor economists have argued over the relationship between earnings and experience. Heckman and Polachek (1974), among others, have argued for a polynomial function. Ullah (1985) examined this assumption by taking the 1971 Canadian Census Public Use Tapes to relate earnings versus experience (age in his application). To be able to illustrate the example in two dimensions, he selected the 205 males in the data set with thirteen years of education.

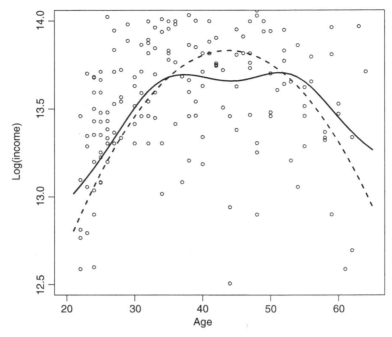

Figure 1.2. Scatterplot of log(income) and age with both local-constant (with rule-of-thumb bandwidth) and quadratic parametric regression fits (1971 Canadian Census Public Use Tapes)

Figure 1.2 is a replica (we additionally include a scatter plot) of that in Pagan and Ullah (1999). The dashed curve is the quadratic fit, whereas the solid line is a nonparametric fit (local-constant kernel fit with a rule-of-thumb bandwidth). The nonparametric fit has a less dramatic increase at lower ages and a less dramatic decrease at higher ages, but the main deviation is the flat portion of the curve from roughly age 35 to 55. If we ignore the slight dip, then this suggests that wages flatten out in mid-career as opposed to continuously changing as is assumed in the quadratic specification. Clearly, both models are simplistic given that there are many other factors which determine wages and hence a more comprehensive analysis is necessary in practice.

1.5.3 Hedonic price function

The final example we give comes from urban economics. Here we consider a hedonic price function for housing. In his seminal work on the theory of hedonic prices, Rosen (1974) suggested that "it is inappropriate to place too many restrictions on [the hedonic price] at the outset." Given that the form of the hedonic price function for housing is unknown (as well as the vast amounts of data available – preferred for nonparametric estimation), this is a great place for nonparametric methods to contribute.

Here we take a portion of the data in Anglin and Gençay (1996). In their paper they model the logarithm of housing price as a semiparametric function of standard

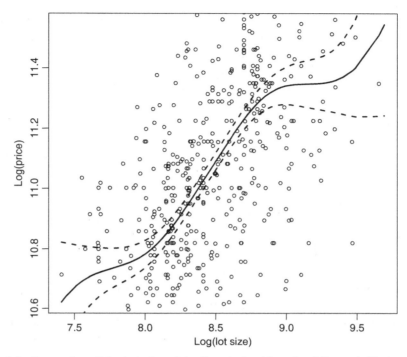

Figure 1.3. Scatterplot of log(price) and log(lot size) with a local-linear (with least-square cross-validation bandwidth) regression fit and confidence intervals (estimated via 399 bootstrap replications)

attributes of a home (number of bedrooms, bathrooms, etc.). The data comprise 546 observations from 1987 in the Windsor (Canada) housing market. Here we take one of their primary variables of interest (logarithm of lot size) as our single explanatory variable.

Figure 1.3 shows the results of a (local-linear) nonparametric regression (with a data-driven bandwidth – the least-squares cross-validation bandwidth is 0.2408). If we were to believe this simple regression, it would suggest that there are plateaus in the price of the home with respect to lot size. In other words, at relatively small and relatively large lot sizes, we see very small changes in price, whereas for intermediate lot sizes we see larger increases in price (which also appears linear in this range). Although this example is simplistic, the function is monotonic (as theory would predict) and we see intuition consistent with hedonic theory. See Parmeter, Henderson, and Kumbhakar (2007) for a full nonparametric examination with the Anglin and Gençay (1996) data.

1.6 Examples in the text

Our approach to present applications illustrating each of the estimators/tests discussed in the text differs from what is typically done. Instead of taking many different applications, we decided to have a singular focus with our illustrations of the methods.

Specifically, we will look at economic growth/output; however, we will be even more specific than that. In the density chapters we will examine the distribution of output per worker and in the regression chapters we will (primarily) look at modeling the worldwide production function.

There are several benefits to this approach, which include the following:

1. The Penn World Table (PWT) is a well-known publicly available data set.
2. Our own research lies in this area and thus we should be able to explain the applications better than we could if we were to examine many different applications.
3. The sample sizes and number of covariates are relatively small and hence replication of our results will not be as time consuming.
4. We are able to uncover findings not previously seen or discussed in the literature.

We feel that this approach will show the methods in their true light (both positive and negative). It is the case that they are not always perfect (as no estimation methodology is). However, the estimators and tests that we discuss are ones that we feel (typically) work well in practice. It also gives authors help on what to do when they are stuck in such a situation. This actually may be more helpful than showing when they do work.

1.6.1 Density

In the beginning of the text, we will focus on the worldwide distribution of labor productivity (output per worker). The main motivation for such an analysis comes from the work of Danny Quah. In a series of papers (Quah, 1993a,b; 1996; 1997), he argues that standard regression methods cannot always address issues relating to aspects of the entire distribution of the world's economies. To assume that the evolution of the distribution of output per worker can be boiled down to a single parameter estimate is naïve (noting that a growth regression with high explanatory power would be very informative regarding the evolution over time). These distributions are often multimodal, and examining the first one or two moments of the distribution is only appropriate when the distribution is Gaussian. He instead advocates examining kernel density estimates where he visually finds two modes in the distribution. These are later confirmed statistically by Bianchi (1997); Henderson, Parmeter, and Russell (2008); and Parmeter (2008), among others.

Our examples in the chapters concerning density estimation examine what was shown in the aforementioned papers, albeit with more recent data, but we also extend the discussion in several dimensions. For example, we look at multidimensional and conditional densities. In other words, we realize that output per worker is related to several other variables and we include some of those in our analysis. We also consider tests for more than just multimodality, including testing for differences between different groups, such as OECD and non-OECD.

1.6.2 Regression

The primary objective in the regression chapters is to attempt to estimate the worldwide production function. Although most research in economic growth has been concerned with growth regressions (Mankiw, Romer, and Weil, 1992), more recent research is concerned with determining the form of the worldwide production function (Duffy and Papageorgiou, 2000). This is another area where nonparametric econometrics may prove useful, as many economists are not comfortable with the standard Cobb–Douglas constant-returns-to-scale production function, which is common in the theoretical literature. There are several researchers who have considered more flexible functions, such as the constant-elasticity-of-substitution production function, but it is quite possible that the worldwide production function is more complicated.

When possible, our plan is to estimate production functions with limited assumptions. First, we generally estimate the models in levels and not in logs. Sun, Henderson, and Kumbhakar (2011) discuss the problems with estimating production functions in logs. Second, we generally will not estimate the models in per-worker terms. In other words, we will not divide output or capital by labor input. The reason for this is that this implies a constant returns production function and we are also interested in testing for this assumption. We will spend time comparing our results to several parametric specifications and between the nonparametric models of different chapters.

As this approach to estimating production functions is relatively new, this process (i.e., the end-of-chapter applications) can be thought of as research in action. When we started this book we were unsure where this approach was going to take us and hence there is a lot of trial and error. This "experiment" to applications may produce some unexpected results (in fact, one of the main results seems to be our Moby Dick), but our belief is that these applications will lead to a better understanding of the methods, which is our primary purpose.

1.7 Outline of the remainder of the book

The remainder of the book can be generally broken down into four sections: (1) density estimation and testing, (2) regression analysis, (3) handling discrete data, and (4) advanced nonparametric methods. The first two sections can be used to teach a semester course if the instructor also dives into the technical appendices. An applied course should probably include the first three sections with selected portions of Section 4 (as desired). It is possible to start a course focusing solely on regression with Section 2, but we recommend spending some time in the first section (say a week or two) to help with intuition.

Chapter 2 outlines univariate density estimation. It is relatively lengthy as it introduces terms, ideas, functions, estimators, and asymptotic properties necessary to develop the intuition of smoothing, which will appear throughout the remainder of the book. We also spend a lot of time describing the smoothing parameter (bandwidth), as it is crucial to nonparametric estimation in any form. We believe that this chapter will be very intuitive and will help with understanding the constructs of later chapters.

Univariate density estimation can be useful in applied settings, but most economic data require methods which can handle multivariate data. Chapter 3 outlines multivariate density estimation. Here you will learn how to estimate and plot multidimensional densities. A lengthy discussion will be devoted to the computational and theoretical concerns when switching from univariate to multivariate data in a nonparametric setting. We also suggest how these methods can be extended in order to perform nonparametric regression.

Chapter 4 introduces various forms of hypothesis tests within the density framework. The understanding of these tests on an intuitive level will lead naturally to testing in other nonparametric realms. For example, we first consider testing a nonparametric density versus a known parametric density. This approach will be useful when trying to compare parametric regression models versus their nonparametric counterparts. We also consider tests for the difference between unknown densities as well as tests for uncovering the number of modes in the underlying density.

Our first real taste of regression analysis is given in Chapter 5 (estimation). We focus on several different estimators of the conditional mean and discuss the role of kernel choice and methods for bandwidth selection. We further discuss how automated bandwidth selectors can tell us something about relevance and linearity in different estimation frameworks. Finally, we consider estimation of the derivative of the conditional mean, which can be used to assess partial effects as well as other interesting economic phenomena (e.g., returns-to-scale).

In Chapter 6, we outline methods for testing in nonparametric regression. We start with methods to test for correct parametric specification. These tests can be used to validate economic theory or discredit past research based on (perhaps) restrictive functional form assumptions. We then consider tests similar to those in the parametric literature, such as tests for omitted variables. Finally, we highlight some tests which are under-utilized, but may be useful.

We start our discussion of discrete data in Chapter 7 by analyzing their role in density estimation. We consider estimation of univariate densities (probability mass functions) with discrete data. We also explain their role in joint densities and conditional densities. We pay special attention to kernel choice here as we cannot use the same kernel functions as before. Bandwidth estimation is also discussed, and we show how automated methods can determine whether or not the discrete data are relevant for prediction. Finally, we detail the analogous testing procedures for univariate and multivariate density estimators with discrete data.

In Chapter 8 we turn to nonparametric regression in the presence of discrete covariates. Using the same estimators as in Chapter 5, we discuss how to incorporate discrete regressors. Implementation is relatively straightforward. We again discuss estimation, bandwidth selection, and testing in a manner similar to what was outlined in Chapters 5 and 6 so that the discussion goes smoothly.

In our advanced topics section (the name of which necessitates that they be taught at a slightly more rigorous level), we decided to discuss four different areas: semiparametric methods, instrumental variable estimation, panel data methods, and constrained regression. There is clearly one very important area of econometrics that we are ignoring: time series data. This may seem to be a mistake to some, as nonparametric time series methods perhaps deserve their own text. We fully acknowledge this, but chose to omit this subject as we do not believe that we would have been able to do it justice, given page constraints and the fact that this is not an area of expertise for either author. We apologize to those of you interested in this area and suggest Gao (2007), Li and Racine (2007), or Lütkepohl and Krätzig (2004) for intuitive nonparametric time series discussion.

Semiparametric models come in a wide variety of shapes and forms, the most famous being the partially linear model. In this model, some regressors enter the conditional mean linearly, while others are allowed to enter in an unknown form. Estimation of these models is common and is often justified as a way to lessen the curse of dimensionality. However, this is not the only way to estimate semiparametric models. Semiparametric is a blanket term used to represent models which have some component parametrically specified *a priori*, while other components are allowed to be unknown. These include single index models, semiparametric smooth coefficient models, and nonparametric additively separable models.

In Chapter 10, we discuss nonparametric instrumental variable estimation. Estimators have existed in the literature for over two decades, but there are very few applications that we are aware of in economics. In this chapter we focus on a particular nonparametric IV estimator that, in our opinion, has been underutilized in the literature and attempt to show how to implement it in practice (including discussing the weak instruments case).

In Chapter 11, we consider estimation of panel data models. Given the nature of available growth data, it only makes sense to consider panel data estimators. Of primary importance in this chapter is how bootstrapping and bandwidth selection differ from what we have seen with cross-sectional estimators.

Our final chapter discusses imposing economic constraints in nonparametric regression (Chapter 12). Nonparametric methods are praised for their flexibility, but often this flexibility comes at a price. It is common for nonparametric estimators to violate economic assumptions, such as monotonicity, even when the true underlying data generating process is monotonic. In this chapter we discuss several methods available in the literature to impose economic constraints, but focus on a particular approach that we have found to work well in the presence of multiple constraints and multiple regressors. We outline how to use the estimator as well as how to perform tests in the presence of imposed constraints.

1.8 Supplemental materials

In addition to what appears in the text, we also have a website that complements the book. On this website we have the data that can be used to replicate the results in the book. This also includes the R language code that we wrote. Finally, we have the technical appendices that are referred to in the text, which derive many of the more difficult results.

Although the data are publicly available (PWT), these data can potentially change over time and therefore we have the exact data we used to help with replication.

We also include the data for the three examples above, as these may also be of interest.

The R language code consists of two types of files. The first type is replication code. This code is the same code that we used to calculate the results in the text. Running this code (which requires calling the second type of code) should give you the results from the text (and sometimes other unreported results). It will be possible to make modifications of this code to look at other types of results within our examples and to use this code with your own data. The second type is procedure code. These are programs that we wrote that can be used to replicate the results of the book or in many different types of applications. We tried to write the code so that it was easy to employ in many other scenarios. We also wrote it so that it was relatively easy to read. What this means is that sometimes we sacrificed efficiency for clarity. We hope that this code will also help the readers of this text to program nonparametric methods. It may be the case that you need to make minor modifications for your particular problem and we hope that we have written it in a way that makes this relatively simple.

The last piece of information available on the textbook's website are the technical appendices, which are available in pdf format. We did this because it is not always obvious how to go from one step to the next in many published proofs. We therefore include as many steps as possible for most of our derivations. We hope that this helps those readers who are trying to learn the methods but may not be experts in mathematics or statistics. We believe it will also be especially useful if you are trying to learn these methods on your own (for instance, without a senior econometrician teaching you). We do not believe that these are necessary for understanding the intuition of the estimators and tests (as we include the intuition in the text), but they may help in various circumstances.

1.9 Acknowledgments

It is impossible to thank all of the people who influenced and helped with this text. It is also highly probable that we will miss someone who was vital. That being said, we would like to thank those who had a profound impact. We first want to thank our mentors and senior colleagues: Subal Kumbhakar, Qi Li, Carlos Martins-Filho, Jeff Racine, Robert Russell (who would often ask the question "you have so many results, why do you simply report the means?" – clearly a motivating factor in the book), and Aman Ullah. We also wish to acknowledge comments made by Oleg Badunenko, Badi Baltagi, Subha Chakraborti, Susan Chen, Meredith Coles, Walter Enders, Brandon Gibb, Darren Grant, William Greene, Arne Henningsen, David Jacho-Chavez, Paan Jindapon, Junsoo Lee, Chris Papageorgiou, Robert Reed, Thanasis Stengos, and Liangjun Su. We wish to single out Jon Temple who painstakingly went through the first five chapters of the book (with as much detail as he does in his editorial duties). It is also the case that our own graduate students (some of whom were in our classes at Southern Methodist University, the State University of New York at Binghamton, the University of Alabama, the University of Miami or Virginia Polytechnic Institute and State University) have shaped our ideas and include: Shahram Amini, Chi-Yang

Chu, Michael Delgado, Sapna Kaul, Nadine McCloud, Deniz Ozabaci, Bisma Sayid, Xianghang Shi, Kai Sun, Le Wang, and Zhiyuan Zheng.

We also want to acknowledge the support of our publishing company, Cambridge University Press, and especially our editors (past and current), Scott Parris and Karen Maloney. It was Mr. Parris who gave us complete control of our text when others wanted us to make major changes to the manuscript. He wanted us to write our book the way we wanted it to be written (likely due in part to strong recommendations given to him by Subal Kumbhakar and Aman Ullah). It is therefore the case that if there are any quarrels about the form of the book that these lie solely on us and not our publisher. Ms. Maloney's input into the processes was also crucial and she made sure the project was finally finished.

Further, both of us acknowledge that we are standing on the shoulders of giants when it comes to writing this book. Many exceptional econometricians have contributed to the exciting field of nonparametric econometrics and we are fortunate to conduct research in such a diverse area. The texts that had the most profound impact on this text (clearly there are influential texts we are not citing here) include: Fan and Gijbels (1996), Härdle (1990), Horowitz (2009), Li and Racine (2007), Pagan and Ullah (1999), Silverman (1986), and Wand and Jones (1995).

Of course the most important people involved in any text are the immediate family members. They are the ones who have to deal with our stresses on a daily basis and it is they who bring us back to reality. Henderson wishes to thank his beautiful wife, Nina, along with his three amazing children: Annmarie, Isaac, and Ethan (I don't think this qualifies as bedtime reading). Parmeter thanks his loving wife, Sandra, without whose support the completion of this book would not have been possible.

2

Univariate density estimation

In this chapter, we discuss univariate density estimation. We are well aware that most interesting applications are with respect to multivariate data, but we must first discuss univariate density estimation so that we can generalize the univariate methods to the multivariate setting. That being said, there are many interesting applications of univariate densities in economics as well as in other fields. The most common application of univariate density estimation in the context of economic growth is the examination of output-per-worker distributions, most commonly attributed to Quah (1993a,b).

We start by considering nonparametric density estimation in the crudest possible way: a histogram. In fact, histograms are nonparametric in nature and can show information that may be hidden (e.g., multimodality) when assuming a pre-specified parametric density (say Gaussian). However, it is well known that the shape of the histogram is determined by the pre-specified binwidth, and hence we spend a large amount of time discussing this "smoothing" parameter. Another problem with this type of approach is that the density is discontinuous, and hence we cannot view gradients and other interesting pieces of information. Although the estimator is simplistic, the discussion of this type of density estimation leads quite naturally to our preferred choice of a smooth, continuous estimator: the kernel density estimator.

Although we focus solely on kernel methods in this book, this does not imply that they are necessarily the best methods for any particular problem or data set. However, these methods are arguably the most popular in the literature, and as such they are the most developed. Here we will discuss how to construct such estimators as well as examine their theoretical properties. For example, we typically give the bias, variance, and mean square error of each estimator. Although this can be found in several existing books, we pay special attention to the choice of kernel function, the role and selection of the smoothing (bandwidth) parameter, and the sample size. Given that we have a specific focus on the application of these methods, we attempt to clarify what is necessary for theoretical purposes and what is necessary for application.

After the methodological section of this chapter, and each subsequent chapter, we will use the methods outlined in real empirical applications. Here we start with simple univariate estimation of the worldwide density of output per worker. We show how kernel choice and the bandwidth play a role in understanding the underlying density and how this relates to uncovering potential multimodality in this density.

2.1 Smoothing preliminaries

Kernel smoothing methods provide a powerful tool for conducting data-driven investigations. Effective use of these methods hinges on the choice of a smoothing parameter. When insufficient smoothing is exacted on the data, the resulting estimates are "rough" and provide spurious information. Alternatively, when excessive smoothing is done, important features of the underlying structure are obscured or completely removed. Thus, it is imperative to understand how the choice of smoothing parameter impacts the findings you uncover from your data.

Consider Figure 2.1, which displays four different densities that all display features that could be interesting when conducting a preliminary data analysis. The upper left figure is the standard normal density, which is symmetric about its mean and unimodal. The upper right figure is a log-normal distribution, which is left skewed but unimodal. The bottom left figure is a student's *t* distribution with 4 degrees of freedom. This density is platykurtic, but symmetric and unimodal. It also does not possess moments of every order. Finally, the bottom right figure is from a 70/30 mixture of a standard normal distribution and a normal distribution with mean 3 and variance 2. This density is bimodal and asymmetric. Each of these features is important in some form for data analysis. Nonparametric methods provide an appealing avenue to assess these properties without direct linkages to a specific distribution family *a priori*.

As we discuss in detail later, while these features are of interest – because they represent the "true" underlying structure of the data generating process – the smoothing

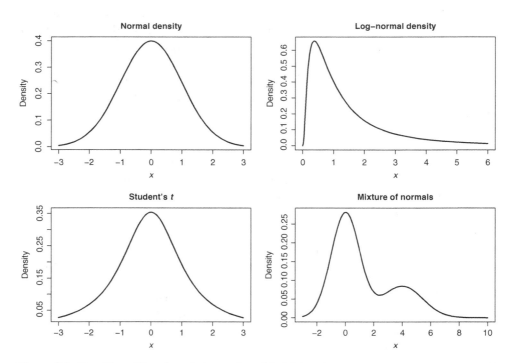

Figure 2.1. Densities with various features of empirical interest

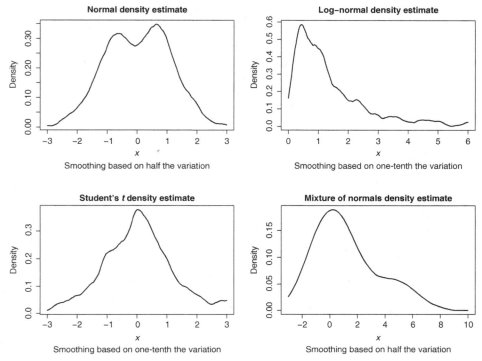

Figure 2.2. Estimated densities with various features of empirical interest obscured based on smoothing

parameter that you control can directly impede your ability to uncover the said features. Smoothing parameter(s) in any nonparametric setting are the *sine qua non* for estimation. Figure 2.2 presents kernel density estimates of single samples of size 250 drawn from each of these densities using a strictly *ad hoc* choice of smoothing parameter based on the overall variation of the density. As we can see, many of the underlying structural features indicative of each of the densities are blurred.

The attractive feature of nonparametric kernel density estimators are that the underlying intuition of them is easy to grasp and carries over to more difficult settings. Think of constructing the sample mean for a given set of data, $\bar{x} = n^{-1} \sum_{i=1}^{n} x_i$. Each observation is weighted *equally* with respect to the other observations. Nonparametric methods seek to adjust the weighting to more adequately characterize the underlying structure of the data generating process. Thus, depending on the object of interest (say a density, $f(x)$), weighting is changed as x changes, thus affording flexibility to the method not present in traditional parametric methods.

We can see this more clearly with a visual illustration. We generate 10 observations from an equal mixture of a $\mathcal{N}(1, 0.65^2)$ and a $\mathcal{N}(-1, 0.65^2)$ whose density is illustrated in Figure 2.3. Using these 10 observations, we construct three different kernel density estimators using different amounts of smoothness. These three density estimates are provided in Figure 2.4. We can see that as the smoothing parameter changes, the amount of weight that each observation carries into the weighted average changes.

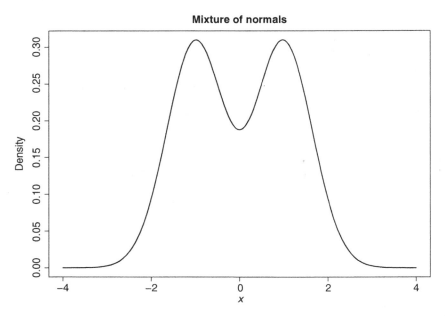

Figure 2.3. Equal mixture of two normal densities

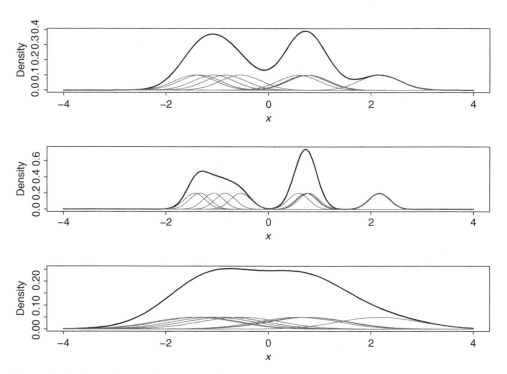

Figure 2.4. Alternative density estimates for our mixture density

The middle graph in Figure 2.4 illustrates the idea of local weighting succinctly. We see that the mode that appears to the right of 2 is completely constructed from the weighting scheme for the observation at 2.16. Thus, if modality is a feature of interest (which it is for the density of interest), it becomes apparent that we have fictitiously created a mode because our weighting scheme is too responsive to the data. Alternatively, the lower figure, which has a smoothing parameter four times the size of the one used in the middle figure, completely veils the true bimodal feature of the density.

While this discussion may seem to suggest that the results of a data analysis are too dependent on the choices made by researchers and as such key insights may be driven by arbitrary choices about the degree of smoothness, we argue that there is no more arbitrariness in this process of statistical estimation than there is in parametric analysis. The choice of parametric model is typically as *ad hoc* as picking the smoothing parameter, sometimes seemingly at random in applied economics. This is because a majority of economic theories rarely yield closed-form solutions about the relationship of interest. It is just as likely that key insights into an important economic relationship are driven via the choice of parametric density assumed for the data or the specification of the conditional mean in a regression study.

2.2 Estimation

2.2.1 A crude estimator

To formalize our discussion on how we can construct a nonparametric estimator of the unknown density, let's first consider a crude way to approximate a density. The simplest way to (nonparametrically) estimate a density is to use a histogram. Specifically, for a univariate random variable x with support $S(x) = [a, b]$, divide $S(x)$ into J equally spaced boxes. In this setup, each box will have width $h = (b - a)/J$ and we will call h our binwidth. The intervals can be described as

$$(a + (j - 1)h, a + jh], \qquad \text{for } j = 1, 2, \ldots, J.$$

Let n_j denote the number of observations from the sample that fall in interval j. This can be summarized as

$$n_j = \sum_{i=1}^{n} 1\{a + (j - 1)h < x_i \le a + jh\},$$

where $1\{A\}$ is the indicator function that takes the value 1 if the event A is true and zero otherwise. The proportion of observations falling into the jth interval (bin) is n_j/n. The expectation of the proportion of observations in the jth interval ($E[n_j]/n$) is then

$$\frac{E[n_j]}{n} = \Pr(a + (j - 1)h < x \le a + jh) = \int_{a+(j-1)h}^{a+jh} f(x)dx, \qquad (2.1)$$

where $f(x)$ is the density of x, which is what we seek to estimate. The first equality in (2.1) follows by the definition of the empirical cumulative distribution function (ECDF), and the second is from the relationship between the cumulative distribution and the probability density function.

Now, if we assume that J is very large (h is very small), then on the interval $(a + (j-1)h, a + jh]$, we can take $f(x)$ to be approximately constant, $f(x) \approx f(c)$ for some $c \in (a + (j-1)h, a + jh]$. We know from univariate calculus that the integral of a constant over the range (a, b) is

$$\int_a^b c\,dx = cx\Big|_a^b = c(b - a).$$

Thus, our expectation is approximately equal to the value of the density function at a point in the interval $(a + (j-1)h, a + jh]$:

$$E[n_j]/n = \int_{a+(j-1)h}^{a+jh} f(x)dx \approx f(c)\,(a + jh - (a + (j-1)h)) = hf(c). \qquad (2.2)$$

Dividing each side of (2.2) by h suggests that a crude estimator of a density function is

$$\widehat{f}(c) = \frac{n_j}{nh} \qquad (2.3)$$

for $c \in (a + (j-1)h, a + jh]$. Unless our point of interest to evaluate the density is exactly the point c (as we show later), we have a biased estimator. Additionally, our estimator is both discontinuous and nondifferentiable. We would like an estimator of our density that is smooth, since we typically think of densities as smooth to begin with.

To better understand the functionality of this estimator, consider the exact bias and precision of our crude approximation to the density of interest. The bias can be formulated as

$$\begin{aligned}
\text{Bias}\left[\widehat{f}(c)\right] &= E[\widehat{f}(c)] - f(c) \\
&= E[n_j]/(nh) - f(c) \\
&= \frac{1}{h}\int_{a+(j-1)h}^{a+jh} f(x)dx - f(c).
\end{aligned}$$

From the mean value theorem for integrals we know that

$$\int_{a+(j-1)h}^{a+jh} f(x)dx = f(\tilde{a})\,(a + jh - (a + (j-1)h)) = hf(\tilde{a})$$

for some $\tilde{a} \in (a + (j-1)h, a + jh]$. Thus, only for $c \equiv \tilde{a}$ will we have an unbiased estimator,

$$\text{Bias}\left[\widehat{f}(c)\right] = E[\widehat{f}(c)] - f(c)$$

$$= \frac{1}{h}\int\limits_{a+(j-1)h}^{a+jh} f(x)dx - f(c)$$

$$= \frac{1}{h}hf(\tilde{a}) - f(c)$$

$$= f(\tilde{a}) - f(c).$$

However, we immediately see that as $h \to 0$, the jth interval collapses, so c must equal $\tilde{a}$ and we will have an unbiased estimator. Notice also that the bias in no way depends on the size of the sample that we have at our disposal. The bias is directly controlled by the binwidth.

Next, consider the variance (precision) of our density estimator,

$$\text{Var}[\widehat{f}(c)] = \text{Var}\left(\frac{n_j}{nh}\right) = \frac{\text{Var}(n_j)}{(nh)^2}.$$

We know that n_j is the number of observations that fall in the rth interval. Moreover, the probability of falling in this interval is $p = f(\tilde{a})h$ for some $\tilde{a} \in (a+(j-1)h, a+jh]$. We also know that n_j is distributed binomial, $Bi(n, p)$. From basic statistics, we know that the variance of a random variable $z \sim Bi(n, p)$ is equal to $np(1 - p)$. Combining all of this information, the variance of our estimator is

$$\text{Var}[\widehat{f}(c)] = \frac{np(1 - p)}{(nh)^2} = \frac{f(\tilde{a})h(1 - f(\tilde{a})h)}{nh^2} = \frac{f(\tilde{a})(1 - f(\tilde{a})h)}{nh}. \qquad (2.4)$$

We see from (2.4), that as $h \to 0$, the variance increases. Notice that our variance is influenced by the sample size, but the bias was not. Thus, if we hold h fixed, we notice that while there is no improvement in the bias, the variance will decrease as the sample size increases. Another thing to point out is that both the bias and the variance of our crude density estimator depend on the design (i.e., $f(\tilde{a})$ appears in our formulae). This implies that for one design, the bias/variance of our estimator may be better than under a different design.

This conflict between controlling the bias and variance of our crude density estimator is at the heart of nonparametric estimation. There is always a delicate interplay between these two that is directly controlled via the binwidth. If we require that $nh \to \infty$ and $h \to 0$, we see that both our bias and variance decrease, suggesting that our estimator converges in the mean square error sense. In essence, as we get more information about the sample (n increases), we can further partition $S(x)$, thus decreasing the binwidth, which lowers bias. At the same time, we cannot lower h so that it offsets the gains in information that we obtain, thus $h/n \to 0$.

When we calculate our density using this crude approximation, we take no stock of where the data are located. Thus, since our density estimate is constant in a given bin, certain points will be estimated more precisely in the bin than others. We can construct a better estimator that takes into account the location of the observations to further reduce the bias that is inherent in our current density estimator. This estimator is known as the naïve density estimator or a centered histogram.

2.2.2 Naïve estimator

Our previous (crude) density estimator placed evenly spaced boxes over $S(x)$, making no distinction of where the data were located. However, we saw that by doing this, the bias varied considerably over each box based on the point of interest. To avoid this issue, we can instead place boxes along $S(x)$ that are centered on each observation. Note that if an observation happens to be centered in one of the original histogram boxes, then these two procedures will produce equivalent estimators (for that specific point). If we label our point of interest as x, then – using boxes that are centered over our sample observations – the number of observations that are within $2h$ (the centered binwidth) of our point of interest is

$$n_x = \sum_{i=1}^{n} \mathbf{1}\{x - h < x_i \le x + h\}.$$

The corresponding probability of falling in this box (centered on x) is n_x/n. A natural estimator of our density is then

$$\widehat{f}(x) = \frac{n_x}{2nh} = \frac{1}{2nh} \sum_{i=1}^{n} \mathbf{1}\{x - h < x_i \le x + h\},$$

where the 2 shows up because we are looking for data both to the right $(x + h)$ and left $(x - h)$ of x. For convenience, we can write our density estimator as

$$\widehat{f}(x) = \frac{1}{nh} \sum_{i=1}^{n} (1/2)\mathbf{1}\left\{\left|\frac{x_i - x}{h}\right| \le 1\right\}. \tag{2.5}$$

Note that our naïve density estimator is equivalent to a density estimator constructed using a *numerical* derivative of the ECDF, $\widehat{F}(x)$. We have

$$\widehat{F}(x) = \frac{1}{n} \sum_{i=1}^{n} \mathbf{1}\{x_i \le x\}$$

and noting that $f(x) = \frac{d}{dx} F(x)$, we can differentiate $\widehat{F}(x)$ to obtain an estimator for $f(x)$. However, $\widehat{F}(x)$ is nonsmooth. Thus, we need to take a numerical derivative. In Technical Appendix 2.1, we show that the numerical derivative is exactly the same as our naïve estimator.

For the discussion that follows, we are going to generalize our estimator slightly. First, we will replace $(1/2)\mathbf{1}\left\{\left|\frac{x_i-x}{h}\right| \le 1\right\}$ in (2.5) with a "kernel" function $k(\psi)$ where

$$k(\psi) = \begin{cases} 1/2 & \text{if } |\psi| \le 1 \\ 0 & \text{otherwise.} \end{cases}$$

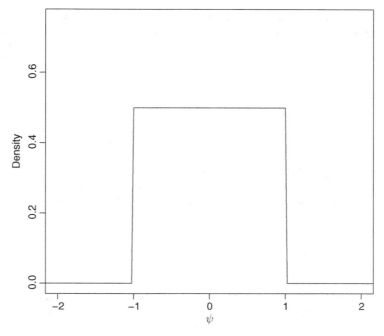

Figure 2.5. Uniform kernel used to construct the naïve kernel density estimator

Note that we have written $k(\psi)$ for notational convenience. In general, you should take ψ to be $(x_i - x)/h$. The term "kernel" stems from spectral analysis, and while it may be somewhat misleading in our context, we will use it without apology. For the sake of nonparametric estimation in our settings, we use kernel as terminology for any one of a variety of weighting functions that are used to construct nonparametric estimators. The kernel used for the naïve estimator is known as the uniform kernel, and this kernel is plotted in Figure 7.2.

We see that one issue with our use of the uniform kernel is that it is discontinuous at -1 and 1 and has derivative 0 everywhere except at these two points (where it is undefined). This suggests that our density estimate will not be smooth. While there exist many nonsmooth densities, typically we think of estimating densities that are smooth. Thus, this feature of the uniform kernel is unappealing. However, the uniform kernel has many nice properties, which we will ask of all of the kernels we employ when smoothing.

A natural question to ask at this stage is if our estimator is indeed a true density function. For a function to be a probability density, it must be nonnegative every-where and integrate to 1. These properties are easily checked with our naïve estimator. First, since $k(\psi) \geq 0 \ \forall \psi$, we see that our estimator must be nonnegative everywhere because the sum of all nonnegative terms must be nonnegative. Thus, for any kernel such that $k(\psi) \geq 0$ (not just the uniform kernel), our density estimate is nonnegative everywhere. Second, Technical Appendix 2.2 shows that our density integrates to 1:

$$\int_{S(x)} \widehat{f}(x)dx = 1.$$

Hence, our estimator is a true density function. These are not restrictive assumptions because the user controls the kernel employed in a statistical analysis. Additionally, as we will see later, other properties of our estimator (such as bias and variance) also depend on the properties of the kernel.

2.2.3 Kernel estimator

We can develop a more general density estimator based on the intuition afforded from our naïve density estimator. Recall that we used the kernel function representation for our naïve density estimator, where the kernel function was equivalent to a uniform weighting function on the interval $[-1, 1]$. To allow for general discussion of density estimation, in what follows, we use the generic definition for a kernel density estimator

$$\widehat{f}(x) = \frac{1}{nh} \sum_{i=1}^{n} k\left(\frac{x_i - x}{h}\right). \tag{2.6}$$

Given the generality of this definition regarding what the kernel function ($k(\psi)$) may look like, we call h a bandwidth as opposed to a binwidth (this practice of referring to h as a bandwidth as opposed to a binwidth again stems from the literature on spectral analysis). In general, we will select kernel functions that are much smoother than the uniform kernel. The bandwidth now corresponds to the smoothness of our estimator instead of the direct width that the kernel covers. We now discuss some basic properties of our kernel estimator to develop intuition for appropriate selection of $k(\psi)$ and h.

We first impose several generic properties on our kernel function involving the moments of the kernel. Letting

$$\kappa_j(k) = \int\limits_{-\infty}^{\infty} \psi^j k(\psi) d\psi,$$

we say a kernel is of second order if $\kappa_0(k) = 1$, $\kappa_1(k) = 0$, and $\kappa_2(k) < \infty$. Imposing $\kappa_0(k) = 1$ means that any weighting function must integrate to unity. This is why we often use probability density functions for kernels. The first moment condition ($\kappa_1(k) = 0$) is satisfied for kernels that are symmetric about zero (i.e., $k(-\psi) = k(\psi)$). In general, both applied and theoretical work on kernel smoothing use symmetric kernels; however, nothing precludes the use of an asymmetric kernel (e.g., see Abadir and Lawford, 2004). The finite variance ($\kappa_2(k)$) condition imposed on the kernel is necessary to obtain meaningful expressions for the bias of various estimators where this quantity will appear prominently. With symmetric kernels, $\kappa_\ell(k) = 0$ for $\ell = 2j + 1$. In other words, all odd moments of our kernel are zero.

Table 2.1 presents several of the most popular kernels employed in kernel density estimation along with their second moments. All of the kernels in Table 2.1 stem from the general polynomial family

$$k_s(\psi) = \frac{(2s + 1)!!}{2^{s+1}s!}(1 - \psi^2)^s \mathbf{1}\{|\psi| \le 1\}, \tag{2.7}$$

Table 2.1. *Common second-order kernels (with their respective second moments)*

Kernel	Formula	$\kappa_2(k)$
Uniform	$k_0(\psi) = \frac{1}{2}\mathbf{1}\{|\psi| \leq 1\}$	1/3
Epanechnikov	$k_1(\psi) = \frac{3}{4}(1 - \psi^2)\mathbf{1}\{|\psi| \leq 1\}$	1/5
Biweight	$k_2(\psi) = \frac{15}{16}(1 - \psi^2)^2\mathbf{1}\{|\psi| \leq 1\}$	1/7
Triweight	$k_3(\psi) = \frac{35}{32}(1 - \psi^2)^3\mathbf{1}\{|\psi| \leq 1\}$	1/9
Gaussian	$k_\phi(\psi) = \frac{1}{\sqrt{2\pi}}e^{-(1/2)\psi^2}$	1

where the double factorial is defined as $(2s + 1)!! = (2s + 1) \cdot (2s - 1) \cdots 5 \cdot 3 \cdot 1$. The biweight kernel ($s = 2$) is occasionally referred to as the quartic kernel (since it is a quartic function in ψ), while the Epanechnikov kernel ($s = 1$) obtained its name from Epanechnikov (1966), who showed several optimality properties for this specific kernel. Notice that as s increases, the kernels possess more derivatives. As $h \to \infty$, $k_s(\psi) \to e^{-(1/2)\psi^2}$. Notice this kernel does not integrate to one. However, if we reweight this kernel by $1/\sqrt{2\pi}$, then we have the common Gaussian kernel ($k_\phi(\psi)$), which has derivatives of all orders (we choose ϕ for the subscript on the Gaussian kernel because the probability density function of a standard normal random variable is commonly denoted in both statistics and econometrics with the lowercase Greek letter ϕ). The four kernels in Table 2.1 (excluding the uniform kernel) are plotted in Figure 2.6.

The discussion on reweighting to obtain the Gaussian kernel suggests that if we use the scaled kernel ($b^{-1}k^*(\psi/b)$) and bandwidth ($h^* = h/b$), we will produce identical density estimates as if we use the kernel $k(\psi)$ and bandwidth h:

$$\widehat{f}(x) = \frac{1}{nh} \sum_{i=1}^{n} k\left(\frac{x_i - x}{h}\right)$$

$$= \frac{1}{nh/b} \sum_{i=1}^{n} b^{-1}k\left(\frac{x_i - x}{bh/b}\right)$$

$$= \frac{1}{nh^*} \sum_{i=1}^{n} k^*\left(\frac{x_i - x}{h^*}\right).$$

Although not an important point theoretically, different authors use different versions of the same kernel, which may cause confusion. For example, Li and Racine (2007, 35) list the Epanechnikov kernel as

$$k_1(\psi) = \frac{3}{4\sqrt{5}}(1 - \psi^2/5)\mathbf{1}\{|\psi| \leq \sqrt{5}\},$$

which will produce identical density estimates as the version of the Epanechnikov kernel listed in Table 2.1, provided you use the bandwidth $h/\sqrt{5}$ ($\kappa_2(k_1) = 1$ for the definition in Li and Racine 2007).

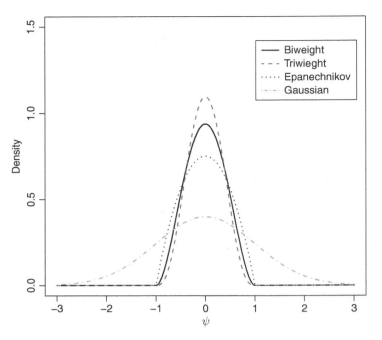

Figure 2.6. Second-order kernels used to construct kernel density estimates

Bias and variance

Using the basic properties of the kernel, we can analyze the bias and variance of the kernel density estimator. While these are not necessarily the most interesting properties of the density estimator which we can establish, they provide intuition for bandwidth and kernel selection. For the discussion that follows, we assume that our data stem from an *iid* process and our density possesses two continuous derivatives (this assumption will be useful when we take a Taylor expansion).

To begin, we analyze the bias of our density estimator given in (2.6). Technical Appendix 2.3 demonstrates that the bias of the kernel density estimator is

$$\text{Bias}[\widehat{f}(x)] = E[\widehat{f}(x)] - f(x) \approx \frac{h^2}{2} f^{(2)}(x)\kappa_2(k), \tag{2.8}$$

where $f^{(2)}(x)$ is defined as the second derivative of $f(\cdot)$ and the approximation is due to the use of a second-order Taylor expansion.[1] Studying the bias reveals several interesting features of nonparametric estimators in general. First, the bias is independent of the sample size. Thus, obtaining more data does not directly imply that the bias will be smaller. Second, the bias depends on the local design, $f^{(2)}(x)$. We see that the bias will change as our point of interest changes based on $f^{(2)}(x)$. This means that certain portions of the density may be able to be estimated with lower bias than other portions. In general, the steeper the density (i.e., larger $f^{(2)}(x)$), the larger the bias. Third, the bias depends on the kernel used via $\kappa_2(k)$. Note that $\kappa_2(k) > 0$ for the kernels

---

[1] It is common in theoretical work to use the little "o" and big "O" notation to capture approximation order. Here we will focus our attention on the primary terms of asymptotic expansions and simply use $\approx$.

previously discussed. Lastly, and most importantly, the bias depends directly on the bandwidth. We see that as the bandwidth decreases, estimation bias decreases. Thus, you can control the bias inherent in nonparametric estimation through manipulation of the bandwidth. As you will see shortly, however, this strategy is not without its costs, as blindly decreasing the bandwidth (to reduce bias) results in increased variance of the density estimator.

Technical Appendix 2.4 gives the derivation of the variance of our density estimator in (2.6) as

$$\text{Var}\left[\widehat{f}(x)\right] \approx \frac{1}{nh} f(x) R(k). \tag{2.9}$$

We use the notation $R(g) = \int g(\psi)^2 d\psi$ for a function g. $R(k)$ can be thought of as the "difficulty" of the kernel function k, with respect to estimating the unknown density. It quantifies the overall shape of the underlying kernel. Larger values of $R(\cdot)$ imply that the kernel function has more shape. We will discuss the difficulty of each of our kernels later in this chapter.

Many of the same features of the bias of our kernel density estimator appear in the variance. The variance depends on the sample size (which the bias does not), the bandwidth, the design, and the kernel employed. As with parametric estimation, as our sample increases, our precision increases (variance decreases). The variance increases as our bandwidth is decreased, which is intuitive because a smaller bandwidth implies that fewer observations (less information) are used to construct the density estimate at a point. This is opposite to how the bandwidth affects the bias. Thus, if you reduce the bandwidth to lower the bias, the variance goes up. The difficulty of the kernel ($R(k)$) impacts the variance as well. An increase in difficulty adds to the variance because a more difficult kernel implies more rapidly changing weights as you obtain observations further away from the point of interest. Also, if $f(x) \approx 0$, we have low variance because no observations are "close" to x. This means we can estimate this point better (in terms of variance) than we can when we have lots of points near x, given that we have to decide which points to smooth over.

We may combine our approximations of the bias (2.8) and variance (2.9) to get the asymptotic mean square error (AMSE) of our density estimator:

$$\text{AMSE}[\widehat{f}(x)] = \text{Bias}[\widehat{f}(x)]^2 + \text{Var}[\widehat{f}(x)]$$

$$\approx \frac{\kappa_2^2(k)}{4} f^{(2)}(x)^2 h^4 + (nh)^{-1} f(x) R(k). \tag{2.10}$$

This measure of the precision of the kernel density estimator stresses the common bias–variance trade-off that arises in applied nonparametric work. The first term is the contribution of the variance and the second term is the contribution of the bias. We see that the bias can be reduced at the expense of the variance. Note that as $n \to \infty$, we can have $h \to 0$, but the bandwidth must decrease slow enough so that $nh \to \infty$. If h decreases too rapidly, in the sense of how fast the sample size grows, then the gains in bias reduction are offset by increases in the variance. This is one of the fundamental issues in nonparametric econometrics. Given that our AMSE decreases with the sample size for all points of the density, we have shown the pointwise consistency of our estimator. If we place further restrictions on the rate of decay of the bandwidth, we can also obtain uniform convergence (Pagan and Ullah, 1999).

Having established the raw form of the precision of our kernel density estimator, one unappealing feature is that it depends on the local design through the bias ($f^{(2)}(x)$) *and* variance ($f(x)$). An alternative measure of precision that depends globally on the design, asymptotic mean integrated squared error (AMISE), is defined as

$$
\begin{aligned}
\text{AMISE}\left[\widehat{f}(x)\right] &= \int\limits_{-\infty}^{\infty} \text{AMISE}\left[\widehat{f}(\psi)\right] d\psi \\
&\approx \frac{h^4 \kappa_2^2(k)}{4} \int f^{(2)}(\psi)^2 d\psi + \frac{R(k) \int f(\psi) d\psi}{nh} \\
&= \frac{h^4 \kappa_2^2(k)}{4} R(f^{(2)}) + \frac{R(k)}{nh},
\end{aligned} \tag{2.11}
$$

where $R(f^{(2)})$ is commonly called the "roughness" of $f(x)$. This stems from the fact that $|g^{(2)}|$ is a measure of the curvature of the function $g(x)$, thus $R(g^{(2)})$ measures the total curvature. We mention here that $R(f^{(2)})$ and $R(k)$ measure different features of the underlying functions and should not be confused with one another. $R(f^{(2)})$ quantifies the overall difficulty in estimating the underlying density. Larger values of $R\left(f^{(2)}\right)$ imply that the density is more "rough" and hence more difficult to estimate.

We see that AMISE only depends on the design through the roughness and not on the specific point of estimation. It was first suggested by Rosenblatt (1956) and is the more commonly studied criterion used to assess kernel smoothers in general because it is independent of the local design. That is, when studying AMSE, we have to account for the point we are considering. However, in general, the focus is on features of the density (e.g., skewness, kurtosis, modality) that are not tied to a specific point, but represent global properties. Thus, AMISE is more in tune with *why* people use kernel density estimators.

We reiterate the trade-off between bias and variance that underlies nonparametric estimation in general. A delicate dance between bias and variance (epitomized in both AMSE and AMISE) occurs via the bandwidth. The common assumption is to require both $nh \rightarrow \infty$ and $h \rightarrow 0$ simultaneously as $n \rightarrow \infty$. You can think of nh as the local information content. As n goes up, we have more information about our design. As h goes down, we have less information. Thus, by asking that n increase faster than h decreases, we ensure that asymptotically we have an infinite amount of information. While this idea is appealing, in practice this is not so simple because h (to the practitioner) is just a number and we will have to decide how best to select it to match the desirable theoretical features of our current discussion.

2.3 Kernel selection

Gains in precision can accrue by appropriate selection of the kernel. Then the question becomes, which kernel results in the lowest AMISE? This amounts to a calculus of variation problem that looks as follows:

$$\min_{k(\psi)} : \text{AMISE}\left[\widehat{f}(x)\right] \text{ s.t. } : \kappa_0(k) = 1, : \kappa_1(k) = 0, : \kappa_2(k) < \infty.$$

Here we note that AMISE depends on the kernel through the term $\left[R(k)^4\kappa_2^2(k)\right]^{1/5}$. Noting that rescaling the kernel does not change AMISE, Technical Appendix 2.5 shows that the above minimization problem can be rewritten as

$$\min_{k(\psi)} : R(k) \text{ s.t. } : \kappa_0(k) = 1, : \kappa_1(k) = 0, : \kappa_2(k) = 1.$$

The first researcher to deal with this issue was Epanechnikov (1969), who determined the optimal kernel which now bears his name (see Serfling, 1980, and Muller, 1984). We now discuss the relative performance of various kernel functions.

2.4 Kernel efficiency

The intuition behind the optimal choice of kernel is relatively straightforward. To understand how gains in precision are achieved, select any kernel – call it $k_\varrho(\psi)$ – along with the Epanechnikov kernel ($k_1(\psi)$) and construct the corresponding density estimators. Then, if both density estimators are constructed using the optimal bandwidth for each, we can determine the relative efficiency of the pair by comparing the ratio of AMISE for each. Technical Appendix 2.6 shows that this efficiency ratio is

$$\text{Eff}(k_\varrho) = \frac{R(k_\varrho)\kappa_2(k_\varrho)^{1/2}}{R(k_1)}. \tag{2.12}$$

If we use a kernel with $\kappa_2(k) = 1$, then the relative efficiency of a kernel is simply $\text{Eff}(k_\varrho) = R(k_\varrho)/R(k_1)$.

Keep in mind that while the use of the Epanechnikov kernel results in the lowest AMISE in the class of second-order kernels, this does not imply that it is the best kernel. There are several reasons for this; the Epanechnikov kernel possesses only one continuous derivative, which may be a problem if you are concerned with derivatives of the density estimator, as opposed to the density estimator itself. The Epanechnikov kernel is optimal in the AMISE sense, but this is by no means the only way to think of the optimality of a kernel. For example, you could be concerned with minimizing alternative metrics such as Kullback–Leibler distance, and it is not obvious that the Epanechnikov kernel is optimal when this metric is used to construct an optimal estimator. Alternatively, we might be interested in the optimal kernel such that the density estimator possesses a given number of continuous derivatives.

To see the gains of the kernels commonly employed (Table 2.1), we list the values of $R(k)$ and $\text{Eff}(k)$ in Table 2.2. We see that there is almost no loss in using the biweight kernel relative to the optimal Epanechnikov kernel. The uniform and Gaussian kernels pay noticeable penalties of over 7% and 5%, respectively. The triweight kernel pays a penalty of about 1.35%.

To think of what these penalties mean, suppose that you have 500 observations at your disposal to construct a density estimate. If the density estimator is constructed using the Epanechnikov kernel, then to obtain the same precision with a different kernel, you would need roughly 538 observations if you deployed the uniform kernel

Table 2.2. *Common second-order kernels (with*
their difficulty factors and their relative
efficiency to the Epanechnikov kernel)

Kernel	$R(k)$	Eff(k)
Uniform	1/2	1.0758
Epanechnikov	3/5	1.0000
Biweight	5/7	1.0061
Triweight	350/429	1.0135
Gaussian	$1/(2\sqrt{\pi})$	1.0513

$(500 \cdot (1.0758))$, 525 observations for the Gaussian kernel, 507 for the triweight, and 504 if the biweight is used. These numbers can be constructed by setting the optimal AMISE for each density estimator equal to one another, but allowing the number of observations to vary. Technical Appendix 2.7 shows that

$$n_\varrho = \text{Eff}(k_\varrho) \cdot n_1.$$

In other words, more observations are needed to estimate a density with the same precision as the Epanechnikov kernel when you use a kernel density estimator with an alternative kernel.

2.5 Bandwidth selection

While the choice of the kernel is important, its overall effect on the results and insights generated from the statistical analysis is limited when compared to the effect of the bandwidth. Thus, it is of the utmost importance to have mechanisms in place to select the bandwidth based on sound statistical theory. Here we discuss several approaches that are common in the literature. The array of methods for selection of the bandwidth do have a unifying theme: they are all based to some degree on estimating/approximating AMISE, but differ in their approach to this approximation. Each has distinct strengths and weaknesses when implementing bandwidth selection.

2.5.1 Optimal selection

Having developed both the AMSE and AMISE of our kernel density estimator, we can determine the optimal amount of smoothing in the sense that AMSE or AMISE is minimized. To determine the optimal bandwidth, we simply need to calculate the minimum for each of our formulae. In Technical Appendix 2.8, we show that our optimal bandwidth with respect to minimizing AMSE is

$$h_{\text{opt}} = \left[\frac{f(x)R(k)}{\kappa_2^2(k)f^{(2)}(x)^2} \right]^{1/5} n^{-1/5}. \tag{2.13}$$

The $n^{-1/5}$ term is a common theme for the optimal bandwidth in univariate settings. This is the rate at which information is used by the bandwidth to decrease the bias.

If we plug this optimal bandwidth back into our formula for AMSE, we can obtain the optimal AMSE in the sense of being minimized via the bandwidth. Straightforward algebra (shown in Technical Appendix 2.8) gives the AMSE for the optimal bandwidth as

$$\text{AMSE}_{\text{opt}}\left[\widehat{f}(x)\right] = \frac{5}{4}\left[f(x)^4 R^4(k)\kappa_2^2(k)f^{(2)}(x)^2\right]^{1/5} n^{-4/5}.$$

In parametric models, it is quite common for information to be processed at the rate $n^{-1/2}$, which is much faster than what we have here. Even though the rate of AMSE is $n^{-4/5}$, keep in mind that this is a squared term, so the actual speed of convergence is $n^{-2/5} = \left(n^{-4/5}\right)^{1/2}$ and this rate is indeed slower than the parametric rate. However, the $n^{-1/2}$ rate is for a *correctly* specified parametric model. Thus, while nonparametric models converge more slowly than their correctly specified parametric counterparts, they converge. In comparison, misspecified parametric models most likely will not converge at any rate. In essence, *correctly* specified parametric models should converge more quickly because the researcher should be rewarded for correct selection of the design, and this information provides a setting that is conducive to better estimation. That is, in a parametric setup, we have an information content of n, instead of nh, given the additional structure imposed on the problem.

Repeating the steps above, we can solve for the optimal h, which minimizes AMISE. Technical Appendix 2.9 shows that the optimal bandwidth is equal to

$$h_{\text{opt}} = \left[\frac{R(k)}{\kappa_2^2(k)R(f^{(2)})}\right]^{1/5} n^{-1/5}. \tag{2.14}$$

This is nearly identical to the previous optimal bandwidth, except that the bandwidth here is globally dependent on the design as opposed to locally (i.e., no $f(x)$ term). This "optimal" bandwidth provides insight into how the bandwidth should work theoretically. Smaller bandwidths are better when n is large, as more information is available, thus allowing the estimator to be more "local." Smaller bandwidths are also desirable when the density itself is rougher, because the effect of the bias is stronger on AMISE.

Replacing the generic h in AMISE with the optimal bandwidth in (2.14), we obtain the minimal AMISE with respect to the bandwidth (shown in Technical Appendix 2.8) as

$$\text{AMISE}_{\text{opt}}\left[\widehat{f}(x)\right] \approx \frac{5}{4}\left[R^4(k)\kappa_2^2(k)R(f^{(2)})\right]^{1/5} n^{-4/5}. \tag{2.15}$$

We notice immediately, from both our minimal AMSE and AMISE, that further reductions can be achieved by selection of the kernel. While these gains may accrue in a finite sample setting, they also appear in the limit, as the asymptotic variance of the kernel density estimator can be reduced through the kernel as well. Asymptotically, these gains in AMSE or AMISE reduction are quite small. However, in applied settings, this could be important because proper kernel selection can result in significant reductions in AMSE (AMISE), depending upon the sample size.

The most basic of "optimal" bandwidth selection rules hinges on replacing the unknown roughness of the underlying density in the asymptotic approximation in

AMISE ($R(f^{(2)})$) with the roughness for a reference distribution. This idea dates to Deheuvels (1977), but was popularized by Silverman (1986). Given that scale is essential for bandwidth choice, but location is not (i.e., $R(f^{(2)})$ is invariant to changes in location), the most natural choice for f is the parametric family of mean zero, normal random variates, $\mathcal{N}(0, \sigma^2) = \sigma^{-1}\phi(\psi/\sigma)$. In Technical Appendix 2.10, we show that the value of $R(f^{(2)})$ for this case is

$$R(f^{(2)}) = (1/\sqrt{2\pi})\sigma^{-10}\left(3\sigma^5/(4\sqrt{2}) - \sigma^5/\sqrt{2} + \sigma^5/\sqrt{2}\right) = \frac{3}{8\sqrt{\pi}\sigma^5}.$$

Assuming a Gaussian kernel, for which $\kappa_2(k) = 1$ and $R(k) = (2\sqrt{\pi})^{-1}$, we can calculate our optimal bandwidth based on minimizing AMISE as

$$h_{\text{opt}} = \left[\frac{R(k)}{\kappa_2^2(k)R(f^{(2)})}\right]^{1/5} n^{-1/5} = \left[\frac{8\sqrt{\pi}\sigma^5}{6\sqrt{\pi}}\right]^{1/5} n^{-1/5} = \left(\frac{4}{3}\right)^{1/5}\sigma n^{-1/5}. \quad (2.16)$$

Given that $\left(\frac{4}{3}\right)^{1/5} \approx 1.06$, we have the popular Silverman rule-of-thumb bandwidth, $h_{\text{rot}} = 1.06\widehat{\sigma}n^{-1/5}$, where $\widehat{\sigma}$ is the standard deviation of the variable for which the density is being estimated.

Noting that the sample standard deviation is not a robust measure of spread, especially for nonnormal data, Silverman (1986) also proposed several modified versions of the rule-of-thumb bandwidth. This intuition led him to replace $\widehat{\sigma}$ with the interquartile range (IQR) in (2.16) and to adjust the constant from 1.06 to 0.79 (note that $0.79 * IQR \approx \sigma$ for a normally distributed random variable). When the data are heavy tailed or skewed, this adjustment will work better than the original rule-of-thumb bandwidth. Unfortunately, if the data are from a bimodal distribution, use of this bandwidth could lead to the bimodal structure being obfuscated, given that this bandwidth tends to oversmooth (which, as mentioned earlier, leads to loss of local information). Thus, to have an adaptive measure of spread, Silverman (1986, Equation (3.29)) proposed the adaptive rule-of-thumb bandwidth

$$h_{\text{arot}} = 1.06An^{-1/5}, \qquad (2.17)$$

where $A = \min\{\widehat{\sigma}, IQR/1.34\}$.

You should notice we have said that if the data are heavy tailed, skewed, or bimodal, you should use this bandwidth or that bandwidth. However, keep in mind that the actual rule-of-thumb bandwidth in (2.16) is *only* optimal for data stemming from a normal distribution. In this setting, we should forgo nonparametric density estimation altogether because the maximum likelihood density estimator is efficient. However, the use of a rule-of-thumb bandwidth is to obtain a preliminary overview of the features of the data and as such, even though it is linked with a normal distribution, its use is mainly for cursory investigation. In general, we do not have *a priori* information on the heaviness of the tails, the skewness of the data or the number of modes and therefore this information is gathered from the kernel density estimate or is tested for in the data.

Table 2.3. *Scaling factors for
rule-of-thumb bandwidth construction*

Kernel	Factor
Uniform	1.843
Epanechnikov	2.345
Biweight	2.778
Triweight	3.154
Gaussian	1.059

Table 3.3 provides the "optimal" rule-of-thumb scale factors for the kernels discussed herein. These "optimal" scale factors (c) are found from the formula

$$c = 2 \left(\frac{\sqrt{\pi} R(k)}{12 \kappa_2^2(k)} \right)^{1/5}.$$

We also mention that the general form of the rule-of-thumb bandwidth is quite similar to how "optimal" bandwidths appear in general. Typically, the bandwidth is composed of the sample size raised to a power reflecting the standard nonparametric rate of convergence times a scaling factor that is dependent in some fashion on the density design and the kernel employed. Even though 1.059 is the optimal scaling factor when the data are normally distributed, in simulations run in Silverman (1986), relatively good performance (in AMISE) can be achieved by reducing the optimal scale to 0.9. Thus, a bevy of easily implementable bandwidths can be used for a preliminary density analysis prior to resorting to more rigorous bandwidth selectors.

Figure 2.7 presents kernel density estimates for a sample of 250 observations generated from a 75/25 mixture of a $\mathcal{N}(1, 1)$ and a $\mathcal{N}(-1, \sqrt{0.65})$, using each of the four Silverman rule-of-thumb bandwidths described previously with a second-order Gaussian kernel. As we can see, the four estimates are visually close and appear to capture the "shoulder" possessed by this density as well as its asymmetric nature. We see that even though the data does not appear to be Gaussian, the bandwidths designed for optimal estimation of normal data provide a fairly accurate representation of the underlying structure. This feature is perhaps one of the main reasons why rule-of-thumb bandwidths are so popular in applied univariate kernel density estimation. We note here that it is not hard to generate data where these rule-of-thumb bandwidths break down and do not provide an accurate representation. However, in general, these bandwidths, if used for preliminary analysis, are typically sufficient to glean important information from the data at hand.

2.5.2 Data-driven methods

While the rule-of-thumb bandwidths discussed above are computationally simple to calculate and may provide accurate insight into the underlying structure of the density of interest, the methods have no formal statistical underpinnings when the design

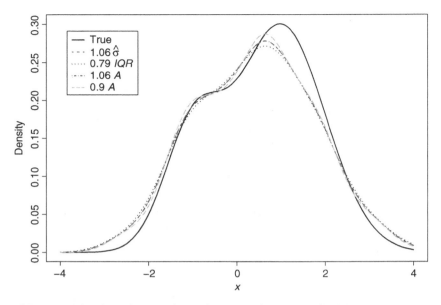

Figure 2.7. Kernel density estimates using various rule-of-thumb bandwidths

density deviates from the assumed density. That is, while (2.16) is the optimal band-width when the true density is normal, it is not clear how well this bandwidth performs (in an optimal sense) when the density is not normal.

Consider the following density (from Wand and Jones 1995, Question 3.2)

$$f_\mu(x) = \frac{1}{2}f(x - \mu) + \frac{1}{2}f(x + \mu),$$

where $\mu > 1$ and $f(\psi) = (35/32)(1 - \psi^2)^3 \mathbf{1}\{|\psi| \le 1\}$. As μ increases, the distance between the modes (2μ) increases. Several variants of $f_\mu(x)$ are plotted in Figure 2.8.

If we were to take random draws from $f_4(x)$ and use any of the Silverman rule-of-thumb bandwidths described earlier, it would be difficult to assess the behavior of the underlying density. Figure 2.9 plots the estimated density for a random sample of size $n = 100$ taken from $f_4(x)$ using the four Silverman rule-of-thumb variants. As evinced by the estimates, the distinct pockets of probability density of $f_4(x)$ are obscured because the rule-of-thumb bandwidths are not tailored to this specific density. Additionally, as μ increases, σ^2 increases and the finite sample performance of these estimators using these bandwidths degrades. This simple example illustrates that while computationally appealing, the rule-of-thumb bandwidths are not practical across all settings. Thus, it is desirable to have access to methods specifically tailored to the underlying design without anchoring yourself to a given probability density family.

Plug-in Methods
A rule-of-thumb bandwidth ignores the unknown roughness of the density (except in the special case of possessing data from a normal distribution). Thus, alternative strategies are required to develop an estimator for the bandwidth to make the kernel

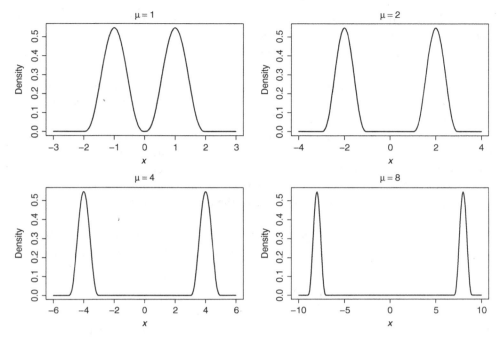

Figure 2.8. Plots for different versions of $f_\mu(x)$

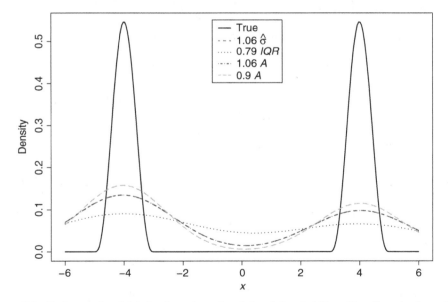

Figure 2.9. Estimates for $f_4(x)$ density using rule-of-thumb bandwidths with a Gaussian kernel

density estimator operational. One of the earliest approaches – due to Scott, Tapia, and Thompson (1977) – involves replacing $R(f^{(2)})$ with an estimate. The most natural choice is to replace $f^{(2)}(\cdot)$ with a kernel density derivative estimate. This will naturally require a bandwidth as well, so Scott, Tapia, and Thompson (1977) developed a fixed-point algorithm that solves for the bandwidth by equating both sides of (2.15) when $R(f^{(2)})$ is replaced with the roughness of the density derivative. However, this type of an approach will produce a biased estimate of $R(f^{(2)})$ as we show in Technical Appendix 2.11.[2]

While the solve-the-equation approach described above offers a convenient alternative to *ad hoc* rule-of-thumb bandwidth selection, it is not computationally appealing. Also, it is somewhat awkward because the same bandwidth is used to estimate the density and the unknown roughness, which depends on the second derivative. As we will see in Section 2.6, the bandwidth, which is optimal for estimating the second derivative of the density, is not optimal for estimating the density itself. To this end, an alternative approach based on the same idea, known as direct plug-in methods, has been proposed in the literature and become one of the more popular methods for obtaining bandwidths.

To understand how direct plug-in approaches work, we note that the difficulty with obtaining optimal bandwidths is the presence of the unknown roughness, $R(f^{(2)})$. Here we can see that

$$R(f^{(2)}) \equiv \int f^{(2)}(x)^2 dx = \int f^{(2)}(x) f^{(2)}(x) dx.$$

Using integration by parts and noting that $df^{(1)}(x) = f^{(2)}(x) dx$, we have

$$R(f^{(2)}) = f^{(2)}(x) f^{(1)}(x) - \int f^{(3)}(x) f^{(1)}(x) dx.$$

If we use integration by parts again and note that $df(x) = f^{(1)}(x) dx$, we have

$$R(f^{(2)}) = f^{(3)}(x) f(x) - \int f^{(4)}(x) f(x) dx = E\left[f^{(4)}(x) \right].$$

More generally, we can repeatedly use integration by parts to show that the unknown roughness for the *r*th order derivative of $f(x)$ is

$$R(f^{(r)}) = (-1)^r \int f^{(2r)}(x) f(x) dx = (-1)^r E\left[f^{(2r)}(x) \right]. \tag{2.18}$$

In our discussion of plug-in bandwidth estimation, r will be even; therefore, $R(f^{(r)}) = E\left[f^{(2r)}(x) \right]$.

A natural estimator of $R(f^{(r)})$ is

$$\widehat{R}(f^{(r)}) = n^{-1} \sum_{i=1}^{n} \widehat{f}^{(r)}(x_i) = n^{-2} \check{h}^{(-1+r)} \sum_{i=1}^{n} \sum_{j=1}^{n} k^{(2r)}\left(\frac{x_i - x_j}{\check{h}} \right). \tag{2.19}$$

This is Jones and Sheather's (1991, 512) $\widehat{S}_{D,m}$, which follows from the discussion in Hall and Marron (1987). We note here that $\check{h}$ is not equivalent to the h we are

---

[2] This result can be generalized to any order (it is not specific to $R\left(\widehat{f}^{(2)} \right)$) and actually is a refinement of lemma 3.2 in Scott and Terrell (1987), who obtained the same result, but with the assumption that $k^{(\ell)}(\pm 1) = 0$ for $0 \leq \ell \leq r - 1$, where r is the maximum number of derivatives assumed to exist for the unknown density.

seeking to determine, nor does $k\,(\cdot)$ have to be the same kernel used in the construction of our density estimator. This suggests that the estimation of $R(f^{(r)})$ is conducted separately from the estimation of $f(x)$. An interesting feature of this estimator is that it also requires a choice of kernel and bandwidth. Jones and Sheather (1991, result 2) show that the optimal bandwidth for estimating $R(f^{(r)})$ (i.e., that which minimizes AMISE) is

$$\check{h} = \left[\frac{(-1)^{r/2} 2k^{(2r)}(0)}{\kappa_2(k) R(f^{(2r+2)})n} \right]^{1/(2r+2+1)}, \qquad (2.20)$$

where $k^{(2r)}(0)$ is the $2r$th derivative of the kernel, evaluated at zero.

While the rule-of-thumb bandwidth replaces $R(f^{(2)})$ with a corresponding roughness from a family of densities (such as the normal), the plug-in approach constructs an estimate of $R(f^{(2)})$. This estimate depends on a bandwidth, which also depends on an unknown roughness. If interest hinges on $R(f^{(2)})$, then in order to obtain an asymptotically valid bandwidth, we need to know (or estimate) $R(f^{(4)})$. If we were to instead estimate $R(f^{(4)})$, this would require a bandwidth $\check{h}$, which in turn would depend on $R(f^{(6)})$. This problem will not go away. At some point, we have to obtain a bandwidth either via a rule-of-thumb argument or using a more sophisticated data-driven method. Thus, the direct plug-in approach can be viewed as an ℓ-step algorithm, where the first step is to construct a bandwidth that is optimal for estimating $R(f^{2\ell+2})$. $R(f^{2\ell+2})$ is then estimated with this bandwidth and the estimate is then "plugged in" to the formula for the optimal bandwidth for estimating $R(f^{(2(\ell-1)+2)})$. This is repeated until an estimate for $R(f^{(2)})$ has been obtained. The purpose of the ℓ steps is to reduce the effect that rule-of-thumb selection has on the final bandwidth. The Sliverman approach to the rule-of-thumb bandwidth selection, described earlier, is a zero-step direct plug-in algorithm, since no steps have been taken to remove the influence of the rule-of-thumb selection on the final density estimate.

As an example, a simple one-step plug-in approach begins by using a rule-of-thumb bandwidth for estimation of $R(f^{(4)})$. This bandwidth can be used to construct $\widehat{R}(f^{(2)})$, which then can be plugged into the formula for the asymptotically optimal bandwidth for our density estimator,

$$h_{\mathrm{DPI},1} = \left[\frac{R(k)}{\kappa_2^2(k) \widehat{R}(f^{(2)})n} \right]^{1/5}. \qquad (2.21)$$

First, we note that the rule-of-thumb bandwidth to begin the algorithm requires anchoring to a parametric family (for instance, Gaussian). The roughness of the $2r$th derivative of a density belonging to the $\mathcal{N}(0, \sigma^2)$ family is

$$R(\phi^{(2r)}) = \frac{(-1)^r (2r)!}{(2\sigma)^{2r+1} r! \sqrt{\pi}}.$$

Here we list the "steps" to obtain the one-step direct plug-in bandwidth in (2.21).

1. Assuming normality, estimate $R(\phi^{(6)})$ via $\widehat{R}(\phi^{(6)}) = -15/\left(16\widehat{\sigma}^7\sqrt{\pi}\right)$, where $\widehat{\sigma}$ is the estimate of the standard deviation of the random variable x. Use this estimate to create the optimal bandwidth for estimating $R(f^{(2)})$, which from (2.20) is

$$\check{h} = \left[\frac{-2k^{(4)}(0)}{\kappa_2(k)\widehat{R}(\phi^{(6)})n}\right]^{1/7}.$$

2. Using $\check{h}$, construct the roughness estimate $\widehat{R}(f^{(2)})$ via (2.19).
3. Finally, use $\widehat{R}(f^{(2)})$ to construct the bandwidth for $\widehat{f}(\cdot)$, which is

$$h_{\text{DPI,opt}} = \left[\frac{R(k)}{\kappa_2^2(k)\widehat{R}(f^{(2)})n}\right]^{1/5}.$$

An alternative one-step plug-in approach can be found in Hall, Sheather, Jones, and Marron (1991). However, Park and Marron (1992) show theoretically that at least two stages should be done for the direct plug-in approach and show that the computation time of the bandwidth selector is essentially linear in the number of stages. Two stage approaches can be found in Sheather and Jones (1991) and Wand and Jones (1995, 72). We do not go into detail here and refer you to the aforementioned references.

Least-squares cross-validation

The most commonly used data-driven bandwidth selection algorithm is least-squares cross-validation (LSCV). The popularity of LSCV stems from numerous theoretical insights regarding bandwidths obtained from this approach. Here we discuss the intuition of the LSCV criterion and several of its properties.

The first proposal of LSCV dates to Rudemo (1982) and Bowman (1984), but additional early work can be found in Hall (1983) and Stone (1984). The goal of LSCV is to minimize the difference between the estimator of the density and the density itself. We define the integrated squared error (ISE) as

$$\text{ISE}(\widehat{f}, f) = \int \widehat{f}(x) - f(x)^2 dx = \int \widehat{f}(x)^2 dx - 2\int \widehat{f}(x)f(x)dx + \int f(x)^2 dx. \tag{2.22}$$

The last term does not depend on the amount of smoothing inherent in our estimator and as such can be taken to be a constant for our purposes. In other words, we have no control over the last term and hence there is no need to consider it when we are trying to minimize $\text{ISE}(\widehat{f}, f)$. An "optimal" bandwidth can be obtained by minimizing $\text{ISE}(\widehat{f}, f)$ with respect to h. This requires selecting h to minimize

$$\text{ISE}^*(\widehat{f}, f) = \int \widehat{f}(x)^2 dx - 2\int \widehat{f}(x)f(x)dx.$$

An estimator of $\text{ISE}^*(\widehat{f}, f)$ is constructed, since $f(x)$ is unknown, and then this is minimized over h. This illustrates the basic principle behind data-driven bandwidth selection. After a distance-based criteria has been selected, a sample estimator for this criteria is constructed and then the bandwidth is selected to minimize this criteria.

An initial guess to constructing a sample estimate for $\text{ISE}^*(\widehat{f}, f)$ would be to replace the unknown $f(x)$ with a kernel density estimator. However, in this case, we would have $\text{ISE}^*(\widehat{f}, \widehat{f}) = -\int \widehat{f}(x)^2 dx$, which would result in a bandwidth of 0 selected no matter what the underlying density is. This is because setting a bandwidth of 0 places weight only on the sample observations and integrating over a fixed number of points will return $-\infty$, the minimum value that $\text{ISE}^*(\widehat{f}, f)$ can take. As an alternative to replacing $f(x)$ with $\widehat{f}(x)$, consider the leave-one-out estimator

$$\widehat{f}_{-i}(x) = \frac{1}{(n-1)h} \sum_{\substack{j=1 \\ j \neq i}}^{n} k\left(\frac{x_j - x}{h}\right),$$

which is the density estimator constructed using all of the observations *except* x_i. At first glance you may feel that there is a typo because i does not appear on the right-hand side of the equation, other than in the summation. Our data vector $(x_1, x_2, \ldots, x_i, \ldots, x_n)$ includes the ith observation, but we only sum over $(x_1, x_2, \ldots, x_{i-1}, x_{i+1}, \ldots, x_n)$ when calculating $\widehat{f}_{-i}(x)$.

By omitting the ith observation, we will prevent the bandwidth from going to 0 in our quest to minimize $\text{ISE}^*(\widehat{f}, f)$. There is no reason to only omit the ith observation. We could have omitted the jth or ℓth observation instead. To avoid any issue with which observation is omitted, we can construct an estimator based on averaging our leave-one-out estimator over all observations. Thus, we construct

$$\bar{f}_{-i}(x) = n^{-1} \sum_{j=1}^{n} \widehat{f}_{-j}(x).$$

In Technical Appendix 2.12, we show that we can think of $\bar{f}_{-i}(x)$ as the finite sample equivalent of $E\left[\widehat{f}_{-i}(x)\right]$.

Partially using these results, Technical Appendix 2.13 shows the most common way to express the LSCV function:

$$\text{LSCV}(h) = \frac{1}{n^2 h} \sum_{i=1}^{n} \sum_{j=1}^{n} \bar{k}\left(\frac{x_i - x_j}{h}\right) - \frac{2}{n(n-1)h} \sum_{i=1}^{n} \sum_{\substack{j=1 \\ j \neq i}}^{n} k\left(\frac{x_i - x_j}{h}\right), \quad (2.23)$$

where $\bar{k}\left(\frac{x_i - x_j}{h}\right)$ is a convolution kernel. The same technical appendix discusses how to obtain the convolution kernels using algebraic software. For the second-order kernels previously introduced, these are defined as

$$\bar{k}_0(\psi) = \frac{1}{4}(2 - |\psi|)\mathbf{1}\{|\psi| \leq 2\}$$

$$\bar{k}_1(\psi) = \frac{3}{160}(2 - |\psi|)^3(\psi^2 + 6|\psi| + 4)\mathbf{1}\{|\psi| \leq 2\}$$

$$\bar{k}_2(\psi) = \frac{5}{3584}(2 - |\psi|)^5(\psi^4 + 10|\psi|^3 + 36x^2 + 40|\psi| + 16)\mathbf{1}\{|\psi| \leq 2\}$$

$$\bar{k}_3(\psi) = \frac{35}{1757184}(2 - |\psi|)^7(5x^6 + 70|\psi|^5 + 404x^4 + 1176|\psi|^3$$
$$+ 1616x^2 + 1120|\psi| + 320)\mathbf{1}\{|\psi| \leq 2\}$$
$$\bar{k}_\phi(\psi) = \frac{1}{\sqrt{4\pi}}e^{-\psi^2/4}. \tag{2.24}$$

Here we note that minimizing LSCV with respect to h is the equivalent to minimizing ISE.[3] Our job is to find the value of h that minimizes this particular function. This bandwidth will minimize the difference between the true density and the estimate of the density. Although this idea is straightforward, it is computationally expensive, especially in the form we have written in (3.13).

To reduce the computation time required to minimize the LSCV function, by exploiting convolution kernels, Technical Appendix 2.14 shows that we can rewrite our LSCV criterion as

$$\text{LSCV}(h) = \frac{1}{n^2 h}\sum_{i=1}^{n}\sum_{j=1}^{n}\check{k}\left(\frac{x_i - x_j}{h}\right). \tag{2.25}$$

In this formulation, we have condensed three separate terms containing different kernel-type arguments into one. This formulation allows us to dispense with the computationally costly leave-one-out construction (notice that the summation over j does not exclude i). In general, most cross-validation routines that use a leave-one-out estimator can be rewritten to avoid this complication. For the normal kernel, using (2.24), we have

$$\check{k}(\psi) = \frac{1}{\sqrt{4\pi}}e^{-\psi^2/4} - \frac{n}{(n-1)\sqrt{\pi}}\left(\sqrt{2}e^{-0.5\psi^2} - \sqrt{2}/n\right).$$

When n is large, $n/(n-1) \approx 1$ and so we can further simplify the expression for $\check{k}(\psi)$. In general, this should not have a noticeable effect on the optimally selected bandwidths. Further, as n increases, the term $\sqrt{2}/n$ collapses to 0, suggesting that the impact of the leave-one-out kernel estimator diminishes.

In a univariate setting, obtaining the optimal h is handled via a standard grid search. You must be careful not to set the lower bound of this grid search too small, since Hall and Marron (1991) have shown that this function has fairly frequent local minima. When numerous minima exist, it is common to use the largest local minima as opposed to the global minima. One reason for this is the established belief that bandwidths obtained via LSCV in the univariate setting are generally smaller than their optimal levels. A useful grid can be obtained from any of the rule-of-thumb bandwidths discussed previously. You can evaluate LSCV(h) on $[h_1, h_2]$ where $h_1 = h_{\text{rot}}/d$ and $h_2 = dh_{\text{rot}}$ for $d > 1$. If d is too large, then evaluation of the cross-validation function will be prone to multiple minima, whereas if d is too small, then the global minimizer

---

[3] We could show that LSCV$(h) + \int f(x)^2 dx$ is an unbiased estimator for AMISE(h). Even though applied researchers typically believe that unbiased estimators are "good" estimators to use, this does not mean that $\widehat{h}$ stemming from the use of LSCV(h) is a good estimator for h_{opt}, the bandwidth that produces the smallest AMISE(h). There are several criteria that can be used to evaluate the usefulness of $\widehat{h}$ obtained via implementation of LSCV.

may be h_1.[4] A useful diagnostic is to plot LSCV(h) against h to see how the performance fluctuates with changes in h. We will define bandwidths obtained via LSCV as $\widehat{h}_{\text{LSCV}}$ or $\widehat{h}$ for brevity.

Another method to select the optimal bandwidth is to define the rate of the bandwidth ahead of time and use LSCV to evaluate the unknown scale factor. That is, instead of finding $\widehat{h}$ directly from LSCV(h), you instead find c, where $h_{\text{opt}} = c\sigma n^{-1/5}$. This approach is useful if you wish to over- or undersmooth your estimate based on theoretical concerns. As we saw with optimal bandwidth selection based on AMISE (see Equation (2.15)), our bandwidth can be characterized as the product of a design component (the scale factor) and the information content (the sample size raised to a "rate"). While you can always find the estimated optimal scale factor by simply multiplying the optimal h by $\sigma^{-1}n^{1/5}$, some software packages calculate bandwidths based on scale factors, so we mention it here.

Likelihood cross-validation

Likelihood cross-validation (LCV) was initially proposed by Duin (1976) and Habbema, Hermans, and van den Broek (1974). It has both a strong intuitive appeal and is computationally more efficient than LSCV. The core idea behind LCV is that a bandwidth that maximizes the LCV criterion is close to the true density in the Kullback–Leibler sense. Kullback–Leibler distance, or information, between the true and estimated densities is defined as

$$\text{KL}(f, \widehat{f}) = \int f(x) \log\{f(x)/\widehat{f}(x)\}dx. \tag{2.26}$$

As its name implies, LCV selects a bandwidth so that if an additional observation of the data becomes available, we want our density estimator to produce the highest likelihood of observing that data point, which in logarithmic terms is $\log(\widehat{f}(x))$. In other words, we treat our observations as fixed and our parameter of interest, the bandwidth, is selected to maximize the likelihood (or log-likelihood). Since we do not have the ability to obtain an additional data point from $f(\cdot)$, we could use any of our original data points. However, as we discussed with leave-one-out estimation, we do not want to have a procedure that relies too heavily on the specific point chosen. Thus, we construct an average over each of the data points. This process yields (the score function)

$$\text{LCV}(h) = n^{-1} \sum_{i=1}^{n} \log \widehat{f}_{-i}(x_i), \tag{2.27}$$

where $\widehat{f}_{-i}(x_i)$ is the now familiar leave-one-out estimator. As with LSCV, we can show that up to a constant, which is independent of our bandwidth, our LCV criterion is an unbiased estimator of the expected Kullback–Leibler distance. Technical Appendix 2.15 shows that the expected value of LCV(h) is

---

[4] An alternative procedure would be to set $h_1 = 0$ and h_2 equal to the maximal possible amount of smoothing as defined in Terrell and Scott (1985) and Terrell (1990) and then select the largest local minimizer. However, since any of the h_{rot} are typically larger than what is optimal, this procedure most likely will result in an unduly wide interval over which to conduct the grid search.

$$E[\text{LCV}(h)] = -E\left[\int \log\{f(x)/\widehat{f}(x)\}f(x)dx\right] + \int f(x)\log\{f(x)\}dx.$$

This expectation exists only under precise conditions on both $f(x)$ and $k(\psi)$, which are both used to construct $\widehat{f}(x)$.

An unfortunate consequence of the simplicity of LCV is that it can produce inconsistent estimates of the underlying density by selecting h such that $h \to \infty$ under certain conditions; this is the opposite behavior we desire of h. This feature has been noted by Schuster and Gregory (1981); Chow, Geman, and Wu (1983); and Hall (1987a,b). In various ways, each of these papers shows how/when bandwidths selected via LCV will produce dramatically different (and inappropriate) bandwidths for estimation of the underlying density. In the simplest argument against the use of LCV, suppose you were constructing $\widehat{f}(x)$ using a kernel with bounded support, such as the Epanechnikov kernel. For any given data set there exists one point that is the farthest from the next closest point. Then, LCV could not select an h smaller than this distance. Otherwise, the density at this point would be zero and the logarithm of this point would be $-\infty$, which would corrupt the bandwidth selection procedure. You would expect that as your sample grows, these gaps between data points would collapse, but this is not always the case. For fat-tailed distributions, such as the Cauchy, these gaps actually widen, leading to bandwidths selected via LCV that diverge to infinity, essentially ignoring any local structure in the data.

The argument here about the breakdown of LCV when using kernels with bounded support may appear to be remedied by selecting kernels with continuous support over the entire real line, such as the Gaussian kernel. However, even in this case, problems arise. Schuster and Gregory (1981) point out that even with the use of an infinite support kernel (e.g., Gaussian), LCV will select bandwidths that diverge to ∞ if the tails of the kernel do not die off slowly, producing an inconsistent estimator. This causes concern since one of the most basic requirements of any estimator is that it is consistent. You might ask why the tail properties of the kernel matter so much in this setting. Hall (1987b) shows that if the kernel's tails die off faster than the density's tails, a "zero" estimate of the density in the tail regions will still occur, thus forcing the bandwidth to be larger (and actually increasing) than necessary. Chow, Geman, and Wu (1983) and Hall (1987b) all recommended the use of fat- or heavy-tailed kernels. One problem with the use of fat-tailed kernels (as we will discuss later) is that they will produce density estimators that are inefficient relative to those produced with the kernels previously discussed.

Hall (1987b) recommends use of the kernel

$$k(\psi) = \varphi e^{-0.5(\log(1+|\psi|))^2} \tag{2.28}$$

as a means to mitigate the problems associated with the selection of the bandwidth in likelihood cross-validation with the use of exponentially decaying tails for the unknown density. Here, φ is a constant of proportionality. If we set $\varphi = [2\Phi(1)\sqrt{2\pi e}]^{-1}$, the kernel will integrate to one. Technical Appendix 2.16 shows that this constant of proportionality is found by integrating the kernel to obtain

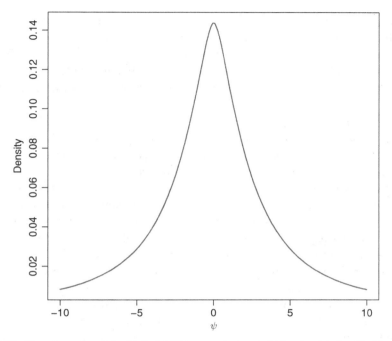

Figure 2.10. Kernel employed by Hall (1987b) to study bandwidth selection for likelihood cross-validation

$\varphi^{-1} = 2\Phi(1)\sqrt{2\pi e}$. Figure 2.10 plots this kernel, which allows bandwidths obtained via LCV to behave properly.

We can calculate the efficiency of this kernel by noting that $\kappa_2 = \int\limits_{-\infty}^{\infty} \psi^2 k(\psi)d\psi =$ 55.39505 and $R(\cdot) = 2e^{1/4}\sqrt{\pi}\,\Phi(1/\sqrt{2})/\varphi^2 = 0.07155708$. Using (2.12), we have Eff$(k) = 1.98482$. We need almost twice as large a sample to achieve the same precision with this kernel in the AMISE sense as we do with the Epanechnikov kernel! Thus, while this kernel allows LCV to work well, it does not effectively use the observations relative to second-order kernels, discussed previously.

2.5.3 Plug-in or cross-validation?

Given the importance of selecting the bandwidth for the performance of the kernel density estimator, the method to obtain the smoothing parameter is undoubtedly important. However, no clear consensus exists on which class (plug-in or cross-validation) to use to obtain bandwidths, nor which method of selection within a class (LSCV vs. LCV, for example) to use. Park and Turlach (1992, 257) remark, "there seems to exist no bandwidth selector which performs consistently well in detecting the modes." We note that even with the discrepancy in opinions regarding the optimal procedure to select bandwidths, in practice there are generally two broadly accepted camps for bandwidth selection. There are those who use LSCV/LCV to obtain bandwidths and those who use direct plug-in methods. A careful inspection of the literature on bandwidth selection procedures tends to paint an unfavorable portrait of data-driven methods, specifically LSCV. For example, Park and Marron (1990, 66) state, "In many simulation studies and real data examples, however, the performance of this method has been often disappointing . . . ," while Jones, Marron, and Sheather (1996, 405) note, "These examples make it clear that first generation (LSCV) methods are not appropriate for widespread use." One of the main criticisms against the use of LSCV in simulation studies is that it displays too much sampling variability in the bandwidths that it selects relative to the true level of smoothing. This has been aptly characterized by Hall, Sheather, Jones, and Marron (1991, 263), who note that "different data sets from the same distribution will all too often give results which are very different."

The progress made on the development of alternative bandwidth selection methods that display superior properties to LSCV throughout the 1990s led some to conclude that LSCV was not an appropriate method to select bandwidths. However, in a seminal paper by Loader (1999), both simulated and theoretical evidence is given to suggest that LSCV is not as inferior as many are led to believe, and that no "optimal" bandwidth selection approach exists for every setting. The easiest way to compare bandwidth selection procedures is to understand how they manifest uncertainty about the underlying density. That is, when presented with data from an unknown distribution, the bandwidth selection procedure, as well as the analyst, has uncertainty about the underlying process. Different bandwidth selection procedures handle this uncertainty in different manners. It is exactly how this uncertainty is dealt with that will allow a deeper understanding of alternative procedures that select the bandwidth.

The key to resolving uncertainty of the bandwidth selectors is to recognize that the bandwidth selector has to decide if the observations passed to it are sufficient to represent a real feature of the underlying process. This is not an easy decision and any selection mechanism will undoubtedly make mistakes from sample to sample. Loader (1999, 417) notes that "variability of cross-validation is not a problem but a symptom of the difficulty of bandwidth selection." That is, alternative bandwidth selectors, such as the class of plug-in methods, deal with this difficulty in the opposite direction: consistently oversmoothing when confronted with data possessing difficult-to-detect features. In practice, the high variability of LSCV is discomfiting when focus resides on global features of the data. For example, in the study of the evolution of the world distribution of cross-country income, a key empirical regularity is the bimodal nature of this distribution. However, as we will see, using LSCV to select the bandwidth produces a density with numerous modes and it is not clear that these modes are "actual" features of the distribution. This raises the question, should we use LSCV to obtain a bandwidth for which to examine this density? It is not that LSCV produces a poor bandwidth, it is the fact that *a priori* assumptions made by the researcher have now drawn doubt on the usefulness of the LSCV selector for a particular data set.

Thus, in simulations, the apparent favoritism towards plug-in methods is how the uncertainty of the different data generating processes are portrayed. If we are to look at the theoretical differences that exist between the different selection methods, it is easy to see two distinct features that actually cause LSCV to appear weak when this is not the case. First, the convergence rate of the LSCV bandwidth towards the optimal bandwidth is $n^{-1/10}$, which is excruciatingly slow, while the Sheather and Jones (1991) plug-in method bandwidth converges at $n^{-4/13}$.

The impression this may give is misleading. Our primary concern is not with the rate of convergence of the bandwidth to its theoretical optimum, but the performance of $\widehat{f}(x)$. If $\widehat{f}(x)$ is an asymptotically inefficient estimator, then it is irrelevant how well the bandwidth selector performs. Loader (1999) points out that the asymptotic analysis of bandwidth selectors hinges on assumptions made regarding the smoothness of the underlying density. Li, Ouyang, and Racine (2006) show optimality of LSCV assuming only two derivatives of the underlying density exist, whereas plug-in selectors require at least four derivatives. As we showed earlier, and also discussed in Li, Ouyang, and Racine (2006), the rate of convergence of $\widehat{f}(x)$ is $n^{-2/5}$ when the bandwidth is proportional to $n^{-1/5}$. However, if we assume that $f(x)$ has four derivatives, then the best possible estimator converges at the $n^{-4/9}$ rate. So even with an asymptotically optimal bandwidth (in terms of estimating the bandwidth), the density estimator is asymptotically inefficient in the sense that it is not converging at the optimal rate, even though it is still consistent.

Loader (1999) notes that while it may not seem like a big difference between $n^{-4/9}$ and $n^{-2/5}$, using a higher-order kernel would provide an estimator that achieves this rate. By allowing the plug-in method to use (assume) additional smoothness, but not the LSCV selector, we are penalizing the LSCV selector for the deficiencies of the plug-in estimator. That is, the plug-in and the LSCV selector are not being compared under the same assumptions and therefore the superior performance of plug-in methods in an asymptotic sense is because these methods require additional assumptions which *should* make them perform better.

We end this section by noting that there is no "best" bandwidth selector and you should use caution when deciding between alternative selection mechanisms. It is important to not blindly rely on a single bandwidth selection procedure in all settings and expect that the bandwidth produced will automatically be optimal. Recalling that plug-in methods reflect uncertainty about the underlying features of the density via oversmoothing, if you prefer smoother estimates then, in the words of Loader (1999, 435), "it is hardly fair to praise plug-in methods (and criticize LSCV), since these methods target AMISE and not smoothness of the estimate. If smoother estimates are preferred, then the AMISE criterion should be acknowledged as inadequate and bandwidth selectors directed towards a more appropriate criterion."

2.6 Density derivatives

In certain settings, interest lies not with the density itself, but with some derivative of the density. For example, our discussion on the optimal bandwidth of the kernel density estimator involving AMISE in (2.11) contained the unknown quantity $R(f^{(2)})$. On the other hand, Silverman's (1978) test graph method requires estimation of the second derivative, whereas Silverman's (1982) modality test and Hall and Simar's (2002) unknown boundary estimation require estimation of the first derivative of the density. Thus, you might consider obtaining the optimal unknown bandwidth by replacing this quantity with an estimator, which requires estimation of the second-order derivative of the unknown density.

A natural estimator of the rth order derivative of the density is the corresponding rth derivative of our initial density estimator given in (2.6):

$$\widehat{f}^{(r)}(x) = \frac{d^r}{dx^r} \widehat{f}(x) = \frac{1}{nh^{r+1}} \sum_{i=1}^{n} k^{(r)} \left(\frac{x_i - x}{h} \right). \tag{2.29}$$

For this estimator to exist, $k^{(r)}(x)$ must exist and not be zero. Additionally, because we typically assume that the rth derivative of our density is continuously differentiable, we also require that the $(r + 1)$th derivative is nonzero everywhere. Thus if $r = 2$, we could not use this definition if we wished to use the Epanechnikov kernel ($k_1(x)$) since its second derivative is a constant (implying that it is not continuously differentiable on its support). As Muller (1984, 768) notes, "Using these kernels, estimated curves are not differentiable and indeed exhibit nasty jumps in practical applications especially if the derivatives are estimated and the number of observations is small."

Figure 2.11 plots the kernel density estimator using the Epanenchnikov kernel with rule-of-thumb bandwidth for a random sample of $n = 500$ from the $Beta(4, 4)$ density along with the estimated first derivative using both the original rule-of-thumb bandwidth (see Table 3.3) as well as the corresponding rule-of-thumb bandwidth for a density derivative (see Table 2.4). We can see that while the density estimate itself

Table 2.4. *Rule-of-thumb constants for second-order kernels used for density derivative estimation*

		\multicolumn{4}{c}{r}			
		1	2	3	4
	1	2.1505			
	2	2.4912	2.4321		
s	3	2.8322	2.7012	2.6911	
	4	3.1421	2.9958	2.9189	2.9312
	5	3.4257	3.2716	3.1837	3.1317
	ϕ	0.9686	0.9397	0.9289	0.9251

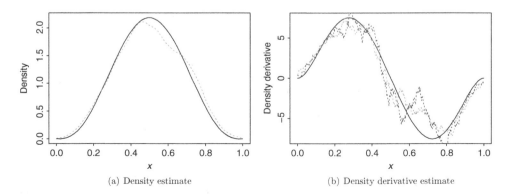

(a) Density estimate   (b) Density derivative estimate

Figure 2.11. Kernel density estimate for $Beta(4, 4)$ density and its first derivative

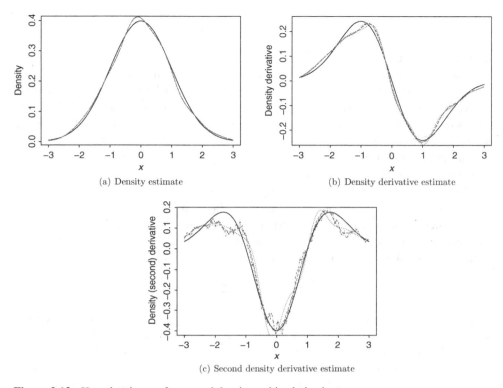

(a) Density estimate   (b) Density derivative estimate

(c) Second density derivative estimate

Figure 2.12. Kernel estimates for normal density and its derivatives

is smooth and reasonably close to the underlying Beta density, both sets of derivative estimates are very rough. This occurs because the first derivative of the Epanechnikov kernel is not continuously differentiable. Recall that it has discontinuities on both boundaries.

In Figure 2.12, we present kernel density estimates along with estimates of the first and second derivatives for a standard normal density. We use a sample of size $n = 2500$ and all four of the density estimates use their corresponding Silverman rule-of-thumb bandwidths. The density plots are presented in panel (a). Notice that with this large sample we do a good job of uncovering the shape of the density. However, progressing from panel (b) to (c), we see that as the order of the derivative increases, our accuracy decreases. When we study the AMISE of density estimators, we will see that, in general, larger samples are needed to achieve the same level of accuracy as that of the density estimator's AMISE.

2.6.1 Bias and variance

Following the same setup as earlier, we can study the bias and variance of our density derivative estimator in (2.29). Technical Appendix 2.17 shows that the bias of our derivative estimator is

$$\text{Bias}[\widehat{f}^{(r)}(x)] \approx \frac{h^2}{2} f^{(r+2)}(x)\kappa_2(k).$$

Studying this bias reveals an interesting feature: the bias is of the same order and identical up to scale with the bias of our initial kernel density estimator in (2.8). That is, the only difference in the bias of the kernel density estimator and that of the rth derivative is the underlying design; $f^{(2)}(x)$ drives the bias of $\widehat{f}(x)$, whereas $f^{(r+2)}(x)$ drives the bias of $\widehat{f}^{(r)}(x)$. In principle, it is no harder to estimate the rth derivative of a density as it is to estimate the density itself with respect to bias. Depending on the design and the point of interest, it may be the case that $|f^{(r+2)}(x)| \leq |f^{(2)}(x)|$, and hence we may be able to reduce the bias relative to that in (2.8).

However, even with the prospect that the rth derivative can be estimated as accurately (in terms of bias) as the initial density, this is not the case when we consider the variance of our kernel density derivative. Following our earlier discussion of the variance of the kernel density estimator, we show in Technical Appendix 2.18 that the variance of our derivative estimator (recalling that our data are assumed to be *iid*) is

$$\text{Var}\left[\widehat{f}^{(r)}(x)\right] \approx \frac{f(x)R(k^{(r)})}{nh^{1+2r}},$$

where $\approx$ shows up because of a second-order Taylor expansion. We can see the difficulty in estimating a derivative of a density that was obscured by looking at the bias. The density derivative estimator has a much larger loss of precision than the density estimator itself. With the density estimator, we had terms of order $(nh)^{-1}$, whereas in the rth derivative setting we have terms of order $n^{-1}h^{(-1+2r)}$, which are much larger.

As can be expected, the AMSE and AMISE will also be of larger order. We have

$$\text{AMSE} \approx \frac{h^4}{4} f^{(r+2)}(x)^2\kappa_2^2(k) + \frac{f(x)R(k^{(r)})}{nh^{1+2r}},$$

$$\text{AMISE} \approx \frac{h^4}{4} R(f^{(r+2)})\kappa_2^2(k) + \frac{R(k^{(r)})}{nh^{1+2r}}.$$

The larger magnitudes of the AMSE and AMISE, as compared to (2.10) and (2.11), suggest that their rates of convergence will be slower than that for general density estimation. This is intuitive. The precision of a density's derivatives should be harder to estimate than the density itself, since no available information on the derivatives exists. We at least have observations that stem from a density, but these observations carry less information regarding derivatives. Moreover, because we do not precisely estimate our density to begin with, these imprecisions carry over to the derivatives, which magnify as we increase the order of the derivative we are interested in estimating.

2.6.2 Bandwidth selection

Technical Appendix 2.19 shows that the asymptotically optimal bandwidth for estimating the rth order density derivative is

$$h_{\text{opt}} = \left[\frac{(1+2r)R(k^{(r)})}{R(f^{(r+2)})\kappa_2^2(k)}\right]^{1/(5+2r)} n^{-1/(5+2r)}.$$

This formulation of the optimal bandwidth is the derivative equivalent to our earlier discussion that focused on the unknown density ($r = 0$) given in (2.14). There we had that the bandwidth decreased to zero at a rate proportional to $n^{-1/5}$. Focusing attention on the rth derivative, we have that our bandwidth converges slower than the $1/5$ rate we had for the density case. For example, for the first derivative ($r = 1$) our rate is $1/7$. Moreover, we see that the higher the derivative of interest, the slower the rate. The reason for the slower decay is that the variance of the kernel density derivative estimator increases as the derivative order increases so we slow the rate of decay of our bandwidth to compensate for this. Since the order of the bias is unaffected by the order of the derivative, we see that more attention is now paid to the variance when investigating the bias–variance trade-off. However, if we use a bandwidth that decays more slowly than the $1/5$ rate, then our bias will actually decay more slowly than the bias of the standard kernel density estimator using an optimal bandwidth because of the difference in rates.

Using this bandwidth, the same technical appendix shows that the asymptotically optimal AMISE is

$$\text{AMISE}_{\text{opt}} \approx \frac{5 + 2r}{4} \left[R(k^{(r)})^4 \left(\frac{\kappa_2^2(k) R\left(f^{(r+2)}\right)}{(1 + 2r)} \right)^{(1+2r)} \right]^{1/(5+2r)} n^{-4/(5+2r)},$$

and when $r = 0$, we have the result in (2.15).

We can obtain a rule-of-thumb bandwidth here as well. Using known results on the roughness of the normal family, we can operationalize our rule-of-thumb bandwidth, assuming that our density is normal with scale σ. We have

$$
\begin{aligned}
h_{\text{rot},r} &= \left[\frac{(1 + 2r)2^{5+2r}\sqrt{\pi}(r + 2)! R(k^{(r)})}{\kappa_2^2(k)(2r + 4)!\widehat{\sigma}^{-(5+2r)}} \right]^{1/(5+2r)} n^{-1/(5+2r)} \\
&= 2\widehat{\sigma} \left[\frac{(1 + 2r)\sqrt{\pi}(r + 2)! R(k^{(r)})}{\kappa_2^2(k)(2r + 4)!} \right]^{1/(5+2r)} n^{-1/(5+2r)} \\
&= c_r(k)\widehat{\sigma} n^{-1/(5+2r)}.
\end{aligned}
$$

The scale factor $c_r(k)$, which we now denote here with a subscript for the rth derivative and note that it is a function of the kernel chosen, are collected in Table 2.4 for density derivatives up to order four for the appropriate kernels.

We notice from this table that as r increases, the rule-of-thumb constant decreases, albeit at a diminishing rate. The Gaussian kernel has scale factors that are roughly equal to unity for derivative orders up to 4, whereas the polynomial kernels have scale factors that are much larger. A separate point to emphasize is that as r increases, we have fewer scale factors. This is, of course, because s not only gives the type of kernel, but it also determines the number of derivatives the kernel possesses.

2.6.3 Relative efficiency

We can determine the relative efficiency of any two kernels for estimating a density derivative much the same way we did for the density itself. To begin, we have to determine the optimal kernel for estimating the rth derivative of our unknown density. Muller (1984) has shown that the most efficient kernel can be found by solving for the minimum of $R(k^{(r)})$, subject to the conditions $\kappa_0 = 1$, $\kappa_1 = 0$, and $\kappa_2 < \infty$. The functional solution is the $s = (r + 1)$th kernel from our polynomial class in (2.7). Thus, if you were estimating the first derivative ($r = 1$) of the density (say, to examine modality), then a biweight kernel ($s = 2$) would be optimal, whereas if you were focusing on the second derivative (say, for estimating $R(f^{(2)})$), then the triweight kernel would be optimal, and so on.

Similar to (2.12), the relative efficiency of a kernel, as derived in Technical Appendix 2.20, is

$$\text{Eff}(k_\varrho, r) = \frac{R(k_\varrho^{(r)})}{R(k_{r+1}^{(r)})} \left(\frac{\kappa_2^2(k_\varrho)}{\kappa_2^2(k_{r+1})} \right)^{(1+2r)/4}. \tag{2.30}$$

Tables 2.5 and 2.6 list the kernel efficiency for the estimation of derivatives for $r = 1, 2, 3, 4$ and the corresponding roughness of the kernel derivative. Note that $R\left(k_\phi^{(r)}\right) = \frac{(2r-1)!!}{2^{r+1}\sqrt{\pi}}$. We see that unlike the standard density estimation case, the Gaussian kernel is much more inefficient when it comes to estimating derivatives of the density.

2.7 Application

Here we see our first (growth) application of nonparametric methods in practice. Specifically, we take data from the Penn World Table (PWT), Version 7.0, to construct estimates of the density of gross domestic product (GDP) per worker (RGDPWOK). The output is measured in 2005 international dollars. We could think of many different variables to plot, but the shape of the cross-country distribution of GDP per worker is

Table 2.5. *Efficiency for second-order kernels used for density derivative estimation (where* s *refers to the type of kernel and* r *refers to the order of the derivative*

		\multicolumn{4}{c}{r}			
		1	2	3	4
	1	1.1596			
	2	1.0000	1.2050		
s	3	1.0185	1.0000	1.2335	
	4	1.0437	1.0290	1.0000	1.2531
	5	1.0651	1.0719	1.0374	1.0000
	ϕ	1.2191	1.4689	1.8119	2.2706

Table 2.6. *Roughness of rth derivative for second-order kernels used for density-derivative estimation*

		r		
	1	2	3	4
1	3/2			
2	15/7	45/2		
s 3	35/11	35	1575/2	
4	630/143	8505/143	14175/11	99225/2
5	24255/4199	20790/221	31185/13	1091475/13
ϕ	$1/4\sqrt{\pi}$	$3/8\sqrt{\pi}$	$15/16\sqrt{\pi}$	$105/32\sqrt{\pi}$

arguably the most interesting application of nonparametric density estimation, and one of the most common, in the study of economic growth/output. We note here that while a univariate density is interesting, only a few results can be teased out of the data, as opposed to estimating in the presence of multivariate data.

It was Quah (1993) who first recognized that the cross-country distribution switched from a unimodal to a bimodal distribution over the period 1960–1990 (noting that his work usually emphasized a tendency to bimodality implied by the ergodic distribution of his estimated transition matrices). Since this influential study, many authors have attempted to examine this phenomenon using a host of nonparametric (as well as parametric) methods. As you have seen earlier in this chapter, the shape of the density depends upon the kernel function and the bandwidth employed. However, the latter matters much more than the former.

What we propose to do here is to informally look at the shape of cross-country GDP per worker over a variety of methods. The goal is to both show how the estimators perform in practice as well as attempt to uncover whether or not – and if so, when – the density of GDP per worker switches from being unimodal to being multimodal. While this phenomenon has been studied in the literature, no article that we are aware of has as much coverage in terms of countries and/or years. Further, many of these bandwidths and kernels employed have not been examined in the literature. Therefore, this can be thought of as the most comprehensive study of the underlying shape of the cross-country distribution of GDP per worker to date. That being said, all of this analysis is informal. We are simply plotting the shape of the density and attempting to make inferences on the number of modes visually. This is far from scientific. In practice, we need to determine the number of modes via statistical tests. We will return to this point in Chapter 4.

2.7.1 Histograms

To begin, reconsider our crude estimator of a density: a histogram. There is no underlying assumption on the data; all we choose here is the binwidth. However, as we discussed with bandwidth estimation, the choice of binwidth is of the utmost importance. That being said, there is little discussion on the choice of the optimal binwidth. A binwidth that is too small will leave a histogram that is too choppy and a bindwidth that is too large will hide underlying features of the density.

Therefore, we generically consider two separate binwidths to examine the cross-country density of real GDP per worker. We consider four years, each spaced fifteen years apart: 1960, 1975, 1990, and 2005. Figure 2.13, panel (a), with 20 equally spaced bins, provides histograms of RGDPWOK (normalized by its mean) for the years 1960, 1975, 1990, and 2005 for 117 countries (note that we only have 96 countries for 1960) that have data for these four years. What we see in each figure is that there is a large mass near zero and a long tail. The skewness is obvious, even in the histogram. What is not obvious from any of the figures is whether or not the density is multimodal. We would argue that there appears to be a single mode (with a long tail) in 1960 and perhaps two modes in 1975, 1990, and 2005. However, many of you may have markedly different opinions on the number of modes present in this figure.

In panel (b), we use 50 bins to construct each histogram. The expectation should be that we will see more of the underlying features, but that some of these features may be spurious if the binwidth is now too small. Our assessment of the histograms is that the story we see above does not change. There appears to be a single mode with a long tail in 1960 and each of the other years appears to have a second mode. In other words, the results here appear to support Quah (1993). However, we know that this estimator is crude and we move to kernel methods.

2.7.2 Kernel densities

Here we examine second-order kernel density estimates of cross-country GDP per worker. We begin with simple rule-of-thumb bandwidths to show their performance, but the resulting densities are clearly not Gaussian. We then examine them under various data-driven bandwidth selection methods. While reading this section, you should pay attention to the number of bumps in the estimates and how they arise with each method. We note here that choice of bandwidth estimation makes a major difference, whereas the kernel used does not have the same effect.

Rule-of-thumb bandwidths
In Figure 2.14, we plot kernel density estimates of cross-country GDP per worker. We plot kernel density estimates using appropriately constructed Silverman rule-of-thumb constants for the Epanechnikov, biweight, triweight, and Gaussian kernels for the years 1960, 1975, 1990, and 2005. The first point to notice is that the distributions are clearly not Gaussian. The second point to note is that the choice of kernel does not appear to be important here. The main difference is that the Gaussian kernel tends to bump the mode up relative to the other kernels, with the Epanenchnikov kernel having the shortest mode. However, the difference is likely not statistically significant (we discuss testing in Chapter 4). The third point to note is the prevalence of modes in the density estimates. There appears to be a shoulder in 1960, but 1975, 1990, and 2005 appear to have a second (shorter) mode. The results here appear to coincide with Quah (1993).

To show this evolution over time, Figure 2.15 plots kernel density estimates using appropriately constructed Silverman rule-of-thumb scale factors for the Epanechnikov

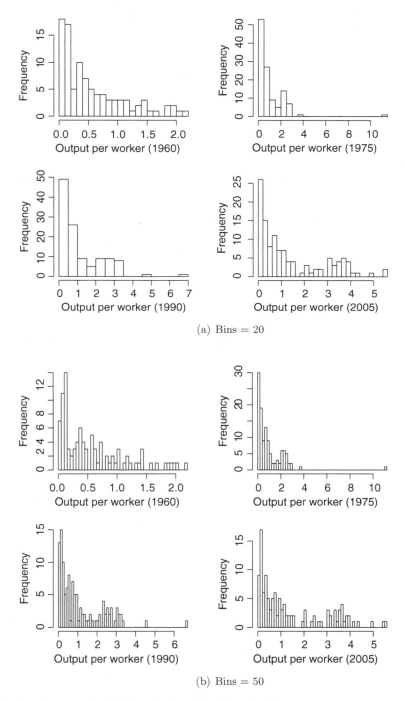

Figure 2.13. Histograms for RGDPWOK from PWT, Version 7.0

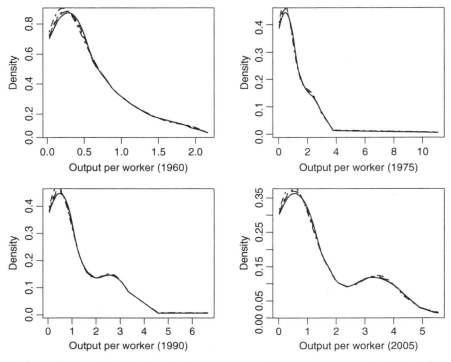

Figure 2.14. Kernel density estimates for RGDPWOK from PWT, Version 7.0 using rule-of-thumb bandwidths

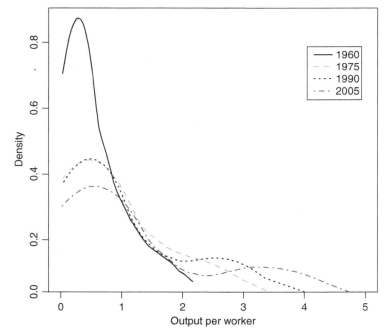

Figure 2.15. Comparison of kernel density estimates across years for RGDPWOK from PWT, Version 7.0 using rule-of-thumb bandwidths (Epanechnikov kernel)

kernels for the years 1960, 1975, 1990, and 2005. We see that a distinct second mode emerges around 1975. This mode appears to become more prevalent over time as some intermediate countries (e.g., the Asian Tigers) have moved towards the richer mode. Henderson, Parmeter, and Russell (2008) discuss mode-jumping over the period 1960–2000 using the trough of the density (estimated by using rule-of-thumb bandwidths) to determine which countries are in the upper and lower modes. We should also note that, when weighting observations by the relative population of the countries, Henderson, Parmeter, and Russell (2008) find the presence of a second mode in 1960. That said, the second mode in 1960 is mostly driven by the presence of a single, rich, highly populated country: the United States.

Data-driven bandwidth

We have argued that rule-of-thumb bandwidths only possess optimal properties when the assumed underlying density holds true. In general, this should not be expected, and we believe that the distribution of output per worker is skewed. Therefore it seems natural to consider data-driven bandwidth methods. Figure 2.16 plots kernel density estimates using data-driven bandwidth selection (LSCV and LCV) for the Epanechnikov and Gaussian kernels for the years 1960, 1975, 1990, and 2005. We see that the LCV bandwidths provide somewhat reasonable portrayals (subject to *a priori* expectations) while the LSCV bandwidths are too small to match previous expectations of

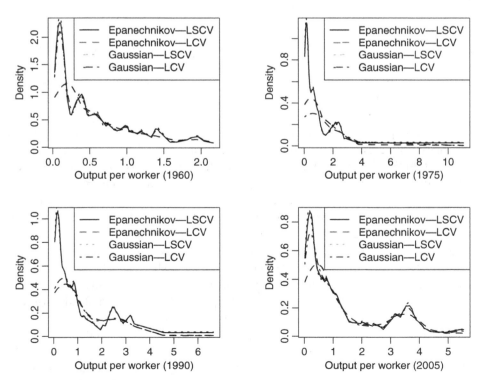

Figure 2.16. Kernel density estimates for RGDPWOK from PWT, Version 7.0 using LCV and LSCV (Epanechnikov and Gaussian second-order kernels)

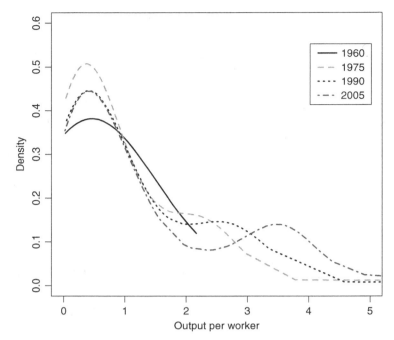

Figure 2.17. Comparison of kernel density estimates across years for RGDPWOK from PWT, Version 7.0 using direct plug-in approach (Gaussian kernel)

the features of the estimated density. This result shows why many authors shy away from LSCV. The density here appears to be more volatile than most of us are willing to believe. The number of modes in each figure is at or above two digits. LCV is less volatile, but it also shows numerous modes in each panel of Figure 2.16. It is unclear whether or not the figures here are more or less helpful than the histograms.

The (one-step) direct plug-in approach is used in Figure 2.17. Here we plot the kernel density estimates using a second-order Gaussian kernel for the years 1960, 1975, 1990, and 2005. The figure is much less volatile than what we saw with LSCV and LCV (likely resulting from the single-step procedure). We also tried a two-step procedure (unreported) and found multiple modes in each year. This puts us in a dilemma. Do we go with the visually appealing rule-of-thumb bandwidths or do we resort to the data-driven methods? It is likely that the rule-of-thumb measures oversmooth the data, but it is also likely the case that the data-driven methods undersmooth the data. We assume that the resulting true density perhaps lies somewhere in between.

To further show the difference between methods, Figure 2.18 plots kernel density estimates using bandwidths obtained from the DPI, LSCV, LCV, and rule-of-thumb for a second-order Gaussian kernel for the year 2005. We see that the bandwidths obtained via LCV, DPI, and ROT all suggest a distinct second mode, whereas the LSCV bandwidth produces a density estimate that is noisy. Although we see some differences, each of the methods appears to suggest that there is a second mode present in the 2005 density. If the goal is to determine whether or not there exists a second mode, as Quah (1993) stressed, then each of these methods appears to show this is true

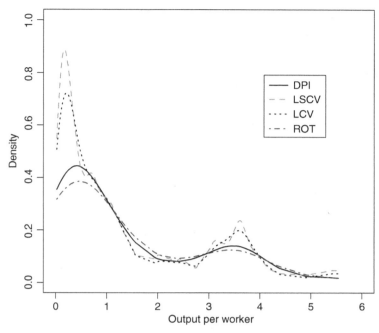

Figure 2.18. Kernel density estimates for RGDPWOK from PWT, Version 7.0 using various bandwidth selection rules (2005)

in 2005 (at least visually). However, if the goal is accuracy of the density estimator, then it is unclear which bandwidth selector achieves this goal. While one bandwidth selector likely is closest to the true underlying density, it need not be the case that this holds true for all densities.

Given this result, and what else we have seen in this chapter, here we emphasize the importance of bandwidth selection methods, but also caution you to question the results that other authors present. Simply using the generic kernel density estimator provided from a statistical software package is probably insufficient. At the very least, you should explicitly state which kernel you are using and which bandwidth method you use to select the smoothing parameter. We also want to emphasize here that visual interpretation should be taken with a large rain of salt. If you have 100 different people examine this figure, we assume you will get 100 different opinions as to its shape. In practice we suggest that you use formal statistical tests, along with graphical evidence, to make inferential statements about your empirical densities.

3

Multivariate density estimation

In traditional applied econometric settings, we typically have access to several variables. For example, in our growth example presented in Chapter 2, not only would a typical analysis have access to output per worker, but also physical and human capital stocks, measures of corruption, natural resource levels, institutional quality, and perhaps many other variables. In this sense, univariate density exploration is limited. For example, suppose you view a univariate density estimate and find bimodality to be a plausible feature. Is this bimodality inherent to the variable of interest, or is there some connection with a secondary variable? Jones, Marron, and Sheather (1996) find exactly this pattern in their research. They have a visually bimodal univariate density (202 observations) of lean body mass. Subsequent analysis shows that the bimodal nature of this density is linked to the gender of the individual. By splitting the data into 100 men and 102 women, each individual density is strongly unimodal. Thus, generically, the lean body mass measurements data was not bimodal, it was combining two different subpopulations into what was believed to be a homogeneous population.

To aptly characterize these types of issues, multivariate nonparametric methods need to be deployed. The natural extension of the univariate kernel density estimator developed in Chapter 2 is the multivariate kernel density estimator. This estimator looks and operates similarly to the univariate estimator and so the intuition built in Chapter 2 will prove useful here. However, there are some conceptual issues. How do we conceive of a kernel function in multiple dimensions? Should we have a bandwidth for each dimension or a single bandwidth which smooths all variables equally? What happens to the statistical properties of our estimator if we incorporate more variables into our density?

In this chapter, we outline both joint and conditional density estimation. We discuss asymptotic properties as well as bandwidth selection and the presence of irrelevant variables. We pay special attention to a problem which arises in multivariate estimation – the curse of dimensionality. We end the chapter by looking at distributions of the Solow (1956) variables (output per worker along with physical and human capital).

3.1 Joint densities

As a basic example of constructing a multivariate kernel density estimator, consider the bivariate normal mixture represented by equal parts of a bivariate normal with mean vector $(1, 1)$ and variance–covariance matrix $\mathrm{diag}(1, 1)$ (where $\mathrm{diag}()$

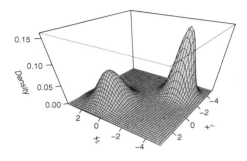

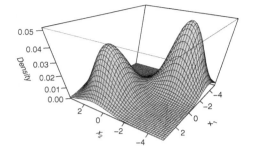

(a) True bivariate normal mixture

(b) Bivariate kernel density estimator with bandwidth vector $\mathbf{h} = (1,1)$ using a normal product kernel

Figure 3.1. Bivariate normal mixture

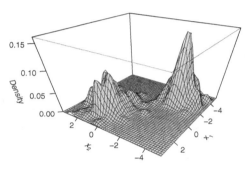

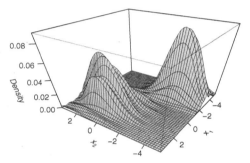

(a) Bivariate kernel density estimator with bandwidth vector $\mathbf{h} = (0.25, 0.25)$ using a normal product kernel

(b) Bivariate kernel density estimator with bandwidth vector $\mathbf{h} = (1, 0.15)$ using a normal product kernel

Figure 3.2. Bivariate normal mixture

represents a diagonal matrix) and bivariate normal with mean vector $(-3, -3)$ and variance–covariance matrix diag$(0.5, 0.5)$. This density is illustrated in the first panel of Figure 3.1. We see that the density is bimodal with distinctly separated modes. Now, if we were to construct an estimate of this using a multivariate kernel density estimator (to be described shortly), we see that our impression of the underlying density changes as we change the smoothness. Figures 3.1 and 3.2 use different sets of bandwidth vectors for this purpose.

The second panel of Figure 3.1 uses large bandwidths (with respect to the underlying variance–covariance matrices). We see that we nearly capture the exact features of the underlying bivariate mixture normal. As we reduce the bandwidths by a factor of 4 (Figure 3.2a), we still capture the overarching features, such as bimodality and the right mode being slimmer than the left mode, but we have introduced more noise into the subtle features.

Figure 3.2b does not use identical bandwidths inside the bivariate kernel density estimator (and there is no requirement to do so). We note that by using a bandwidth which may be viewed as "small" in one direction, we still obscure certain stylistic features of the bivariate density. More importantly, the bandwidth used for a specific dimension can have consequences on what we uncover in alternative dimensions.

Smoothing in higher-dimensional spaces is done through a multivariate kernel. As with the traditional univariate kernel, a multivariate kernel is taken as a multivariate probability density function that assigns nonnegative weights to points nearby via a vector of bandwidths. The reason we use a vector of bandwidths as opposed to a singular bandwidth is that having different levels of smoothness in different dimensions offers a more general setting and it also recognizes that the individual variables may have different scales. In applied work the most common forms of a multivariate kernel are either a full-fledged kernel which is not multiplicatively separable in its elements or the product kernel. If we have a q vector of data, $\mathbf{x} = \{x_1, x_2, \ldots, x_q\}$, then a full-fledged multivariate kernel is any function $K(\mathbf{x})$ on $\mathbb{R}^q \to \mathbb{R}$ such that

$$K(\mathbf{x}) \geq 0, \quad \forall \mathbf{x} \in \mathbb{R}^q, \quad \text{and} \quad \int_{\mathbb{R}^q} K(\mathbf{x})d\mathbf{x} = 1.$$

A simple kernel which satisfies this requirement and is easy to construct is the product kernel, defined as

$$K_h(\mathbf{x}_i, \mathbf{x}) = \prod_{d=1}^{q} k\left(\frac{x_{id} - x_d}{h_d}\right).$$

In this case, $k(\cdot)$ could be selected as any of the univariate kernels discussed in Chapter 2.

Our multivariate kernel density estimator is then constructed as

$$\widehat{f}(\mathbf{x}) = (n|\mathbf{h}|)^{-1} \sum_{i=1}^{n} K(|\mathbf{h}|^{-1}(\mathbf{x}_i - \mathbf{x})), \tag{3.1}$$

where $|\mathbf{h}| = h_1 h_2 \cdots h_q$ and $|\mathbf{h}|^{-1}$ is taken to imply element wise inversion. If we use the product kernel, our multivariate kernel density estimator becomes

$$\widehat{f}(\mathbf{x}) = (n|\mathbf{h}|)^{-1} \sum_{i=1}^{n} K_h(\mathbf{x}_i, \mathbf{x}). \tag{3.2}$$

There is no consensus for selection of the appropriate multivariate kernel, either for a full-fledged multivariate density function or the product kernel (which is itself a multivariate density function). However, the product kernel is the dominant choice in the applied literature.

The product kernel basically constructs the multivariate kernel, assuming independence among each covariate. Clearly this would be a tenuous assumption to make in general. However, this "assumption" of independence used to construct the kernel does not transfer over to the density estimator. That is, if we use a product kernel in the construction of the unknown multivariate density, dependence may still be present in the density estimator. The reason for this is the averaging that is conducted over the n sample points. The perceived naïvety of using a product kernel with data that may possess dependence is purely illusory.

Before developing our intuition for the bias, variance, and AMSE of the multivariate kernel density estimator, we focus on the concept of smoothing in higher dimensions.

Just as in the univariate case, our estimator is constructed by leveraging information from *nearby* points, with "nearness" indicated by the bandwidth. As opposed to the univariate setting where weighting is done over the real line, in higher dimensions, weighting is done over the q-dimensional manifold where the data resides. If we use a uniform kernel, in the univariate case, we construct weights based on points' distance from the center of the box. In two dimensions, these weights are constructed by basing location relative to the cube whose center is the point of interest. With kernels that take more flexible shapes, the areas receiving weight appear more ellipsoidal in nature (though other shapes are certainly possible if we use kernels outside of those discussed in Chapter 2).

3.2 Bias, variance, and AMISE

To better understand the statistical properties of our multivariate kernel density estimator, we first place several assumptions on our multivariate kernel. Recall from Chapter 2 that two key aspects of the kernel that influence the statistical properties of the kernel density estimator were the order of the kernel (specifically, the second moment) and the difficulty factor of the kernel. As we will see, these two properties are where the multivariate kernel exerts influence on the statistical properties of the multivariate kernel density estimator. A multivariate second-order kernel is defined as

$$\kappa_0(K) = \int_{\mathbb{R}^q} K(\mathbf{x}) d\mathbf{x} = 1$$

$$\kappa_1(K) = \int_{\mathbb{R}^q} \mathbf{x} K(\mathbf{x}) d\mathbf{x} = 0$$

$$\kappa_2(K) = \int_{\mathbb{R}^q} \mathbf{x}\mathbf{x}' K(\mathbf{x}) d\mathbf{x} < \infty.$$

With a product kernel we have

$$\kappa_2(K) = \int_{\mathbb{R}^q} \mathbf{x}\mathbf{x}' K(\mathbf{x}) d\mathbf{x} = \kappa_2(k) I,$$

where $\prime$ denotes transposition of a matrix.

For the product kernel, if we use second-order kernels for each dimension of the data, then the product kernel will also be a multivariate second-order kernel. The difficulty factor of the multivariate kernel is defined as

$$R(K) = \int_{\mathbb{R}^q} K(\mathbf{x})^2 d\mathbf{x},$$

which for the product kernel is $R(K) = R(k)^q$, assuming the identical kernel is used in each direction (which is common). With this notation in hand, we are now ready to investigate the asymptotic bias, variance, and AMSE of our multivariate kernel density estimator.

For the derivations that follow, we will assume that a product kernel is used for the multivariate kernel. Technical Appendix 3.1 derives the bias of the multivariate kernel density estimator to be

$$\text{Bias}\left[\widehat{f}(\mathbf{x})\right] \approx \frac{\kappa_2(k)}{2} \sum_{d=1}^{q} \frac{\partial^2 f(\mathbf{x})}{\partial x_d^2} h_d^2. \tag{3.3}$$

The intuition here is nearly identical to that in the univariate case. First, the bias is not directly influenced by the sample size, only indirectly via the vector of bandwidths linked to the sample size. Second, the kernel influences the bias through its variance. Third, the second partial derivatives of the underlying density impacts the bias. As the density becomes more dispersed around $\mathbf{x}$ (i.e., greater fluctuations in the density), the second partial derivatives are higher and this leads to more uncertainty of the shape of the density, producing a larger bias. Notice that decreasing *all* of the bandwidths will reduce the pointwise bias.

In Technical Appendix 3.2, it is shown that the variance of the multivariate kernel density estimator is

$$\text{Var}\left[\widehat{f}(\mathbf{x})\right] \approx \frac{f(\mathbf{x})R(k)^q}{n|\mathbf{h}|}. \tag{3.4}$$

As with the variance of the univariate density estimator, we have that as the sample size increases, the variance of the multivariate kernel density estimator decreases. Outside of this direct dependence on the sample size, the bandwidths also play a role in reducing the variance of our estimator. As the bandwidths increase, this leads to smoother estimates, resulting in lower pointwise variance. However, this reduction in the variance comes at the expense of increased bias. We need the bandwidths to all shrink to zero to eliminate the pointwise bias, thus again illustrating the bias–variance tradeoff that exists. We also see that the kernel influences the variance through its difficulty factor and the density itself places a design-dependent component on the variance of the multivariate kernel density estimator. Note that the difficulty factor of the kernel is symmetric in all dimensions given the use of a product kernel with identical univariate kernels.

As with the univariate setting, constructing a measure that balances the trade-off between bias and variance will allow insights into the performance of the multivariate kernel density estimator and offers opportunities for investigating selection of bandwidths. The AMSE of the multivariate kernel density estimator is constructed by adding together the squared bias and the variance. This results in

$$\text{AMSE}\left[\widehat{f}(\mathbf{x})\right] \approx \frac{\kappa_2^2(k)}{4}\left[\sum_{d=1}^{q} \frac{\partial^2 f(\mathbf{x})}{\partial x_d^2} h_d^2\right]^2 + \frac{f(\mathbf{x})R(k)^q}{n|\mathbf{h}|}. \tag{3.5}$$

As before, we see that the AMSE is dependent upon the design point. To mitigate the effects of a particular point, the AMISE provides a global measure of performance of the multivariate kernel density estimator. This is found by integrating AMSE over all support points of $\mathbf{x}$. Technical Appendix 3.3 shows that this is

$$\text{AMISE}\left[\widehat{f}(\mathbf{x})\right] \approx \frac{\kappa_2^2(k)}{4} \int_{\mathbb{R}^q} \left[\sum_{d=1}^{q} \frac{\partial^2 f(\mathbf{x})}{\partial x_d^2} h_d^2\right]^2 d\mathbf{x} + \frac{R(k)^q}{n|\mathbf{h}|}. \qquad (3.6)$$

Given that AMISE depends on the kernel only through $\kappa_2^2(k)$ and $R(k)$, the optimal kernel for multivariate density estimation will be exactly the same as for the univariate density estimator, the Epanechnikov kernel. A closed-form solution for each of the q bandwidths which minimize AMISE does not exist. However, what we can see starkly is that the optimal bandwidths must balance the squared bias (the h_d^4 component) against the variance (the $n|\mathbf{h}|$ component). This gives us some insight that the optimal bandwidths must be of the order $h_{\text{opt}} \sim n^{-1/(4+q)}$. We will discuss various alternatives to selecting optimal bandwidths in Section 3.4. With bandwidths of this order, we have that as $n \to \infty$, $h_d \to 0\ \forall d$, and $n|\mathbf{h}| \to \infty$, guaranteeing that both the integrated squared bias component and the integrated variance component decay to zero. Moreover, looking at the rate of decay of the bandwidths, $n^{-1/(4+q)}$, we see that as the dimensionality increases, the bandwidths proceed more slowly towards 0. This is commonly referred to as the curse of dimensionality.

3.3 The curse of dimensionality

The curse of dimensionality is credited to Richard Bellman, who referred to the difficulty of exhaustive enumeration over all grid points in high dimensions in optimization problems. In nonparametric estimation, the curse refers to the difficulty in detecting the structure of high-dimensional data generating processes (DGPs) without excessive parametric assumptions. The curse of dimensionality must be recognized as a drawback of nonparametric estimation methods, yet it must be judged against the likely alternative, a misspecified parametric model, which has no natural connection to the dimensionality of the problem, but will produce estimates that do not improve in accuracy as the sample size increases. As the econometrician Carlos Martins-Filho quips, "Is it better to be mostly right or precisely wrong?"

Figure 3.3 helps to illustrate the curse of dimensionality. Here we provide a scatterplot of ten data points generated from a uniform distribution ($\mathcal{U}[0, 1]$) in one dimension and then using those points, append a second draw of ten data points, again generated from a uniform distribution ($\mathcal{U}[0, 1]$). The univariate points appear as a + while the bivariate points appear as ∘. Consider the points A and B in the plot. The distance between these points is simply the difference in their x-coordinates. In two dimensions, the distance between the new points, A' and B', increases. While the x_1-coordinate distance remains the same, we have added another dimension on which they differ, and this must increase the distance between them (or at the very least keep the distance the same). The point C' (the filled circle in the figure) represents the latter scenario. The distance between C' and B' represents the one-dimensional distance between A and B, while the distance between C' and A' represents the difference between A' and B' captured by the addition of the second dimension to the data. Alternatively, consider the two points directly to the left of A. In one dimension they are extremely close, nearly indistinguishable from one another. However, with the addition of the second dimension, these two points are considerably more distant.

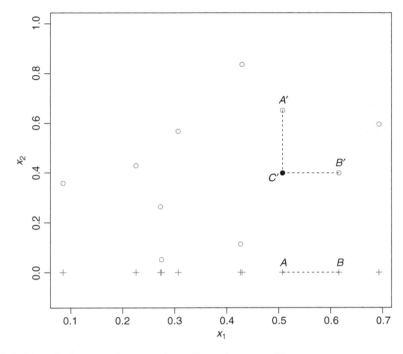

Figure 3.3. Data dispersement in one and two dimensions, $n = 10$

Another way to think about the curse of dimensionality is filling space. For example, let's consider that our variables (regardless of dimension) always lie in [0, 1]. In one dimension, the space to be filled has length 1. In two dimensions the space has length $\sqrt{2}$, while in three dimensions the space has length $\sqrt{3}$ (calculated as the Euclidean distance between the points farthest away). For a q-dimensional data set, the distance to fill has length $\sqrt{q}$, which never decreases as the dimensionality increases. Further, if we think of points as taking up space in our domain (i.e., a measure of volume), then consider what happens to the volume of a q-dimensional space if the data has dimension $[-1, 1]$. In this setting the one-dimensional volume is 2, the two-dimensional volume is 4 and the three-dimensional volume is 8. For q-dimensional data, the volume is 2^q, which is increasing exponentially in q. This suggests that the higher the dimension, the harder it becomes to fill the space. Or, to fill the space equally from one dimension to the next, you need more points in the higher dimension. Figures 3.4 and 3.5 show this phenomenon from the same DGP set-up as Figure 3.3, but with additional observations.

The curse of dimensionality refers to the simple fact that as your dimensionality increases, it becomes harder to detect structure without *a priori* assumptions. It is natural to think that, regardless of dimension, draws from a multivariate density should be clustered around the "center" of the distribution: for the normal, say, we would expect many of our observations to be near the mean vector. However, this is misleading. For exposition only, assume that our data have mean μ. Suppose we wish to draw a hypersphere around this center of the data with radius r. The volume of such a hypersphere

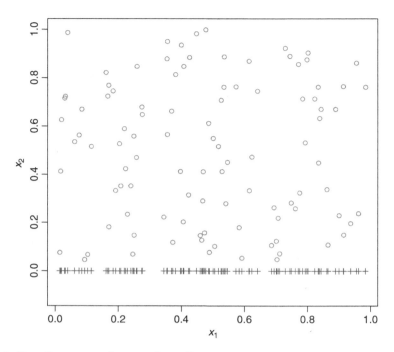

Figure 3.4. Data dispersement in one and two dimensions, $n = 100$

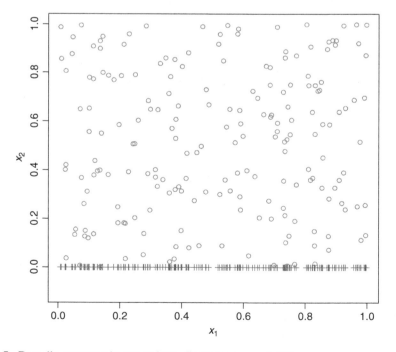

Figure 3.5. Data dispersement in one and two dimensions, $n = 1,000$

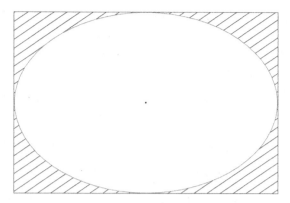

Figure 3.6. Nonoverlapping "volume" of a hypercube and a hypersphere

in q dimensions is $V_s(q) = C_q r^q$, where $C_q = \pi^{q/2}/\Gamma(q/2+1)$. Alternatively, if we were to draw a hypercube of length $2r$ around μ, it would have volume $V_c(q) = (2r)^q$. If we look at the ratio of these two volumes we have

$$\frac{V_s(q)}{V_c(q)} = \frac{\pi^{q/2} r^q}{\Gamma(q/2+1)(2r)^q} = \frac{\pi^{q/2}}{2^{q-1} q \Gamma(q/2)} \longrightarrow 0 \quad \text{as } q \to \infty.$$

The area close to the center of the data has no volume relative to the rest of the space. Figure 3.6 illustrates this phenomenon in two dimensions. Here the center of the data is $(0.5, 0.5)$ and we draw a circle of radius 0.5 around this point and a cube with sides of length 1 such that $(0.5, 0.5)$ is at the center of this cube. The shaded area represents the points not near the center. The previous result tells us that as q increases, this shaded "volume" increases relative to the "volume" of the points "near" the center. This is the operation of the curse of dimensionality, and from a data perspective it suggests that as we go into higher dimensions, draws from the distribution will reside in the tails instead of the middle. By assuming a specific parametric structure, we circumvent the problems related to the curse, given sparseness concerns. However, the likely accuracy of a mean vector or covariance matrix estimate is also likely to be poor, since most data will lie in the tails. So the parametric assumptions do not represent a panacea for high dimensions when the sample size is small.

Table 3.1 helps illustrate the numerical precision that can be lost as the dimensionality of your data increases. Recall that we have stated that *correctly specified* parametric models converge at a rate proportional to $n^{-1/2}$, that is, the order of the error in estimation. This implies a trade-off in accuracy of roughly 3 ($\sqrt{10} = 3.1623 \approx 3$) for a ten-fold increase in the sample size. Thus, reading the column labelled "Parametric" in Table 3.1, we have that the relative error for a sample size of 100 is 0.1, while increasing the sample to 1,000 provides a relative error of 0.0316. Contrast this with a nonparametric model with a single covariate. We need a sample of 100,000 to have the same relative error in estimation as a *correctly specified* parametric model of size 100. This clearly illustrates how nonparametric methods pale in comparison with their correctly specified parametric counterparts. Furthermore, consider that a nonparametric

Table 3.1. *Accuracy as dimensionality increases relative to correctly specified parametric model*

n	Parametric	q							
		1	2	3	4	5	6	7	8
10	0.3162	0.6310	0.6813	0.7197	0.7499	0.7743	0.7943	0.8111	0.8254
50	0.1414	0.4573	0.5210	0.5719	0.6132	0.6475	0.6762	0.7007	0.7218
100	0.1000	0.3981	0.4642	0.5179	0.5623	0.5995	0.6310	0.6579	0.6813
500	0.0447	0.2885	0.3550	0.4116	0.4599	0.5013	0.5372	0.5684	0.5958
1,000	0.0316	0.2512	0.3162	0.3728	0.4217	0.4642	0.5012	0.5337	0.5623
5,000	0.0141	0.1821	0.2418	0.2962	0.3448	0.3882	0.4267	0.4610	0.4918
10,000	0.0100	0.1585	0.2154	0.2683	0.3162	0.3594	0.3981	0.4329	0.4642
50,000	0.0045	0.1149	0.1648	0.2132	0.2586	0.3005	0.3389	0.3740	0.4059
100,000	0.0032	0.1000	0.1468	0.1931	0.2371	0.2783	0.3162	0.3511	0.3831

model with dimension six requires 100,000 observations to achieve the same accuracy as the correctly specified parametric model with ten observations!

While we discussed these issues in Chapter 2, the trade-off between parametric and nonparametric modeling should now be clear. Parametric models offer greater accuracy with less data at the expense of potential model misspecification. Nonparametric models assuage concerns of specification error at the expense of much larger data requirements and slower convergence rates than correctly specified parametric models. However, keep in mind that if a parametric model is misspecified, then this draws into question not only the accuracy of the numerical estimates, but the consistency (and other statistical properties) of the parametric estimator being used.

3.4 Bandwidth selection

The selection of the vector of bandwidths is of great importance for the multivariate kernel density estimator, both from a theoretical and an applied perspective. To obtain the intuition for how to construct our optimal bandwidth vector, we temporarily think of having identical bandwidths across our data, $h_1 = h_2 = \cdots = h_q = h$ and refer back to (3.6). If we use the notation $\nabla^2 f(\mathbf{x}) = \sum_{d=1}^{q} \frac{\partial^2 f(\mathbf{x})}{\partial x_d^2}$, we have that AMISE with identical bandwidths is

$$\text{AMISE}\left[\widehat{f}(\mathbf{x})\right] \approx \frac{\kappa_2^2(k)h^4}{4} R\left(\nabla^2 f\right) + \frac{R(k)^q}{nh^q}. \tag{3.7}$$

We can think of $R\left(\nabla^2 f\right)$ as the total roughness of the second derivative of the unknown multivariate density. Solving this for the optimal bandwidth (vector), Technical Appendix 3.4 shows that

$$h_{\text{opt}} = \left(\frac{q R(k)^q}{\kappa_2^2(k) R(\nabla^2 f)}\right)^{1/(4+q)} n^{-1/(4+q)}. \tag{3.8}$$

Table 3.2. *Kernel efficiency (relative to the Epanechnikov kernel) as the dimensionality increases*

Kernel	Dimension									
	$q=1$	$q=2$	$q=3$	$q=4$	$q=5$	$q=6$	$q=7$	$q=8$	$q=9$	$q=10$
Biweight	1.006	1.012	1.019	1.025	1.031	1.037	1.044	1.050	1.057	1.063
Triweight	1.013	1.027	1.041	1.055	1.069	1.084	1.098	1.113	1.128	1.143
Gaussian	1.051	1.105	1.162	1.222	1.284	1.350	1.419	1.492	1.569	1.649

The traditional features of a bandwidth are evident in (3.8). We have the canonical description, which is a scale component and a rate of decay dependent upon the sample size. As discussed previously, the individual bandwidths decay to zero more slowly as the dimensionality of the problem increases. We also have that the roughness and variance of the kernel offset one another within the scale component. As the total roughness of the second derivative increases, the density becomes more choppy and the optimal bandwidth necessarily becomes smaller.

The choice of kernel has a more important role in higher dimensional settings than in the univariate case. The reason for this is the use of a product kernel compounds any perceived deficiencies that exist between the selected kernel and the Epanechnikov kernel. To see this, Technical Appendix 3.5 derives the efficiency of any univariate kernel used within the product kernel ($k_\varrho(\cdot)$) against the Epanechnikov kernel

$$\text{Eff}(k_\varrho) = \frac{\kappa_2(k_\varrho)^{q/2} R(k_\varrho)^q}{\kappa_2(k_1)^{q/2} R(k_1)^q}.$$

While the general form of a kernel's efficiency is the same, depending upon the variance and the difficulty factor of the kernel, the dimensionality of the analysis has now entered. Note that if we were to use standardized kernels ($\kappa_2(k) = 1$), the efficiency of a kernel depends entirely upon the proportion of the difficulty factors, raised to the power q, $\text{Eff}(k_\varrho) = \left(R(k_\varrho)/R(k_1)\right)^q$. If we consider the univariate case, this ratio is always greater than one (see Table 3.2), since the Epanechnikov kernel is optimal with respect to AMISE, and so increasing the dimension further corrupts the efficiency that any given kernel has with respect to the optimal kernel.

While kernel choice is a more important aspect of an empirical analysis in high-dimensional settings, the selection of bandwidths remains the prime focus. In almost parallel fashion to the univariate setup, we can construct optimal bandwidths in a variety of ways, ranging from rule-of-thumb bandwidths which adhere to a pre-specified parametric family, to cross-validation and plug-in methods. We elect to focus on both rule-of-thumb and cross-validation approaches as plug-in methods can become computationally cumbersome as the dimensionality of the problem increases. While cross-validation methods are computationally burdensome as well, the plug-in methods require more sophisticated calculations of model primitives, whereas cross-validation methods require more time. Our belief is that the clarity gained in a

Table 3.3. *Scaling factors for rule-of-thumb bandwidth construction for given dimensionality*

Kernel	Dimension								
	$q = 2$	$q = 3$	$q = 4$	$q = 5$	$q = 6$	$q = 7$	$q = 8$	$q = 9$	$q = 10$
Epanechnikov	2.1991	2.1200	2.0730	2.0437	2.0246	2.0121	2.0037	1.9982	1.9947
Biweight	2.6073	2.5150	2.4604	2.4263	2.4044	2.3900	2.3805	2.3744	2.3705
Triweight	2.9636	2.8606	2.8000	2.7624	2.7383	2.7226	2.7124	2.7059	2.7020
Gaussian	1.0000	0.9686	0.9506	0.9397	0.9330	0.9289	0.9265	0.9251	0.9245

multivariate setting with cross-validation bandwidth selection more than compensates for the sacrifice of computer run time when bandwidths are estimated.

3.4.1 Rule-of-thumb bandwidth selection

Following the insight of Silverman, a simple rule-of-thumb bandwidth can be constructed by replacing the unknown density in (3.8) with a well known density, such as the multivariate normal. The standard q-variate normal probability density is defined as

$$\phi(\mathbf{x}) = \prod_{d=1}^{q} \phi(x_d) = (2\pi)^{-q/2} e^{-(1/2)\mathbf{x}'\mathbf{x}}.$$

Here $\phi(x)$ is the traditional, univariate standard normal density function. Using the standard q-variate normal probability density function as a reference family, we have (see Technical Appendix 3.6)

$$R(\nabla^2 f) = \frac{q}{\pi^{q/2} 2^{q+2}} (4!! + (q-1)) = \frac{q(q+2)}{\pi^{q/2} 2^{q+2}}. \tag{3.9}$$

The scale factors in Table 3.3 (defined as $c(q)$) can be used to construct bandwidths for each individual variable as

$$h_d^{\text{ROT}} = c(q)\hat{\sigma}_d n^{-1/(4+q)}. \tag{3.10}$$

These provide a quick approach for construction of the vector of bandwidths for exploratory data analysis. However, as with the univariate setting, the concept of selecting bandwidths based on a reference parametric family is dubious, given the original aim of deploying nonparametric methods to avoid arbitrary and tenuous parametric assumptions. Thus, while rule-of-thumb bandwidth construction exists in the multivariate setting, we recommend that more rigorous methods be used to select optimal bandwidths. Next, we discuss the main tool used to find optimal bandwidths within the community of data-driven methods.

3.4.2 Cross-validation bandwidth selection

We can easily transfer our understanding of both LSCV and LCV in the univariate setting to the multivariate setting. Regardless if we have one or q variables, LSCV selects the bandwidth(s) to minimize a sample version of ISE

$$\text{ISE}(\widehat{f}, f) = \int \left[\widehat{f}(\mathbf{x}) - f(\mathbf{x})\right]^2 dx. \tag{3.11}$$

As before, the form of $\text{ISE}(\widehat{f}, f)$ requires replacing the unknown density $(f(\cdot))$ with a leave-one-observation-out estimator to prevent the pathological case of $h_1 = h_2 = \cdots = h_q = 0$ occurring. The multivariate, leave-one-observation-out kernel density estimator is

$$\widehat{f}_{-i}(\mathbf{x}_i) = \frac{1}{(n-1)|\mathbf{h}|} \sum_{\substack{j=1 \\ j \neq i}}^{n} K_h(\mathbf{x}_j, \mathbf{x}_i). \tag{3.12}$$

Using (3.12), we have our empirical counterpart to (3.11) as

$$\text{LSCV}(\mathbf{h}) = \frac{1}{n^2|\mathbf{h}|} \sum_{i=1}^{n} \sum_{j=1}^{n} \bar{K}_h(\mathbf{x}_i, \mathbf{x}_j) - \frac{2}{n(n-1)|\mathbf{h}|} \sum_{i=1}^{n} \sum_{\substack{j=1 \\ j \neq i}}^{n} K_h(\mathbf{x}_j, \mathbf{x}_i), \tag{3.13}$$

where $\bar{K}_h(\mathbf{x}_i, \mathbf{x}_j)$ is the product convolution kernel.[1] Using the same set of manipulations as in Chapter 2, Technical Appendix 3.7 shows that the LSCV criterion can be written as

$$\text{LSCV}(\mathbf{h}) = \frac{1}{n^2|\mathbf{h}|} \sum_{i=1}^{n} \sum_{j=1}^{n} \check{K}_h(\mathbf{x}_i, \mathbf{x}_j). \tag{3.14}$$

In this formulation, we have again condensed different kernels into a single kernel for notational ease. The virtues of the product kernel should be readily apparent. Given its form, the use of a product kernel typically implies that in a multivariate setting, even things such as multivariate convolution kernels are constructed simply as the products of individual convolution kernels. So the univariate kernel we derived in Chapter 2 succinctly captures the LSCV criterion function $(\tilde{k}(\psi))$, converting to product kernel form in the multivariate LSCV setting. This makes implementation relatively easy.

Aside from LSCV as a selection mechanism for optimal bandwidths, we can also leverage LCV. Recall that LCV selects optimal bandwidths using a data-based surrogate for Kullback–Leibler distance. The same mechanics that are worked out for the univariate case can be repeated in the multivariate setting to show that the empirical score function to be maximized over the vector of bandwidths is

$$\text{LCV}(\mathbf{h}) = n^{-1} \sum_{i=1}^{n} \log \widehat{f}_{-i}(\mathbf{x}_i). \tag{3.15}$$

As with the univariate case, using LCV to select optimal bandwidths can produce undesired consequences because the leave-one-out estimate for the unknown multivariate density may be zero, and taking the logarithm of this will lead to bandwidths being selected that are potentially larger than necessary. One way to eschew this effect is to use univariate kernels inside the product kernel that have infinite support, such as the

---

[1] Recall that we presented the forms of the convolution kernels for popular kernels within our polynomial class of kernels in Chapter 2.

standard normal kernel or the theoretically consistent kernel proposed by Hall (1987b), which does not have exponentially decaying tails. This is an important point to be cognizant of, given our earlier discussion on the curse of dimensionality. As we saw, increasing the dimensionality of the problem tends to compound the issue of having points that are far away from one another and this is exactly the reason that LCV breaks down as a viable mechanism for selecting bandwidths. Given this, consumers of cross-validation methods will undoubtedly gravitate towards LSCV as the main bandwidth selector.

An important observation to make regarding the empirical implementation of data-driven bandwidth selection mechanisms is that in dimensions greater than two, you will not be able to visually construct the criterion function. As the work of Hall and Marron notes, the cross-validation criterion (specifically LSCV) produces local minima. To ensure that the bandwidths used from a cross-validation procedure locate a global minimum, it is generally advisable to run repeated evaluations of the criterion function. Each set of runs is commonly referred to as a "multistart." There is a distinct trade-off between the number of multistarts deployed and the overall time it takes to determine the optimal set of bandwidths. For more advanced users, an alternative to using numerous multistarts would be to use search algorithms with excellent properties in high-dimensional settings. Genetic algorithms such as differential evolution (Storn and Price, 1997) and particle swarm optimization (Parsopoulos and Vrahatis, 2002) represent attractive options.

3.5 Conditional density estimation

While studying the univariate and multivariate kernel density estimators is informative, we often desire more direct knowledge of various features of the outcome of interest. As such, the conditional distribution (and density) becomes a key object of interest. From the conditional density, we can investigate the first moment (conditional mean or regression model), quantiles (such as the conditional median), or the second moment (conditional heteroskedasticity model) to name a few. The conditional kernel density estimator will combine our univariate estimator with the multivariate estimator to create a conditional density.

Let $f_{\mathbf{x},y}(\cdot)$ denote the joint density of $(\mathbf{x}, y)$ and $f_{\mathbf{x}}(\cdot)$ denote the marginal density of $\mathbf{x}$. Our discussion here focuses on univariate y but could be generalized to multivariate settings. We denote our estimators of the joint and marginal densities, $\widehat{f}_{\mathbf{x},y}(\mathbf{x}, y)$ and $\widehat{f}_{\mathbf{x}}(\mathbf{x})$ as

$$\widehat{f}_{\mathbf{x},y}(\mathbf{x}, y) = (n|\mathbf{h}|h_y)^{-1} \sum_{i=1}^{n} K_h(\mathbf{x}_i, \mathbf{x}) k\left(\frac{y_i - y}{h_y}\right),$$

$$\widehat{f}_{\mathbf{x}}(\mathbf{x}) = (n|\mathbf{h}|)^{-1} \sum_{i=1}^{n} K_h(\mathbf{x}_i, \mathbf{x}),$$

where h_y is the smoothing parameter associated with y and $k(\cdot)$ is a univariate kernel.

From a pure statistical perspective, the conditional density of y given $\mathbf{x}$ is defined as $f_{y|\mathbf{x}}(y|\mathbf{x}) = f_{\mathbf{x},y}(\mathbf{x}, y)/f_{\mathbf{x}}(\mathbf{x})$. We estimate the conditional density as

$$\widehat{f}_{y|\mathbf{x}}(y|\mathbf{x}) = \widehat{f}_{\mathbf{x},y}(\mathbf{x}, y)/\widehat{f}_{\mathbf{x}}(\mathbf{x}). \tag{3.16}$$

A more succinct way to write the conditional density of y is

$$\widehat{f}_{y|\mathbf{x}}(y|\mathbf{x}) = (nh_y)^{-1} \sum_{i=1}^{n} A_i(\mathbf{x})k\left(\frac{y_i - y}{h_y}\right),$$

where

$$A_i(\mathbf{x}) = \frac{K_h(\mathbf{x}_i, \mathbf{x})}{n^{-1}\sum_{j=1}^{n} K_h(\mathbf{x}_j, \mathbf{x})}.$$

Writing the conditional density in this form reveals that it is constructed as a local average, with weights determined by the relative density of the point $\mathbf{x}$ and averaging over the smoothed y. In essence we are constructing the unconditional density of y and then smoothing this density over the covariate support, again using the idea of "localness." Without the presence of $A_i(\mathbf{x})$, we would just have the standard univariate kernel density estimator. However, with the conditioning, we have two sources of local averaging taking place, one in the y direction and another in the $\mathbf{x}$ domain.

3.5.1 Bias, variance, and AMSE

The bias and variance (and subsequently the AMSE) of the conditional density estimator take on more complex forms than those of the unconditional kernel density estimator do. This stems from the fact that we have a denominator that is random. While these statistical features of the conditional kernel density estimator are complex, we will attempt to provide an intuitive explanation of each component.

We first focus on the bias. Technical Appendix 3.8 shows that the bias of our conditional density estimator is

$$\text{Bias}\left[\widehat{f}_{y|\mathbf{x}}(y|\mathbf{x})\right] \approx \kappa_2 \sum_{d=0}^{q} h_d^2 B_d,$$

where

$$B_0 = (1/2)\frac{\partial^2 f_{y|\mathbf{x}}(y|\mathbf{x})}{\partial y^2}$$

and

$$B_d = (1/2)\frac{\partial_{y|\mathbf{x}}^2 f(y|\mathbf{x})}{\partial x_d^2} + f_{\mathbf{x}}(\mathbf{x})^{-1}\frac{\partial f_{y|\mathbf{x}}(y|\mathbf{x})}{\partial x_d}\frac{\partial f_{\mathbf{x}}(\mathbf{x})}{\partial x_d}, \quad d = 1, \ldots, q.$$

Each B_d can be thought of as a measure of the curvature of $f_{y|\mathbf{x}}(y|\mathbf{x})$ in the x_d (or y) direction. We still see the main aspects of the bias of a nonparametric estimator. First, the bias does not depend upon the sample size except through the vector of bandwidths. Second, the "rougher" the conditional density, the greater the bias. Notice how each bandwidth has the ability to contain roughness in a specific direction (in terms of its effect on bias), much the same as with the multivariate kernel density estimator. In this case, increased "roughness" in a given x direction tends to suggest that the given bandwidth decreases. However, this comes at the expense of the overall variance of the estimator.

Next we focus on variance. Technical Appendix 3.9 shows that the variance of our conditional density estimator is

$$\text{Var}\left[\widehat{f}_{y|x}(y|\mathbf{x})\right] \approx \frac{R(k)^{q+1} f_{y|\mathbf{x}}(y|\mathbf{x})}{n|\mathbf{h}| f_{\mathbf{x}}(\mathbf{x})}.$$

Interestingly, this variance looks almost identical to that of the multivariate kernel density estimator. Using a more difficult kernel increases the variance of the estimator, as do conditioning points with little density (i.e., low probability). Also, as $n|\mathbf{h}| \to \infty$, we see that the variance decreases. One important thing to note here is that $f_{y|\mathbf{x}}(y|\mathbf{x}) = f_{\mathbf{x},y}(\mathbf{x}, y)/f_{\mathbf{x}}(\mathbf{x})$, so conditioning points with little density grossly inflate the variance of the conditional density estimator. This stems from the division that takes place when a conditional density is constructed.

The AMSE of our conditional density estimator is

$$\text{AMSE}\left[\widehat{f}_{y|x}(y|\mathbf{x})\right] \approx \kappa_2^2 \sum_{d=0}^{q} \sum_{\ell=0}^{q} h_d^2 h_\ell^2 B_d B_\ell + \frac{R(k)^{q+1} f_{y|\mathbf{x}}(y|\mathbf{x})}{n|\mathbf{h}| f_{\mathbf{x}}(\mathbf{x})}.$$

As with the multivariate kernel estimator, the Epanechnikov kernel is the optimal kernel because the MSE depends on the kernel in the same way as in the unconditional setting. This is comforting, since it suggests that as we move across estimation objects, the optimality properties of the Epanechnikov kernel transfer.

3.5.2 Bandwidth selection

There is no proposed rule-of-thumb bandwidth for estimating a conditional density beyond that of the Silverman rule-of-thumb for each variable. In multivariate settings, rule-of-thumb bandwidths serve as useful diagnostic tools to get a rough idea of what is happening, but ideally we would progress to data-driven methods. To this end, we again discuss LSCV. While the intuition behind LSCV for the conditional density estimator mimics that for the multivariate and univariate density estimators discussed earlier, an important feature of this bandwidth selection mechanism will emerge that does not exist in the unconditional setting. This feature is important for applied research.

To describe the LSCV approach for obtaining bandwidths for the conditional density estimator, we follow the work of Hall, Racine, and Li (2004). The optimal bandwidths are found by minimizing the sample analog of integrated squared error:

$$\begin{aligned}
\text{ISE} &= \int \left\{\widehat{f}_{y|\mathbf{x}}(y|\mathbf{x}) - f_{y|\mathbf{x}}(y|\mathbf{x})\right\}^2 f_{\mathbf{x}}(\mathbf{x}) d\mathbf{x} dy \\
&= \int \widehat{f}_{y|\mathbf{x}}^2(y|\mathbf{x}) f_{\mathbf{x}}(\mathbf{x}) d\mathbf{x} dy - 2\int \widehat{f}_{y|\mathbf{x}}(y|\mathbf{x}) f_{\mathbf{x},y}(\mathbf{x}, y) d\mathbf{x} dy + \int f_{y|\mathbf{x}}^2(y|\mathbf{x}) f_{\mathbf{x}}(\mathbf{x}) d\mathbf{x} dy,
\end{aligned}$$

where $f_{\mathbf{x},y}(\mathbf{x}, y)$ arises in the second term because of a cancellation with $f_{\mathbf{x}}(\mathbf{x})$ and the second term does not depend upon the bandwidth. The first term can be estimated with

$$\widehat{\text{ISE}}_1 = \frac{1}{n} \sum_{i=1}^{n} \frac{\frac{1}{n^2} \sum_{j=1}^{n} \sum_{l=1}^{n} K_h(\mathbf{x}_j, \mathbf{x}_i) K_h(\mathbf{x}_l, \mathbf{x}_i) \int k\left(\frac{y_j - y}{h_y}\right) k\left(\frac{y_l - y}{h_y}\right) dy}{\left[\widehat{f}_{-i,\mathbf{x}}(\mathbf{x}_i)\right]^2},$$

where $\widehat{f}_{-i,\mathbf{x}}(\cdot)$ is the leave-one-out estimator of $f_{\mathbf{x}}(\cdot)$. Similarly, ISE_2 can be estimated with

$$\widehat{\text{ISE}}_2 = \frac{1}{n} \sum_{i=1}^{n} \frac{\widehat{f}_{-i,\mathbf{x},y}(\mathbf{x}_i, y_i)}{\widehat{f}_{-i,\mathbf{x}}(\mathbf{x}_i)},$$

where $\widehat{f}_{-i,\mathbf{x},y}(\cdot, \cdot)$ is the leave-one-out estimator of $f_{\mathbf{x},y}(\cdot, \cdot)$. The LSCV objective function is thus given as

$$\text{LSCV}(h_y, \mathbf{h}) = \widehat{\text{ISE}}_1(h_y, \mathbf{h}) - 2\widehat{\text{ISE}}_2(h_y, \mathbf{h}).$$

Once the bandwidths have been determined, the conditional density can be estimated at any given level of the covariates.

3.5.3 Inclusion of irrelevant variables

In a seminal contribution, Hall, Racine, and Li (2004) discuss the relative attractiveness of LSCV to determine optimal bandwidths for the conditional density estimator. They show the ability of LSCV to *remove* irrelevant variables from the conditioning set. Keep in mind that the rate of convergence of the conditional density estimator depends upon the number of variables within the conditioning set. If erroneous variables are included, then plug-in or rule-of-thumb bandwidths only serve to compound the problem. LSCV, on the other hand, can determine asymptotically which variables belong in the conditioning set.

This is important in several aspects. First, it lessens the curse of dimensionality. Second, it is fully automatic: no choice of test or alternative dimension reduction methods need be implemented prior to final construction of the conditional density estimator. Perhaps even more important is that this ability to remove irrelevant variables from the conditional density carries over to the estimation of moments and quantiles of the estimator as well. Thus, irrelevant variables can be removed from a mean regression (or quantile regression). This has far-reaching consequences for empirical analysis.

A further virtue of LSCV and the ability to correctly document asymptotically the conditioning set is that there are no obvious peers for selecting bandwidths. So while the use of rule-of-thumb and plug-in methods may possess desirable features, such as ease of construction and fast rates of convergence, they lack this dimension reduction benefit of LSCV (which is useful in practice).

To understand how LSCV works from an applied perspective, consider the form of
the weights within the conditional density estimator:

$$A_i(\mathbf{x}) = \frac{K_h(x_i, x)}{n^{-1} \sum\limits_{j=1}^{n} K_h(x_j, x)} = \frac{\prod\limits_{d=1}^{q} k(\frac{x_{id} - x_d}{h_d})}{n^{-1} \sum\limits_{j=1}^{n} \prod\limits_{d=1}^{q} k(\frac{x_{jd} - x_d}{h_d})}.$$

Suppose we can split our set of covariates into two groups—those that we know to be
relevant and those that we know to be irrelevant. To do so we will use q_r and q_{irr} as
the number of relevant and irrelevant covariates where $q_r + q_{irr} = q$. Notationally, our
set of covariates are separated as

$$\mathbf{x} = \{x_1, x_2, \ldots, x_q\} = \left\{ \overbrace{x_1, x_2, \ldots, x_{q_r}}^{q_r \text{ relevant covariates}}, \underbrace{x_{q_r+1}, x_{q_r+2}, \ldots, x_q}_{q_{ir} \text{ irrelevant covariates}} \right\}.$$

By focusing our attention on the weights and paying attention to the distinct nature
of our covariates, we have that

$$A_i(\mathbf{x}) = \frac{\prod\limits_{d=1}^{q_r} k(\frac{x_{id} - x_d}{h_d}) \prod\limits_{d=q_r+1}^{q} k(\frac{x_{id} - x_d}{h_d})}{n^{-1} \sum\limits_{j=1}^{n} \prod\limits_{d=1}^{q_r} k(\frac{x_{jd} - x_d}{h_d}) \prod\limits_{d=q_r+1}^{q} k(\frac{x_{jd} - x_d}{h_d})}.$$

When LSCV detects an irrelevant variable, the bandwidth diverges to ∞ instead of
collapsing to 0. As $h_d \to \infty$, we have that $k(\frac{x_{jd} - x_d}{h_d}) \to k(0)$, which is independent
of j. This lack of an index implies that we can pull the second set of product kernels
through the summation in the denominator. Doing so results in

$$A_i(\mathbf{x}) = \frac{k(0)^{q_{ir}} \prod\limits_{d=1}^{q_r} k(\frac{x_{id} - x_d}{h_d})}{n^{-1} k(0)^{q_{ir}} \sum\limits_{j=1}^{n} \prod\limits_{d=1}^{q_r} k(\frac{x_{jd} - x_d}{h_d})} = \frac{\prod\limits_{d=1}^{q_r} k(\frac{x_{id} - x_d}{h_d})}{n^{-1} \sum\limits_{j=1}^{n} \prod\limits_{d=1}^{q_r} k(\frac{x_{jd} - x_d}{h_d})} = A_i(\mathbf{x}_{q_r}).$$

It is as if the irrelevant variables did not enter in the first place. For an interesting
empirical example where these methods can improve upon their misspecified parametric counterparts, see the paper by Li and Racine (2004a) regarding the determinants of
extramarital affairs.

3.6 Application

Here we look at three different bivariate kernel density estimates by appending our
output per worker data from Chapter 2 with two of the classic Solow (1956) variables,
namely, physical and human capital stocks (noting that Solow didn't actually look at
human capital in his paper). We look at the bivariate densities of the capital variables
as well as conditional densities. This will give us a good overview of how adding
dimensionality to the problem can lead to different insights over a purely univariate
approach.

Our data on output (Y), physical (K), and human (H) capital come from the Penn World Table, Version 7.0 (Heston, Summers, and Aten, 2011) and Barro and Lee (2013), respectively. Output is obtained by multiplying RGDPCH (per capita GDP computed via the chain method) by POP (population). The output is in 2005 international dollars. Real aggregate investment in international dollars is computed as RGDPL $*$ POP $*$ KI, where RGDPL is the real GDP computed via the Laspeyres index and KI is the investment share of real GDP.

Following standard practice, we compute the capital stock using the perpetual inventory method (see Caselli and Feyrer, 2007). For human capital, we employ the updated Barro and Lee (2010) education data. We adopt the Hall and Jones (1999) construction of human capital, which in turn is based on the Psacharopoulos (1994) survey of wage equations evaluating returns to education. Specifically, let e_{it} represent the average number of years of education of the adult population in country i at time t and define human capital labor in country i at time t by

$$H_{it} = Q\left(e_{it}\right) = \exp\left[\vartheta\left(e_{it}\right)\right]$$

where $\vartheta\left(\cdot\right)$ is a piecewise linear function, with a zero intercept and a slope of 0.134 through the fourth year of education, 0.101 for the next four years, and 0.068 for education beyond the eighth year. The rate of return to education (where $\vartheta\left(\cdot\right)$ is differentiable) is

$$\frac{\partial Q\left(e_{it}\right)}{\partial e_{it}} = \vartheta'\left(e_{it}\right)$$

and $Q(0) = 1$.

Beyond two covariates, there is no accepted practice for presenting and discussing multivariate kernel density estimates. For our purposes we will scale each variable by its respective mean and present kernel density estimates and contour plots using likelihood cross-validated bandwidths. We will see that over time the data become heavily nonnormal.

Figures 3.7 and 3.8 present the bivariate kernel density estimates and the corresponding contour plots. Given the three-dimensional nature of bivariate kernel density estimates, the contour plots help to distill this information in a concise two-dimensional form. By presenting the subsequent plots and contours from a fit with a normal, any departures from normality will show up quickly.

There are several features that we immediately notice. The kernel density estimates do not appear normal, with the contours not displaying the common elliptical pattern. Moreover, while the correlation between physical and human capital is roughly 0.67, the nonparametric density estimate appears to display more independence than the normal density; this is seen in the slant that the contours take for the bivariate normal density estimate.

Another interesting feature of the nonparametric bivariate density estimate is that it appears that there is some probability mass forming in the upper right tails. That is, there is some formation of countries with both high levels of physical and human capital beyond the regular contours. To see if this is a pattern consistent over time or simply a phenomenon of the data in 1960, Figure 3.8 presents the same set of density

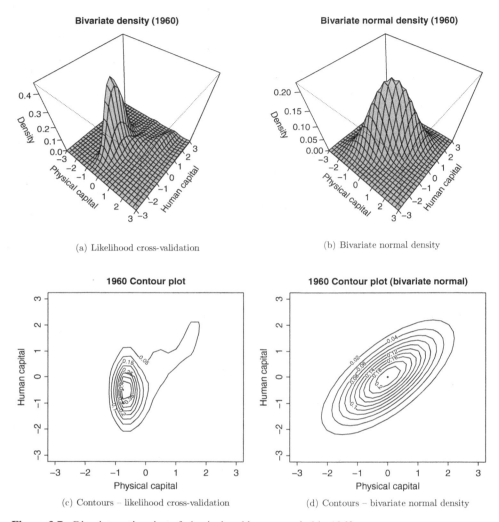

Figure 3.7. Bivariate estimation of physical and human capital in 1960

and contour plots for the year 2000 data. Again we present both bivariate kernel and normal density estimates.

We see the appearance of a second mode in the year 2000 joint density of physical and human capital. This potential feature is completely overlooked with the normal density. Moreover, this finding is consistent with that of Battisti and Parmeter (2013), who look at the trivariate density of output, physical, and human capital over time. We again see that it appears that the nonparametric density estimate suggests a density that is closer to displaying independent marginals than the bivariate normal density estimates do. This is not to say that the marginal densities of physical and human capital are independent (we will discuss testing in the next chapter), but that the contours display a less slanted distribution than the elliptical normal contours.

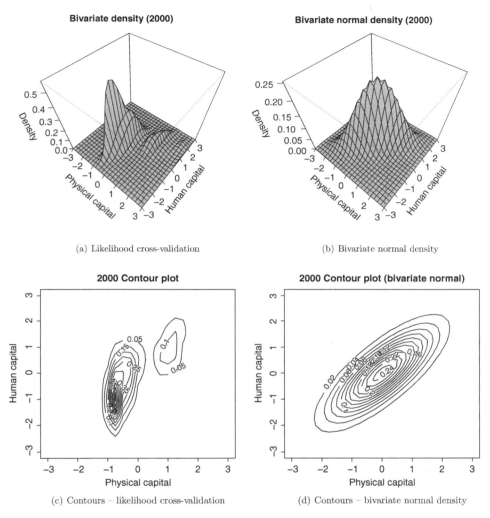

Figure 3.8. Bivariate estimation of physical and human capital in 2000

We now turn our attention to conditional kernel density estimates. Again, in multiple dimensions, there does not exist a simple way to visualize results without fixing the level of the conditioning variables. In this case we will present conditional density plots in both 1960 and 2000 with physical and human capital held fixed (together) at their lower, middle, and upper quartiles.

Using bandwidths selected via LCV, Figures 3.9 and 3.10 present our conditional density estimates. Several noticeable features appear. First, in 1960, there is little difference in the conditional density estimates when human and physical capital are held fixed at either the 25th or 50th quantile. When both are held fixed at the 75th quantile, however, there is a large shift in the probability mass to the right. This suggests that (at low levels of physical and human capital) minor increases in physical and human capital may have little effect on output per worker (assuming there is a causal relationship).

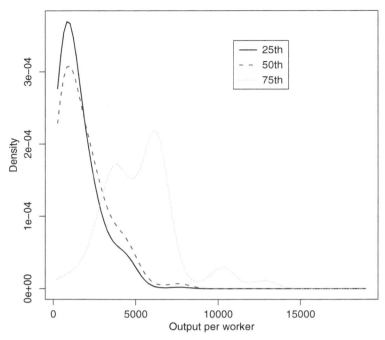

Figure 3.9. Conditional density plot of output conditioned on physical and human capital per worker in 1960 using likelihood cross-validated bandwidths

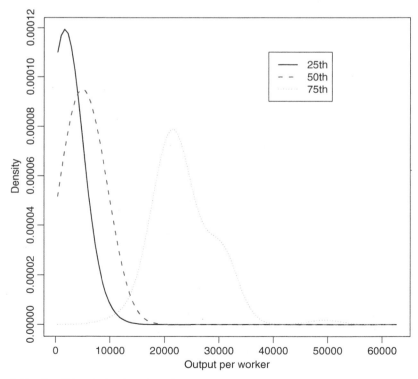

Figure 3.10. Conditional density plot of output conditioned on physical and human capital per worker in 2000 using likelihood cross-validated bandwidths

This may be indicative of a threshold or severe nonlinear effect in the conditional density of output per worker. Second, the conditional density of output per worker in 1960 for the capital variables held fixed at the 75th quantile has multiple modes, distinctly different from the lower quantile conditional density estimates that have a sharp peak near 0 and a long decaying right tail.

Progressing to 2000, we see a difference (where physical and human capital are held fixed at their 25th and 50th quantiles, respectively) between the conditional densities. Further, consistent with what we saw in Chapter 2, the entire distribution of output per worker has shifted to the right, suggesting at all places in the distribution countries are becoming more productive over time. Further, the multimodality inherent in the estimates fixed at the 75th quantile of the 1960 conditional density estimate is nonexistent in the year 2000 estimate. Again, we notice that there appears to be a strong threshold effect in the impact of human and physical capital with the 25th and 50th quantiles have similar (though different) effects on the density, with a perceivably large effect at the 75th quantile. Once we introduce regression methods, we can more rigorously study this effect.

4

Inference about the density

Estimation of univariate and multivariate densities and examining their plots is of direct interest to practitioners. However, as is the case with a photograph, a thousand people viewing an estimated density may have a thousand different opinions on its shape. Therefore, it is imperative to conduct formal statistical tests for various phenomena of interest. In this chapter, we consider common and useful tests for both estimated univariate and multivariate densities.

Given that a correctly specified parametric model is efficient, it is important to test the nonparametric model versus a parametric alternative. For instance, if the density is normally distributed, it would be advantageous to exploit this fact when conducting an empirical analysis. For some economic problems, theory may provide information on the underlying distribution and hence this test could be used to validate theory with empirical data. Alternatively, this test can be used to test the assumptions other practitioners have used in the past. A test of interest for multivariate data is a test for joint normality. It is known that if two variables, say y and $\mathbf{x}$, are jointly normal, then the conditional mean of y given $\mathbf{x}$ is linear. In other words, $E(y|\mathbf{x}) = \mathbf{x}\beta$. Hence, we can use this test to determine whether or not OLS would be an appropriate estimator in a regression framework.

In addition to the test for a correctly specified parametric distribution, we consider tests for equality between two unknown densities. This is common in the growth and development literature, where testing for equality of income densities of two different regions (Western and Central Europe), groups (WTO and non-WTO), or time periods is insightful. Another useful test in practice is that of symmetry around a particular point, most commonly zero. For example, in the nominal wage rigidity literature, symmetry of the wage-change distribution is key (e.g., Christofides and Stengos, 2001).

A test which requires multivariate data is the test for independence. Here we can check to see if the joint density of two variables is equal to the product of their marginal densities. Although determining independence can be important from an economic point of view, we can also benefit from independence on the empirical side. As noted previously, multivariate data is subject to the curse of dimensionality, and the ability to separate variables can lead to substantial gains in the accuracy of estimated densities for a given sample size. Separating the variables will also lead to large decreases in computation time.

A unifying theme of these types of tests are that they fit into a standard setup, which makes their underlying intuition and implementation straightforward. Given this, we will focus attention on the general testing environment and then provide specific details for each test. There are three primary ways to perform tests about distributions. The most popular is probably a Kolmogorov-Smirnov type test. These tests are based on the empirical distribution function (ECDF). These tests have been around for a long time, work quite well and are easy to implement in a univariate setting. Tests based on probability density functions are also very popular. Here, kernel-based tests are widely used in the applied nonparametric literature. A third way to perform these types of null hypotheses is to use characteristic functions. We will center our discussion around kernel-based tests. For those of you interested in the other tests, we suggest you consult texts such as Gibbons and Chakraborti (2010).

The final test we outline in this chapter is a test for multimodality. Cluster analysis or bump hunting, as these modality tests are often referred to, have become very popular in the cross-country growth literature. Bianchi (1997) popularized these methods, uncovering a shift in the cross-country distribution of income per capita from a unimodal to a multimodal density over time. This paper led to a host of articles trying to detect club convergence via modality tests (e.g., Zelli and Pittau, 2006). Although the story has been criticized, the idea of clustering can still be identified with multimodality tests, assuming the groups are sufficiently well separated. This test is constructed in a different manner from the first four and hence deserves separate attention.

Each of these tests is useful in practice, but implementing them is another issue. It is well known that kernel-based tests do not perform well in finite samples when using asymptotic distributions. Therefore we consider bootstrap versions for each of our test statistics. We therefore spend a fair amount of time discussing bootstrap methods.

Our applications in this section should already be apparent to you. Our primary goal is to analyze the distribution of output per worker and assess whether or not it comes from a particular parametric density, whether or not it is skewed and whether or not it is multimodal. We are also interested in whether or not this density differs among groups, regions and/or over time.

4.1 Fundamentals

We consider many tests in this chapter, but most of them boil down to a simple hypothesis. Consider two possible candidates for the density of a random variable. Let's call these two densities $f(\mathbf{x})$ and $g(\mathbf{x})$ and assume that they are absolutely continuous. For the moment, without lack of generality, let's assume that each is a univariate density. With the observed data $\{x_i\}_{i=1}^{n_1}$ and $\{y_i\}_{i=1}^{n_2}$ we can conduct tests for whether or not these two densities are different from one another. Formally, the null hypothesis is $H_0: f(x) = g(x)$ almost everywhere versus the alternative $H_1: f(x) \neq g(x)$ on a set of positive measure. Almost everywhere implies that $f(x)$ and $g(x)$ can be different, but that the places where these two densities differ is made up of a set of points which do not jointly cover area. If these points were to jointly cover area, then we say that they have positive measure.

This is illustrated in Figures 4.1 and 4.2, respectively. Note that while we use the data $\{x_i\}_{i=1}^{n_1}$ and $\{y_i\}_{i=1}^{n_2}$ to construct $f(x)$ and $g(x)$, respectively, both of these are

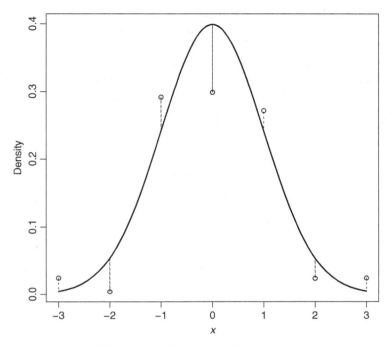

Figure 4.1. Two densities which are equal almost everywhere

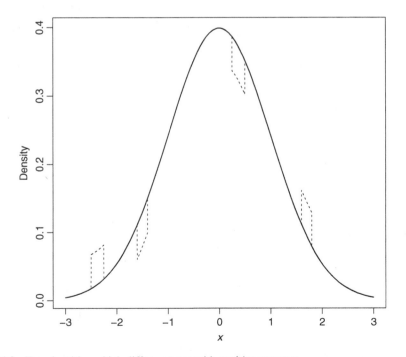

Figure 4.2. Two densities which differ on a set with positive measure

being evaluated at x in the test. In other words, it would not make sense to evaluate $f(x_1)$ versus $g(y_1)$ as there is no reason to believe that $f(\cdot)$ evaluated at x_1 is equal to $g(\cdot)$ evaluated at y_1 even if $f(x) = g(x)$.

This null hypothesis is quite flexible and can be used for an assortment of tests. Here we focus on four specific forms of this general hypothesis: a test for whether two unknown densities are different from one another, whether an unknown density is equal to a parametric density, the symmetry about a point of the density, and if two random variables are independent.

4.1.1 Consistent test

It is important to note that these types of tests can reject for a variety of reasons. For example, we will reject the null if the means of two densities are the same, but their variances are not, and vice versa. We may also reject if both the means and variances are the same, but higher order moments differ. Recall that if a distribution is normal, the first two moments characterize the entire distribution, so if you fail to reject that the mean and variance are equal between the two distributions, you can conclude that the data come from the same distribution. However, when distributions are nonnormal, which we certainly want to allow for in practice, simple tests on the first two moments are typically insufficient.

To visualize this, consider Figure 4.3. In this figure we plot both a normal and log-normal distribution, both of which have mean and variance equal to unity. If we were to randomly sample from each distribution and test if the first two moments were different from one another, we would likely fail to reject the null. However, when we analyze

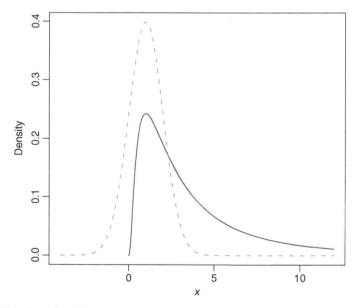

Figure 4.3. Two densities with the same mean and variance (each equal to unity), but from different distributions (normal vs. log-normal)

the figure, it is obvious that these two distributions are different from one another. This is a benefit of nonparametric tests. A nonparametric test is not based on a subsample of the moments. In our tests we compare the density over a set of points on the support of the data. Hence, we would reject the null that random samples taken from the two distributions in Figure 4.3 are equal with probability 1 as the sample size tends towards infinity. This is what is meant by a consistent test. Formally, we know that our test is consistent if

$$P\,(\text{reject } H_0 \mid H_0 \text{ is false}) \to 1 \text{ as } n \to \infty.$$

We want to emphasize here that even though we consider consistent tests, in finite samples, different tests will have varying levels of performance. In other words, we may have more finite sample power in certain directions (i.e., different alternatives) and some nonparametric tests will reject a false null more often than others.

4.1.2 Distance measures

Many measures of distance are in the literature and we summarize some of them here. For those interested in a more thorough treatment of distance measures for use in economic research, we suggest you consult Ullah (1996).

Integrated squared error
Perhaps the most popular – and the one we adopt throughout the text – is a global measure of distance between two densities measured via integrated squared error (the perceived popularity for this metric is probably more for mathematical convenience than anything else). Analogous to what we saw in our discussion of bandwidth selection in Chapter 2, the ISE between two densities is

$$\text{ISE}(f, g) = \int_x \left[f\,(x) - g\,(x) \right]^2 dx.$$

This measure is equal to zero under the null and is positive under the alternative hypothesis. This makes it a proper candidate for testing the null. ISE can be estimated by replacing $f\,(x)$ and $g\,(x)$ with their nonparametric kernel density estimates.

The upper left-hand panel of Figure 4.4 plots two separate densities from the gamma distribution. The solid line has both shape and scale parameters equal to 2 and the dashed line has a scale parameter equal to 3. It is obvious from the figure that these densities are similar around the values of x equal to zero, five, and twenty. The upper right-hand panel constructs ISE (the cumulative difference over x between the two densities – $\widehat{\text{ISE}}\,(\cdot, \cdot) = 0.2042$). We can see that this cumulative difference starts near zero and then drastically increases between zero and five. This is expected as the difference between the two densities is greatest in this range. Next notice that the curve flattens near $x = 5$ as the densities are nearly identical in the neighborhood of five. We then see a gradual increase and another plateau once $x > 15$. This again reflects that the curves depart after $x = 5$ and are similar once $x > 15$.

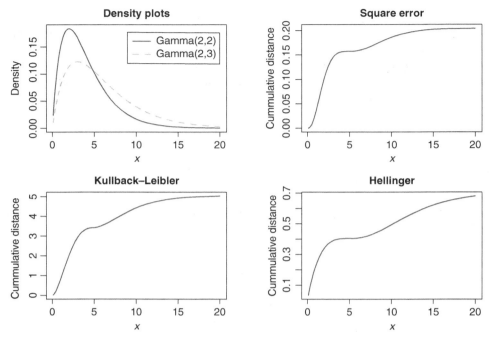

Figure 4.4. Density plots of a gamma(2,2) versus gamma (2,3) along with the construction of corresponding distance metrics (integrated square error, Kullback–Leibler, and Hellinger)

Kullback–Leibler

Another popular method to determine distance is to use a Kullback–Leibler information measure. This method is commonly used to determine the distance between two probability distributions. Recall that in Chapter 2, we used it to motivate likelihood cross-validation. Although it is often intuited as a distance metric, KL divergence is not a true metric as it is an asymmetric measure of distance. Specifically, the distance between $f(x)$ and $g(x)$ is not necessarily the same as the distance between $g(x)$ and $f(x)$ when measured by this method. Nevertheless, this method is common in the literature. Formally, KL distance is defined as

$$\mathrm{KL}\,(f, g) = \int_{x} g(x) \log \left\{ \frac{f(x)}{g(x)} \right\} dx.$$

The asymmetric nature of this distance measure is obvious here. However, we note that under the null this distance is zero and it is strictly positive under the alternative. This also serves as a proper candidate for testing the null hypothesis. Similar to above, the values of $f(x)$ and $g(x)$ can be replaced by their kernel density estimators.

Hellinger distance

The final distance measure we present here is Hellinger distance. In probability theory, it is also used to quantify the distance between two probability distributions. This is less popular with kernel methods, but is popular in empirical likelihood (Owen, 2000). Formally, the squared Hellinger distance can be expressed as

$$\mathrm{HD}^2\left(f, g\right) = \frac{1}{2} \int_x \left[\sqrt{f\left(x\right)} - \sqrt{g\left(x\right)}\right]^2 dx.$$

The Hellinger distance itself $\mathrm{HD}\left(f, g\right) = \sqrt{\mathrm{HD}^2\left(f, g\right)}$ lies between zero and unity and is equal to zero when the null hypothesis is true. It is strictly positive under the alternative hypothesis. Thus, this also serves as a proper candidate for testing the null. This method has also been used to calculate bandwidths in the kernel framework (e.g., see Ahmad and Mugdadi, 2006).

These are only three possibilities for distance metrics and one is not necessarily uniformly better than the others. Looking at Figure 4.4, we can see that the Kullback–Leibler and Hellinger distances look very much like ISE. This is not always the case, but it shows that changing distance metrics may not make a major difference in many applications. We discuss the use of ISE for testing features of kernel density estimates in this chapter.

4.1.3 Centering terms

One common issue throughout this chapter is the presence of centering terms. As you will see later, these centering terms can lead to finite sample biases. Further, a nonzero centering term often does not disappear as the sample size tends towards infinity. Specifically, many nonparametric test statistics require a double summation, and inclusion of the diagonal terms ($j = i$) leads to this nonzero center term (i.e., $k\left(\frac{x_i - x_j}{h}\right) = k\left(\frac{x_i - x_i}{h}\right) = k\left(0\right) \neq 0 \ \forall h$). The easiest way to take care of this is to continue to use the double summation, but to exclude the case where $j = i$ in the second summation. Our summations are generally of the form

$$\sum_{i=1}^{n} \sum_{\substack{j=1 \\ j \neq i}}^{n}.$$

In many cases this is sufficient to remove the centering term and leads to a test with a zero asymptotic mean. An alternative is to calculate the centering term and subtract it from the test statistic so that the asymptotic mean of the differenced test statistic is zero. These are equivalent asymptotically, but some authors (e.g., Li, 1996) have found that the "center-free" test has better finite-sample size and power than the "center-subtracted" test. One reason for this better performance is that a center-subtracted test requires you to estimate the center term. This is also estimated with some amount of finite sample bias, which carries over to the estimation of the center-subtracted test statistic.

4.1.4 Degenerate U-statistics

The primary tool needed to derive the asymptotic distribution of the kernel-based test statistics discussed in this chapter is the central limit theorem for degenerate U-statistics given in Theorem 1 of Hall (1984). A statistic of the form

$$U_n = \binom{n}{j}^{-1} \sum_{(n,j)} \psi(x_{i_1}, x_{i_2}, \ldots, x_{i_j}), \tag{4.1}$$

where the sum is taken over all permutations of $(i_1, i_2, \ldots, i_j)$ and of $\{1, 2, \ldots, j\}$, such that $1 \leq i_1 < \cdots < i_j \leq n$ is termed a U-statistic of degree j note that here and through the remainder of the book that j is a counter and is distinct from j. The function $\psi(\cdot)$ is symmetric in its arguments and is known as the kernel of the U-statistic, which should not be confused with our main use of a kernel function, which is used to smooth across data points. U-statistics have a long history in statistical theory, dating to Hoeffding (1948). The U stands for "unbiased," as both Halmos (1946) and Hoeffding (1948) showed that (4.1) is an unbiased estimator for the population characteristic $\theta(F) = \int \cdots \int \psi(x_1, \ldots, x_j) dF(x_1) \cdots dF(x_j)$. Many common estimators in practice are indeed U-statistics: for example, the sample mean[1] and the sample variance. A degenerate U-statistic is simply a U-statistic that has a mean of 0. Degenerate U-statistics are popular in nonparametric econometrics, as they give a simple framework to prove asymptotic normality for a wide range of (test) statistics.

The most common case in the literature is a second-order degenerate U-statistic given by

$$U_n = \binom{n}{2}^{-1} \sum_{i=1}^{n} \sum_{j>i}^{n} H_n(x_i, x_j)$$

$$= \frac{2}{n(n-1)} \sum_{i=1}^{n} \sum_{j>i}^{n} H_n(x_i, x_j),$$

where

$$2 \sum_{i=1}^{n} \sum_{j>i}^{n} = \sum_{i=1}^{n} \sum_{\substack{j=1 \\ j \neq i}}^{n}$$

and the terms in the binomial coefficient represent both the sample size and the number of elements (otherwise known as the order) in $H_n(x_i, x_j)$ and x_i is *iid* Further, $H_n(x_i, x_j)$ must be symmetric ($H_n(x_i, x_j) = H_n(x_j, x_i)$) with expected value zero, degenerate ($E[H_n(x_i, x_j)|x_i] = 0$) almost surely and its variance $E[H_n^2(x_i, x_j)]$ must be finite for each n. The term $H_n(x_i, x_j)$ will typically consist of (s-class) kernel functions in our problems, but this is not necessary.

---

[1] The mean functional for a distribution F (whose mean exists) is

$$\theta(F) = \int_{-\infty}^{\infty} x \, dF(x)$$

and the U-statistic that estimates $\theta(F)$ is just the sample mean

$$\bar{x}_n = \binom{n}{1}^{-1} \sum_{(n,1)} \psi(x_{i_1}) = \frac{1}{n} \sum_{i=1}^{n} x_i.$$

For this estimator $j = 1$ and the kernel function $\psi(x_{i_1})$ is the identity function.

Hall (1984) and Technical Appendix 4.1 outline that in the limit

$$\frac{U_n}{\sigma_n} \xrightarrow{d} N(0, 1),$$

where $\sigma_n^2 = 2E\left[H_n^2\left(x_i, x_j\right)\right]$ (Fan and Li, 1996, extend the result to allow for higher-order U-statistics). For the first test we will go slowly through the construction of the distance measure and the test statistic, including deriving the variance term. For later tests we will try to avoid repetitiveness and relegate most of the relevant derivations to the technical appendix.

4.1.5 Bootstrap

The bootstrap is a useful tool which can be used to evaluate test statistics when calculating the asymptotic distribution is difficult. It is also quite useful for nonparametric kernel-based tests because the test statistics converge at a slow rate. It has been shown by many authors (e.g., Mammen, 1992) that kernel-based tests perform poorly in finite samples when using the asymptotic distribution. Hence, we encourage you to use bootstrap methods when performing inference.

The basic idea behind the bootstrap is to obtain an asymptotic refinement for the distribution of the test statistic. In order to do this, you resample from the original data. This essentially allows you to treat the data as if it were the true population and you resample from your "population." In other words, you use the data you have at hand in order to get what you need – the sampling distribution of your test statistic. Therefore, the phrase "pulling yourself up by your own bootstraps," as we believe Efron (1979) envisioned, seems appropriate here.

Under fairly standard regularity conditions, the sampling distribution obtained from the bootstrap procedure is essentially as accurate as an approximation obtained from first-order asymptotic theory. In fact, it is sometimes more accurate and it does not require going through (potentially) difficult theory.

The conditions for which the bootstrap estimator is consistent are given in Beran and Ducharme (1991). We outline their proof in Technical Appendix 4.2. Necessary and sufficient conditions for consistent estimation for the bootstrap are given in Mammen (1992). Similar to the case with degenerate U-statistics, we can check the conditions in Mammen (1992) to ensure that our bootstrap is consistent. However, the conditions that cause inconsistency in econometrics are uncommon. Thus the bootstrap, when performed correctly, is consistent for most economic problems.

The key to performing any bootstrap in practice is to make sure that you generate data under the null hypothesis. Recall that the goal is to evaluate the distribution of the test statistic under the null hypothesis. Therefore, when reconstructing your test statistic, in order for this reconstruction to be valid, the null hypothesis must hold. Each test requires a specific bootstrap procedure to ensure that the null hypothesis holds. While our discussion of each bootstrap may appear repetitive, our goal is to outline a set of resampling instructions such that you can confidently implement these tests in practice and potentially see how to construct a bootstrap for a different null hypothesis that you wish to test.

4.2 Equality

Perhaps the most commonly applied nonparametric density-based test is a test for whether or not two random samples are from the same distribution. For example, it can be used to determine whether income distributions are equal across different groups of countries or across time periods (e.g., Henderson and Russell, 2005). Here we consider the case where we have two sets of data drawn at random that may or may not be correlated and may or may not be of the same length. However, they must be of the same dimension.

Not only will this test be useful for testing whether or not two variables come from the same distribution, we will also exploit it in regression. For example, it is common to compare the distributions of the gradients between two different groups. We will exploit this test as well as other tests in this chapter when examining the results from a regression model later in the text.

The kernel-based test we consider is attributed to Li (1996, 1999) for the *iid* case, but in the aforementioned papers he notes that it also will hold for correlated data. Using the extension of the Hall (1984) central limit theorem given in Fan and Li (1996), Fan and Ullah (1999) give several extensions of the tests for differences between densities for correlated data. For the purposes of this section, we note their generalization of the Li (1996) test. Formally, assume that we have two data (potentially multivariate) sets drawn at random where $\{\mathbf{x}_i\}_{i=1}^{n_1}$ and $\{\mathbf{y}_i\}_{i=1}^{n_2}$ have the pdfs $f(\cdot)$ and $g(\cdot)$, respectively. Although we allow for different sample sizes for each, we need n_1/n_2 to go to a constant as n_1 goes to infinity. In other words, both n_1 and n_2 must grow at the same speed (the reason for which will be obvious later).

Formally, we wish to test the hypothesis that

$$H_0: f(\mathbf{x}) = g(\mathbf{x})$$

for almost all $\mathbf{x}$ versus the alternative that

$$H_1: f(\mathbf{x}) \neq g(\mathbf{x})$$

on a set of positive measure. Under the null hypothesis we have

$$
\begin{aligned}
\text{ISE}(f, g) &= \int_{\mathbf{x}} \left[f(\mathbf{x}) - g(\mathbf{x}) \right]^2 d\mathbf{x} \\
&= \int_{\mathbf{x}} \left[f^2(\mathbf{x}) + g^2(\mathbf{x}) - f(\mathbf{x}) g(\mathbf{x}) - g(\mathbf{x}) f(\mathbf{x}) \right] d\mathbf{x} \\
&= \int_{\mathbf{x}} \left[f(\mathbf{x}) dF(\mathbf{x}) + g(\mathbf{x}) dG(\mathbf{x}) - f(\mathbf{x}) dG(\mathbf{x}) - g(\mathbf{x}) dF(\mathbf{x}) \right] \\
&= \int_{\mathbf{x}} f(\mathbf{x}) dF(\mathbf{x}) + \int_{\mathbf{x}} g(\mathbf{x}) dG(\mathbf{x}) - \int_{\mathbf{x}} f(\mathbf{x}) dG(\mathbf{x}) - \int_{\mathbf{x}} g(\mathbf{x}) dF(\mathbf{x}),
\end{aligned}
$$

where $f^2(\mathbf{x}) d\mathbf{x}$ can be written as $f(\mathbf{x}) f(\mathbf{x}) d\mathbf{x} = f(\mathbf{x}) dF(\mathbf{x})$.

To obtain a consistent estimator of this distance for a particular sample of data, the simplest thing to do is replace $f(\cdot)$, $g(\cdot)$, $F(\cdot)$, and $G(\cdot)$ with their nonparametric counterparts (kernel estimators for the pdf and ECDF, respectively). For example, the first term can be replaced by

$$\frac{1}{n_1} \sum_{i=1}^{n_1} \widehat{f}(\mathbf{x}_i) = \frac{1}{n_1} \sum_{i=1}^{n_1} \frac{1}{n_1 |\mathbf{h}|} \sum_{j=1}^{n_1} K_h (\mathbf{x}_i, \mathbf{x}_j)$$

$$= \frac{1}{n_1^2 |\mathbf{h}|} \sum_{i=1}^{n_1} \sum_{j=1}^{n_1} K_h (\mathbf{x}_i, \mathbf{x}_j),$$

where

$$K_h (\mathbf{x}_i, \mathbf{x}_j) = \prod_{d=1}^{q} k \left(\frac{x_{di} - x_{dj}}{h_d} \right)$$

is our notation for the standard product kernel and $|\mathbf{h}| = (h_1 h_2 \cdots h_q)$ is the product of the q different bandwidths associated with each corresponding element of $\mathbf{x}$. Following this approach for each of the remaining terms, we then have that

$$\widehat{\mathrm{ISE}}_n^c = \frac{1}{n_1} \sum_{i=1}^{n_1} \widehat{f}(\mathbf{x}_i) + \frac{1}{n_2} \sum_{i=1}^{n_2} \widehat{g}(\mathbf{y}_i) - \frac{1}{n_1} \sum_{i=1}^{n_1} \widehat{f}(\mathbf{y}_i) - \frac{1}{n_2} \sum_{i=1}^{n_2} \widehat{g}(\mathbf{x}_i)$$

$$= \frac{1}{n_1^2 |\mathbf{h}|} \sum_{i=1}^{n_1} \sum_{j=1}^{n_1} K_h (\mathbf{x}_i, \mathbf{x}_j) + \frac{1}{n_2^2 |\mathbf{h}|} \sum_{i=1}^{n_2} \sum_{j=1}^{n_2} K_h (\mathbf{y}_i, \mathbf{y}_j)$$

$$- \frac{1}{n_1 n_2 |\mathbf{h}|} \sum_{i=1}^{n_1} \sum_{j=1}^{n_2} K_h (\mathbf{x}_i, \mathbf{y}_j) - \frac{1}{n_1 n_2 |\mathbf{h}|} \sum_{i=1}^{n_2} \sum_{j=1}^{n_1} K_h (\mathbf{y}_i, \mathbf{x}_j),$$

where the superscript c denotes that we have centering term. Note that we use the subscript n to denote that this statistic depends upon the sample size (in this case both n_1 and n_2). Notice that we do not specify the bandwidth with respect to $\mathbf{x}$ or $\mathbf{y}$. This issue is not resolved (or typically mentioned) in the literature. Most articles simply state a generic bandwidth that works for both variables. Under the null hypothesis the difference is minor, but this is an issue for applied econometricians who use this test in practice. It would be possible to have a bandwidth vector for $\mathbf{x}$ and another bandwidth vector for $\mathbf{y}$ for the first and second terms, respectively. However, it is unclear what bandwidth should be used for the third and fourth terms. A safe but very time-consuming option is to check the value of the test for all possible combinations. If you wish to avoid this, we advocate using a bandwidth scaled for $\mathbf{x}$ for the first and fourth terms and a bandwidth scaled for $\mathbf{y}$ for the second and third terms. Our justification for this argument is that we are looking at the distance from $\mathbf{x}$ in the first and fourth terms and the distance from $\mathbf{y}$ in the second and third terms. In subsequent tests the choice of bandwidth is more obvious.

A separate issue with this proposed test statistic is the double summation used to calculate it. Recall that we argued that the double summation may lead to a nonzero centering term. Leaving out the ith observation in the second summation for the first term gives

$$\frac{1}{n_1} \sum_{i=1}^{n_1} \widehat{f}_{-i}(\mathbf{x}_i) = \frac{1}{n_1} \sum_{i=1}^{n_1} \frac{1}{(n_1 - 1) |\mathbf{h}|} \sum_{\substack{j=1 \\ j \neq i}}^{n_1} K_h (\mathbf{x}_i, \mathbf{x}_j)$$

$$= \frac{1}{n_1 (n_1 - 1) |\mathbf{h}|} \sum_{i=1}^{n_1} \sum_{\substack{j=1 \\ j \neq i}}^{n_1} K_h (\mathbf{x}_i, \mathbf{x}_j).$$

This can be expanded to each of the terms above. Li (1996) shows that the center-free test statistic is

$$\widehat{\text{ISE}}_n = \frac{1}{n_1} \sum_{i=1}^{n_1} \widehat{f}_{-i} (\mathbf{x}_i) + \frac{1}{n_2} \sum_{i=1}^{n_2} \widehat{g}_{-i} (\mathbf{y}_i) - \frac{1}{n_1} \sum_{i=1}^{n_1} \widehat{f}_{-i} (\mathbf{y}_i) - \frac{1}{n_2} \sum_{i=1}^{n_2} \widehat{g}_{-i} (\mathbf{x}_i)$$

$$= \frac{1}{n_1 (n_1 - 1) |\mathbf{h}|} \sum_{i=1}^{n_1} \sum_{\substack{j=1 \\ j \neq i}}^{n_1} K_h (\mathbf{x}_i, \mathbf{x}_j) + \frac{1}{n_2 (n_2 - 1) |\mathbf{h}|} \sum_{i=1}^{n_2} \sum_{\substack{j=1 \\ j \neq i}}^{n_2} K_h (\mathbf{y}_i, \mathbf{y}_j)$$

$$- \frac{1}{n_1 (n_2 - 1) |\mathbf{h}|} \sum_{i=1}^{n_1} \sum_{\substack{j=1 \\ j \neq i}}^{n_2} K_h (\mathbf{x}_i, \mathbf{y}_j) - \frac{1}{n_2 (n_1 - 1) |\mathbf{h}|} \sum_{i=1}^{n_2} \sum_{\substack{j=1 \\ j \neq i}}^{n_1} K_h (\mathbf{y}_i, \mathbf{x}_j),$$

and the center term is given in Technical Appendix 4.3. Ignoring potentially different sample sizes (we will return to this point later), under the null ($f (\mathbf{x}) = g (\mathbf{x})$), the first term is equal to the fourth term and the second term is equal to the third. Hence, under the null, ISE is equal to 0. Further note that some authors use the terms n_1 and n_2 in place of $(n_1 - 1)$ and $(n_2 - 1)$ for notational simplification and this does not make any difference asymptotically. This difference is similar to calculating a sample variance by dividing by the sample size instead of the degrees of freedom.

Now that we have a viable test statistic, we want to know its distribution. The application of Theorem 1 of Hall (1984) requires that $\widehat{\text{ISE}}_n$ can be written as a degenerate U-statistic. First, we rewrite $\widehat{\text{ISE}}_n$ as

$$\widehat{\text{ISE}}_n = \frac{2}{n_1 (n_1 - 1) |\mathbf{h}|} \sum_{i=1}^{n_1} \sum_{j<i}^{n_1} K_h (\mathbf{x}_i, \mathbf{x}_j) + \frac{2}{n_2 (n_2 - 1) |\mathbf{h}|} \sum_{i=1}^{n_2} \sum_{j<i}^{n_2} K_h (\mathbf{y}_i, \mathbf{y}_j)$$

$$- \frac{2}{n_1 (n_2 - 1) |\mathbf{h}|} \sum_{i=1}^{n_1} \sum_{j<i}^{n_2} K_h (\mathbf{x}_i, \mathbf{y}_j) - \frac{2}{n_2 (n_1 - 1) |\mathbf{h}|} \sum_{i=1}^{n_2} \sum_{j<i}^{n_1} K_h (\mathbf{y}_i, \mathbf{x}_j),$$

where each numerator now contains a 2 due to the change in the summation as discussed earlier. To simplify the discussion, we follow Section 2.2 of Li (1996) and rewrite $\widehat{\text{ISE}}_n$ as

$$\widehat{\text{ISE}}_n = \frac{2}{|\mathbf{h}|} \sum_{i=1}^{n_1} \sum_{j<i}^{n_2} H_{n_1, n_2} (z_i, z_j),$$

where

$$H_{n_1, n_2} (z_i, z_j) = \frac{1}{n_1 (n_1 - 1)} K_h (\mathbf{x}_i, \mathbf{x}_j) + \frac{1}{n_2 (n_2 - 1)} K_h (\mathbf{y}_i, \mathbf{y}_j)$$

$$- \frac{1}{n_1 (n_2 - 1)} K_h (\mathbf{x}_i, \mathbf{y}_j) - \frac{1}{n_2 (n_1 - 1)} K_h (\mathbf{y}_i, \mathbf{x}_j).$$

To prove that $H_{n_1,n_2}(z_i, z_j)$ is a degenerate U-statistic, we must show:

1. $H_{n_1,n_2}(z_i, z_j)$ is symmetric
2. $E\left[H_{n_1,n_2}(z_i, z_j)|z_i\right] = 0$
3. $E\left[H_{n_1,n_2}^2(z_i, z_j)\right] < \infty$

Technical Appendix 4.4 shows that each of these conditions holds. However, we must note that in a finite sample we cannot actually show that $H_{n_1,n_2}(z_i, z_j)$ is a degenerate U-statistic. Note that most papers in this area assume that $n_1 = n_2$ and in this case it is relatively simple to show that we have a degenerate U-statistic. Most of these papers also argue that their tests can be extended when the sample sizes differ. What they also say, or at least must be implying, is that asymptotically this will not matter assuming that n_1/n_2 converges to a constant as n_1 goes to infinity.

Now that we have (somewhat successfully) demonstrated that we have a degenerate U-statistic, we know that $(n_1 n_2 |\mathbf{h}|)^{1/2} \widehat{\text{ISE}}_n/\hat{\sigma}_n$ is standard normal asymptotically and the estimator of our variance term is

$$
\begin{aligned}
\hat{\sigma}_n^2 &= \frac{2}{|\mathbf{h}|} E\left[H_{n_1,n_2}^2(z_i, z_j)\right] \\
&= \frac{2}{|\mathbf{h}|} E\left\{\left[\begin{array}{c} K_h(\mathbf{x}_i, \mathbf{x}_j) + K_h(\mathbf{y}_i, \mathbf{y}_j) \\ -K_h(\mathbf{x}_i, \mathbf{y}_j) - K_h(\mathbf{y}_i, \mathbf{x}_j) \end{array}\right]^2\right\} \\
&= \frac{2}{|\mathbf{h}|}\left[\begin{array}{c} \frac{1}{n_1(n_1-1)} \sum\limits_{\substack{i=1}}^{n_1} \sum\limits_{\substack{j=1 \\ j\neq i}}^{n_1} K_h^2(\mathbf{x}_i, \mathbf{x}_j) + \frac{1}{n_2(n_2-1)} \sum\limits_{\substack{i=1}}^{n_2} \sum\limits_{\substack{j=1 \\ j\neq i}}^{n_2} K_h^2(\mathbf{y}_i, \mathbf{y}_j) \\ + \frac{1}{n_1(n_2-1)} \sum\limits_{\substack{i=1}}^{n_1} \sum\limits_{\substack{j=1 \\ j\neq i}}^{n_2} K_h^2(\mathbf{x}_i, \mathbf{y}_j) + \frac{1}{n_2(n_1-1)} \sum\limits_{\substack{i=1}}^{n_2} \sum\limits_{\substack{j=1 \\ j\neq i}}^{n_1} K_h^2(\mathbf{y}_i, \mathbf{x}_j) \end{array}\right],
\end{aligned}
$$

where $K_h^2(\mathbf{x}_i, \mathbf{x}_j)$ is the square of $K_h(\mathbf{x}_i, \mathbf{x}_j)$ and the term $|\mathbf{h}|$ in the denominator appears because our test statistic is written as $1/|\mathbf{h}|$ times a degenerate U-statistic. A consistent estimator of the variance can also be obtained by including the diagonal terms. This leads to a more compact form (for example, n_1^{-2} instead of $[n_1(n_1-1)]^{-1}$ in the first term). However, note that each method is consistent and will give the same result asymptotically. Further, given our advocacy of bootstrap-based tests, this difference is irrelevant for inference. We will continue to exclude the diagonal for the remaining test statistic variance terms without discussion.

Thus, our test statistic can be written as

$$
\widehat{T}_n = (n_1 n_2 |\mathbf{h}|)^{1/2} \frac{\widehat{\text{ISE}}_n}{\hat{\sigma}_n} \xrightarrow{d} N(0, 1),
$$

where the issue of which bandwidth (one based on $\mathbf{x}$ or $\mathbf{y}$) to use in order to scale the test is also relevant here. In our own work we generally use one or the other, but have also seen authors use a geometric mean.

Although we see that the test statistic is distributed as a standard normal under the null hypothesis, nonparametric tests using the asymptotic distribution perform poorly

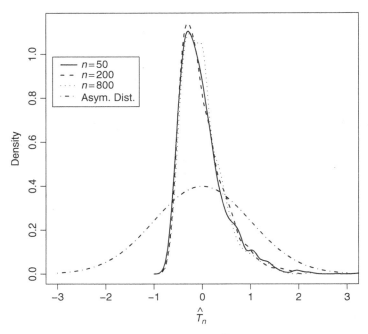

Figure 4.5. Finite sample and asymptotic distribution of $\widehat{T}_n$ for 1,000 Monte Carlo replications

in finite samples. A simple explanation for this is that while they tend towards particular distributions asymptotically, their slow rates of convergence imply that in finite samples the exact distribution may not look much like the asymptotic distribution. This is illustrated in Figure 4.5. Here we generate samples of size 50, 200, and 800 from standard normal densities and test the null of equality using rule-of-thumb bandwidths for each density. We report the finite sample densities of $\widehat{T}_n$ for 1000 Monte Carlo replications. It is quite obvious from this plot that the densities do not look like their asymptotic counterpart. Thus we suggest using a bootstrap procedure.

The basic idea here is to generate data under the null hypothesis many times and construct the sampling distribution of the test statistic. This is done by randomly sampling from the null distribution and constructing the test statistic over and over. Repeating this process a large number of times will provide us with the sampling distribution of the test statistic. We then compare the value of the original estimated test statistic to that distribution to see if we lie in the upper tail. Recall that under the null hypothesis, ISE is equal to zero and it is strictly positive under the alternative. Thus, under the null hypothesis $T_n = 0$, and it is strictly positive under the alternative. That being said, it is possible for the test statistic to be negative in any particular sample and a negative value would generally point to a failure to reject the null.

The scaling terms are relevant in terms of the asymptotic distribution, but these are not of extreme importance when using bootstrap-based methods to calculate p-values. It is feasible, and perhaps worthwhile, when bootstrapping the test statistics to consider the p-value for both $\widehat{T}_n$ and $\widehat{\text{ISE}}_n$. This can be done in the same computer program by simply saving both the estimates of $\widehat{T}_n$ and $\widehat{\text{ISE}}_n$ and the bootstrapped versions of each.

Li (1999) developed our preferred bootstrap for this particular test. Given that the null assumes that both samples come from the same distribution, we can pool the data and randomly sample with replacement from the pooled data set. The bootstrap we suggest for this particular test is as follows:

1. Compute the test statistics $\widehat{T}_n$ for the original sample of $\{x_1, x_2, \ldots, x_{n_1}\}$ and $\{y_1, y_2, \ldots, y_{n_2}\}$.
2. Define the pooled sample as $\Psi = \{x_1, x_2, \ldots, x_{n_1}, y_1, y_2, \ldots, y_{n_2}\}$. Randomly sample, with replacement from Ψ, n_1 observations for the construction of $f(\cdot)$ and call this sample $\{x_i^*\}_{i=1}^{n_1}$. Similarly, randomly sample, with replacement from Ψ, n_2 observations for the construction of $g(\cdot)$ and call this sample $\{y_i^*\}_{i=1}^{n_2}$.
3. Calculate $\widehat{T}_n^*$ where $\widehat{T}_n^*$ is calculated the same way as $\widehat{T}_n$ except that x_i and y_i are replaced by x_i^* and y_i^*, respectively.
4. Repeat steps 2 and 3 a large number (B) of times and then construct the sampling distribution of the bootstrapped test statistics. We reject the null of equality if the estimated test statistic $\widehat{T}_n$ is greater than the upper α-percentile of the bootstrapped test statistics.

4.3 Parametric specification

Here we consider the problem of testing a known parametric density versus a non-parametric alternative. We assume that $f(x)$ is unknown and $g(x) = g(x, \theta)$ is a known parametric density with known or unknown parameter vector θ. This test was previously studied by Bickel and Rosenblatt (1973) and Rosenblatt (1975). However, these tests can handle at most two dimensions and require that the data are under-smoothed, so the kernel estimator is suboptimal. Fan (1994), taking an idea similar to that in Härdle and Mammen (1993), presents a test that does not require the data to be undersmoothed.

Formally, the null hypothesis is that the unknown density is equal to some known parametric density

$$H_0 : f(x) = g(x, \theta)$$

for almost all x versus the alternative that

$$H_1 : f(x) \neq g(x, \theta)$$

on a set of positive measure. The basic idea is to estimate each model, the unknown by kernel estimation and the parametric by maximum likelihood, and then test the difference between the two. Fan (1994) considers ISE to test this difference. Formally, we have

$$\text{ISE}^*(f, g) = \int_{\mathbf{x}} [f(x) - g(x, \theta)]^2 \, dx.$$

The asymptotic distribution of ISE (f, g) can be derived and this was studied by Bickel and Rosenblatt (1973) among others. Fan (1994) shows that the distribution of this test statistic depends upon the level of smoothing. To avoid this complicaiton, she compares $\widehat{f}(\mathbf{x})$ to $K_h(\cdot) * g(\mathbf{x}, \widehat{\theta})$. In other words, she replaces the maximum likelihood estimator with a smoothed version. The integrated squared error becomes

$$\text{ISE}(f, g) = \int_{\mathbf{x}} \left[f(\mathbf{x}) - K_h(\cdot) * g(\mathbf{x}, \theta) \right]^2 d\mathbf{x},$$

where

$$K_h(\cdot) * g(\mathbf{x}, \theta) = \int_{\mathbf{x}} \frac{1}{|\mathbf{h}|} K_h(\mathbf{x}, u) g(u, \theta) du.$$

Given the above information, Technical Appendix 4.5 shows that we construct our test statistic as

$$\widehat{T}_n = (n |\mathbf{h}|)^{1/2} \frac{\widehat{\text{ISE}}_n}{\widehat{\sigma}_n} \xrightarrow{d} N(0, 1),$$

where (noting that we follow Li and Racine (2007) and remove the diagonal terms) ISE equals

$$\widehat{\text{ISE}}_n = \frac{1}{n(n-1)|\mathbf{h}|} \sum_{i=1}^{n} \sum_{\substack{j=1 \\ j \neq i}}^{n} K_h(\mathbf{x}_i, \mathbf{x}_j) + \int_{\mathbf{x}} \left[K_h(\cdot) * g(\mathbf{x}, \widehat{\theta}) \right]^2 d\mathbf{x}$$

$$- \frac{2}{n} \sum_{i=1}^{n} K_h(\mathbf{x}_i, \mathbf{x}) * g(\mathbf{x}_i, \widehat{\theta}),$$

and

$$\widehat{\sigma}_n^2 = \frac{2}{n(n-1)|\mathbf{h}|} \sum_{i=1}^{n} \sum_{\substack{j=1 \\ j \neq i}}^{n} K_h^2(\mathbf{x}_i, \mathbf{x}_j).$$

Notice that we only have one sample of data and hence do not need to worry about the problems associated with different sample sizes and bandwidths as we did in the test of equality.

Calculation of the second and third terms in $\widehat{\text{ISE}}_n$ are slightly more involved. In some cases, integration of the second term is not necessary. For example, if you have a Gaussian kernel and the assumed distribution of $g(\mathbf{x}, \theta)$ is also normal, then a closed form solution for the second and third terms exists. Fan (1994, 333) shows how to calculate ISE* in the aforementioned (univariate) case. For $\widehat{\text{ISE}}_n$, Technical Appendix 4.6 shows that this can be written as

$$\widehat{\text{ISE}}_n = \frac{1}{n(n-1)h} \sum_{i=1}^{n} \sum_{\substack{j=1 \\ j \neq i}}^{n} k\left(\frac{x_i - x_j}{h} \right) + \frac{1}{2\sqrt{\pi}(h^2 + \widehat{\sigma}^2)^{1/2}}$$

$$- \frac{2}{n\sqrt{2\pi}(h^2 + \widehat{\sigma}^2)^{1/2}} \sum_{i=1}^{n} \exp\left[-\frac{(x_i - \widehat{\mu})^2}{2(h^2 + \widehat{\sigma}^2)} \right],$$

where $\widehat{\mu}$ and $\widehat{\sigma}^2$ are the sample mean and variance estimates of the random sample $\{x_i\}_{i=1}^n$. This is a bit cumbersome to program, but it is a closed-form solution. Even if a closed-form solution does not exist, if you have a univariate data set, these terms are relatively easy for a computer to handle. However, for some combinations of kernels and densities, this may be a very difficult problem and given the number of possibilities, we omit any further discussion here.

We now turn our attention to a bootstrap procedure. The basic idea is to generate data from the hypothesized parametric density. For example, assuming the distribution was normal with estimated mean $\widehat{\mu}$ and variance $\widehat{\sigma}^2$, you would use a random number generator to take draws from that distribution with corresponding mean and variance. Note that many programs only offer a standard normal random number generator. In this case you would multiply that by $\widehat{\sigma}$ and add $\widehat{\mu}$. Other null hypotheses may be more complicated. Here we formally outline a simple four-step bootstrap procedure to perform a test that the unknown distribution is equal to the assumed parametric distribution.

1. Compute the test statistics $\widehat{T}_n$ for the original sample $\{\mathbf{x}_1, \mathbf{x}_2, \ldots, \mathbf{x}_n\}$ of data.
2. Draw $i = 1, 2, \ldots, n$ bootstrap observations $\{\mathbf{x}_i^*\}_{i=1}^n$ from the null distribution $g\left(\mathbf{x}, \widehat{\theta}\right)$.
3. Use the bootstrap sample to construct the bootstrap test statistic $\widehat{T}_n^*$, where $\widehat{T}_n^*$ is calculated in the same way as $\widehat{T}_n$, but $\mathbf{x}_i$ is replaced by $\mathbf{x}_i^*$.
4. Repeat steps 2 and 3 a large number (B) of times and then construct the sampling distribution of the bootstrapped test statistics. We reject the null of the hypothesized parametric density if the estimated test statistic $\widehat{T}_n$ is greater than the upper α-percentile of the bootstrapped test statistics.

You may also be interested in a separate test for an unknown conditional pdf versus a parametric conditional pdf. The first kernel-based test we are aware of was developed by Zheng (2000) for continuous data. This test was later extended by Fan, Li, and Min (2006) for discrete data.

4.4 Independence

For some applications it may be important to determine whether or not two (potentially sets of) variables are independent of one another. For example, Wilson (2003) documents how the independence assumption between efficiency and output is important for bootstrapping data envelopment analysis estimators. Alternatively, recall the curse of dimensionality problem touched upon in Chapter 3. If we can determine that two variables are independent when estimating a bivariate density, then we can lessen the curse of dimensionality by estimating the marginal densities separately to construct the bivariate density. Here we present a kernel-based test for independence (Ahmad and Li, 1997a). The basic idea behind the test is to see if the joint distribution is different from the product of the marginal distributions. It is relatively straightforward as compared to the previous tests, but follows a similar structure to those as well. Su and

White (2008) consider using a Hellinger distance to construct a test for independence, but we omit further discussion on this test and direct those interested to their paper.

We begin by considering the random variables $\mathbf{x}$ and $\mathbf{y}$ where each may be multidimensional and they need not be of the same dimension. Call their joint density $f_{\mathbf{x},\mathbf{y}}(\mathbf{x}, \mathbf{y})$ and their marginal densities $f_{\mathbf{x}}(\mathbf{x})$ and $f_{\mathbf{y}}(\mathbf{y})$, respectively. Our goal here is to test the null that the random vectors $\mathbf{x}$ and $\mathbf{y}$ are independent of one another. Our null hypothesis is thus

$$H_0 : f_{\mathbf{x},\mathbf{y}}(\mathbf{x}, \mathbf{y}) = f_{\mathbf{x}}(\mathbf{x}) \, f_{\mathbf{y}}(\mathbf{y})$$

for almost all $\mathbf{x}$ and $\mathbf{y}$, versus the alternative that

$$H_1 : f_{\mathbf{x},\mathbf{y}}(\mathbf{x}, \mathbf{y}) \neq f_{\mathbf{x}}(\mathbf{x}) \, f_{\mathbf{y}}(\mathbf{y})$$

on a set of positive measure.

The distance between the joint and marginal distributions can be written as

$$\text{ISE}\left(f_{\mathbf{x}.\mathbf{y}}, f_{\mathbf{x}}f_{\mathbf{y}}\right) = \int_{\mathbf{y}} \int_{\mathbf{x}} \left[f_{\mathbf{x},\mathbf{y}}(\mathbf{x}, \mathbf{y}) - f_{\mathbf{x}}(\mathbf{x}) \, f_{\mathbf{y}}(\mathbf{y}) \right]^2 d\mathbf{x} d\mathbf{y}.$$

We note that when $\mathbf{x}$ and $\mathbf{y}$ are independent of one another, $f_{\mathbf{x},\mathbf{y}}(\mathbf{x}, \mathbf{y}) = f_{\mathbf{x}}(\mathbf{x}) \, f_{\mathbf{y}}(\mathbf{y})$ and $\text{ISE}\left(f_{\mathbf{x},\mathbf{y}}, f_{\mathbf{x}}f_{\mathbf{y}}\right)$ will be equal to zero.

Technical Appendix 4.7 shows that our test statistic can be written as

$$\widehat{T}_n = n \left(|\mathbf{h_x}| \, |\mathbf{h_y}| \right)^{1/2} \frac{\widehat{\text{ISE}}_n}{\widehat{\sigma}_n} \overset{d}{\to} N(0, 1),$$

where

$$\widehat{\text{ISE}}_n = \frac{1}{n(n-1)|\mathbf{h_x}| \, |\mathbf{h_y}|} \sum_{i=1}^{n} \sum_{\substack{j=1 \\ j \neq i}}^{n} K_{h_{\mathbf{x}}}\left(\mathbf{x}_i, \mathbf{x}_j\right) K_{h_{\mathbf{y}}}\left(\mathbf{y}_i, \mathbf{y}_j\right)$$

$$+ \frac{1}{n^2(n-1)^2 |\mathbf{h_x}| \, |\mathbf{h_y}|} \sum_{i=1}^{n} \sum_{\substack{j=1 \\ j \neq i}}^{n} K_{h_{\mathbf{x}}}\left(\mathbf{x}_i, \mathbf{x}_j\right) \sum_{r=1}^{n} \sum_{\substack{l=1 \\ r \neq l}}^{n} K_{h_{\mathbf{y}}}\left(\mathbf{y}_r, \mathbf{y}_l\right)$$

$$- \frac{2}{n(n-1)^2 |\mathbf{h_x}| \, |\mathbf{h_y}|} \sum_{i=1}^{n} \sum_{\substack{j=1 \\ j \neq i}}^{n} \sum_{\substack{l=1 \\ l \neq j}}^{n} K_{h_{\mathbf{x}}}\left(\mathbf{x}_i, \mathbf{x}_j\right) K_{h_{\mathbf{y}}}\left(\mathbf{y}_j, \mathbf{y}_l\right),$$

where $|\mathbf{h_x}| = \left(h_{x_1} h_{x_2} \cdots h_{x_q} \right)$ and $|\mathbf{h_y}| = \left(h_{y_1} h_{y_2} \cdots h_{y_q} \right)$ and

$$\widehat{\sigma}_n^2 = \frac{2}{n(n-1)|\mathbf{h_x}| \, |\mathbf{h_y}|} \sum_{i=1}^{n} \sum_{\substack{j=1 \\ j \neq i}}^{n} K_{h_{\mathbf{x}}}^2\left(\mathbf{x}_i, \mathbf{x}_j\right) K_{h_{\mathbf{y}}}^2\left(\mathbf{y}_i, \mathbf{y}_j\right).$$

Given that we have our feasible test statistic, we can proceed to the bootstrap. The null hypothesis here is that $\mathbf{x}$ and $\mathbf{y}$ are independent of one another. This must be reflected in the bootstrap. Under the null our data are assumed to be independent and we suggest that you randomly draw from each vector separately. In other words, we are no longer sampling $(\mathbf{x}, \mathbf{y})$ "pairs" of the data. This should lead to an independent sample. Our proposed four-step procedure for the bootstrap is as follows:

1. Compute the test statistics $\widehat{T}_n$ for the original sample pairs $\{(\mathbf{x}_1, \mathbf{y}_1), (\mathbf{x}_2, \mathbf{y}_2), \ldots, (\mathbf{x}_n, \mathbf{y}_n)\}$.
2. Draw $i = 1, 2, \ldots, n$ bootstrap observations (with or without replacement) $\{\mathbf{x}_i^*\}_{i=1}^n$ from the original data $\{\mathbf{x}_i\}_{i=1}^n$. Then (separately) draw $i = 1, 2, \ldots, n$ bootstrap observations (with or without replacement) $\{\mathbf{y}_i^*\}_{i=1}^n$ from the original data $\{\mathbf{y}_i\}_{i=1}^n$. Combine the data as $\{(\mathbf{x}_i^*, \mathbf{y}_i^*)\}_{i=1}^n$ and call this the bootstrap sample.
3. Use the bootstrap sample to construct the bootstrap test statistic $\widehat{T}_n^*$, where $\widehat{T}_n^*$ is calculated in the same way as $\widehat{T}_n$, but using $\{(\mathbf{x}_i^*, \mathbf{y}_i^*)\}_{i=1}^n$ instead of $\{(\mathbf{x}_i, \mathbf{y}_i)\}_{i=1}^n$.
4. Repeat steps 2 and 3 a large number (B) of times and then construct the sampling distribution of the bootstrapped test statistics. We reject the null of independence if the estimated test statistic $\widehat{T}_n$ is greater than the upper α-percentile of the bootstrapped test statistics.

4.5 Symmetry

Symmetry is of interest in many areas of economics. For example, it is used in constructing predictive regions for nonlinear time series (Polonik and Yao, 2000). Here we will focus on the case of symmetry about zero, but this can be modified if needed. To keep consistent with the methodology above, we present the test of Ahmad and Li (1997b). We will only consider the univariate case, but note that Ahmad and Li (1997b) consider a bivariate case as well. Su (2006) provides a test which allows for multivariate data, but the symmetry hypothesis is restricted to a single variable.

The null for our test of symmetry is

$$H_0 : f(x) = f(-x)$$

almost always, versus the alternative

$$H_1 : f(x) \neq f(-x) .$$

on a set with positive measure. Note here that our hypothesis focuses on the classic case of symmetry about the origin. If you are interested in the less common notion of symmetry about a particular point, everything will hold suit if you first re-center your data around that point. For this hypothesis we have

$$\text{ISE}(f, f_-) = \int_x [f(x) - f(-x)]^2 \, dx, \text{ where we use the notation } f_- \text{ to denote } f(-x).$$

We note that when the density is symmetric $f(x) = f(-x)$, $\text{ISE}(f, f_-)$ will be equal to zero.

Technical Appendix 4.8 shows that we can write our test statistic as

$$\widehat{T}_n = (nh)^{1/2} \frac{\widehat{\text{ISE}}_n}{\widehat{\sigma}_n} \xrightarrow{d} N(0, 1),$$

where

$$\widehat{\text{ISE}}_n = \frac{1}{n(n-1)h} \sum_{i=1}^{n} \sum_{\substack{j=1 \\ j \neq i}}^{n} \left[k\left(\frac{x_i - x_j}{h}\right) - k\left(\frac{x_i + x_j}{h}\right) \right],$$

and where the main departure from previous test statistics is that we have $(x_i + x_j)$ in the numerator of the second kernel function. Also recall that we are looking at a univariate kernel function; hence, the notation $k(\cdot)$ instead of $K_h(\cdot)$ and h instead of $|\mathbf{h}|$. Further,

$$\widehat{\sigma}_n^2 = \frac{2}{n(n-1)h} \sum_{i=1}^{n} \sum_{\substack{j=1 \\ j \neq i}}^{n} \left[k^2\left(\frac{x_i - x_j}{h}\right) + k^2\left(\frac{x_i + x_j}{h}\right) \right.$$
$$\left. -2k\left(\frac{x_i - x_j}{h}\right) k\left(\frac{x_i + x_j}{h}\right) \right].$$

To use the data at hand to construct a finite sample null distribution, Henderson and Parmeter (2013) propose a bootstrap procedure. Again, the goal is to bootstrap the data under the null hypothesis. Given that our null is symmetry around zero, Henderson and Parmeter (2013) suggest that you take your data as well as the negation of your data (i.e., multiply each of your points by -1) and have a pool of $2n$ observations. Then randomly select n observations from this symmetric sample of data. Formally, their four-step procedure for the bootstrap is as follows:

1. Compute the test statistic $\widehat{T}_n$ for the original sample $\{x_1, x_2, \ldots, x_n\}$ of data.
2. Take your original data $\{x_1, x_2, \ldots, x_n\}$, append $\{-x_1, -x_2, \ldots, -x_n\}$, and draw n observations from $\{x_1, x_2, \ldots, x_n, -x_1, -x_2, \ldots, -x_n\}$ with replacement and call $\{x_i^*\}_{i=1}^{n}$ the bootstrap sample.
3. Use the bootstrap sample to construct the bootstrap test statistic $\widehat{T}_n^*$, where $\widehat{T}_n^*$ is calculated in the same way as $\widehat{T}_n$, but x_i is replaced by x_i^*.
4. Repeat steps 2 and 3 a large number (B) of times and then construct the sampling distribution of the bootstrapped test statistics. We reject the null of symmetry if the estimated test statistic $\widehat{T}_n$ is greater than the upper α-percentile of the bootstrapped test statistics.

4.6 Silverman test for multimodality

As we discussed in the application section of Chapter 2, modality is often of interest in economic applications. Here we outline a popular kernel-based test used in economics. Further discussion of this test and alternative tests of modality can be found in Henderson, Parmeter, and Russell (2008).

Silverman (1981) showed that, for a given sample of data, if we use the Gaussian kernel to construct the kernel density estimator, the number of modes of the corresponding univariate kernel density estimate is nonincreasing in h.[2] Intuitively, the greater the degree of smoothing that is imposed, the fewer the number of modes in the estimated density. Silverman proposed the test statistic

$$\widehat{h}_{crit}^m = \inf\{h : \widehat{f}(x) \text{ has precisely } m \text{ modes}\},$$

which is well defined when $k(\cdot)$ is the Gaussian kernel. Large values of $\widehat{h}_{crit}^m$ are taken as evidence against the null hypothesis that $f(\cdot)$ has only m modes. Intuitively, a larger value of $\widehat{h}_{crit}^m$ means that more smoothing is required to eliminate the appearance of a "true" mode in a density estimate. One issue that arises in practice is the detection of spurious modes. In order to account for the existence of spurious modes in the extrema of the data set, we defer to Cheng and Hall (1998), who suggest considering only those modes that have height greater than $1.5k(0)/nh$.

The bootstrap for the Silverman test is more involved than those we previously discussed. The reason for this is that it is not *a priori* obvious how to resample in order to impose the null of m modes. Silverman's approach was to use what is known as a smooth bootstrap. The smooth bootstrap involves resampling from the original data, but with a small perturbation added to the resampled points. The nature of the perturbation corresponds to the specific null hypothesis that we are testing.

To think of this more clearly, consider resampling from a bimodal density. For a given sample size it is not guaranteed that every resample will produce an estimated bimodal density. Sometimes the estimated density could be unimodal or trimodal. However, the point is that the data need to be resampled as though they came from a bimodal density. Recall Silverman's (1981, Theorem 1) result on the monotonic relationship between the number of modes of $\widehat{f}(x)$ and the bandwidth. Thus, the larger the perturbation, the fewer the modes of the underlying density we are sampling from. The key is to make the size of the perturbation depend on the amount of smoothing necessary for $\widehat{f}(x)$ to have m modes.

Formally, the "largeness" of the $\widehat{h}_{crit}^m$ statistic can be assessed via bootstrap methods. The procedure is as follows:

1. Compute the critical bandwidth $\widehat{h}_{crit}^m$ for the original sample $\{x_1, x_2, \ldots, x_n\}$ of data.

2. Take your original data $\{x_1, x_2, \ldots, x_n\}$ and construct

$$x_i^* = (1 + (\widehat{h}_{crit}^m)^2/\widehat{\sigma}^2)(x_{(i)} + \widehat{h}_{crit}^m \varepsilon_i), \tag{4.2}$$

   where $\widehat{\sigma}^2$ is the sample variance, ε_i is a random draw from a standard normal density (unrelated to the fact that we use a Gaussian kernel), and $x_{(i)}$ is sampled uniformly with replacement from $\{x_1, x_2, \ldots, x_n\}$. Call $\{x_i^*\}_{i=1}^n$ the (smoothed) bootstrap sample. The appearance of the factor $(\widehat{h}_{crit}^m)^2/\widehat{\sigma}^2$ in (4.2) appears so that the resampled data has variance equal to the sample data.

3. Use the bootstrap sample to construct the bootstrap density $\widehat{f}^*(x)$ using $\widehat{h}_{crit}^m$ and x_i^* and determine the number of modes of $\widehat{f}^*(x)$.

---

[2] This condition is not true for the Epanechnikov kernel. This follows given the discontinuous nature of the first derivative of the Epanechnikov kernel.

4. Repeat steps 2 and 3 a large number (B) of times and then construct the sampling distribution of the bootstrapped test statistics. We the null of m modes

$$\widehat{P} = \big(\# \text{ of occurrences in which } \widehat{f}^{*}(x) \text{ has more than } m \text{ modes}\big)\,/\,B.$$

Rejection of the null hypothesis that $f\,(\cdot)$ has m modes against the alternative hypothesis that $f\,(\cdot)$ has more than m modes at the α confidence level is then determined by $\widehat{P} \geq 1 - \alpha$.

Note that this test is conducted in a conservative manner (Mammen, Marron, and Fisher, 1992). The smoothed bootstrap, by using a perturbation based on $\widehat{h}^{m}_{crit}$, in essence samples data from the most m-modal distribution possible. Sampling from a less extreme m-modal distribution could lead to a different conclusion. Recall that the bootstrap should resample from the null hypothesis, which in this case is that the true distribution has m modes. However, there is more than one m-modal distribution to sample from. Silverman's suggestion was to resample from the most m-modal distribution, which is why the underlying test is conservative.

To understand this conservativeness visually, consider Figure 4.6. Here, for a sample of 250 drawn at random from a standard normal distribution, we plot three different estimated densities. The density with the solid line is constructed using the rule-of-thumb bandwidth described in Chapter 2, while the dashed line is $h^{1}_{crit} = 0.20$ and the dotted line smooths the data with twice the rule-of-thumb bandwidth. Silverman's test resamples from the dashed density, which is the most extreme unimodal distribution

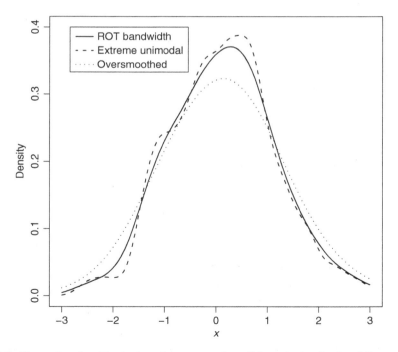

Figure 4.6. Competing densities to draw from to test the null hypothesis of unimodality

for this data. However, if the data were truly unimodal, it is unlikely that they would stem explicitly from this density. As such, sampling from either the solid or dotted densities would also represent resampling under the null. The fact that we may sample from an array of unimodal densities leads to the conservative performance of the test.

To combat the conservative nature of this test, Hall and Huang (2001) calibrate the Silverman test to obtain the correct asymptotic level. Theoretically they show that it can be calibrated to test for any number of modes, but they are only able to calculate the calibration factors numerically for the null hypothesis of unimodality (with multimodality as the alternative hypothesis).

Hall and York (2001) show that the Silverman test is appropriately modified by setting $h = \lambda_\alpha \widehat{h}^m_{crit}$ in (4.2), where λ_α is chosen so that the test has asymptotic level α. They determine λ_α for testing the null of one mode versus the alternative of more than one mode from the bootstrap distribution of $\widehat{h}^{1*}_{crit}/\widehat{h}^1_{crit}$, where $\widehat{h}^{1*}_{crit}$ is the infimum of all bandwidths h such that (4.2) has exactly one mode. They set up an α-level test that rejects the null hypothesis if

$$\widehat{P} = P\left(\widehat{h}^{1*}_{crit}/\widehat{h}^1_{crit} \le \lambda_\alpha\right)$$
$$= P\left(\widehat{h}^{1*}_{crit} \le \lambda_\alpha \widehat{h}^1_{crit}\right) \ge 1 - \alpha.$$

The calibration factor (λ_α) corrects for the fact that the distribution of $P\left(\widehat{h}^{1*}_{crit} \le \widehat{h}^1_{crit}\right)$ is not uniform on the interval $(0, 1)$. Hall and York (2001) show that the bootstrap distribution function

$$\widehat{G}_n(\lambda) = P\left(\widehat{h}^{1*}_{crit}/\widehat{h}^1_{crit} \le \lambda_\alpha\right),$$

converges in probability to a stochastic process for which the distribution is independent of unknowns. This property allows them to determine λ_α uniquely, for every α, as

$$\lambda_\alpha = \frac{a_1\alpha^3 + a_2\alpha^2 + a_3\alpha + a_4}{\alpha^3 + a_5\alpha^2 + a_6\alpha + a_7},$$

where $a_1 = 0.94029$, $a_2 = -1.59914$, $a_3 = 0.17695$, $a_4 = 0.48971$, $a_5 = -1.77793$, $a_6 = 0.36162$, and $a_7 = 0.42423$. For standard-sized tests, the corresponding λ results in approximately a 15% inflation of the critical bandwidth being tested.

The bootstrap for the calibrated version of the Silverman test only requires one minor modification. In step 2, replace $\widehat{h}^1_{crit}$ with $\lambda_\alpha \widehat{h}^1_{crit}$, wherever it occurs, again noting that the calibrated version of the test considers the case of unimodality versus multimodality ($m = 1$).

4.7 Testing in practice

For the tests described here, there are several practical issues to keep in mind. These focus on the use of tests with or without center terms, the use of a bootstrap version of the test versus the asymptotic distribution, and the appropriate selection of the bandwidth. With regards to centering terms, the theoretical literature is unambiguous. Test statistics without center terms should be used to prevent an asymptotic bias. For the decision to deploy a bootstrap, the vast majority of empirical researchers concur. However, for which bandwidths to use, there is less consensus. Very few papers (theoretical or applied) discuss bandwidth selection (other than specifying the rate of decay that the bandwidth vector must satisfy).

4.7.1 Bootstrap versus asymptotic distribution

While electing to use a bootstrap version of the tests discussed above is computationally expensive relative to using the asymptotic distribution, many of the normalized test statistics converge slowly and the normal distribution is a poor approximation for the sample sizes common in empirical applications. Acknowledging the computational cost of the bootstrap, we require that the number of bootstraps is such that $\alpha(B + 1)$ is an integer. The reason for this is that if $\alpha(B + 1)$ were not an integer, then the bootstrap p-value can never equal α. Consider $\alpha = 0.05$ with $B = 9$. In this case, the bootstrap p-values could only be $\{0, 0.1, 0.2, 0.3, 0.4, 0.5, 0.6, 0.7, 0.8, 0.9, 1\}$. Here, if we obtained a bootstrap p-value of 0.1, it is not clear whether we are failing to reject our null hypothesis because it is actually representative of the data generating process (DGP) or if we simply did not use enough bootstrap replications to be able to reject 5% of the time. In this example, for α=5%, 19 bootstraps would suffice (though we do not recommend such a small number). One issue with selecting B too small is that power loss can occur, and in some settings the loss of power can be dramatic.

Alternatively, Davidson and MacKinnon (2000) propose obtaining a sequence of bootstrap p-values based on an increasing number of bootstraps until the estimated p-value can be statistically differentiated from α. Consider that for an α-level test, if $\widehat{T}_n > \widehat{T}_n^*$ for all B of the bootstrap samples, the probability of observing this by pure chance is $(1-\alpha)^B$. If we had 49 bootstrap samples and were testing at the 1% level, this probability is 0.61, whereas using 99 bootstrap replications at the 5% level, the same probability is 0.006. Effectively, what Davidson and MacKinnon (2000) point out is that we can calculate the probability of observing B' out of B resamples where $\widehat{T}_n^* > \widehat{T}_n$, under the null hypothesis, by pure chance via the binomial distribution. By way of example, the probability of observing 5 bootstrap test statistics larger than $\widehat{T}_n$ using 99 bootstrap replications for $\alpha = 0.05$ is 0.375, whereas the probability of observing 7 bootstrap test statistics larger than $\widehat{T}_n$ is 0.122. Thus, with relatively few bootstrap replications, we can quickly determine if the null hypothesis should be rejected.

For more advanced users, if you are still concerned that bootstrapping may pose too great a computational burden, we mention that the bootstrap is an embarrassingly parallel problem (the loops in the program with respect to the bootstraps do not depend upon one another), which means it is ideally suited to parallel processing. We direct the reader to Delgado and Parmeter (2013) for more insight on embarrassingly parallel problems and how they can be tackled in the software language R.

4.7.2 Role of bandwidth selection on reliability of tests

As with estimation, bandwidth selection plays an important role in testing hypotheses about the underlying density (or densities). The simplest approach would be to select

Table 4.1. *Bandwidths used for Monte Carlo simulations of proposed tests*

Study	$\widehat{h}$	δ	C
Fan (1994)	$C\widehat{\sigma}n^{-\delta}$	$\{1/4, 2/7\}$	$\{1.80 - 2.4\}$
Li (1996)	$Cn^{-\delta}$	$\{1/5\}$	$\{0.8, 1, 1.2\}$
Ahmad and Li (1997a)	$\widehat{\sigma}n^{-\delta}$	$\{1/5, 1/4, 1/3, 1/2\}$	–
Ahmad and Li (1997b)	$Cn^{-\delta}$	$1/5$	$\{0.8, 1, 1.2\}$
Li (1999)	$\min\{\widehat{\sigma}_x n^{-\delta}, \widehat{\sigma}_y n^{-\delta}\}$	$1/5$	–

bandwidths that are optimal for estimation of the densities. One complication with this approach is that it is not clear that this method of selecting the bandwidths maximizes the power of the test. In fact, very little empirical guidance exists in the kernel density literature on bandwidth selection for testing. In Chapter 6 we will discuss a recent approach to bandwidth selection when testing correct functional form of the regression model.

For our purposes here, we mention that the papers that develop these tests study the performance of the test statistics under a variety of scenarios for a variety of bandwidths. Table 4.1 documents the range of bandwidths deployed in each of the tests we discussed previously (aside from modality). One notable feature from the table is that none of the papers use data-driven bandwidth selection mechanisms. This most likely occurs for two reasons. First, when conducting simulations, adding in data-driven bandwidth selection can be computationally costly when performing hundreds, if not thousands, of simulations. Second, data-driven bandwidth selection, as discussed in Chapter 2, has the tendency to produce poorly estimated bandwidths, in the sense that the bandwidths are smaller than what is theoretically required, in finite samples, which carries over to the testing environment.

We note that most papers use either optimal smoothing or undersmoothing. Both Fan (1994) and Ahmad and Li (1997b) report that their proposed test displays better size properties when using a bandwidth that undersmooths the data relative to the optimal ($\delta > 1/5$). Aside from Li (1999), all of the above paper's simulations are conducted using the asymptotic distribution. The undersmoothing could help alleviate the slow convergence of the test statistic we described above. What is clear, however, is that there is no uniform approach to selecting bandwidths prior to conducting a hypothesis test. Our recommendation is to perform your test using several different bandwidths to determine if your results are sensitive to the selected amount of smoothing. Alternatively, the test could be performed over a range of bandwidths based on some simple criteria (such as picking the scale factor range to be between one fourth and four times the standard deviation of the data). If the results of the test statistic were consistent across this range, we can be reasonably confident that the insights were a product of the null hypothesis reflecting features of the DGP and not the level of smoothing. Optimal bandwidth selection for these kernel-density tests remains an open area.

4.8 Application

In this section we perform tests related to claims made in the application sections of Chapters 2 and 3 as well as other tests proposed in this chapter. We begin by testing equality between specific densities and also test for normality, independence, symmetry, and the number of modes. In each case we set the number of bootstrap replications to 999. This is both to ensure that the results are robust and to allow you to run them relatively quickly on your own machine. Given the discussion above (and to decrease computation time), we limit our bandwidth choice to the most basic Silverman rule-of-thumb ($c = 1.06$) and only consider Gaussian kernels. We will also only consider normalized test statistics here, as the results for the ISE-type statistics do not differ in almost every case (and none substantially). We will consider more interesting comparisons (say with different bandwidths, types of test statistics, etc.) in our regression testing chapter (Chapter 6) as we find more differences arise in this context (in our applications). That being said, it is feasible to slightly modify the code given on this text's website to validate these claims.

4.8.1 Equality

For the test of equality, we can consider many types of comparisons, but here we examine two of specific interest. The first is in the time-series dimension. Specifically, we are interested in whether the 1960 distribution of output per worker is equal to the 2005 distribution of output per worker. Both common sense and visual inspection of Figure 4.7 would lead us to believe that they are different (the output measure in each year is divided by its respective mean – as are all figures in this application). This difference is confirmed by the p-value in Table 4.2, which is less than 0.01.

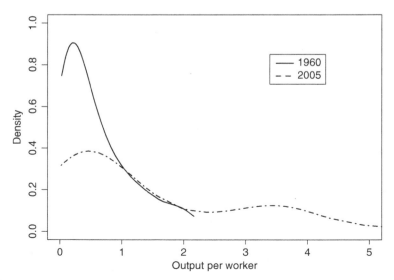

Figure 4.7. Kernel density estimates of normalized output per worker in 1960 and 2005 using Silverman rule-of-thumb bandwidths

Table 4.2. *Various tests presented in the chapter (equality, correct*
specification, independence, symmetry, and modality) – each
element in the table represents the p-value (for the normalized test
statistic) for a given test – all p-values are computed via 999
bootstrap replications

	p-value
Equality	
y_{1960} vs. y_{2005}	0.0020
y_{OECD} vs. $y_{non\text{-}OECD}$	0.0000
Normality	
y_{2005}	0.0000
k_{2005}	0.0000
h_{2005}	0.0000
Independence	
k_{2005} vs. h_{2005}	0.0020
y_{1990} vs. y_{2005}	0.0000
Symmetry	
y_{1960}	0.0000
y_{1975}	0.0000
y_{1990}	0.0000
y_{2005}	0.0000
Unimodality (calibrated)	
y_{1960}	0.3734
y_{1975}	0.2182
y_{1990}	0.1892
y_{2005}	0.0000

A separate test of interest is to see whether or not two groups of countries differ in terms of their distribution of output per worker. In Figure 4.8, we look at the distributions for OECD and non-OECD countries. As expected, these distributions differ substantially. We would expect OECD countries to have higher output per worker, as this is a prerequisite for joining the organization (of course the process is more complicated than just having higher income). Note that we are looking over all years here as we would not have much faith in a test with $n_1 = 20$ observations (the number of OECD nations in a given year) even with a larger number in n_2 (the number of non-OECD countries). The p-value in Table 4.2 supports this difference, as it is zero to four decimal places.

4.8.2 Correct parametric specification

In our test for correct parametric specification, we consider the case where our null hypothesis is that the density of interest is normally distributed. Specifically, we consider three densities in 2005: output, physical capital and human capital (all in per-worker terms). These three densities are overlaid (all mean of unity) in Figure 4.9. The solid line is the 2005 density of output per worker shown in Figure 4.7. It is fairly obvious that each of these densities differs from the normal distribution substantially.

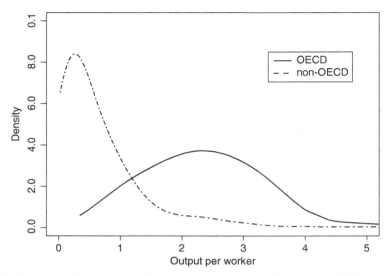

Figure 4.8. Kernel density estimates of output per worker for OECD and non-OECD nations for all years using Silverman rule-of-thumb bandwidths

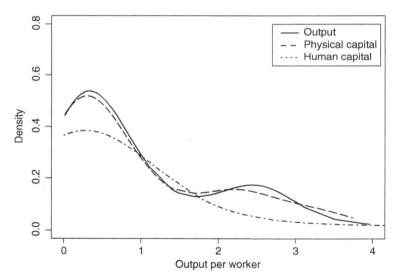

Figure 4.9. Kernel density estimates of output, physical capital, and human capital per worker in 2005 using Silverman rule-of-thumb bandwidths

This is confirmed with the formal statistical tests in Table 4.2, which reject the null in each case.

What is perhaps more interesting from this figure is the possibility of a second mode in the distribution of physical capital. We will return to this point later.

4.8.3 Independence

For the tests of independence, we again consider cases where we expect to reject the null. For the first test we look at the joint distribution of physical and human capital. We saw these joint distributions in Chapter 3. We were able to see the interplay between the two, one point of interest being the smaller mode for larger amounts of physical and human capital mode developing over time. These figures, as well as common sense, suggested that there is a link between the level of physical and human capital within a given country. The formal statistical tests confirm this as we reject the null (p-value = 0.0020).

The second test we consider is whether or not the labor productivity distributions in 1990 and 2005 are independent of one another (another interesting test would be to compare 1960 to 2005, but the number of observations differ here and recall that this test requires the sample sizes to be equal). Similar figures are shown in Chapter 2. Again, we would assume that countries that were relatively rich in 1990 would also be relatively rich in 2005. The same likely holds true for relatively poor countries. Although movement has occurred over time (mostly from relatively poor to relatively rich), we still expect to see a high level of dependence. The formal statistical test again confirms this, as we did not find a single case (in our 999 bootstraps) where the bootstrapped test statistic was larger than the test statistic. In fact, the largest boot-strapped test statistic was 1.4388 and our test statistic for this particular test is 15.8103. This result appears to support Quah's finding that the diagonal elements in an esti-mated transition matrix (lack of movement from one income group to another) are high.

4.8.4 Symmetry

It will be equally unsurprising if our distributions are asymmetric. In Figure 4.10, we plot the density of output per capita centered at zero (sample mean subtracted). We see a large mode to the left of zero and a smaller mode to the right of zero. The formal test

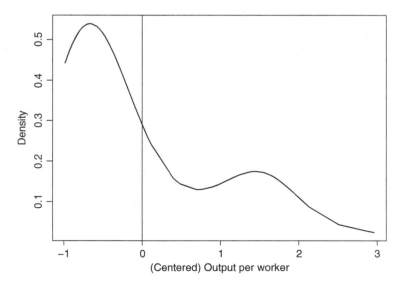

Figure 4.10. Kernel density estimate of (mean zero) output per worker in 2005 using a Silverman rule-of-thumb bandwidth – vertical line at zero shows the point around which we are testing for symmetry

confirms the asymmetry for the 2005 density as well as for the 1960, 1975, and 1990 distributions of output per worker.

4.8.5 Modality

Perhaps the most relevant tests of this chapter are for multimodality. In Chapter 2 we saw the densities in different time periods with different kernels and bandwidth selectors. Some distributions appeared unimodal, while others appeared multimodal. It was also clear that the perceived multimodality depended on the bandwidth. It therefore makes sense to consider tests that do not assume a particular bandwidth. Figure 4.7 shows the densities in the 1960 and 2005 periods with a Silverman rule-of-thumb bandwidth (optimal for Gaussian data). Similar figures for 1975 and 1990 are again in Chapter 2. As noted before, a mode appears to emerge over time, but the timing is in question. Table 4.2 gives the p-values from the calibrated version of the Silverman test for multimodality (the conclusions from the uncalibrated test do not differ) for the distribution of output per worker in each of the aforementioned years. The test fails to reject a unimodal distribution in 1960, 1975, and 1990. However, it rejects the null (p-value = 0.0000) in 2005. This result is in contrast with Henderson, Parmeter, and Russell (2008), who find multimodality (using the calibrated Silverman test and nearly identical code) as early as 1980 for real GDP per worker (note that they find multimodality as early as 1970 with output per capita). One possible explanation for this is that our data are more recent (they use the Penn World Table, Version 6.2) and include more countries.

In addition to output, Henderson, Parmeter, and Russell (2008) look at potential multimodality in the distribution of development accounting measures (capital per unit of output, marginal product of capital, human capital and total factor productivity). Here we consider the density of physical capital per worker given the possible mode in Figure 4.9. If we run the calibrated version of the Silverman test we reject the null of unimodality (p-value = 0.0070), but note that we do not observe this in earlier periods. This emergence of a bimodal distribution of physical capital accumulation could be one explanation for the emergence of a second mode in the 2005 distribution of output per worker.

5

Regression

Regression is the backbone of applied econometric research. Although regression is widespread, the vast majority of economic research assumes that regressors enter the conditional mean linearly and that each regressor is separable without any theoretical justification. Here were discuss how to estimate regression functions where we are unsure of the underlying functional form.

The nonparametric regression estimators that we will describe in this chapter will construct an estimate of the unknown function in much the same way that we constructed the unknown density: by using a local sample for each point. Whereas parametric estimators are considered global estimators (using all data points), nonparametric kernel regression estimators are local estimators, using a local sample of nearby data points to fit a specific parametric model (typically a constant or a line) and then "smooth" each of these local fits to construct the global function estimator. This allows you to focus on the local peculiarities inherent in your data set while estimating the unknown function without judicious choice of parametric functional form.

We first motivate regression through explanation of the conditional mean via its connection to conditional and joint densities. Then, similar to our discussion of the construction of kernel densities, we also consider a simplistic (nonparametric) estimator of the conditional mean. We choose a method that uses indicator functions to evaluate the conditional mean at various points. Specifically, we calculate the average value of the dependent variable at specific values of the covariates. This method is crude, but does not require us to specify the functional form *a priori*. As we also saw with density estimation, we will use our crude estimator to gain intuition and motivate kernel estimators.

Within kernel regression, there are several existing estimators which seek to estimate the unknown smooth function of interest. Here we will primarily discuss three of the most popular methods. The oldest, local-constant least-squares (LCLS), has seen less use in recent years, but is still being used, despite its shortcomings. The idea behind LCLS is that it is simply a weighted average of the left-hand-side variable. The estimate of the conditional mean is obtained by locally averaging those values of the left-hand-side variable that are "close" in terms of the values taken on by the regressors. As expected, the amount of local information used to construct the average is controlled by the bandwidth.

A popular alternative to the LCLS estimator is the local-linear least-squares (LLLS) estimator, which has dominated the theoretical literature. The basic idea behind LLLS is that we fit a line local to **x**. Again, the amount of local information used to construct the estimator is controlled by the bandwidth. The LLLS estimator possesses an array of theoretical advantages over the LCLS estimator, generally provides more accurate measurement of the conditional mean, and simultaneously provides an estimator of the first derivatives of the conditional mean.

In many cases, the gradients of the conditional mean are of primary interest to economists. These are the partial effects that are commonly examined in a linear **x** parametric setting. For example, in a production function, the gradient with respect to the capital variable is the marginal product of capital. Although the gradients come directly from LLLS, they can also be obtained from the LCLS estimator.

As before, bandwidths here are simply not a means to an end. Within different regression frameworks, the bandwidths can tell us something about the relevance or the behavior of the regressors. For instance, with LCLS, using automatic bandwidth selection criteria, when the bandwidth hits its upper bound, the regressor is deemed irrelevant. On the other hand, when performing LLLS using automatic bandwidth selection criteria, when the bandwidth hits its upper bound, the regressor enters the model linearly.

To assess the precision of our estimates, we use bootstrap methods to calculate standard errors. We outline how to perform and obtain bootstrap estimates of standard errors for both the conditional mean as well as the derivative estimates. These methods are computationally expensive, but are more reliable than the asymptotic formulas.

In the application of this chapter, we set out to estimate the worldwide production function. We attempt to model output (not its per-worker version) as a function of physical capital and human-capital-augmented labor. Our goal is to try to estimate this function while at the same time highlighting various estimators and their complications. We pay special attention to presenting results from nonparametric regressions, as this is seldom discussed in the literature.

5.1 Smoothing preliminaries

To build some intuition before jumping into specifics, suppose that the conditional mean of our joint density is $E(y|x) = x + 2e^{-16x^2}$. In Figure 5.1, we generate 100 data points via $y = x + 2e^{-16x^2} + u$ assuming that x is distributed standard normal and our error term (u) is distributed normal with mean zero and standard deviation equal to 0.4. We can see from the figure that globally this function is essentially linear. However, we see that near $x = 0$ there is local structure that is inconsistent with a linear-in-x model. To show how standard parametric modeling can fail, we plot out the fitted values using linear, quadratic, cubic, and quartic polynomials of x to estimate the unknown function.

Next, consider Figure 5.2, which plots the same data points and function, except we have removed the four low-order fits and replaced them with a 10th-order polynomial. While this function provides a more accurate fit (relative to the other polynomial functions we presented earlier) of the local structure around 0, it has done so at the expense of the global linear structure that is apparent when moving in either direction away

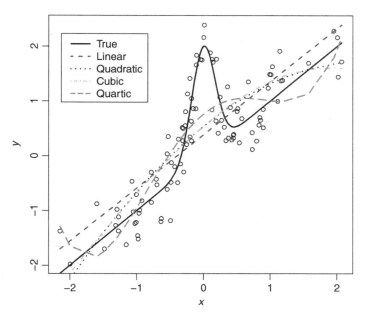

Figure 5.1. Difficulty of common parametric models fitting local structure

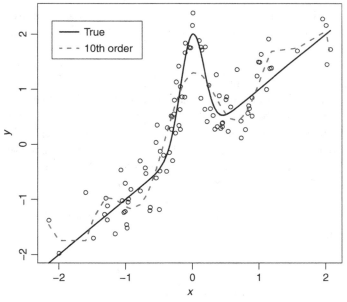

Figure 5.2. Tenth-order polynomial fit for sample with conditional mean $m(x) = x + 2e^{-16x^2}$

from 0. This represents a challenge for parametric modeling, as the selected functional form will always involve a trade-off between global and local structure.

Even though the 10th-order fit detects the hump in the unknown function, it still does not uncover the shape of the function all that well, suggesting too much variability

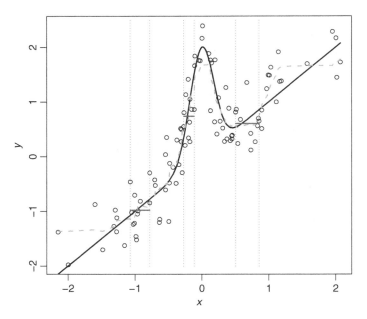

Figure 5.3. Local averaging to detect latent structure

in the linear portions of the function due to the need to fit the hump by a polynomial. To consider a naïve nonparametric estimator instead of fitting a parametric model, suppose we were to construct the function at a point as the average of the 10 points surrounding a given point. That is, we take the five closest points on each side of x and average those corresponding y values to construct an estimate of the unknown function. We repeat this for each point (noting that some points do not have five observations on each side). The end result of this process is shown in Figure 5.3 along with three channels to more clearly illustrate the windows over which the averaging is taking place. While admittedly crude, this graph is the essence of kernel-based smoothing. The key difference is in how the weights within each of these channels is constructed.

To lay the general foundation we assume that we have a response variable y and a matrix of covariates, which are used to predict the response, $\mathbf{x}$. y and $\mathbf{x}$ are related through the additive error model

$$y_i = m(\mathbf{x}_i) + u_i, \qquad i = 1, \ldots, n,$$

where $\mathbf{x}_i$ is the $1 \times q$ vector of responses ($\mathbf{x}_i = (x_{1i}, x_{2i}, \ldots, x_{qi})$). For simplicity, we will assume that the sample realizations are distributed *iid* for our discussion.

In general parametric analysis, a functional form for $m(\cdot)$ is assumed known up to a finite-dimensional number of unknown parameters. If we assume that $m(\mathbf{x}_i) = \alpha + \mathbf{x}_i \beta$, then our model can be estimated via ordinary least squares (OLS). However, if our parametric specification of the conditional mean deviates from $\alpha + \mathbf{x}_i \beta$, then the OLS estimator will likely be biased and inconsistent. Regardless of the exact form of $m(\mathbf{x})$, we can interpret it as the the conditional mean of y, $E(y|\mathbf{x})$. Doing so will allow us to develop a simple, nonparametric estimator for this quantity using our results on the conditional density estimator discussed in Chapter 3.

5.2 Local-constant estimator

Here we discuss three distinct approaches to deriving a nonparametric kernel estimator of the conditional mean. All three approaches will yield an identical estimator. We do this to help provide intuition for the conditional mean estimator and to provide insight into the potential for deriving alternative estimators. The first approach exploits results from the univariate and multivariate density chapters to construct the conditional mean estimator. The second begins with indicator functions (much like we started with for the univariate density estimation case), while the final approach considers minimizing a kernel weighted least-squares regression of y on a constant. It is the third approach from which this estimator takes its commonly used name (LCLS). The local-constant estimator is also referred to as the Nadaraya–Watson estimator after Nadaraya (1964, 1965) and Watson (1964), who independently proposed this estimator.

5.2.1 Derivation from density estimators

Recall the estimated joint density of $(y, \mathbf{x})$ in Chapter 3,

$$\widehat{f}_{y,x}(y, \mathbf{x}) = \frac{1}{nh_y |\mathbf{h}|} \sum_{i=1}^{n} k\left(\frac{y_i - y}{h_y}\right) K_h(\mathbf{x}_i, \mathbf{x}),$$

where $|\mathbf{h}| = h_1 h_2 \cdots h_q$ and

$$K_h(\mathbf{x}_i, \mathbf{x}) = \prod_{d=1}^{q} k\left(\frac{x_{id} - x_d}{h_d}\right)$$

is the product kernel. The conditional mean of y is defined as

$$E(y|\mathbf{x}) = \frac{\int y f(y, \mathbf{x}) dy}{f(\mathbf{x})}.$$

Technical Appendix 5.1 shows that our nonparametric estimator of the conditional mean is

$$\widehat{E}(y|\mathbf{x}) = \widehat{m}(\mathbf{x}) = \frac{\frac{1}{n|\mathbf{h}|} \sum_{i=1}^{n} K_h(\mathbf{x}_i, \mathbf{x}) y_i}{\frac{1}{n|\mathbf{h}|} \sum_{i=1}^{n} K_h(\mathbf{x}_i, \mathbf{x})} = \frac{\sum_{i=1}^{n} K_h(\mathbf{x}_i, \mathbf{x}) y_i}{\sum_{i=1}^{n} K_h(\mathbf{x}_i, \mathbf{x})} = \sum_{i=1}^{n} A_i(\mathbf{x}) y_i, \quad (5.1)$$

where $|\mathbf{h}| = h_1 h_2 \cdots h_q$ is the product of the q bandwidths. We see that our conditional mean is simply a weighted average of our regressand, with weights that depend on the covariates. All of the local estimators we will discuss in this chapter can be put in this form. The only aspect of the estimator that will change is the form of $A_i(\mathbf{x})$.

5.2.2 An indicator approach

There is a more intuitive way to arrive at the nonparametric estimator of the conditional mean in (5.1). Suppose for the moment that we have a single regressor. If we think of constructing a naïve estimator for the conditional mean of y, $m(x)$, we could average over the observations that are close to x. That is, our naïve estimator is

$$\widehat{m}(x) = \frac{1}{n_x} \sum_{i \in S(x)} y_i,$$

where $S(x)$ is the set of observations that are close to x and n_x is the cardinality of $S(x)$. The elements of $S(x)$ can be represented with a uniform kernel as $\mathbf{1}\{x - h < x_i \le x + h\} = \mathbf{1}\{|x_i - x| \le h\}$ and the cardinality as $n_x = \sum_{i=1}^{n} \mathbf{1}\{|x_i - x| \le h\}$. Thus, our naïve conditional mean estimator is

$$\widehat{m}(x) = \frac{\sum_{i=1}^{n} \mathbf{1}\{|x_i - x| \le h\} y_i}{\sum_{i=1}^{n} \mathbf{1}\{|x_i - x| \le h\}}.$$

Recognizing that we have used a uniform kernel, we can arrive at our kernel estimator in (5.1) by replacing the uniform kernel with the general kernel form, $k\left(\frac{x_i - x}{h}\right)$. Finally, in relation to our formulation in Equation (5.1), $A_i(x) = \mathbf{1}\{|x_i - x| \le h\}/n_x$.

5.2.3 Kernel regression on a constant

A third derivation for the nonparametric conditional mean estimator will shed light into its common name, the LCLS estimator. Instead of explicitly deriving the conditional mean from the nonparametric estimator of the conditional density, we can think of estimating the unknown function $(m(\mathbf{x}))$ as that which minimizes the weighted squared distance between the function itself and y. This is a weighted average where the weights vary by $\mathbf{x}$.

Think of how we construct the OLS estimator. We solve

$$\min_{\alpha, \beta} \sum_{i=1}^{n} (y_i - \alpha - \mathbf{x}_i \beta)^2,$$

by setting the first-order conditions equal to zero and obtaining the slope and intercept estimators.

If we instead replace $\alpha + \mathbf{x}_i \beta$ with $m(\mathbf{x})$ and introduce kernel weights, we have

$$\min_{a} \sum_{i=1}^{n} \left[y_i - m(\mathbf{x})\right]^2 K_h(\mathbf{x}_i, \mathbf{x}),$$

which has first-order condition

$$-2 \sum_{i=1}^{n} (y_i - a) K_h(\mathbf{x}_i, \mathbf{x}) = 0.$$

Solving this yields

$$a = \widehat{m}(\mathbf{x}) = \frac{\sum_{i=1}^{n} K_h(\mathbf{x}_i, \mathbf{x}) y_i}{\sum_{i=1}^{n} K_h(\mathbf{x}_i, \mathbf{x})}$$

which is identical to (5.1). We essentially regress a constant, locally, on y to determine our function at a point, hence LCLS. In matrix form, the estimator can be written as

$$\widehat{m}(\mathbf{x}) = \left(\iota' K(\mathbf{x})\iota\right)^{-1} \iota' K(\mathbf{x}) y,$$

where ι is an $n \times 1$ vector of ones and

$$K(\mathbf{x}) = \begin{bmatrix} K_h(\mathbf{x}_1, \mathbf{x}) & 0 & \cdots & 0 \\ 0 & K_h(\mathbf{x}_2, \mathbf{x}) & \cdots & 0 \\ \vdots & \vdots & \ddots & \vdots \\ 0 & 0 & \cdots & K_h(\mathbf{x}_n, \mathbf{x}) \end{bmatrix}.$$

An illustration of LCLS is displayed in Figure 5.4. This is the same data set used in the construction for Figures 5.1 to 5.3. Here we estimate the unknown curve using a bandwidth of $h = 0.15$. As opposed to our crude measure of local averaging depicted in Figure 5.3, we see the weights decrease exponentially (due to the use of a Gaussian kernel) away from the point of interest; points further away from $x = -1$ receive less weight to construct the (unknown) conditional mean than points "close" to -1. We have drawn the effective window that the LCLS estimator uses to construct the local

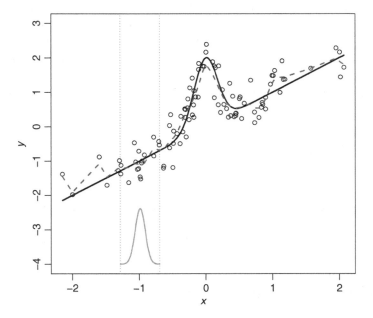

Figure 5.4. Local averaging for the LCLS estimator to detect unknown functional form

average. Given that the Gaussian kernel is nonnegative everywhere, we simply present the window as those points where the weighting is larger than 0.00001. Notice how the LCLS estimator is smoother than our crude averaging idea.

5.3 Bias, variance, and AMISE of the LCLS estimator

Here we discuss several of the asymptotic properties of the LCLS estimator. The derivations can be found in Technical Appendices 5.2-5.4.

The bias of the LCLS estimator is

$$\text{Bias}\,[\widehat{m}(\mathbf{x})] \approx \frac{\kappa_2}{2f(\mathbf{x})} \sum_{d=1}^{q} h_d^2 B_d(\mathbf{x}), \tag{5.2}$$

where $\approx$ shows up because we are ignoring smaller order terms (as we did in the density case) and where $B_d(\mathbf{x}) = 2m_d(\mathbf{x})f_d(\mathbf{x}) + m_{dd}(\mathbf{x})f(\mathbf{x})$, where $m_d(\mathbf{x})$ and $m_{dd}(\mathbf{x})$ are the first and second partial derivatives of the conditional mean with respect to the dth regressor, respectively. This equation has some intuitive properties that are worth examining. First, we notice that the bias is independent of the sample size except through the presence of the bandwidths, a common feature of nonparametric estimators. Second, our estimator has no bias when we estimate a constant (i.e., $m_d(\mathbf{x}) = m_{dd}(\mathbf{x}) = 0 \;\; \forall x$). In that case a nonparametric estimator is inappropriate to begin with. Thus, even if the data come from a linear relationship, a bias still exists for the LCLS estimator.

When we (later) consider local-polynomial least-squares, the $2m_d(\mathbf{x})f_d(\mathbf{x})$ term will not appear in the bias derivation, meaning that we will have an unbiased nonparametric estimator for linearly generated data. Further, an interesting (and somewhat unappealing) feature of LCLS is that its bias is design-dependent (the bias depends upon the distribution of the data, $f(\mathbf{x})$) and hence the distribution of the data can have an effect on the theoretical performance of the LCLS estimator. Thus, the estimator will not only depend upon the curvature of the unknown function, $m_{dd}(\mathbf{x})$, but also on the sparseness of the data. For certain data designs the estimator will perform much better than alternative designs (e.g., uniform data versus normally distributed data). We will discuss design dependency later in this chapter.

Next we consider the variance of the LCLS estimator. Our variance is

$$\text{Var}\,[\widehat{m}(\mathbf{x})] \approx \frac{\sigma^2}{f(\mathbf{x})(n\,|\mathbf{h}|)} \int K(\mathbf{t})^2 d\mathbf{t} = \frac{\sigma^2 R(k)^q}{f(\mathbf{x})(n\,|\mathbf{h}|)}.$$

See that the variance of our LCLS estimator depends on the error variance, σ^2, (inversely on) the sample size, (inversely on) the bandwidths and on the kernel chosen. What is not in the variance is any explicit feature of the function's being estimated. This is intuitive. Since we have a nonparametric estimator, we can estimate any (continuous) function arbitrarily well with a large enough data set. What causes variance in our estimator is not the function itself, but the variance of the errors that cause deviations from the function. This is a desirable feature because it implies that for highly nonlinear functions, our variance is not arbitrarily increasing simply due to the function that we are estimating. Note that this is not true for the bias and we again witness the bias–variance trade-off.

Note one important difference with the form of the variance for the LCLS estimator as opposed to the kernel density estimator of Chapter 2. The variance of the regression estimator is inversely related to the design density, whereas the variance of the density estimator is directly proportional to the design density. This has important implications for AMISE, as the integration *removed* the design from the variance component in the density setting. In the regression context this is not the case. The difference in the occurrence of the design density is intuitive. Recall that in the density setting, since we were trying to discern local structure from global structure, a higher density in a region necessarily led to a higher variance of the density estimator. Here, we need covariates to appear in a given region to be able to discern structure of the underlying conditional mean. Thus, a lower-density region will lead to higher variation in our estimator given the (relative) lack of information to work with.

Combining the results above, we can obtain the asymptotic mean integrated squared error (AMISE) of our local-constant estimator. Mathematically, AMISE $= \int E\left[(m(\mathbf{x}) - \widehat{m}(\mathbf{x}))^2\right] d\mathbf{x} = \int \text{Var}(\widehat{m}(\mathbf{x})) d\mathbf{x} + \int \text{Bias}(\widehat{m}(\mathbf{x}))^2 d\mathbf{x}$. Using the results above, we find that

$$
\text{AMISE} \approx \int \left(\frac{\kappa_2}{2f(\mathbf{x})} \sum_{d=1}^{q} h_d^2 B_d(\mathbf{x}) \right)^2 d\mathbf{x} + \int \frac{\sigma^2 R(k)^q}{f(\mathbf{x})(n\,|\mathbf{h}|)} d\mathbf{x}
$$

$$
= \frac{\kappa_2^2}{4} \sum_{d=1}^{q} \sum_{r=1}^{q} h_d^2 h_r^2 \int \frac{B_d(\mathbf{x}) B_r(\mathbf{x})}{f(\mathbf{x})^2} d\mathbf{x} + \frac{\sigma^2 R(k)^q}{n\,|\mathbf{h}|} \int f^{-1}(\mathbf{x}) d\mathbf{x}.
$$

As in the density estimation case, we see the standard bias–variance trade-off with respect to the bandwidth parameter(s). Consistency is again achieved by noting that as the sample size tends towards infinity, the bandwidths shrink, but more slowly than the sample size, so an infinite number of points are used in estimation of the unknown function at any given value of **x**.

5.4 Bandwidth selection

We plan to advocate data-driven bandwidth procedures for regression estimation, but will first start with a discussion about optimal bandwidths. To help with intuition, we first start with a univariate regression and then move to the general q-variate case.

5.4.1 Univariate digression

Our AMISE for the single dimension ($q = 1$) case is

$$
\text{AMISE} \approx \frac{\kappa_2^2 h^4}{4} \int \frac{B(x)^2}{f(x)^2} dx + \frac{\sigma^2 R(k)}{nh} \int f^{-1}(x) dx.
$$

Focusing only on the terms pertaining to the kernel chosen, the AMISE for the univariate LCLS estimator looks almost identical to the AMISE for the univariate kernel density estimator. This suggests that the choice of kernel in the regression setting is equivalent to the choice of kernel in the density setting (i.e., the Epanechnikov kernel is optimal in terms of relative efficiency). Further, we can see that developing a rule-of-thumb bandwidth is slightly more involved than in the density setting. Technical Appendix 5.5 shows that the optimal h for the univariate case is

$$\frac{\partial \text{AMISE}}{\partial h} = h^3 \kappa_2^2 \int \frac{B(x)^2}{f(x)^2} dx - \frac{\sigma^2 R(k)}{nh^2} \int f^{-1}(x)dx = 0$$

$$\rightarrow \quad h_{\text{opt}} = \left[\frac{\sigma^2 R(k) \int f^{-1}(x)dx}{\kappa_2^2 \int \frac{B(x)^2}{f(x)^2}dx} \right]^{1/5} n^{-1/5}.$$

Note (as in the density case) that the optimal level of smoothing is inversely related to the sample size augmented by a constant, which depends upon the kernel, the unknown function, the error variance, and the data design.

To see how an optimal bandwidth could be derived in practice, we consider a simple example. Suppose that the true underlying conditional mean is quadratic, $m(x) = \alpha + \beta x + \gamma x^2$, the data are distributed uniformly, $f(x) = \mathcal{U}[a, b]$, and the error process is homoskedastic, $\text{Var}(u) = \sigma_u^2$. In this setting we have $m'(x) = \beta + 2\gamma x$, $m''(x) = 2\gamma$ and $f'(x) = 0$. Therefore, $B(x) = 2\gamma$. Noting that $\int_a^b dx = b - a$, our optimal bandwidth is

$$h_{\text{opt}} = \left[R(k)/4\kappa_2^2 \right]^{1/5} \left[\sigma_u/\gamma \right]^{2/5} (b - a)^{1/5} n^{-1/5}.$$

We see here that our rule-of-thumb bandwidth depends on five different features. It depends upon the sample size, the range of the x values, $b - a$, which in turn stems from the design density $f(x)$, the variance of the errors from the regression, the quadratic coefficient (γ), and the choice of kernel. In the density case, the bandwidth depended upon the kernel, the sample size, and the unknown density. Here we have two additional aspects of our data generating process determining the ideal level of smoothing.

A useful strategy for constructing a rule-of-thumb bandwidth in the spirit of the Silverman density estimator bandwidth would be to first estimate a quadratic model via OLS to obtain $\widehat{\gamma}$ and $\widehat{u}$ (where $\widehat{u}$ is the residual). Next, the residuals can be used to construct $\widehat{\sigma}_u$. Finally, $b - a$ can be estimated as $x_{\text{max}} - x_{\text{min}}$ (or, to avoid outliers, either $x_{0.90} - x_{0.10}$, the difference in the extreme deciles or the interquartile range of the covariate). In this very specific case, if we are using the Gaussian kernel, then our rule-of-thumb regression bandwidth would be

$$h_{\text{rot}} = 0.6306 \left[\widehat{\sigma}_u/\widehat{\gamma} \right]^{2/5} (x_{0.90} - x_{0.10})^{1/5} n^{-1/5}.$$

Even in this simple case, we can see why authors often resort to data-driven bandwidths. It is common in applied work to use the univariate (Gaussian kernel) Silverman rule-of-thumb bandwidth for the LCLS estimator in the form $h_{\text{rot}} = 1.06 \widehat{\sigma}_x n^{-1/5}$, where $\widehat{\sigma}_x$ is the standard deviation of the covariate being smoothed (but there is no theoretical justification for this). If we think of $x_{0.90} - x_{0.10}$ as a measure of the variance of x, then our rule-of-thumb bandwidth for our toy case above can be seen in this form, except now the 1.06 is really a catchall for $0.6306 \left[\widehat{\sigma}_u / \widehat{\gamma}\right]^{2/5}$.

5.4.2 Optimal bandwidths in higher dimensions

For the discussion of optimal bandwidths in higher dimensions, we first consider the case of $q = 2$. If we minimize AMISE for each bandwidth, we can completely solve for the asymptotically optimal bandwidths that we should use in smoothing our unknown function. Our optimality conditions are

$$\frac{\partial \text{AMISE}}{\partial h_1} = \left(4\mathcal{B}_1 h_1^3 + 2\mathcal{B}_2 h_1 h_2^2\right) - \frac{\mathcal{V}}{nh_1^2 h_2} = 0,$$

and

$$\frac{\partial \text{AMISE}}{\partial h_2} = \left(4\mathcal{B}_2 h_2^3 + 2\mathcal{B}_1 h_2 h_1^2\right) - \frac{\mathcal{V}}{nh_1 h_2^2} = 0,$$

where $\mathcal{B}_1$, $\mathcal{B}_2$, and $\mathcal{V}$ are constants referring to the specific bias and variance components of AMISE, respectively. Lets solve for h_1 first and then find h_2. Solving for h_1 yields

$$\left(4\mathcal{B}_1 h_1^3 + 2\mathcal{B}_2 h_1 h_2^2\right) - \frac{\mathcal{V}}{nh_1^2 h_2} = 0$$

$$\left(4\mathcal{B}_1 h_1^3 + 2\mathcal{B}_2 h_1 h_2^2\right) = \frac{\mathcal{V}}{nh_1^2 h_2}$$

$$h_1^2 h_2 \left(4\mathcal{B}_1 h_1^3 + 2\mathcal{B}_2 h_1 h_2^2\right) = \mathcal{V} n^{-1}$$

$$4\mathcal{B}_1 h_1^5 h_2 + 2\mathcal{B}_2 h_1^3 h_2^3 = \mathcal{V} n^{-1}. \tag{5.3}$$

Unfortunately, there is no closed form solution for determining h_d when $q > 1$. However, when we engage in nonparametric regression, we want all of the bandwidths to be of the same rate (analogous to the multivariate density case). Thus, if we have $h_1 \sim h_2 \sim n^{-1/8}$, then we can determine that in the q-variate setting $\delta = 4 + q$ will allow for the equivalence in (5.3).

It is common to condense the notation inherent with the optimal bandwidths, which depend on the setup and kernel, terms such as $B_d(\mathbf{x})$, $f(\mathbf{x})$, σ, κ_2, and $R(k)$ into a scale factor c_d, for the dth covariate. Then, bandwidths are commonly expressed as the scale factor times the variance of the covariate times the theoretically desired rate, in our case $n^{-1/(4+q)}$. Specifically, our bandwidth for the dth regressor is

$$h_d = c_d \sigma_{x_d}^2 n^{-1/(4+q)}.$$

The rationale for this specific expression of the bandwidths is that the size of a given bandwidth relative to that variable's standard deviation provides important insight to us depending upon which regression estimator we use. Thus, writing the bandwidth such that it depends on the variance of the covariate makes this assessment clear. Note that we can assess the "size" of the bandwidth relative to $\sigma_{x_d}^2$ by considering $c_d \cdot n^{-1/(4+q)}$.

5.4.3 Least-squares cross-validation

Standard applied nonparametric papers rarely consider asymptotically optimal bandwidths (see Gasser, Kniep, and Köhler, 1991, and Ruppert, Sheather, and Wand, 1995, for plug-in bandwidth selection methods designed for kernel regression and see Chai and Moneta, 2012, for a recent example that uses plug-in bandwidth selection to estimate Engel curves nonparametrically). Instead they typically rely on cross-validation to determine the appropriate amount of smoothing for a given data set. The most common method of cross-validation is least-squares cross-validation (LSCV), defined as

$$\text{LSCV}(h) = \sum_{i=1}^{n} \left[y_i - \widehat{m}_{-i}(\mathbf{x}_i) \right]^2,$$

where the leave-one-out estimator is defined as

$$\widehat{m}_{-i}(\mathbf{x}_i) = \frac{\sum\limits_{\substack{j=1 \\ j \neq i}}^{n} y_j K_h \left(\mathbf{x}_j, \mathbf{x}_i \right)}{\sum\limits_{\substack{j=1 \\ j \neq i}}^{n} K_h \left(\mathbf{x}_j, \mathbf{x}_i \right)}.$$

We would like to note two points of interest. First, $m(\cdot)$ is replaced with the left-hand-side variable y. This replacement occurs because we do not observe $m(\cdot)$, but rather a noise corrupted version ($y = m(x) + u$). However, with the assumption that $E(u|\mathbf{x}) = 0$, on average, y_i equals $m(\mathbf{x}_i)$. Second, the presence of the leave-one-out estimator may make it appear to you as if an algorithm would require n^2 calculations per evaluation of the cross-validation function. While this is true, our cross-validation function may be rearranged so that it only involves n calculations.

To dispense with the leave-one-out estimator inside our cross-validation function, consider that many cross-validation objective functions can be written as $\sum_{i=1}^{n} \left[y_i - \widehat{m}(\mathbf{x}_i) \right]^2 \pi(\mathbf{x}_i)$ where $\pi(\cdot)$ is a weight function designed to increase with the roughness of the function (or, alternatively, $\pi(\cdot)$ is designed to decrease with the smoothness of the function). For LSCV, Technical Appendix 5.6 shows that

$$\pi(\mathbf{x}_i) = \left(\frac{\sum\limits_{j=1}^{n} K_h \left(\mathbf{x}_j, \mathbf{x}_i \right)}{\sum\limits_{\substack{j=1 \\ j \neq i}}^{n} K_h \left(\mathbf{x}_j, \mathbf{x}_i \right)} \right)^2,$$

the squared ratio of the kernel sum against the leave-one-out kernel sum. The closer this ratio is to one (regardless of bandwidth), the more points there are near $\mathbf{x}_i$ to smooth over. The further the ratio is from one (regardless of bandwidth), the fewer points there are near $\mathbf{x}_i$ to smooth over. Note what happens as $h \to 0$. In this case, the kernel function forces all points to be "far" from $\mathbf{x}_i$, essentially giving them no weight. Thus, for $h = 0$ we have $\pi(\mathbf{x}_i) = k(0)^q/0 = \infty \; \forall i$ forcing LSCV to diverge to ∞.

We can also see what would happen if we failed to use a leave-one-observation-out estimator in this setting, i.e., $\pi(\mathbf{x}_i) = 1 \; \forall i$. In this case ($h \to 0$), we see from our definition of the local-constant estimator that the only point in the local average used to construct the conditional mean is the ith point. That gives us

$$\widehat{m}(\mathbf{x}_i) = \frac{\sum_{j=1}^{n} K_h(\mathbf{x}_j, \mathbf{x}_i) y_j}{\sum_{j=1}^{n} K_h(\mathbf{x}_j, \mathbf{x}_i)} = \frac{k(0)^q y_i}{k(0)^q} = y_i.$$

In this case the LSCV function will achieve its optimal minimum value, 0. Since we do not want to interpolate the data, the weight function is introduced to provide a further balance between bias and variance. Intuitively, if we were to interpolate our data ($h = 0$) then we have no bias, but infinite variance. Cross-validation functions, including the LSCV function, are designed to select bandwidths which balance this trade-off. While LSCV is well understood, it is not the only means to obtain bandwidths. That is, we could select a different $\pi(\mathbf{x}_i)$ instead of the one deployed by LSCV, which may provide bandwidths with more desirable finite sample properties.

5.4.4 Cross-validation based on Akaike information criteria

Another increasingly popular method of cross-validation is known as improved AIC (AIC$_c$), proposed by Hurvich, Simonoff, and Tsai (1998). This type of cross-validation is similar to Kullback–Leibler information criterion that was the basis for likelihood cross-validation in density estimation. It also falls under the spectrum of what is known as generalized cross-validation (Craven and Wahba, 1979). Our criterion is constructed as

$$\text{AIC}_c(h) = \ln(\widehat{\sigma}^2) + \frac{1 + tr(\mathbf{H})/n}{1 - (tr(\mathbf{H}) + 2)/n},$$

where

$$\widehat{\sigma}^2 = \frac{1}{n} \sum_{i=1}^{n} \left[y_i - \widehat{m}(\mathbf{x}_i) \right]^2,$$

and

$$\mathbf{H} = \begin{bmatrix} \frac{K(\mathbf{x}_1, \mathbf{x}_1)}{\widehat{f}(\mathbf{x}_1)} & \frac{K(\mathbf{x}_1, \mathbf{x}_2)}{\widehat{f}(\mathbf{x}_1)} & \cdots & \frac{K(\mathbf{x}_1, \mathbf{x}_n)}{\widehat{f}(\mathbf{x}_1)} \\ \frac{K(\mathbf{x}_2, \mathbf{x}_1)}{\widehat{f}(\mathbf{x}_2)} & \frac{K(\mathbf{x}_2, \mathbf{x}_2)}{\widehat{f}(\mathbf{x}_2)} & \cdots & \frac{K(\mathbf{x}_2, \mathbf{x}_n)}{\widehat{f}(\mathbf{x}_2)} \\ \vdots & \vdots & \ddots & \vdots \\ \frac{K(\mathbf{x}_n, \mathbf{x}_1)}{\widehat{f}(\mathbf{x}_n)} & \frac{K(\mathbf{x}_n, \mathbf{x}_2)}{\widehat{f}(\mathbf{x}_n)} & \cdots & \frac{K(\mathbf{x}_n, \mathbf{x}_n)}{\widehat{f}(\mathbf{x}_n)} \end{bmatrix}.$$

The trace of $\mathbf{H}$ may be interpreted as a loose measure of the number of parameters that exist in the nonparametric model (Hastie and Tibshirani, 1993). One important point we mention here is that the AIC$_c$ criterion can be viewed as a variant of the cross-validation results discussed previously. Specifically, we can use the cross-validation notation if we write the weighting factor as

$$\pi\left(\cdot\right) = \exp\left(\frac{1 + tr(\mathbf{H})/n}{1 - [tr(\mathbf{H}) + 2]/n}\right).$$

The AIC_c criterion typically provides bandwidths that are larger than those provided by LSCV, leading to less variability of the estimates of the conditional mean. Li and Racine (2004b) show that in finite samples, using AIC_c provides bandwidths that deliver improved performance of the conditional mean estimator relative to using bandwidths selected via LSCV. They also find that as the sample size increases, these gains disappear. AIC_c often performs well in finite samples because it uses a global weight based on $tr(\mathbf{H})/n$, when there are sparse data or outliers (i.e., it does not have to compromise on smoothness the way the LSCV does). Given that LSCV has an observation-specific weighting scheme, the bandwidths need to adjust more to balance fitting errors for these points than those close to the cluster. In this manner, AIC_c avoids this problem because the weights are altered in a global fashion, as opposed to local, thus helping to achieve more smoothness, which we would expect when considering the function from a global standpoint as opposed to a local one.

5.4.5 Interpretation of bandwidths for LCLS

Historically, large-sample theory in the nonparametric literature assumes that the bandwidths gravitate towards zero at a rate slow enough so that it does not dominate the fact that the sample size is growing towards infinity. What this implies (in large samples) is that we should see bandwidths that are close to zero. In finite samples, it is impossible to know how "close" to zero we are. However, we can get a good sense of a large bandwidth by comparing it to the standard deviation of the regressor. If the bandwidth of a particular variable (when using a Gaussian kernel) is, say, 3 times its standard deviation, then we can be pretty confident that this is a large bandwidth.

The intuition is that for a really big bandwidth, the term within the kernel $(x_{id} - x_d)/h_d$ is very small and so we can treat it as 0. Thus, the term does not depend on i and hence it cancels from both the numerator and the denominator. This signifies that the variable is irrelevant in terms of smoothing the function. It does not suggest that the variable is statistically insignificant. This is something that would need to be formally tested, which we discuss in Chapter 6. That being said, we now have a means of quantifying bandwidths. When they are (relatively) small, a variable can be deemed relevant for smoothing, while when they are (relatively) large, the variable is removed from the smoothing procedure. This is commonly referred to as "automatic dimensionality reduction" (Hall, Li, and Racine, 2007).

To more formally show what a large bandwidth does, suppose we have $q_{ir} > 0$ irrelevant regressors and $q_r > 0$ relevant regressors in our model. We will denote the relevant covariates as $\mathbf{w}$ and the irrelevant covariates as $\mathbf{z}$, giving $\mathbf{x} \equiv (\mathbf{w}, \mathbf{z})$. Our product kernel can now be written as $K_h(\mathbf{x}_i, \mathbf{x}) = K_{h_w}(\mathbf{w}_i, \mathbf{w}) K_{h_z}(\mathbf{z}_i, \mathbf{z}) = \prod_{d=1}^{q_r} k\left(\frac{w_{id} - w_d}{h_d}\right) \prod_{d=1}^{q_{ir}} k\left(\frac{z_{id} - z_d}{h_{z_d}}\right)$. Moreover, for $h_{z_d} = \infty$ for $d = 1, \ldots, q_{ir}$, we have

$k\left(\frac{z_{id}-z_d}{h_{z_d}}\right) = k(0)$, yielding $K_h(\mathbf{x}_i, \mathbf{x}) = K_{h_w}(\mathbf{w}_i, \mathbf{w})K_{h_z}(\mathbf{z}_i, \mathbf{z}) = k(0)^{q_{ir}}K_{h_w}(\mathbf{w}_i, \mathbf{w})$.
The estimator of the conditional mean becomes

$$\widehat{m}(\mathbf{x}) = \frac{\sum_{i=1}^{n} K_h(\mathbf{x}_i, \mathbf{x})y_i}{\sum_{i=1}^{n} K_h(\mathbf{x}_i, \mathbf{x})} = \frac{\sum_{i=1}^{n} K_{h_z}(\mathbf{z}_i, \mathbf{z})K_{h_w}(\mathbf{w}_i, \mathbf{w})y_i}{\sum_{i=1}^{n} K_{h_z}(\mathbf{z}_i, \mathbf{z})K_{h_w}(\mathbf{w}_i, \mathbf{w})}$$

$$= \frac{k(0)^{q_{ir}} \sum_{i=1}^{n} K_{h_w}(\mathbf{w}_i, \mathbf{w})y_i}{k(0)^{q_{ir}} \sum_{i=1}^{n} K_{h_w}(\mathbf{w}_i, \mathbf{w})} = \frac{\sum_{i=1}^{n} K_{h_w}(\mathbf{w}_i, \mathbf{w})y_i}{\sum_{i=1}^{n} K_{h_w}(\mathbf{w}_i, \mathbf{w})}$$

$$= \widehat{m}(\mathbf{w}).$$

Simulation results in Hall, Li, and Racine (2007); Henderson, Papageorgiou, and Parmeter (2012); and Parmeter, Zheng, and McCann (2009) show that for small samples, bandwidths obtained via LSCV perform admirably in removing variables included erroneously in the modeling procedure. However, the results of Parmeter, Zheng, and McCann (2009) also show that (for a fixed n) as both q_r and q_{ir} increase, the ability of LSCV to correctly remove irrelevant variables diminishes. This is to be expected, as this result is similar to the parametric setting where including irrelevant variables does not affect the OLS parameter estimator in terms of bias, but does increase its variance. Here, including many irrelevant variables leads to LSCV not having the ability to remove all the irrelevant variables (i.e., there is too much variation). In practice, formal testing may be necessary to determine which variables are irrelevant.

5.5 Gradient estimation

If we wish to take the analytical derivative with respect to a particular regressor (Equation 5.1), we simply take the partial derivative. Without any loss of generality, let's assume we take a partial derivative with respect to a particular regressor, x_d. Thus, our estimated gradient ($\widehat{\beta}(x_d)$) is calculated as

$$\widehat{\beta}(x_d) = \frac{\partial \widehat{m}(\mathbf{x})}{\partial x_d}$$

$$= \frac{\left(\sum_{i=1}^{n} y_i \frac{\partial K_h(\mathbf{x}_i, \mathbf{x})}{\partial x_d}\right)\left(\sum_{i=1}^{n} K_h(\mathbf{x}_i, \mathbf{x})\right) - \left(\sum_{i=1}^{n} y_i K_h(\mathbf{x}_i, \mathbf{x})\right)\left(\sum_{i=1}^{n} \frac{\partial K_h(\mathbf{x}_i, \mathbf{x})}{\partial x_d}\right)}{\left(\sum_{i=1}^{n} K_h(\mathbf{x}_i, \mathbf{x})\right)^2}.$$

Assuming we have a Gaussian kernel, we can show that

$$\frac{\partial K_h(\mathbf{x}_i, \mathbf{x})}{\partial x_d} = \left(\frac{x_{id} - x_d}{h_d^2}\right) K_h(\mathbf{x}_i, \mathbf{x}).$$

This procedure is repeated for each gradient of interest. It is possible to take higher-order derivatives as well and these would be obtained in a similar fashion.

As we saw with density derivatives, the rate of convergence is slower for the derivatives ($n^{-1/(6+q)}$) and hence we should change the rate on the bandwidths. In practice, we would typically estimate the bandwidths for the conditional mean model via a cross-validation technique. If we instead calculate the scale factors, then the bandwidths for the gradient estimates can be obtained by multiplying the estimated scale factor (for the conditional mean) by the standard deviation of the dth regressor and then by $n^{-1/(6+q)}$. If the bandwidths themselves and not the scale factor are calculated, all that needs to be done is to multiply each bandwidth by $n^{1/(4+q)(6+q)}$.

5.6 Limitations of LCLS

As we saw with our discussion of kernel density estimation, our local-constant estimator is biased, which is a drawback compared to a correctly specified parametric regression model. However, recall that the bias depends upon the first and second derivatives of the conditional mean in the univariate setting. What this suggests is that when our true underlying function is a constant, our LCLS estimator will be unbiased in finite samples. However, if we knew our underlying function was a constant, we would not engage in nonparametric modeling. Further, even if our true underlying function is linear, the LCLS estimator is biased in finite samples except when the data are distributed uniformly (something not common for economic data).

In fact, think of the following heuristic. Suppose that we observe our data with no error (i.e., our points lie along a straight line). In this case, the variance of the LCLS estimator is zero. We would expect in this setting that determining the functional form would be easy. However, from (5.2) we will not detect this relationship because we have a biased estimator (unless we have uniformity). The reason for this is that instead of locally fitting a line, we are fitting a constant and this procedure of constructing the unknown (deterministic) relationship causes a bias, given that the weights are not equal around the point of interest. In general, the local-constant estimator will produce an estimated curve that is nonlinear. At first glance it might seem appropriate to increase the bandwidth to reduce variability; however, keep in mind that increasing the bandwidth of a nonparametric estimator tends to lead to a larger bias, not a smaller one. What happens is that our estimated curve progresses towards a flat line (i.e., slope of zero), and fails to detect the linear relationship between y and x. Since we have a local-constant estimator, as we increase the bandwidth, we are focusing less on local aspects of the data and more on global (in terms of weighting). Therefore, as the weights essentially become constant over x, we are left with a constant fit (zero slope).

We illustrate this in Figure 5.5. Here we generate data from the relationship $y = 1 + 2x$ where x is distributed standard normal. There is no model error here so our hope is that the local-constant estimator would pin down this relationship. We generate 50 points and each of the four plots uses a different bandwidth. For small bandwidths, we have an estimated nonlinear relationship, whereas for large bandwidths, our estimated curve tends towards a flat line near the average value of y ($\bar{y} = 1$). Figure 5.6 zooms in on the upper left plot from Figure 5.5. Clearly, while the LCLS estimator is easy to interpret and work with, it is not without its flaws. We would obtain a perfect estimated

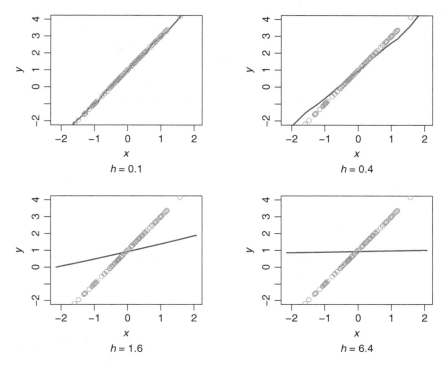

Figure 5.5. Illustration of bias of the LCLS estimator with no noise

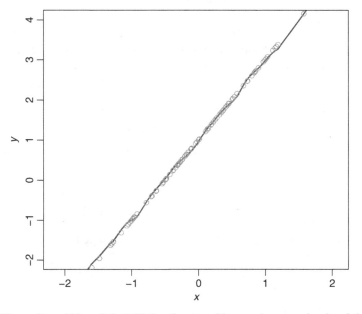

Figure 5.6. Illustration of bias of the LCLS estimator with no noise; zooming in of the upper left plot in Figure 5.5 ($h = 0.1$)

fit if we set our bandwidth to zero in this case, given that there is no error variance. However, if there were noise present, this ploy would have dramatic consequences on the plot, essentially interpolating the data, which would further introduce spurious nonlinearities.

To gain some more intuition for this flatness problem, recall the (univariate) "least-squares" type setup discussed at the beginning of the chapter,

$$\widehat{m}(x) = \min_a \sum_{i=1}^n (y_i - a)^2 k\left(\frac{x_i - x}{h}\right).$$

As $h \to \infty$, $k\left(\frac{x_i - x}{h}\right) \to k(0)$, which is a constant, rendering our minimization problem to be

$$\widehat{m}(x) = \min_a \sum_{i=1}^n (y_i - a)^2 k(0) = \min_a \sum_{i=1}^n (y_i - a)^2.$$

This is exactly the least-squares setup if we were regressing on a constant, which we know will produce for all x the estimated function $\bar{y}$.

5.7 Local-linear estimation

We can use the same intuition of the LCLS estimator to think of fitting alternative functional forms locally. As it will turn out, locally fitting a line, as opposed to a constant, provides desirable theoretical and applied features. The local-linear approximation can be viewed as the equivalent of a local Taylor expansion at any point $\mathbf{x}$. That is, for the relationship $y = m(\mathbf{x}) + u$, we have data for $(y_1, \mathbf{x}_1), (y_2, \mathbf{x}_2), \ldots, (y_n, \mathbf{x}_n)$ and as such, for each point $\mathbf{x}_i$, we can take a linear Taylor approximation for the point $\mathbf{x}$. Naturally, points far away from $\mathbf{x}$ would be expected to provide poor approximations of $m(\mathbf{x})$. However, by limiting our attention locally, via kernel weighting, we can mitigate the influence of the poor approximation of points far off.

To begin, we consider a Taylor expansion about $\mathbf{x}$ for observation i as

$$y_i = m(\mathbf{x}_i) + u_i$$
$$\approx m(\mathbf{x}) + (\mathbf{x}_i - \mathbf{x})\beta(\mathbf{x}) + u_i,$$

where $(\mathbf{x}_i - \mathbf{x})$ is a $1 \times q$ vector and $\beta(\mathbf{x})$ is the gradient (column) vector of dimension q. By ignoring the higher-order terms and treating $m(\mathbf{x})$ and $\beta(\mathbf{x})$ as parameters, we have

$$y_i = a + (\mathbf{x}_i - \mathbf{x})b + u_i = \begin{pmatrix} 1, & (\mathbf{x}_i - \mathbf{x}) \end{pmatrix} \begin{pmatrix} a \\ b \end{pmatrix} + u_i.$$

Our minimization problem for the full set of n observations is

$$\min_{a,b} \sum_{i=1}^n \left[y_i - a - (\mathbf{x}_i - \mathbf{x})b\right]^2 K_h(\mathbf{x}_i, \mathbf{x}).$$

In matrix notation this is

$$\min_\delta (y - \mathbf{X}\delta)' \, K(\mathbf{x}) \, (y - \mathbf{X}\delta),$$

where $\delta \equiv (a, b)'$, $\mathbf{X}$ is a $n \times (q+1)$ matrix with ith row equal to $\left(\ 1,\ \ (\mathbf{x}_i - \mathbf{x})\ \right)$ and $K(\mathbf{x})$ is a $n \times n$ diagonal matrix with ith element equal to $K_h(\mathbf{x}_i, \mathbf{x})$. This is simply the nonparametric generalization of least-squares. Notice that if $K(\mathbf{x})$ is an identity matrix, then we have the OLS estimator. If it is equal to the variance–covariance matrix of the errors (typically notated as Ω), we have a generalized least-squares estimator. Minimizing this objective function with respect to δ gives us

$$
\begin{aligned}
\widehat{\delta}(\mathbf{x}) &= \begin{pmatrix} \widehat{m}(\mathbf{x}) \\ \widehat{\beta}(\mathbf{x}) \end{pmatrix} \\
&= \left[\sum_{i=1}^{n} K_h(\mathbf{x}_i, \mathbf{x}) \begin{pmatrix} 1 \\ \mathbf{x}_i - \mathbf{x} \end{pmatrix} \left(\ 1,\ \ (\mathbf{x}_i - \mathbf{x})\ \right) \right]^{-1} \sum_{i=1}^{n} K_h(\mathbf{x}_i, \mathbf{x}) \begin{pmatrix} 1 \\ \mathbf{x}_i - \mathbf{x} \end{pmatrix} y_i \\
&= \left(\mathbf{X}' K(\mathbf{x}) \mathbf{X} \right)^{-1} \mathbf{X}' K(\mathbf{x}) y.
\end{aligned}
$$

Technical Appendix 5.7 shows that the leading term of the bias of the LLLS estimator of $m(\mathbf{x})$ is

$$
\mathrm{Bias}\,[\widehat{m}(\mathbf{x})] \approx \frac{\kappa_2}{2} \sum_{d=1}^{q} h_d^2 m_{dd}(\mathbf{x}),
$$

where m_{dd} for $d = 1, 2, \ldots, q$ are the second derivatives of the conditional mean. The leading term of the variance of the LLLS estimator of $m(\mathbf{x})$ is

$$
\mathrm{Var}\,[\widehat{m}(\mathbf{x})] \approx \frac{R(k)^q \sigma^2}{n\,|\mathbf{h}|\,f(\mathbf{x})}.
$$

Regardless of the sample size and the bandwidths, if the underlying function is linear in all arguments (i.e., $m_{dd}(\mathbf{x}) = 0$, $\forall \mathbf{x}$, for each $d = 1, 2, \ldots, q$), then our bias is zero. This was not the case with the local-constant estimator, which depended upon the gradient. Further, both the local-linear and local-constant estimators have the same variance. On the surface this might seem to suggest that the LLLS estimator has a smaller mean square error than the LCLS estimator. However, without explicit assumptions on both $m(\mathbf{x})$ and $f(\mathbf{x})$, it is impossible to know if one bias dominates the other.

An appealing feature of the LLLS estimator is that it provides information on the function itself as well as its gradient for each $\mathbf{x}$ under consideration. Recall that the LCLS estimator does not automatically provide this information on the gradients. We note here that the estimates $\widehat{\beta}(\mathbf{x})$ are not equivalent to the actual, numerical gradients of $\widehat{m}(\mathbf{x})$, due to the fact that we are only approximating $m(\mathbf{x})$ with a Taylor expansion. However, in the limit, the approximation error stemming from the Taylor expansion disappears. Technical Appendix 5.8 shows that the numerical and analytical gradients from the LLLS estimator are indeed different.

5.7.1 Choosing LLLS over LCLS

There are some cases where LCLS may be preferable over LLLS. For example, when estimating the nonparametric equivalent of a linear probability model (dummy variable on the left hand side), the LCLS will ensure that the fitted values (estimated conditional probabilities) will be bounded by zero and one, whereas the LLLS estimator will not. Also, when estimating conditional volatility (say in a time series model), the LCLS estimator ensures that the estimates are nonnegative. However, in practice, most authors employ the LLLS estimator. The two main areas where the LLLS estimator improves over the LCLS smoother are in a simpler bias term and minmax efficiency.[1] We discuss each in turn.

Simpler bias

The LLLS estimator has two "bias" features that make it desirable compared to the LCLS smoother. First, if the true underlying function is linear (i.e., $m(\mathbf{x}) = \alpha + \mathbf{x}\beta$), then the LLLS estimator is unbiased and the LCLS estimator is not. Formally, we have

$$y_i = \alpha + \mathbf{x}_i \beta + u_i = \alpha + \mathbf{x}\beta + (\mathbf{x}_i - \mathbf{x})\beta + u_i = \left(1, \quad (\mathbf{x}_i - \mathbf{x}) \right) \left(\begin{array}{c} \alpha + \mathbf{x}\beta \\ \beta \end{array} \right) + u_i.$$

Recalling the formal definition of the LLLS estimator, we have

$$\left(\begin{array}{c} \widehat{m}(\mathbf{x}) \\ \widehat{\beta}(\mathbf{x}) \end{array} \right) = \left[\sum_{i=1}^{n} K_h\left(\mathbf{x}_i, \mathbf{x}\right) \left(\begin{array}{c} 1 \\ \mathbf{x}_i - \mathbf{x} \end{array} \right) \left(1, \quad (\mathbf{x}_i - \mathbf{x}) \right) \right]^{-1} \sum_{i=1}^{n} K_h\left(\mathbf{x}_i, \mathbf{x}\right) \left(\begin{array}{c} 1 \\ \mathbf{x}_i - \mathbf{x} \end{array} \right) y_i$$

$$= \left[\sum_{i=1}^{n} K_h\left(\mathbf{x}_i, \mathbf{x}\right) \left(\begin{array}{c} 1 \\ \mathbf{x}_i - \mathbf{x} \end{array} \right) \left(1, \quad (\mathbf{x}_i - \mathbf{x}) \right) \right]^{-1}$$

$$\sum_{i=1}^{n} K_h\left(\mathbf{x}_i, \mathbf{x}\right) \left(\begin{array}{c} 1 \\ \mathbf{x}_i - \mathbf{x} \end{array} \right) \left[\left(1, \quad (\mathbf{x}_i - \mathbf{x}) \right) \left(\begin{array}{c} \alpha + \mathbf{x}\beta \\ \beta \end{array} \right) + u_i \right]$$

$$= \left(\begin{array}{c} \alpha + \mathbf{x}\beta \\ \beta \end{array} \right) + \left[\sum_{i=1}^{n} K_h\left(\mathbf{x}_i, \mathbf{x}\right) \left(\begin{array}{c} 1 \\ \mathbf{x}_i - \mathbf{x} \end{array} \right) \left(1, \quad (\mathbf{x}_i - \mathbf{x}) \right) \right]^{-1}$$

$$\sum_{i=1}^{n} K_h\left(\mathbf{x}_i, \mathbf{x}\right) \left(\begin{array}{c} 1 \\ \mathbf{x}_i - \mathbf{x} \end{array} \right) u_i.$$

Taking expectations conditional on x for the second term produces an unbiased estimator, $E\left[\widehat{m}(\mathbf{x})\right] = \alpha + \mathbf{x}\beta = m(\mathbf{x})$ and $E\left[\widehat{\beta}(\mathbf{x})\right] = \beta = \beta(\mathbf{x})$ ($\beta(\mathbf{x})$ is constant) because the conditional mean is linear and $E(u|\mathbf{x}) = 0$.

5.7.2 *Efficiency of the local-linear estimator*

In parametric regression, if the underlying model is correctly specified, then – subject to several additional assumptions – the Gauss–Markov theorem informs us that the OLS estimator is the best linear unbiased estimator of the conditional mean. Best is meant to imply smallest variance, which is commonly referred to as efficiency. In a similar vein, Fan (1992, 1993) has shown a similar type of efficiency

---

[1] A further benefit of the LLLS estimator is automatic boundary correction. We do not discuss this issue here, but direct the interested reader to Hastie and Loader (1993), Fan and Marron (1994), and Fan and Gijbels (1996) for more insight on this.

(minimax efficiency) of the local-linear estimator (also subject to some additional assumptions – Fan, 1992, 1000). In other words, Fan (1992) establishes that the local-linear estimator is the best linear smoother over all linear smoothers – satisfying several nonrestrictive assumptions – of the underlying conditional mean. More importantly, the local-constant kernel regression estimator is found to have 0 efficiency relative to the local-linear smoother.

The efficiency result of Fan (1992) also shows that the Epanechnikov kernel is the optimal kernel for the local-linear estimator (in terms of relative efficiency). In much the same way that we found a small, but perceptible loss in efficiency when using a kernel other than Epanechnikov kernel in the density setting, the same insight holds here. As an example, Fan (1992) shows that the relative efficiency of the local-linear estimator using a Gaussian kernel is 95.12% compared to the same estimator with the Epanechnikov kernel. Recall from Table 2.2 in Chapter 2 that the relative efficiency of the kernel density estimator with Gaussian kernel was 95.12% as well (1/1.0513).

The intuition here is clear. In the local-constant setup, a locally parametric model that only fits a constant would implicitly act as though no covariates enter the model, whereas with a locally parametric model that fits a line, the model is acting as though the covariates enter the model in a meaningful manner. It is this result that can be seen as the primary basis for using the LLLS over the LCLS as the primary kernel-based nonparametric regression estimator.

5.8 Local-polynomial estimation

We saw how fitting a line as opposed to a constant led to better performance. We obtained the local-linear estimator by taking a first-order Taylor expansion about the point $\mathbf{x}$. This begs the question: why not take higher-order Taylor expansions? The most popular higher-order expansion is what is known as local-quadratic least-squares (LQLS). This, as you would expect, comes from a second-order Taylor expansion. With this estimator, we estimate the conditional mean, gradient, and Hessian simultaneously.

The choice of how many expansions to take is important. More expansions will lead to a reduction in the bias, but at a cost of an increase in variability. This is caused by the increase in the number of local parameters which must be estimated. Fan and Gijbels (1996) have an in-depth discussion of this issue, but we will limit ours to the following insight. It is often argued that if we are interested in the pth gradient, then we should use the $(p + 1)$th-order expansion. For example, if we are interested in the conditional mean, the local-linear estimator is preferable. On the other hand, if we are interested in the gradient(s) of the conditional mean, the local-quadratic estimator is preferable, and so on. That being said, when we have a relatively large number of regressors and a relatively small number of observations, the higher expansions come with substantial variation and we should be concerned with the numerical stability and performance of higher-order local-polynomial estimators.

In this section we will begin with the general case, but will focus our attention on the LQLS estimator. For the general (univariate) case, if we are interested in the pth order Taylor expansion, and we assume that the $(p + 1)$th derivative of the conditional mean at the point x exists, then we can write our equation as

$$y_i \approx m(x) + (x_i - x)\frac{\partial m(x)}{\partial x} + (x_i - x)^2 \frac{\partial^2 m(x)}{\partial x^2}\frac{1}{2!} + \cdots + (x_i - x)^p \frac{\partial^p m(x)}{\partial x^p}\frac{1}{p!} + u_i.$$

Our kernel weighted least-squares problem can be written as

$$\min_{a_0, a_1, \ldots, a_p} \sum_{i=1}^{n} \left[y_i - a_0 - (x_i - x)a_1 - (x_i - x)^2 a_2 - \cdots - (x_i - x)^p a_p \right]^2 K_h(x_i, x).$$

In matrix notation this looks nearly identical to LLLS (the case where $p = 1$) and our objective function becomes

$$\min_{\delta} (y - \mathbf{X}\delta)' K(x)(y - \mathbf{X}\delta),$$

where the difference is now that the ith row of $\mathbf{X}$ is equal to $\left[1, (x_i - x), (x_i - x)^2, \ldots, (x_i - x)^p\right]$ and $\delta = (a_0, a_1, \ldots, a_p)'$. The local-polynomial least-squares estimator is given by

$$\widehat{\delta}(x) = \left(\widehat{m}(x), \frac{\partial \widehat{m}(x)}{\partial x}, \frac{\partial^2 \widehat{m}(x)}{\partial x^2}, \cdots, \frac{\partial^p \widehat{m}(x)}{\partial x^p} \right)'$$

$$= \left[\mathbf{X}' K(x) \mathbf{X} \right]^{-1} \mathbf{X}' K(x) y.$$

One important point that is not typically discussed is the role of kernel choice. Fan and Gijbels (1996, Table 3.3) show that as the order of the polynomial increases, the variability of the estimate of the conditional mean increases regardless of kernel choice, as expected. However, they also show that the longer the effective support of the kernel function (i.e., how many observations are included in the "local" estimate), the larger the increase in variability with respect to increases in the order of the polynomial. Effectively this means that the uniform kernel will give the highest increase (Epanechnikov being the next highest) in variability and the Gaussian kernel will exhibit the lowest increase in variability. This may partially help explain why so many economists use Gaussian kernels even though they are aware of the "optimality" of the Epanechnikov kernel in terms of MSE (in the LCLS case).

For the case where $q > 1$, as q increases the number of local estimates increases, even if p remains constant. This is a curse-of-dimensionality problem. Table 5.1 yields the number of parameters for local-constant through local-quintic fitting anywhere from 1 to 5 regressors. In general the number of parameters involved in a local-polynomial fit is $\binom{p+q}{p} = \frac{(p+q)!}{p!q!}$.

The main point that is illustrated by this table is that while higher-order polynomials may pick up the shape of the unknown function better, it is done so at an increasing cost. Assuming more derivatives means more parameters to estimate, and adding more covariates (q) increases the number of parameters even more quickly (except in the local-constant setting). So there is the well known trade-off between flexibility and overfitting. The properties of local-polynomial smoothers are well known (for single equation estimation) and are not discussed further (see Masry, 1996a, b for full details).

Table 5.1. *Dimension of local parameter vector*

Covariate dimension	$q = 1$	$q = 2$	$q = 3$	$q = 4$	$q = 5$
$p = 0$ (local-constant)	1	1	1	1	1
$p = 1$ (local-linear)	2	3	4	5	6
$p = 2$ (local-quadratic)	3	6	10	15	21
$p = 3$ (local-cubic)	4	10	20	35	56
$p = 4$ (local-quartic)	5	15	35	70	126
$p = 5$ (local-quintic)	6	21	56	126	252

In our own work we have typically found that estimation with anything past a second-order Taylor expansion leads to results which have far too much variability (this undoubtedly is due to the relative sizes of our samples and number of regressors). Therefore, we are going to focus the remainder of this section on the second-order expansion. For the more common multivariate case, what follows below are the results for the LQLS estimator. Our second-order Taylor expansion gives us the equation

$$y_i \approx m(\mathbf{x}) + (\mathbf{x}_i - \mathbf{x}) \frac{\partial m(\mathbf{x})}{\partial \mathbf{x}} + \frac{1}{2} vec\left[(\mathbf{x}_i - \mathbf{x})(\mathbf{x}_i - \mathbf{x})'\right]' vec\left[\frac{\partial^2 m(\mathbf{x})}{\partial \mathbf{x}'\mathbf{x}}\right] + u_i,$$

where $vec(A)$ represents the (column) vectorization of the matrix A. Further, $\partial^2 m(\mathbf{x})/\partial \mathbf{x}'\mathbf{x}$ includes not only second derivatives, but also the cross-partial derivatives ($q^2 - q$ estimates in total, owing to the fact that $\frac{\partial^2 m(\mathbf{x})}{\partial x_i \partial x_j} = \frac{\partial^2 m(\mathbf{x})}{\partial x_j \partial x_i}$, and this carries over into the definition of the data vector $vec\left[(\mathbf{x}_i - \mathbf{x})(\mathbf{x}_i - \mathbf{x})'\right]$). The minimization problem for the full set of n observations is

$$\min_{a_0, a_1, a_2} \sum_{i=1}^{n} \left[y_i - a_0 - (\mathbf{x}_i - \mathbf{x}) a_1 - vec\left[(\mathbf{x}_i - \mathbf{x})(\mathbf{x}_i - \mathbf{x})'\right]' a_2\right]^2 K_h(\mathbf{x}_i, \mathbf{x}).$$

The $((q^2 + 1) \times 1)$-dimensional estimator is

$$\widehat{\delta}(x) = \left(\widehat{m}(\mathbf{x}), \frac{\partial \widehat{m}(\mathbf{x})}{\partial \mathbf{x}}, vec\left[\frac{\partial^2 \widehat{m}(\mathbf{x})}{\partial \mathbf{x}'\mathbf{x}}\right]\right)'$$

$$= \left[\mathbf{X}'K(x)\mathbf{X}\right]^{-1} \mathbf{X}'K(x) y,$$

where now the ith row of $\mathbf{X}$ is defined as $\mathbf{X}_i \equiv \left(1, (\mathbf{x}_i - \mathbf{x}), vec\left[(\mathbf{x}_i - \mathbf{x})(\mathbf{x}_i - \mathbf{x})'\right]'\right)$. It is easy to see that as q increases, the number of local estimates increases quickly.

5.9 Gradient-based bandwidth selection

Suppose that interest hinges explicitly on the slope (gradient) of the unknown regression function as opposed to the function itself. We know that gradient estimates obtained from $\widehat{m}(\mathbf{x})$, using a bandwidth determined through LSCV is (asymptotically) too small for estimating $\partial \widehat{m}(\mathbf{x})/\partial \mathbf{x}$. Consider the one-dimensional case. Here the optimal bandwidth for estimating $m(x)$ is $\sim n^{-1/5}$, whereas the optimal bandwidth for estimating $\partial m(x)/\partial x$ is $\sim n^{-1/7}$. Ignoring this fact will lead to estimates that in finite samples are most likely too variable (given that a smaller bandwidth reduces bias but increases variance). Ideally, we want to select a bandwidth that has the appropriate rate required for estimating $\partial m(x)/\partial x$. However, it is not immediately apparent how this is accomplished.

Consider the naïve approach where the user performs LSCV to obtain bandwidths that are appropriate for estimating $\widehat{m}(\mathbf{x})$ and then rate adjusts these bandwidths by an amount such that the new bandwidths have the appropriate rate for estimating $\partial \widehat{m}(\mathbf{x})/\partial \mathbf{x}$. In the case where $\mathbf{x}$ is q-dimensional, the optimal rate for estimating the regression function is $n^{-1/(4+q)}$, whereas the optimal rate for estimating a derivative of the regression function is $n^{-1/(6+q)}$. This implies that the rate adjustment to the LSCV bandwidths (or any bandwidth selected to estimate the regression function) is $n^{2/(24+10q+q^2)}$. In the single dimension case, the rate adjustment is $n^{2/35}$. However, while this is a simple and quick way to obtain bandwidths with appropriate rates for estimating gradients, in finite samples it is expected that this approach will not work well. Not only is the rate of the bandwidth important, but also the unknown constant that depends on the model primitives, and this is different if your interest is the function rather than the gradient of the function.

We now discuss an approach to estimate rate appropriate bandwidths for constructing gradients of the regression function. To keep the description simple, we initially focus on a single regressor. The main idea to facilitate determination of the bandwidth for estimating the gradient is

$$\min_h \sum_{i=1}^n \left[\beta(x_i) - \widehat{\beta}_{-i}(x_i) \right]^2. \tag{5.4}$$

This criterion is identical to our LSCV criterion, except that now we are minimizing the squared difference between the estimated and true gradients and the fact that $\beta(x_i)$ is unobserved. Note that in the LSCV setting $m(x_i)$ is also unobserved, but we have a noise-corrupted observation of it, y_i. It would seem that this approach is infeasible. A literature dating back to Rice (1986) proposes replacing $\beta(x_i)$ with an estimate based on first differences of the data (given that we are in a single dimension). Müller, Stadtmüller, and Schmitt (1987) and Charnigo, Hall, and Srinivasan (2011) implement Rice's insight using different methods of estimating the derivatives.

As opposed to using first differences to calculate noise-corrupted versions of $\beta(x_i)$, Henderson, Li, Parmeter, and Yao (2014) propose to use a local-polynomial estimator to replace $\beta(x_i)$ in (5.4), a procedure they term gradient-based cross-validation (GBCV). Their cross-validation function is

$$\min_h \sum_{i=1}^n \left[\widetilde{\beta}(x_i) - \widehat{\beta}_{-i}(x_i) \right]^2, \tag{5.5}$$

where $\widetilde{\beta}(x_i)$ is a local-polynomial estimator and $\widehat{\beta}_{-i}(x_i)$ is the leave-one-out local-linear estimator. There are (at least) two benefits to this approach. First, the use of a local-polynomial estimator allows the method to work in higher dimensional settings, as it is difficult to use first differences in more than a univariate setting. Second,

Henderson, Li, Parmeter, and Yao (2014) prove that using the local-cubic estimator for $\widetilde{\beta}(x_i)$ in (5.5) coupled with the use of the local-linear estimator for $\widehat{\beta}_{-i}(x_i)$ asymptotically produces bandwidths that are identical (up to a constant depending on the kernel) to the bandwidths we would obtain if we directly observed $\beta(x_i)$ and used (5.4). This is a powerful result and hinges on the fact that the bias of the local-cubic estimator is much smaller than that of the local-linear estimator and so in the limit, the local-cubic estimator behaves like the truth from the perspective of the local-linear estimator. Naturally, we can think that using any higher-order local-polynomial estimator would work, but as we add more polynomial terms, the finite sample complications that are introduced may eliminate any asymptotic gains.

In the q-dimensional setting, the gradient based cross-validation function is

$$\min_{h} \sum_{i=1}^{n} \left[\widetilde{\beta}(x_i) - \widehat{\beta}_{-i}(x_i)\right]' \left[\beta(x_i) - \widehat{\beta}_{-i}(x_i)\right], \tag{5.6}$$

where again we would use the local-linear estimator for $\widehat{\beta}(x_i)$ and the local-cubic estimator for $\widetilde{\beta}(x_i)$. One operational caveat we mention here is that even though it appears there are two stages at play here (estimate the local-cubic estimator, then solve for the bandwidths), there is only one set of bandwidths that are necessary. That is, the bandwidths used to construct $\widetilde{\beta}(x_i)$ are done within the confines of the minimization routine; they are not fixed outside.

5.10 Standard errors and confidence bounds

Here we consider estimation of standard errors and confidence bounds via bootstrap procedures. The type of bootstrap you choose to estimate standard errors and confidence bounds will depend upon whether or not your data homoskedastic. If your data are homoskedastic, then either the pairs bootstrap or a residual bootstrap should work. However, in the presence of heteroskedasticity, we typically recommend a wild bootstrap.

We note here that these bootstrap procedures are valid for each estimation procedure. The one mistake that many beginners make is to include the derivatives (which come from Taylor expansions) as well. It is important only to include the estimated conditional mean when obtaining residuals $\widehat{u}_i = y_i - \widehat{m}(\mathbf{x}_i)$.

We also wish to note that our description of confidence bounds is simplistic; constructing confidence bounds is often more complicated. We suggest you consult a book such as Hall (1992) for more technical details.

5.10.1 Pairs bootstrap

One popular method for obtaining standard errors is to use a pairs bootstrap. The basic idea here is to randomly sample pairs with replacement for a particular observation $\{y, \mathbf{x}\}$ and repeat this process n times $\{y_i^*, \mathbf{x}_i^*\}_{i=1}^{n}$. Although the pairs bootstrap is valid for inference in the heteroskedastic case (as it permits the conditional variance of the errors to vary with the regressors), it does not offer an asymptotic refinement, as it does not assume that the conditional mean of the errors given the set of regressors is equal to zero.

The one issue that arises with the pairs bootstrap is how to estimate the model. As the goal is to obtain standard errors for the fitted values and gradients specific to $\mathbf{x}$, you still need to evaluate the model at those same points $\mathbf{x}$, but with the bootstrapped data. For example, for the pooled LCLS estimator, you will estimate the bootstrapped model as

$$\widehat{m}^* (\mathbf{x}) = \frac{\sum\limits_{i=1}^{n} y_i^* K_h \left(\mathbf{x}_i^*, \mathbf{x} \right)}{\sum\limits_{i=1}^{n} K_h \left(\mathbf{x}_i^*, \mathbf{x} \right)}$$

where y_i^* and $\mathbf{x}_i^*$ are the bootstrapped values of y_i and $\mathbf{x}_i$, respectively (noting that y_i^* and $\mathbf{x}_i^*$ likely do not come from the ith individual). The main point to note is that we are comparing $\mathbf{x}_i^*$ to $\mathbf{x}$, not $\mathbf{x}^*$. You have new data, but you still evaluate the function at the same values of $\mathbf{x}$ you used to estimate the initial estimate (say, $\widehat{m}(\mathbf{x})$). For completeness we list the steps of the pairs bootstrap to obtain standard errors:

1. For each $i = 1, 2, \ldots, n$ randomly sample, with replacement pairs from $\{y_i, \mathbf{x}_i\}_{i=1}^{n}$ and call the resulting sample $\left\{ y_i^*, \mathbf{x}_i^* \right\}_{i=1}^{n}$ the bootstrap sample.
2. Using the bootstrap sample, estimate the unknown function $\widehat{m}^*(\mathbf{x})$ and/or derivative $\widehat{\beta}^*(\mathbf{x})$ via the initial estimator where y_i and $\mathbf{x}_i$ are replaced by y_i^* and $\mathbf{x}_i^*$, respectively. Remember to evaluate each estimator at the same values of $\mathbf{x}$.
3. Repeat steps 1 and 2 a large number (B) of times and then construct the sampling distribution of the bootstrapped estimates. Standard errors can be obtained by taking the standard deviation of the sampling distribution for each particular estimate. Confidence bounds can be obtained (for example) by taking the $\alpha/2\%$ and $(1 - \alpha/2)\%$ estimates from the vector of B for each estimate of $\widehat{m}(\mathbf{x})$ and/or $\widehat{\beta}(\mathbf{x})$.

5.10.2 Residual bootstrap

The steps for the residual bootstrap are very similar except that we re-sample n (centered, i.e., mean subtracted) residuals with replacement in order to construct our bootstrap sample. The steps to construct a residual bootstrap in order to obtain standard errors are as follows:

1. For $i = 1, 2, \ldots, n$, randomly sample, with replacement, centered residuals from $\left\{ u_i^* = \widehat{u}_i - \overline{\widehat{u}} \right\}_{i=1}^{n}$ (where $\overline{\widehat{u}}$ is the sample average of u) and construct the bootstrap left-hand-side variable $y_i^* = \widehat{m}(\mathbf{x}_i) + u_i^*$ for $i = 1, 2, \ldots, n$. The resulting sample $\left\{ y_i^*, \mathbf{x}_i \right\}_{i=1}^{n}$ is the bootstrap sample.
2. Using the bootstrap sample, estimate the unknown function $\widehat{m}^*(\mathbf{x})$ and/or derivative $\widehat{\beta}^*(\mathbf{x})$ via the initial estimator where y_i is replaced by y_i^* wherever it occurs. Remember that we use the data $\mathbf{x}_i$ and evaluate at the same values of $\mathbf{x}$.

3. Repeat steps 1 and 2 a large number (B) of times and then construct the sampling distribution of the bootstrapped estimates. Standard errors can be obtained by taking the standard deviation of the sampling distribution for each particular estimate. Confidence bounds can be obtained (for example) by taking the $\alpha/2\%$ and $(1 - \alpha/2)\%$ estimates from the vector of B for each estimate of $\widehat{m}(\mathbf{x})$ and/or $\widehat{\beta}(\mathbf{x})$.

5.10.3 Wild bootstrap

We typically recommend a wild bootstrap, as it is consistent under both homoskedasticity and heteroskedasticity. That being said, it is not applicable in all areas of econometrics and you should make sure that it is asymptotically valid. For example, Yu (2012) shows that when conducting inference regarding a threshold parameter, the wild bootstrap is invalid. The steps to implement the wild bootstrap are similar to that of the residual bootstrap, but the ith (centered) residual is not shared by the other observations. The basic idea is that for each residual, you multiply by one of two values, and the value that is used is chosen at random. These numbers can take many forms, but most are chosen so that the mean of the bootstrapped residuals is equal to zero (noting that our centering of residuals is now redundant) and that the second and third moments of the bootstrapped residuals remain unchanged. The three-step procedure is as follows:

1. Compute the two-point wild bootstrap errors from the re-centered residuals by $u_i^* = \frac{1-\sqrt{5}}{2}\left(\widehat{u}_i - \overline{\widehat{u}}\right)$ with probability $(1+\sqrt{5})/(2\sqrt{5})$ and $u_i^* = \frac{1+\sqrt{5}}{2}\left(\widehat{u}_i - \overline{\widehat{u}}\right)$ with probability $1 - (1 + \sqrt{5})/(2\sqrt{5})$. Generate y_i^* via $y_i^* = \widehat{m}(\mathbf{x}_i) + u_i^*$. Call $\{y_i^*, \mathbf{x}_i\}_{i=1}^n$ the bootstrap sample.
2. Using the bootstrap sample, estimate the unknown function $\widehat{m}^*(\mathbf{x})$ and/or derivative $\widehat{\beta}^*(\mathbf{x})$ via the initial estimator where y_i is replaced by y_i^* wherever it occurs. Remember that we use the data $\mathbf{x}_i$ and evaluate at the same values of $\mathbf{x}$.
3. Repeat steps 1 and 2 a large number (B) of times and then construct the sampling distribution of the bootstrapped point estimates. Standard errors can be obtained by taking the standard deviation of the sampling distribution for each particular estimate. Confidence bounds can be obtained (for example) by taking the $\alpha/2\%$ and $(1 - \alpha/2)\%$ estimates from the vector of B for each estimate of $\widehat{m}(\mathbf{x})$ and/or $\widehat{\beta}(\mathbf{x})$.

5.11 Displaying estimates

There are a variety of methods that you can deploy after estimation of the regression surface to visualize the regression estimates. Unlike a traditional parametric analysis with a finite number of parameters, a nonparametric analysis does not have (standard) parameter estimates. Thus, no exact comparison with the standard approach of presenting parametric estimates in a table with standard errors can be made. However, there are similar avenues you can pursue. The most generic approach is to present a table with the quartile and or decile estimates of the estimated gradients. Given that in a linear (in $\mathbf{x}$) regression $\beta = \partial y / \partial \mathbf{x}$ is the object of interest and $\beta_j(\cdot) = \partial m(\mathbf{x}) / \partial x_j$, the gradient estimates at each observation are the most similar "estimate" to compare. However, these gradient estimates will be observation specific, so interpretation of them can be somewhat tricky.

Aside from presenting results in tabular form, two popular visual approaches are partial mean plots and 45° plots (Henderson, Kumbhakar, and Parmeter, 2012). The partial mean plot graphs the relationship, either the conditional mean or the gradient of the conditional mean, against one of the covariates, holding all of the remaining covariates fixed at their mean levels (or some other arbitrary value). As noted by Henderson, Kumbhakar, and Parmeter (2012), in more than two dimensions it is not clear that holding the remaining variables fixed at their means represents an interesting point of comparison from an economic perspective. Further, it is not clear that the same relationship would hold if the points were held fixed at a different point. Consider a setting with three covariates and the option of holding two of the three variables fixed at the lower, middle, or upper quartile. Allowing each variable to be held fixed at a particular quantile would result in $3^2 = 9$ different combinations for each partial mean plot (in a model with four variables, holding three variables fixed will result in 27 plots). While constructing these plots is easily handled with available software, it is not clear that these plots will convey useful information nor is it clear what values are to be held fixed.

To combat this tyranny of choices facing the practitioner, Henderson, Kumbhakar, and Parmeter (2012) propose the 45° plot. These plots do not have the simple one-to-one link between a given covariate and the conditional mean (or gradient of). However, they do convey useful information pertaining to the estimated nonparametric model. The intuition of the plots is simple. For each estimate (either the function itself or a given gradient), plot the estimate (say, gradient) against itself (resulting in a 45° line). Next, plot upper and lower $(1 - \alpha)\%$ confidence intervals around each of the estimated points on the 45° line. These graphs then allow you to discern both the spread of the estimates (to assess heterogeneous effects) and the statistical significance of effects (by seeing which confidence intervals contain 0).

Still another alternative graphical approach that has been deployed in empirical settings is to plot the kernel density of the estimated gradients (e.g., Henderson, 2010; Henderson, Papageorgiou, and Parmeter, 2012, 2013). These densities can be taken a step further and subdivided according to another variable. For example, in a growth setting we could estimate the return of physical and human capital on economic growth, then compare the estimated gradients for human capital by subdividing based on each observation's level of physical capital (above/below the median, for example). Then the Li (1996) test can be used to determine if the estimated density of estimated gradients differ based on physical capital.

It is clear that each approach has costs and benefits and given the observation-specific nature of nonparametric estimators, (in multivariate settings) no singular method is likely to dominate. However, with the array of methods comes the ability to present results in numerous ways and to investigate links that might be obscured or less readily detected in parametric models.

5.12 Assessing fit

Applied researchers often take comfort in the R^2 of their parametrically specified models. A similar measure can be conceived in nonparametric regression models. Regardless of the estimator deployed, once the model has been estimated, we can use

$$R^2 = \frac{\left[\sum_{i=1}^{n} (y_i - \bar{y})(\widehat{y}_i - \bar{y}) \right]^2}{\sum_{i=1}^{n} (y_i - \bar{y}) \sum_{i=1}^{n} (\widehat{y}_i - \bar{y})}.$$

This measure is the analog of the traditional R^2 defined for a linear projection from an n-dimensional space to a subspace. It is simply the squared correlation between the observed and estimated outcome variable. In the case of a simple linear regression with an intercept, this is the standard R^2 measure. As with the standard measure, this measure will always lie in $[0, 1]$. This is not true of other measures that have been proposed in the literature (e.g., Anglin and Gençay, 1996).

5.13 Prediction

Another approach to assessing a nonparametric model, a parametric versus a nonparametric model, or even a set of nonparametric models, is to compare their predictive ability. This could be as simple as comparing the R^2 across the competing models. However, it is widely known that R^2 does not account for model complexity. Alternative in-sample measures of fit, such as adjusted R^2 or AIC, also have known flaws for comparing nonparametric models (see Ye, 1998; Shen and Ye, 2002). One approach to comparing nonparametric models (or any set of models) is to use out-of-sample prediction. In a cross-sectional setting it is not obvious how you would go about such an exercise given that additional data does not exist.

Racine and Parmeter (2013) propose using random sample splits of the available data to construct evaluation and training data sets, estimating the competing models with the training data sets and then engaging in out-of-sample prediction with the evaluation data. To avoid cherry-picking favorable splits of the data, the process is repeated a large number of times and then the average out-of-sample squared prediction error (ASPE) is used to compare across models. The model with the smallest ASPE is deemed the model with the lowest average prediction error.

The approach of Racine and Parmeter (2013) can be described as follows: for concreteness denote one model "Model 1" and the other "Model 2." Assuming the data represent independent draws (as they would in a standard cross-sectional setup), the steps are:

1. Resample without replacement pairwise from $\{y_i, \mathbf{x}_i\}_{i=1}^{n}$ and call these resamples $\{y_i^*, \mathbf{x}_i^*\}_{i=1}^{n}$.
2. Let the first n_1 of the resampled observations represent the training sample, $\{y_i^*, \mathbf{x}_i^*\}_{i=1}^{n_1}$, those observations which will be used to smooth over. The remaining $n_2 = n - n_1$ observations represent the evaluation sample, $\{y_i^*, \mathbf{x}_i^*\}_{i=n_1+1}^{n}$.

3. Fit Model 1 and Model 2 using only the training observations ($\{y_i^*, \mathbf{x}_i^*\}_{i=1}^{n_1}$) and then obtain predicted values from the evaluation observations ($\{y_i^*, \mathbf{x}_i^*\}_{i=n_1+1}^{n}$).

4. Compute the ASPE of each model as $\text{ASPE}^1 = n_2^{-1} \sum_{i=n_1+1}^{n} y_i^* - \widehat{m}_{n_1}^1 (\mathbf{x}_i^*)^2$ and $\text{ASPE}^2 = n_2^{-1} \sum_{i=n_1+1}^{n} y_i^* - \widehat{m}_{n_1}^2 (\mathbf{x}_i^*)^2$.

5. Repeat steps 1–3 a large number of times (B), yielding B draws, $\{\text{ASPE}_b^1, \text{ASPE}_b^2\}_{b=1}^{B}$. Use a paired t-test to assess $H_0 : \overline{ASPE}^1 = \overline{ASPE}^2$ against a one-sided alternative.

In step two the bandwidths for the competing models do not need to be recalculated. We advocate, as in Racine and Parmeter (2013), that you use the scaling factors from the cross-validated bandwidths used to estimate Models 1 and 2. This approach will ensure that the same degree of smoothing is applied to each of the training samples as the full sample (Racine, 1993). The rationale for this is that if we did not rescale the cross-validated bandwidths for subsamples of size $n_1 < n$ then we would have a different amount of smoothing for the training samples and so our interpretation of Models 1 and 2 would be different than Models 1 and 2, which use the full sample. The choice of B in step 5 is somewhat arbitrary and we suggest a large number of resamples. See Racine and Parmeter (2013) for a more detailed discussion and several examples illustrating this approach in a cross-sectional framework.

5.14 Application

In this section we take our first shot at applied nonparametric regression. Our goal here (as well as at several other points in the text) is to estimate a cross-country production function. We have several reasons for choosing such a function: (1) there is still no consensus on the appropriate form of the cross-country production function, (2) the production function is the basis for many growth studies and hence estimating this correctly is of the utmost importance, (3) given the relatively few inputs necessary for the standard case (physical capital and human-capital-augmented labor), it is relatively easy to obtain data on a wide range of countries, and (4) estimation with fewer variables makes nonparametric estimation both more reliable (considering the curse of dimensionality) and computationally faster (fewer bandwidths to estimate). The last two points are especially important when trying to learn applied nonparametric regression.

Here we are going to attempt to estimate the production function in its purest form with as few assumptions as possible. The most common way to estimate a production function in the literature is to assume that it is Cobb–Douglas (CD) and to measure it in log-per-worker terms with the assumption of constant returns to scale (CRS). This is obtained from the raw production function

$$Y = A K^\alpha (HL)^{1-\alpha},$$

where Y is output, A is the technology parameter, K is physical capital, HL is human-capital-augmented labor, and α is the elasticity of (output with respect to) physical capital. Ignoring the error term, to obtain a simple regression model we would first divide by labor

$$y = Ak^\alpha H^{1-\alpha},$$

where $y = Y/L$ and $k = K/L$. We then would take logarithms of both sides in order to be able to estimate the model by OLS. The model becomes

$$\ln y = \ln A + \alpha \ln k + (1 - \alpha) \ln H.$$

The beauty of this form is that it only requires estimation of two parameters (the intercept and the elasticity of physical capital) and can be estimated via OLS. The problem with this model is that it makes several assumptions. First, (and most relevant to our book) is the assumption that the model is truly CD. Second, OLS estimation of a CD production function requires us to log each side of the equation and this can lead to biases as pointed out in Sun, Henderson, and Kumbhakar (2011) (inspired by the related work of Santos Silva and Tenreyro, 2004). Finally, the homogeneity assumption with respect to labor (i.e., CRS) need not hold. In other words, $m(K, HL)/L$ is not necessarily equal to $m(k, H)$.

We consider parametric and nonparametric production functions where output and input measures enter in level form. Our general production function will be

$$Y = m(K, HL) + u,$$

where u is an additive error term which is assumed to be mean zero. In the parametric models we drop the CRS assumption, but will assume the form of $m(\cdot)$ and we will need to estimate a parameter vector. In the nonparametric models, we will let the data tell us the form of $m(\cdot)$.

This type of formulation is desirable, but leads to computational issues. Logs not only allow a CD production function to be estimated by OLS, they also reduce the variability of the data. The reduced variability is perhaps more important with nonlinear estimators, as minimization of a criterion function becomes difficult when no closed form solution exists. To combat this problem we will estimate our models by scaling our output and inputs by their respective means. In other words, we will be regressing $Y/\overline{Y}$ on $K/\overline{K}$ and $HL/\overline{HL}$ where the bar over the variable represents its sample mean. This will have no impact on the estimated elasticities, but will upon the gradients themselves (of lesser economic importance in this problem). We do this not only to minimize issues with numerical optimization, but also so that the resulting estimates are easier to visualize.

5.14.1 Data

The data used for output (Y), physical capital (K), and labor (L) are derived from the Penn World Tables (PWT), Version 7.0 (Heston, Summers, and Aten, 2011). The number of workers is obtained as RGDPCH * POP/RGDPWOK, where RGDPCH is per-capita GDP computed via the chain method, POP is the population, and RGDPWOK is real GDP per worker. The measure of output is calculated as RGDPWOK multiplied by the number of workers; the resulting output is in 2005 international dollars. Real aggregate investment in international dollars is computed as RGDPL ∗ POP ∗ KI, where RGDPL is the real GDP computed via the Laspeyres index and KI is the investment share of real GDP.

Following standard practice, we compute the capital stock using the perpetual inventory method (see Caselli and Feyrer, 2007). For human capital, we employ the updated Barro and Lee (2010) education data. We adopt the Hall and Jones (1999) construction of human capital, which in turn is based on the Psacharopoulos (1994) survey of wage equations evaluating returns to education. Specifically, let e_{it} represent the average number of years of education of the adult population in country i at time t and define human-capital-augmented labor (recall that we only looked at human capital, H, in Chapter 3) in country i at time t by

$$HL_{it} = Q(e_{it}) L_{it} = \exp[\vartheta(e_{it})] L_{it}$$

where $\vartheta(\cdot)$ is a piecewise linear function, with a zero intercept and a slope of 0.134 through the fourth year of education, 0.101 for the next four years, and 0.068 for education beyond the eighth year. The rate of return to education (where $\vartheta(\cdot)$ is differentiable) is

$$\frac{\partial Q(e_{it})}{\partial e_{it}} = \vartheta'(e_{it})$$

and $h(0) = 1$.

To maximize the number of observations, we take the largest number of countries possible in each year, which results in an unbalanced panel. Due to the frequency of the human capital data set, we consider five-year intervals from 1950–2005. In 1950 we have 49 countries, 65 in 1955, 96 in 1960, 98 in 1965, and 117 from 1970 onward. Thus, the total number of observations is 1244. We note that this is a much larger sample than most existing growth studies.

5.14.2 Results

In this section we discuss the results from our regressions. We start with the CD model, but also estimate several flexible parametric models. We do this for two reasons. First, we wish to compare them to our nonparametric models. Second, one potential benefit of using nonparametric methods is to help correctly identify (or at least find a good approximation of) the true underlying structure of the data. As we already know, a correctly specified parametric model is preferable.

Note that our goal is to estimate the parametric models so that they do not fall victim to potential biases due to homogeneity assumptions or logging the model. Hence, these results are (as far as we are aware) new in the literature.

After we estimate a set of flexible parametric functional forms, we move to nonparametric estimation. We consider estimation by each method discussed (LCLS, LLLS, and LQLS) as well as different bandwidth selection criteria (LSCV and AIC$_c$) and different kernel functions (Epanachenikov, biweight, triweight, and Gaussian). We hope to achieve two goals here. The first is to show how to analyze nonparametric estimates. As there is no single way to analyze the data, we give a sample of some of the most popular as well as some other useful (in our view) ways to examine the results. Second, we want to better understand cross-country production functions. As is the case in the parametric models, the nonparametric models here avoid many potential biases and are novel as well.

Finally, we would like to note that even with the reduced number of potential biases, that the estimates in this chapter are also not without their own faults. For example, we have an unbalanced panel and we do not control for region or time effects. Also, there is potentially omitted variable bias and our inputs are likely endogenous. We plan to address each of these issues (and others) later in the book.

Parametric

Here we consider two standard and two less common (but flexible) parametric production functions. First, we look at the CD production function in levels:

$$Y_{it} = A K_{it}^{\alpha} (HL_{it})^{\beta} + u_{it}, \quad i = 1, 2, \ldots, n, t = 1, 2, \ldots, T_i,$$

where T_i is the total number of observations for country i, α and β are the elasticities of physical capital and human-capital-augmented labor (respectively), and they are not required to sum to one. Again, the log-linearized per-worker CRS version of this model is the standard in the literature.

The second most common model in the literature is the constant elasticity of substitution (CES) production function:

$$Y_{it} = A \left(\delta K_{it}^{-\rho} + (1 - \delta) HL_{it}^{-\rho} \right)^{-\upsilon/\rho} + u_{it}, \quad i = 1, 2, \ldots, n, t = 1, 2, \ldots, T_i,$$

where δ is the distribution parameter (which, in the CRS case, help explain relative factor shares), ρ is the substitution parameter, and υ is the returns to scale (RTS). A log-linearized version of this production function with CRS can be found in Duffy and Papageorgiou (2000), among others. Both of these models are nonlinear in parameters and can be estimated via nonlinear least-squares (NLS). That being said, we would like to note that CES models in levels are particularly difficult to estimate (one well written reliable package in R is micEconCES by Henningsen and Henningsen, 2011).

Here we also consider two other parametric specifications. These are less popular, but have the benefit of allowing for nonlinearities and complementaries while at the same time can be estimated via OLS. The downfall of these approaches (as compared to CD and CES) is that they do not impose convexity *a priori* (something which many economists believe – this is also true for most nonparametric models). First, we consider the generalized quadratic (GQ) production function. Here we include each of the inputs in levels as well as their squares and interactions. In our two-input model the GQ production function is

$$Y_{it} = A + \alpha_1 K_{it} + \alpha_2 HL_{it} + \alpha_{11} K_{it}^2 + \alpha_{22} (HL_{it})^2 + \alpha_{12} K_{it} HL_{it} + u_{it},$$
$$i = 1, 2, \ldots, n, t = 1, 2, \ldots, T_i,$$

where we drop the constant 1/2 on the higher-order terms for simplicity. This model allows for nonlinearities and interactions.

The final parametric model is similar to the GQ model except that the terms come in as square roots. The Generalized Leontief (GL) model within our scenario is

$$Y_{it} = A + \alpha_1 K_{it} + \alpha_2 HL_{it} + \alpha_{12} K_{it}^{1/2} (HL_{it})^{1/2} + u_{it}, \ i = 1, 2, \ldots, n, t = 1, 2, \ldots, T_i.$$

This is the original formulation (plus an intercept, as this often leads to more reliable results) for the two-input case as given in Diewert (1971). Note that this model requires the regressors to be nonnegative. This is not an issue in our application.

For each model listed, we estimate the parameters and then calculate the elasticities of both physical capital and human-capital-augmented labor. These are obtained by taking the partial derivative of the estimated function with respect to a given input and then multiplying that number by the value of the input and then dividing by the fitted value. These are commonly interpreted in the growth literature as factor shares, but this is only true under perfect competition and constant returns to scale. We are not comfortable with either assumption and will refer to them as elasticities. Finally, we use the elasticities to calculate the RTS (typically defined as the sum of the elasticities), but we do not assume that they are equal to unity in any of the models.

The elasticities and RTS can be found in Table 5.2. Note that we only have a single estimate for each object of interest in the CD model. Even though this model is nonlinear in its parameters, the elasticities are constant across i and t (which is consistent with Kaldor's 1957 stylized facts). This is also true for RTS in the CES model. For the remaining functional forms, we get elasticities and RTS, which are specific to each observation. Instead of listing each value for each i and t, we take the vector of results and extract the first, second (median), and third quartile estimates. Listed below each quartile estimate is its corresponding (wild) bootstrapped standard error.

The first point of interest is the relatively large elasticities being attributed to physical capital and the relatively small elasticities being attributed to human-capital-augmented labor. In US data, we would expect roughly 1/3 and 2/3, respectively. Given the less developed capital markets across developing countries, we may expect that in a cross-country study the share of physical capital should be less than 1/3 and the share devoted to human-capital-augmented labor to be greater than 2/3. In fact, we find the opposite. Although we are able to estimate models that avoid several potential biases, we do not get elasticities that are in line with conventional wisdom. We will also see that this is a problem (to a lesser extent) with our nonparametric models in this chapter. This suggests that something else is missing. For example, as noted before, we failed to include region and time effects. We also may have an omitted variable bias. These points and others will be addressed later in the book.

The results on RTS are the second point of interest. In general, we are unable to reject CRS across estimators (GL being the exception). This suggests that assuming CRS could actually be correct. We will consider nonparametric production functions with economic constraints in Chapter 12.

Finally, we want to note that the R^2 for each model is very high. Each of our R^2 measures (squared correlation coefficient between Y and the fitted value of Y) are in

Table 5.2. *Summary of elasticities and returns to scale from various parametric models*

	Cobb–Douglas	CES			Generalized quadratic			Generalized Leontief		
	Q_2	Q_1	Q_2	Q_3	Q_1	Q_2	Q_3	Q_1	Q_2	Q_3
K	0.945	0.911	0.972	1.001	0.332	0.687	0.866	0.258	0.592	0.862
	(0.040)	(0.047)	(0.034)	(0.066)	(0.079)	(0.079)	(0.074)	(0.081)	(0.065)	(0.020)
HL	0.054	0.010	0.039	0.100	0.196	0.404	0.803	−0.069	0.008	0.056
	(0.061)	(0.062)	(0.044)	(0.075)	(0.058)	(0.121)	(0.088)	(0.058)	(0.022)	(0.059)
RTS	0.999		1.011	1.013	1.052	1.215	0.173	0.528	0.899	
	(0.024)		(0.030)	(0.008)	(0.152)	(1.025)	(0.077)	(0.104)	(0.041)	
R^2	0.945		0.951		0.956		0.946			

excess of 0.90. This suggests that the parametric models are doing a relatively good job at fitting the data (noting the issues with the elasticities). This implies that it may be difficult to reject the parametric functional forms using the test statistics we will present in Chapter 6, even if they are incorrectly specified.

Nonparametric

Although the parametric models have high goodness-of-fit measures, we did see counter-intuitive results for the elasticities. Further, each of these production functions is potentially misspecified. It makes sense to look at alternative estimators. Here we consider the nonparametric regression model

$$Y_{it} = m (K_{it}, HL_{it}) + u_{it}, \quad i = 1, 2, \ldots, n, t = 1, 2, \ldots, T_i,$$

where $m (\cdot)$ is the unknown smooth production function. We consider a host of different methods for which to estimate the cross-country production function as well as many different ways to present the results.

Bandwidths. As we stress throughout the book, bandwidth selection is the most salient factor when performing applied nonparametric estimation. Not only can the bandwidth parameter(s) greatly affect the shape of the function (and hence gradients), they also can tell us something about how the variables enter the function. In Table 5.3 we give six sets of bandwidths for K and HL. We estimate the bandwidths via both LSCV and AIC_c for the LCLS, LLLS, and LQLS estimators. In each case we use a Gaussian kernel, but note that the results are qualitatively similar when we use other kernel functions.

The results of Hall, Li, and Racine (2007) suggest an effective upper bound can be set as a few standard deviations of the regressor. The upper bound here is calculated as two times the standard deviation of the regressor, but we would suggest you be cautious in your interpretation of bandwidths near these (somewhat) arbitrary upper bounds.

As we noted before, the bandwidths from the LCLS estimator determine whether or not a variable is relevant in the prediction of the left-hand-side variable. In both

Table 5.3. *Summary of bandwidths (Gaussian kernel)*

	K	HL	Interpretation
LSCV			
LCLS	1.1255	0.9538	Relevant, Relevant
LLLS	2.6311	1.8536	Nonlinear, Nonlinear
LQLS	4.6981	8.1206	Not quadratic, Possibly quadratic
AIC_c			
LCLS	0.1976	0.8248	Relevant, Relevant
LLLS	0.7113	0.2652	Nonlinear, Nonlinear
LQLS	0.6928	0.3027	Not quadratic, Not quadratic
Upper bound	7.5850	7.9586	

bandwidth selection procedures (LSCV and AIC_c) and for both inputs (K and HL) our bandwidths suggest that each is a relevant input. We would have been worried if this were not the case.[2]

The bandwidths from the LLLS estimator indicate whether or not a variable enters the production function linearly. Here we also see that the corresponding bandwidths for each regressor for each bandwidth selection criterion are less than two times their respective standard deviations. Hence, we argue that both variables affect output in a nonlinear manner. This result is also expected.

Finally, the bandwidths on the inputs for the LQLS estimator can determine whether or not the variables enter in quadratically. If so, this would suggest that a quadratic production function may not be far off the mark. In three of the four cases we see that the bandwidth is less than the upper bound and in one case (LSCV for HL) it is slightly above two standard deviations of the input. Thus we conclude that while there is some evidence to suggest that HL enters in quadratic form, we do not believe this to be the case for physical capital and hence it does not appear likely that the GQ model sufficiently captures the functional form. That being said, we will perform formal tests in the next chapter.

Conditional mean. Perhaps the most popular way to present a nonparametric regression is to plot the conditional mean estimate (and its confidence interval) versus a single input. In the case where there is only one regressor, this type of figure can be very enlightening. However, when more than one input exists, in order to plot the conditional mean in two dimensions, it is necessary to hold all of the other inputs fixed. In Figure 5.7 we run a LCLS regression with bandwidths selected via LSCV with a Gaussian kernel and plot the conditional mean of output versus physical capital holding human-capital-augmented labor fixed at its median value. The dashed lines above and below the conditional mean represent the confidence interval (the conditional mean estimate plus or minus two times the standard deviation of the conditional mean at a given value of K).

We see that for a fixed level of human-capital-augmented labor, increases in physical capital lead to increases in output. This result is expected. However, this figure hides any potential complementarities between the inputs. Further, this result is counterfactual and it need not represent any particular observation. In fact, for some estimation methods and for some fixed values of HL, we sometimes find plots that are not intuitive. Some authors attempt to look at figures like these at several values of the fixed inputs (say at $Q1$, $Q2$, and $Q3$), but these are counterfactual as well. In general, we find that the results from such figures are often unreliable when the number of inputs is greater than one and generally do not recommend them (see Henderson, Kumbhakar, and Parmeter, 2012).

A similar approach for conditional means can be done in three dimensions. This approach is useful when there are two inputs as we have in our particular problem. Plotting three dimensional figures with more than two regressors will require holding

---

[2] See Delgado, Henderson, and Parmeter (2014) for a more detailed investigation of cross-country growth regressions and the impact that physical and human capital have on it in a fully nonparametric setting.

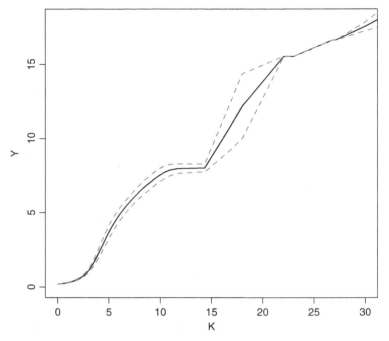

Figure 5.7. Two-dimensional counterfactual conditional mean plot of output versus physical capital with human-capital-augmented labor fixed at its median value (LCLS with LSCV bandwidths and Gaussian kernel)

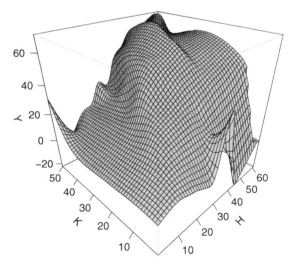

Figure 5.8. Three-dimensional conditional mean plot of output versus physical capital and human-capital-augmented labor (LQLS with LSCV bandwidths and Gaussian kernel)

all the remaining variables fixed as well. In Figure 5.8 we perform such an exercise. It is important to note that to obtain such a figure we need to evaluate the function over a grid of points (this is also common in two-dimensional plots, but is not necessary there).

In the figure we see that increases in K or HL lead to increases in Y, but we also see the complementarity between the two inputs that is masked with the counterfactual plot. One point which is interesting in this figure is that the slope appears to be steep for low levels of physical capital regardless of the level of human-capital-augmented labor. In other words, small increases in physical capital lead to large increases in output when physical capital is relatively scarce. At the same time, large increases are needed to bring about increases in output for given levels of physical capital when human-capital-augmented labor is relatively scarce (the less steep slope in the direction of larger amounts of HL).

Gradients. In a typical study we are interested in the gradients. Here the gradients are less important than the elasticities (which we obtain from the gradients), but it is worthwhile to examine them here as a teaching tool. For simplicity, we look at the gradients by using perhaps the most common method to obtain them. Specifically, we use the LLLS estimator with LSCV to select the bandwidths with various kernel functions.

The results of this experiment can be found in Table 5.4. There are at least three things you should take from this table. First, the gradients are generally significant. This should be expected, given economic intuition as well as the bandwidth estimates we saw earlier. Second, the results do not differ much across kernels (when considering the standard errors). This is also expected, given our past experience with kernel functions.

The final point of interest from the table is the R^2 measure in each case. Here we see that the goodness-of-fit measure is higher for the nonparametric models. That being said, the fit was already very high with the parametric methods and now we should begin to worry about overfitting the data. Nonparametric methods are known for very strong in-sample fit. However, any (continuous) function can be interpolated with a sufficiently high-order polynomial. It is also important to conduct out-of-sample predictions to determine whether or not a model predicts well. There are cases in the literature where the nonparametric model does a better (Henderson and Kumbhakar, 2006) or a worse (Henderson and Millimet, 2008) job at out-of-sample prediction. We will address this issue later.

Table 5.4. *Summary of gradients (LLLS with LSCV)*

	K			HL			R^2
	$Q1$	$Q2$	$Q3$	$Q1$	$Q2$	$Q3$	
Epanechnikov	0.7601	0.7662	0.7676	0.2813	0.2831	0.2989	0.9942
	(0.0300)	(0.0200)	(0.0198)	(0.0263)	(0.0292)	(0.0306)	
Biweight	0.7493	0.7513	0.7565	0.2976	0.3044	0.3094	0.9943
	(0.0167)	(0.0169)	(0.0180)	(0.0312)	(0.0254)	(0.0256)	
Triweight	0.7508	0.7532	0.7600	0.2985	0.3110	0.3174	0.9955
	(0.0159)	(0.0161)	(0.0171)	(0.0285)	(0.0252)	(0.0250)	
Gaussian	0.8336	0.8343	0.8378	0.2489	0.2494	0.2495	0.9855
	(0.0283)	(0.0290)	(0.0354)	(0.0562)	(0.0547)	(0.0537)	

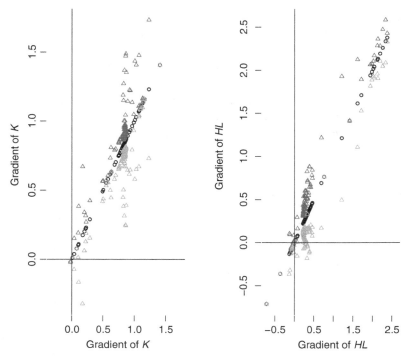

Figure 5.9. 45° plot of the gradient with respect to physical capital and human capital augmented labor (LLLS with LSCV and Gaussian kernel)

These types of tables are informative, but they only show three points in the sample (for each regressor). It is possible that any one of these points may be associated with a relatively large (or small) standard error and this could influence our perception of the overall behavior of the data. Further, it only spans the interquartile range and at most characterizes 50% of the data. An alternative way to present the gradients (or other estimates from a nonparametric or nonlinear parametric model) is to plot the gradients and their upper and lower bounds against themselves (our 45° plot).

We have conducted such an exercise for the Gaussian kernel estimates in Table 5.4 in Figure 5.9. It is easy to see where the majority of the estimates lie. We also see from both panels in the figure that there appear to be two groups of gradients, large and small, with very little in between. In a similar ilk, Henderson (2010) finds some evidence of bimodality in the gradients of his nonparametric LLLS estimates (AIC_c bandwidths and Gaussian kernels) of growth regressions, but not to the same degree.

In Table 5.5 we calculated the percentage of each gradient that is positive and the percentage that is negative as well as the percentage that is positive and significant or negative and significant. Very few are negative. Given the large amount of variability generally associated with nonparametric models, this is a particularly good sign. In practice you may find less extreme percentages.

Table 5.5. *Percentage of gradients which are positive (or negative) and percentage which are positive (or negative) and significant (LLLS with LSCV and a Gaussian kernel)*

	Percent positive (and significant)	Percent negative (and significant)
K	0.9992	0.0008
	(0.9775)	(0.0008)
HL	0.9879	0.0121
	(0.9815)	(0.0080)

Elasticities. In the case of production functions, elasticities are generally more interesting than the gradients themselves. These are calculated as the gradient times the corresponding input to predicted output ratio. Formally, the elasticity of physical capital is calculated as

$$elasticity\,(K_{it}) = \widehat{\beta}\,(K_{it})\,K_{it}/\widehat{Y}_{it},$$

for each it, where $\widehat{\beta}\,(K)$ is the gradient of the conditional mean with respect to physical capital, and $\widehat{Y}_{it}$ is the fitted value. The elasticity of human-capital-augmented labor is calculated similarly. The benefit of using elasticities is that they are directly comparable to one another. Further, under the assumption of CRS the elasticities can be interpreted as the percentage base of a given input used in the production process. Thus, an estimated elasticity of 0.3 for human-capital-augmented labor would tell us that it accounts for 30% of the inputs used to produce output. Again, we wish to emphasize that these are elasticities and can be interpreted as shares only under perfect competition and constant returns to scale.

Table 5.6 gives the nonparametric elasticities as well as RTS for the LCLS, LLLS, and LQLS estimators via LSCV and AIC_c bandwidth selection (all using Gaussian kernels). Beneath each quartile estimate is the corresponding (wild) bootstrapped standard error. In the final column we list the goodness-of-fit measure for each of the six regressions.

There are several points worth emphasizing in Table 5.6. The elasticities from the LCLS estimator are much more variable than the LLLS or LQLS estimates. We have found this result in other empirical work. This could be due to the difference in the gradient calculation between the LCLS estimator and both the LLLS and LQLS estimators. Gradients obtained from the LCLS estimator are analytical, taken as the direct derivative of the estimator, whereas derivatives from both the LLLS and LQLS estimators are approximations stemming from the Taylor expansion.

Also notice that while the elasticities of physical capital are larger than the elasticities of human-capital-augmented labor, they are generally to a lesser degree than what we saw with the parametric estimates. This shows that potential functional form misspecification can only explain some of additional weight devoted to the elasticity of physical capital. Even though we find large changes in the elasticities between the

Table 5.6. *Summary of elasticities and returns to scale (Gaussian kernel)*

	K			HL			RTS			R^2
	Q1	Q2	Q3	Q1	Q2	Q3	Q1	Q2	Q3	
LSCV										
LCLS	0.0061	0.0268	0.2026	0.0142	0.0503	0.1529	0.0243	0.0861	0.4353	0.9784
	(0.0002)	(0.0011)	(0.0092)	(0.0006)	(0.0022)	(0.0081)	(0.0009)	(0.0038)	(0.0210)	
LLLS	0.4162	0.7469	0.8954	0.1431	0.3274	0.7095	1.0092	1.0427	1.1540	0.9855
	(3.1729)	(0.0320)	(0.0215)	(0.0475)	(0.0421)	(0.1136)	(0.0082)	(0.0351)	(0.1563)	
LQLS	0.3702	0.7150	0.8710	0.1834	0.3621	0.7477	1.0192	1.0495	1.2045	0.9838
	(0.0504)	(1.5337)	(0.0319)	(0.0635)	(0.1124)	(0.1844)	(0.0158)	(0.0945)	(0.4009)	
AIC$_c$										
LCLS	0.0224	0.1196	0.7857	0.0094	0.0281	0.0700	0.0431	0.1718	0.8873	0.9911
	(0.0009)	(0.0050)	(0.0331)	(0.0008)	(0.0027)	(0.0078)	(0.0017)	(0.0105)	(0.1043)	
LLLS	0.3070	0.6579	0.8353	0.1932	0.4292	0.7836	1.0128	1.0674	1.2059	0.9963
	(0.0183)	(0.0202)	(0.0134)	(0.0169)	(0.0678)	(0.0334)	(0.0056)	(0.0222)	(0.0670)	
LQLS	0.3086	0.6274	0.7647	0.2699	0.4239	0.7018	0.9777	1.0632	1.1954	0.9968
	(0.0002)	(0.0526)	(0.0034)	(0.0067)	(0.0004)	(0.0027)	(0.0148)	(0.0041)	(0.0013)	

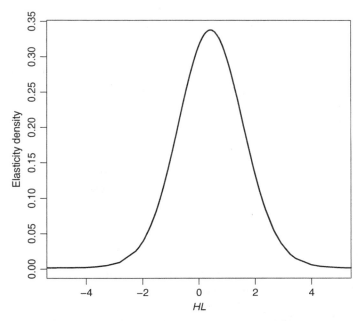

Figure 5.10. Density plot of the estimated elasticities of human-capital-augmented labor. Estimates are from the LLLS estimator with bandwidths obtained via LSCV using a Gaussian kernel

parametric and nonparametric estimates, the median RTS for the LLLS and LQLS are not different from unity. This implies we fail to reject CRS for these median estimates. That being said, we see substantial variation in RTS as well as for the elasticities.

To show the variation in elasticities, we employ the popular technique of plotting the kernel densities. In Figure 5.10 we plot the density of elasticities from human-capital-augmented labor. This density is useful, but has two disadvantages as compared to the 45° plots we showed for the gradients. First, there is no way to assess significance from this figure. For example, we find some very large and small elasticities, but it is unclear from the figures how much variation is associated with these estimates. Second, the shape of this density also depends upon a bandwidth. For simplicity, and because most authors who use this approach do so, we use the Silverman rule-of-thumb bandwidth for a Gaussian kernel function (1.06) to plot the densities without any justification.

If we try to make economic sense of these plots, it seems that while we find bimodality in the gradients, we see that the elasticity densities are unimodal. However, recall that the 1.06 scale factor assumes a unimodal density. That being said, (unreported) 45° plots of these estimates of the elasticities appear unimodal. Although unimodal, we see a large dispersion in the estimates. Comparing these estimates to our parametric estimates, we find far more heterogeneity with the nonparametric approach (as expected). The polynomial approaches such as GQ and GL do not uncover the same degree of heterogeneity. However, it is likely the case that these nonparametric models show too much variation. Our subsequent goal will be to use more advanced nonparametric techniques to try to obtain more reliable estimates of the production function and its elasticities.

Prediction

Finally, we are interested in examining the out-of-sample prediction power of our non-parametric estimators versus themselves and the parametric estimators. We see that the goodness-of-fit measures for the nonparametric estimators are similar to one another and uniformly higher than the parametric estimators. That being said, we worry that the fit is too good and perhaps this is a case of overfitting, which sometimes arises with data-driven bandwidth selection methods.

To examine this, we run a simple out-of-sample prediction scheme (given that we have panel data). Here our in-sample data is all observations up to 2000 (1127 observations) and the out-of-sample data are the year 2005 observations (117 observations). We estimate the parametric and nonparametric models using the in-sample data and then use the out-of-sample inputs to predict the out-of-sample (year 2005) output values. We present four alternative measures of out-of-sample performance (R^2, mean square error, mean absolute error, and mean absolute percentage error) in Table 5.7.

The parametric estimators not only have a high R^2 for in-sample fit, they also have high values for out-of-sample fit. Of these, the CD model is the highest, followed by GL. The other measures are only interesting when compared across methods, and it appears as if the CD model dominates here as well.

The results for the nonparametric estimators are less than desirable. Other than for the LCLS, the out-of-sample R^2 measure for the nonparametric estimators is relatively small. Similarly, they have relatively large values for MSE and MAE.

As we hinted earlier, our data-driven bandwidth procedures lead to undersmoothing in this application. In fact, if we generically double the bandwidths for any of the estimation procedures, we often get much better performance (even when compared to the parametric estimators). For example, if we multiply each of the bandwidths for the LLLS case by two, we obtain an $R^2 = 0.9846$, MSE $= 84.6380$, MAE $= 0.3127$, and MAPE $= 0.5400$. With the exception of MAPE, each of these measures is better than any of the nonparametric or parametric estimators in Table 6. As we saw with bandwidth selection for density estimation, LSCV tends to undersmooth the data. This leads to gains in in-sample fit, but this comes at the cost of out-of-sample fit.

Table 5.7. *Out-of-sample prediction performance
summary (LSCV and Gaussian kernel)*

	R^2	MSE	MAE	MAPE
Parametric				
CD	**0.9696**	**228.3651**	**0.3533**	**0.2580**
CES	0.9490	248.6175	0.3875	0.2793
GQ	0.9386	514.1515	0.5072	0.6984
GL	0.9635	256.2792	0.4237	0.9901
Nonparametric				
LCLS	0.9623	284.7541	0.6279	2.9666
LLLS	0.1226	4347.304	1.0272	0.5715
LQLS	0.1143	4396.463	1.0270	0.6383

As noted by Racine and Parmeter (2013), any given subset of the data can potentially give different conclusions and if we were to use a different split of the data we may end up with a different conclusion on the dominant model (in terms of prediction). However, our goal here is to illustrate the use of out-of-sample prediction to consider the performance of several competing models. A more detailed examination could be done as an exercise at the expense of more lengthy computations.

6

Testing in regression

In regression, estimation is only one component of an empirical analysis. It is incumbent upon the researcher to conduct inference regarding various features underlying the unknown data generating process. The story is no different for nonparametric methods. Many of the tests discussed in this chapter will be analogous to tests performed with parametric estimators. The tests here are similar to those in Chapter 4 and we suggest that you familiarize yourself with the fundamentals discussed in that section before proceeding further if you have not done so already.

As with inference in the density setting, the use of nonparametric testing facilities offers the opportunity to deploy consistent tests. Our main discussion here will be on goodness-of-fit and nonparametric conditional-moment tests. While there are numerous testing approaches, conditional-moment tests serve the same purpose here as the ISE-based tests in Chapter 4. Conditional-moment tests have a rich history in applied econometrics and they are sufficiently general to offer tests for an array of important hypotheses within the regression framework.

Our discussion sets out with perhaps the most common nonparametric regression testing problem, that of correct functional form specification. Recall that a *correctly* specified parametric regression model will always produce more efficient estimates of the unknown model parameters than a nonparametric model will. Thus, testing the functional form of an empirical model is important for applied econometric research. Another popular inferential concern in the regression context is that of variable significance (either individual or joint). This type of inference can also be supported with the conditional-moment tests discussed here. Finally, we show how a test for heteroskedasticity of the error term can also be cast as a conditional-moment test. Testing for heteroskedasticity is important because knowledge of the presence of it may be used to construct more efficient nonparametric estimators.

Implementation of these tests faces similar hurdles that our ISE tests in Chapter 4 encountered, namely, issues related to appropriate selection of the bandwidths to be used when constructing the test statistic, as well as the choice between using the limiting distribution versus a bootstrap approximation. We cover the appropriate steps for using a bootstrap approximation for each of our hypotheses discussed here. Furthermore, we devote additional discussion on recent research of how to select the appropriate bandwidth in conditional-moment tests.

We apply these tests to many of the regressions estimated in Chapter 5. For example, we test whether the four parametric specifications we proposed in Chapter 5 are correctly specified. We also consider tests for relevance of inputs as well as for the presence of heteroskedasticity. Finally, we look at the elasticities and returns to scale across different groups of countries and use the tests discussed in Chapter 4 for testing differences across groups.

6.1 Testing preliminaries

A variety of testing facilities exist for investigating the validity of a given hypothesis. For example, in the realm of maximum likelihood, many hypotheses can be tested using Wald, Lagrange multiplier (Rao's score), and/or likelihood ratio statistics. In a nonparametric framework, a variety of test statistics also exist. Here our discussion focuses on two relatively simple methods: goodness-of-fit statistics and conditional-moment tests.

6.1.1 Goodness-of-fit tests

Ullah (1985) provides a discussion of a goodness-of-fit test statistic that is similar to a standard F-test in the parametric literature. Recall that for a standard F-statistic, we compare a restricted model to an unrestricted model. Here, we have the same setup, except that our unrestricted residuals come from a nonparametric model. The restricted model could be parametric or nonparametric, depending upon the hypothesis that is being tested. For example, in a test of variable significance, both models would be non-parametric, whereas in a test of correct parametric specification, the restricted model would be parametric.

More specifically, the general test is outlined as follows. Define the residuals obtained from the restricted model as $\widehat{u}_i$ and those from the unrestricted model as $\widetilde{u}_i$. It is expected that the sum of squared residuals from the unrestricted model should be smaller than those from the restricted model. When the (relative) difference is large, this is evidence against the null, while when the difference is small, there is not enough evidence to reject the null (the same intuition as with standard F-statistics). Formally, the goodness-of-fit statistic proposed by Ullah (1985) is

$$\widehat{I}_n = \frac{\sum_{i=1}^{n} \widehat{u}_i^2 - \sum_{i=1}^{n} \widetilde{u}_i^2}{\sum_{i=1}^{n} \widetilde{u}_i^2}. \tag{6.1}$$

This test statistic is popular because it is easy to grasp and can be applied in other dimensions (e.g., semiparametric vs. nonparametric models), but issues persist. First, in a parametric model, this statistic is necessarily greater than or equal to zero, but this is not necessarily true for this test statistic. Second, this test statistic requires estimation of both the restricted and unrestricted models. While this may not be a major burden to construct the test statistic, it can be computationally expensive to estimate both models (especially nonparametric models) in a bootstrap procedure. Third, Hong and Lee (2013) argue that this test does not have optimal power, and propose in its place a general testing procedure based on loss functions. Finally, Lee and Ullah (2001) show that this test statistic has a degenerate distribution. Fan and Jiang (2007) show that the test is not optimal without rescaling. "Pretending that the error distribution is normal," Fan and Jiang (2005, 892) show that a generalized likelihood ratio (GLR) statistic can be written in a similar manner. Proper scaling (which is dependent, for example, upon the kernel and distribution of the regressors) leads to a test statistic that is distributed as chi-squared. That being said, Fan and Jiang (2007, 427) do not use the scaling factor in their bootstrap and hence we omit it and any additional discussion on the asymptotic distribution. We have found in our own work that the bootstrapped version of the Ullah (1985) test works relatively well (see also Cai, Fan, and Li, 2000 and Cai, Fan, and Yao, 2000, among others).

6.1.2 Conditional-moment test

An alternative to a goodness-of-fit test is a conditional-moment test. Conditional-moment tests have a long history in the econometrics literature (e.g., see Bierens, 1990 and Newey, 1985). Newey (1985, sec. 3), in the context of testing for correct functional form, suggested using moment conditions of the form

$$E[u w_J(x)] = 0, \tag{6.2}$$

for $J = 1, \dots, J$ weighting functions, $w_J(\cdot)$. The errors (u) stem from a model based on the hypothesis of interest, and the weighting functions are chosen such that under the alternative hypothesis at least one of the J conditions will not hold. As more moment conditions are used, the more likely one or more moment conditions will be violated under the alternative hypothesis. However, given that only a finite number of conditions can be imposed, this style of test will not possess power in all directions from the null hypothesis.

Bierens (1990) demonstrated how to convert the finite set of moment conditions in (6.2) to an infinite set of moment conditions in order to have power for all departures from the null. Lemma 1 in Bierens (1990) shows that a family of exponential functions can generate an infinite number of moment conditions required for the consistency of the conditional-moment test. Unfortunately, the calculation of the test statistic with these exponential weighting functions can impose a major computational burden in practice. To overcome this problem, we can use a random subset of these exponential weighting functions. Unfortunately, this means that implementation of Bierens' (1990) test relies on arbitrary selection of moment conditions and, based on different moment conditions, different conclusions can be reached.

Zheng (1996) was perhaps the first to use a nonparametrically specified weighting function. He considers replacing $w_J(\cdot)$ with $E(u|x)$ (the conditional expectation of the null models errors, given the regressors). This type of formulation serves at least two purposes. First, *any* departure from the null ($E(u|x) = 0$) will lead to a violation of the moment condition as

$$
\begin{aligned}
E[uE(u|x)] &= E[E[uE(u|x)|x]] \\
&= E[E(u|x)E(u|x)] \\
&= E\left[E(u|x)^2\right] > 0,
\end{aligned}
$$

where the first equality holds by the law of iterated expectations. Given that $E(u|x) \neq 0$ when the null hypothesis fails, the conditional moment cannot be 0.

Although useful for testing correct parametric specification, this type of test is more general than what we have described above. The general form for a density-weighted conditional-moment test takes the form

$$E\left[\varepsilon E\left(\varepsilon|\mathbf{x}\right)f\left(\mathbf{x}\right)\right] = 0, \tag{6.3}$$

under a general null hypothesis ($H_0 : E(\varepsilon|\mathbf{x}) = 0$). Here ε is some aspect of the data generating process we are interested in testing. The appearance of $f(\mathbf{x})$ in the weighting function inside the conditional moment is to cancel the random denominator that will arise from estimating $E(\varepsilon|\mathbf{x})$. A further benefit of using $E(\varepsilon|\mathbf{x})$ as the weighting function is that it becomes relatively straightforward to show that the test statistic based on the conditional moment is a second-degree degenerate U-statistic and Hall's (1984) central limit theorem can be invoked to ascertain the limiting distribution of the test statistic.

6.2 Correct parametric specification

A test for correct parametric specification compares a parametric model to a nonparametric alternative. This is quite different from tests performed in the parametric world. Typical parametric tests compare one model versus a specific alternative. When the null is rejected, the test points to the alternative model. However, it need not be the case that the alternative is true. In this case we argue that the test is inconsistent (in some directions). In other words, the probability that the test is rejected given that the null is false does not necessarily tend towards one as the sample size grows. In our nonparametric tests, we compare the assumed parametric model to a nonparametric alternative. Here our alternative need not be specified and we possess power in all directions.

Assume we observe data from n individuals, each with a single response variable y and q explanatory variables $\mathbf{x} = (x_1, x_2, \ldots, x_q)$. Consider some pre-specified parametric model, perhaps linear, which we define as $m(\mathbf{x}; \beta)$, where β is a p-dimensional parameter vector. Note that q need not be equal to p. For example, we could have each regressor enter in both levels and quadratics in our model and hence $p = 2q + 1$ (+1 being the intercept).

Consider a simple example. Suppose we are testing the null hypothesis of correct functional form and the data generating process is quadratic

$$y_i = \alpha + \beta x_i + \gamma x_i^2 + v_i,$$

but the model you propose is linear

$$y_i = \alpha + \beta x_i + u_i.$$

It is clear here that

$$u_i = \gamma x_i^2 + v_i.$$

We can see that the residual sum of squares from restricted and unrestricted models should differ significantly and that $E\left(u_i|x_i\right) \neq 0$ (both assuming $\gamma \neq 0$).

More generally, our null hypothesis is that the parametric model is correctly specified

$$H_0 : P\left[E\left(y|\mathbf{x}\right) = m\left(\mathbf{x}; \beta\right)\right] = 1$$

for some β versus the alternative that

$$H_1 : P\left[E\left(y|\mathbf{x}\right) = m\left(\mathbf{x}; \beta\right)\right] \neq 1$$

for any β. We describe both a goodness-of-fit and conditional-moment version of the test for correct parametric specification.

6.2.1 Goodness-of-fit test

One of the first papers to consider a parametric specification versus a nonparametric alternative in econometrics is Ullah (1985, 200-201).[1] Ullah's (1985) goodness-of-fit test takes the restricted model as the assumed parametric specification and the unrestricted model is the nonparametric specification.

For simplicity, consider the simple case of a single regressor. If we assume our model is linear, this can be written as

$$y_i = \alpha + \beta x_i + u_i$$

and our nonparametric alternative is written as

$$y_i = m\left(x_i\right) + u_i.$$

Under the null hypothesis, $E\left(y|x\right) = m\left(x; \beta\right) = \alpha + \beta x$. However, under the alternative, these will differ. The basic idea behind the Ullah (1985) test is to estimate each model by the corresponding method and then to look at the relative difference of the sum of the squared residuals across both models.

We first define the parametric residuals (i.e., restricted model) obtained from a least-squares regression as

$$\widehat{u}_i = y_i - \widehat{\alpha} - \widehat{\beta} x_i.$$

Similarly, our residuals from a nonparametric regression (i.e., unrestricted model), say LCLS, are defined as

$$\widetilde{u}_i = y_i - \widetilde{m}\left(x_i\right).$$

In general, we suspect that the sum of the squared residuals from the nonparametric model will be less than those from the parametric model. The resulting test statistic is thus

$$\widehat{I}_n = \frac{\sum_{i=1}^{n} \widehat{u}_i^2 - \sum_{i=1}^{n} \widetilde{u}_i^2}{\sum_{i=1}^{n} \widetilde{u}_i^2}.$$

---

[1] See Bierens (1982) for a consistent nonsmoothing test.

Given the discussion in Chapter 4, as well as the discussion of calculating standard errors via a bootstrap in nonparametric regression, you may think that the bootstrap would involve taking random draws from the data. The idea of resampling $\{y_i, x_i\}$ pairs of data with replacement, better known as the pairs bootstrap, is often inconsistent. Although it works well for calculating standard errors when the data are homoskedastic, the basic issue with this type of bootstrap for testing is that it typically does not impose the null hypothesis. For example, let's assume the data generating process is quadratic, but the assumed model is linear. Randomly sampling $\{y, x\}$ pairs still leads to a data generating process that is quadratic. We therefore need to approach the bootstrap from a different angle (Mammen, 1992). We give two popular methods below.

The first bootstrap procedure we discuss is the naïve bootstrap. This is also often referred to as a residual bootstrap as we bootstrap from the parametric residuals. We prefer the term naïve bootstrap here as the wild bootstrap also requires resampling from the parametric residuals. We again note that this method is only valid for testing when we have an additive error and the data are homoskedastic. The basic idea is to resample the residuals with replacement, add them to the parametric fitted values and then obtain the bootstrapped left-hand-side variables. These are then regressed against the original $\mathbf{x}$ values in order to obtain a bootstrapped test statistic. This test statistic preserves the null hypothesis, as the parametric fitted values are used to calculate the bootstrapped values of y. Formally, the steps (for the general q-variate case) are as follows:

1. Compute the test statistic $\widehat{I_n}$ for the original sample of $\{\mathbf{x}_1, \mathbf{x}_2, \ldots, \mathbf{x}_n\}$ and $\{y_1, y_2, \ldots, y_n\}$.
2. Randomly sample, with replacement from the centered parametric residual vector $\widehat{u}_i - \overline{\widehat{u}}$, where $\widehat{u}_i = y_i - m\left(\mathbf{x}_i; \widehat{\beta}\right)$ and $\overline{\widehat{u}}$ is the average (over n) residual (needed to keep the mean zero assumption), n bootstrapped residuals $\{u_i^*\}_{i=1}^n$. Then construct the bootstrapped left-hand-side variable as $y_i^* = m\left(\mathbf{x}_i; \widehat{\beta}\right) + u_i^*$ for $i = 1, 2, \ldots, n$. Call $\{y_i^*, \mathbf{x}_i\}_{i=1}^n$ the bootstrap sample.
3. Calculate $\widehat{I_n^*}$ where $\widehat{I_n^*}$ is calculated the same way as $\widehat{I_n}$, except that y_i is replaced by y_i^*.
4. Repeat steps 2 and 3 a large number (B) of times and then construct the sampling distribution of the bootstrapped test statistics. We reject the null that the parametric model is correctly specified if the estimated test statistic $\widehat{I_n}$ is greater than the upper α-percentile of the bootstrapped test statistics.

We mentioned in Chapter 5 that one of the problems with the naïve bootstrap is that it is only valid when the data are homoskedastic. Leads to invalid standard errors in regression and a similar story holds here. The basic problem is that when you randomly sample the residuals with replacement and then add them to the parametric fitted values, you generally mix errors with large variances with $\mathbf{x}$ values associated with smaller variances and vice versa. The alternative that we use to construct standard errors in the presence of heteroskedasticity is the wild bootstrap. Not only does this method allow for heteroskedasticity in an unknown form, but it generally has better performance in kernel-based tests in finite samples (Li and Wang, 1998). In simulations it is often found that using a naïve bootstrap leads to size distortions, especially under heteroskedasticity. On the other hand, a wild bootstrap works well compared to other methods even when there is no heteroskedasticity. Therefore, we will only discuss the wild bootstrap in subsequent tests.

The basic idea behind the wild bootstrap is to randomly rescale the residual of each individual observation; there is no sharing of residuals across observations. The question, of course, becomes, "how do we vary the residual?" As we showed in Chapter 5, the construction of two-point wild-bootstrap errors are popular in practice. The basic idea is that for each residual, you multiply by one of two values, and the value that is used is chosen at random. These numbers can take many forms, but most are chosen so that the mean of the bootstrapped residuals is equal to zero (noting that our centering of residuals is now redundant) and that the second and third moments of the bootstrapped residuals remain unchanged. Formally, the steps for the two-point wild bootstrap procedure are as follows:

1. Compute the test statistic $\widehat{I}_n$ for the original sample of $\{\mathbf{x}_1, \mathbf{x}_2, \ldots, \mathbf{x}_n\}$ and $\{y_1, y_2, \ldots, y_n\}$.
2. For each observation i, construct the centered bootstrapped residual u_i^*, where $u_i^* = \frac{1-\sqrt{5}}{2}\left(\widehat{u}_i - \overline{\widehat{u}}\right)$ with probability $\frac{1+\sqrt{5}}{2\sqrt{5}}$ and $u_i^* = \frac{1+\sqrt{5}}{2}\left(\widehat{u}_i - \overline{\widehat{u}}\right)$ with probability $1 - \frac{1+\sqrt{5}}{2\sqrt{5}}$. Then construct the bootstrapped left-hand-side variable as $y_i^* = m\left(\mathbf{x}_i; \widehat{\beta}\right) + u_i^*$ for $i = 1, 2, \ldots, n$. Call $\left\{y_i^*, \mathbf{x}_i\right\}_{i=1}^n$ the bootstrap sample.
3. Calculate $\widehat{I}_n^*$ where $\widehat{I}_n^*$ is calculated the same way as $\widehat{I}_n$, except that y_i is replaced by y_i^*.
4. Repeat steps 2 and 3 a large number (B) of times and then construct the sampling distribution of the bootstrapped test statistics. We reject the null that the parametric model is correctly specified if the estimated test statistic $\widehat{I}_n$ is greater than the upper α-percentile of the bootstrapped test statistics.

Given that we use the same $\mathbf{x}$'s in each bootstrap iteration, when programming it may be useful (here and elsewhere) to save the kernel matrices from the estimation of the original test statistic for use in the bootstrap. This leads to fewer calculations in your program at the cost of additional memory requirements.

Many test statistics have since been described which improved upon Ullah's (1985) test. In addition, a majority of the more current testing proposals contain asymptotic results regarding the limiting distribution of the proposed test statistic, the validity of the bootstrap, and/or the power of the test in certain directions away from the null hypothesis. See Fan and Li (1996), González-Manteiga and Cao (1993), Gozalo (1995, 1997), Härdle and Mammen (1993), Hong (1993), Hong and Lee (2013), Horowitz and Härdle (1994), Staniswalis and Severini (1991), Whang (2000), Wooldridge (1992), and Yatchew (1992) for discussion on various tests for correct model specification.

However, a majority of these tests require estimation of both the parametric and non-parametric models and hence are computationally burdensome. We now consider a test for correct parametric specification which does not suffer from this computational burden.

6.2.2 Conditional-moment test

We consider a conditional-moment test for the null hypothesis of correct specification (Zheng, 1996; Li and Wang, 1998). Formally, under the null, since $E(u_i | \mathbf{x}_i) = 0$, we have, by the law of iterated expectations,

$$I = E\left[u E(u|\mathbf{x}) f(\mathbf{x})\right] = 0.$$

The sample moment condition is taken by averaging over the observations as

$$I_n = \frac{1}{n} \sum_{i=1}^{n} u_i E(u_i | \mathbf{x}_i) f(\mathbf{x}_i). \tag{6.4}$$

The errors can be replaced by the parametric residuals, the conditional mean can be replaced with the LCLS estimator of u on $\mathbf{x}$ and a kernel density estimator will comprise the third term. Defining $\widehat{u}_i = y_i - m(\mathbf{x}_i; \widehat{\beta})$, where the estimator $\widehat{\beta}$ is obtained, say, via nonlinear least-squares, a feasible test statistic is given as

$$
\widehat{I}_n = \frac{1}{n} \sum_{i=1}^{n} \widehat{u}_i \left[\frac{\frac{1}{n|\mathbf{h}|} \sum_{j=1}^{n} \widehat{u}_j K_h(\mathbf{x}_i, \mathbf{x}_j)}{\frac{1}{n|\mathbf{h}|} \sum_{j=1}^{n} K_h(\mathbf{x}_i, \mathbf{x}_j)} \right] \frac{1}{n|\mathbf{h}|} \sum_{j=1}^{n} K_h(\mathbf{x}_i, \mathbf{x}_j)
$$

$$
= \frac{1}{n} \sum_{i=1}^{n} \widehat{u}_i \frac{1}{n|\mathbf{h}|} \sum_{j=1}^{n} \widehat{u}_j K_h(\mathbf{x}_i, \mathbf{x}_j)
$$

$$
= \frac{1}{n^2 |\mathbf{h}|} \sum_{i=1}^{n} \sum_{j=1}^{n} \widehat{u}_i \widehat{u}_j K_h(\mathbf{x}_i, \mathbf{x}_j),
$$

where $K_h(\cdot)$ is the product kernel function and $|\mathbf{h}|$ is defined as the product of each of the q bandwidth parameters $(h_1 h_2 \cdots h_q)$. The appearance of $f(\mathbf{x})$ in (6.4) should now be clear: it is included to eliminate the denominator stemming from the LCLS estimator for the regression of u on $\mathbf{x}$. Thus, theoretically no random denominator term needs to be analyzed when considering the asymptotic behavior of $\widehat{I}_n$. Keep in mind that the form of the kernel density estimator is such that it eliminates the random denominator when a LCLS estimator is used. If we were to use a LPLS estimator, then this form of the weighting would not remove the random denominator.

As was the case in Chapter 4, the double summation leads to an asymptotically nonnegligible center term. Leaving out the diagonal terms leads to our feasible test statistic

$$\widehat{I}_n = \frac{1}{n\,(n-1)\,|\mathbf{h}|} \sum_{i=1}^{n} \sum_{\substack{j=1 \\ j \neq i}}^{n} \widehat{u}_i \widehat{u}_j K_h\left(\mathbf{x}_i, \mathbf{x}_j\right).$$

$\widehat{I}_n$ can be rewritten as a degenerate U-statistic, much like we saw in Chapter 4. Formally, we have

$$U_n = \frac{1}{n\,(n-1)\,|\mathbf{h}|} \sum_{i=1}^{n} \sum_{\substack{j=1 \\ j \neq i}}^{n} \widehat{u}_i \widehat{u}_j K_h\left(\mathbf{x}_i, \mathbf{x}_j\right) = \frac{2}{n\,(n-1)\,|\mathbf{h}|} \sum_{i=1}^{n} \sum_{j>i}^{n} H\left(\mathbf{x}_i, \mathbf{x}_j\right).$$

Technical Appendix 6.1 shows the conditions for which $H\left(\mathbf{x}_i, \mathbf{x}_j\right)$ is a degenerate U-statistic hold. Thus, with proper normalization we can show that U_n tends towards the standard normal in distribution. Given that we have a degenerate U-statistic, as we showed in Chapter 4, we can obtain the estimator of the variance of the test statistic as

$$\begin{aligned}
\widehat{\sigma}_n^2 &= \frac{2}{|\mathbf{h}|} E\left[H^2\left(\mathbf{x}_i, \mathbf{x}_j\right)\right] \\
&= \frac{2}{|\mathbf{h}|} E\left[\widehat{u}_i^2 \widehat{u}_j^2 K_h^2\left(\mathbf{x}_i, \mathbf{x}_j\right)\right] \\
&= \frac{2}{n\,(n-1)\,|\mathbf{h}|} \sum_{i=1}^{n} \sum_{\substack{j=1 \\ j \neq i}}^{n} \widehat{u}_i^2 \widehat{u}_j^2 K_h^2\left(\mathbf{x}_i, \mathbf{x}_j\right).
\end{aligned}$$

Given these results, the test statistic is constructed as

$$\widehat{T}_n = n\,|\mathbf{h}|^{1/2}\,\frac{\widehat{I}_n}{\widehat{\sigma}_n}$$

and converges to the standard normal distribution under the null. Similar to before, we recommend a bootstrap procedure for use of this test in practice. The steps for the two-point wild bootstrap procedure are as follows:

1. Compute the test statistic $\widehat{T}_n$ for the original sample of $\{\mathbf{x}_1, \mathbf{x}_2, \ldots, \mathbf{x}_n\}$ and $\{y_1, y_2, \ldots, y_n\}$.
2. For each observation i, construct the centered (wild) bootstrapped residual u_i^*, where $u_i^* = \frac{1-\sqrt{5}}{2}\left(\widehat{u}_i - \overline{\widehat{u}}\right)$ with probability $\frac{1+\sqrt{5}}{2\sqrt{5}}$ and $u_i^* = \frac{1+\sqrt{5}}{2}\left(\widehat{u}_i - \overline{\widehat{u}}\right)$ with probability $1 - \frac{1+\sqrt{5}}{2\sqrt{5}}$. Then construct the bootstrapped left-hand-side variable as $y_i^* = m\left(\mathbf{x}_i; \widehat{\beta}\right) + u_i^*$ for $i = 1, 2, \ldots, n$. Call $\{y_i^*, \mathbf{x}_i\}_{i=1}^{n}$ the bootstrap sample.
3. Calculate $\widehat{T}_n^*$ where $\widehat{T}_n^*$ is calculated the same way as $\widehat{T}_n$ except that y_i is replaced by y_i^*.
4. Repeat steps 2 and 3 a large number (B) of times and then construct the sampling distribution of the bootstrapped test statistics. We reject the null that the parametric model is correctly specified if the estimated test statistic $\widehat{T}_n$ is greater than the upper α-percentile of the bootstrapped test statistics.

6.3 Irrelevant regressors

Testing for the statistical significance of a specific covariate (or a group of the covariates) is imperative both economically and statistically. Economically, a variable's significance provides insight into the mechanisms through which our regressand is influenced. Statistically, removing irrelevant covariates produces more desirable properties of our estimators. In a nonparametric setting, this is especially important, as the curse of dimensionality is an overarching concern. Determining statistically irrelevant variables should help mitigate these effects.

Informally, we can look at whether or not the confidence bound of a gradient estimate includes zero, but this is specific to each value of $\mathbf{x}$. Also, this type of approach will only state whether or not a specific point estimate is statistically significant; it cannot definitively suggest if a regressor possesses predictive power. In Chapter 5, we discussed bandwidths that attained their upper bound for the LCLS estimator when the regressor is irrelevant. In practice, this is unlikely to occur, but we did provide a rule of thumb for when the regressor is likely irrelevant. As an alternative, formal statistical tests can be performed to determine the statistical relevance of one or a set of regressors in a nonparametric framework.

Assume we observe data from n individuals, each with a single response variable y and q explanatory variables $\mathbf{x} = (x_1, x_2, \ldots, x_q)$. Let $\mathbf{w} \subset \mathbf{x}$ be a vector of length q_r, where $q_r < q$. The null hypothesis for variable relevance is

$$H_0 : P\left[E\left(y|\mathbf{w}\right) = E\left(y|\mathbf{x}\right)\right] = 1$$

almost surely versus

$$H_1 : P\left[E\left(y|\mathbf{w}\right) = E\left(y|\mathbf{x}\right)\right] < 1$$

on a set with measure 0. Although there exists a handful of approaches to assess statistical significance in a nonparametric regression (e.g., Fan and Li, 1996; Gozalo, 1993; Lavergne and Vuong, 1996; Yatchew, 1992), we first describe a goodness-of-fit test and then discuss one of the most popular methods deployed in practice based on the conditional-moment framework. Further, we describe appropriate bootstrapping techniques for both tests.

6.3.1 Goodness-of-fit test

It is possible to construct a goodness-of-fit test for variable relevance. That being said, given the existence of a popular conditional-moment test (which is computuationally less demanding), our discussion here will be terse. Similar to the parametric case, we construct the restricted model ($E\left(y|\mathbf{w}\right)$) where the variable(s) in question are assumed irrelevant (i.e., removed from the model). The estimated residual sum of squares from that model is compared to the unrestricted model ($E\left(y|\mathbf{x}\right)$), where all the variables are included. In the nonparametric case, each model is estimated via the same nonparametric technique (say, LCLS). The resulting estimates can be plugged into Equation (6.1). If we were interested in the asymptotic distribution, we could scale the test statistic (as in Fan and Jiang, 2005), but simply suggest a bootstrap procedure.

Here we propose a wild bootstrap procedure. The idea is similar to the test for correct parametric specification. We first estimate the test statistic and then create a bootstrapped data set which imposes the null hypothesis (i.e., the variables in question are irrelevant). Formally, the steps for the two-point wild bootstrap procedure are as follows:

1. Compute the test statistic $\widehat{I}_n$ for the original sample of $\{x_1, x_2, \ldots, x_n\}$ and $\{y_1, y_2, \ldots, y_n\}$.
2. For each observation i, construct the centered bootstrapped residual u_i^*, where $u_i^* = \frac{1-\sqrt{5}}{2}\left(\widehat{u}_i - \overline{\widehat{u}}\right)$ with probability $\frac{1+\sqrt{5}}{2\sqrt{5}}$ and $u_i^* = \frac{1+\sqrt{5}}{2}\left(\widehat{u}_i - \overline{\widehat{u}}\right)$ with probablity $1 - \frac{1+\sqrt{5}}{2\sqrt{5}}$, where $\widehat{u}_i$ is the residual from the restricted model $(\widehat{u}_i = y_i - \widehat{E}\left(y_i|w_i\right))$. Then construct the bootstrapped left-hand-side variable as $y_i^* = \widehat{E}\left(y_i|w_i\right) + u_i^*$ for $i = 1, 2, \ldots, n$. Call $\left\{y_i^*, x_i\right\}_{i=1}^{n}$ the bootstrap sample.
3. Calculate $\widehat{I}_n^*$ where $\widehat{I}_n^*$ is calculated the same way as $\widehat{I}_n$ except that y_i is replaced by y_i^*.
4. Repeat steps 2 and 3 a large number (B) of times and then construct the sampling distribution of the bootstrapped test statistics. We reject the null that the elements are (jointly) irrelevant if the estimated test statistic $\widehat{I}_n$ is greater than the upper α-percentile of the bootstrapped test statistics.

As is the case with standard F-tests, if we reject the null, it implies that at least one regressor is relevant. We do not know from the test which variable(s) are irrelevant. Further testing is required to identify the variables which are relevant/irrelevant.

6.3.2 Conditional-moment test

The form of the conditional-moment test for assessing variable significance is based on Lavergne and Vuong (2000). It is computationally more expensive than the conditional-moment test for correct parametric specification, as it does not rely on parametric residuals, but it still possesses desirable properties. Their test does not require the errors to be normally distributed or homoskedastic. They also argue that it does not require much more additional demand on the bandwidths past those which are needed for general regression. The basic idea behind the test is to check whether or not the residuals have a conditional mean equal to zero when the assumed irrelevant regressors are not included in the estimation.

Consider a nonparametric regression model of the form

$$y_i = m\left(w_i, z_i\right) + u_i,$$

where x is the union of the regressors w and z. Let w be a set of regressors that we believe are relevant and of dimension q_r and z is a vector of potentially irrelevant regressors that are of dimension $q - q_r$. The null hypothesis is that the conditional mean of y does not depend on z

$$H_0 : E(y|\mathbf{w}, \mathbf{z}) = E(y|\mathbf{w}).$$

Under this null hypothesis, we define our error as $u = y - E(y|\mathbf{w})$. It is relatively easy to show that under the null, the expectation of the error term conditional on the vector $\mathbf{x}$ is equal to zero

$$
\begin{aligned}
E(u|\mathbf{x}) &= E\left[y - E(y|\mathbf{w})|\mathbf{x}\right] \\
&= E(y|\mathbf{w}, \mathbf{z}) - E\left[E(y|\mathbf{w})|\mathbf{w}, \mathbf{z}\right] \\
&= E(y|\mathbf{w}) - E(y|\mathbf{w}) \\
&= 0
\end{aligned}
$$

and that it is different from zero under the alternative. Therefore, it is a proper candidate for testing the null hypothesis. This result holds because if the true regression function included $\mathbf{z}$, then u would include both the idiosyncratic disturbance and $\mathbf{z}$, and hence it would be correlated with $\mathbf{x}$.

As our (estimated) errors ($u = y - E(y|\mathbf{w})$) will be obtained from a nonparametric regression (which has a random denominator), we consider a weighted conditional-moment test as

$$I = E\left[u f_\mathbf{w}(\mathbf{w}) E\left[u f_\mathbf{w}(\mathbf{w})|\mathbf{x}\right] f(\mathbf{x})\right]$$

where $f_\mathbf{w}(\mathbf{w})$ and $f(\mathbf{x})$ are the densities of $\mathbf{w}$ and $\mathbf{x} = (\mathbf{w}, \mathbf{z})$, respectively. Notice here that in addition to weighting by the density of $\mathbf{x}$, we also weight the residuals by the density of $\mathbf{w}$ (recalling the discussion surrounding Equation (6.3), we have here that $\varepsilon = u f_\mathbf{w}(\mathbf{w})$), to remove the random denominator that will be present in the estimate of u. Note that these additional densities did not appear in the test for correct parametric specification because the residuals came from a *parametric* model. Here the residuals come from a nonparametric model and so asymptotic arguments relying on the first moments of the residuals need to remove (or trim) the random denominator. The sample moment condition is taken by averaging over the observations as

$$I_n = \frac{1}{n} \sum_{i=1}^{n} u_i f_\mathbf{w}(\mathbf{w}_i) E\left[u_i f_\mathbf{w}(\mathbf{w}_i)|\mathbf{x}_i\right] f(\mathbf{x}_i).$$

Again, many of these terms are unknown and must be estimated. We will replace the errors with the residuals from the nonparametric regression of y on $\mathbf{w}$ and the densities will be replaced by kernel-density estimates. Using LCLS, our regression estimator is

$$\widehat{E}(y|\mathbf{w}) = \frac{\frac{1}{n|\mathbf{h_w}|} \sum_{i=1}^{n} y_i K_{h_\mathbf{w}}(\mathbf{w}_i, \mathbf{w})}{\frac{1}{n|\mathbf{h_w}|} \sum_{i=1}^{n} K_{h_\mathbf{w}}(\mathbf{w}_i, \mathbf{w})},$$

where $K_{h_\mathbf{w}}(\mathbf{w}_i, \mathbf{w})$ is a product kernel for the regressors $\mathbf{w}$, $|\mathbf{h_w}|$ is the product of the q_r bandwidths, which correspond to the r elements in $\mathbf{w}$, and we note that the denominator is $\widehat{f}_\mathbf{w}(\mathbf{w})$. Our sample moment condition (that removes the center term) becomes

$$\widehat{I}_n = \frac{1}{n(n-1)|\mathbf{h}|} \sum_{i=1}^{n} \sum_{\substack{j=1 \\ j \neq i}}^{n} \widehat{u}_i \, \widehat{f}_{\mathbf{w}}(\mathbf{w}_i) \, \widehat{u}_j \, \widehat{f}_{\mathbf{w}}(\mathbf{w}_j) \, K_h(\mathbf{x}_i, \mathbf{x}_j),$$

where $\widehat{u}_i = y_i - \widehat{E}(y_i|\mathbf{w}_i)$. We should mention here that while h includes the bandwidths for both $\mathbf{w}$ and $\mathbf{z}$, the estimation of the density of $\mathbf{w}$, $f_{\mathbf{w}}(\mathbf{w})$, requires a separate set of bandwidths.

Following the same steps as before, our variance term is calculated as

$$\widehat{\sigma}_n^2 = \frac{2}{n(n-1)|\mathbf{h}|} \sum_{i=1}^{n} \sum_{\substack{j=1 \\ j \neq i}}^{n} \widehat{u}_i^2 \, \widehat{f}_{\mathbf{w}}^2(\mathbf{w}_i) \, \widehat{u}_j^2 \, \widehat{f}_{\mathbf{w}}^2(\mathbf{w}_j) \, K_h^2(\mathbf{x}_i, \mathbf{x}_j).$$

As expected, with this information we can construct a test statistic that is asymptotically normal with mean zero and unit variance under the null hypothesis. This test statistic is given as

$$\widehat{T}_n = n \, |\mathbf{h}|^{1/2} \frac{\widehat{I}_n}{\widehat{\sigma}_n}.$$

As an alternative to using the asymptotic distribution, we can employ a bootstrap procedure to test the null hypothesis. Gu, Li, and Liu (2007) propose a wild bootstrap procedure and show its asymptotic validity. Formally, the steps for the two-point wild bootstrap procedure are as follows:

1. Compute the test statistic $\widehat{T}_n$ for the original sample of $\{\mathbf{x}_1, \mathbf{x}_2, \ldots, \mathbf{x}_n\}$ and $\{y_1, y_2, \ldots, y_n\}$.
2. For each observation i, construct the centered bootstrapped residual u_i^*, where $u_i^* = \frac{1-\sqrt{5}}{2}(\widehat{u}_i - \overline{\widehat{u}})$ with probability $\frac{1+\sqrt{5}}{2\sqrt{5}}$ and $u_i^* = \frac{1+\sqrt{5}}{2}(\widehat{u}_i - \overline{\widehat{u}})$ with probablity $1 - \frac{1+\sqrt{5}}{2\sqrt{5}}$, where $\widehat{u}_i = y_i - \widehat{E}(y_i|\mathbf{w}_i)$. Then construct the bootstrapped left-hand-side variable as $y_i^* = \widehat{E}(y_i|\mathbf{w}_i) + u_i^*$ for $i = 1, 2, \ldots, n$. Call $\{y_i^*, \mathbf{x}_i\}_{i=1}^{n}$ the bootstrap sample.
3. Calculate $\widehat{T}_n^*$, where $\widehat{T}_n^*$ is calculated the same way as $\widehat{T}_n$ except that y_i is replaced by y_i^*.
4. Repeat steps 2 and 3 a large number (B) of times and then construct the sampling distribution of the bootstrapped test statistics. We reject the null that the elements of $\mathbf{z}$ are (jointly) irrelevant if the estimated test statistic $\widehat{T}_n$ is greater than the upper α-percentile of the bootstrapped test statistics.

6.4 Heteroskedasticity

At many points in this text we argue that most economic data are heteroskedastic. However, we have yet to provide a formal test for the presence of heteroskedasticity in a nonparametric regression. The first test we are aware of in the literature, Eubank and Thomas (1993), uses smoothing splines and diagnostic plots. While their test may be useful in the univariate regressor case, we prefer a test that can handle multivariate data. The aforementioned test also requires a normally distributed error, which is less desirable. Other tests have been proposed in the literature that improve upon Eubank and Thomas (1993) in many directions. These tests include Dette (2002), Dette and Marchlewski (2010), Dette and Munk (1998), Liero (2003), Su and Ullah (2013), and You and Chen (2005).

Given the lack of an obvious restricted and unrestricted model, we focus our attention on the conditional-moment test by Zheng (2009). We are unaware of any economic applications of this test (other than the one appearing in Zheng, 2009), but believe that economists should consider using this test. Not only is identifying heteroskedasticity important for conducting inference, but if you are able to determine the type of heteroskedasticity present in your application, it is possible to employ a more efficient estimator. For example, you could consider switching to some type of nonparametric feasible generalized least-squares estimator (Martins-Filho and Yao, 2009).

To begin, consider the nonparametric regression model

$$y_i = m(\mathbf{x}_i) + u_i,$$

where y is still our left-hand-side variable, $\mathbf{x}$ is a $1 \times q$ vector of regressors and $m(\cdot)$ is an unknown smooth function. Here, u_i represents our errors, which we assume are mean zero, but we make no specific assumption on the form of the variance. Our goal here is to check whether or not the variance of u varies with $\mathbf{x}$. Formally, the null hypothesis is that the errors are homoskedastic

$$H_0 : V(u|\mathbf{x}) = V(u),$$

versus the alternative that they are heteroskedastic

$$H_1 : V(u|\mathbf{x}) \neq V(u).$$

Note that we do not make any particular assumptions on the form of the heteroskedasticity and hence it encompasses all possible departures from homoskedasticity.

In the popular parametric test by White (1980), the moment condition is

$$E\left[\left(u^2 - \sigma^2\right)\varphi(\mathbf{x})\right] = 0,$$

where $\varphi(\mathbf{x})$ is a vector of second and cross moments of the regressors (the lower triangular elements of $\mathbf{X}_i'\mathbf{X}_i$, where $\mathbf{X}_i = (1, \mathbf{x}_i)$). Under the null hypothesis, the term in parentheses is zero. However, in practice, if the form of the heteroskedasticity is more complicated than polynomial terms of the regressors, this test will be unable to detect heteroskedasticity.

Zheng (2009) considers a variant of $\varphi(\mathbf{x})$ such that the test can detect any form of heteroskedasticity with respect to $\mathbf{x}$. Specifically, his choice for $\varphi(\mathbf{x})$ is

$$\varphi(\mathbf{x}) = E\left[\left(u^2 - \sigma^2\right)|\mathbf{x}\right]f(\mathbf{x}),$$

where $f(\mathbf{x})$ is the density of $\mathbf{x}$. Plugging this into the original moment condition, we obtain

$$I = E\left[\left(u^2 - \sigma^2\right)E\left[\left(u^2 - \sigma^2\right)|\mathbf{x}\right]f(\mathbf{x})\right] = 0$$

and this conditional moment looks much like the others given in this chapter (from Equation (6.3), we have here that $\varepsilon = u^2 - \sigma^2$). The sample moment condition is given as

$$I_n = \frac{1}{n} \sum_{i=1}^{n} \left(u_i^2 - \sigma^2 \right) E \left[\left(u_i^2 - \sigma^2 \right) | \mathbf{x}_i \right] f(\mathbf{x}_i).$$

The residuals are obtained from the nonparametric regression of y on $\mathbf{x}$ as $\widehat{u}_i = y_i - \widehat{m}(\mathbf{x}_i)$ and the variance term is calculated by averaging over the squares of these residuals as

$$\widehat{\sigma}^2 = \frac{1}{n} \sum_{i=1}^{n} \left[y_i - \widehat{m}(\mathbf{x}_i) \right]^2.$$

The conditional expectation can be estimated by performing a LCLS regression of $\left(\widehat{u}^2 - \widehat{\sigma}^2 \right)$ on $\mathbf{x}$. Finally, the density of $\mathbf{x}$ can be obtained using a standard kernel density estimator. Our feasible test statistic, where the diagonal terms are dropped, is given by

$$\widehat{I}_n = \frac{1}{n(n-1)|\mathbf{h}|} \sum_{i=1}^{n} \sum_{\substack{j=1 \\ j \neq i}}^{n} \left(\widehat{u}_i^2 - \widehat{\sigma}^2 \right) \left(\widehat{u}_j^2 - \widehat{\sigma}^2 \right) K_h(\mathbf{x}_i, \mathbf{x}_j).$$

Following the same steps as above, our variance term is calculated as

$$\widehat{\sigma}_n^2 = \frac{2}{n(n-1)|\mathbf{h}|} \sum_{i=1}^{n} \sum_{\substack{j=1 \\ j \neq i}}^{n} \left(\widehat{u}_i^2 - \widehat{\sigma}^2 \right)^2 \left(\widehat{u}_j^2 - \widehat{\sigma}^2 \right)^2 K_h^2(\mathbf{x}_i, \mathbf{x}_j).$$

It is important to remember that $\widehat{\sigma}_n^2$ is different from $\widehat{\sigma}^2$ and you should not use the two interchangeably.

Given these results, our test statistic is constructed as

$$\widehat{T}_n = n |\mathbf{h}|^{1/2} \frac{\widehat{I}_n}{\widehat{\sigma}_n}$$

and converges to the standard normal distribution under the null. Following our previous format, we also give a bootstrap procedure for testing this null in practice. Here we follow the bootstrap given in Zheng (2009). The basic idea is to perform a two-point wild bootstrap on $\{\widehat{u}_i^2 - \widehat{\sigma}^2\}_{i=1}^{n}$. Subtracting $\widehat{\sigma}^2$ may seem strange, but this ensures that the bootstrapped values are mean zero and homoskedastic. This is intuitive since $I = 0$ can only occur under the null, which cannot happen if $u_i^2 - \sigma^2$ is not mean zero. Moreover, we always bootstrap from the null hypothesis, which in this case is homoskedasticity, and the re-centering here ensures this holds. It may also seem strange that the bootstrap proposed by Zheng (2009) does not re-estimate the function. This is not necessary here, as we are concerned with the squared residuals (which are consistently obtained from the nonparametric regression) and not the function itself. Thus, he bootstraps from the residuals as if they represent the underlying data. The four-step procedure outlined in Zheng (2009) is as follows:

1. Compute the test statistic $\widehat{T}_n$ for the original sample of $\{\mathbf{x}_1, \mathbf{x}_2, \dots, \mathbf{x}_n\}$ and $\{y_1, y_2, \dots, y_n\}$.
2. For each observation i, construct the bootstrapped squared differenced residual $\left(\widehat{u}_i^2 - \widehat{\sigma}^2\right)^* = \frac{1-\sqrt{5}}{2}\left(\widehat{u}_i^2 - \widehat{\sigma}^2\right)$ with probability $\frac{1+\sqrt{5}}{2\sqrt{5}}$ and $\left(\widehat{u}_i^2 - \widehat{\sigma}^2\right)^* = \frac{1+\sqrt{5}}{2}\left(\widehat{u}_i^2 - \widehat{\sigma}^2\right)$ with probablity $1 - \frac{1+\sqrt{5}}{2\sqrt{5}}$. Call $\left\{\left(\widehat{u}_i^2 - \widehat{\sigma}^2\right)^*\right\}_{i=1}^{n}$ the bootstrap sample.
3. Calculate $\widehat{T}_n^*$, where $\widehat{T}_n^*$ is calculated the same way as $\widehat{T}_n$ except that $\left(\widehat{u}_i^2 - \widehat{\sigma}^2\right)$ is replaced by $\left(\widehat{u}_i^2 - \widehat{\sigma}^2\right)^*$.
4. Repeat steps 2 and 3 a large number (B) of times and then construct the sampling distribution of the bootstrapped test statistics. We reject the null that the error term is homoskedastic if the estimated test statistic $\widehat{T}_n$ is greater than the upper α-percentile of the bootstrapped test statistics.

The careful reader will have noticed that $\widehat{u}$ is obtained from a nonparametric regression and hence has a random denominator problem. Zheng (2009) avoids this issue by assuming that $f(\mathbf{x})$ has compact support as well as continuous and bounded second derivatives (his Assumption B2, 286). In practice (for our test statistic), it may be necessary to multiply $\left(\widehat{u}_i^2 - \widehat{\sigma}^2\right)$ and $\left(\widehat{u}_j^2 - \widehat{\sigma}^2\right)$ by $\widehat{f}^2(\mathbf{x}_i)$ and $\widehat{f}^2(\mathbf{x}_j)$, respectively, where each estimated density is squared to cancel out its corresponding squared denominator in the estimate of $\widehat{u}^2$.

6.5 Testing in practice

6.5.1 Bootstrap versus asymptotic distribution

Given that much of the discussion of the bootstrap versus the asymptotic distribution is similar to that in Chapter 4, we provide limited details here. While we have shown that each of the standardized conditional-moment test statistics is asymptotically standard normal, we caution against using the normal quantiles to construct cut-offs for assessment of the validity of the null hypothesis. The reason for this is that the convergence rate of the standardized test statistics are slow, implying that for small samples, the accuracy of the asymptotic approximation may not be reliable. This inaccuracy surfaces through the size of the test, often leading to undersized tests. Given that the bootstrap is an asymptotic refinement, it provides desirable accuracy at the expense of an increased computational burden.

The term asymptotic refinement is taken to imply that the order of approximation for an asymptotically pivotal test statistic using the asymptotic distribution is larger than that of the bootstrap approximation. See Hall (1992, 1995) and Horowitz (2001) for detailed treatments of the order-of-approximation issue between the bootstrap and the asymptotic distribution. Unless extensive simulations bear out the accuracy of an asymptotic distribution providing correctly sized tests, it is recommended that boot-strapping be used to construct the distribution of the test statistic to calculate p-values and quantiles.

6.5.2 Role of bandwidth selection on reliability of tests

A key issue which we have been silent on heretofore is which bandwidth should be used in the construction of the test. Many of the papers that introduce test statistics typically demonstrate the performance of the test using simplified data generating processes with a narrow range of bandwidths and only one or two covariates. This is unpalatable on several dimensions. First, it is highly unlikely that the data generating processes used as the basis for simulations will mimic real-life conditions. Second, the range of bandwidths provided in the simulations typically only have theoretical under-pinnings with respect to the appropriate rate on the bandwidth in accordance with the asymptotic theory of the test. For example, if a test requires that the bandwidth converge to zero at the rate $n^{-1/6}$, then a common approach is to use bandwidths of the form $h_{\text{test}} = c\sigma n^{-1/6}$ where $c \in \{a_1, a_2, \ldots, a_J\}$ where the a's are a string of constants, such as $\{0.5, 0.75, 1, 1.25, 1.5\}$. It is likely that in practice these "scale factors" will not suffice. Both Lavergne and Vuong's (2000) and Gu, Li, and Lu's (2009) test of significance for a regressor require different bandwidths under the null and alternative, and use/propose using bandwidths of the form $c\sigma n^{-1/\delta}$ where δ is under the user's control to ensure appropriate smoothing.

An alternative approach is to use cross-validation. However, even this avenue is rocky. First, cross-validation is computationally intensive and for several tests (such as the inclusion of irrelevant variables) more than a single bandwidth is required. Additionally, it has been shown in finite samples that bandwidths selected via data-driven methods (such as cross-validation) lead to overfitting. In this case, undesirable impacts on the performance of the test are likely to occur. To address the specific issue of which bandwidth to use in practice, Gao and Gijbels (2008) propose an approach that selects a bandwidth that maximizes power while holding size constant through the use of Edgeworth expansions. Their approach was designed for testing correct functional form, but the intuition carries over to any of the conditional-moment tests described here.

Gao and Gijbels (2008) develop Edgeworth expansions for the Li and Wang (1998) conditional-moment test to select bandwidths that maximize power for a given significance level. Through their statistical analysis, they are able to obtain a closed-form solution for the optimal bandwidth for the Li and Wang test. The optimal bandwidth ensures that as $n \to \infty$, the power of the test converges to 1. This optimal bandwidth takes the form

$$\hat{h}_{ew} = \hat{a}^{-1/(2q)}\hat{t}_n^{-3/(2q)}, \tag{6.5}$$

where q is the number of regressors and

$$\hat{a} = \frac{\sqrt{2}K^{(3)}(0)}{3\left(\sqrt{R(k)}\right)^3}\hat{c}(f) \quad \text{and } \hat{t}_n = n\hat{C}_n^2,$$

with

$$\hat{C}_n^2 = \frac{n^{-1} \sum_{i=1}^{n} \hat{\Delta}_n^2(\mathbf{x}_i) \hat{f}(\mathbf{x}_i)}{\hat{\mu}^2 \sqrt{2 \hat{v}_2 R(k)}}, \quad \hat{c}(f) = \frac{n^{-1} \sum_{i=1}^{n} \hat{f}(\mathbf{x}_i)^2}{\left(\sqrt{n^{-1} \sum_{i=1}^{n} \hat{f}(\mathbf{x}_i)} \right)^3},$$

$$\widehat{\Delta}_n(\mathbf{x}) = \frac{\sum_{i=1}^{n} K_{h_{cv}}(\mathbf{x}_i, \mathbf{x}) \left(y_i - g(\mathbf{x}_i, \hat{\beta}) \right)}{\sum_{i=1}^{n} K_{h_{cv}}(\mathbf{x}_i, \mathbf{x})},$$

and

$$\hat{\mu}_2 = \overline{\hat{u}_i}; \quad \hat{v}_2 = \overline{\hat{f}(\mathbf{x}_i)^2}; \quad \hat{f}(\mathbf{x}) = (n \hat{h}_{cv}^d)^{-1} \sum_{i=1}^{n} K_{h_{cv}}(\mathbf{x}_i, \mathbf{x}).$$

Recall from Table 2.2 in Chapter 2 that $R(k) = \int k^2(v) dv$. In this setup, $\hat{h}_{cv}$ is the cross-validated bandwidth selected for estimating the density of the data. $K^{(3)}(0)$ is the thrice-convoluted kernel. For the standard normal kernel, $K^{(3)}(\mathbf{x}) = \frac{e^{-\mathbf{x}'\mathbf{x}/6}}{\sqrt{6\pi}}$ so that $K^{(3)}(0) = 1/\sqrt{6\pi} \approx 0.23$. For the Epanechnikov, biweight, and triweight kernels, $K^{(3)}(0) = 9/20, 475/784,$ and $9205/13728$, respectively. In the framework of Gao and Gijbels (2008), the same bandwidth is used for each regressor. If this is unappealing, you can rescale the optimal bandwidth by the individual scale factors obtained when constructing $\hat{h}_{cv}$.

To formally implement the Zheng (1996) and Li and Wang (1998) conditional-moment test for correct functional form, using the bandwidth of Gao and Gijbels (2008), the following procedure may be used:

1. Determine $\hat{h}_{cv}$ through cross-validation for $f(\mathbf{x})$. Once $\hat{h}_{cv}$ has been constructed, use (6.5) to create $\hat{h}_{ew}$.
2. Compute the test statistic $\widehat{T}_n$ for the original sample of $\{\mathbf{x}_1, \mathbf{x}_2, \ldots, \mathbf{x}_n\}$ and $\{y_1, y_2, \ldots, y_n\}$, using $\hat{h}_{ew}$.
3. For each observation i, construct the centered bootstrapped residual u_i^*, where $u_i^* = \frac{1-\sqrt{5}}{2} \left(\hat{u}_i - \overline{\hat{u}} \right)$ with probability $\frac{1+\sqrt{5}}{2\sqrt{5}}$ and $u_i^* = \frac{1+\sqrt{5}}{2} \left(\hat{u}_i - \overline{\hat{u}} \right)$ with probability $1 - \frac{1+\sqrt{5}}{2\sqrt{5}}$. Then construct the bootstrapped left-hand-side variable as $y_i^* = m(\mathbf{x}_i; \hat{\beta}) + u_i^*$ for $i = 1, 2, \ldots, n$. Call $\{y_i^*, \mathbf{x}_i\}_{i=1}^{n}$ the bootstrap sample.
4. Calculate $\widehat{T}_n^*$ where $\widehat{T}_n^*$ is calculated the same way as $\widehat{T}_n$, except that y_i is replaced by y_i^*.
5. Repeat steps 3 and 4 a large number (B) of times and then construct the sampling distribution of the bootstrapped test statistics. We reject the null that the parametric model is correctly specified if the estimated test statistic $\widehat{T}_n$ is greater than the upper α-percentile of the bootstrapped test statistics.

This same approach can be followed to implement the conditional-moment tests for variable significance and heteroskedasticity as well. However, in those settings, the Edgeworth expansions will not be the same as those derived in Gao and Gijbels (2008). This means that the h_{ew} will be different. This is an open area of research that certainly deserves more attention given the importance of the bandwidth on the performance of the conditional-moment tests in practice.

6.6 Application

In Chapter 5, we estimated cross-country production functions and examined elasticities and returns to scale. Here we plan to test various features of these cross-country production functions. First, we will test for correct parametric specification. Second, we will test the relevance of the inputs in the production function. Third, we will test for the presence of heteroskedasticity. Finally, we will look at the estimated elasticities across regions and use the density tests discussed in Chapter 4.

In addition to performing tests to uncover features of the underlying function, we also hope to review some of the nuances of the tests. Specifically, for each test we will try to isolate a particular attribute of the test besides simply giving the p-value. For example, for the Li and Wang (1998) test we will look at the difference between using normalized and nonnormalized test statistics. As you will see, we will sometimes have conflicts regarding whether or not to reject a null hypothesis. While this may be concerning, it is even more concerning if you ignore it and blindly trust the results for a particular set-up.

6.6.1 Correct functional form

We considered four different parametric specifications in the application section of Chapter 5 (CD, CES, GQ, and GL). We improved upon previous attempts in the literature by removing several potential biases. The question we now pose is whether or not these improvements are sufficient to approximate the true underlying functional form. To test these hypotheses we perform both functional form tests we discussed in this chapter: Ullah (1985) and Li and Wang (1998).

In addition to the choice of which test to use, you must also consider several other issues: kernel choice, bandwidth choice, regression estimator, asymptotic versus bootstrapped critical value, and, where relevant, whether to use a normalized or non-normalized test statistic. In our experience, kernel choice rarely matters and hence we will solely employ the Gaussian kernel. However, as you will see, bandwidth choice and regression estimator are very important. In some cases, the conclusions using the asymptotic and bootstrapped critical values are the same, but we highly recommend using a bootstrap. Finally, the choice between a normalized and nonnormalized test statistic do not matter much. However, given that a majority of the literature uses normalized test statistics, we generally use them (when available) in our own work for comparability.

Goodness-of-fit tests
We consider the Ullah (1985) goodness-of-fit test in Table 6.1. In the table we report the p-values for each test, for each functional form (CD, CES, GQ, and GL), for

Table 6.1. *Ullah (1985) test for correct functional form – each element in table represents the p-value for a given test*

	CD	CES	GQ	GL
ROT				
LCLS	0.1125	0.2575	0.2275	0.1425
LLLS	0.4800	0.3650	0.5650	0.4200
LQLS	0.4875	0.4300	0.5750	0.4100
LSCV				
LCLS	0.1700	0.2525	0.2400	0.1650
LLLS	0.0525	0.0075	0.0025	0.0000
LQLS	0.0075	0.0300	0.0025	0.0100
AIC_c				
LCLS	0.5300	0.5025	0.3375	0.4925
LLLS	0.2550	0.2675	0.2850	0.2500
LQLS	0.2100	0.2875	0.2475	0.1975

various bandwidths. Specifically, we obtain the bandwidths by using rule-of-thumb, LSCV or AIC_c from a LCLS, LLLS, or LQLS regression (noting that this style of test does not limit the type of estimator) of output (Y) on physical capital (K) and human-capital-augmented labor (HL). As you can see, the conclusion depends on the estimation procedure and bandwidth. For LSCV with LLLS or LQLS, we reject the null of a correctly specified parametric model at the 10% level (for each case). However, in the other cases (e.g., rule-of-thumb bandwidths) we fail to reject the null of a correctly specified parametric model. At this point it is premature to cast a decision on whether or not a given parametric model is correctly specified.

To look for differences across estimation procedures, in Figure 6.1 we plot the bootstrap test statistic distributions for the null that the true underlying form is CD for LSCV-selected bandwidths with LCLS, LLLS, and LQLS. The LCLS and LQLS densities have a substantial amount of overlap, but this is not the case for LLLS.

Conditional-moment tests

We now consider the Li and Wang (1998) test for correct functional form. The results for the Li and Wang (1998) tests can be found in Table 6.2. Specifically, we give the p-values for both the normalized and nonnormalized test statistics (bandwidths are estimated via LSCV). The results often conflict with the Ullah (1985) tests, but we note that we look at other estimation procedures with the Ullah test. Given the conflicting evidence, we choose to hold off on a conclusion about whether or not any of the parametric models are correctly specified.

Given that we only show the results for LSCV in the table, we decided to plot several of the bootstrap normalized test statistics in Figure 6.2. Specifically, we plot the 399 wild-bootstrap-generated densities for the test for which the null model is CES. All estimations are conducted via LCLS and bandwidths are chosen via rule-of-thumb, LSCV, and AIC_c. There is point we would like you to take away from this

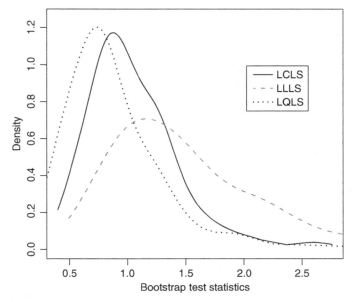

Figure 6.1. Bootstrap test statistics from the Ullah (1985) test for a CD model versus a nonparametric alternative; all bandwidths estimated via LSCV. Estimation conducted via LCLS, LLLS, and LQLS; 399 wild bootstraps used to construct each distribution; Gaussian kernel with rule-of-thumb bandwidths used to generate densities

Table 6.2. *Li and Wang (1998) test for correct functional form (with and without normalization) – bandwidths selected via LSCV, each element in the table represents the p-value for a given test*

	CD	CES	GQ	GL
$\widehat{I}_n$	0.1275	0.0975	0.6150	0.0200
$\widehat{T}_n$	0.1850	0.1025	0.6375	0.0425

figure. The tails of these bootstrapped densities are much thicker than that of a standard normal. We will examine this more with the Lavergne and Vuong (2000) test, but we can easily see how employing the asymptotic distribution could lead to improper inferential conclusions.

The conflicting results in Table 6.2 may seem disheartening, but they allow us to emphasize several points. First, statistical tests can and do conflict in practice. This could either be due to the test itself or the fact that the model is incomplete. Recall that these are panel data and we have failed to account for this. This lack of consistency could reflect our simplification of the model. Second, the specific bandwidth we have deployed could be influencing our test results. We believe it is important to use both statistical tests and economic reasoning when examine a parametric model. As we saw in Chapter 5, the elasticities from the parametric models were not economically intuitive, despite each model's proclivity for a high fit.

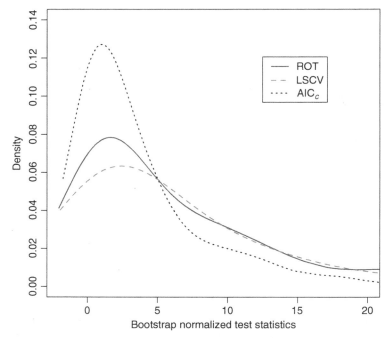

Figure 6.2. Bootstrap test statistics from the Li and Wang (1998) test for a CES model versus a non-parametric alternative; all estimation conducted via LCLS; bandwidths obtained via rule-of-thumb, LSCV, and AIC_c; Gaussian kernel with rule-of-thumb bandwidths used to generate densities (399 wild bootstraps)

6.6.2 Relevance

In contrast to the functional form tests, there is far less conflict for the tests of relevance. This should be expected, as we have a very simple production function with two inputs, which (presumably) all economists consider to be vital. When using the Lavergne and Vuong (2000) test to investigate the relevance of physical capital and human-capital-augmented labor, we obtain p-values that are zero to four decimal places when using either bootstrapped or asymptotic distributions (all bandwidths are calculated via LSCV and the test statistics are normalized). The unreported test statistics are generally much larger than their critical values. Figure 6.3 plots the bootstrap and asymptotic distribution along with the (very different) 95% critical values (for the null K is). In conclusion, we argue that both of our inputs are relevant. Both economic intuition and the test statistics support our position.

6.6.3 Heteroskedasticity

The presence of heteroskeasticty in economic data is often the default assumption. However, homoskedasticity is a testable assumption that can and should be performed. If heteroskedasticity is shown to hold, then we can consider using GLS-type estimators to potentially improve efficiency.

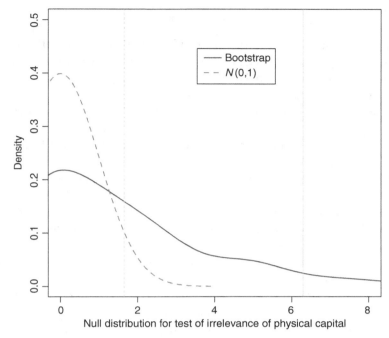

Figure 6.3. Bootstrap test statistic for irrelevance of physical capital via the Lavergne and Vuong (2000) test versus the asymptotic distribution (standard normal); bandwidths for the test estimated via LSCV; estimation conducted via LCLS. 399 wild bootstraps used to construct the bootstrap distribution; Gaussian kernel with rule-of-thumb bandwidths used to generate the density; critical values (95th percentiles) shown as vertical lines

Table 6.3. *Zheng (2009) test for heteroskedasticity – bandwidths*
selected via rule-of-thumb, LSCV, and AIC$_c$, critical value is
defined as the 95th percentile of the bootstrapped test statistics

	$\widehat{T}_n$	$\widehat{T}_{n,\mathrm{crit}}$	p-value
ROT	108.2343	1.4697	0.0000
LSCV	88.2418	1.6208	0.0000
AIC$_c$	16.3724	1.3701	0.0000

Table 6.3 gives the results for the Zheng (2009) test for each bandwidth procedure. In this table we give the value of the normalized test statistic, the 95th percentile of the bootstrapped test statistics (which we use as our critical value), and the p-value of the test. In each case we see very large test statistics and we reject the null of homoskedasticity. This is as expected.

One point we should examine are the critical values. Note that these are substantially larger than the critical values from the asymptotic distribution. However, this is not an issue here.

6.6.4 Density tests

One benefit of nonparametric kernel methods is that they give a plethora of results. Observation-specific estimates can be obtained for each regressor in a nonparametric regression. An increasingly popular method for presenting the results is to plot kernel densities of the estimates. This allows you to examine the entire set (or subset) of estimates for a particular regressor in one simple-to-view figure. One hypothesis of interest is to see whether or not the marginal effects from one group are different from another. For example, are the marginal products of capital different between OECD and non-OECD countries?

For the most part, these tests are variants of the tests discussed in Chapter 4. For some tests, all that is required is to replace the data being analyzed. For example, instead of comparing $f(\mathbf{x})$ to $g(\mathbf{x})$, we compare the densities of the partial effects for pre-specified groups. Technical Appendix 6.2 discusses how to estimate the densities and perform several of the tests in practice. The theoretical justification for this is taken from Fan and Ullah (1999), who show that the Li (1996) test goes through for dependent data.

In what follows, we will take a look at heterogeneity in the elasticities of the inputs as well as returns to scale. Specifically, our goal is to separate the estimates by group and then compare various aspects of these group estimates. We examine equality of the densities of the estimates of interest via the Li (1996) test.

Table 6.4 lists the seven distinct groups. With the exception of the OECD group (Group 1), most of these groupings are geographical. Again, Group 1 is made up of (some, but not all of the) OECD economies, Group 2 is Sub-Saharan Africa, Group 3 is Latin America, Group 4 is Middle Eastern and North African economies, Group 5 is East Asia, Group 6 is Central (commonly referred to as Eastern) Europe, and Group 7 is South Asia.

In Table 6.5 we report the median share of physical capital and human-capital-augmented labor as well as returns to scale for each group along with their associated standard error.[2] Specifically, we present the results for the LLLS estimator with LSCV bandwidths. It is interesting to note that the median values of RTS are indistinguishable from 1 except for Sub-Saharan African countries where the RTS are greater than one. If this is true, it is relevant information for foreign direct-investment decisions. On the other hand, we see big differences across groups (at the median values) for the elasticities.

We see that the elasticities for physical capital are highest for OECD and Middle Eastern and North African countries. At the same time, the median elasticities of human-capital-augmented labor are highest for Sub-Saharan African and South Asian countries. In fact, for each of these groups the median share of physical capital is less

---

[2] For the median share of physical capital for groups 1 and 5 we insert the 51st percentile, as the median estimate's standard errors are uncommonly large for observations in the "center" of the data. As you can see from the 45° plots in the previous chapter, we occasionally observe very large standard errors for specific observations, which often arise due to too few bootstrap resamples. Here we use 399 wild bootstraps and in practice it would seem prudent to use at least 999 in this example. We do not do so here because we do not want to burden you in case you wish to replicate the results of this chapter.

Table 6.4. *Region classifications (seven distinct groups)*

	1	2	3	4	5	6	7
1	Australia	Benin	Argentina	Algeria	Brunei	Albania	Bangladesh
2	Austria	Botswana	Barbados	Bahrain	Cambodia	Bulgaria	India
3	Belgium	Burundi	Bolivia	Egypt	China	Cyprus	Maldives
4	Canada	Cameroon	Brazil	Iran	Fiji	Greece	Nepal
5	Denmark	Central African Republic	Chile	Israel	Hong Kong	Hungary	Pakistan
6	Finland	Congo	Colombia	Jordan	Indonesia	Poland	Sri Lanka
7	France	Côte d'Ivoire	Costa Rica	Malta	Japan	Romania	
8	Iceland	Gabon	Cuba	Morocco	Korea	Turkey	
9	Ireland	Gambia	Ecuador	Syria	Laos		
10	Italy	Ghana	El Salvador	Tunisia	Macao		
11	Luxembourg	Kenya	Guatemala		Malaysia		
12	Netherlands	Lesotho	Guyana		Mongolia		
13	New Zealand	Liberia	Haiti		Papua New Guinea		
14	Norway	Malawi	Honduras		Philippines		
15	Portugal	Mali	Jamaica		Singapore		
16	Spain	Mauritius	Mexico		Taiwan		
17	Sweden	Mozambique	Nicaragua		Thailand		
18	Switzerland	Namibia	Panama		Vietnam		
19	United Kingdom	Niger	Paraguay				
20	United States	Rwanda	Peru				
21		Senegal	Trinidad and Tobago				
22		Sierra Leone	Uruguay				
23		South Africa	Venezuela				
24		Sudan					
25		Swaziland					
26		Tanzania					
27		Togo					
28		Uganda					
29		Zambia					
30		Zimbabwe					

than that of human-capital-augmented labor. This is the expected result and we have found this for a subset of the countries.

The median results are interesting, but they only explain behavior at the center of the distribution. We have the elasticity of each input for each country in each time period. This allows us to compare the densities of elasticities and RTS between groups.

Table 6.6 gives the p-values for the Li (1996) test for equality of estimated densities. Specifically, we test the null that the elasticities of physical capital and human-capital-augmented labor as well as RTS are different between OECD and all other groups of countries. The first element in each column is the test of equality between Group 1

Table 6.5. *Median elasticities and returns-to-scale estimates for*
each group (with standard errors), obtained via a
nonparametric regression of output on physical capital and
human-capital-augmented labor (LLLS with LSCV)

	Elasticity (K)	Elasticity (HL)	RTS
OECD	0.8864	0.1226	1.0106
	(0.0441)	(0.0187)	(0.1605)
Sub-Saharan Africa	0.4274	0.7318	1.1491
	(0.0653)	(0.0344)	(0.0253)
Latin America	0.7951	0.2893	1.0618
	(0.0459)	(0.0265)	(0.1843)
Middle East and North Africa	0.8713	0.1727	1.0321
	(0.0512)	(0.0209)	(0.0272)
East Asia	0.6429	0.4412	1.0195
	(0.0344)	(0.0393)	(0.0256)
Central Europe	0.7755	0.2437	1.0147
	(0.0355)	(0.0355)	(0.0461)
South Asia	0.3975	0.5444	1.0131
	(0.0085)	(0.0209)	(0.0255)

Table 6.6. *Li (1996) test for equality of densities – differences in*
estimates between Group 1 (OECD) and all other groups (2–7)
obtained via a nonparametric regression of output on physical
capital and human-capital-augmented labor (LLLS with LSCV
used for regressions, rule-of-thumb bandwidths and Gaussian
kernels used for densities)

	Elasticity (K)	Elasticity (HL)	RTS
OECD	1.0000	1.0000	1.0000
Sub-Saharan Africa	0.0000	0.0000	0.0000
Latin America	0.0000	0.0000	0.0000
Middle East and North Africa	0.0000	0.0000	0.0050
East Asia	0.0000	0.0000	0.0000
Central Europe	0.0000	0.0000	0.7900
South Asia	0.0000	0.0000	0.0000

and Group 1. The p-value is necessarily equal to unity. The second row of numbers
gives the p-value for the test that the estimated densities of estimates of Group 1 are
different from those of Group 2. Here we reject the null that the elasticities of physical
capital, human-capital-augmented labor and RTS are equal between the two groups. In
fact, we only find one case where we fail to reject the null hypothesis (RTS between
Group 1 and Group 6 are equal). There are two possible explanations for the failure to
reject this null. The first is that they truly are similar. If we look at the median values in

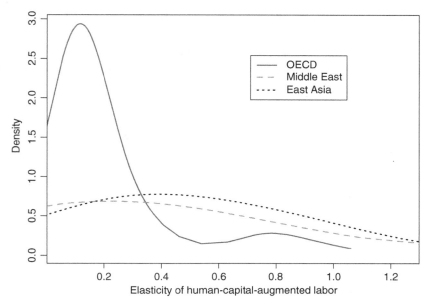

Figure 6.4. Kernel density plots for elasticities of human-capital-augmented labor for OECD, Middle East and North Africa, and East Asian countries, respectively; all densities are calculated with a Gaussian kernel and rule-of-thumb bandwidth

Table 6.6, we see that they are quite close. However, a more cynical view is that given that the number of observations is relatively small in the latter group, it could just be a case of not having enough data to reject the null.

In fact, this test is quite restrictive. It requires that both the mean and variance (and in the case of nonnormal distributions, higher-order moments) to be equal. Slight changes in any of these moments will necessarily lead to rejection as the sample size tends towards infinity.

Partly for this reason, we plot kernel-estimated densities of the elasticities of human-capital-augmented labor for OECD, Middle Eastern and North African as well as East Asian economies (Figure 6.4). We can see that the elasticities for OECD economies are generally relatively small with a mode near 0.20. On the other hand, the variation in elasticities across Middle Eastern and North African as well as East Asian countries are quite large. This figures shows at least two things. First, there is a big difference between the human-capital-augmented labor share distributions between OECD economies and the other two groups. This confirms the p-values. Second, it shows that, in addition to variation across groups, there is substantial variation within groups. As stated before, simple intercept-shift terms in a regression would fail to find this type of variation.

So, what have we learned from this mountain of test statistics? The most important lesson is that the conclusion of the test can depend upon the bandwidth selection mechanism and the estimator. Therefore we suggest you should be cautious before making strong statements on the results of a test. As always, you should use your better economic judgement in conjunction with test statistics. With this in mind, we also see how some tests do not waver with respect to these differences. For example, the tests for relevance of inputs and homoskedasticity were convincing. Finally, we have shown how tests from the density chapter can be useful when looking at output from a nonparametric regression. Specifically, the pdf-based tests were able to shed light on differences in estimates between geographic groups.

7

Smoothing discrete variables

In this chapter, we discuss the intuition underlying the smoothing of discrete variables in the context of a probability density. In virtually all applied economic milieus, many variables will be discrete (also termed categorical), which is to say the variables take on a countable number of outcomes. For example, when we include a regional indicator in a growth regression, this variable takes on anywhere from four to eight distinct values depending upon how finely we wish to partition the globe. Alternatively, a variable categorizing membership into the OECD would present itself as a classic dummy variable, taking only two values. In these instances, smoothing with traditional kernels – such as the s-class of kernels described in Chapter 2 – is inappropriate. Here we outline kernels that are appropriate for smoothing discrete variables. We discuss the interpretation of these smoothing parameters. However, we must delineate between two types of discrete variables: unordered (such as a region indicator) and ordered (say, year).

The elegance of the inclusion of categorical variables to the empirical analysis is that while the interpretation and handling of the variables requires some care beyond what we covered with continuous variables, the mechanics of the estimators do not vary greatly, requiring nothing more than some additional notation and a generalization of the product kernel. The beauty of discrete variables is that (with respect to data requirements) their addition to the model does not lead to severe consequences as was the case with the addition of continuous variables. As with all nonparametric estimation, bandwidth selection is of primary importance and the presence of categorical variables does nothing to change this perception.

We end the chapter incorporating region and time into our investigation of cross-country output. We investigate the distribution of cross-country output looking both over time (ordered discrete) and across regions (unordered discrete). This allows us to document how smoothing these variables aids our understanding of the global distribution of cross-country output without resorting to the common frequency approach, which simply splits the data by each individual category. Lastly, we mention that although a number of authors have provided key insights into the smoothing of discrete data (e.g., Ahmad and Cerrito, 1994; Bierens, 1983, 1987), the more recent work of Qi Li and Jeffrey Racine has been paramount. They have made repeated contributions that have enhanced these methods and made them accessible to applied researchers. Our hope here is to discuss these methods in a manner that reflects their comprehensive insights.

7.1 Estimation of a density

Prior to the development of rigorous statistical methods to smooth discrete variables, the standard approach was to use a nonparametric frequency estimator to handle them. In essence, researchers would engage in sample splitting, pooling continuous variables of interest into groups based on specific outcomes of the discrete variable they wished to analyze. For example, in a study of the distribution of wages, the density of wages for men would be estimated separately from the distribution of wages for women. The frequency approach is a consistent way to estimate the density across various categories; however, its appeal breaks down in the presence of many categories. For example, suppose we also had access to a worker's union status and his or her number of dependents. In this case, the frequency approach would dictate splitting the sample into distinct cells based on all possible combinations of all the discrete variables. Assuming the number of dependents ranged from zero to four, this would lead to a total of $5 \cdot 2^2 = 20$ distinct groups. With a uniform distribution of 1000 observations, this would suggest roughly 50 observations per cell. This problem worsens as the number of categories increases. The smoothing approach introduces bias to help reduce the variance that is likely to occur with the frequency method. Recall from Chapter 2 that the bias of the kernel-density estimator does not depend on the sample size directly, whereas the variance does; thus, it is intuitive that the frequency estimator will have a large variance (relative to the bias) given the small number of observations used per cell (on average).

The intuition behind smoothing discrete variables is that by using information from nearby cells, the construction of the density for a cell can be improved in an MSE sense. Even with the introduction of bias, the variance from the frequency approach has the potential to dominate, so the smoothing method can dramatically reduce MSE. Additionally, the smoothing approach does not necessitate estimating densities for each cell independently. Both of these features make smoothing discrete variables appealing in empirical settings.

Before we dig into the details of the kernels and estimators, consider a simple (elementary statistics book type) example. Suppose we have two six-sided dice. If we roll the two dice simultaneously and sum the values, the possible outcomes are $S = (2, 3, \ldots, 12)$. The probability of the outcome 2 on an given roll is $1/36$. Suppose we were unaware of this and decide to roll the two dice fifty times in order to estimate the probabilities. The chance that we do not roll a 2 over those fifty rolls is $(35/36)^{50}$ or roughly 24.44 percent. If we were going to estimate the probabilities based upon the frequency of observations that fall into a given outcome (say 2), then there is almost a 25 percent chance that we would assign a probability of zero to the outcome 2. However, with a kernel density estimator for discrete data, even in the case where none of the outcomes were equal to 2, we would still assign a positive probability to the value 2.

7.1.1 Kernels for smoothing discrete variables

To understand why alternative kernels are needed to smooth discrete variables, consider the *s*-class of kernels from Chapter 2. For a variable that only takes the values

$\{0, 1\}$, the Epanechnikov $(s = 1)$ kernel would deliver weights of 0 $(x_i = x)$ and 0.75 $(x_i \neq x)$. Notice that these weights do not represent a proper density. This generically suggests that if we were to use a continuous variable kernel, such as the s-class kernel, to estimate a pure discrete density, the resulting estimated density will fail to satisfy the most basic requirement of a density, namely, that the probabilities sum to 1. Here we consider kernels specifically designed for both unordered and ordered discrete variables.

Unordered

As far as we are aware, Aitchison and Aitken (1976) were the first to introduce a kernel function for discrete variables. Consider a discrete variable that takes values in $\mathcal{S} = \{0, 1, \ldots, C\}$. Then, an appropriate kernel function is

$$l\,(x_i, x, \lambda) = \begin{cases} 1 - \lambda & \text{if } x_i = x \\ \lambda/C & \text{if } x_i \neq x \end{cases}. \tag{7.1}$$

Notice that this kernel function only takes on two values: $1 - \lambda$ and λ/C (regardless of the number of categories).[1] It is verifiable that the kernel weights from this function will sum to 1, so that a proper density is produced (see Technical Appendix 7.1).

Notice how the weighting function is similar to that of a continuous variable. When $\lambda = 0$, $\ell\,(x_i, x, 0)$ is nothing more than an indicator function. When the kernel function is an indicator function, this is identical to frequency estimation, splitting the sample on each cell and engaging in nonparametric analysis on only observations in a cell, as opposed to smoothing across cells. Thus, $\lambda = 0$ suggests that neighboring cells are not considered. Alternatively, when $\lambda = C/(C + 1)$, we have that the weights for the case $x_i = x$ and $x_i \neq x$ are identical, $1/(C+1)$. This case can be seen as uniform weighting and provides insight into the nature of the categorical data. From these two extreme cases we notice that the bandwidth for the discrete kernel introduced here is bounded between $\left[0, C/(C + 1)\right]$. With continuous variables, we have an infinite upper bound on the bandwidth (zero is the lower bound).

Note the similarities for a zero bandwidth across both continuous and discrete data. In both cases a bandwidth of zero implies that the local neighborhood is effectively a point mass. The difference is, in the discrete setting, likely more than a single observation will make up that point mass, whereas in a continuous setting the point mass will have a single observation (have measure zero). It is more palatable to have a (finite sample) zero bandwidth for a discrete variable than a continuous one, given the implications.

Ordered

The kernel we just described ignores any natural ordering in the discrete variable. It is likely in applied work that we will also have variables that possess a natural order. A common example is a time trend, but survey data where respondents are asked for a ranking or placing income into bins is also common. In these cases the discrete kernel

---

[1] This kernel introduced by Aitchison and Aitken (1976) was the counterpart to the Gaussian kernel for discrete data.

in Equation (7.1) will not exploit this known ordinal relationship. The reason underlying this is that for the Aitchison and Aitken (1976) kernel, a constant weight is assigned to all values of the variable that do not equal the value under study (x). However, with an ordered variable, we can see that cells closer to the cell of interest should naturally be seen as "closer" than cells further away, as is the case in the continuous setting. In the time trend example, we might expect that the years 1999 and 2001 have more information to offer when smoothing for the year 2000 than the years 1990 and 2010.

Both Aitchison and Aitken (1976, 419) and Wang and van Ryzin (1981, 302) suggest kernels appropriate for estimating densities of an ordered discrete variable. Aitchison and Aitken (1976) do not provide a general formula for an ordered, discrete kernel function: they provide a single kernel function (for the case $C = 2$). While Wang and van Ryzin (1981) only discuss the case where the discrete variable is countable. The kernel proposed by Aitchison and Aitken (1976) has the form

$$\ell(x_i, x, \lambda) = \binom{C}{|x_i - x|} \lambda^{|x_i - x|} (1 - \lambda)^{C - |x_i - x|}, \qquad (7.2)$$

where $\binom{a}{b}$ is the binomial coefficient. Technical Appendix 7.2 verifies that these kernel weights sum to one. The ordered kernel still has the appearance of an indicator function when $\lambda = 0$, meaning that the frequency method is also contained in this approach. However, it is not clear how distance between ordered categories manifests itself in the frequency approach and as such, the smoothing method is a more meaningful characterization of this problem. One downside to the ordered kernel presented here is that, for $C > 2$, no λ exists such that a uniform weighting scheme exists. This is unfortunate since we have started to build intuition on interpreting bandwidths as they increase to imply that less information is localized.

7.1.2 Generalized product kernel

The (univariate) discrete kernel-density estimator, with either unordered or ordered univariate discrete data, is

$$\widehat{f}(x) = n^{-1} \sum_{i=1}^{n} \ell(x_i, x, \lambda).$$

Notice that we do not divide by λ here as we did with h for continuous data. The reason for this is a direct consequence of the discrete nature of the data. Recall our first discussion on the kernel function in Chapter 2. The univariate continuous kernel is often written as $h^{-1} k \left(\frac{x_i - x}{h} \right)$. The appearance of the h^{-1} is to ensure that the kernel-density estimator integrates to one. This occurs given the change of variables inside the integral. However, there is no such λ^{-1} because the kernel is already constructed such that the kernel weights allow proper integration of the discrete density estimator to one. Further, given the lack of a λ^{-1}, this necessarily implies that the discrete kernel-density estimator is not scale invariant, as was the case with the continuous kernel-density estimator.

It is likely that we will have mixed data, data that is composed of both continuous and discrete data, with the discrete data possessing both ordered and unordered variables. To allow for easy description, we introduce the generalized product kernel (Li and Racine, 2003). This form of the kernel provides a clean and transparent notation regarding the smoothing of mixed data.

Our data $\mathbf{x}$ can be decomposed as $\mathbf{x} = [\mathbf{x}^c, \mathbf{x}^D]$, where $\mathbf{x}^c$ contains the continuous variables and $\mathbf{x}^D = [\mathbf{x}^u, \mathbf{x}^o]$ contains the discrete data, further partitioned as unordered and ordered data. Next we will distinguish our discrete bandwidths in the same manner, allowing $\lambda = [\lambda^u, \lambda^o]$ to contain the vectors of bandwidths for the unordered and ordered data. Our continuous kernel(s) will still use the familiar $k(\cdot)$ notation, but our discrete kernels will be delineated as $\ell^u(\cdot)$ and $\ell^o(\cdot)$ to clarify the type of kernel being used. Finally, the total number of covariates can be decomposed as $q = q_c + q_D = q_c + (q_u + q_o)$. This notation will allow us to construct a product kernel that is easy to work with and readily provides intuition for smoothing mixed data.

The product kernel function can be constructed as

$$
\begin{aligned}
W_{ix} &= K_h \left(\mathbf{x}_i^c, \mathbf{x}^c \right) L_{\lambda^u}^u \left(\mathbf{x}_i^u, \mathbf{x}^u \right) L_{\lambda^o}^o \left(\mathbf{x}_i^o, \mathbf{x}^o \right) \\
&= \prod_{d=1}^{q_c} k \left(\frac{x_{id}^c - x_d^c}{h_d} \right) \prod_{d=1}^{q_u} \ell^u(x_{id}^u, x_d^u, \lambda_d^u) \prod_{d=1}^{q_o} \ell^o(x_{id}^o, x_d^o, \lambda_d^o).
\end{aligned}
$$

This gives rise to the generalized product kernel density estimator

$$
\widehat{f}(\mathbf{x}) = \frac{1}{n\,|\mathbf{h}|} \sum_{i=1}^{n} W_{ix},
$$

where $|\mathbf{h}|$ is the product of the bandwidths for just the continuous variables $(h_1 h_2 \cdots h_{q_c})$.

7.2 Finite sample properties

It is interesting to study the properties of the mixed-data kernel-density estimator to understand how the statistical properties of the estimator differ in the presence of discrete data. We first present the finite sample properties for the discrete data estimator. The intuition underlying the bias, variance, and mean-squared error are essentially identical when considering ordered or unordered data we will generically refer to both types of variables as discrete.

7.2.1 Discrete-only bias

With discrete data, the bias of the discrete (only) kernel probability density estimator is

$$
\begin{aligned}
\text{Bias}\left[\widehat{f}(\mathbf{x}) \right] &\approx \sum_{d=1}^{q} \lambda_d \left[\sum_{z \in \mathcal{S}} \frac{1\{x_d = z_d\}}{C_d} f(z) - f(x) \right] \\
&= \sum_{d=1}^{q} \lambda_d B_d,
\end{aligned}
$$

where $z \in \mathcal{S}$, C_d corresponds to the distinct values taken on by the dth discrete regressor and in the discrete-only case, $q = q_D$. There are two key differences between the bias of the discrete-only density estimator and the bias of the continuous kernel density estimator. First, the approximation error appears in the bias only as a means for conserving notation. There is no second-order Taylor approximation that is being taken of either the kernel or the unknown density. We could always write out the exact form of the bias (for finite C_d) for the discrete density estimator. Second, and more importantly, the bias depends on the bandwidth through λ_d, whereas in the continuous only case the bias depends on the bandwidth through h_d^2 (the emphasis, of course, on the squared term). This subtle difference has important consequences for the limiting behavior of the estimator.

7.2.2 Discrete-only variance

The variance of the discrete-only kernel probability density estimator is

$$\text{Var}\left[\widehat{f}(\mathbf{x})\right] \approx \frac{f(\mathbf{x})\left[1 - f(\mathbf{x})\right]}{n}.$$

Again, the two main differences with the variance of the discrete estimator and that of the continuous estimator are the approximation error (to simplify notation) and the appearance (or lack thereof) of the bandwidth. In the continuous case, the variance of the kernel density estimator is of order $(n\,|\mathbf{h}|)^{-1}$, whereas in the discrete case the variance is of order n^{-1}. This suggests that the bandwidth only operates through the bias. While this may seem strange, it is intuitive. The sole purpose of smoothing discrete data is to introduce bias to mitigate finite sample variance that undoubtedly occurs from the use of the frequency method with a large number of cells. In small samples, the variance of the frequency estimator will be large, not because the estimator is bad, but because there is not enough information in the sample to reliably extract a cell probability (think of our dice example). As the sample size increases, this concern dissipates.

7.2.3 Discrete-only MSE

Combining the squared bias and the variance of the discrete-kernel probability density estimator, we have that the MSE is

$$\text{MSE}\left[\widehat{f}(\mathbf{x})\right] \approx \left(\sum_{d=1}^{q} \lambda_d B_d\right)^2 + \frac{f(\mathbf{x})(1 - f(\mathbf{x}))}{n}.$$

Here the bandwidth decays to zero so that the squared bias and the variance are balanced, implying $\lambda_d \sim n^{-1/2}$, which is much faster than the $n^{-1/(4+q)}$ we witnessed in the continuous density case.

A few observations are important here. First, when $\lambda_d \sim n^{-1/2}$, this implies that the discrete data kernel-density estimator converges at the parametric rate. Second, the rate of decay is independent of the number of discrete variables that we have, suggesting that the curse of dimensionality does *not* have an impact on the performance of the estimator. In fact, in the discrete-only setting, it could be argued that the frequency estimator suffers from a type of curse-of-dimensionality problem given that increasing the dimensionality of the problem while holding the sample size fixed makes it more difficult to extract information. The ability to smooth over cells allows the kernel-density estimator to enjoy an advantage over a traditional parametric estimator that is not witnessed with continuous data.

7.2.4 Mixed-data bias

With mixed continuous-discrete data, the bias of the kernel-density estimator is (Li and Racine, 2003; Theorem 3.1)

$$\text{Bias}\left[\widehat{f}(\mathbf{x})\right] \approx \frac{\kappa_2(k)}{2} \sum_{d=1}^{q_c} h_d^2 \frac{\partial^2 f(\mathbf{x})}{\partial x_j^2} + \sum_{d=1}^{q_D} \lambda_d B_d^D,$$

where $B_d^D = C_d^{-1} 1\left\{|z^D - x^D| = 1\right\} \left(f(\mathbf{x}^c, z^D) - f(\mathbf{x}^c, \mathbf{x}^D)\right)$. This bias is quite intuitive. It is essentially the combination of the bias from the continuous-only and the discrete-only kernel-density estimators. This stems from the use of the product kernel. Larger bandwidths increase bias and smaller bandwidths decrease bias. Instead of a second derivative appearing in the bias contributed from the discrete component, we have the difference in probabilities assigned between points in the support that differ by 1, akin to a first difference. The greater the discrepancy in these differences, the more bias is contributed from the discrete component. However, in the case that the discrete data are distributed uniformly, $f(\mathbf{x}^c, z^D) = f(\mathbf{x}^c, \mathbf{x}^D) \; \forall z^D$, no bias is contributed from the discrete component of the joint density.

7.2.5 Mixed-data variance

The variance of the mixed-data kernel-density estimator is

$$\text{Var}\left[\widehat{f}(\mathbf{x})\right] \approx \frac{f(\mathbf{x}) R(k)^{q_c}}{n|\mathbf{h}|}.$$

The main difference between the variance of the kernel-density estimator in the mixed-data case and in the discrete-only case is that the presence of discrete data does not add to the overall variance, aside from the presence of $f(\mathbf{x})$. In the discrete-only setting, we have a binomial variance contribution, $f(\mathbf{x}^D)\left[1 - f(\mathbf{x}^D)\right]$. The variance is influenced by the vector of continuous bandwidths in the standard way: as they decrease (to decrease bias), the variance increases.

7.2.6 Mixed-data MSE

Combining the squared bias and the variance of the mixed-data kernel-density estimator, we have that the MSE is

$$\text{MSE}\left[\widehat{f}(\mathbf{x})\right] \approx \frac{\kappa_2^2(k)}{4} \left(\sum_{d=1}^{q_c} h_d^2 \frac{\partial^2 f(\mathbf{x})}{\partial x_j^2}\right)^2 + \left(\sum_{d=1}^{q_D} \lambda_d B_d^D\right)^2$$

$$+ \left(\frac{\kappa_2(k)}{2} \sum_{d=1}^{q_c} h_d^2 \frac{\partial^2 f(\mathbf{x})}{\partial x_j^2}\right) \left(\sum_{d=1}^{q_D} \lambda_d B_d^D\right) + \frac{f(\mathbf{x}) R(k)^{q_c}}{n|\mathbf{h}|}. \tag{7.3}$$

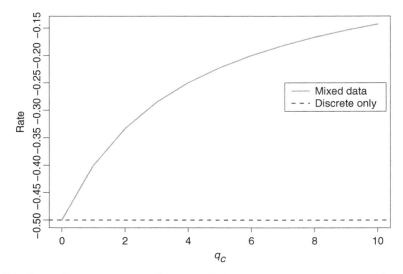

Figure 7.1. Rate of convergence on discrete-variable bandwidth in the presence of continuous variables

By assuming that all of the continuous-variable bandwidths have the same rate of decay and that all the discrete-variable bandwidths have the same rate of decay (but potentially different than that of the continuous variables), we can establish the optimal rates for both. Technical Appendix 7.3 shows that $h_{\mathrm{opt}} \sim n^{-1/(4+q_c)}$ and $\lambda_{\mathrm{opt}} \sim n^{-2/(4+q_c)}$. One reason for the differing rates of decay for h_{opt} and λ_{opt} stems from the interaction term (the third term) in (7.3). This interaction term requires $\lambda \sim h^2$ when solving for the optimal smoothing parameters. It is precisely this interaction term in the mixed-data setting that degrades the rate of convergence relative to the discrete-only case and leads to the dependence of the optimal λ on the number of continuous variables in the data.

Immediately these rates suggest that the presence of discrete data does not influence the rate of the continuous variable bandwidths, consistent with the fact that smoothing over discrete data does not contribute to the curse of dimensionality. However, the presence of continuous variables does impede the rate of decay of the discrete-variable bandwidths. In fact, the parametric rate of decay enjoyed in the discrete-only setting has evaporated. Compare the rates with even a single continuous variable present: $n^{-1/2}$ versus $n^{-2/5}$. Figure 7.1 shows the difference in the rate of convergence for fixed n as q_c increases.

To summarize, while the presence of additional discrete data does not harm performance on the continuous side, the presence of continuous data does impede performance on the discrete side.

7.3 Bandwidth estimation

To ensure that we are using the appropriate amount of smoothing, we need to develop methods to optimally estimate the bandwidth. Currently, limited research has studied either rule-of-thumb or plug-in selection of bandwidths in the discrete-only or mixed-data setting. However, a healthy literature has developed, focusing on data-driven selection of the optimal bandwidths in both discrete-only and mixed-data settings. We discuss each in turn.

7.3.1 Discrete-data only

Ouyang, Li, and Racine (2006) provided an in-depth analysis of the performance of data-driven bandwidth selection in the discrete-only case ($q = q_D$). They suggest selecting the bandwidths $\lambda_1, \ldots, \lambda_q$, which minimize the squared difference between $\widehat{f}(\mathbf{x})$ and $f(\mathbf{x})$. Given the discrete nature of the data, we sum over the support instead of integrating, providing

$$\mathrm{CV}^D(\lambda) = \min_{\lambda_1,\ldots,\lambda_q} \sum_{\mathbf{x}\in\mathcal{S}} \left[\widehat{f}(\mathbf{x}) - f(\mathbf{x})\right]^2.$$

This cross-validation function is equivalent to minimizing

$$\mathrm{CV}_1^D(\lambda) = \min_{\lambda_1,\ldots,\lambda_q} \sum_{\mathbf{x}\in\mathcal{S}} \widehat{f}(\mathbf{x})^2 - 2\sum_{\mathbf{x}\in\mathcal{S}} \widehat{f}(\mathbf{x})f(\mathbf{x}),$$

given that the term depending on $f(\mathbf{x})^2$ does not depend on λ_d. We see that $2\sum_{\mathbf{x}\in\mathcal{S}} \widehat{f}(\mathbf{x})f(\mathbf{x}) = 2E[\widehat{f}(\mathbf{x})]$. As with continuous data, we need to replace $f(\mathbf{x})$ in $\mathrm{CV}_1^D(\lambda)$ with a leave-one-out estimator to prevent the cross-validation function from setting $\lambda_d = 0 \ \forall d$. This leads to

$$\mathrm{CV}_1^D(\lambda) = \min_{\lambda_1,\ldots,\lambda_q} n^{-2}\sum_{i=1}^{n}\sum_{j=1}^{n} L_{\lambda,ijx}^{(2)} - \frac{2}{n(n-1)}\sum_{i=1}^{n}\sum_{\substack{j=1\\j\neq i}}^{n} L_{\lambda,ijx}, \qquad (7.4)$$

where $L_{\lambda,ijx}^{(2)} = \sum_{\mathbf{x}\in\mathcal{S}} L_\lambda(\mathbf{x}_i, \mathbf{x}) L_\lambda(\mathbf{x}_j, \mathbf{x})$ is the discrete convolution kernel (Li and Racine, 2003). Notice that we replace $2\sum_{\mathbf{x}\in\mathcal{S}} \widehat{f}(\mathbf{x})f(\mathbf{x})$ with $\frac{2}{n(n-1)}\sum_{i=1}^{n}\sum_{\substack{j=1\\j\neq i}}^{n} L_\lambda(\mathbf{x}_i, \mathbf{x}_j)$ in (7.4) (i.e., we replace the population mean with the sample mean). Thus, we average our leave-one-out kernel-density estimator over all sample realizations, $n^{-1}\sum_{i=1}^{n} \widehat{f}_{-i}(\mathbf{x}_i)$.

The results of Ouyang, Li, and Racine (2006) are based on two different scenarios. The first occurs when none of the variables are uniformly distributed. They define a variable as being uniformly distributed when

$$f(x^1, \ldots, x^{d-1}, x^d, x^{d+1}, \ldots, x^q)$$
$$= f(x^1, \ldots, x^{d-1}, z^d, x^{d+1}, \ldots, x^q), \quad \forall x^d, z^d \in \mathcal{S}^D.$$

In cases where smoothing occurs over a uniformly distributed variable, we would expect to see that λ_d does not converge to 0, but rather converges to its upper bound

$C_d/(C_d + 1)$. With unordered discrete data, all points are weighted equally, which is how we typically think of a uniform variable. When $\lambda_d = C_d/(C_d + 1)$, the estimated density will satisfy the uniform property.

From an applied point of view, this is a desirable feature, as $f(\mathbf{x})$ is invariant with respect to uniformly distributed variables and we should not engage in sample splitting with these variables since it only complicates the problem (which is exactly what the frequency method does). The ideal strategy is to remove them from the analysis by smoothing them out. Ouyang, Li, and Racine (2006) show that the selection of bandwidths via cross-validation can produce estimated bandwidths that correctly smooth out the irrelevant discrete regressors a little over 60 percent of the time. This implies, in the discrete-only case, that cross-validation may fail to assign a bandwidth that smooths this variable out of the analysis, even though it should.

The uniformity property is an important feature in applied analysis and will show up more prevalently when we discuss conditioning. The uniformity property is equivalent to a variable being irrelevant in a regression model in that the value of a given covariate does not influence the value of the conditional mean across all potential outcomes. Intuitively, the uniform distribution provides the least amount of information regarding the variable of interest. This is where the smoothing of categorical variables really possesses an advantage over traditional frequency methods, which have no way to account for the potential uniformity of a random variable.

The second case that Ouyang, Li, and Racine (2006) study is one in which no variables are uniformly distributed. In this case, cross-validation produces bandwidths that converge to 0 at the appropriate n^{-1} rate for each component.

7.3.2 Mixed data

Li and Racine (2003) discuss data-driven bandwidth selection in the mixed-data case. Following Li and Racine (2003), we introduce the notation $\int dv = \sum_{\mathbf{x}^D \in \mathcal{S}} \int dx^c$. Li and Racine (2003) suggest estimating optimal smoothing parameters for the mixed-data kernel density estimator by minimizing the integrated squared difference between the estimated density and the true density. This yields

$$\text{CV}^m(h, \lambda) = \min_{h_1, \ldots, h_{qc}\lambda_1, \ldots, \lambda_{qD}} \int \left[\widehat{f}(v) - f(v)\right]^2 dv.$$

Following similar logic, we can decompose CV^m into two components: one that depends on (h, λ) and one that does not. This yields

$$\text{CV}_1^m(h, \lambda) = \min_{h_1, \ldots, h_{qc}\lambda_1, \ldots, \lambda_{qD}} \int \widehat{f}(v)^2 dv - 2 \int \widehat{f}(v) f(v) dv.$$

Again, the second piece in CV_1^m is equivalent to $2E[\widehat{f}(v)]$ and we can replace this population moment with a sample moment using a leave-one-out estimator to avoid redundancy. Technical Appendix 7.4 shows that

$$\mathrm{CV}_1^m(h, \lambda) = \min_{h_1,\ldots,h_{qc}\lambda_1,\ldots,\lambda_{qD}} \left[\frac{1}{n^2 |\mathbf{h}|^2} \sum_{i=1}^n \sum_{j=1}^n W_{ijx}^{(2)} - \frac{2}{n(n-1) |\mathbf{h}|^2} \sum_{i=1}^n \sum_{\substack{j=1 \\ j \neq i}}^n W_{ijx} \right],$$

where W_{ijx} is the generalized product kernel (where j represents the point x_j where the kernel function is being evaluated) and $W_{ijx}^{(2)} = K_{h,ijx}^{(2)} L_{\lambda,ijx}^{(2)}$ is the convolution kernel with mixed discrete (see above) and continuous (see Chapter 2) kernels.

7.4 Why the faster rate of convergence?

The intriguing aspect of discrete data in nonparametric analysis is that they do not contribute to the curse of dimensionality. Rather, they behave in a manner entirely consistent with a parametric approach. The intuition underlying this feature is straightforward. As more discrete variables are added to a problem, the number of potential outcomes increases (as with continuous variables). However, the number of outcomes added is countable; with a continuous variable, the number of potential outcomes is infinite. Thus, the local sample size for a discrete variable is going to be larger than that of a continuous variable for any given sample size.

Consider Figures 7.2 and 7.3. They demonstrate in one and two dimensions the difference in the local neighborhoods for discrete (pluses) and continuous (ovals) variables (to make the figures clearer, the discrete data observations are slightly displaced). Figure 7.2 presents univariate data. Notice how for even small sample sizes the closeness of continuous data points resonates. When we look at Figure 7.3,

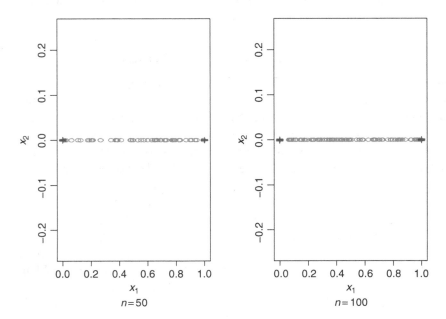

Figure 7.2. Localness between univariate discrete and continuous variables

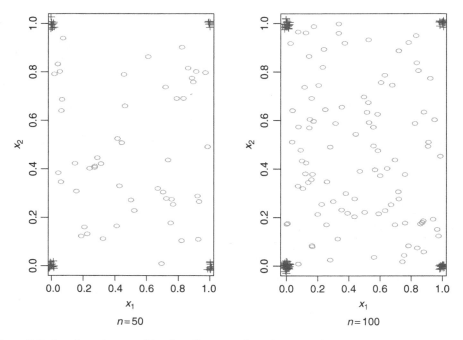

Figure 7.3. Localness between bivariate discrete and continuous variables

we see that the one added dimension places numerous gaps between continuous data points, yet the discrete data points have many "close" observations. This stems from the fact that although new data points were added, going from $\{0, 1\}$ to $\{(0, 0), (0, 1), (1, 0), (1, 1)\}$, this is far less than the number of potential points added in a second dimension for a continuous variable.

7.5 Alternative discrete kernels

The unordered discrete kernel function of Aitchison and Aitken (1976) requires knowledge of the support of the data (i.e., we must know C). In most cases this is not untenable, as with a binary variable. However, it is certainly possible that we may not know C *a priori* (e.g., number of distinct years of tenure with a firm). To avoid this support knowledge, Ouyang, Li, and Racine (2006) suggest an alternative kernel function for unordered discrete variables. Specifically, their kernel function is

$$l^u \left(x_i^u, x^u, \lambda \right) = \lambda^{1\{x_i^u \neq x^u\}}$$

for the univariate case, where $\lambda \in [0, 1]$. This kernel has the same limiting behavior in λ as our previously introduced kernel function. When $\lambda = 0$, we resort back to an indicator function (frequency estimator) and when $\lambda = 1$, the kernel function becomes a constant, ensuring the possibility of having uniform smoothing. The problem is that the kernel weights no longer sum to one, which implies that the kernel density estimator will no longer be a proper probability density. This is not overly worrisome because we can always normalize their density estimator as $\widetilde{f}(\mathbf{x}) = \widehat{f}(\mathbf{x}) / \sum_{z \in \mathcal{S}} \widehat{f}(z)$.

With ordered discrete variables, Ouyang, Li, and Racine suggest using a slight modification of their unordered kernel, with the indicator function being replaced with the absolute difference between two points. Specifically, their ordered kernel function is

$$l^o\left(x_i^o, x^o, \lambda\right) = \lambda^{|x_i^o - x^o|}.$$

This kernel function enjoys the benefit of having the ability to uniformly smooth the data when $\lambda = 1$, unlike the ordered kernel proposed by Aitchison and Aitken (1976) when $C > 2$. However, both kernels contain the frequency method when $\lambda = 0$. This alternative kernel also does not produce a proper density, but we could construct one by normalizing.

An additional ordered kernel is given in Wang and van Ryzin (1981),

$$l^o\left(x_i^o, x^o, \lambda\right) = \left\{ \begin{array}{ll} \frac{1-\lambda}{2}\lambda^{|x_i^o - x^o|} & \text{for } |x_i^o - x^o| > 0 \\ 1 - \lambda & \text{for } |x_i^o - x^o| = 0 \end{array} \right. .$$

They proposed this kernel for countable discrete data. Thus, if we were to use this kernel to smooth over a variable with a finite number of categories, the kernel weights would not sum to one. Moreover, as with the Aitchison and Aitken (1976) ordered kernel, this kernel cannot produce uniform weighting. It is therefore recommended that the Ouyang, Li, and Racine (2006) kernel be deployed when we are concerned that some of the ordered discrete components may be uniformly distributed.

7.6 Testing

There are surprisingly few kernel-based tests for densities in the presence of discrete. One explanation for this is that many nonsmoothing (Kolmogorov-Smirnov) and entropy tests exist that are often sufficient for existing problems (see, for example Anderson, 2001, Hong and White, 2005 and Racine and Maasoumi, 2007). Another explanation is that, in the presence of mixed data, the extension of existing tests will require little more than modifying the product kernel in order to allow for mixed data types (that being said, the theoretical aspects are often nontrivial). Two such tests can be found in Li, Maasoumi, and Racine (2009). In their paper they consider tests for equality of conditional and unconditional densities in the presence of mixed data types.

In this section, we will briefly outline the test for equality of unconditional densities, which can be thought as an extension of the Li (1996) test discussed in Chapter 4. Formally, assume that we have two mixed variable data sets drawn at random where $\{\mathbf{x}_i\}_{i=1}^{n_1}$ and $\{\mathbf{y}_i\}_{i=1}^{n_2}$ have the pdfs $f\left(\cdot\right)$ and $g\left(\cdot\right)$, respectively. Our null hypothesis is

$$H_0 : f\left(\mathbf{x}\right) = g\left(\mathbf{x}\right)$$

for almost all x versus the alternative that

$$H_1 : f\left(\mathbf{x}\right) \neq g\left(\mathbf{x}\right)$$

on a set of positive measure.

Using the ISE measure of distance, Technical Appendix 7.5 shows that we can write our normalized test statistic as

$$\widehat{T}_n = (n_1 n_2 \, |\mathbf{h}|)^{1/2} \frac{\widehat{\text{ISE}}_n}{\widehat{\sigma}_n},$$

where $|\mathbf{h}| = (h_1 h_2 \cdots h_{q_c})$ is the product of the q_c continuous bandwidths,

$$\widehat{\text{ISE}}_n = \frac{1}{n_1 (n_1 - 1) \, |\mathbf{h}|} \sum_{i=1}^{n_1} \sum_{\substack{j=1 \\ j \neq i}}^{n_1} W_{ijx} + \frac{1}{n_2 (n_2 - 1) \, |\mathbf{h}|} \sum_{i=1}^{n_2} \sum_{\substack{j=1 \\ j \neq i}}^{n_2} W_{ijy}$$

$$- \frac{1}{n_1 (n_2 - 1) \, |\mathbf{h}|} \sum_{i=1}^{n_1} \sum_{\substack{j=1 \\ j \neq i}}^{n_2} W_{ijxy} - \frac{1}{n_2 (n_1 - 1) \, |\mathbf{h}|} \sum_{i=1}^{n_2} \sum_{\substack{j=1 \\ j \neq i}}^{n_1} W_{ijyx},$$

and

$$\widehat{\sigma}_n^2 = \frac{2}{|\mathbf{h}|} \left[\begin{array}{c} \frac{1}{n_1(n_1-1)} \sum_{i=1}^{n_1} \sum_{\substack{j=1 \\ j \neq i}}^{n_1} W_{ijx}^2 + \frac{1}{n_2(n_2-1)} \sum_{i=1}^{n_2} \sum_{\substack{j=1 \\ j \neq i}}^{n_2} W_{ijy}^2 \\ + \frac{1}{n_1(n_2-1)} \sum_{i=1}^{n_1} \sum_{\substack{j=1 \\ j \neq i}}^{n_2} W_{ijxy}^2 + \frac{1}{n_2(n_1-1)} \sum_{i=1}^{n_2} \sum_{\substack{j=1 \\ j \neq i}}^{n_1} W_{ijyx}^2 \end{array} \right],$$

where

$$W_{ijx} = K_h \left(\mathbf{x}_i^c, \mathbf{x}_j^c \right) L_{\lambda^u}^u \left(\mathbf{x}_i^u, \mathbf{x}_j^u \right) L_{\lambda^o}^o \left(\mathbf{x}_i^o, \mathbf{x}_j^o \right)$$

$$W_{ijy} = K_h \left(\mathbf{y}_i^c, \mathbf{y}_j^c \right) L_{\lambda^u}^u \left(\mathbf{y}_i^u, \mathbf{y}_j^u \right) L_{\lambda^o}^o \left(\mathbf{y}_i^o, \mathbf{y}_j^o \right)$$

$$W_{ijxy} = K_h \left(\mathbf{x}_i^c, \mathbf{y}_j^c \right) L_{\lambda^u}^u \left(\mathbf{x}_i^u, \mathbf{y}_j^u \right) L_{\lambda^o}^o \left(\mathbf{x}_i^o, \mathbf{y}_j^o \right)$$

$$W_{ijyx} = K_h \left(\mathbf{y}_i^c, \mathbf{x}_j^c \right) L_{\lambda^u}^u \left(\mathbf{y}_i^u, \mathbf{x}_j^u \right) L_{\lambda^o}^o \left(\mathbf{y}_i^o, \mathbf{x}_j^o \right).$$

As expected, Li, Maasoumi, and Racine (2009) show that the test is distributed as a standard normal and offer a bootstrap for use in practice. For completeness we list the steps below. Note that these steps are identical to those from Chapter 4 regarding the Li (1996) test (see, Li, 1999). The bootstrap is as follows:

1. Compute the test statistics $\widehat{T}_n$ for the original sample of $\{\mathbf{x}_1, \mathbf{x}_2, \ldots, \mathbf{x}_{n_1}\}$ and $\{\mathbf{y}_1, \mathbf{y}_2, \ldots, \mathbf{y}_{n_2}\}$.
2. Define the pooled sample as $\Psi = \{\mathbf{x}_1, \mathbf{x}_2, \ldots, \mathbf{x}_{n_1}, \mathbf{y}_1, \mathbf{y}_2, \ldots, \mathbf{y}_{n_2}\}$. Randomly sample, with replacement from Ψ, n_1 observations for the construction of $f(\cdot)$ and call this sample $\{\mathbf{x}_i^*\}_{i=1}^{n_1}$. Similarly, randomly sample, with replacement from Ψ, n_2 observations for the construction of $g(\cdot)$ and call this sample $\{\mathbf{y}_i^*\}_{i=1}^{n_2}$.
3. Calculate $\widehat{T}_n^*$ where $\widehat{T}_n^*$ is calculated the same way as $\widehat{T}_n$ except that $\mathbf{x}_i$ and $\mathbf{y}_i$ are replaced by $\mathbf{x}_i^*$ and $\mathbf{y}_i^*$, respectively.

4. Repeat steps 2 and 3 a large number (B) of times and then construct the sampling distribution of the bootstrapped test statistics. We reject the null of equality if the estimated test statistic $\widehat{T}_n$ is greater than the upper $\dot{\alpha}$-percentile of the bootstrapped test statistics.

7.7 Application

Here we consider conditional densities where a subset (not necessarily proper) of the variables are discrete. Let $f_{\mathbf{x},\mathbf{y}}(\cdot)$ denote the joint density of $(\mathbf{x},\mathbf{y})$ and $f_{\mathbf{x}}(\cdot)$ denote the marginal density of $\mathbf{x}$, our kernel estimators are thus

$$\widehat{f}_{\mathbf{x},\mathbf{y}}(\mathbf{x},\mathbf{y}) = (n|\mathbf{h}_x||\mathbf{h}_y|)^{-1} \sum_{i=1}^{n} W_{ix} W_{iy},$$

$$\widehat{f}_{\mathbf{x}}(\mathbf{x}) = (n|\mathbf{h}|)^{-1} \sum_{i=1}^{n} W_{ix},$$

where

$$W_{ix} = K_h\left(\mathbf{x}_i^c, \mathbf{x}^c\right) L_{\lambda^u}^u\left(\mathbf{x}_i^u, \mathbf{x}^u\right) L_{\lambda^o}^o\left(\mathbf{x}_i^o, \mathbf{x}^o\right)$$
$$W_{iy} = K_h\left(\mathbf{y}_i^c, \mathbf{y}^c\right) L_{\lambda^u}^u\left(\mathbf{y}_i^u, \mathbf{y}^u\right) L_{\lambda^o}^o\left(\mathbf{y}_i^o, \mathbf{y}^o\right)$$

where $|\mathbf{h}_x|$ and $|\mathbf{h}_y|$ are the products of the bandwidths of the continuous regressors in $\mathbf{x}$ and $\mathbf{y}$, respectively. The conditional density of $\mathbf{y}$ given $\mathbf{x}$ is defined as $f_{\mathbf{y}|\mathbf{x}}(\mathbf{y}|\mathbf{x}) = f_{\mathbf{x},\mathbf{y}}(\mathbf{x},\mathbf{y})/f_{\mathbf{x}}(\mathbf{x})$ and we estimate the conditional density as

$$\widehat{f}_{\mathbf{y}|\mathbf{x}}(\mathbf{y}|\mathbf{x}) = \widehat{f}_{\mathbf{x},\mathbf{y}}(\mathbf{x},\mathbf{y})/\widehat{f}_{\mathbf{x}}(\mathbf{x}).$$

In the special case where we have a (continuous) univariate y, our estimators of the joint and marginal densities, $\widehat{f}_{\mathbf{x},y}(\mathbf{x},y)$ and $\widehat{f}_{\mathbf{x}}(\mathbf{x})$ are

$$\widehat{f}_{\mathbf{x},y}(\mathbf{x},y) = (n|\mathbf{h}_x|h_y)^{-1} \sum_{i=1}^{n} W_{ix} k\left(\frac{y_i - y}{h_y}\right),$$

$$\widehat{f}_{\mathbf{x}}(\mathbf{x}) = (n|\mathbf{h}_x|)^{-1} \sum_{i=1}^{n} W_{ix}.$$

The conditional density estimate of y given $\mathbf{x}$ is similarly given as

$$\widehat{f}_{y|\mathbf{x}}(y|\mathbf{x}) = \widehat{f}_{\mathbf{x},y}(\mathbf{x},y)/\widehat{f}_{\mathbf{x}}(\mathbf{x}).$$

Here we consider two empirical examples of the conditional density estimators. In the first case y will be discrete, and in the second, x will be discrete. In each case we use a Gaussian kernel for the continious variable and the Ouyang, Li, and Racine (2006) kernel for the discrete variable. In the first example, we consider the conditional density of OECD status (we cheat here slightly as we are actually looking at whether or not the country is in Region 1 – described in Chapter 6 – as this includes nearly all the OECD nations) on average years of schooling (ays). More formally, we estimate the conditional density

$$\widehat{f}_{\mathrm{OECD|ays}}\,(\mathrm{OECD|ays}) = \frac{\widehat{f}_{\mathrm{OECD,ays}}\,(\mathrm{OECD, ays})}{\widehat{f}_{\mathrm{ays}}\,(\mathrm{ays})},$$

which can be interpreted as the probability that OECD takes on a particular value (either zero or one) given the average years of schooling. Figure 7.4 plots the conditional probabilities for each outcome (OECD = 0 and OECD = 1) versus average years of schooling. The overall results are as expected. For low levels of schooling (less than two years), the probability of not belonging to the OECD is nearly 100%. As the years of schooling increase, the probability of not being in the OECD decreases, slowly at first and then sharply once the average years of schooling exceeds approximately six years. Similarly, for low levels of schooling, the probability of belonging to the OECD is relatively low, but increases as the average years of schooling nears twelve years. In fact, at twelve years of schooling, the conditional probability of being a member of the OECD is in excess of 90%.

For the second example we switch the order of the conditional probability. Instead of looking at the conditional probability of OECD status on average years of schooling, we look at the conditional density of average years of schooling conditional on OECD status. Note that we are simply looking at conditional probabilities and are not implying any form of causation at this point. Here we are going to consider three different values for our bandwidth parameter on OECD status to highlight its importance. Specifically, we artificially set the bandwidth on OECD equal to zero (sample splitting – i.e., the frequency approach), one-half (smoothing) and one (irrelevance). The corresponding conditional densities can be found in Figures 7.5 – 7.7.

In Figure 7.5, we set the bandwidth on OECD status equal to zero. This is equivalent to splitting the sample based on OECD status and estimating two separate densities.

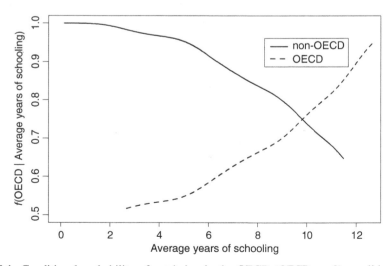

Figure 7.4. Conditional probability of not being in the OECD (OECD = 0) – solid curve – or being in the OECD (OECD = 1) – dashed curve; conditional on the average years of schooling plotted against the average years of schooling; OECD here is defined as being in Region 1 from the application in Chapter 6

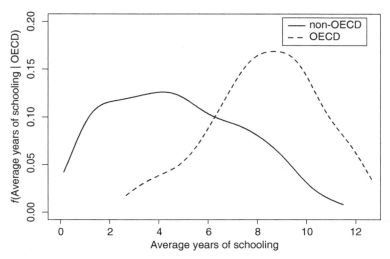

Figure 7.5. Conditional probability (bandwidth on OECD equal to zero) of average years of schooling conditional of OECD status plotted against the average years of schooling; OECD here is defined as being in Region 1 from the application in Chapter 6

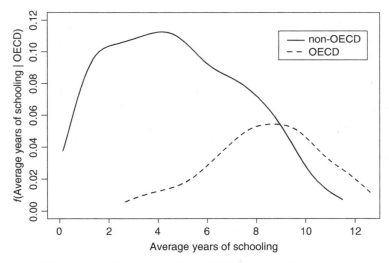

Figure 7.6. Conditional probability (bandwidth on OECD equal to 0.5) of average years of schooling conditional of OECD status plotted against the average years of schooling; OECD here is defined as being in Region 1 from the application in Chapter 6

The solid line is the estimated density of average years of schooling for non-OECD nations and the dashed line is the estimated densities of average years of schooling for OECD nations. As expected, the density for OECD nations is shifted to the right of non-OECD nations.

Instead of estimating the densities separately, Figure 7.6 shows what happens when we use kernel weighting. In this figure, we generically set the bandwidth equal to 0.5. The OECD nations still have a larger mean in terms of average years of schooling, but

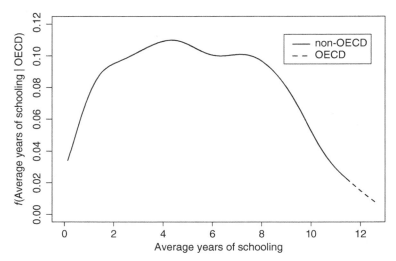

Figure 7.7. Conditional probability (bandwidth on OECD equal to unity) of average years of school-ing conditional of OECD status plotted against the average years of schooling; OECD here is defined as being in Region 1 from the application in Chapter 6

now the non-OECD density has a thicker right-hand tail (likely due to the weighting of OECD results). At the same time we see that left-hand tail is larger for the OECD density and that the height of the mode is smaller (as we are no longer splitting the sample).

In the final figure, we set the bandwidth on OECD status equal to unity. Recall that a bandwidth equal to one implies that the weights are equal across categories. In other words, OECD is an irrelevant variable in the conditional probability. To put it yet another way, in our particular case the conditional probability becomes an uncon-ditional probability. Figure 7.7 is simply the kernel-density estimate of average years of schooling across all countries in the sample (note that the right-hand tail is dashed, as only OECD countries have average years of schooling in excess of 12).

8

Regression with discrete covariates

In this chapter, we outline how to construct nonparametric estimators for a regression model in the presence of discrete regressors. Estimating a regression model when either all of the covariates are discrete or there is mixed data is relatively straightforward, given our earlier discussion in Chapter 5. The key is that we must use kernels appropriate for smoothing discrete data, as discussed in Chapter 7. As with density estimation we will need to modify the kernel weights. Aside from this modification from the continuous-only setting, the intuition and construction of the estimators follow. We feel that you will have little trouble following the arguments in this chapter (assuming you understand the previous chapters). We leave our treatment of estimation with a discrete left-hand-side variable for the presentation of semiparametric methods (Chapter 9).

After discussing estimation, we focus on derivative estimation. Estimating derivatives for the continuous regressors (when discrete regressors are present) proceeds exactly as in the continuous-variable-only setting. What requires more care is obtaining the "derivatives" for the discrete variables, but this should be expected. We use the term "derivative" loosely given that it is clear our conditional mean estimator is no longer continuous in the discrete variables. Similar to the case for a discrete regressor in a parametric model, we obtain our partial effect as the difference between the conditional mean evaluated at one value for the discrete regressor minus value of the discrete regressor, holding everything else constant.

As in all nonparametric estimation, bandwidth selection is of primary importance. We discuss how to select the bandwidths for our discrete variables. The methodology is essentially the same as that in Chapter 5. After selecting our bandwidths and running regressions, we subject our models to formal statistical tests. Here we examine tests that are designed specifically for discrete data. We start with a test for correct parametric specification and also examine tests for variable relevance in the presence of discrete regressors.

We end the chapter using both ordered and unordered discrete variables in our estimation of a cross-country production function. The growth literature has seen a handful of studies use discrete regressors in nonparametric regression (e.g., Henderson, Papageorgiou, and Parmeter, 2012, 2013). While the majority of these studies simply control for region and time effects, the methods are more generally applicable. In our application we estimate the models with region and time effects, analyze the bandwidths and gradients (for both discrete and continuous regressors), and employ the tests proposed in the chapter. We find substantial differences between regions and (unexpectedly) a minor impact from the year variable.

8.1 Estimation of the conditional mean

The smoothing of discrete variables in applied nonparametric regression has only recently seen use. As with the density case, the most common approach to handling discrete data was either the frequency approach or to use a semiparametric framework (treating the discrete regressors as linear).[1] It is quite possible that the discrete variables enter the regression model nonlinearly and interact with the continuous regressors. When this is the case, the semiparametric estimators that have been deployed are likely to be inconsistent. Alternatively, using the frequency approach can introduce unnecessary variance into many applied settings where there are a number of discrete variables (think of a wage regression with race, gender, education, marital status, age, and experience). Therefore, in general, we advocate for a nonparametric smoothing approach.

8.1.1 Local-constant least-squares

While it is possible to use the Aitchison and Aitken (1976) kernel function for discrete regressors, we follow Racine and Li (2004) and use the alternative discrete kernel for unordered data presented in Section 7.5. Recall that this kernel did not sum to 1 and as such it was inappropriate for direct estimation of a probability density function. This does not pose an issue in the regression setting, as the conditional mean depends on the kernel in both the numerator and denominator, hence rescaling becomes unnecessary.

We again consider a nonparametric regression function, but now allow for some of the regressors to be discrete in nature. Our nonparametric regression model, as given in Racine and Li (2004), is

$$y_i = m(\mathbf{x}_i) + u_i, \quad i = 1, 2, \ldots, n.$$

The difference is that we consider three types of regressors: continuous, unordered, and ordered. Using the notation from Chapter 7, we define our regression vector as $\mathbf{x}_i = (\mathbf{x}_i^c, \mathbf{x}_i^u, \mathbf{x}_i^o)$, where $\mathbf{x}_i^c = (x_{i1}^c, x_{i2}^c, \ldots, x_{iq_c}^c)$ is a $1 \times q_c$ vector of continuous regressors, $\mathbf{x}_i^u = (x_{i1}^u, x_{i2}^u, \ldots, x_{iq_u}^u)$ is a $1 \times q_u$ vector of unordered discrete regressors and $\mathbf{x}_i^o = (x_{i1}^o, x_{i2}^o, \ldots, x_{iq_o}^o)$ is a $1 \times q_o$ vector of discrete ordered regressors. Again u_i is our mean zero additive error term, which we assume is uncorrelated with the $1 \times q$ regressor vector $\mathbf{x}_i$, where $q = (q_c + q_u + q_o)$.

Using the mixed data (Li–Racine) product kernel described in Chapter 7, it is relatively easy to construct kernel-regression estimators. In the case of the LCLS estimator, we simply replace the continuous-product kernel we saw in Chapter 5 with the product kernel for mixed continuous and discrete data. Our LCLS estimator thus becomes

$$\widehat{m}(\mathbf{x}) = \frac{\sum_{i=1}^{n} y_i W_{ix}}{\sum_{i=1}^{n} W_{ix}}, \tag{8.1}$$

---

[1] See the discussion on the partly linear model in Chapter 9.

where

$$W_{ix} = K_h \left(\mathbf{x}_i^c, \mathbf{x}^c\right) L_{\lambda^u}^u \left(\mathbf{x}_i^u, \mathbf{x}^u\right) L_{\lambda^o}^o \left(\mathbf{x}_i^o, \mathbf{x}^o\right)$$

and recall from Chapter 7 that the Li–Racine kernels for each type are

$$L_{\lambda^u}^u \left(\mathbf{x}_i^u, \mathbf{x}^u\right) = \prod_{d=1}^{q_u} \left(\lambda_d^u\right)^{1\{x_{di}^u \neq x_d^u\}}$$

and

$$L_{\lambda^o}^o \left(\mathbf{x}_i^o, \mathbf{x}^o\right) = \prod_{d=1}^{q_u} \left(\lambda_d^o\right)^{|x_{di}^o - x_d^o|}.$$

Again note that the (univariate) continuous kernel is often written as $\frac{1}{h} k \left(\frac{x_i - x}{h}\right)$, but we choose to only list the kernel function (without h) as h drops out of the regression estimator due to its appearance in both the numerator and denominator.

The intuition behind this estimator is identical to that of the LCLS estimator we described in Chapter 5, taking the form of a weighted mean. However, in addition to weighting observations that are more like $\mathbf{x}$ for continuous regressors, we also weight observations that are more like $\mathbf{x}$ in terms of the discrete regressors. In other words, if we were estimating the expected log wage for an individual, we would place more weight on male observations if the point $\mathbf{x}$ were for a male than we would for female observations. Similarly, we would place more weight on individuals with higher levels of education if the point $\mathbf{x}$ were for an individual with a college degree than we would for observations who dropped out of high school (noting that we only need a single categorical variable for level of education and not multiple dummies as in a parametric model).

The asymptotic properties of the LCLS estimator in the presence of mixed data can be found in Racine and Li (2004), and we will only highlight those which we feel are most important to the practitioner. As was the case for density estimation with mixed discrete and continuous data, we require the conditions that each bandwidth $h \to 0$, $nh_1 h_2 \cdots h_{q_c} \to \infty$ and each bandwidth $\lambda \to 0$ as $n \to \infty$. As the sample size gets larger, each bandwidth shrinks to zero, but it shrinks slow enough so that $nh_1 h_2 \cdots h_{q_c} \to \infty$. The intuition is the same as we saw earlier for continuous regressors and we do not repeat it here. For the discrete regressors, the intuition is that as the sample size gets larger, we do not need to smooth over other groups.

An important part of their theory discusses the rate of convergence of the nonparametric estimate of the condition mean. Specifically, Theorem 2.3 of Racine and Li (2004) shows that the rate of the convergence of $\widehat{m}(\mathbf{x})$ in the mixed data setting is the same as the case where there are only continuous regressors (see Technical Appendix 8.1). In other words, the rate of convergence is tied to q_c and not to $(q_c + q_u + q_o)$. This is almost a free lunch, as additional discrete regressors do not slow down the rate of convergence and hence do not add to the curse of dimensionality (one cost is that we must calculate additional bandwidths). Given that many economic regressors are discrete in nature or are measured discretely (e.g., age), we can see many gains associated with their result.

The intuition here is a combination of that from the discrete density and regression chapters. Suppose we add a binary discrete regressor to the right-handside of our equation. The data vector is either zeros or ones. In other words, the support of the discrete regressor is finite. Thus, we are only adding a 0 or a 1 to the support of the data. Thus, adding a zero or one does not leave "holes" in the data for the nonparametric model to get lost as would happen when we add a continuous variable. A separate way to describe this is that asymptotically we have an infinite sample size and therefore we have an infinite amount of data for each group. We recognize that as $n \rightarrow \infty$ that $\lambda \rightarrow 0$ and hence we are only looking at observations for that particular group and the rate of convergence will depend only upon the continuous regressors in that group.

A further intuitive insight of the local-constant mixed-data regression estimator is that it is a weighted combination of the frequency estimator and the local-constant, continuous-data-only regression estimator. Technical Appendix 8.2 and Kiefer and Racine (2009) provide a clear Bayesian perspective of the estimator, a combination between the no-discrete-data global mean (a uniform prior) and the frequency estimator of a given cell (the posterior). We see that as $\lambda \rightarrow 1$, we obtain the continuous-data-only regression estimator and as $\lambda \rightarrow 0$, we obtain the frequency estimator for a given value of the discrete regressor. Kiefer and Racine (2009) show that this Bayesian form for the discrete-data-only estimator (discussed later) is similarly constructed. The Bayesian flavor of the smooth estimator is that as the groups are thought to be more homogeneous, λ should be larger and when the groups are thought to be more heterogeneous, λ should be smaller, approaching the frequency estimator.

8.1.2 Local-linear least-squares

The LLLS estimator with mixed data has an identical extension from its continuous-only form, but there are several nuances that deserve proper attention. We follow the approach in Li and Racine (2004b) and consider the nonparametric regression function

$$y_i = m(\mathbf{x}_i) + u_i, \quad i = 1, 2, \ldots, n$$

with mixed discrete and continuous regressors. As in Chapter 5, we take a first-order Taylor expansion. The first thing to note is that we cannot take analytical derivatives of the discrete regressors. Hence, we are only going to take the Taylor expansion with respect to the continuous regressors as

$$y_i \approx m(\mathbf{x}) + \left(\mathbf{x}_i^c - \mathbf{x}^c\right) \beta(\mathbf{x}) + u_i, \tag{8.2}$$

where $\beta(\mathbf{x}) \equiv \partial m(\mathbf{x}) / \partial \mathbf{x}^c$. We can rewrite Equation (8.2) as

$$y_i \approx \left[1, \left(\mathbf{x}_i^c - \mathbf{x}^c\right)\right] m(\mathbf{x}) \beta(\mathbf{x}) + u_i$$
$$\equiv \mathbf{X}\delta(\mathbf{x}) + u_i,$$

where the ith row of $\mathbf{X}$ is $\left[1, \left(\mathbf{x}_i^c - \mathbf{x}^c\right)\right]$ and $\delta(\mathbf{x}) \equiv \left[m(\mathbf{x}), \beta(\mathbf{x})'\right]'$.

We obtain our kernel regression estimates of $\delta(\mathbf{x})$ by solving the kernel-weighted objective function

$$\min_{\delta(\mathbf{x})} \left[y - \mathbf{X}\delta(\mathbf{x})\right]' W(\mathbf{x}) \left[y - \mathbf{X}\delta(\mathbf{x})\right],$$

where $W(\mathbf{x})$ is a $n \times n$ diagonal matrix with ith element W_{ix}. The primary difference between the LLLS estimator here and that in Chapter 5 is that we have a kernel function for mixed-discrete and continuous data. Minimization of the objective function leads to the LLLS estimator

$$\widehat{\delta}(\mathbf{x}) = \begin{pmatrix} \widehat{m}(\mathbf{x}) \\ \widehat{\beta}(\mathbf{x}) \end{pmatrix} = \left[\sum_{i=1}^{n} W_{ix} \begin{pmatrix} 1 \\ \mathbf{x}_i^c - \mathbf{x}^c \end{pmatrix} (1, \ (\mathbf{x}_i^c - \mathbf{x}^c)) \right]^{-1} \sum_{i=1}^{n} W_{ix} \begin{pmatrix} 1 \\ (\mathbf{x}_i^c - \mathbf{x}^c) \end{pmatrix} y_i$$

$$= \left[\mathbf{X}' W(\mathbf{x}) \mathbf{X} \right]^{-1} \mathbf{X}' W(\mathbf{x}) y.$$

This again looks like our LLLS estimator for the continuous case. The difference is in the product kernel. If we look closer, we can see that this estimator treats the continuous regressors in a local-linear fashion and the discrete variables in a local-constant fashion. Estimation of the gradients for the continuous variables are given by $\widehat{\beta}(\mathbf{x})$. Estimation of the gradients for the discrete variables have to be calculated in a separate step. We consider this problem.

Asymptotic normality of the LLLS estimator in the mixed-data setting is proven in Li and Racine (2004b) and mimics the asymptotic normality of the LCLS estimator given in Racine and Li (2004). As expected, the rate of convergence of both estimators depends upon the number of continuous regressors. We omit the precise details here, but note that they can be found in Technical Appendix 8.3.

The LQLS estimator is similarly constructed. By adding squares and interactions to the column space of $\mathbf{X}$, our estimators of the conditional mean, gradient, and Hessian are given by $\left[\mathbf{X}' W(\mathbf{x}) \mathbf{X} \right]^{-1} \mathbf{X}' W(\mathbf{x}) y$, where the ith row of $\mathbf{X}$ is now $\mathbf{X}_i = \left[1, (\mathbf{x}_i^c - \mathbf{x}^c), vec \left[(\mathbf{x}_i^c - \mathbf{x}^c)(\mathbf{x}_i^c - \mathbf{x}^c)' \right]' \right]$, where $vec(A)$ is the column vectorization of the matrix A.

8.2 Estimation of gradients

In this section we are going to primarily focus on estimation of the gradients for the discrete covariates, but we will quickly discuss the estimator of the gradients for the continuous variables first.

8.2.1 Continuous covariates

The local-linear case is obvious from the above discussion and the local-constant case is quite similar to what we saw in Chapter 5. The primary difference, as expected, is in the kernel function.

Without any loss of generality, let's assume we take a partial derivative with respect to x_d^c. Thus, our estimated gradient, $\widehat{\beta}(x_d^c)$, is calculated as

$$\widehat{\beta}(x_d^c) = \frac{\partial \widehat{m}(\mathbf{x})}{\partial x_d^c}$$

$$= \frac{\left(\sum_{i=1}^{n} y_i \frac{\partial W_{ix}}{\partial x_d^c} \right) \left(\sum_{i=1}^{n} W_{ix} \right) - \left(\sum_{i=1}^{n} y_i W_{ix} \right) \left(\sum_{i=1}^{n} \frac{\partial W_{ix}}{\partial x_d^c} \right)}{\left(\sum_{i=1}^{n} W_{ix} \right)^2},$$

where

$$\frac{\partial W_{ix}}{\partial x_d^c} = \frac{\partial K_h\left(\mathbf{x}_i^c, \mathbf{x}^c\right)}{\partial x_d^c} L_{\lambda^u}^u\left(\mathbf{x}_i^u, \mathbf{x}^u\right) L_{\lambda^o}^o\left(\mathbf{x}_i^o, \mathbf{x}^o\right).$$

You can see that the discrete kernels do not play a major role in the partial derivative (only being part of the product kernel) and thus the gradient is estimated similar to before. The calculation of standard errors of the gradients for continuous covariates is the same as before, and presentation of these gradients need not change either. We now move to the case of discrete regressors.

8.2.2 Discrete covariates

Estimating the gradient for discrete regressors is more computationally expensive as we cannot take analytical gradients. Here we are forced to take numerical gradients. The procedures from both the LCLS and LLLS (or local-quadratic, for that matter) estimators are essentially the same and we will explain them simultaneously. The basic idea is similar to what we do in basic parametric regression models. The goal is to estimate the conditional mean both at the point with known data as well as a counterfactual point. In other words, we want to see the effect on the estimated conditional mean of moving from one group to the next, holding everything else constant.

Let's first consider the case of a simple linear parametric model consisting of two groups. Our basic parametric model with both an intercept and slope shift can be written as

$$y_i = \alpha + \beta x_i + \gamma x_i D_i + \delta D_i + u_i \quad i = 1, 2, \ldots, n$$

where (the dummy variable) $D_i = 1$ implies that observation i belongs to group 1 and $D_i = 0$ implies that observation i belongs to group 0. Let's consider the equation for each group. When $D_i = 1$, we have

$$y_i = (\alpha + \delta) + (\beta + \gamma) x_i + u_i,$$

and when $D_i = 0$ we have

$$y_i = \alpha + \beta x_i + u_i.$$

If we are interested in the numerical difference between the two groups, we can look at the difference in the conditional means at a given point x. Formally, the marginal effect of moving from group 0 to group 1 given a specific value of x is

$$E\left(y|x, D = 1\right) - E\left(y|x, D = 0\right) = \left[(\alpha + \delta) + (\beta + \gamma) x\right] - \left[\alpha + \beta x\right]$$
$$= \delta + \gamma x,$$

which is unique to the point x. This numerical gradient estimate is made operational by replacing the unknown parameters by their OLS estimates.

We use the same logic to construct the nonparametric estimator of the gradient for discrete regressors. The difference (in the general case) is that we replace $E\left(y|\mathbf{x}, D = 1\right)$ and $E\left(y|\mathbf{x}, D = 0\right)$ with their nonparametric counterparts. In other words, for each observation where $D = 1$, we obtain the estimate of the conditional mean $\widehat{E}(y|\mathbf{x}, D = 1)$ by our preferred method (say LCLS) and then counterfactually estimate the conditional mean $\widehat{E}(y|\mathbf{x}, D = 0)$ by that same method assuming that $D = 0$ instead of 1, holding all other values of $\mathbf{x}$ constant. This is not difficult, but it is time consuming. Below we give a specific example for the LCLS estimator.

Recall that we can evaluate the conditional mean at any point $\mathbf{x}$ for LCLS. For the moment let's assume we have one continuous regressor and one binary regressor. If we have n data points on y, x^c, and x^u, we can construct our LCLS estimator of the conditional mean as

$$\widehat{E}\left(y|x^c, x^u\right) = \widehat{m}(\mathbf{x})$$

$$= \frac{\sum_{i=1}^{n} y_i k\left(\frac{x_i^c - x^c}{h}\right) l^u\left(x_i^u, x^u, \lambda^u\right)}{\sum_{i=1}^{n} k\left(\frac{x_i^c - x^c}{h}\right) l^u\left(x_i^u, x^u, \lambda^u\right)},$$

where in practice we will need to replace our bandwidths h and λ^u with estimates. Let's assume we are interested in calculating the change in the expected conditional mean of going from group 0 to group 1 (the gradient) for a particular observation, say observation j. Suppose for observation j, $x_j^c = 3$, and $x_j^u = 1$. Our estimate of the gradient is thus

$$\widehat{\beta}\left(x_j^u\right) = \widehat{E}\left(y|x^c = x_j^c, x^u = x_j^u\right) - \widehat{E}\left(y|x^c = x_j^c, x^u = 0\right)$$

$$= \widehat{E}\left(y|x^c = 3, x^u = 1\right) - \widehat{E}\left(y|x^c = 3, x^u = 0\right)$$

$$= \frac{\sum_{i=1}^{n} y_i k\left(\frac{x_i^c - 3}{h}\right) l^u\left(x_i^u, 1, \lambda^u\right)}{\sum_{i=1}^{n} k\left(\frac{x_i^c - 3}{h}\right) l^u\left(x_i^u, 1, \lambda^u\right)} - \frac{\sum_{i=1}^{n} y_i k\left(\frac{x_i^c - 3}{h}\right) l^u\left(x_i^u, 0, \lambda^u\right)}{\sum_{i=1}^{n} k\left(\frac{x_i^c - 3}{h}\right) l^u\left(x_i^u, 0, \lambda^u\right)}.$$

This is our gradient estimate for this particular observation.

We can also perform this for every other observation in the sample if we are interested in knowing the gradient for each observation. However, it is important to note that you only need to perform this task for those observations where $x^u \neq 0$ as 0 is the base category. The logic here is the same as in the parametric world. We need to compare each group to a base group. The base group need not be the group where $x^u = 0$, but this is generally the default value.

For an ordered discrete variable, the process is the same, and we can compare each group to the base group. It may also be of interest to compare each group to the group that directly precedes it. For example, you might be more interested in what happens when you move from a less-developed to a developed country, as opposed to knowing what happens when moving from a developing to a developed country. In this scenario the ordered categorical variable takes three distinct values $x^o \in \{0, 1, 2\}$. Let's take the simple example we had above ($x_j^c = 3$ and $x_j^u = 1$) and add the single-ordered discrete regressor x^o. If we are interested in the effect on observation j from going from less-developed (group 1) to developed (group 2), our gradient estimate is

$$\widehat{\beta}\left(x_j^o\right) = \widehat{E}\left(y|x^c = x_j^c, x^u = x_j^u, x^o = x_j^o\right) - \widehat{E}\left(y|x^c = x_j^c, x^u = x_j^u, x^o = 1\right)$$

$$= \widehat{E}\left(y|x^c = 3, x^u = 1, x^o = 2\right) - \widehat{E}\left(y|x^c = 3, x^u = 1, x^o = 1\right)$$

$$= \frac{\sum\limits_{i=1}^{n} y_i k\left(\frac{x_i^c - 3}{h}\right) l^u\left(x_i^u, 1, \lambda^u\right) l^o\left(x_i^u, 2, \lambda^o\right)}{\sum\limits_{i=1}^{n} k\left(\frac{x_i^c - 3}{h}\right) l^u\left(x_i^u, 1, \lambda^u\right) l^o\left(x_i^u, 2, \lambda^o\right)}$$

$$- \frac{\sum\limits_{i=1}^{n} y_i k\left(\frac{x_i^c - 3}{h}\right) l^u\left(x_i^u, 1, \lambda^u\right) l^o\left(x_i^u, 1, \lambda^o\right)}{\sum\limits_{i=1}^{n} k\left(\frac{x_i^c - 3}{h}\right) l^u\left(x_i^u, 1, \lambda^u\right) l^o\left(x_i^u, 1, \lambda^o\right)}.$$

Notice that we also held $x_j^u = 1$ fixed. We are interested in the effect of the ordered discrete variable's going from 1 to 2 in this case, holding everything else constant (including all other discrete variables). The extension to multiple regressors of each type is simple, but notationally burdensome. We can also consider other types of estimators as we mentioned before, but this just requires replacing the conditional expectation with an estimator other than the LCLS estimator.

Estimation of standard errors here is no different from what we saw in Chapter 5. In the heteroskedastic case, we use a two-point wild bootstrap to resample the residuals and obtain a new left-hand-side variable, which is constructed by adding the bootstrapped residuals to the conditional mean. Then we estimate the conditional mean and gradients as outlined above and repeat this process many times. The standard deviation of the bootstrapped gradients for a particular **x** is the standard error for that gradient for that observation.

8.3 Bandwidth selection

Our focus here will be solely on data-driven measures and the properties of the bandwidths produced with these methods. Rule-of-thumb bandwidths do not currently exist for discrete data and we are unaware of plug-in methods. Bandwidth selection for discrete regressors was first discussed in Ahmad and Cerrito (1994), but they only consider the LCLS case and do not discuss the theoretical properties associated with cross-validation methods; therefore, we are going to focus our discussion on the papers by Racine and Li (2004), Li and Racine (2004b), and Hall, Li, and Racine (2007).

Technical appendix 8.4 shows that the optimal bandwidth for each regression type is proportional to the sample size. Specifically, we see that

$$h \sim n^{-\frac{1}{4+q_c}}$$
$$\lambda^u \sim n^{-\frac{2}{4+q_c}}$$
$$\lambda^o \sim n^{-\frac{2}{4+q_c}}.$$

As in the density case, each bandwidth type tends towards zero as the sample size increases, and this rate does not depend upon the number of discrete covariates. The only difference in the rate between the continuous and discrete types is the "2" for the discrete bandwidths. The explanation here is the same as we saw in the density case.

In practice, we must also adjust the continuous bandwidths depending upon the variation in $\mathbf{x}^c$. As in the density-estimation case, we do not have an adjustment factor for the discrete regressors. Hence, our bandwidths take the form

$$h_d = c_d \sigma_{x_d} n^{-\frac{1}{4+q_c}}$$
$$\lambda_j^u = c_j n^{-\frac{2}{4+q_c}}$$
$$\lambda_l^o = c_l n^{-\frac{2}{4+q_c}},$$

where c_d is the scale factor for the dth continuous variable, c_j is the scale factor for the jth unordered variable and c_l is the scale factor for the lth ordered variable. Again, the discrete bandwidths are not scaled because they are bounded between 0 and 1, so the sample variance plays no role in understanding the size of the bandwidth like it does with the continuous variables. That being said, we could write a discrete-variable bandwidth as a product of a scale factor, a variance parameter, and a rate. However, the form presented above is the dominant description of bandwidths in both the theoretical and applied literature.

8.3.1 Automatic bandwidth selection

The extension of cross-validation methods to the case with mixed discrete and continuous data is relatively simple. Ahmad and Cerrito (1994) and Racine and Li (2004) consider the LCLS case and Li and Racine (2004b) give the results for the LLLS case. Instead of solely looking for the continuous bandwidths $h_1, h_2, \ldots, h_{q_c}$, we must also simultaneously estimate both the unordered and ordered discrete bandwidths ($\lambda_1^u, \lambda_2^u, \ldots, \lambda_{q_u}^u$ and $\lambda_1^o, \lambda_2^o, \ldots, \lambda_{q_o}^o$). Again, the goal is to produce the set of bandwidths that minimize the cross-validation function

$$\text{CV}\left(h, \lambda^u, \lambda^o\right) = \sum_{i=1}^n \left[y_i - \widehat{m}_{-i}\left(\mathbf{x}_i\right)\right]^2,$$

where $\widehat{m}_{-i}\left(\mathbf{x}_i\right)$ is the leave-one-out estimator. For the LCLS estimator, this is defined as

$$\widehat{m}_{-i}\left(\mathbf{x}_i\right) = \frac{\sum_{\substack{j=1 \\ j \neq i}}^n y_j W_{jix}}{\sum_{\substack{j=1 \\ j \neq i}}^n W_{jix}},$$

and is similarly constructed for the LLLS estimator as the first element of the vector obtained from

$$\left[\sum_{\substack{j=1 \\ j \neq i}}^n W_{jix}\begin{pmatrix} 1 \\ \mathbf{x}_j^c - \mathbf{x}_i^c \end{pmatrix}\left(1, \ \left(\mathbf{x}_j^c - \mathbf{x}_i^c\right)\right)\right]^{-1} \sum_{\substack{j=1 \\ j \neq i}}^n W_{jix}\begin{pmatrix} 1 \\ \mathbf{x}_j^c - \mathbf{x}_i^c \end{pmatrix} y_j,$$

where

$$W_{jix} = K_h \left(\mathbf{x}_j^c, \mathbf{x}_i^c\right) L_{\lambda^u}^u \left(\mathbf{x}_j^u, \mathbf{x}_i^u\right) L_{\lambda^o}^o \left(\mathbf{x}_j^o, \mathbf{x}_i^o\right).$$

It is also possible to use the AIC_c bandwidth selector. Li and Racine (2004b) show that the AIC_c bandwidth selector performs well in finite samples, as it tends to reduce the undersmoothing that often happens with LSCV. They do not show any asymptotic properties for this selection method, but it is typically assumed that these two are equivalent asymptotically.

8.3.2 *Upper and lower bounds for discrete bandwidths*

The behavior of the bandwidths for the continuous regressors is the same as we saw in Chapter 5. Recall that $h \in [0, \infty)$. Depending upon the estimation procedure, when the bandwidth hits its upper bound we learn something about the relationship between the regressor and the left-hand-side variable. Hall, Li, and Racine (2007) show that with the LCLS estimator, when the bandwidth tends towards infinity, the continuous kernel becomes a constant in both the numerator and denominator of the estimator and cancels out. In other words, when the bandwidth procedure selects a very large bandwidth, it is as if the regressor never entered in the first place. For the LLLS estimator, we again see that when the bandwidth on a continuous regressor gets very large, the estimator treats the variable as if it enters linearly. Finally, for the LQLS estimator, when the bandwidth is very large, the variable enters in a quadratic fashion.

The intuition for upper and lower bounds for discrete variables is relatively simple given that we have seen how our estimators treat the discrete variables. We showed for the LCLS and LLLS estimators that we treat discrete variables in a local-constant way (it holds more generally for the LPLS estimator). Therefore, whenever the bandwidth on a discrete variable hits its upper bound (for any of the three estimators), it is deemed to be irrelevant.

The other interesting case is when the cross-validation procedure selects the bandwidth on a discrete regressor equal to zero. When this happens, the discrete kernel becomes an indicator function (frequency estimator). In essence, it splits the sample based on the group(s) associated with that discrete variable. For example, suppose we have a single continuous variable and a single binary variable. We have one regression function for where $x_i^u = x^u$ and one regression function for where $x_i^u \neq x^u$. The same logic extends to discrete unordered variables with more than two groups. If we have three groups $x^u \in \{0, 1, 2\}$ and $\lambda^u = 0$, then the sample would be split into three distinct groups. This can similarly be shown for ordered discrete variables as well.

When the sample size is very large, a bandwidth equal to zero makes sense. In relatively small samples, when a bandwidth on a discrete regressor tends towards zero, it is likely that there will be high variability in your estimates, especially in cases where the number of observations in a group is relatively small. We have found in our own work that we often get cases where the bandwidth on a discrete regressor is very small even when the sample size is relatively small. This often leads to gradient estimates with far too much variation to have any economic meaning. This is most common with the LSCV selection method, and in cases like this it may make sense to switch to the AIC_c bandwidth selector.

8.4 Testing

Here we consider three different tests related to discrete covariates. Two of these tests are similar to those we discussed in Chapter 6 and we will refer to them when we can to avoid redundant derivations and discussion. The first test – attributed to Hsiao, Li, and Racine (2007) – is a test for correct parametric specification that is similar in spirit to the test by Li and Wang (1998). We consider a test for the relevance of continuous regressors in a mixed-data framework similar in spirit to the tests by Gu, Li, and Liu (2007) and Lavergne and Vuong (2000), but note that neither of these papers uses discrete kernels. That being said, Gu, Li, and Liu (2007) mention that their estimator can be extended to consider this case. Finally, we examine the test for the relevance of discrete regressors in a mixed-data framework attributed to Racine, Hart, and Li (2006).

8.4.1 Correct parametric specification

Here we discuss the test for correct parametric specification in the presence of mixed discrete and continuous regressors. This test (developed by Hsiao, Li, and Racine, 2007) is closely related to the tests by Fan and Li (2001), Li and Wang (1998), and Zheng (1996). We start by assuming that we observe data from n individuals, each with a single response variable y and $q = (q_c + q_u + q_o)$ explanatory variables $\mathbf{x} = (\mathbf{x}^c, \mathbf{x}^u, \mathbf{x}^o) = (x_1, x_2, \ldots, x_q)$. Consider some pre-specified parametric model (perhaps linear) which we will define as $m(\mathbf{x}; \beta)$, where β is a p dimensional parameter vector. Note that q need not be equal to p. Our null hypothesis is that the parametric model is correctly specified. Formally, we wish to the test the null that

$$H_0 : P\left[E\left(y|\mathbf{x}\right) = m\left(\mathbf{x}; \beta\right)\right] = 1$$

for some β versus the alternative that

$$H_1 : P\left[E\left(y|\mathbf{x}\right) = m\left(\mathbf{x}; \beta\right)\right] \neq 1$$

for any β.

Following the results in Technical Appendix 8.5, we can write our normalized test statistic as

$$\widehat{T}_n = n\,|\mathbf{h}|^{1/2}\,\frac{\widehat{I}_n}{\widehat{\sigma}_n},$$

where

$$\widehat{I}_n = \frac{1}{n\,(n-1)} \sum_{i=1}^{n} \sum_{\substack{j=1 \\ j \neq i}}^{n} \widehat{u}_i\,\widehat{u}_j\,W_{jix}$$

and

$$\widehat{\sigma}_n^2 = \frac{2}{n(n-1)|\mathbf{h}|} \sum_{i=1}^{n} \sum_{\substack{j=1 \\ j \neq i}}^{n} \widehat{u}_i^2 \widehat{u}_j^2 W_{jix}^2,$$

where the parametric residuals $\widehat{u}_i = y_i - m(\mathbf{x}_i; \widehat{\beta})$ are obtained, say, via nonlinear least-squares.

Hsiao, Li, and Racine (2007) show that the test statistic converges to the standard normal distribution under the null. Hsiao, Li, and Racine (2007) note that when all the regressors are relevant, there do not exist asymptotic gains in power over existing tests.

The bootstrap procedure for using the test in practice is identical to that discussed in Chapter 6, except that we have mixed data for our regressors, $\mathbf{x} = (\mathbf{x}^c, \mathbf{x}^u, \mathbf{x}^o)$. For completeness we list the steps of the two-point wild bootstrap procedure here:

1. Compute the test statistic $\widehat{T}_n$ for the original sample of $\{\mathbf{x}_1, \mathbf{x}_2, \ldots, \mathbf{x}_n\}$ and $\{y_1, y_2, \ldots, y_n\}$.
2. For each observation i, construct the centered bootstrapped residual u_i^*, where $u_i^* = \frac{1-\sqrt{5}}{2}(\widehat{u}_i - \overline{\widehat{u}})$ with probability $\frac{1+\sqrt{5}}{2\sqrt{5}}$ and $u_i^* = \frac{1+\sqrt{5}}{2}(\widehat{u}_i - \overline{\widehat{u}})$ with probability $1 - \frac{1+\sqrt{5}}{2\sqrt{5}}$. Then construct the bootstrapped left-hand-side variable as $y_i^* = m(\mathbf{x}_i; \widehat{\beta}) + u_i^*$ for $i = 1, 2, \ldots, n$. Call $\{y_i^*, \mathbf{x}_i\}_{i=1}^{n}$ the bootstrap sample.
3. Calculate $\widehat{T}_n^*$ where $\widehat{T}_n^*$ is calculated the same way as $\widehat{T}_n$ except that y_i is replaced by y_i^*.
4. Repeat steps 2 and 3 a large number (B) of times and then construct the sampling distribution of the bootstrapped test statistics. We reject the null that the parametric model is correctly specified if the estimated test statistic $\widehat{T}_n$ is greater than the upper α-percentile of the bootstrapped test statistics.

8.4.2 Significance of continuous regressors

We are unaware of a theoretical paper which proposes a test for the significance of continuous regressors in the presence of mixed discrete and continuous data. We assume that this is the case because it is a straightforward extension of Gu, Li, and Liu (2007) and Lavergne and Vuong (1996). We therefore briefly discuss how this test would be performed, assuming you were interested in solely testing that a subset of continuous regressors is irrelevant.

Consider a nonparametric regression model of the form

$$y_i = m(\mathbf{w}_i, \mathbf{z}_i^c) + u_i,$$

where $\mathbf{x}$ is the union of the regressors $\mathbf{w}$ and $\mathbf{z}^c$. Let $\mathbf{w} = (\mathbf{w}^c, \mathbf{w}^u, \mathbf{w}^o)$ be a set of mixed-type regressors which are relevant of dimension r and $\mathbf{z}^c$ is a vector of potentially irrelevant continuous regressors which are of dimension $q - q_r$. The null hypothesis is that the conditional mean of y does not depend on $\mathbf{z}^c$:

$$H_0 : E(y|\mathbf{w}, \mathbf{z}^c) = E(y|\mathbf{w}),$$

which can be recast as $H_0 : E(u|\mathbf{x}) = 0$, where $u = y - E(y|\mathbf{w})$. The conditional expectation of u given $\mathbf{x}$ is zero under the null and it is different from zero under the alternative. Therefore it is a proper candidate for testing the null hypothesis.

Technical Appendix 8.6 shows that our normalized test statistic is

$$\widehat{T}_n = n\,|\mathbf{h}|^{1/2}\,\frac{\widehat{I}_n}{\widehat{\sigma}_n},$$

where

$$\widehat{I}_n = \frac{1}{n(n-1)} \sum_{i=1}^{n} \sum_{\substack{j=1 \\ j \neq i}}^{n} \widehat{u}_i\,\widehat{f}_{\mathbf{w}}(\mathbf{w}_i)\,\widehat{u}_j\,\widehat{f}_{\mathbf{w}}(\mathbf{w}_j)\,W_{jix}$$

and

$$\widehat{\sigma}_n^2 = \frac{2}{n(n-1)|\mathbf{h}|} \sum_{i=1}^{n} \sum_{\substack{j=1 \\ j \neq i}}^{n} \widehat{u}_i^2\,\widehat{f}_{\mathbf{w}}^2(\mathbf{w}_i)\,\widehat{u}_j^2\,\widehat{f}_{\mathbf{w}}^2(\mathbf{w}_j)\,W_{jix}^2,$$

where the residuals come from a nonparametric (LCLS) regression of y on $\mathbf{w}$.

We conjecture that with this information we can construct a test statistic that is asymptotically normal with mean zero and unit variance under the null hypothesis. We suggest using a two-point wild bootstrap. Gu, Li, and Liu (2007) propose this bootstrap procedure and show its asymptotic validity in the continuous only case. We do not formally prove its validity, but note that similar arguments in Hsiao, Li, and Racine (2007) can be used to justify its use. Formally, the steps for the two-point wild bootstrap procedure are as follows:

1. Compute the test statistics $\widehat{T}_n$ for the original sample of $\{\mathbf{x}_1, \mathbf{x}_2, \ldots, \mathbf{x}_n\}$ and $\{y_1, y_2, \ldots, y_n\}$.
2. For each observation i, construct the centered bootstrapped residual u_i^*, where $u_i^* = \frac{1-\sqrt{5}}{2}(\widehat{u}_i - \overline{\widehat{u}})$ with probability $\frac{1+\sqrt{5}}{2\sqrt{5}}$ and $u_i^* = \frac{1+\sqrt{5}}{2}(\widehat{u}_i - \overline{\widehat{u}})$ with probability $1 - \frac{1+\sqrt{5}}{2\sqrt{5}}$, where $\widehat{u}_i = y_i - \widehat{E}(y_i|\mathbf{w}_i)$. Then construct the bootstrapped left-hand-side variable as $y_i^* = \widehat{E}(y_i|\mathbf{w}_i) + u_i^*$ for $i = 1, 2, \ldots, n$. Call $\{y_i^*, \mathbf{x}_i\}_{i=1}^{n}$ the bootstrap sample.
3. Calculate $\widehat{T}_n^*$ where $\widehat{T}_n^*$ is calculated the same way as $\widehat{T}_n$ except that y_i is replaced by y_i^*.
4. Repeat steps 2 and 3 a large number (B) of times and then construct the sampling distribution of the bootstrapped test statistics. We reject the null that each of the elements of $\mathbf{z}^c$ are (jointly) irrelevant if the estimated test statistic $\widehat{T}_n$ is greater than the upper α-percentile of the bootstrapped test statistics.

8.4.3 Significance of discrete regressors

Different from the first two tests we discussed in this chapter, the test for significance of discrete variables is like nothing we have seen before and deserves separate attention.

The Racine, Hart, and Li (2006) test can determine whether a single discrete variable or a set of discrete variables is relevant in a nonparametric regression. The test proposed in their paper is also different from others we have seen, as they do not normalize their test statistic and there currently is no formal demonstration of the limiting distribution of the test statistic. The basic idea behind the test is to see if the random assignment of values for the discrete regressors significantly changes the difference in the estimated conditional mean by measuring the sum of the squared difference between the estimated and counterfactually estimated conditional means. They propose a bootstrap procedure to test the null hypothesis.

Consider a nonparametric regression model of the form

$$y_i = m\left(\mathbf{w}_i, \mathbf{z}_i^u, \mathbf{z}_i^o\right) + u_i,$$

where $\mathbf{x} = (\mathbf{w}, \mathbf{z}^u, \mathbf{z}^o)$. The null hypothesis is that the conditional mean of y does not depend on the categorical variables $\mathbf{z}^u$ or $\mathbf{z}^o$. The irrelevant variables can either be scalars or vectors; $\mathbf{w}$ is allowed to contain both continuous and discrete regressors. Formally, the null hypothesis is

$$H_0 : E\left(y|\mathbf{w}, \mathbf{z}^u, \mathbf{z}^o\right) = E\left(y|\mathbf{w}\right).$$

We note that the null hypothesis is equivalent to saying

$$H_0 : m\left(\mathbf{w}, \mathbf{z}^u, \mathbf{z}^o\right) = m\left(\mathbf{w}, \mathbf{z}^u = \mathbf{0}, \mathbf{z}^o = \mathbf{0}\right),$$

for all $\mathbf{w}$ and all possible values of $\mathbf{z}^u$ and $\mathbf{z}^o$, where $\mathbf{0}$ is a vector of zeros (the base categories of each for simplicity). Our test statistic for the general case is

$$I_n = \sum_{i=1}^{n} \sum_{\mathbf{z}^u} \sum_{\mathbf{z}^o} \left[m\left(\mathbf{w}_i, \mathbf{z}_i^u = \mathbf{z}^u, \mathbf{z}_i^o = \mathbf{z}^o\right) - m\left(\mathbf{w}_i, \mathbf{z}_i^u = \mathbf{0}, \mathbf{z}_i^o = \mathbf{0}\right)\right]^2,$$

where $\sum_{\mathbf{z}^u}$ and $\sum_{\mathbf{z}^o}$ denote the summation over all possible values of the vectors $\mathbf{z}^u$ and $\mathbf{z}^o$, respectively. Under the null hypothesis, $I_n = 0$ and it is greater than zero under the alternative. The logic behind the test statistic is that if the discrete variables are in fact relevant, we would expect the conditional mean to differ across different cells of the discrete variable. If these variables are instead irrelevant, then there should be no impact on the conditional mean as different cells are considered. A feasible test statistic is given by

$$\widehat{I}_n = \sum_{i=1}^{n} \sum_{\mathbf{z}^u} \sum_{\mathbf{z}^o} \left[\widehat{m}\left(\mathbf{w}_i, \mathbf{z}_i^u = \mathbf{z}^u, \mathbf{z}_i^o = \mathbf{z}^o\right) - \widehat{m}\left(\mathbf{w}_i, \mathbf{z}_i^u = \mathbf{0}, \mathbf{z}_i^o = \mathbf{0}\right)\right]^2,$$

where the estimator of the unknown function can be replaced with the LCLS, LLLS, or LQLS estimator.

For illustration purposes, let's assume we have a case where we believe there is one irrelevant unordered regressor that takes on $(C_u + 1)$ distinct values $z^u \in \{0, 1, \ldots, C_u\}$ and one irrelevant ordered regressor that takes on $(C_o + 1)$ distinct values $z^o \in \{0, 1, \ldots, C_o\}$. The test statistic for this estimator is

$$I = \sum_{d_u=1}^{C_u} \sum_{d_o=1}^{C_o} E\left\{\left[m\left(\mathbf{w}, z^u = d_u, z^o = d_o\right) - m\left(\mathbf{w}, z^u = 0, z^o = 0\right)\right]^2\right\},$$

where the summation counter begins at one and not zero because summing over the base category would equate to summing values equal to zero. A feasible test statistic is given by

$$\widehat{I}_n = \sum_{i=1}^{n} \sum_{d_u=1}^{C_u} \sum_{d_o=1}^{C_o} \left[\widehat{m}\left(\mathbf{w}_i, z_i^u = d_u, z_i^o = d_o\right) - \widehat{m}\left(\mathbf{w}_i, z_i^u = 0, z_i^o = 0\right) \right]^2.$$

It should be apparent that this test will be relatively computationally expensive to implement relative to the test of variable significance for continuous variables. The form of the test statistic requires that you estimate a counterfactual for each observation for each variable being tested for each value that the discrete regressor can take. For example, consider a setting with n observations and two discrete regressors being tested for statistical significance. If the first discrete regressor takes on three distinct values and the other takes on four distinct values, you must calculate $n \times 2 \times 3$ counterfactual estimates. As the number of cells increases or the number of discrete regressors in question increases, the number of counterfactual estimates increases rapidly.

The asymptotic distribution here is quite complex because the estimated discrete bandwidths have an effect on the limiting distribution of the test statistic. A bootstrap procedure is suggested instead. We follow the bootstrap procedure outlined in Racine, Hart, and Li (2006, 530). As usual, the goal is to develop a bootstrap that imposes the null hypothesis. The null hypothesis here is that the discrete variables $\mathbf{z}^u$ and $\mathbf{z}^o$ are irrelevant. This particular bootstrap randomly selects $\mathbf{z}^u$ and $\mathbf{z}^o$ with replacement and re-estimates the model. Formally, the steps for the bootstrap procedure are as follows:

1. Compute the test statistic $\widehat{I}_n$ for the original sample of $\left\{y_i, \mathbf{w}_i, \mathbf{z}_i^u, \mathbf{z}_i^o\right\}_{i=1}^n$.
2. Randomly select $\mathbf{z}_i^{u*}$ and $\mathbf{z}_i^{o*}$ from $\left\{\mathbf{z}_i^u, \mathbf{z}_i^o\right\}_{i=1}^n$ with replacement and call $\left\{y_i, \mathbf{w}_i, \mathbf{z}_i^{u*}, \mathbf{z}_i^{o*}\right\}_{i=1}^n$ the bootstrap sample.
3. Calculate $\widehat{I}_n^*$ where $\widehat{I}_n^*$ is calculated the same way as $\widehat{I}_n$ except that $\mathbf{z}_i^u$ and $\mathbf{z}_i^o$ are replaced by $\mathbf{z}_i^{u*}$ and $\mathbf{z}_i^{o*}$.
4. Repeat steps 2 and 3 a large number (B) of times and then construct the sampling distribution of the bootstrapped test statistics. We reject the null that each of the elements in $\mathbf{z}^u$ and $\mathbf{z}^o$ is (jointly) irrelevant if the estimated test statistic $\widehat{I}_n$ is greater than the upper α-percentile of the bootstrapped test statistics.

There is an alternative bootstrap in Racine, Hart, and Li (2006) that is much more computationally expensive, as well as an additional alternative bootstrap in Li and Racine (2007). We are unaware of any systematic comparison of the three bootstrap procedures against one another and hence we suggest using the consistent bootstrap described above, which is less difficult to implement and less computationally expensive. However, should you have a case where the p-value is close to the nominal level, it makes sense to also consider the other procedures as a robustness check.

We assume that you have noticed that we only test for continuous or discrete regressors being irrelevant and not a combination of the two. If you are interested in a case where you can test for irrelevance of mixed-data types, one option is to resort to an Ullah (1985)-type test.

8.5 All discrete regressors

It may be the case that you have a set of regressors that are completely discrete.[2] When this is the case, estimation is similar, but both theory and practice are different compared to the mixed-data case. Li and Racine (2007), as well as Ouyang, Li, and Racine (2009), give an in-depth discussion of regression with only discrete regressors. In this section we discuss the differences between this discrete-only case and the mixed-data case. We keep theoretical derivations to a minimum and focus on the intuition afforded from Ouyang, Li, and Racine (2009).

Estimation is performed as expected. We can again use LCLS, but we no longer have any continuous regressors. In the LCLS case, we have our typical product kernel, but we no longer have any continuous-kernel functions. Hence, our LCLS estimator becomes

$$\widehat{m}(\mathbf{x}) = \frac{\sum_{i=1}^{n} y_i L_{\lambda^u}^u \left(\mathbf{x}_i^u, \mathbf{x}^u\right) L_{\lambda^o}^o \left(\mathbf{x}_i^o, \mathbf{x}^o\right)}{\sum_{i=1}^{n} L_{\lambda^u}^u \left(\mathbf{x}_i^u, \mathbf{x}^u\right) L_{\lambda^o}^o \left(\mathbf{x}_i^o, \mathbf{x}^o\right)}.$$

An LLLS estimator is infeasible, as we cannot take a first-order Taylor expansion if we do not have any continuous regressors. Cross-validation is straightforward as we look to minimize

$$\mathrm{CV}\left(\lambda^u, \lambda^o\right) = \sum_{i=1}^{n} \left[y_i - \widehat{m}_{-i}\left(\mathbf{x}_i\right)\right]^2,$$

where $\widehat{m}_{-i}\left(\mathbf{x}_i\right)$ is the leave-one-out estimator of $m\left(\mathbf{x}_i\right)$.

The primary difference between the mixed-data case and the discrete-only case is the asymptotic performance of the conditional mean as well as the behavior of the bandwidths. In the case where all regressors are relevant, the bandwidths converge to zero at the rate n^{-1} and the conditional mean is estimated without bias asymptotically (there will still be a finite sample bias). The conditional expectation will be root-n consistent because the bandwidths tend towards zero asymptotically. For example, consider the case with a single binary regressor. As n tends towards infinity, the bandwidth goes to zero and we have an indicator function. Our estimated conditional mean takes on two values. The first is the sample average of y when the discrete variable takes value 1 and the other is the sample average of y when the discrete variable is equal to 0.

In the case where we only have discrete regressors and at least one regressor is irrelevant, there are some issues that arise. The bandwidths for the relevant discrete regressors now converge to zero at the rate $n^{-1/2}$. Notice that this is a much slower rate than in the case where all of the discrete regressors are relevant. A natural question to ask is why this happens. As Ouyang, Li, and Racine (2009) show, in the asymptotic expansions of the estimator, when irrelevant discrete regressors are included, there are terms that no longer cancel that converge to 0 at the rate $n^{-1/2}$. These terms do not

---

[2] This is common in the meta-analysis literature (see Kaul, Boyle, Kuminoff, Parmeter, and Pope, 2013, for a recent application in the study of the accuracy of benefit transfers where nearly all variables are categorical in nature).

exist when only relevant discrete regressors are included and the main terms in the asymptotic expansions converge to 0 at the rate n^{-1}.

More simplistically, we can see that while $\lambda \to 0$ at the n^{-1} rate when we include only relevant regressors, the inclusion of irrelevant regressors requires that the estimator use more "local information" and this impedes the performance of the bandwidths because it is not known *a priori* which variables are relevant. Thus, λ must converge more slowly to 0 to allow for correct information processing of the added dimensions. Consider a setting where there are three relevant binary variables and a single irrelevant binary variable. In the relevant regressor-only case there are $2^3 = 8$ cells to smooth over. By including the additional irrelevant regressor, we now must smooth over 16 cells. The additional cells are not the real problem, but the fact that it takes larger samples for enough data to accrue in each of these additional cells in order to discern that this variable is irrelevant. In the irrelevant case, this information accrual slows down the bandwidth's progression towards 0. This is akin to a correctly specified model where an additional but irrelevant variable is added. In this case, while the parametric estimator converges at that same $\sqrt{n}$ rate, the variance of the estimator increases. Here, the bandwidth suffers in terms of its convergence rate (for the relevant regressors).

A second problem stemming from the inclusion of irrelevant variables is the fact that while the bandwidths for the irrelevant discrete regressors have a positive probability of hitting their upper bound, this probability is not one asymptotically. In other words, when we have irrelevant regressors in the discrete-only case, we have no guarantee that they are smoothed out asymptotically. Again, this stems from the theoretical expansion of the cross-validation function. In the presence of irrelevant regressors, an additional term enters this expansion and this term is not minimized for $\lambda = 1$ with probability 1. Instead, this term is a random variable whose minimum value occurs when $\lambda = 1$ with some probability. The exact probability is a complicated function of the distribution of both the regressors and the error term of the model, but Ouyang, Li, and Racine (2009) show that this term is mean zero and this gives reason to believe the probability is larger than 0.5.

In limited simulations, Ouyang, Li, and Racine (2009) find that when the error is symmetrically distributed around zero and is independent of the regressors, the probability of smoothing out the irrelevant regressor is greater than 1/2 and is usually around 60%. Finally, when estimating the conditional mean in the presence of irrelevant discrete regressors, Ouyang, Li, and Racine (2009) show that the conditional mean is estimated with an asymptotic bias. Luckily, they show the form of the bias as well as how to estimate it. However, you will need to know the set of relevant variables (ex post). If you have a large data set, it is possible to look at the bandwidths to get a sense of whether or not the variables are irrelevant (say values near one). A separate way to determine relevance would be to use the test of Racine, Hart, and Li (2006).

In summary, if you have a case where you only have discrete regressors, you should use caution. If you are sure that all of your regressors are relevant, perhaps according to economic theory, then the results of your estimation are likely reliable. However, should some of these regressors be irrelevant, the results require more scrutiny. Further, it is difficult to determine which variables are relevant and which are irrelevant in this case. In contrast, if you have at least a single continuous regressor, we know that asymptotically the irrelevant regressors will be smoothed out, although now the bandwidths for the discrete variables converge at a slower rate to zero. It is often the case that we will have a combination of both discrete and continuous regressors (at least in the cross-country output setting). However, there do exist settings where all the regressors are discrete and so the work of Ouyang, Li, and Racine (2009) has appeal beyond their important theoretical insights (e.g., Kaul, Boyle, Kuminoff, Parmeter, and Pope, 2013).

8.6 Application

In past chapters we have essentially ignored that we have observations for each country over several time periods. To showcase discrete variables as well as attempt to account for this type of data, we now include both a region (we will consider a categorical variable for country in the panel data chapter) and a year variable into our production functions.

Here we hope to show how these methods work, as well as compare our results to those from previous chapters. We first look at the bandwidths and then move onto elasticities and RTS. Although arguably less interesting here, we discuss the gradients from the discrete variables as well. Finally, we employ the tests discussed in this chapter to our production functions.

In order to minimize the amount of repetitiveness, we only show the results for LCLS and LLLS with bandwidths selected via LSCV. Both LCLS and LLLS are popular in the literature and the bandwidths from each convey useful information about the regressors. LQLS is less common and the computing time is increased and so we omit it here. AIC_c is a useful bandwidth selection procedure, but we omit it here as well. Those of you who are interested in the results from such experiments can modify the code provided (on the manuscript's website) accordingly.

8.6.1 Bandwidths

Table 8.1 shows the LSCV-estimated bandwidths for LCLS and LLLS regressions of output on physical capital and human-capital-augmented labor with and without discrete regressors controlling for region and year. The results without the discrete regressors are identical to those found in Chapter 5.

The first thing to note is that the bandwidths for the continuous regressors only change slightly. They go up for both of the LCLS regressors and down for both of the LLLS regressors and hence we do not see a clear pattern here, nor need there be one. It is important to note that the interpretation does not change for each of these bandwidths. For each of the LCLS bandwidths, we see that they are relevant, and they are nonlinear for the LLLS case, whether or not we include the region and year variables.

Turning our attention to the discrete regressors, we see that each is below the upper bound of unity. In other words, each of the discrete regressors plays a role in the estimation of output. That being said, the bandwidths for region are near zero and the bandwidths for year are much larger. In fact, the bandwidth for year for the LCLS case is near one. We will formally test for its relevance with the Hart, Racine, and Li (2006) test later.

Table 8.1. *Bandwidths both with and without discrete*
regressors – LCLS and LLLS estimation with bandwidths
estimated via LSCV

	Without	With	UB	Interpretation
LCLS				
K	1.1255	1.3151	7.5850	Relevant
HL	0.9538	1.0333	7.9586	Relevant
Region		0.0017	1.0000	Relevant
Year		0.9700	1.0000	Relevant
LLLS				
K	2.6311	1.7039	7.5850	Nonlinear
HL	1.8536	1.3020	7.9586	Nonlinear
Region		0.0141	1.0000	Relevant
Year		0.8449	1.0000	Relevant

While the relevance of year is in question, the relevance of region is not. The near-zero bandwidth suggests that the majority of weight we place on any particular observation is with respect to observations from that same region. This suggests that there are major differences across regions and questions the legitimacy of regressions that ignore this (Temple, 1998).

8.6.2 Elasticities

Given that each of our bandwidths for the discrete regressors is less than unity, this implies that each has a role in the prediction of output. In a typical parametric model with dummy variables, these only shift the intercept and do not have an impact on the elasticities of the production function. With our nonparametric methods, we allow the discrete covariates to interact with the continuous regressors in an unknown way. Hence, adding region and year variables can have significant impacts on the elasticities of the production function.

Table 8.2 gives the median elasticities and RTS for the LCLS and LLLS estimators with and without region and year. The results without region and year are identical to those in Chapter 5. The results for LCLS look equally poor with or without the discrete regressors. The median elasticities and RTS are economically infeasible. That being said, we do not see major differences at the median.

The results for LLLS show some differences in the elasticities, but similar median values for RTS (near unity). In fact, we see that the elasticities for physical capital fall at the median and rise for human-capital-augmented labor. Although the median share of human-capital-augmented labor is still smaller than the median share of physical capital, the change is in the right direction.

8.6.3 Numerical gradients

In this particular scenario the (numerical) gradients of the discrete regressors are of (relatively) little importance. The gradient on region will tell us, all else constant, what

Table 8.2. *Median elasticities both with and without discrete regressors – LCLS and LLLS estimation with bandwidths estimated via LSCV*

	Elasticity (K)	Elasticity (HL)	RTS
LCLS			
without	0.0268	0.0503	0.0861
	(0.0011)	(0.0022)	(0.0038)
with	0.0226	0.0634	0.1054
	(0.0085)	(0.0093)	(0.0069)
LLLS			
without	0.7469	0.3274	1.0427
	(0.0320)	(0.0421)	(0.0351)
with	0.6566	0.3759	1.0412
	(0.0357)	(0.1002)	(0.0216)

Table 8.3. *Percentage of gradients that are positive (or negative) and percentage that are positive (or negative) and significant (LLLS with LSCV) – region and time do not sum to one, as a given percentage are exactly equal to zero*

	Percent positive (and significant)	Percent negative (and significant)
K	0.9976	0.0024
	(0.9960)	(0.0024)
HL	0.9686	0.0314
	(0.9566)	(0.0225)
Region	0.3963	0.4116
	(0.0161)	(0.0137)
Year	0.4823	0.4767
	(0.0177)	(0.0185)

going from Region 1 (OECD) to another region will do to estimated output. The estimates here are expected to be negative. For year (1950 is our base category), this is sometimes used as a measure of technological innovation. In such a case, we would expect the gradients to be positive.

As opposed to plotting the numerical gradients, we simply summarize the percent positive (and significant) and percent negative (and significant). Table 8.3 gives the results for each regressor in the LLLS case. As expected, the gradients for physical capital and human-capital-augmented labor are primarily positive and significant. However, for our discrete regressors, we find very little significance. In fact, less than five percent of either are significant (combining negative and positive cases). Note that the percentages for the discrete regressors do not sum to one, as the gradient for the base category is zero by design and hence is neither negative or positive.

The large amount of insignificance needs some justification. We believe that at least two factors may be at work. First, there was already a very high fit and the addition of the region and year variables did very little to change that. In each case the goodness-of-fit measure went from approximately 0.97 and 0.98 to 0.99. In other words, the variation in physical capital and human-capital-augmented labor explains most of the variation in output across countries. Second, the bandwidths for year are relatively large, and in the case of LCLS, very close to unity. Hence, the relevance of year is in question.

The relevance of year begs another question: if year captures technological changes, why do we find few significant results from 1950 to 2005? One explanation stems from recent research which suggests that technological change only happens for highly capitalized countries. Hence, this effect could be picked up by the inputs in the production function (e.g., Henderson and Russell, 2005).

8.6.4 Testing

Finally, we consider the tests discussed in this chapter. Most of these tests are straightforward extensions of tests from Chapter 6 and so we will only highlight the results. We consider each of the three tests: Hsiao, Li, and Racine (2007); augmented for discrete variables Lavergne and Vuong (2000); and Hart, Racine, and Li (2006). The p-values for each of the tests can be found in Table 8.4.

The first number is for the correct functional form test of Hsiao, Li, and Racine (2007). Here we only compare our results to the GQ model (with dummies for region and year). We reject the GQ production function. Recall that we failed to reject the null of the GQ model at the 10% level in the case with no discrete covariates with the analogous Li and Wang (1998) test. Here our p-value is zero to four decimal places. In other words, we find a much stronger case for rejection of the parametric model.

Table 8.4. *p-values from the Hsiao, Li, and Racine (2007) test (HLR), discrete-modified Lavergne and Vuong (2000) test (LV), and Hart, Racine, and Li (2006) test (HRL) – estimation via LCLS with bandwidths estimated via LSCV*

HLR	
GQ	0.0000
LV	
K	0.0000
HL	0.0000
HRL	
Region	0.0275
Year	0.7100

The tests for relevance of the inputs are similar to those in Chapter 6. The test of irrelevance of physical capital and human-capital-augmented labor are rejected when using the Lavergne and Vuong (2000) influenced test, with or without the presence of region and year variables. These results are as expected, as each input is vital in a cross-country production function.

The final test we consider is the Hart, Racine, and Li (2006) test for the presence of irrelevant discrete variables. This test is quite different from what we have seen before. It is not in the same spirit as our conditional-moment tests and we do not have an asymptotic distribution from which to compare. This test relies solely on a bootstrap null distribution for testing. Given that we typically argue for bootstrap-based tests, this should not be an issue, but this test is very computationally expensive, especially when the number of categories is large and/or the number of regressors being tested is large.

The results for this test can also be found in Table 8.4. These are perhaps the most interesting results from the table. Even though many of the numerical gradients for region are indistinguishable from zero, we reject the null that the variable is irrelevant at the five-percent level. This complements the relatively small bandwidth we uncovered with both the LCLS and LLLS estimators. On the other hand, we fail to reject the null that year is irrelevant for the LCLS case. The p-value here is relatively large (0.6975) and complements the relatively large bandwidth found via LSCV. Although there is mixed evidence on the relevance of year, most economists would tend to argue that it is relevant. We therefore suggest that some control for year be included in practice. Note that we can also use LLLS with the Hart, Racine, and Li (2006) test. In this particular case the p-values are equal to 0.0450 and 0.0025, respectively. In other words, we fail to reject the null of irrelevance for each (our prior belief).

9

Semiparametric methods

Nonparametric methods are often criticized because of their need for large amounts of data. The study of economic growth is a prime example of where nonparametric methods are being stretched to their limits (Henderson, Papageorgiou, and Parmeter, 2012, 2013). Here a wide variety of covariates exist and at best the available sample size is moderate. Thus, issues regarding the accuracy and insightfulness of the results from nonparametric estimation/inference are in question. In the presence of dimensionality issues, we often resort to semiparametric methods, which place additional structure on the model.

While a variety of semiparametric methods exist, perhaps the most famous is the partially linear model (PLM), popularized in econometrics by Robinson (1988). In this model, some of the variables enter the conditional mean nonparametrically, while others enter in linearly. It is assumed that the groups of variables are separable from one another and estimation of each part can be obtained as a combination of OLS and the estimators from Chapter 5. The estimator for the nonparametric component generally converges at the standard nonparametric rate, albeit faster because we have fewer regressors, while the parametric estimator converges at the standard $\sqrt{n}$ rate. It is this result that is the most appealing empirically regarding the PLM.

Both the statistical and econometric literature is rich in treatises on semiparametric estimation and inference. Our goal here is to provide a simple overview of many of the most common methods, paying careful attention to empirical implementation issues. We start with the aforementioned PLM and then discuss single-index models. The latter of these methods is often used for discrete-choice models, where you may be uncomfortable assuming a distribution for the errors, such as Gaussian (for probit), but are comfortable with the single-index framework. Afterwards we discuss semiparametric smooth coefficient models (SPSCMs). Here the functional form is assumed to be linear in a given set of covariates while the coefficients are allowed to depend on another set of covariates in an unknown way. These methods are becoming increasingly popular in many applied economic milieus. They are also perhaps the easiest to compute in practice and are relatively easy to interpret. Finally, we will consider additively separable nonparametric models. These estimators avoid the curse of dimensionality at the cost of assuming the variables enter the model in an additively separable fashion.

Overall, semiparametric methods are attractive for their faster convergence rates, but unless the structure imposed on the model is correct, the subsequent estimators will be inconsistent. Thus, users need to be aware that these methods present their own sets of assumptions, which need to be statistically validated. We present tests of correct parametric and semiparametric specification to allow applied users a direct avenue to adjudicate between estimators.

For our empirical application of cross-country output, we deploy each of the four methods discussed here. We begin by estimating semiparametric production functions. We then perform tests for parametric models versus semiparametric models, as well as tests for semiparametric models versus nonparametric models.

9.1 Semiparametric efficiency

A semiparametric estimator introduces some loss of efficiency relative to a parametric model that characterizes the truth. This stems from the fact that it should not be any easier to estimate a semiparametric model relative to the true parametric model. The extent of the inefficiency can then be used as a benchmark to decide if it is desirable to use a semiparametric estimator.

A natural question, then, is how can we know the loss of the semiparametric estimator without knowing the correct parametric model. We are able to define this via semiparametric efficiency bounds. To understand how this works, consider a simple example. Suppose the data are generated from a parametric model that satisfies a set of assumptions. In the linear regression setting, we could assume a linear functional form $y_i = \mathbf{x}_i \beta + u_i$ and that the conditional mean of the error is zero $E(u_i | \mathbf{x}_i) = 0$. Any distribution for u_i that satisfies the zero conditional mean assumption would represent a valid parametric model. These parametric models are referred to as parametric submodels by Newey (1990). For a given parametric submodel, maximum likelihood could be implemented to determine the Cramer–Rao lower bound. The semiparametric efficiency bound is the supremum over the Cramer–Rao lower bounds for all parametric submodels that satisfy the set of assumptions alluded to above. We have purposely left out a rigorous explanation of these methods for each estimator in this chapter, but direct interested readers to the relatively intuitive discussion given in Newey (1990) and the references within for further details.

9.2 Partially linear models

The PLM specifies the conditional mean of y as two separate components, one that is parametric and another that is nonparametric. Formally, our model is

$$y_i = \mathbf{x}_i \beta + m(\mathbf{z}_i) + u_i, \quad i = 1, 2, \dots, n \tag{9.1}$$

where $\mathbf{x}$ is a $1 \times p$ vector of regressors and β is a $p \times 1$ vector of parameters. The $1 \times q$ vector of regressors $\mathbf{z}$ enter solely through the unknown smooth function $m(\cdot)$. The additive mean zero error term u is assumed to be uncorrelated with each regressor vector, and it may or may not have a heteroskedastic variance that depends on $\mathbf{x}$ and/or $\mathbf{z}$. Robinson (1988) demonstrated that estimation of the finite dimensional parameter vector β can be estimated at the parametric rate ($\sqrt{n}$) while the nonparametric component (the infinite dimensional parameter) is estimated at the standard nonparametric rate.

It is important to note that Robinson (1988) was not the only author to propose the PLM, though this is the most commonly cited reference for this model. A similar PLM estimator that uses kernel methods is found in Stock (1989). This paper is more concerned with the nonparametric component, whereas Robinson (1988) focuses more attention on the rate of convergence of the parametric component. Earlier work by Schick (1986) uses kernel methods for the same problem, but for a scalar random variable in the unknown function. Other early examples of work on this problem can also be found in Chen (1988), Heckman (1986), Rice (1986), Shiller (1984), and Speckman (1988). Only the last of these references uses kernel methods.

9.2.1 Estimation

Estimation of Equation (9.1) is generally performed in two steps. First the model is transformed to eliminate the unknown function. Once this is accomplished, β is estimated using OLS. Following the estimation of β, standard nonparametric methods can be applied to recover the unknown function. Our discussion here will focus on the setting where the error term is assumed to be homoskedastic. It is possible to construct a weighted least-squares version of the PLM for the heteroskedastic case developed by Schick (1996), where the variance is known up to a multiplicative constant (also see Li and Stengos, 1993).

We must mention that (typically) in order to identify the parameter vector β, we cannot include an intercept term in $\mathbf{x}$. The reason for this is that an intercept term cannot be identified separately from the unknown function $m(\cdot)$. In other words, as $m(\cdot)$ is an unknown smooth function, it is allowed to have an intercept and hence we cannot identify a parametric intercept without some restrictions on the unknown function. For example, Schick (1986) shows that we can identify an intercept term if we are willing to impose the assumption that the unknown function integrates to zero. However, as the intercept is generally of second-order importance in applied work, we focus our discussion on the setting where no intercept is present in the parametric component of the PLM.

The parametric component
We estimate β via a two-step process by first isolating the parametric component. Once this is achieved, we can use OLS to estimate the parameter vector β. The way we do this is to take the conditional expectation of each side of (9.1) with respect to $\mathbf{z}$. This leads to

$$
\begin{aligned}
E\left(y_i|\mathbf{z}_i\right) &= E\left[\mathbf{x}_i\beta + m\left(\mathbf{z}_i\right) + u_i|\mathbf{z}_i\right] \\
&= E\left(\mathbf{x}_i\beta|\mathbf{z}_i\right) + E\left(m\left(\mathbf{z}_i\right)|\mathbf{z}_i\right) + E\left(u_i|\mathbf{z}_i\right) \\
&= E\left(\mathbf{x}_i|\mathbf{z}_i\right)\beta + m\left(\mathbf{z}_i\right),
\end{aligned}
$$

which we subtract from (9.1) to obtain

$$
\begin{aligned}
y_i - E\left(y_i|\mathbf{z}_i\right) &= \mathbf{x}_i\beta + m\left(\mathbf{z}_i\right) + u_i - \left[E\left(\mathbf{x}_i|\mathbf{z}_i\right)\beta + m\left(\mathbf{z}_i\right)\right] \\
&= \left[\mathbf{x}_i - E\left(\mathbf{x}_i|\mathbf{z}_i\right)\right]\beta + u_i.
\end{aligned}
\tag{9.2}
$$

If we knew $E\left(y_i|\mathbf{z}_i\right)$ and $E\left(\mathbf{x}_i|\mathbf{z}_i\right)$, we could proceed with OLS to estimate β.

In practice these conditional means are unknown and must be estimated. Robinson's (1988) suggestion was to use LCLS to estimate each conditional mean separately. As we learned in Chapter 5, we can estimate these conditional expectations as

$$\widehat{E}(y_i|\mathbf{z}_i) = \frac{\sum_{i=1}^{n} K_{h_z}(\mathbf{z}_i, \mathbf{z})\, y_i}{\sum_{i=1}^{n} K_{h_z}(\mathbf{z}_i, \mathbf{z})}, \quad \widehat{E}(x_{ji}|\mathbf{z}_i) = \frac{\sum_{i=1}^{n} K_{h_z}(\mathbf{z}_i, \mathbf{z})\, x_{ji}}{\sum_{i=1}^{n} K_{h_z}(\mathbf{z}_i, \mathbf{z})},$$

for $J = 1, \ldots, p$, where

$$K_{h_z}(\mathbf{z}_i, \mathbf{z}) = \prod_{d=1}^{q} k\left(\frac{z_{id} - z_d}{h_{zd}}\right)$$

is the product kernel function and the bandwidth vector h_z uses the subscript term to note that the bandwidths are for the regressors in $\mathbf{z}$. We will discuss how to estimate these bandwidths below.

Once these conditional means have been estimated, we can plug them into (9.2) to obtain

$$y_i - \widehat{E}(y_i|\mathbf{z}_i) = \left[\mathbf{x}_i - \widehat{E}(\mathbf{x}_i|\mathbf{z}_i)\right]\beta + u_i.$$

Noting that $\mathbf{x} - \widehat{E}(\mathbf{x}|\mathbf{z})$ does not contain a column of ones, our estimator of the parameter vector β is obtained by OLS regression of $y - \widehat{E}(y|\mathbf{z})$ on $\mathbf{x} - \widehat{E}(\mathbf{x}|\mathbf{z})$ as

$$\widehat{\beta}_{SP} = \left\{\sum_{i=1}^{n}\left[\mathbf{x}_i - \widehat{E}(\mathbf{x}_i|\mathbf{z}_i)\right]'\left[\mathbf{x}_i - \widehat{E}(\mathbf{x}_i|\mathbf{z}_i)\right]\right\}^{-1}\sum_{i=1}^{n}\left[\mathbf{x}_i - \widehat{E}(\mathbf{x}_i|\mathbf{z}_i)\right]'\left[y_i - \widehat{E}(y_i|\mathbf{z}_i)\right].$$

Using higher-order kernels, Robinson (1988) proved that $\widehat{\beta}_{SP}$ converges to the true population parameter vector at the parametric rate ($\sqrt{n}$) and is asymptotically normally distributed. The idea is that even though the nonparametric estimators converge more slowly than $\sqrt{n}$, because these are averaged in the OLS estimator this makes it possible for the parametric components estimator to exhibit the same rate of convergence as in a typical parametric model. Li (1996) later showed that a second-order kernel can be used to give the same rate of convergence if $p < 6$. Note that this is solely for the parametric component and not the number of elements in $\mathbf{z}$. We skip the technical arguments underlying this result but refer interested readers to Li (1996). Further, in applied settings, the PLM is typically deployed with fewer than $p = 6$ regressors in the unknown function (e.g., $p = 4$ in Anglin and Gençay, 1996).

The nonparametric component
Having constructed an estimator for β, we now discuss estimation of the nonparametric component of the PLM. We discuss two potential avenues to estimate $m(\cdot)$ and then provide details on estimating the gradients of our unknown function.

Recall that the expected value of y with respect to $\mathbf{z}_i$ is

$$E(y_i|\mathbf{z}_i) = E(\mathbf{x}_i|\mathbf{z}_i)\beta + m(\mathbf{z}_i),$$

which can be rewritten as

$$m\left(\mathbf{z}_i\right) = E\left(y_i | \mathbf{z}_i\right) - E\left(\mathbf{x}_i | \mathbf{z}_i\right)\beta.$$

Our previous discussion demonstrated that we could obtain consistent estimators of each component on the right-handside. Therefore we can construct an estimator of the unknown function at observation i as

$$\widehat{m}\left(\mathbf{z}_i\right) = \widehat{E}\left(y_i | \mathbf{z}_i\right) - \widehat{E}\left(\mathbf{x}_i | \mathbf{z}_i\right)\widehat{\beta}_{SP}.$$

The more common approach to estimating the unknown function is to replace β with $\widehat{\beta}_{SP}$ back in (9.1). Doing this gives us

$$y_i = \mathbf{x}_i\widehat{\beta}_{SP} + m\left(\mathbf{z}_i\right) + u_i,$$

and since $\mathbf{x}_i\widehat{\beta}_{SP}$ is known, we can subtract it from each side as

$$y_i - \mathbf{x}_i\widehat{\beta}_{SP} = m\left(\mathbf{z}_i\right) + u_i.$$

It should be clear that we can now nonparametrically regress $\left(y_i - \mathbf{x}_i\widehat{\beta}_{SP}\right)$ on $\mathbf{z}_i$ to obtain our estimator of the unknown function. For example, LCLS leads to the estimator of the conditional mean as

$$\widehat{m}\left(\mathbf{z}\right) = \frac{\sum\limits_{i=1}^{n} K_{h_z}\left(\mathbf{z}_i, \mathbf{z}\right)\left(y_i - \mathbf{x}_i\widehat{\beta}_{SP}\right)}{\sum\limits_{i=1}^{n} K_{h_z}\left(\mathbf{z}_i, \mathbf{z}\right)}. \tag{9.3}$$

We know that nonparametric estimators converge at much slower rates than parametric estimators and since our estimator of $\widehat{\beta}_{SP}$ is $\sqrt{n}$-consistent, we can treat it as if it were known when determining the rate of convergence of $\widehat{m}\left(\mathbf{z}\right)$. Thus, what we are left with is a nonparametric regression of a "known" value on $\mathbf{z}$ and hence we obtain the same rate of convergence for the unknown smooth function, as we saw for the LCLS estimator in Chapter 5.

One point which may not be clear is that the bandwidths for estimating $\widehat{m}\left(\mathbf{z}\right)$ are likely different from those which we use to estimate $E\left(y_i | \mathbf{z}_i\right)$ and which are likely different from the p sets of bandwidths we use to estimate $E\left(\mathbf{x}_i | \mathbf{z}_i\right)$. In practice you are going to need to calculate a separate set of bandwidths for each conditional mean (including $E\left(y_i - \mathbf{x}_i\widehat{\beta}_{SP} | \mathbf{z}_i\right)$). As you may expect, this is very computationally expensive and so (later) we also consider an alternative approach.

For reasons that we do not quite understand, the gradient vector for the unknown function is often an afterthought in applied econometric papers, even though this may be of separate importance. It is not difficult to estimate the gradient vector. Perhaps the easiest method would be to use LLLS in the second-stage estimation. As expected, the LLLS estimator of $m\left(\mathbf{z}\right)$ and its gradient vector are obtained as

$$\begin{pmatrix} \widehat{m}\left(\mathbf{z}\right) \\ \frac{\partial\widehat{m}\left(\mathbf{z}\right)}{\partial\mathbf{z}} \end{pmatrix} = \left[Z'K\left(\mathbf{z}\right)Z\right]^{-1} Z'K\left(\mathbf{z}\right)\left(y - \mathbf{x}\widehat{\beta}_{SP}\right),$$

where $(1, \mathbf{z}_i - \mathbf{z})$ is the ith column of the $n \times (q+1)$ matrix Z, $K\left(\mathbf{z}\right)$ is the diagonal $n \times n$ kernel-weighting matrix and the ith row of $y - \mathbf{x}\widehat{\beta}_{SP}$ is equal to $y_i - \mathbf{x}_i\widehat{\beta}_{SP}$.

Note that we are treating $\widehat{\beta}_{SP}$ as fixed when we recover $\widehat{m}(\mathbf{z})$. Alternatively, you could take the analytical derivative of the LCLS estimator (9.3) with respect to $\mathbf{z}$ to obtain the gradients, as we saw in Chapter 5 for the traditional LCLS estimator.

Similarly, standard errors can be obtained for both the parametric and nonparametric components (both the unknown function and its gradient vector) via bootstrap techniques. The approach is the same as we saw in Chapter 5 in that we use a wild bootstrap (as we generally do not expect economic data to be homoskedastic) to resample the residuals. Formally, the steps are as follows:

1. Let $\widehat{u}_i = y_i - \mathbf{x}_i \widehat{\beta}_{SP} - \widehat{m}(\mathbf{z}_i)$ be the residual from the PLM. Save the re-centered residuals from the null model $\widehat{u}_i - \overline{\widehat{u}}, i = 1, 2, \ldots, n$ where $\overline{\widehat{u}} = n^{-1} \sum_{i=1}^{n} \widehat{u}_i$. Compute the two-point wild bootstrap errors using the re-centered residuals by $u_i^* = \{(1 - \sqrt{5})/2\} \left(\widehat{u}_i - \overline{\widehat{u}}\right)$ with probability $(1 + \sqrt{5})/(2\sqrt{5})$ and $u_i^* = \{(1 + \sqrt{5})/2\} \left(\widehat{u}_i - \overline{\widehat{u}}\right)$ with probability $1 - (1 + \sqrt{5})/(2\sqrt{5})$. Generate y_i^* via $y_i^* = \mathbf{x}_i \widehat{\beta}_{SP} + \widehat{m}(\mathbf{z}_i) + u_i^*$. Call $\{y_i^*, \mathbf{x}_i, \mathbf{z}_i\}_{i=1}^{n}$ the bootstrap sample.
2. Using the bootstrap sample, estimate the parametric parameter vector $\widehat{\beta}_{SP}^*$, the unknown function $\widehat{m}^*(\mathbf{z})$ and/or its derivative $\partial \widehat{m}^*(\mathbf{z})/\partial \mathbf{z}$ via the PLM estimator, where y_i is replaced by y_i^* wherever it occurs. Remember that we use the data $\mathbf{x}_i$ and $\mathbf{z}_i$ and evaluate at the same values of $\mathbf{x}$ and $\mathbf{z}$ that we did initially.
3. Repeat steps 1 and 2 a large number (B) of times and then construct the sampling distribution of the bootstrapped point estimates. Standard errors can be obtained by taking the standard deviation of the sampling distribution for each particular estimate.

9.2.2 Bandwidth selection

Given that we have a two-step procedure that requires bandwidths specified in each step, the issue of bandwidth selection for this estimator requires extra attention. Recall that we must first estimate the expected value of y as well as each element of $\mathbf{x}$ conditional on $\mathbf{z}$. Thus, this requires $(p + 1)$ sets of bandwidths, each of dimension q. Formally, the bandwidths for the conditional expectation of y given $\mathbf{z}$ are calculated via the cross-validation function

$$\text{CV}(h_z) = \sum_{i=1}^{n} \left[y_i - \widehat{E}_{-i}(y_i|\mathbf{z}_i)\right]^2,$$

where $\widehat{E}_{-i}(y_i|\mathbf{z}_i)$ is the leave-one-out estimator of $E(y_i|\mathbf{z}_i)$. Formally, the leave-one-out estimator is defined as

$$\widehat{E}_{-i}(y_i|\mathbf{z}_i) = \frac{\sum_{\substack{j=1 \\ j \neq i}}^{n} K_{h_z}(\mathbf{z}_j, \mathbf{z}_i) y_i}{\sum_{\substack{j=1 \\ j \neq i}}^{n} K_{h_z}(\mathbf{z}_j, \mathbf{z}_i)}. \tag{9.4}$$

Similarly, the q bandwidths for each of the p conditional expectations of $\mathbf{x}$ given $\mathbf{z}$ are calculated via

$$\mathrm{CV}\left(h_z\right) = \sum_{i=1}^{n} \left[x_{ji} - \widehat{E}_{-i}\left(x_{ji}|\mathbf{z}_i\right)\right]^2,$$

where $\widehat{E}_{-i}\left(x_{ji}|\mathbf{z}_i\right)$ is the leave-one-out estimator of $E\left(x_{ji}|\mathbf{z}_i\right)$ for the jth element of $\mathbf{x}$ and is defined similarly for $\widehat{E}_{-i}(y_i|\mathbf{z}_i)$ in Equation (9.4).

Once we have used these bandwidths to estimate each conditional expectation, we employ them to estimate the parametric parameter vector $\widehat{\beta}_{SP}$ as described above. We can then estimate the q bandwidths for estimation of the unknown function as

$$\mathrm{CV}\left(h_z\right) = \sum_{i=1}^{n} \left[y_i - \mathbf{x}_i\widehat{\beta}_{SP} - \widehat{m}_{-i}\left(\mathbf{z}_i\right)\right]^2,$$

where $\widehat{m}_{-i}\left(\mathbf{z}_i\right)$ is the leave-one-out estimator of $m\left(\mathbf{z}_i\right)$. Note that if we use the set-up where we construct the unknown function from our first stage conditional means, cross-validation is unnecessary for the third step.

We mention several issues which may arise in implementation of the cross-validation procedure. First, given the preliminary conditional expectations that need to be estimated (which require bandwidths), this approach can be computationally demanding depending on the dimensionality of the model. However, we do not recommend rule-of-thumb bandwidths in empirical applications (other than for exploratory analysis). Second, and perhaps more important, the bandwidths we select to estimate each conditional expectation may not be the best bandwidths to estimate the parametric vector or the unknown function. In other words, the cross-validation functions look for the best out-of-sample prediction of the variables y and $\mathbf{x}$ and not necessarily the best estimates of β and $m(\cdot)$.

As an alternative, we can consider selecting $\widehat{\beta}$ and h_z (for the unknown function) simultaneously. The cross-validation function for this problem would be

$$\mathrm{CV}\left(\widehat{\beta}, h_z\right) = \sum_{i=1}^{n} \left[y_i - \mathbf{x}_i\widehat{\beta} - \widehat{m}_{-i}\left(\mathbf{z}_i\right)\right]^2.$$

Computation time diminishes drastically and it is not much more difficult to implement than the previous cross-validation criteria. That being said, we introduce this approach here with the caveat that it has not been analyzed in a theoretically rigorous manner.

9.2.3 Testing

Here we consider two separate tests for correct specification. The first is the test for a parametric model versus a PLM. The second is a test for a PLM versus a nonparametric model. Each test is likely of interest as we go from the most restrictive to the least restrictive. Recall that the PLM is somewhere in-between and we want to make sure use of this model does not come at the cost of inefficiency or inconsistency.

Perhaps the easiest way (and one you should be familiar with) to compare each of these models would be to use a goodness-of-fit (Fan, Zhang, and Zhang, 2001 or

Ullah, 1985) or conditional-moment (Li and Wang, 1998) type test. These tests were discussed in detail in Chapter 6 and form the foundation of our discussion of inference for the PLM here.

Parametric versus semiparametric
In our first test our null hypothesis is

$$H_0 : E\,(y|\mathbf{x}, \mathbf{z}) = \mathbf{x}\beta + \mathbf{z}\gamma$$

versus the alternative

$$H_1 : E\,(y|\mathbf{x}, \mathbf{z}) = \mathbf{x}\beta + m\,(\mathbf{z})$$

for testing a parametric model versus a PLM.

Goodness-of-fit test. To perform the goodness-of-fit test, we first estimate each model. We estimate the null model via parametric regression, such as an OLS regression of y on $\mathbf{x}$ and $\mathbf{z}$. Once each model is estimated, we calculate the residual sum of squares for the null model as

$$\sum_{i=1}^{n}\widehat{u}_i^2 = \sum_{i=1}^{n}\left(y_i - \mathbf{x}_i\widehat{\beta} - \mathbf{z}_i\widehat{\gamma}\right)^2$$

and for the alternative model as

$$\sum_{i=1}^{n}\widetilde{u}_i^2 = \sum_{i=1}^{n}\left[y_i - \mathbf{x}_i\widetilde{\beta}_{SP} - \widetilde{m}\,(\mathbf{z}_i)\right]^2.$$

The test statistic is then calculated as

$$\widehat{J}_n = \frac{\displaystyle\sum_{i=1}^{n}\widehat{u}_i^2 - \sum_{i=1}^{n}\widetilde{u}_i^2}{\displaystyle\sum_{i=1}^{n}\widetilde{u}_i^2}.$$

We suggest using a bootstrap-based test in practice. Formally, our (wild) bootstrap procedure is as follows:

1. Compute the test statistic $\widehat{J}_n$ for the original sample of $\{\mathbf{x}_1, \mathbf{x}_2, \ldots, \mathbf{x}_n\}$, $\{\mathbf{z}_1, \mathbf{z}_2, \ldots, \mathbf{z}_n\}$ and $\{y_1, y_2, \ldots, y_n\}$ and save the re-centered residuals from the null model $\widehat{u}_i - \overline{\widehat{u}}$, $i = 1, 2, \ldots, n$ where $\widehat{u}_i = y_i - \mathbf{x}_i\widehat{\beta} - \mathbf{z}_i\widehat{\gamma}$ and $\overline{\widehat{u}} = n^{-1}\sum_{i=1}^{n}\widehat{u}_i$.
2. For each observation i, construct the bootstrapped residual u_i^*, where $u_i^* = \frac{1-\sqrt{5}}{2}\left(\widehat{u}_i - \overline{\widehat{u}}\right)$ with probability $\frac{1+\sqrt{5}}{2\sqrt{5}}$ and $u_i^* = \frac{1+\sqrt{5}}{2}\left(\widehat{u}_i - \overline{\widehat{u}}\right)$ with probability $1 - \frac{1+\sqrt{5}}{2\sqrt{5}}$. Construct the bootstrapped left-hand-side variable by adding the bootstrapped residuals to the fitted values under the null as $y_i^* = \mathbf{x}_i\widehat{\beta} + \mathbf{z}_i\widehat{\gamma} + u_i^*$. Call $\left\{y_i^*, \mathbf{x}_i, \mathbf{z}_i\right\}_{i=1}^{n}$ the bootstrap sample.
3. Calculate $\widehat{J}_n^*$ where $\widehat{J}_n^*$ is calculated the same way as $\widehat{J}_n$ except that y_i is replaced by y_i^*.

4. Repeat steps 2 and 3 a large number (B) of times and then construct the sampling distribution of the bootstrapped test statistics. We reject the null that the parametric model is correctly specified if the estimated test statistic $\widehat{J}_n$ is greater than the upper α-percentile of the bootstrapped test statistics.

Conditional-moment test

Defining $\widehat{u}_i = y_i - \mathbf{x}_i \widetilde{\beta}_{SP} - \mathbf{z}\widehat{\gamma}$, where the estimator $\widehat{\gamma}$ is obtained using OLS, a feasible test statistic for the null of correct parametric specification (vs. a PLM alternative) is given as (Equation 5 of Li and Wang, 1998)

$$\widehat{I}_n = \frac{1}{n(n-1)\,|\mathbf{h}|} \sum_{i=1}^{n} \sum_{\substack{j=1 \\ j \neq i}}^{n} \widehat{u}_i \widehat{u}_j K_h\left(\mathbf{z}_i, \mathbf{z}_j\right).$$

The use of $\widetilde{\beta}_{SP}$ instead of the standard OLS estimator is required so that the test statistic does not converge to zero under the alternative without requiring further technical assumptions. Technical Appendix 9.1 shows the conditions for which $\widehat{I}_n$ is a degenerate U-statistic hold. Thus, with proper normalization we can show that $\widehat{I}_n$ tends towards the standard normal in distribution. Given that we have a degenerate U-statistic, as we showed in Chapter 6, we can obtain the estimator of the variance of the test statistic as

$$\widehat{\sigma}_n^2 = \frac{2}{n(n-1)\,|\mathbf{h}|} \sum_{i=1}^{n} \sum_{\substack{j=1 \\ j \neq i}}^{n} \widehat{u}_i^2 \widehat{u}_j^2 K_h^2\left(\mathbf{z}_i, \mathbf{z}_j\right).$$

Given these results, the test statistic is constructed as

$$\widehat{T}_n = n\,|\mathbf{h}|^{1/2}\, \frac{\widehat{I}_n}{\widehat{\sigma}_n}$$

and converges to the standard normal distribution under the null. Li and Wang (1998) note that we could use $\widehat{\beta}_{OLS}$ to construct the residuals and still obtain this result. Similar to the other conditional-moment tests we have described, we recommend a bootstrap procedure for use of this test in practice. The steps for the two-point wild bootstrap procedure are as follows:

1. Compute the test statistics $\widehat{T}_n$ for the original sample of $\{\mathbf{x}_1, \mathbf{x}_2, \ldots, \mathbf{x}_n\}$, $\{\mathbf{z}_1, \mathbf{z}_2, \ldots, \mathbf{z}_n\}$ and $\{y_1, y_2, \ldots, y_n\}$ and save the re-centered residuals from the null model $\widehat{u}_i - \overline{\widehat{u}}$, $i = 1, 2, \ldots, n$ where $\widehat{u}_i = y_i - \mathbf{x}_i\widetilde{\beta}_{SP} - \mathbf{z}_i\widehat{\gamma}$ and $\overline{\widehat{u}} = n^{-1}\sum_{i=1}^{n}\widehat{u}_i$.
2. For each observation i, construct the bootstrapped residual u_i^*, where $u_i^* = \frac{1-\sqrt{5}}{2}\left(\widehat{u}_i - \overline{\widehat{u}}\right)$ with probability $\frac{1+\sqrt{5}}{2\sqrt{5}}$ and $u_i^* = \frac{1+\sqrt{5}}{2}\left(\widehat{u}_i - \overline{\widehat{u}}\right)$ with probability $1 - \frac{1+\sqrt{5}}{2\sqrt{5}}$. Construct the bootstrapped left-hand-side variable by adding the bootstrapped residuals to the fitted values under the null as $y_i^* = \mathbf{x}_i\widetilde{\beta}_{SP} + \mathbf{z}_i\widehat{\gamma} + u_i^*$. Call $\left\{y_i^*, \mathbf{x}_i, \mathbf{z}_i\right\}_{i=1}^{n}$ the bootstrap sample.

3. Calculate $\widehat{T}_n^*$ where $\widehat{T}_n^*$ is calculated the same way as $\widehat{T}_n$ except that y_i is replaced by y_i^*.

4. Repeat steps 2 and 3 a large number (B) of times and then construct the sampling distribution of the bootstrapped test statistics. We reject the null that the parametric model is correctly specified if the estimated test statistic $\widehat{T}_n$ is greater than the upper α-percentile of the bootstrapped test statistics.

Semiparametric versus nonparametric

Here we suggest a very similar bootstrap-based test to test between a PLM and a nonparametric alternative. Here our null hypothesis of interest is

$$H_0 : E\,(y|\mathbf{x}, \mathbf{z}) = \mathbf{x}\beta + m\,(\mathbf{z})$$

versus the alternative

$$H_1 : E\,(y|\mathbf{x}, \mathbf{z}) = \theta\,(\mathbf{x}, \mathbf{z}),$$

which tests a PLM versus the nonparametric model $\theta\,(\cdot)$, where $\theta\,(\cdot)$ is an unknown smooth function containing both $\mathbf{x}$ and $\mathbf{z}$.

Goodness-of-fit test

Similar to before, we estimate both the null and alternative models and obtain their respective residual sum of squares. For the null model this is

$$\sum_{i=1}^n \widehat{u}_i^2 = \sum_{i=1}^n \left[y_i - \mathbf{x}_i \widehat{\beta}_{SP} - \widehat{m}\,(\mathbf{z}_i) \right]^2$$

and for the alternative we have

$$\sum_{i=1}^n \widetilde{u}_i^2 = \sum_{i=1}^n \left[y_i - \widetilde{\theta}\,(\mathbf{x}_i, \mathbf{z}_i) \right]^2 .$$

Our test statistic is again calculated as

$$\widehat{J}_n = \frac{\displaystyle\sum_{i=1}^n \widehat{u}_i^2 - \sum_{i=1}^n \widetilde{u}_i^2}{\displaystyle\sum_{i=1}^n \widetilde{u}_i^2}.$$

The bootstrap procedure is identical to above except that the null model is now the PLM. Formally, the bootstrap procedure is as follows:

1. Compute the test statistics $\widehat{J}_n$ for the original sample of $\{\mathbf{x}_1, \mathbf{x}_2, \ldots, \mathbf{x}_n\}$, $\{\mathbf{z}_1, \mathbf{z}_2, \ldots, \mathbf{z}_n\}$ and $\{y_1, y_2, \ldots, y_n\}$ and save the re-centered residuals from the null model $\widehat{u}_i - \overline{\widehat{u}}, i = 1, 2, \ldots, n$ where $\widehat{u}_i = y_i - \mathbf{x}_i \widehat{\beta}_{SP} - \widehat{m}\,(\mathbf{z}_i)$ and $\overline{\widehat{u}} = n^{-1} \sum_{i=1}^n \widehat{u}_i$.

2. For each observation i, construct the bootstrapped residual u_i^*, where $u_i^* = \frac{1-\sqrt{5}}{2}\left(\widehat{u}_i - \overline{\widehat{u}}\right)$ with probability $\frac{1+\sqrt{5}}{2\sqrt{5}}$ and $u_i^* = \frac{1+\sqrt{5}}{2}\left(\widehat{u}_i - \overline{\widehat{u}}\right)$ with probability

$1 - \frac{1+\sqrt{5}}{2\sqrt{5}}$. Construct the bootstrapped left-hand-side variable by adding the bootstrapped residuals to the fitted values under the null as $y_i^* = \mathbf{x}_i \widehat{\beta}_{SP} + \widehat{m}(\mathbf{z}_i) + u_i^*$. Call $\{y_i^*, \mathbf{x}_i, \mathbf{z}_i\}_{i=1}^n$ the bootstrap sample.

3. Calculate $\widehat{J}_n^*$ where $\widehat{J}_n^*$ is calculated the same way as $\widehat{J}_n$ except that y_i is replaced by y_i^*.

4. Repeat steps 2 and 3 a large number (B) of times and then construct the sampling distribution of the bootstrapped test statistics. We reject the null that the semiparametric is correctly specified if the estimated test statistic $\widehat{J}_n$ is greater than the upper α-percentile of the bootstrapped test statistics.

Conditional-moment test

Following Li and Wang (1998), we can construct a conditional-moment test for assessing correct specification of the PLM versus a nonparametric alternative (noting that we are unaware of an application of this in the literature). The key difference is the form of the residuals that are passed to the test statistic. Other tests with a completely nonparametric alternative hypothesis in the literature include Delgado and González Manteiga (2001), Härdle, Mammen, and Müller (1998), Whang (2000), Whang and Andrews (1993) and Yatchew (1992).

Defining $\widehat{u}_i = y_i - \mathbf{x}_i \widehat{\beta}_{SP} - \widehat{m}(\mathbf{z}_i)$ as the residuals from the PLM, $|\mathbf{h}| = h_1 \cdots h_q \cdots h_{p+q}$ as the product of the bandwidths from both $\mathbf{x}$ and $\mathbf{z}$, and $\mathbf{w}_i = (\mathbf{x}_i, \mathbf{z}_i)$ as the union of $\mathbf{x}$ and $\mathbf{z}$, a feasible test statistic is given as

$$\widehat{I}_n = \frac{1}{n(n-1)\,|\mathbf{h}|} \sum_{i=1}^n \sum_{\substack{j=1 \\ j \neq i}}^n \widehat{u}_i \widehat{u}_j K_h(\mathbf{w}_i, \mathbf{w}_j),$$

which Technical Appendix 9.2 demonstrates is a degenerate U-statistic. Following our discussions in Chapters 4 and 6, we can obtain the estimator of the variance of the test statistic as

$$\widehat{\sigma}_n^2 = \frac{2}{n(n-1)\,|\mathbf{h}|} \sum_{i=1}^n \sum_{\substack{j=1 \\ j \neq i}}^n \widehat{u}_i^2 \widehat{u}_j^2 K_h^2(\mathbf{w}_i, \mathbf{w}_j).$$

Given these results, the test statistic is constructed as

$$\widehat{T}_n = n\,|\mathbf{h}|^{1/2} \frac{\widehat{I}_n}{\widehat{\sigma}_n}$$

and converges to the standard normal distribution under the null. Similar to before, we recommend a bootstrap procedure for use of this test in practice. The steps for the two-point wild bootstrap procedure are as follows:

1. Compute the test statistics $\widehat{J}_n$ for the original sample of $\{\mathbf{x}_1, \mathbf{x}_2, \ldots, \mathbf{x}_n\}$, $\{\mathbf{z}_1, \mathbf{z}_2, \ldots, \mathbf{z}_n\}$, and $\{y_1, y_2, \ldots, y_n\}$ and save the re-centered residuals from the null model $\widehat{u}_i - \overline{\widehat{u}}$, $i = 1, 2, \ldots, n$ where $\widehat{u}_i = y_i - \mathbf{x}_i \widehat{\beta}_{SP} - \widehat{m}(\mathbf{z}_i)$ and $\overline{\widehat{u}} = n^{-1} \sum_{i=1}^n \widehat{u}_i$.

2. For each observation i, construct the bootstrapped residual u_i^*, where $u_i^* = \frac{1-\sqrt{5}}{2}\left(\widehat{u}_i - \overline{\widehat{u}}\right)$ with probability $\frac{1+\sqrt{5}}{2\sqrt{5}}$ and $u_i^* = \frac{1+\sqrt{5}}{2}\left(\widehat{u}_i - \overline{\widehat{u}}\right)$ with probability $1 - \frac{1+\sqrt{5}}{2\sqrt{5}}$. Construct the bootstrapped left-hand-side variable by adding the bootstrapped residuals to the fitted values under the null as $y_i^* = \mathbf{x}_i\widehat{\beta}_{SP} + \widehat{m}(\mathbf{z}_i) + u_i^*$. Call $\left\{y_i^*, \mathbf{x}_i, \mathbf{z}_i\right\}_{i=1}^n$ the bootstrap sample.

3. Calculate $\widehat{T}_n^*$ where $\widehat{T}_n^*$ is calculated the same way as $\widehat{T}_n$ except that y_i is replaced by y_i^*.

4. Repeat steps 2 and 3 a large number (B) of times and then construct the sampling distribution of the bootstrapped test statistics. We reject the null that the parametric model is correctly specified if the estimated test statistic $\widehat{T}_n$ is greater than the upper α-percentile of the bootstrapped test statistics.

9.3 Single-index models

One of the main draws of the PLM is that it is able to reduce the dimension of the problem. In other words, we are not faced with the full force of the curse of dimensionality. An alternative way to reduce the dimension of the model that is nonparametric is a single-index model. In this type of model we have a single dimensioned index that enters the unknown function nonparametrically. The popularity of single-index models is that they function in a similar fashion to many parametric models you are most likely already familiar with. For example, normal regression, logit, probit, and (both censored and truncated) Tobit as well as Poisson regression and duration models are all examples of single-index models.

Here, one of the elegant features of the single-index model is that a distributional assumption is not required to operationalize the model, as is often the case in the parametric setting. A further benefit of the single-index model is that the parametric component of the model can often be estimated at the parametric rate, as was the case with the PLM. These benefits do not come without costs: most notably, it is difficult – if not impossible – to incorporate discrete variables (common in applied work) in the index (Horowitz and Härdle, 1996).

The general form of a single-index model with an additive error is

$$y_i = m\left(\varphi\left(\mathbf{x}_i, \beta\right)\right) + u_i, i = 1, 2, \ldots, n,$$

where $m\left(\cdot\right)$ is an unknown smooth function, $\varphi\left(\cdot, \cdot\right)$ is a known parametric function with q regressors $\mathbf{x}$ and $p \times 1$ parameter vector β. u is our usual additive error term, which we assume is uncorrelated with $\mathbf{x}$. Even though $\varphi\left(\mathbf{x}_i, \beta\right)$ may be a nonlinear function, it is deemed single index because $\varphi\left(\mathbf{x}_i, \beta\right)$ is a scalar. The majority of economic research assumes that we have a linear single index and we will thus assume that the function $\varphi\left(\cdot, \cdot\right)$ is equal to

$$\varphi\left(\mathbf{x}_i, \beta\right) = \beta_1 x_{1i} + \beta_2 x_{2i} + \cdots + \beta_q x_{qi},$$

where we have the same number of regressors and parameters and hence $p = q$. In matrix form, our single index model is given as

$$y_i = m\left(\mathbf{x}_i\beta\right) + u_i, i = 1, 2, \ldots, n, \tag{9.5}$$

where $\mathbf{x}_i = (x_{1i}, x_{2i}, \ldots, x_{qi})$ and $\beta = (\beta_1, \beta_2, \ldots, \beta_q)'$. Note that, similar to the PLM case, we do not have a constant term in $\mathbf{x}$, as an intercept cannot be identified without restrictions on the unknown function, and β generally cannot be identified without a normalization (similar to logit and probit models). Two normalizations are popular in the literature. The first is to set the first regressors coefficient equal to unity (assuming the true parameter is different from zero) and the second is to assume that the vector β has unit length. In other words, the Euclidian norm is one. More details on normalization of parameters in single-index models can be found in, for example, Cameron and Trivedi (2005).

Given that the main difference between the parametric and the semiparametric case is $m(\cdot)$, we spend some time discussing this "link" function. In the parametric world $m(\cdot)$ is known and we can use nonlinear least-squares or maximum likelihood estimation. In the semiparametric world, it is unknown and must be estimated. If we look closer, we can see that $m(\cdot)$ is essentially the conditional mean of y with respect to $\mathbf{x}\beta$. Thus, the obvious choice would be to run a nonparametric regression of y on $\mathbf{x}\beta$. If β were known, this is trivial, but in practice β is unknown and hence we must estimate both $m(\cdot)$ and β.

Here we will focus on the general estimation procedure attributed to Ichimura (1993). We will discuss estimation, bandwidth selection, and relevant hypothesis tests. We highlight the use of the estimator to the case of discrete choice models, primarily with respect to binary choice models. Whereas the Ichimura (1993) estimator may not be optimal in any given scenario, its wide generality is the reason we choose to focus on this particular estimator.

Although these types of semiparametric estimators are popular in the literature to estimate discrete choice models, they are not the only way to estimate them nonparametrically. If you are willing to take the full brunt of the curse of dimensionality, it is possible to use nonparametric conditional density estimation in the presence of discrete variables. Recent advances in kernel estimation allow us to estimate a wide range of discrete-choice models fully nonparametrically. We believe that these methods are underutilized, but we proceed with single-index models given their ability to reduce the curse of dimensionality as well as for their popularity.

9.3.1 Estimation

As we mentioned before, if $m(\cdot)$ were known, we could estimate β via nonlinear least squares. Formally, our goal would be to minimize the least-squares objective function

$$\frac{1}{n} \sum_{i=1}^{n} \left[y_i - m(\mathbf{x}_i \beta) \right]^2$$

with respect to β. Given that $m(\cdot)$ is unknown, we must estimate both terms. We could think of a two-step procedure, but this would be inefficient.

Ichimura (1993) suggests using a leave-one-out estimator of the conditional mean of y given $\mathbf{x}\beta$ while minimizing the sum-of-squared residuals with respect to the q-dimensional parameter vector β. We first define our leave-one-out estimator of the conditional mean of y given $\mathbf{x}\beta$ as

$$E_{-i}\left(y_i|\mathbf{x}_i\beta\right) = \frac{\sum\limits_{\substack{j\neq i}}^{n} y_j K_h\left(\mathbf{x}_j\beta, \mathbf{x}_i\beta\right)}{\sum\limits_{\substack{j\neq i}}^{n} K_h\left(\mathbf{x}_j\beta, \mathbf{x}_i\beta\right)},$$

where

$$K_h\left(\mathbf{x}_j\beta, \mathbf{x}_i\beta\right) = \prod_{d=1}^{q} k\left(\frac{\mathbf{x}_{dj}\beta_d - \mathbf{x}_{di}\beta_d}{h_d}\right)$$

is our product kernel function. We note here that Ichimura (1993) needs higher-order kernels to obtain $\sqrt{n}$-consistent estimators of β, but the very similar estimator of Härdle, Hall, and Ichimura (1993) allows for second-order kernels. We will discuss this latter estimator in the bandwidth selection section. With this estimator in hand, the least-squares criterion becomes

$$\frac{1}{n}\sum_{i=1}^{n}\left[y_i - \frac{\sum\limits_{\substack{j\neq i}}^{n} y_j K_h\left(\mathbf{x}_j\beta, \mathbf{x}_i\beta\right)}{\sum\limits_{\substack{j\neq i}}^{n} K_h\left(\mathbf{x}_j\beta, \mathbf{x}_i\beta\right)}\right]^2. \tag{9.6}$$

The estimator of β is defined as the value of $\widehat{\beta}$ that minimizes the objective function. This objective function may look complicated, but it can be coded by plugging this function into a minimization routine and asking it to solve for $\widehat{\beta}$.

In theoretical research on the single-index model, this objective function generally differs in two respects. First, given that the LCLS estimator only converges uniformly over compact sets, a trimming function is needed to remove small values in the denominator. This turns out to be important in developing asymptotic theory, but some consider it to be less important in practice, we omit it here. The second difference is that we often see the objective function estimated by a weighting function as well. Ichimura (1993) suggests using the inverse of the heteroskedastic variance term for a weighting function. The weighting function is not necessary in order to achieve the $\sqrt{n}$-convergence rate of the slope coefficients when the error term is heteroskedastic, but it is required to achieve the semiparametric efficiency bound on the estimates. In order to use a weighting function, we must use a two-step procedure, which can be computationally costly. Again, the presence of heteroskeasticity does not lead to an inconsistent estimator, only an inefficient one. Hence, we omit this here as well, but recommend that those who are interested read the corresponding references.

Partial effects

Here we consider how to estimate the partial effects for single-index models. We are unaware of any papers in the literature that attempt to do this. The basic idea is to look at the change in the unknown function with respect to a particular regressor evaluated at the estimate of β. The approach will be similar to the case of a parametric single-index model (for instance, probit) because we are assuming that we have a linear single index, but it will differ in one key respect because we do not assume the unknown function is a CDF.

Formally, our suggested approach to calculate the partial effects is as follows. If we take the estimate of β obtained from minimizing (9.6) as given, we can rewrite the conditional mean as

$$\widehat{m}\left(\mathbf{x}_i\widehat{\beta}\right) = \frac{\sum\limits_{j=1}^{n} y_j K_h\left(\mathbf{x}_j\widehat{\beta}, \mathbf{x}_i\widehat{\beta}\right)}{\sum\limits_{j=1}^{n} K_h\left(\mathbf{x}_j\widehat{\beta}, \mathbf{x}_i\widehat{\beta}\right)}.$$

Then our analytical gradient with respect to the regressor x_d is defined as

$$\frac{\partial \widehat{y}}{\partial x_d} = \frac{\partial \widehat{m}\left(\mathbf{x}_i\widehat{\beta}\right)}{\partial x_{di}}\widehat{\beta}_d$$

$$= \left\{\frac{\left[\sum\limits_{j=1}^{n} y_j \frac{\partial K_h(\mathbf{x}_j\widehat{\beta},\mathbf{x}_i\widehat{\beta})}{\partial x_{di}}\right]\sum\limits_{j=1}^{n} K_h\left(\mathbf{x}_j\widehat{\beta}, \mathbf{x}_i\widehat{\beta}\right) - \left[\sum\limits_{j=1}^{n} y_j K_h\left(\mathbf{x}_j\widehat{\beta}, \mathbf{x}_i\widehat{\beta}\right)\right]\sum\limits_{j=1}^{n}\frac{\partial K_h(\mathbf{x}_j\widehat{\beta},\mathbf{x}_i\widehat{\beta})}{\partial x_{di}}}{\left[\sum\limits_{j=1}^{n} K_h\left(\mathbf{x}_j\widehat{\beta}, \mathbf{x}_i\widehat{\beta}\right)\right]^2}\right\}\widehat{\beta}_d,$$

and if we use a Gaussian kernel, then

$$\frac{\partial K_h\left(\mathbf{x}_j\widehat{\beta}, \mathbf{x}_i\widehat{\beta}\right)}{\partial x_{di}} = \left(\frac{x_{dj} - x_{di}}{h^2}\right)\widehat{\beta}_d K_h\left(\mathbf{x}_j\widehat{\beta}, \mathbf{x}_i\widehat{\beta}\right).$$

Note that for the LCLS estimator, this is nothing more than replacing $\mathbf{x}$ with $\mathbf{x}\widehat{\beta}$ in our formula for the in Chapter 5 coupled with the change in the kernel derivative.

The important difference from typical parametric single-index models is that we have not assumed that $m\left(\cdot\right)$ is a monotonically increasing function. When $m\left(\cdot\right)$ is monotonically increasing (say a CDF), the sign of $\widehat{\beta}$ is the same as the sign of the partial effect. However, our method does not assume that the unknown function is monotonically increasing. Hence, the sign of the partial effect need not be the same as the sign of the parametric coefficient. The good news is that we are still dealing with a single-index model. This simplifies the procedure to check for monotonicity. Here, we can simply plot $\widehat{m}\left(\mathbf{x}\widehat{\beta}\right)$ versus $\mathbf{x}\widehat{\beta}$, as each is a scalar value. Although informal, this works for any dimension q.

Standard errors can be obtained for partial effects via bootstrap techniques. The approach is the same as we saw above in that we use a wild bootstrap to resample the residuals. Formally, the steps are as follows:

1. Let $\widehat{u}_i = y_i - \widehat{m}\left(\mathbf{x}_i\widehat{\beta}\right)$ be the residual from the single-index model. Compute the two-point wild-bootstrap errors from the re-centered residuals by $u_i^* = \{(1 - \sqrt{5})/2\}\left(\widehat{u}_i - \overline{\widehat{u}}\right)$ with probability $(1 + \sqrt{5})/(2\sqrt{5})$ and $u_i^* = \{(1 + \sqrt{5})/2\}\left(\widehat{u}_i - \overline{\widehat{u}}\right)$ with probability $1 - (1 + \sqrt{5})/(2\sqrt{5})$. Generate y_i^* via $y_i^* = \widehat{m}\left(\mathbf{x}_i\widehat{\beta}\right) + u_i^*$. Call $\{y_i^*, \mathbf{x}_i\}_{i=1}^{n}$ the bootstrap sample.
2. Using the bootstrap sample, estimate the partial effect via the semiparametric single-index model where y_i is replaced by y_i^* wherever it occurs. Remember that we use the data $\mathbf{x}_i$ and evaluate at the same values of $\mathbf{x}$ that we did initially.

3. Repeat steps 1 and 2 a large number (B) of times and then construct the sampling distribution of the bootstrapped point estimates. Standard errors can be obtained by taking the standard deviation of the sampling distribution for each particular estimate.

Binary outcome models

Perhaps the most popular use of single-index models in semiparametric estimation is for limited dependent-variable models. The approach mimics that found in most graduate econometrics textbooks and thus we will be brief. First, consider a latent variable model defined as

$$y_i^* = \mathbf{x}_i \beta + u_i^*$$

where y_i^* is the (unobserved) latent variable. Note that u_i^* will differ from the error term in our regression model as y_i^* is unobserved. Several special cases of parametric latent-variable models include logit, probit, and Tobit.

To show how this works, let's consider a binary outcome model. The observed value of y takes value one when the latent variable is positive and zero otherwise. Formally,

$$y_i = 1 \text{ if } y_i^* > 0, \quad 0 \text{ if } y_i^* \le 0,$$

where the threshold of zero is simply a normalization. As in the parametric world, the expected value of y given $\mathbf{x}$ is equal to the probability that y takes value one given $\mathbf{x}$. This in turn is equal to the probability that y^* is positive. The conditional mean is thus equal to

$$
\begin{aligned}
E\left(y|\mathbf{x}\right) &= 1 \cdot P\left(y_i = 1|\mathbf{x}\right) + 0 \cdot P\left(y_i = 0|\mathbf{x}\right) \\
&= P\left(y_i = 1|\mathbf{x}\right) \\
&= P\left(y_i^* > 0\right) \\
&= P\left(\mathbf{x}_i \beta + u_i^* > 0\right) \\
&= P\left(u_i^* > -\mathbf{x}_i \beta\right) \\
&= 1 - P\left(u_i^* < -\mathbf{x}_i \beta\right) \\
&= 1 - F\left(-\mathbf{x}_i \beta\right) \\
&= m\left(\mathbf{x}_i \beta\right),
\end{aligned}
$$

where $F\left(\cdot\right)$ is the CDF of the error term u_i^*. If this error term is symmetric, then $F\left(-\mathbf{x}_i \beta\right) = m\left(\mathbf{x}_i \beta\right)$. If the function $F\left(\cdot\right)$ is the logistic CDF, then we have the logit model; if it is the standard normal CDF, then we have the probit model. Note that consistent estimation of $E\left(y|\mathbf{x}\right)$ relies heavily on the assumed form of $F\left(\cdot\right)$. Unlike the simple linear regression model, if we incorrectly specify $F\left(\cdot\right)$, our parameter estimator will be inconsistent. This amplifies the importance of the semiparametric method, assuming you believe the linear single-index specification.

We note here that this is not the only way to estimate a binary-choice model semiparametrically. Other examples in the literature include, but are not limited to, Cosslett (1983), Horowitz (1992), Ichimura and Lee (1991), Lee (1995), Lewbel (2000), and Manski (1975). However, the most popular estimator for this problem is the estimator presented in Klein and Spady (1993). In their paper they suggest a semiparametric likelihood approach. Their log-likelihood (for the Bernoulli distributed outcome) is given by

$$L\left(m\left(\cdot\right),\beta\right)=\sum_{i=1}^{n}\left\{y_{i}\ln m\left(\mathbf{x}_{i}\beta\right)+\left(1-y_{i}\right)\ln\left[1-m\left(\mathbf{x}_{i}\beta\right)\right]\right\}.$$

The goal here, as expected, is to maximize the log-likelihood function with respect to $m\left(\cdot\right)$ and β. They suggest using a leave-one-out estimator for $m(\cdot)$ as well as a trimming function, but do not require a weighting function. It is perhaps this difference that makes the Klein and Spady (1993) estimator more popular. This estimator is efficient without needing to perform a second step. We are not restricted to binary left-hand-side variables in either framework, either. For example, Lee (1995) generalizes the Klein and Spady (1993) estimator to the estimation of polychotomous-choice and sequential-choice models. For an extension of the Ichimura (1993) estimator, see Ichimura and Lee (1991).

Here we want to highlight two other ways to estimate discrete-choice models. First, in the presence of a binary left-hand-side variable, it is possible to use LCLS to estimate a nonparametric probability model. This is analogous to the linear probability model you learned in introductory econometrics where the binary variable is regressed on the right-hand-side variables via OLS. Recall that one problem with the linear probability model was that it often led to probabilities that were greater than one or less than zero. This is not true when we use a LCLS estimator. Second, we can also use discrete conditional density estimation to estimate a host of discrete-choice models as well (using the methods discussed in Chapter 7).

Semiparametric single-index models can also be used to estimate other types of limited dependent-variable models. One example also considered in Ichimura (1993) is censored regression models. A censored sample occurs when we have a sample where we record only those values of y^* that are in excess of a particular value, say zero. Note that this is different from truncated samples where no observations are drawn for which $y^* < 0$. Lee (1994) considers the case of truncated Tobit. Other semiparametric sample selection models include a dummy variable approach by Cosslett (1991), a maximum likelihood approach by Gallant and Nychka (1987) and a kernel estimator by Powell (1984). Further discussion of these types of models can also be found in Pagan and Ullah (1999, Chapter 8).

Computational issues
When reading the above description of the single-index model, it almost seems too good to be true. We can obtain $\sqrt{n}$-consistent and even efficient estimates of the parametric components without making any distributional assumptions. This is important as misspecification of the distribution in these types of models often leads to inconsistency.

Of course there is always a catch. The problem with the single-index model, especially the Ichimura (1993) estimator, is that there are many computational hurdles.

Recall the objective function (9.6). Each time this objective is evaluated, n nonparametric regressions must be computed. It is possible to reduce the computational burden if we feed the optimization-function analytical gradients, but these methods can also be problematic. Specifically, the objective function likely has local minima and saddle points.

Some of these problems can be avoided by using average derivative estimators. These require a two-step procedure. The first step requires a multidimensional nonparametric estimation and then this estimator is averaged over all the sample points in the second stage. It is possible to show that these estimators are $\sqrt{n}$-consistent. The parametric rate again emerges, given that we are averaging over n. Several interesting average derivative estimators can be found in Härdle, Hart, Marron, and Tsybakov (1992); Härdle and Stoker (1989); Horowitz and Härdle (1996); Li, Lu, and Ullah (2003); Newey and Stoker (1993); and Powell, Stock, and Stoker (1989). The use of the average derivative estimator also comes at a price. First, average derivative estimators have more stringent technical conditions than those required for the estimators in Ichimura (1993) or Klein and Spady (1993). Second, these estimators require multidimensional nonparametric estimation. Finally, we are taking observation-specific estimates and then condensing them down to a single parameter estimate. We get a parametric rate, but at the cost of essentially ignoring the heterogeneity present in the estimates.

9.3.2 Bandwidth selection

Bandwidth selection here is somewhat tricky, as it is in the PLM. It is not obvious that the bandwidths best suited to estimate the conditional mean are the best bandwidths to estimate the parametric parameters. It is also not clear whether or not we should estimate our bandwidths in one step or two. A two-step approach would be to construct a preliminary estimator of the conditional mean so that β could be estimated and then construct a final estimator of the conditional mean. Ichimura (1993) simply talks of ranges of bandwidths which are satisfactory, but does not explicitly come up with a data-driven criterion.

We suggest using the bandwidth-selection mechanism in Härdle, Hall, and Ichimura (1993). Not only do they suggest a bandwidth-selection procedure, but this procedure estimates the bandwidths as well as the finite and infinite dimensional parameters simultaneously. They show that this simultaneous approach for estimating both (the bandwidth) h and β is very much like minimizing the residual sum of squares and the usual cross-validation function separately. In fact, it leads to $\sqrt{n}$-consistent estimates of β as well as asymptotically optimal estimates of the bandwidths.

Formally, their cross-validation function is

$$\mathrm{CV}\left(\widehat{\beta}, h\right) = \frac{1}{n} \sum_{i=1}^{n} \left[y_i - \widehat{m}_{-i}\left(\mathbf{x}_i \widehat{\beta}\right) \right]^2,$$

where the terms $\widehat{\beta}$ and h on the left-hand side denote that we are minimizing the objective function with respect to both. To show how this method works, Härdle, Hall, and Ichimura (1993, 169) and Technical Appendix 9.3 show that you can rewrite the cross-validation function as

$$
\mathrm{CV}\left(\widehat{\beta}, h\right) = \frac{1}{n} \sum_{i=1}^{n} \left[y_i - \widehat{m}_{-i}\left(\mathbf{x}_i \widehat{\beta}\right)\right]^2
$$

$$
\approx \frac{1}{n} \sum_{i=1}^{n} \left[y_i - m\left(\mathbf{x}_i \widehat{\beta}\right)\right]^2 + \frac{1}{n} \sum_{i=1}^{n} \left[\widehat{m}_{-i}\left(\mathbf{x}_i \beta\right) - m\left(\mathbf{x}_i \beta\right)\right]^2 .
$$

Closer examination shows that the first term is a least-squares problem for estimating the parametric vector when $m(\cdot)$ is known and the second term is a least-squares problem for estimating the bandwidths of the unknown function, assuming the parametric vector is known. Thus, we see how this cross-validation function acts as if it is estimating each component separately.

9.3.3 Testing

Here we can think of several tests for a semiparametric single-index model (e.g., Fan and Liu, 1997). The first would be that a parametric single-index model is correctly specified versus a semiparametric single-index model alternative. Recall that there are no gains in rates of convergence or reduced variances if the weighted version of the optimization function is employed. However, if we reject the null, then this suggests that we can use the computationally simple parametric model and avoid many of the other issues listed above.

There are several possible ways to test for this, but an interesting test is developed in Horowitz and Härdle (1994). In their paper they develop a test for a parametric versus a semiparametric single-index model. However, as we will argue later, their test is much more general. Their null hypothesis for the test under discussion is

$$
H_0 : E\left(y|\mathbf{x}\right) = m_P\left(\mathbf{x}\beta\right),
$$

where $m_P(\cdot)$ is our hypothesized (parametric) form. For example, in the binary choice problem, if we have a probit model, then $m_P(\cdot)$ is the standard normal CDF. The alternative hypothesis is that $m_P(\cdot)$ is incorrectly specified

$$
H_1 : E\left(y|\mathbf{x}\right) = m\left(\mathbf{x}\beta\right),
$$

where $m(\cdot)$ is our unknown smooth function. A conditional-moment test of the null versus the alternative hypothesis can be based on the following conditional moment:

$$
J = E\left\{\left[y - m_P\left(\mathbf{x}\beta\right)\right]\left[m\left(\mathbf{x}\beta\right) - m_P\left(\mathbf{x}\beta\right)\right]\right\} = 0,
$$

which is assumed to hold under the null (i.e., $m\left(\mathbf{x}\beta\right) = m_P\left(\mathbf{x}\beta\right)$).

The sample moment condition is taken by averaging over the observations as

$$
J_n = \frac{1}{n} \sum_{i=1}^{n} \left[y_i - m_P\left(\mathbf{x}_i \beta_P\right)\right]\left[m\left(\mathbf{x}_i \beta\right) - m_P\left(\mathbf{x}_i \beta\right)\right]. \tag{9.7}
$$

Note here that this test is two-sided. As usual, many of these terms must be estimated and we obtain a feasible test statistic by replacing the unknown values with their estimated counterparts as

$$\widehat{J}_n = \frac{1}{n} \sum_{i=1}^{n} \left[y_i - m_P \left(\mathbf{x}_i \widehat{\beta}_P \right) \right] \left[\widehat{m} \left(\mathbf{x}_i \widehat{\beta}_{SP} \right) - m_P \left(\mathbf{x}_i \widehat{\beta}_P \right) \right],$$

and Horowitz and Härdle (1994) show that after proper normalization that this test is distributed as a standard normal under the null hypothesis. Horowitz and Härdle (1994) suggest multiplying the terms to the right of the summation by a weighting function to improve power, but we prefer to rely on the bootstrap method, for which the weighting is not essential. In fact, Proença (1993) shows that there are size distortions when using the asymptotic distribution and the test is sensitive to the choice of the weighting function. She also found that using a bootstrap improved the size of the test in finite samples.

Before turning to the bootstrap procedure, we want to emphasize that this test is much more general. In a well cited working paper, Rodriguez and Stoker (1993) argue that it is feasible that we can test between a parametric and semiparametric single-index estimator (as shown above), a parametric versus a nonparametric estimator, or a semiparametric single index versus a nonparametric estimator. Each of the three tests only requires replacing the estimates of the conditional mean in (9.7) with the appropriate estimates. Then a bootstrap can be performed by resampling under the null distribution as we discuss below.

As we have done so repeatedly, we suggest using a two-point wild bootstrap for constructing p-values in practice. We write the steps in a very general format. What is left is for you to choose the null and alternative models and then place the corresponding elements into the procedure. The bootstrap is as follows:

1. Compute the test statistics $\widehat{J}_n$ for the original sample of $\{\mathbf{x}_1, \mathbf{x}_2, \ldots, \mathbf{x}_n\}$ and $\{y_1, y_2, \ldots, y_n\}$ and save the re-centered residuals $\widehat{u}_i - \overline{\widehat{u}}, i = 1, 2, \ldots, n$ from the model estimated under the null.
2. For each observation i, construct the bootstrapped residual u_i^*, where $u_i^* = \frac{1-\sqrt{5}}{2} \left(\widehat{u}_i - \overline{\widehat{u}} \right)$ with probability $\frac{1+\sqrt{5}}{2\sqrt{5}}$ and $u_i^* = \frac{1+\sqrt{5}}{2} \left(\widehat{u}_i - \overline{\widehat{u}} \right)$ with probability $1 - \frac{1+\sqrt{5}}{2\sqrt{5}}$. Construct the bootstrapped left-hand-side variable by adding the bootstrapped residuals to the fitted values under the null. Call $\left\{ y_i^*, \mathbf{x}_i \right\}_{i=1}^{n}$ the bootstrap sample.
3. Calculate $\widehat{J}_n^*$ where $\widehat{J}_n^*$ is calculated the same way as $\widehat{J}_n$, except that y_i is replaced by y_i^*.
4. Repeat steps 2 and 3 a large number (B) of times and then construct the sampling distribution of the bootstrapped test statistics. We reject the null hypothesis if the (absolute value of the) estimated test statistic $\left| \widehat{J}_n \right|$ is greater than the upper α-percentile of the bootstrapped test statistics.

Finally, it is possible to eschew semiparametric single-index models altogether and resort to conditional density estimation for discrete-choice models. In this case, a bootstrap-based test is available in Fan, Li, and Min (2006). Their test is designed to be an extension of Zheng's (2000) test to allow for discrete left-hand-side variables (as well as mixed conditioning variables). Their test allows you to compare, for example, a probit model versus a completely nonparametric alternative. The difference is that we are using a nonparametric conditional-density estimator. This may appear strange, but the primary benefit is that the nonparametric estimator here explicitly takes into account that the dependent variable is binary. The test above for the case of probit versus a completely nonparametric alternative estimated via a regression would not.

9.4 Semiparametric smooth coefficient models

SPSCM are becoming an increasingly popular form of semiparametric regression. The basic motivation for these models is that you may be comfortable with the linear in **x** structure of your model, but not the homogeneity of the coefficients in the model. For example, you may be willing to accept the Cobb–Douglas specification, but do not believe that the elasticities are constant across countries, varying perhaps with institutional quality or the amount of foreign direct investment in the country. While allowing the coefficients to depend in an unspecified fashion on a set of covariates may seem to complicate the understanding of the model, as noted in Asaftei and Parmeter (2010), the SPSCM allows you to think of your model as being conditionally parametric.

The smooth coefficient model is also intuitive from an economic theory standpoint. For example, assume you wanted to estimate a production function. We typically model output as a function of inputs, such as physical capital and labor. What we often see in the literature is a production function being modeled as output versus both inputs (physical capital, labor, etc.) and control variables (R&D expenditure, environmental regulation, etc.). We often see this model because authors are worried about omitted variable bias. However, we learned in basic microeconomics that output is function of inputs, but we never recall R&D expenditure being an input in the production function. Here we argue that R&D expenditure can affect output indirectly through the coefficients on physical capital and labor. In other words, the marginal productivities of physical capital and labor may depend on R&D expenditure. A fully nonparametric model does not distinguish from the outset which variables are inputs and which are "conditioning variables" in the production function, and a PLM would treat physical capital and labor as inputs and would only allow R&D expenditure to shift the production function (with no interactions between the inputs and R&D expenditure).

We start our discussion with the most general model presented in Hastie and Tibshirani (1993). In their model they assume that the regressors enter linearly, but the coefficients are allowed to vary. The most general smooth coefficient model is

$$y_i = \alpha(\mathbf{z}_{0i}) + x_{1i}\beta_1(\mathbf{z}_{1i}) + x_{2i}\beta_2(\mathbf{z}_{2i}) + \cdots + x_{pi}\beta_p(\mathbf{z}_{pi}) + u_i,$$

for the p regressors $\mathbf{x} = \{x_1, x_2, \ldots, x_p\}$ and $(p+1)$ "conditioning" variables $\{\mathbf{z}_0, \mathbf{z}_1, \ldots, \mathbf{z}_p\}$, where the dth element $\mathbf{z}_d$ is a $(1 \times q_d)$ vector. The dependence of $\beta(\cdot)$ on the conditioning variables can be viewed as a type of interaction between the conditioning variables and the regressors. The conditioning variables here are allowed to vary in each smooth coefficient and it also allows the conditioning variables and regressors to be nested, but this makes estimation difficult.

Li, Huang, Li, and Fu (2002) consider a simplification of the Hastie and Tibshirani (1993) model. In their model they do not allow the variables to be nested and they further assume that the conditioning variables are the same vector for all smooth coefficients. In other words, the simplest model of Li, Huang, Li, and Fu (2002) assumes that $z_0 = z_1 = \cdots = z_p = z$. This more familiar smooth coefficient model is

$$y_i = \alpha(z_i) + x_{1i}\beta_1(z_i) + x_{2i}\beta_2(z_i) + \cdots + x_{pi}\beta_p(z_i) + u_i,$$

which in matrix form is

$$y_i = X_i\delta(z_i) + u_i, \tag{9.8}$$

where $X_i = \left(1, x_{1i}, x_{2i}, \ldots, x_{pi}\right)$ and $\delta(z_i) = \left(\alpha(z_i), \beta_1(z_i), \beta_2(z_i), \ldots, \beta_p(z_i)\right)'$, where $z_i = \left(z_{1i}, z_{2i}, \ldots, z_{qi}\right)'$ is a $(q \times 1)$ vector. The curse of dimensionality still applies here, but it is with respect to q and not p.

Prior to discussing estimation of the SPSCM in (9.8), we note here that parametric versions are common and many of you most likely have familiarity with this style of model. Consider the simple example of a bivariate regression model in x and z that contains an interaction. Here we have

$$y_i = \alpha_0 + \alpha_1 x_i + \alpha_2 z_i + \alpha_3 x_i z_i + u_i,$$

which can be rewritten as

$$y_i = (\alpha_0 + \alpha_2 z_i) + (\alpha_1 + \alpha_3 z_i) x_i + u_i = \alpha(z_i) + \beta_1(z_i)x_i + u_i.$$

Notice that for a fixed value of z_i, we can interpret our model as we would with a standard linear-in-parameters model. Our SPSCM in (9.8) merely drops the functional form for the coefficients of the model, but retains the parametric flavor that many applied researchers desire.

We note here that these methods are widely used in statistics (see Cleveland, Grosse, and Shyu, 1991, and Hastie and Tibshirani, 1993) and have been extended in many directions. Of particular interest to some of you may be the time series case discussed in Robinson (1989) and Chen and Tsay (1993) or the more efficient estimation procedures in Cai, Fan, and Li (2000) and Fan and Zhang (1999). Partially linear smooth coefficient models have been developed in Ahmad, Leelahanon, and Li (2005); Fan and Huang (2005); and Zhang, Lee, and Song (2002). Cai, Das, Xiong, and Wu (2006) allow for endogenous regressors in a smooth coefficient model and develop a semiparametric IV estimator for the varying coefficients. Finally, Li and Racine (2010) and Su, Chen, and Ullah (2009) consider smooth coefficient models in the presence of discrete data. This is but a mere subsample of the extensions which exist, but we believe these are some of the most relevant citations for use in applied econometric work. Note that we are unaware of economic applications for several of these references.

9.4.1 Estimation

Coefficient estimation

To estimate the SPSCM in (9.8) we use a kernel-weighted least-squares approach. The goal is to minimize the kernel-weighted sum of squared residuals as

$$\sum_{i=1}^{n} \widehat{u}_i^2 K_{h_z}(\mathbf{z}_i, \mathbf{z}) = \sum_{i=1}^{n} \left[y_i - X_i \widehat{\delta}(\mathbf{z}) \right]^2 K_{h_z}(\mathbf{z}_i, \mathbf{z}),$$

where the $\mathbf{z}$ variables enter in the product kernel function. Taking the first-order condition with respect to the $(p+1) \times 1$ varying coefficient vector and solving for $\widehat{\delta}(\mathbf{z})$ yields

$$\widehat{\delta}(\mathbf{z}) = \left[\sum_{i=1}^{n} X_i' X_i K_{h_z}(\mathbf{z}_i, \mathbf{z}) \right]^{-1} \sum_{i=1}^{n} X_i' y_i K_{h_z}(\mathbf{z}_i, \mathbf{z}).$$

In matrix notation, we have

$$\widehat{\delta}(\mathbf{z}) = \left[X' K(\mathbf{z}) X \right]^{-1} X' K(\mathbf{z}) y,$$

where X is the $n \times (p+1)$ matrix of regressors, $K(\mathbf{z})$ is the diagonal matrix of kernel weights with ith element $K_{h_z}(\mathbf{z}_i, \mathbf{z})$ and y is the $n \times 1$ vector of responses. Notice that if we re-write X as a column of ones, we have a LCLS regression of y on $\mathbf{z}$. If instead, the kernel matrix is an identity matrix (no smoothing), we have the OLS estimator of y on X.

The conditions for consistency of the varying coefficients are similar to what we saw with nonparametric regression. Li, Huang, Li, and Fu (2002) show that when $h_z \to 0$ and $n h_{z_1} h_{z_2} \cdots h_{z_q} \to \infty$ as $n \to \infty$, that the the SPSCM model is consistent and asymptotically normal in distribution. Notice that this is a LCLS approach as we only obtain the coefficients and not their gradients.

We now turn our attention to a LLLS estimator of the smooth coefficients. As we know, local-linear estimators have many nice properties, such as higher efficiency and good boundary behavior. Further, for application purposes, we can estimate the gradient of $\widehat{\delta}(\mathbf{z})$ directly, which will be useful when we want to examine partial effects with respect to $\mathbf{z}$. Following papers such as Cai, Fan, and Li (2000), Cai, Fan, and Yao (2000) and Lee and Ullah (2001), if we take a first-order Taylor expansion of (9.8) with respect to $\mathbf{z}$ we obtain

$$y_i \approx X_i \left[\delta(\mathbf{z}) + (\mathbf{z}_i - \mathbf{z}) \frac{\partial \delta(\mathbf{z})}{\partial \mathbf{z}} \right] + u_i$$

$$= [X_i, (\mathbf{z}_i - \mathbf{z}) \otimes X_i] \begin{bmatrix} \delta(\mathbf{z}) \\ \frac{\partial \delta(\mathbf{z})}{\partial \mathbf{z}} \end{bmatrix} + u_i,$$

where $\otimes$ is the Kroneker product. The LLLS estimator is thus given as

$$\begin{bmatrix} \delta(\mathbf{z}) \\ \frac{\partial \delta(\mathbf{z})}{\partial \mathbf{z}} \end{bmatrix} = \left[\mathcal{X}' K(\mathbf{z}) \mathcal{X} \right]^{-1} \mathcal{X}' K(\mathbf{z}) y,$$

where $\mathcal{X}_i \equiv [X_i, (\mathbf{z}_i - \mathbf{z}) \otimes X_i]$ is the ith row of $\mathcal{X}$. The only difference between the two procedures is that the LLLS estimator also includes the additional elements

$(\mathbf{z}_i - \mathbf{z}) \otimes X_i$. This will only require minor modifications in programming code. Although the LCLS estimator is more popular in the literature, we recommend the LLLS estimator in practice.

Partial effects

The discussion of partial effects is somewhat more complicated in the SPSCM world, as we have an additional dimension of complexity. We not only need to look over $\mathbf{x}$, but we also need to look over $\mathbf{z}$. Our goal here will be to look at two separate types of partial effects. Specifically, we are interested in the effects of a change in $\mathbf{x}$ on $\widehat{y}$, $\partial \widehat{y}/\partial \mathbf{x}$, as well as the effect of a change in $\mathbf{z}$ on $\widehat{y}$, $\partial \widehat{y}/\partial \mathbf{z}$. The former is trivial. The latter also requires us to estimate $\partial \widehat{\delta}(\mathbf{z})/\partial \mathbf{z}$.

We have seen how to estimate the gradient of the varying coefficient for the LLLS estimator, so we first describe how to calculate this for the LCLS estimator of the SPSCM. If we are interested in obtaining $\partial \widehat{\delta}(\mathbf{z})/\partial \mathbf{z}$ for a particular element of $\mathbf{z}$, say z_d, we begin by defining the first-order derivative of the kernel function for a particular $\mathbf{z}$, say z_d, at a point i. If we assume we have a Gaussian kernel, this is defined as

$$\frac{\partial K_{h_z}(\mathbf{z}_i, \mathbf{z})}{\partial z_d} = \left(\frac{\mathbf{z}_{di} - \mathbf{z}_d}{h_d^2}\right) K_{h_z}(\mathbf{z}_i, \mathbf{z})$$

For the diagonal matrix $K(\mathbf{z})$, this becomes

$$\frac{\partial K(\mathbf{z})}{\partial z_d} = \mathrm{diag}\left[\left(\frac{z_{d1} - z_d}{h_d^2}\right) K_{h_z}(\mathbf{z}_1, \mathbf{z}), \left(\frac{z_{d2} - z_d}{h_d^2}\right) K_{h_z}(\mathbf{z}_2, \mathbf{z}),\right.$$
$$\left. \cdots, \left(\frac{z_{dn} - z_d}{h_d^2}\right) K_{h_z}(\mathbf{z}_n, \mathbf{z})\right],$$

where *diag* denotes the diagonal elements of the diagonal matrix $K(\mathbf{z})$. We can now define the first-order derivative of the smooth coefficient as

$$\frac{\partial \widehat{\delta}(\mathbf{z})}{\partial z_d} = \frac{\partial \left[X'K(\mathbf{z})X\right]^{-1} X'K(\mathbf{z})y}{\partial z_d}$$

$$= \frac{\partial \left[X'K(\mathbf{z})X\right]^{-1}}{\partial z_d} \left[X'K(\mathbf{z})y\right] + \left[X'K(\mathbf{z})X\right]^{-1} \frac{\partial X'K(\mathbf{z})y}{\partial z_d}$$

$$= \left\{-\left[X'K(\mathbf{z})X\right]^{-1} \left[X'\frac{\partial K(\mathbf{z})}{\partial z_d}X\right] \left[X'K(\mathbf{z})X\right]^{-1}\right\} \left[X'K(\mathbf{z})y\right]$$

$$+ \left[X'K(\mathbf{z})X\right]^{-1} \left[X'\frac{\partial K(\mathbf{z})}{\partial z_d}y\right].$$

Now that we have shown how to obtain the gradient vector of the smooth coefficients with respect to both the LCLS and LLLS estimators, we can proceed to look at the partial effects. If we are interested in the change in the (estimate of the) expected value of y with respect to a change in a particular element of $\mathbf{x}$, say x_d, the partial effect is defined as

$$\frac{\partial \widehat{y}}{\partial x_d} = \widehat{\beta}_d (\mathbf{z}),$$

which is a function of $\mathbf{z}$, but not of x_d (or any other $\mathbf{x}$, for that matter).

The options for reporting the results for these partial effects mirror those we looked at in Chapter 5. We can report the mean and/or quartiles, or we can plot the kernel density of the n partial effects evaluated at the values of $\mathbf{z}$ for each observation i. In the case of a univariate $\mathbf{z}$, it is possible to plot $\widehat{\beta}_d (\mathbf{z})$ versus $\mathbf{z}$ to see how the coefficient changes over $\mathbf{z}$.

The more complicated partial effect comes from estimating the effect of a change in a particular $\mathbf{z}$, say z_d, on $\widehat{y}$,

$$\frac{\partial \widehat{y}}{\partial z_d} = X \frac{\partial \widehat{\delta} (\mathbf{z})}{\partial z_d}.$$

Recall that the restricted model of Li, Huang, Li, and Fu (2002) assumes that the $\mathbf{z}$s are the same in each of the $p + 1$ varying coefficients. Therefore, it is necessary to look at each element of $\partial \widehat{\delta} (\mathbf{z}) / \partial z_d$ when calculating the partial effect.

Although this is relatively straightforward, it is more complicated when you want to present the partial effects because this partial effect depends both on $\mathbf{x}$ and $\mathbf{z}$. In fact, it depends upon each element of $\mathbf{x}$ and each element of $\mathbf{z}$. Specifically, we suggest calculating

$$\frac{\partial \widehat{y}_i}{\partial z_{id}} = X_i \frac{\partial \widehat{\delta} (\mathbf{z}_i)}{\partial z_{id}}$$

$$= \frac{\partial \widehat{\alpha} (\mathbf{z}_i)}{\partial z_d} + x_{1i} \frac{\partial \widehat{\beta}_1 (\mathbf{z}_i)}{\partial z_d} + x_{2i} \frac{\partial \widehat{\beta}_2 (\mathbf{z}_i)}{\partial z_d} + \cdots + x_{pi} \frac{\partial \widehat{\beta}_p (\mathbf{z}_i)}{\partial z_d},$$

as this leaves us with n partial effects, which is relatively manageable.

If you decide to report the mean and/or quartile estimates, it will also be important to calculate the wild bootstrapped standard errors. The steps are as follows:

1. Let $\widehat{u}_i = y_i - X_i \widehat{\delta} (\mathbf{z}_i)$ be the residual from the SPSCM (either LCLS or LLLS). Construct the re-centered residual as $\widehat{u}_i - n^{-1} \sum_{i=1}^n \widehat{u}_i = \widehat{u}_i - \overline{\widehat{u}}$.
2. Compute the two-point wild bootstrap errors by $u_i^* = \{(1 - \sqrt{5})/2\} (\widehat{u}_i - \overline{\widehat{u}})$ with probability $(1 + \sqrt{5})/(2\sqrt{5})$ and $u_i^* = \{(1 + \sqrt{5})/2\} (\widehat{u}_i - \overline{\widehat{u}})$ with probability $1 - (1 + \sqrt{5})/(2\sqrt{5})$. Generate y_i^* via $y_i^* = X_i \widehat{\delta} (\mathbf{z}_i) + u_i^*$. Call $\{y_i^*, \mathbf{x}_i, \mathbf{z}_i\}_{i=1}^n$ the bootstrap sample.
3. Using the bootstrap sample, estimate the smooth coefficient $\widehat{\delta}^* (\mathbf{z}_i)$, its gradient $\partial \widehat{\delta}^* (\mathbf{z}_i) / \partial \mathbf{z}_i$, as well as each of the partial effects via the SPSCM where y_i is replaced by y_i^* wherever it occurs. Remember that we use the data $\mathbf{x}_i$ and $\mathbf{z}_i$ and evaluate at the same values of $\mathbf{x}$ and $\mathbf{z}$ that we did initially.
4. Repeat steps 2 and 3 a large number (B) of times and then construct the sampling distribution of the bootstrapped point estimates. Standard errors can be obtained by taking the standard deviation of the sampling distribution for each particular estimate.

9.4.2 Bandwidth selection

Automated bandwidth selection is relatively straightforward. The goal is to minimize the cross-validation function with respect to the bandwidths $h_{z_1}, h_{z_2}, \ldots, h_{z_q}$. Formally, the cross-validation function is given as

$$\text{CV}(h_z) = \sum_{i=1}^{n} \left(y_i - X_i \widehat{\delta}_{-i}(\mathbf{z}_i) \right)^2,$$

where $\widehat{\delta}_{-i}(\cdot)$ is the leave-one-out estimator of $\delta(\cdot)$ and is defined as

$$\widehat{\delta}_{-i}(\mathbf{z}_i) = \left[\sum_{\substack{j=1 \\ j \neq i}}^{n} X_j' X_j K_{h_z}(\mathbf{z}_j, \mathbf{z}_i) \right]^{-1} \sum_{\substack{j=1 \\ j \neq i}}^{n} X_j' y_j K_{h_z}(\mathbf{z}_j, \mathbf{z}_i)$$

for the LCLS estimator. The leave-one-out estimator is similarly defined for the LLLS case.

9.4.3 Testing

When considering tests of the SPSCM for correct functional form specification, it is possible to think of at least three types of tests. The first is for a correctly specified parametric varying coefficient model versus the SPSCM. Li, Huang, Li, and Fu (2002) provide a test for the first null hypothesis, while Li and Racine (2010) consider a similar test in the mixed-discrete and continuous-variable case. Fan, Zhang, and Zhang (2001) consider a goodness-of-fit test along the lines of what was proposed by Cai, Fan, and Yao (2000) and Ullah (1985).

The second test would be for whether or not the true coefficients actually vary with $\mathbf{z}$. Cai, Fan, and Li (2000) consider a test for this hypothesis using a likelihood ratio test, but we did not discuss their estimator. However, we can think of a similar test along the lines of the goodness-of-fit tests in Cai, Fan, and Yao (2000) or Ullah (1985). The Li and Racine (2010) approach to detecting irrelevant $\mathbf{z}$ variables (in this case all of them) is not valid here because they require at least one relevant continuous $\mathbf{z}$. It is unclear what happens when all of the $\mathbf{z}$ variables are irrelevant.

The third test would be for a correctly specified SPSCM versus a nonparametric model. However, we are unaware of a formal test designed specifically for this null hypothesis in the literature. That being said, it is not difficult to apply the goodness-of-fit test here or to use the Li and Wang (1998) test in this scenario. Here we will consider goodness-of-fit tests to test all three types.

To begin, let's specify each particular null and alternative hypothesis. For the first test the null is that the parametric varying coefficient model is correctly specified versus the alternative that it is a SPSCM. Formally, our null is

$$H_0 : \delta(\mathbf{z}) = \delta(\mathbf{z}, \eta),$$

versus the alternative that

$$H_1 : \delta\left(\mathbf{z}\right) \neq \delta\left(\mathbf{z}, \eta\right),$$

where $\delta\left(\mathbf{z}, \eta\right)$ is a specific parametric form. For example, let's assume that there is (a scalar x and) a simple interaction term z with coefficient ψ. Our parametric model becomes

$$
\begin{aligned}
y &= \alpha + \beta x + \psi x z + u \\
&= (\iota, x)\,\delta\left(z, \eta\right) + u,
\end{aligned}
$$

where ι is an $n \times 1$ vector of ones and $\delta\left(z, \eta\right) = [\alpha, \beta + \psi z]'$. We recognize that this is only one particular way that the coefficient can depend upon z, which emphasizes that this test only corresponds to the null of whether or not a particular parametric specification is correct.

The second null hypothesis is that each of the varying coefficients is fixed. In other words, we are interested in testing whether $\delta\left(\mathbf{z}\right) = \left(\alpha\left(\mathbf{z}\right), \beta_1\left(\mathbf{z}\right), \beta_2\left(\mathbf{z}\right), \ldots, \beta_p\left(\mathbf{z}\right)\right)'$ $= \left(\alpha, \beta_1, \beta_2, \ldots, \beta_p\right) = \delta$. Formally, our null hypothesis is

$$H_0 : \delta\left(\mathbf{z}\right) = \delta,$$

versus the alternative that

$$H_1 : \delta\left(\mathbf{z}\right) \neq \delta$$

on a set with positive measure. The null hypothesis corresponds to a simple linear regression of y on $\mathbf{x}$.

Finally, we may be interested in knowing whether the SPSCM model is correctly specified as compared to a nonparametric alternative. In this scenario the null hypothesis is that the conditional mean is a SPSCM. Formally, the null hypothesis is

$$H_0 : E\left(y|\mathbf{x}, \mathbf{z}\right) = X\delta\left(\mathbf{z}\right),$$

versus the alternative that

$$H_1 : E\left(y|\mathbf{x}, \mathbf{z}\right) = \theta\left(\mathbf{x}, \mathbf{z}\right),$$

where recall that $\theta\left(\mathbf{x}, \mathbf{z}\right)$ is the unknown smooth function which, is estimated via a nonparametric regression of y on $\mathbf{x}$ and $\mathbf{z}$. There are many reasons why we may reject the SPSCM. First, the additive structure of the regressors may be inappropriate. Second, the smooth coefficients may not be multiplicative. For example, we could envision a scenario where the $\mathbf{x}$s should be raised to the power of $\beta\left(\mathbf{z}\right)$. Regardless of the reason, this alternative is consistent in each direction.

If we denote the residuals under the null hypothesis as $\widehat{u}$ and the residuals under the alternative as $\widetilde{u}$, then we can formulate our test statistic as

$$\widehat{J}_n = \frac{\sum_{i=1}^{n} \widehat{u}_i^2 - \sum_{i=1}^{n} \widetilde{u}_i^2}{\sum_{i=1}^{n} \widetilde{u}_i^2}.$$

Here we discuss the generic bootstrap procedure for the goodness-of-fit test. Formally, the steps for the two-point wild bootstrap procedure are as follows:

1. Compute the test statistics $\widehat{J}_n$ for the original sample of $\{\mathbf{x}_1, \mathbf{x}_2, \ldots, \mathbf{x}_n\}$, $\{\mathbf{z}_1, \mathbf{z}_2, \ldots, \mathbf{z}_n\}$ and $\{y_1, y_2, \ldots, y_n\}$ and save the re-centered residuals $\widehat{u}_i - \overline{\widehat{u}}$, $i = 1, 2, \ldots, n$ from the model estimated under the null.
2. For each observation i, construct the bootstrapped residual u_i^*, where $u_i^* = \frac{1-\sqrt{5}}{2}\left(\widehat{u}_i - \overline{\widehat{u}}\right)$ with probability $\left(1 + \sqrt{5}\right)/2\sqrt{5}$ and $u_i^* = \frac{1+\sqrt{5}}{2}\left(\widehat{u}_i - \overline{\widehat{u}}\right)$ with probability $1 - \left(1 + \sqrt{5}\right)/2\sqrt{5}$. Construct the bootstrapped left-hand-side variable by adding the bootstrapped residuals to the fitted values under the null. Call $\left\{y_i^*, \mathbf{x}_i, \mathbf{z}_i\right\}_{i=1}^n$ the bootstrap sample.
3. Calculate $\widehat{J}_n^*$ where $\widehat{J}_n^*$ is calculated the same way as $\widehat{J}_n$, except that y_i is replaced by y_i^*.
4. Repeat steps 2 and 3 a large number (B) of times and then construct the sampling distribution of the bootstrapped test statistics. We reject the null that the parametric model is correctly specified if the estimated test statistic $\widehat{J}_n$ is greater than the upper α-percentile of the bootstrapped test statistics.

9.5 Additive models

For our final form of semiparametric regression, we look at additive nonparametric models. Even though the name includes the term "nonparametric," we think of it as a semiparametric model because it places structure on the model to lessen the nonparametric dimension. Specifically, we make the assumption that the regressors enter the model in an additively separable fashion. That is, we assume that there are no interactions among the regressors.

Additively separable nonparametric models allow regressors to enter nonparametrically, but separate from each other, hence avoiding the curse of dimensionality. Here we focus on the oracle nonparametric additive estimator of Kim, Linton, and Hengartner (1999). This estimator gets its name from its achievement of the "oracle-efficiency" level, which means each additive component can be estimated with the same asymptotic accuracy as if all the other components were known except a scalar and the function of interest (Horowitz, 2009). We consider both LCLS and LLLS estimators of both the conditional mean and gradients.

In addition to estimation, we also discuss bandwidth selection, calculating standard errors, and testing (albeit in a terse manner as to avoid too much repetitiveness). Although we focus on the estimator attribed to Kim, Linton, and Hengartner (1999), alternative estimators exist and include Martins-Filho and Yang (2007), who suggest modifications to Kim, Linton, and Hengartner's (1999) conditional mean estimator in the identically distributed multi dimensional case; Linton and Mammen (2008), who consider the conditional mean estimator in the weakly dependent single-dimensional case; and Cai (2002), who uses a two-step conditional-mean estimator in the weakly dependent case (noting that his estimator is closer to Linton 1997, 2000). For those interested in a recent review article (which includes extensions to existing models), we suggest Mammen, Park, and Schienle (2014).

9.5.1 Estimation

Assuming additive separability of the unknown conditional mean implies

$$m(\mathbf{x}) = c + m_1(x_1) + m_2(x_2) + \cdots + m_q(x_q),$$

where the left-hand side is the conditional mean function, c is a constant term, each scalar element in $\mathbf{x} \equiv (x_1, x_2, \ldots, x_q)$ is a continuous variable and each element in $m(\cdot)$ on the right-hand side is a smooth function of the corresponding element of $\mathbf{x}$. Stone (1985) proved that the optimal rate of convergence in the additive model is independent of the number of regressors. This circumvents the curse-of-dimensionality problem.

The two most common kernel-based methods used for estimating models of this kind are marginal integration (Linton and Nielsen, 1995; Newey, 1994; Tjøstheim and Auestad, 1994) and backfitting methods (Buja, Hastie, and Tibshirani, 1989). The estimator in Kim, Linton, and Hengartner (1999) is a combination of these two methods. This method is efficient and possesses computational advantages over marginal integration methods.

In short, this method requires two steps: the first is marginal integration and the second is backfitting. The first step estimator is consistent, but not efficient. The second stage estimator allows for efficient estimation. In other words, we estimate each component as if we knew the true values of the other components.

Conditional mean

In the additive model, the left-hand-side variable is a smooth additive function of the right-hand-side variables

$$y = c + m_1(x_1) + m_2(x_2) + \cdots + m_q(x_q) + u,$$

where we separate x_1 from all other regressors for ease in exposition. In what follows we will use the notation $\mathbf{x}_{-1} \equiv (x_2, x_3, \ldots, x_q)$ to represent all regressors, except for x_1 and similarly, $m_{-1}(\mathbf{x}_{-1}) \equiv m_2(x_2) + \cdots + m_q(x_q)$. u is our mean zero additive error. For identification, it is typically assumed that $E[m_1(x_1)] = E[m_{-1}(\mathbf{x}_{-1})] = 0$ (where each element in $m_{-1}(\mathbf{x}_{-1})$ is assumed to be zero in expectation) and hence $E(y) = c$, our intercept term.

First stage. If we estimate the conditional mean of y given x_1 in a nonparametric fashion, we have that

$$E(y|x_1) = c + m_1(x_1) + E[m_{-1}(\mathbf{x}_{-1})|x_1].$$

The final term $E[m_{-1}(\mathbf{x}_{-1})|x_1]$ creates a bias in the estimation. In order to eliminate this bias, Kim, Linton, and Hengartner (1999) propose an instrument function, $w(x_1, \mathbf{x}_{-1})$, such that

$$E\left[w\left(x_1, \mathbf{x}_{-1}\right)|x_1\right] = 1$$
$$E\left[w\left(x_1, \mathbf{x}_{-1}\right)m_{-1}\left(\mathbf{x}_{-1}\right)|x_1\right] = 0.$$

If we have such an instrument, then it can be shown that

$$E\left[w(x_1, \mathbf{x}_{-1})y|x_1\right] = c + m_1(x_1). \tag{9.9}$$

The exact instrument they propose is

$$w(x_1, \mathbf{x}_{-1}) = \frac{f_{x_1}\left(x_1\right) f_{\mathbf{x}_{-1}}\left(\mathbf{x}_{-1}\right)}{f_{x_1, \mathbf{x}_{-1}}\left(x_1, \mathbf{x}_{-1}\right)} = \frac{f_{x_1}\left(x_1\right) f_{\mathbf{x}_{-1}}\left(\mathbf{x}_{-1}\right)}{f_{\mathbf{x}}\left(\mathbf{x}\right)},$$

where $f_{x_1}\left(x_1\right)$, $f_{\mathbf{x}_{-1}}\left(\mathbf{x}_{-1}\right)$ and $f_{\mathbf{x}}\left(\mathbf{x}\right)$ are the marginal, leave-one-variable-out and joint-probability densities, respectively. We can think of these instruments as a measure of the degree of independence between the regressors. Note that in the case where x_1 is independent from $\mathbf{x}_{-1}$, $w(\cdot, \cdot) = 1$.

$w(x_1, \mathbf{x}_{-1})$ is a valid instrument given that

$$\int w\left(x_1, \mathbf{x}_{-1}\right) \frac{f_{x_1, \mathbf{x}_{-1}}\left(x_1, \mathbf{x}_{-1}\right)}{f_{x_1}\left(x_1\right)} d\mathbf{x}_{-1} = \int f_{\mathbf{x}_{-1}}\left(\mathbf{x}_{-1}\right) d\mathbf{x}_{-1} = 1$$

and

$$\int w\left(x_1, \mathbf{x}_{-1}\right) m_{-1}\left(\mathbf{x}_{-1}\right) \frac{f_{x_1, \mathbf{x}_{-1}}\left(x_1, \mathbf{x}_{-1}\right)}{f_{x_1}\left(x_1\right)} d\mathbf{x}_{-1} = \int m_{-1}\left(\mathbf{x}_{-1}\right) f_{\mathbf{x}_{-1}}\left(\mathbf{x}_{-1}\right) d\mathbf{x}_{-1} = 0.$$

In practice, we estimate the instruments with standard kernel-density estimators. We estimate (9.9) by choosing a method that eliminates the random denominator term. Formally, if we have n observations for y, x_1 and $\mathbf{x}_{-1}$, $\{y_i, x_{1i}, \mathbf{x}_{-1i}\}_{i=1}^n$, our estimator of (9.9), which we define as $\gamma_1\left(\cdot\right)$ is

$$\widehat{\gamma_1}\left(x_{1i}\right) = \frac{1}{nh_{11}} \sum_{j=1}^n k\left(\frac{x_{1j} - x_{1i}}{h_{11}}\right) \frac{\widehat{f}_{\mathbf{x}_{-1}}\left(\mathbf{x}_{-1j}\right)}{\widehat{f}_{\mathbf{x}}\left(\mathbf{x}_j\right)} y_j, \tag{9.10}$$

where $k\left(\cdot\right)$ is our univariate kernel function with scalar bandwidth h_{11} (where the 1 and 1 in the subscript signifies that this is the first stage estimator with respect to the first right-hand-side variable (x_1) and our kernel estimators of the leave-one-out and joint densities are

$$\widehat{f}_{\mathbf{x}_{-1}}\left(\mathbf{x}_{-1j}\right) = \frac{1}{n\left|\mathbf{h}_{1-1}\right|} \sum_{i=1}^n K_{h_{1-1}}\left(\mathbf{x}_{-1i}, \mathbf{x}_{-1j}\right)$$

and

$$\widehat{f}_{\mathbf{x}}\left(\mathbf{x}_j\right) = \frac{1}{n\left|\mathbf{h}\right|} \sum_{i=1}^n K_h\left(\mathbf{x}_i, \mathbf{x}_j\right),$$

where $K_{h_{1-1}}\left(\mathbf{x}_{-1j}, \mathbf{x}_{-1}\right)$ is the product kernel for the data $\mathbf{x}_{-1}$ and $\left|\mathbf{h}_{1-1}\right| \equiv \left(h_{12}h_{13}\cdots h_{1q}\right)$ is the product of the remaining $q - 1$ bandwidths for the first stage regression.

Each element of $\widehat{\gamma}_{-1}(\mathbf{x}_{-1})$ is similarly estimated by interchanging terms as necessary. For example, the first-stage estimator of $\gamma_2(x_2)$ (at the point x_{2i}) is

$$\widehat{\gamma}_2(x_{2i}) = \frac{1}{nh_{12}} \sum_{j=1}^{n} k\left(\frac{x_{2j} - x_{2i}}{h_{12}}\right) \frac{\widehat{f}_{\mathbf{x}_{-2}}(\mathbf{x}_{-2j})}{\widehat{f}_{\mathbf{x}}(\mathbf{x}_j)} y_j,$$

where $\mathbf{x}_{-2} \equiv (x_1, x_3, x_4, \ldots, x_q)$.

Martins-Filho and Yang (2007) note that this estimator does not produce an equivalent kernel vector that sums to one. They propose an alternative first-stage estimator, which they show has better finite sample performance. In short, this requires that the estimator subtract the sample average of y ($\overline{y}$). The first stage estimator of $\gamma_1(x_1)$ then becomes

$$\widetilde{\gamma}_1(x_1) = \frac{1}{nh_{11}} \sum_{j=1}^{n} k\left(\frac{x_{1j} - x_1}{h_{11}}\right) \frac{\widehat{f}_{\mathbf{x}_{-1}}(\mathbf{x}_{-1j})}{\widehat{f}_{\mathbf{x}}(\mathbf{x}_j)} (y_j - \overline{y}).$$

Second stage. Regardless of what method you choose to estimate each component of $\gamma(\cdot)$, to obtain an efficient estimator, we require an additional step. The idea of the second-step (backfitting) originates from the oracle efficiency principle. Our backfitting procedure proceeds as follows. Assume that we know $m_{-1}(\mathbf{x}_{-1})$. In order to estimate $m_1(x_1)$ efficiently, we first construct y_1^{oracle}, which is a partial residual obtained assuming $m_{-1}(\mathbf{x}_{-1})$ is known,

$$y_{1i}^{oracle} = y_i - m_{-1}(\mathbf{x}_{-1i}) - c.$$

We would then run a nonparametric regression of y_1^{oracle} (or $y_1^{oracle} - \overline{y}$ under the advice of Martins-Filho and Yang, 2007) on x_1 (say via LCLS) as

$$\widehat{m}_1^{oracle}(x_1) = \frac{\sum_{j=1}^{n} k\left(\frac{x_{1j} - x_1}{h_{21}}\right) y_{1j}^{oracle}}{\sum_{j=1}^{n} k\left(\frac{x_{1j} - x_1}{h_{21}}\right)}$$

and this is our oracle estimator (where h_{21} is our second-stage bandwidth for x_1). The LLLS estimator can be calculated similarly (a LLLS regression of y_1^{oracle} on x_1).

Of course $m_{-1}(\mathbf{x}_{-1})$ and c are unknown, and thus this estimator is infeasible. We can replace c with the sample mean of y and $m_{-1}(\mathbf{x}_{-1}) + c$ with $\widehat{\gamma}_{-1}(\mathbf{x}_{-1})$. The feasible version of y_1^{oracle} (y_1^{2-step}) is constructed as

$$y_{1i}^{2-step} = y_i - \widehat{\gamma}_{-1}(\mathbf{x}_{-1i}). \tag{9.11}$$

This leads to our second-step estimator of $m_1(x_1)$ as

$$\widehat{m}_1(x_1) = \frac{\sum_{j=1}^{n} k\left(\frac{x_{1j} - x_1}{h_{21}}\right) y_{1j}^{2-step}}{\sum_{j=1}^{n} k\left(\frac{x_{1j} - x_1}{h_{21}}\right)}. \tag{9.12}$$

Again, a LLLS estimator can be similarly constructed via a LLLS regression of y_1^{2-step} on x_1. The estimator of each element of $\widehat{m}_{-1}(\mathbf{x}_{-1})$ is similarly obtained. With the full q set of estimates, we can obtain the fitted values for our additive regression as

$$\widehat{m}(x_{1i}, \mathbf{x}_{-1i}) = \overline{y} + \widehat{m}_1(x_{1i}) + \widehat{m}_{-1}(\mathbf{x}_{-1i}) = \overline{y} + \widehat{m}_1(x_{1i}) + \widehat{m}_2(x_{2i}) + \cdots + \widehat{m}_q(x_{qi}).$$

Gradients

Here we discuss how to obtain the gradients in the additive setting. The additive structure of $m(\mathbf{x})$ implies that $\partial \widehat{m}(\mathbf{x})/\partial x_1 = \partial \widehat{m}_1(x_1)/\partial x_1$. The gradients from the LLLS regression stem directly from the second-stage estimator. For the LCLS estimator, Ozabaci and Henderson (2014) show that

$$\frac{\partial \widehat{m}(\mathbf{x})}{\partial x_1} = \frac{\sum_{j=1}^n k^{(1)}\left(\frac{x_{1j}-x_1}{h_{21}}\right) y_{1j}^{2-step} \sum_{j=1}^n k\left(\frac{x_{1j}-x_1}{h_{21}}\right) - \sum_{j=1}^n k\left(\frac{x_{1j}-x_1}{h_{21}}\right) y_{1j}^{2-step} \sum_{j=1}^n k^{(1)}\left(\frac{x_{1j}-x_1}{h_{21}}\right)}{\left[\sum_{j=1}^n k\left(\frac{x_{1j}-x_1}{h_{21}}\right)\right]^2},$$

where $k^{(1)}(\cdot)$ is the first derivative of the kernel function with respect to x_1. The first derivative with respect to x_d is obtained similarly.

Standard errors for the fitted values or gradients can be obtained via bootstrap techniques. The steps are as follows:

1. Let $\widehat{u}_i = y_i - \widehat{m}(\mathbf{x}_i)$ be the residual from the additively separable model. Save the re-centered residuals as $\widehat{u}_i - \overline{\widehat{u}}$, $i = 1, 2, \ldots, n$ where $\overline{\widehat{u}} = n^{-1}\sum_{i=1}^n \widehat{u}_i$. Compute the two-point wild bootstrap errors using the re-centered residuals by $u_i^* = \{(1-\sqrt{5})/2\}(\widehat{u}_i - \overline{\widehat{u}})$ with probability $(1+\sqrt{5})/(2\sqrt{5})$ and $u_i^* = \{(1+\sqrt{5})/2\}(\widehat{u}_i - \overline{\widehat{u}})$ with probability $1 - (1+\sqrt{5})/(2\sqrt{5})$. Generate y_i^* via $y_i^* = \widehat{m}(\mathbf{x}_i) + u_i^*$. Call $\{\mathbf{x}_i, y_i^*\}_{i=1}^n$ the bootstrap sample.
2. Using the bootstrap sample, estimate (via the two-step procedure) the unknown functions and/or their derivatives where y_i is replaced by y_i^* wherever it occurs. Remember that we use the data $\mathbf{x}_i$ and evaluate at the same values of $\mathbf{x}$ that we did initially.
3. Repeat steps 1 and 2 a large number (B) of times and then construct the sampling distribution of the bootstrapped point estimates. Standard errors can be obtained by taking the standard deviation of the sampling distribution for each particular estimate.

9.5.2 Bandwidth selection

The discussion of bandwidth selection in additively separable models typically involves plug-in methods. For example, several different plug-in strategies can be found in Martins-Filho and Yang (2007). Our personal preference would be for a cross-validation procedure. That being said, we are unaware of any theoretical work here and hence more research is needed. The complication here occurs because we have bandwidths in each stage for each regression

$(h_1, h_2 = h_{11}, h_{12}, \ldots, h_{1q}, h_{21}, h_{22}, \ldots, h_{2q})$ and it is not obvious how we would create a cross-validation procedure. We leave this topic to future research.

Here we present the simplest method, which comes from Kim, Linton, and Hengartner (1999). In their paper they use the same bandwidth vector for each stage (i.e., $h_1 = h_2$). The specific form of their bandwidth is

$$h_1 = h_2 = 0.5\widehat{\sigma}_\mathbf{x} n^{-1/(4+q)}.$$

Although simple, this bandwidth selection method is dominated in simulations (in terms of average square error) by the data-driven methods given in Martins-Filho and Yang (2007, 42).

9.5.3 Testing

There are at least two tests that we would find interesting in the case of additively separable models. The first is for correct parametric specification versus the nonparametric additive model. The second is for the additive nonparametric model versus the standard nonparametric model. This latter test is for the null of additive separability.

Here we consider the Ullah (1985) type goodness-of-fit tests. For the first test our null is that the parametric model is correctly specified

$$H_0 : E\,(y|\mathbf{x}) = \mathbf{x}\beta$$

versus the alternative of a nonparametric additive model. Our null residuals are defined as

$$\widehat{u}_i = y_i - \mathbf{x}_i\widehat{\beta}$$

and our residuals under the alternative are

$$\widetilde{u}_i = y_i - \widetilde{c} - \widetilde{m}_1\,(x_{1i}) - \widetilde{m}_2\,(x_{2i}) - \cdots - \widetilde{m}_q(x_{qi}).$$

Our test statistic is calculated as

$$\widehat{J}_n = \frac{\sum\limits_{i=1}^{n} \widehat{u}_i^2 - \sum\limits_{i=1}^{n} \widetilde{u}_i^2}{\sum\limits_{i=1}^{n} \widetilde{u}_i^2}.$$

The bootstrap procedure is as follows:

1. Compute the test statistics $\widehat{J}_n$ for the original sample of $\{\mathbf{x}_1, \mathbf{x}_2, \ldots, \mathbf{x}_n\}$ and $\{y_1, y_2, \ldots, y_n\}$ and save the re-centered residuals from the null model $\widehat{u}_i - \overline{\widehat{u}}$, $i = 1, 2, \ldots, n$ where $\widehat{u}_i = y_i - \mathbf{x}_i\widehat{\beta}$ and $\overline{\widehat{u}} = n^{-1}\sum_{i=1}^{n}\widehat{u}_i$.
2. For each observation i, construct the bootstrapped residual u_i^*, where $u_i^* = \frac{1-\sqrt{5}}{2}\left(\widehat{u}_i - \overline{\widehat{u}}\right)$ with probability $\frac{1+\sqrt{5}}{2\sqrt{5}}$ and $u_i^* = \frac{1+\sqrt{5}}{2}\left(\widehat{u}_i - \overline{\widehat{u}}\right)$ with probability $1 - \frac{1+\sqrt{5}}{2\sqrt{5}}$. Construct the bootstrapped left-hand-side variable by adding the bootstrapped residuals to the fitted values under the null as $y_i^* = \mathbf{x}_i\widehat{\beta} + u_i^*$. Call $\left\{y_i^*, \mathbf{x}_i\right\}_{i=1}^{n}$ the bootstrap sample.

3. Calculate $\widehat{J}_n^*$ where $\widehat{J}_n^*$ is calculated the same way as $\widehat{J}_n$ except that y_i is replaced by y_i^*.
4. Repeat steps 2 and 3 a large number (B) of times and then construct the sampling distribution of the bootstrapped test statistics. We reject the null that the semiparametric model is correctly specified if the estimated test statistic $\widehat{J}_n$ is greater than the upper α-percentile of the bootstrapped test statistics.

For the second test, we consider testing the additive model versus a nonparametric model. This can be conducted via a Li and Wang (1998) type test, but here consider a goodness-of-fit test. Our null is that the nonparametric additive model is correctly specified

$$H_0 : E\,(y|\mathbf{x}) = c + m_1\,(x_1) + m_2\,(x_2) + \cdots + m_q(x_q)$$

versus the alternative of a nonparametric model. Our null residuals are defined as

$$\widehat{u}_i = y_i - \widehat{c} - \widehat{m}_1\,(x_{1i}) - \widehat{m}_2\,(x_{2i}) - \cdots - \widehat{m}_q(x_{qi})$$

and our residuals under the alternative are

$$\widetilde{u}_i = y_i - \widetilde{m}\,(\mathbf{x}_i)\,,$$

where $\mathbf{x}_i$ is the $1 \times q$ vector of regressors (and $\widetilde{m}\,(\cdot)$ is obtained via the methods discussed in Chapter 5). Our test statistic is calculated as

$$\widehat{J}_n = \frac{\sum\limits_{i=1}^{n} \widehat{u}_i^2 - \sum\limits_{i=1}^{n} \widetilde{u}_i^2}{\sum\limits_{i=1}^{n} \widetilde{u}_i^2}.$$

The bootstrap procedure is as follows:

1. Compute the test statistics $\widehat{J}_n$ for the original sample of $\{\mathbf{x}_1, \mathbf{x}_2, \ldots, \mathbf{x}_n\}$ and $\{y_1, y_2, \ldots, y_n\}$ and save the re-centered residuals from the null model $\widehat{u}_i - \overline{\widehat{u}}$, $i = 1, 2, \ldots, n$ where $\widehat{u}_i = y_i - \widehat{c} - \widehat{m}_1\,(x_{1i}) - \widehat{m}_2\,(x_{2i}) - \cdots - \widehat{m}_q(x_{qi})$ and $\overline{\widehat{u}} = n^{-1} \sum_{i=1}^{n} \widehat{u}_i$.
2. For each observation i, construct the bootstrapped residual u_i^*, where $u_i^* = \frac{1-\sqrt{5}}{2}\,\left(\widehat{u}_i - \overline{\widehat{u}}\right)$ with probability $\frac{1+\sqrt{5}}{2\sqrt{5}}$ and $u_i^* = \frac{1+\sqrt{5}}{2}\,\left(\widehat{u}_i - \overline{\widehat{u}}\right)$ with probability $1 - \frac{1+\sqrt{5}}{2\sqrt{5}}$. Construct the bootstrapped left-hand-side variable by adding the bootstrapped residuals to the fitted values under the null as $y_i^* = \widehat{c} + \widehat{m}_1\,(x_{1i}) + \widehat{m}_2\,(x_{2i}) + \cdots + \widehat{m}_q(x_{qi}) + u_i^*$. Call $\left\{y_i^*, \mathbf{x}_i\right\}_{i=1}^{n}$ the bootstrap sample.
3. Calculate $\widehat{J}_n^*$ where $\widehat{J}_n^*$ is calculated the same way as $\widehat{J}_n$ except that y_i is replaced by y_i^*.
4. Repeat steps 2 and 3 a large number (B) of times and then construct the sampling distribution of the bootstrapped test statistics. We reject the null that the semiparametric model is correctly specified if the estimated test statistic $\widehat{J}_n$ is greater than the upper α-percentile of the bootstrapped test statistics.

9.6 Application

In this application we highlight some of the semiparametric estimators. While there exist many (including growth) empirical papers that apply semiparametric methods, we are unaware of any that look specifically at production functions. That being said, the types of models we employ here are simplistic. We wanted to keep the models in this chapter relatively simple and these should be thought of more as learning tools than realistic production functions. Therefore, for the PLM, we simply have a linear structure for physical capital and human-capital-adjusted labor, and then let a time trend (treated as a continuous variable) enter nonparametrically. Specifically, our model is

$$y = \alpha K + \beta HL + m(t) + u,$$

where $m(t)$ can be thought of a time-varying technology parameter. Our single-index model employs the estimator of Ichimura (1993) with the same linear introduction of the variables of interest. This model is of the form

$$y = m(\alpha K + \beta HL) + u,$$

where we exclude a time trend. For the SPSCM model, we employ a linear structure, but allow the coefficients on our regressors to vary with time. Here our model takes the form

$$y = A(t) + \alpha(t) K + \beta(t) HL + u,$$

where our parameter $A(\cdot)$ is also a function of time. Finally, our additive nonparametric regression model treats each input separately and is of the form

$$y = m_1(K) + m_2(HL) + u,$$

where we exclude a time trend.

9.6.1 Bandwidths

The bandwidths for each model are found in Table 9.1. What you will notice first is that each model has a scalar bandwidth. This is the expectation in the single-index model, but not necessarily for the other two. In each of the other two models we have a single component (the time trend) that enters nonlinearly. Additional covariates could be added, but a single covariate makes it possible for us to introduce figures that do not require counterfactual estimates.

For the PLM we have bandwidths estimated via rule of thumb and LSCV (for LCLS and LLLS). The rule-of-thumb bandwidth is the same for each model (LCLS and LLLS) as we have a single regressor ($1.06\sigma_t n^{-1/5}$, where σ_t is the standard deviation of the time trend). It turns out that we also obtain the same bandwidth for LCLS and LLLS estimation via LSCV. This was somewhat surprising. In our code we minimized the function with respect to the final estimates, as opposed to estimating each bandwidth for each element separately. It appears as though the first-stage estimates (which are LCLS for both models) dominate. We could alternatively estimate the bandwidths separately for each step, in which case we would obtain different bandwidths for each model. That being said, the second-stage estimates of the models still differ.

Table 9.1. *Bandwidths for each*
semiparametric model

	t	$g\,(\cdot)$	K	HL
PLM				
ROT	4.0924			
LCLS	25.1536			
LLLS	25.1536			
SPSCM				
ROT	4.0924			
LCLS	8.2438			
LLLS	24.0072			
Single index				
ROT		0.9062		
LCLS		1.3363		
Additive				
Kim et al.			0.4560	0.4784

For the SPSCM model, we see much larger bandwidths. The rule-of-thumb bandwidth is the same, as the formula does not change. The bandwidth is twice as large for LCLS and roughly six times as large for LLLS. Note that each of these bandwidths is less than the upper bounds and hence we still see relevance and nonlinearity in our estimates with respect to the time trend variable.

Finally, for the single-index model, our bandwidths are for the unknown function with respect to $\mathbf{x}\widehat{\beta}$. There is no time trend in this model. Here our rule-of-thumb estimate is 0.9062. We searched the literature and were unable to find a rule of thumb and are proposing one here. Specifically, we used a linear model (in essence assumed that $m\,(\cdot) = 1$) and estimated it via OLS. We then took their fitted values from that model and calculated the standard deviation. This led to the rule-of-thumb bandwidth

$$1.06\sigma_{\widehat{y}}n^{-1/5},$$

where $\sigma_{\widehat{y}}$ is obtained from the fitted values of the linear regression. We fed this rule-of-thumb estimate as our initial value in our LSCV function and obtained a data-driven bandwidth equal to 1.3363.

Finally, for the additively separable model, we obtain a separate bandwidth for each regressor. However, unlike a fully nonparametric model, the additive model has bandwidths that decrease at the single dimensional rate. We follow the simulation results in Kim, Linton, and Hengartner (1999), and use bandwidths of the form

$$0.50\widehat{\sigma}_{x}n^{-1/5}.$$

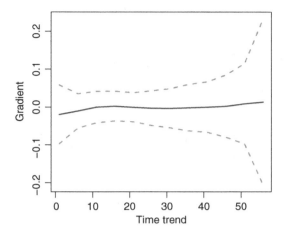

Figure 9.1. Gradient estimates with respect to time in the PLM versus time

Notice that the scale is less than half that of a standard rule-of-thumb estimate and hence we may expect more variation in our estimates.

9.6.2 Plotting estimates

Semiparametric models often give us a unique opportunity to view figures in two dimensions without resorting to counterfactual estimates. Here we consider two cases where we can plot our estimates in a two-dimensional figure. In the first case we examine the PLM where we model output as a linear function of physical capital and human-capital-augmented labor and allow a time trend to enter nonparametrically (i.e., our time varying technology parameter). In Figure 9.1 we look at the gradient of the technology parameter versus time itself (where the second stage is estimated via LLLS with the rule-of-thumb bandwidth). We see both positive and negatives values, but the confidence bounds (obtained via 399 bootstraps) include zero over the entire time period. In other words, we do not find a significant change in the technology over time and hence a constant technology parameter may be acceptable.

In the second case (SPSCM), we regress output as a linear function of physical capital and human-capital-augmented labor, but allow their coefficients to be a function of time. Even though time is a continuous variable, it is measured discretely and hence the estimated coefficients only take a finite number of values. In this figure we plot the returns to scale, which is obtained by summing the "slope" coefficients of the model $(\alpha(t) + \beta(t))$. Figure 9.2 shows the result of this exercise by plotting returns to scale over time. The returns to scale start off very large in earlier time periods, but then move towards unity in later time periods. Given that a large percentage of macroeconomic models assume constant returns to scale, these later time periods seem plausible, while the earlier time periods have increasing returns to a degree that most economists would consider unbelievable. It is feasible that there are data problems in earlier time periods (or it could be due to missing observations for some countries) and this may be one explanation for the large returns earlier in the sample.

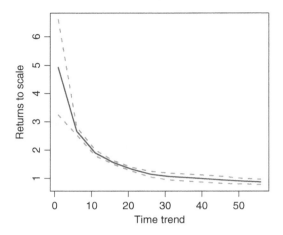

Figure 9.2. Returns-to-scale estimates from the SPSCM model versus time

9.6.3 Specification testing

Finally, while there exist many tests for semiparametric models, we are going to look at two general types of specification tests. We will first employ the Ullah (1985) test to compare parametric to semiparametric and then semiparametric to nonparametric models (for each of our four types of semiparametric estimators). We will then compare each of these to the similar test in Horowitz and Härdle (1994). Recall that these estimators look for "closeness" between two competing methods. The Ullah (1985) test looks for differences in residuals, whereas the Horowitz and Härdle (1994) test looks for differences in fitted values. We would suspect that they typically give the same conclusions and hence we are also looking for empirical evidence of this here.

Table 9.2 gives the p-values for each of the aforementioned tests. The first column of numbers is the p-values for the test that the parametric model is correctly specified versus the semiparametric alternative. This type of test is popular in semiparametric papers. It is often argued that if we reject the null, the semiparametric model is preferable. While this may be true in many cases, similar to what we discussed in Chapter 6, this type of test is only consistent in the direction of the alternative. It is possible that the semiparametric model is also misspecified. While we agree that this type of test is useful, if we want to argue for a semiparametric specification, it is also prudent to test the semiparametric model versus a nonparametric alternative. The second column of numbers in Table 9.2 does exactly that. Here we test each semiparametric specification versus a nonparametric alternative (LCLS estimators with rule-of-thumb bandwidths).

The first thing to notice from the table is that the results are relatively similar between the Ullah (1985) and Horowitz and Härdle (1994) tests (even for a relatively small sample size), which is expected. We see clear rejections of the parametric and semiparametric specifications for the SPSCM model. The sum of these two tests suggests that a nonparametric model would be preferable. In each specification we let output be a separable function of physical capital and human-capital-augmented labor. In other words, we are forcing the inputs to be substitutes and do not allow for any interactions, whereas the nonparametric model makes no such restrictions.

Table 9.2. *p-values for tests of correct specification (399 wild bootstrap replications) – estimation is performed via LCLS estimators with rule-of-thumb bandwidths*

	P vs. SP	SP vs. NP
Ullah		
PLM	0.1303	0.0000
Single index	1.0000	0.0000
SPSCM	0.0025	0.0000
Additive	0.0727	0.0000
Horowitz and Härdle		
PLM	0.5464	0.0000
Single index	0.9799	0.0326
SPSCM	0.0025	0.0000
Additive	0.1003	1.0000

We also see a few cases of failure to reject the parametric model versus the semiparametric alternative. This is not surprising either, given that we simply include a time trend nonlinearly in the PLM model and the single-index model (which does not include a time trend in either the parametric or semiparametric specification) and these are only slightly different from the corresponding parametric models (this may also be a function of us using an inflated rule-of-thumb bandwidth – 2.06 scale factor – generated from a linear model in the single-index case). If we stopped here, we would argue that these parametric models are correctly specified. However, in most cases, we reject the semiparametric specifications (and unreported parametric specifications) versus nonparametric alternatives. Each of these three cases suggests that the nonparametric model is preferable. While we admit that there likely exist parametric and semiparametric models that are consistent and more efficient than a nonparametric model, it is up to the user to find that model. We simply wish to outline that employing a semiparametric model for the sake of "efficiency" is insufficient (or at least should be considered suspect) unless a formal test versus a nonparametric model is employed.

As a final statement, as we previously emphasized in Chapter 6, bandwidth selection in nonparametric testing has not been studied enough. Some of our results depend upon the chosen bandwidth and we encourage research such that the conclusions of tests are not so dependent on user-chosen bandwidths.

10

Instrumental variables

Many situations in applied econometric work require knowledge of a structural or *causal* relationship in order to guide policy recommendations. Aside from possessing valid instrumental variables to correctly capture endogeneity, uncovering the structural relationship of interest usually requires specifying a utility or cost function or the distribution of preferences in order to derive a reduced form model that can be estimated. Unfortunately, this route is unappealing, as it is uncommon to know the underlying distribution or specification of the model primitives necessary for deriving the corresponding reduced form. Moreover, economic theory rarely provides tight correspondence between the model primitives and their functional forms. However, turning directly to a nonparametric approach has not been a common choice among empiricists, as the methods necessary to provide consistent estimates in the face of endogeneity have only recently been developed and may present complications for implementation (see Newey, Powell, and Vella, 1999; Pinske, 2000; Newey and Powell, 2003; Horowitz and Hall, 2005; Su and Ullah, 2008; and Darolles, Fan, Florens, and Renault, 2011; Martins-Filho and Yao, 2012; Ozabaci, Henderson, and Su, 2014).

A key difficulty with the implementation of instrumental variable nonparametric methods is that, in their most general form, they require inversion of an integral equation, and this inversion does not represent a continuous mapping: the so-called ill-posed inverse problem. Thus, the typical analog estimation routines (replacing population expectations with sample ones) that we have seen in previous chapters are unlikely to work here. That is, replacing an unknown (smooth) mean with a sample analog will not guarantee consistent estimation of the object of interest in this setting. One approach to avoiding the ill-posed inverse problem is to use a control function approach. From an applied standpoint, the control function approach produces estimators that are easier to implement in practice.

In this chapter, we outline the inherent difficulty induced by endogeneity in a nonparametric framework. We then discuss why a control function approach is suitable for dealing with endogeneity. It turns out that the control function approach is not a nested case of the nonparametric instrumental variable setting. This offers appeal for deploying the control function approach in practice, given its relative ease of implementation. The main estimator we describe is based on local-polynomial least-squares, and readers familiar with the material in Chapter 5 will find using this estimator to control for endogeneity attractive. We also discuss the case of a discrete endogenous regressor, which turns our nonparametric model into a semiparametric smooth coefficient model (see Chapter 9). Lastly, we detail implementation issues for this estimator, which include bandwidth selection, bootstrap-based standard errors, and weak instruments.

For our empirical example, we examine potential endogeneity in physical capital stock. A common criticism in models of cross-country economic growth is that the covariates are endogenous. Here, exploiting the panel nature of the data set, we use a lagged value of the capital stock as an instrument. We compare the returns to each input with and without controlling for potential endogeneity. We find small changes in the returns to physical capital, but relatively large changes in the return to human-capital-augmented labor.

10.1 The ill-posed inverse problem

Consider the nonparametric regression model

$$y_i = m(x_i) + u_i, \text{ where } E(u_i|z_i) = 0. \tag{10.1}$$

If $z_i = x_i$, this is the standard nonparametric regression model detailed in Chapter 5. For simplicity, we assume that both x and z are scalars (to be relaxed later). To illustrate the difficulty in constructing an estimator of $m(x)$ in (10.1), consider that

$$E(u_i|z_i) = E\left[y_i - m(x_i)|z_i\right] = 0.$$

This yields

$$E(y_i|z_i) = E[m(x_i)|z_i] = \int m(x)f(x|z_i)dx. \tag{10.2}$$

The integral in (10.2) is known as a Fredholm integral of the first kind (Kress, 1999). The study of these integral equations is common in the signal-processing literature and a large body of research exists on methods to solve these integrals (Ramm, 2005; Ivanov, Vasin, and Tanana, 2002; Morozov, 1984). With data on the triplet (y_i, x_i, z_i), we can estimate $E(y_i|z_i)$ and $f(x_i|z_i)$ nonparametrically. However, we cannot recover $m(x_i)$ by inverting the relationship in (10.2). Even though $E[y_i|z_i]$ is well behaved for small changes in $m(x_i)$, the converse is not true. This is the ill-posed inverse problem. While the integral relationship in (10.2) is continuous in $m(x_i)$, the inverse relationship is discontinuous. This discontinuity results in the inability to recover $m(x_i)$ without further restrictions on the model or regularization of the inversion of the integral relationship.

To provide a simple illustration of regularization of the inverse integral relationship, consider estimating a probability density function. The probability density function $(f(x))$ is defined as

$$f(x) \equiv \frac{dF(x)}{dx}, \tag{10.3}$$

where $F(x)$ is the cumulative distribution function. This equivalence follows via the inverse integral relationship of the definition of the cumulative distribution function from the probability density function

$$F(x) = \int 1\{v \le x\} f(v)dv.$$

To place this estimation problem in the context of the ill-posed inverse problem, consider that with data on x, we can use the ECDF, $\widehat{F}(x) = n^{-1} \sum_{i=1}^{n} 1 \{x \le x_i\}$ to estimate $F(x)$. Moreover, this is a uniformly consistent estimator of $F(x)$. However, we cannot use $\widehat{F}(x)$ to construct an estimator of $f(x)$ from the inverse integral relationship in (10.3). This is because for all nonstep points of $\widehat{F}(x)$, the derivative is zero, while for the step points of $\widehat{F}(x)$, the derivative is infinite. Thus, as $n \to \infty$, even though $\widehat{F}(x) \to F(x) \ \forall x$, $\widehat{f}(x)$ does not converge to $f(x)$.

Figures 10.1 and 10.2 illustrate this issue. We generate data from a standard normal distribution and estimate $F(x)$ using the ECDF, and estimate $f(x)$ as the derivative of the ECDF. The left panel of each figure plots the ECDF against the true cumulative distribution function and the right panel plots the estimated probability distribution function against the actual probability distribution function. The blotted line in the right panel represents the estimated curve, where nonstep points of the ECDF are black (at zero) and the step points are white (at infinity). In both panels the dashed lines are the true objects of interest. Figure 10.1 is for 100 observations and Figure 10.2 is for 1,000 observations. As the sample size increases, the ECDF converges everywhere towards the normal cumulative distribution function. However, the probability density function does not converge anywhere.

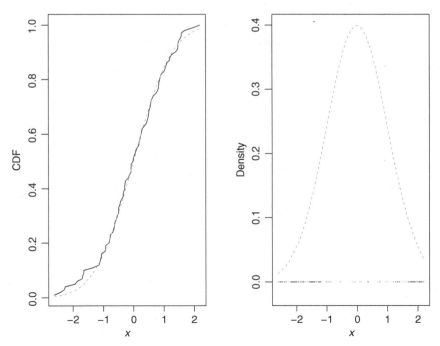

Figure 10.1. Illustration of inconsistency of the estimated probability distribution function as the derivative of the empirical cumulative distribution function, $n = 100$ observations, dashed line is the truth, solid line is the estimate

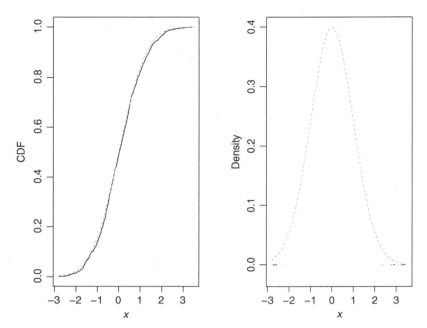

Figure 10.2. Illustration of inconsistency of the estimated probability distribution function as the derivative of the empirical cumulative distribution function, $n = 1000$ observations, dashed line is the truth, solid line is the estimate

10.2 Tackling the ill-posed inverse

In the previous example, the inverse integral solution did not provide a consistent estimator because the ECDF was discontinuous. It turns out that even with a smooth objective function, an inverse Fredholm integral equation of the first kind will not produce a smooth continuous solution. The two main approaches to solving the integral equation in (10.2) are to resort to further restrictions or to use regularization. Further restrictions can be additional moment conditions or parametric restrictions on the unknown object of interest. Regularization amounts to removing the discontinuity that exists in the inverse mapping, restricting the smoothness of the function through use of a smoothing parameter.

Regularization

To gain intuition for how regularization works, we again focus on the density estimation case. We know from Chapter 2 how to construct a consistent nonparametric estimator of the probability density function using kernels. It turns out that the construction of the kernel density estimator stems from regularization of the integral equation in (10.2). Note that we can write our probability density function as

$$\breve{f}(x) = h^{-1} \int k\left(\frac{x - z}{h}\right) f(z) dz,$$

where h is our bandwidth parameter and $k(\cdot)$ is our kernel function. Bochner's Theorem (see Theorem 1A in Parzen, 1962) suggests that $\breve{f}(x) \rightarrow f(x)$ as $n \rightarrow \infty$

provided $h \to 0$ (with the requirement that $k(\cdot)$ integrates to 1). This setup is not particularly useful to us, given that $f(z)$ is unknown. However, we can rewrite this equation as

$$\check{f}(x) = h^{-1} \int k\left(\frac{x-z}{h}\right) dF(z),$$

using the definition of the probability density function. We can replace $F(z)$ in this integral equation with the ECDF. Technical Appendix 10.1 shows that

$$\widehat{f}(x) = h^{-1} \int k((x-z)/h) d\widehat{F}(z) = (nh)^{-1} \sum_{i=1}^{n} k\left(\frac{x_i - x}{h}\right), \tag{10.4}$$

which is our kernel density estimator. While our discussion in Chapter 2 eschewed the ill-posed inverse problem, the kernel density estimator is perhaps one of the simplest regularized estimators that exists. The regularization occurs through smoothing the discontinuities that exist in the ECDF. Further, replacing the unknown distribution function with the ECDF allows consistent estimation of $\check{f}(x)$ via Helly's second theorem (see Lukacs, 1975, 16). Thus, we have $\widehat{f}(x) \to \check{f}(x) \to f(x)$ as $n \to \infty$ and $h \to 0$.

We now see how regularization works. The discontinuous nature of the inverse integral equation requires smoothing (regularizing) the integral prior to inversion. The *smoothness* that is induced by the kernel mitigates the discontinuity, allowing estimation of the density. However, this smoothing (regularization) prevents consistent estimation of the object of interest. Note that neither $\check{f}(x)$ nor $\widehat{f}(x)$ consistently estimates $f(x)$ if h does not converge to 0. Therefore, less regularization is required as the sample size increases. However, we must also recognize that h must not decrease too fast, or the induced smoothness cannot appropriately displace the discontinuity.

Control function approach

As an alternative to regularization, additional restrictions/assumptions can be placed on the model that can eliminate the "ill-posedness" of the problem. One approach is to adopt a parametric structure, as would be the case if we deployed two-stage least-squares (2SLS). However, this is unappealing for our purposes. Instead, at the expense of imposing several additional moment conditions, we will remain entrenched in a nonparametric setting. Consider the following regression framework (again we focus on scalar x and z)

$$y_i = m(x_i) + u_i \tag{10.5}$$

$$x_i = g(z_i) + \varepsilon_i, \tag{10.6}$$

with conditions $E(\varepsilon_i | z_i) = 0$ and $E(u_i | z_i, \varepsilon_i) = E(u_i | \varepsilon_i)$. The first of these conditions is innocuous if $g(z) = E(x|z)$ and implies that z_i is a valid instrument for x_i. What allows identification of $m(x)$ and avoidance of the ill-posed inverse problem is the second condition. This condition requires the conditional expectation of u_i to depend on x_i only through ε_i. As stated earlier, once ε is controlled for, x is no longer viewed as endogenous.

To see how identification of $m(x_i)$ is obtained, we note that

$$
\begin{aligned}
E\,(y_i|x_i, \varepsilon_i) &= m(x_i) + E\,(u_i|x_i - \varepsilon_i, \varepsilon_i) \\
&= m(x_i) + E\,(u_i|z_i, \varepsilon_i) \\
&= m(x_i) + E\,(u_i|\varepsilon_i) \\
&= m(x_i) + r(\varepsilon_i).
\end{aligned}
$$

Then, $m(x_i) = E\,(y_i|x_i, \varepsilon_i) - r(\varepsilon_i)$ and both of the terms on the right-hand side can be estimated nonparametrically. The elimination of the ill-posed inverse problem follows, given that the relationship between $m(x_i)$ and the conditional mean is continuous. $r(\varepsilon_i)$ is termed the control function. In essence, the presence of $r(\varepsilon_i)$ acts as a proxy variable, which captures an unobserved variable; controlling for this eliminates endogeneity in the model (see Blundell and Powell, 2003, for a more detailed discussion of the control function approach).

While it might seem that the control function approach is more restrictive than our model in (10.1), this is not the case. The model in (10.1) and those in (10.5) and (10.6) are not nested. Neither is more general than the other. It is possible for $E\,(u|z_i) = 0$ to be valid, but $E\,(u|x_i, \varepsilon_i) \neq E\,(u|\varepsilon_i)$. The converse may also be true: $E\,(u|x_i, \varepsilon_i) = E\,(u|\varepsilon_i)$ may hold, but $E\,(u|z = z_i) = 0$ may not. It is also possible that both conditions hold. Thus, in practice it is not possible to distinguish between these two models if both conditions hold (see Horowitz, 2012, for a test of $E\,(u|z_i) = 0$). Our preference is for the control-function approach, as simple nonparametric estimators for $m(x_i)$ exist and are relatively easy to implement.

10.3 Local-polynomial estimation of the control-function model

In this section we describe local polynomial estimation of the unknown smooth function in the presence of both endogenous and exogenous covariates. Our previous discussion excluded exogenous (included) covariates for simplicity. Here we describe estimation of the general nonparametric triangular model

$$
y_i = m(x_i, \mathbf{z}_{1i}) + u_i \tag{10.7}
$$

$$
x_i = g(\mathbf{z}_i) + \varepsilon_i, \tag{10.8}
$$

where x is the endogenous regressor; $\mathbf{z}_i = (\mathbf{z}_{1i}, \mathbf{z}_{2i})$ where $\mathbf{z}_{1i}$ and $\mathbf{z}_{2i}$ are $1 \times q_1$ and $1 \times q_2$ vectors of (included and excluded) instrumental variables, respectively; $g(\cdot)$ is an unknown smooth function of the instruments $(\mathbf{z})$; and u and ε are disturbances. We assume that $E\,(\varepsilon|\mathbf{z}) = 0$, and $E\,(u|\mathbf{z}, \varepsilon) = E\,(u|\varepsilon)$. These assumptions are more general than the strict requirement of $\mathbf{z}$ being independent of (u, ε) and allow both u and ε to be heteroskedastic.

We follow the approach of Su and Ullah (2008) and use local-polynomial least-squares to estimate the unknown function $m(x_i, \mathbf{z}_{1i})$. Similar to the discussion above, we have that

$$E(y|x, \mathbf{z}, \varepsilon) = m(x, \mathbf{z}_1) + E(u|x, \mathbf{z}, \varepsilon)$$
$$= m(x, \mathbf{z}_1) + E\left[u|x - g(\mathbf{z}), \mathbf{z}, \varepsilon\right]$$
$$= m(x, \mathbf{z}_1) + E(u|\mathbf{z}, \varepsilon)$$
$$= m(x, \mathbf{z}_1) + E(u|\varepsilon).$$

It thus follows by the law of iterative expectations that

$$w(x, \mathbf{z}_1, \varepsilon) \equiv E(y|x, \mathbf{z}, \varepsilon) = m(x, \mathbf{z}_1) + r(\varepsilon),$$

where $r(\varepsilon) \equiv E(u|\varepsilon)$. Following the procedure outlined in Su and Ullah (2008), this additive structure provides consistent estimates of $m(x, \mathbf{z}_1)$, up to an additive constant $(E(u|\varepsilon))$, without further restrictions. To fully identify $m(x, \mathbf{z}_1)$, we need to assume that $E(u) = 0$.

Let h_1 be a $(q_1 + q_2)$ vector of bandwidths and h_2 be a $(q_1 + 2)$ (the q_1 exogenous covariates, the single endogenous covariate, and the estimated residual that enters the control function) vector of bandwidths. The Su and Ullah (2008) approach to estimate $m(x, \mathbf{z}_1)$ requires three steps:

1. Obtain a consistent estimator of $g(\cdot)$ by running a local-p_1 polynomial regression of x on $\mathbf{z}$ with kernel function $K_{h_1}(\cdot)$ and bandwidth vector h_1 (this can be extended to the mixed-data case). Denote the estimates of the unknown function as $\widehat{g}(\mathbf{z})$ and obtain the residuals $\widehat{\varepsilon}_i = x_i - \widehat{g}(\mathbf{z}_i)$, for $i = 1, 2, \ldots, n$.
2. Obtain a consistent estimator of $w(\cdot)$ by running a local-p_2 polynomial regression of y on x, $\mathbf{z}_1$, and $\widehat{\varepsilon}$ with kernel function $K_{h_2}(\cdot)$ and bandwidth vector h_2. Denote the estimates of the unknown function as $\widehat{w}(x, \mathbf{z}_1, \varepsilon)$.
3. Assuming that $E(u) = 0$, we can obtain a consistent estimator of $m(\cdot)$ as

$$\widehat{m}(x, \mathbf{z}_1) = n^{-1} \sum_{i=1}^{n} \widehat{w}(x, \mathbf{z}_1, \widehat{\varepsilon}_i),$$

where $\widehat{w}(x, \mathbf{z}_1, \widehat{\varepsilon}_i)$ is the counterfactual estimator of the unknown function obtained using the bandwidths from the local-p_2 polynomial regression in step 2. The derivatives of $m(\cdot)$ can be obtained similarly as

$$\widehat{m}'(x, \mathbf{z}_1) = n^{-1} \sum_{i=1}^{n} \widehat{w}'(x, \mathbf{z}_1, \widehat{\varepsilon}_i),$$

where $\widehat{w}'(x, \mathbf{z}_1, \widehat{\varepsilon}_i)$ is the counterfactual derivative of $w(\cdot)$. Notice that this last step is estimating the value of the function $\widehat{w}(x, \mathbf{z}_1, \cdot)$ at each value of $\widehat{\varepsilon}$ and then averaging over the sample. Thus, the estimator consists of two estimation stages and a final step consisting of counterfactual estimation to average out the error term since we are assuming it to be mean zero.

The kernel functions used for estimation of $g(\cdot)$ and $w(\cdot)$ in steps 1 and 2 can be the same (i.e., $K_{h_1}(\cdot) = K_{h_2}(\cdot)$). Further, the polynomial orders in steps 1 and 2 can be the same (i.e., $p_1 = p_2$), depending upon the number of exogenous covariates that are in the model (to be discussed below).

Su and Ullah (2008, Theorem 2.2) prove that this local-p_2 polynomial estimator is asymptotically normal. Further, there are two useful pieces of information from their large sample theory that are potentially important in applied work. First, even though ε is unknown and must be estimated, this first stage estimation does not impact the bias of the second stage estimator (there is still a bias, but it is the usual bias for a local-p_2 polynomial estimator). This is due to the counterfactual nature of the estimator. Second, the first-stage estimation does not impact the asymptotic variance of the second-stage estimator. This result is surprising compared to the common parametrically specified instrumental variables estimator, which does have an increased asymptotic variance given the first-stage estimation. This result is also important in light of the series-based estimator of Newey, Powell, and Vella (1999) where the first-stage estimation impacts the second-stage estimator's asymptotic variance (unless further assumptions are imposed on the problem). Thus, the Su and Ullah (2008) two-stage estimator is a powerful device to cope with endogeneity.

10.3.1 Multiple endogenous regressors

Our discussion thus far has restricted x to be scalar, but this need not hold true. Suppose that there exists $q_x > 1$ endogenous regressors $\mathbf{x} \equiv (x_1, x_2, \ldots, x_{q_x})$. The steps for the Su and Ullah (2008) estimator are similar. The one major difference is that we must estimate q_x first-stage regressions. Our model becomes

$$y_i = m(\mathbf{x}_i, \mathbf{z}_{1i}) + u_i$$
$$x_{1i} = g_1(\mathbf{z}_i) + \varepsilon_{1i}$$
$$x_{2i} = g_2(\mathbf{z}_i) + \varepsilon_{2i}$$
$$\vdots$$
$$x_{q_x i} = g_{q_x}(\mathbf{z}_i) + \varepsilon_{q_x i}.$$

The four-step estimation process is as follows:

1. Obtain consistent estimates of $g_1(\cdot)$, $g_2(\cdot), \ldots, g_{q_x}(\cdot)$ by running a (separate) local-p_1 polynomial regression for each element of $\mathbf{x}$ on $\mathbf{z}$ with kernel function $K_{h_1}(\cdot)$ and bandwidth vector h_{h_1}. Here p_1, $K_{h_1}(\cdot)$, and h_1 are fixed across the q_x local-polynomial regressions. Denote the estimates of the unknown function as $\widehat{g}_j(\mathbf{z})$ and obtain the residuals $\widehat{\varepsilon}_{ji} = x_{ji} - \widehat{g}_j(\mathbf{z}_i)$, for $i = 1, 2, \ldots, n$ and $J = 1, 2, \ldots, q_x$.
2. Obtain a consistent estimator of $w(\cdot)$ by running a local-p_2 polynomial regression of y on $\mathbf{x}$, $\mathbf{z}_1$ and $\widehat{\varepsilon}_{1i}, \widehat{\varepsilon}_{2i}, \ldots, \widehat{\varepsilon}_{q_x i}$ with kernel function $K_{h_2}(\cdot)$ and bandwidth vector h_2. Denote the estimates of the unknown function as $\widehat{w}(\mathbf{x}, \mathbf{z}_1, \varepsilon)$.
3. Assuming that $E(u) = 0$, we can obtain a consistent estimator of $m(\cdot)$ as

$$\widehat{m}(\mathbf{x}, \mathbf{z}_1) = n^{-1} \sum_{i=1}^{n} \widehat{w}(\mathbf{x}, \mathbf{z}_1, \widehat{\varepsilon}_{1i}, \widehat{\varepsilon}_{2i}, \ldots, \widehat{\varepsilon}_{q_x i}),$$

where $\widehat{w}\left(\mathbf{x}, \mathbf{z}_1, \widehat{\varepsilon}_{1i}, \widehat{\varepsilon}_{2i}, \ldots, \widehat{\varepsilon}_{qxi}\right)$ is the counterfactual estimator of the unknown function obtained using the bandwidths from the local-p_2 polynomial regression in Step 2. The derivatives of $m(\cdot)$ can be obtained similarly as

$$\widehat{m}'(\mathbf{x}, \mathbf{z}_1) = n^{-1} \sum_{i=1}^{n} \widehat{w}'\left(\mathbf{x}, \mathbf{z}_1, \widehat{\varepsilon}_{1i}, \widehat{\varepsilon}_{2i}, \ldots, \widehat{\varepsilon}_{qxi}\right),$$

where $\widehat{w}'\left(\mathbf{x}, \mathbf{z}_1, \widehat{\varepsilon}_{1i}, \widehat{\varepsilon}_{2i}, \ldots, \widehat{\varepsilon}_{qxi}\right)$ is the counterfactual derivative of $w(\cdot)$.

10.3.2 Bandwidth selection

Bandwidth estimation is important in both stages. Here we discuss the conditions the first-stage bandwidths need to satisfy in order for the control function estimator to be consistent. We then propose a simple data-driven bandwidth selection approach. We mention that the optimal rates of the bandwidths are important in this setting, given that we do not observe ε and must approximate it with a first-stage local-polynomial regression. If the approximation error does not decay quickly enough, this can impede consistent estimation of the second stage.

Assumption A5 in Su and Ullah (2008) details the necessary requirements for the behavior of both bandwidth vectors as it pertains to the performance of the estimator of $\widehat{m}(\mathbf{x}, \mathbf{z}_1)$. While these conditions are technical, they do suggest that h_2 converge at the optimal local-polynomial rate, which is $h_2 \propto n^{-1/\gamma_2}$, where $\gamma_2 = 2*(p_2 + 1) + q_1 + 1$. The same optimal rate for h_1 for the first-stage local-polynomial estimator is not required. That is, selecting h_1 optimally for estimation of $g(\mathbf{z})$ does not ensure optimal performance for estimation of $m(\mathbf{x}, \mathbf{z}_1)$.

If we were purely concerned with optimal estimation of $g(\mathbf{z})$, then the rate on the bandwidths would be that $h_1 \propto n^{-1/\gamma_1}$, where $\gamma_1 = 2*(p_1 + 1) + (q_1 + q_2)$. However, Assumption A5 in Su and Ullah (2008) places the restriction $h_1 \propto n^{-\alpha}$ where, assuming a single endogenous variable, we have

$$\underline{\alpha} = \gamma_2^{-1} \max \left\{ \frac{p_2 + 1}{p_1 + 1}, \frac{p_2 + 3}{2(p_1 + 1)} \right\} < \alpha < \gamma_2^{-1} \frac{p_2 + q_1}{q_1 + q_2} = \bar{\alpha}, \qquad (10.9)$$

where $\bar{\alpha}$ and $\underline{\alpha}$ are the upper and lower bounds (respectively) on the rate of the optimal bandwidths for the first-stage local-polynomial regression. Any first-stage bandwidth that decays to zero within these bounds will suffice for consistent estimation of the unknown conditional mean.

An interesting theoretical finding of the local-polynomial estimator of Su and Ullah (2008) is that the asymptotic distribution of $\widehat{m}(\cdot)$ does not depend on h_1, provided it decays at a rate consistent with the bounds in (10.9). This suggests a simple approach to developing a data-driven bandwidth selection procedure based on least-squares cross-validation. We propose the following LSCV criterion function:

$$\mathrm{CV}(h_2) = \operatorname*{argmin}_{h_2} \frac{1}{n} \sum_{i=1}^{n} \left[y_i - \widehat{m}_{-i}(\mathbf{x}_i, \mathbf{z}_{1i})^2 \right], \qquad (10.10)$$

where $\widehat{m}_{-i}(\mathbf{x}_i, \mathbf{z}_{1i})$ is the leave-one-out estimator. The first-stage bandwidths are constructed as

$$\widehat{h}_1 = \widehat{h}_2 n^{-(\bar{\alpha}-\underline{\alpha})/2}. \tag{10.11}$$

This shows that we can fix the bandwidths in the first-stage regressions.

10.3.3 Choice of polynomial order

Not only does Equation (10.9) provide bounds on the rate of the optimal bandwidths, it also provides checks on the admissible combinations of local-polynomial regression estimators in stages one and two. For example, with a single instrument and one exogenous regressor ($q_1 = 1$, $q_2 = 1$), we can not deploy local-constant estimation in both stages, as we have the fallacy max$\{1, 3/2\} < 1/2$.

Figures 10.3 to 10.5 plot the bounds on the rate for h_1 across differing numbers of exogenous covariates, assuming a single instrument and a single endogenous regressor. The thin solid line is the optimal rate if we estimate bandwidths specifically for the regression of x on $\mathbf{z}$. The thick dashed lines are the bounds on the necessary rate for consistency of the second-stage local-polynomial control function regression. In Figure 10.3 we have the first stage as a local-cubic, while the second stage is local-linear. Here we can use the optimal, first-stage bandwidths. Compare this to the case where both the first and second stages use local-cubic estimators (Figure 10.4). In this case the bandwidth using the first-stage optimal rate is exactly the (strictly lower) bound. In other words, we need a bandwidth that undersmooths in the first stage, inducing less bias for the first-stage estimator.

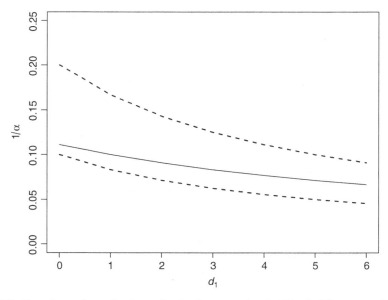

Figure 10.3. Bounds on the optimal rate for the first-stage bandwidths, holding $p_1 = 3$, $p_2 = 1$, and $q_2 = 1$

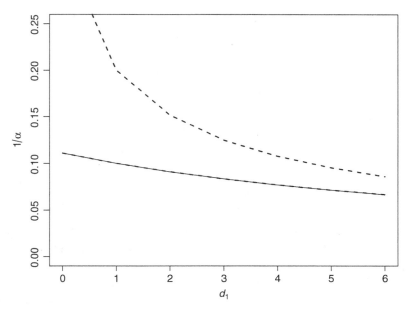

Figure 10.4. Bounds on the optimal rate for the first-stage bandwidths, holding $p_1 = 3$, $p_2 = 3$, and $q_2 = 1$

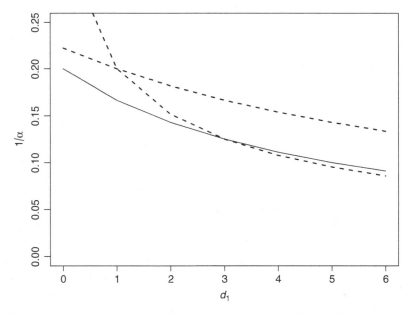

Figure 10.5. Bounds on the optimal rate for the first-stage bandwidths, holding $p_1 = 1$, $p_2 = 3$, and $q_2 = 1$

In Figure 10.5, we allow the local-polynomial estimator in the second stage to be larger than in the first stage, $p_2 = 3$ with $p_1 = 1$. Here we see that the optimal first-stage rate can only be used if $q_1 \geq 4$. Further, if $q_1 \leq 1$ we can not use the configuration of local linear in the first stage and local-cubic in the second, as no bandwidth will satisfy the rate restrictions.

Table 10.1. *Admissible combinations of polynomial orders for
the Su and Ullah (2008) estimator assuming a single
endogenous variable with a single excluded instrument*

		p_2				
		1	2	3	4	5
	1	–	–	–	–	–
	2	$q_1 \geq 0$	$q_1 \geq 0$	$q_1 \leq 4$	$q_1 \leq 3$	$q_1 \leq 2$
p_1	3	$q_1 \geq 0$	$q_1 \geq 0$	$q_1 \geq 0$	$q_1 \leq 10$	$q_1 \leq 6$
	4	$q_1 \geq 0$	$q_1 \geq 0$	$q_1 \geq 0$	$q_1 \geq 0$	$q_1 \leq 18$
	5	$q_1 \geq 0$	$q_1 \geq 0$	$q_1 \geq 0$	$q_1 \geq 0$	$q_1 \geq 0$

Table 10.1 presents admissible combinations of local-polynomial estimators, up to fifth order, that can be used for the common setting of a single endogenous regressor with a single excluded instrument based on (10.9). Two features emerge from this table. First, local-linear estimation will not be viable, regardless of q_1, in the first stage of the estimator. Second, for the lowest odd polynomial setting ($p_1 = 3$, $p_2 = 1$), all reasonable values of q_1 will satisfy the necessary conditions required in the large sample theory of Su and Ullah (2008). This suggests that in practice we adopt the local-cubic–local-linear estimation framework in the presence of a just-identified single endogenous regressor.

10.3.4 *Simulated evidence of the counterfactual simplification*

For large sample sizes, it is reasonable to expect that step 3 will be computationally expensive. Several alternatives to consistently estimate $\widehat{m}(x, \mathbf{z}_1)$ in a computationally feasible manner would be to use a fixed grid over the support of $\widehat{\varepsilon}$ or to use a random sample of size $n_1 < n$. When using a random sample, the *same* subset of $\widehat{\varepsilon}$ would be used for each evaluation point. This idea is similar to the cross-validation simplification for bandwidth selection suggested by Racine (1993). In essence, a smaller subsample can be used to conduct the counterfactual construction, given that the estimator is consistent. Alternatively, we can exploit the embarrassingly parallel nature of the counterfactual and use parallel programming methods to construct the counterfactual estimate (see Delgado and Parmeter, 2013).

Here we conduct a simple Monte Carlo simulation to illustrate the computational gains when we reduce the number of points over which to estimate the counterfactual to obtain $\widehat{m}(x, \mathbf{z}_1)$. These gains can be expected to pay off for data-driven bandwidth selection as well.

We follow the simulations in Su and Ullah (2008). Specifically, we use sample sizes of $n = 100$ and 400 for the following data generating process:

$$y_i = \ln(|x_i - 1| + 1) \cdot \text{sign}(x_i - 1) + u_i$$
$$x_i = z_i + \varepsilon_i,$$

where $(u_i, \varepsilon_i, z_i)$ is generated as *iid* multivariate normal with mean vector $(0, 0, 0)$ and variance–covariance matrix

Table 10.2. *Median RMSE and computation times (in seconds) for differing
subsample sizes for the counterfactual analysis of the Su and Ullah (2008) estimator
(values in brackets are the lower and upper extreme deciles) – the results in the
column 1.00 represent the "full sample" Su and Ullah (2008) estimator*

	$n = 100$			$n = 400$		
	0.25	0.50	1.00	0.25	0.50	1.00
RMSE	0.256	0.245	0.239	0.168	0.169	0.167
	[0.198,0.318]	[0.192,0.306]	[0.193,0.313]	[0.135,0.205]	[0.132,0.205]	[0.132,0.205]
Time (secs.)	8.72	17.36	34.74	161.24	330.24	683.59
	[8.70,8.74]	[17.34,17.39]	[34.69,34.82]	[161.06,161.43]	[329.76,330.62]	[682.24,684.52]

$$\Sigma = \begin{bmatrix} 1 & 0.2 & 0 \\ 0.2 & 1 & 0 \\ 0 & 0 & 1 \end{bmatrix}.$$

The sign function is defined as $\text{sign}(b) = 1$ for $b > 0$, $= -1$ for $b < 0$, and $= 0$ for
$b = 0$. We set $p_1 = 3$, $p_2 = 1$ and use random samples of size $n_1 = 0.25n$, $0.50n$, and
$1.00n$, where $1.00n$ represents the "full sample" Su and Ullah (2008) estimator. We
compare root mean square error (RMSE) as our performance metric of the different
estimators and for each simulation we document the time it takes to construct the
estimator over the n data points. We use a total of 250 simulations.

Lastly, our bandwidths are calculated as follows: we use $\widehat{h}_2 = 2\widehat{\sigma}_x n^{-1/5}$ as our
second-stage bandwidth for both x and $\widehat{\varepsilon}$, while $\widehat{h}_1 = \widehat{h}_2 n^{-1/20}$, consistent with the
rule provided in (10.11). While Su and Ullah (2008) use an Epanechnikov kernel for
their simulations, we deploy a Gaussian kernel here.

Table 10.2 presents the median and extreme quartile values of the relative RMSE
and run times of our random counterfactual approach to that of the "full sample" Su
and Ullah (2008) estimator across the simulations. As expected, regardless of sample size, the time gains are proportional to the percentage of included observations.
However, the loss in precision of the estimator is less impacted by the choice of this
percentage than you would think. For $n_1 = 0.25n$, we have a median RMSE ratio of
$0.245/0.239 \approx 1.07$, when $n = 100$, while for $n = 400$, we have $0.168/0.167 \approx$
1.006. Contrast this to the time gains, and the counterfactual nature of the Su and
Ullah (2008) estimator is less daunting. This approach is also useful for data-driven
bandwidth selection in this setting, as the gains in constructing the counterfactual
are further amplified given the repeated evaluation of the estimator across different
bandwidths.

10.3.5 A valid bootstrap procedure

While Su and Ullah (2008) provide the limiting distribution of their local-polynomial
control-function estimator, our earlier discussion regarding slow convergence to the
asymptotic distribution holds here as well. Resampling methods that preserve the endogeneity are required to consistently provide inferential statements. A simple bootstrap
approach in the current setting is the pairs bootstrap proposed by Blundell, Chen, and

Kristensen (2007). The bootstrap in Blundell, Chen, and Kristensen (2007) is for a semiparametric version of the nonparametric instrumental variable model of Newey and Powell (2003), which uses the condition $E(u|\mathbf{z}) = 0$ for identification. Our use of the control function approach necessitates a slightly different version of the bootstrap, which we propose here. Recall from Chapter 5 that we must evaluate the unknown conditional mean at the sample points to construct standard errors.

1. For each $i = 1, 2, \ldots, n$ randomly sample, with replacement pairs from $\{y_i, \mathbf{x}_i, \mathbf{z}_{1i}, \mathbf{z}_{2i}\}_{i=1}^{n}$ and call the resulting sample $\{y_i^*, \mathbf{x}_i^*, \mathbf{z}_{1i}^*, \mathbf{z}_{2i}^*\}_{i=1}^{n}$ the bootstrap sample.
2. Using the bootstrap sample, estimate the unknown function $\widehat{g}^*(\cdot)$ and obtain the bootstrapped residuals from the equation, $\widehat{\varepsilon}_i^* = \mathbf{x}_i^* - \widehat{g}^*(\mathbf{z}_i)$ (in the multivariate $\mathbf{x}$ case, we will do this for each $\mathbf{x}$). Remember to evaluate at the original data points $(\mathbf{z}_i)$. We can use the same first-stage bandwidth as the initial estimator.
3. Using the bootstrap residuals, estimate the unknown control-function regression, $\widehat{w}^*(\mathbf{x}_i, \mathbf{z}_{1i}, \widehat{\varepsilon}_i^*)$. Remember to evaluate at the original data points $(\mathbf{x}_i, \mathbf{z}_{1i})$. Here we can use the same second-stage bandwidths as the initial estimator.
4. Calculate the counterfactual estimates (and gradients) at the sample points as

$$\widehat{m}^*(\mathbf{x}, \mathbf{z}_1) = n^{-1} \sum_{i=1}^{n} \widehat{w}^*(\mathbf{x}, \mathbf{z}_1, \widehat{\varepsilon}_i^*).$$

5. Repeat steps 1–4 a large number (B) of times and then construct the sampling distribution of the bootstrapped estimates. Standard errors can be obtained by taking the standard deviation of the sampling distribution for each particular estimate.

A wild bootstrap approach that simply resamples from the residuals from the control function equation $(\widehat{u}_i)$ will not properly mimic the underlying triangular setup in (10.7) and (10.8). An alternative "wild" resampling algorithm would be to jointly resample from $(\widehat{u}, \widehat{\varepsilon})$, using $\widehat{\varepsilon}$ and $\widehat{g}(\mathbf{z})$ to construct new values of $\mathbf{x}$. These new values of $\mathbf{x}$ can then be used to construct new values of y and the entire model can then be estimated with this new data.

10.4 Weak instruments

In the parametric instrumental variable literature, a large body of work has studied the impact, both empirically and theoretically, of the presence of weak instruments. However, to date, little research exists studying this phenomenon in the nonparametric setting. Our discussion here focuses on the recent work of Han (2013), who provides a formal definition of weak instruments in the control-function setting and provides a series-based estimator to tackle the problem. We will present a kernel-based solution to this problem.

To begin, we focus on identification of the unknown function of interest in (10.7), $m(\mathbf{x}_i, \mathbf{z}_{1i})$. Newey, Powell, and Vella (1999) provide a sufficient condition for identification: the rank of the vector of derivatives of $g(\mathbf{z})$ on the instruments ($\mathbf{z}_2$) is equal to the dimension of the endogenous variables in $m(\cdot)$, which is the nonparametric equivalent to the parametric rank condition, which effectively requires as many instruments as endogenous variables. Formally, they require

$$\Pr\left\{\operatorname{rank}\left(\frac{\partial g(\mathbf{z})}{\partial \mathbf{z}_2'}\right) = q_x\right\} = 1.$$

In the setting, where $q_1 = 0$ and there is a single instrument and endogenous variable, this condition effectively requires that the relationship between x and $\mathbf{z}_2$ is not constant. Again, this condition is the nonparametric generalization of the rank condition for linear models. However, as noted by Han (2013), this condition is not enough to understand what a weak instrument is, since it may be possible to identify the model if $0 < \Pr\left\{\operatorname{rank}\left(\frac{\partial g(\mathbf{z})}{\partial \mathbf{z}_2'}\right) = q_x\right\} < 1$.

To develop a formal notion of weak instruments in this setting, Han (2013) developed the necessary and sufficient conditions to identify $m(\mathbf{x}, \mathbf{z}_1)$. To describe these conditions, we need to introduce a key set. This set, termed the relevant set, is the region where the rank condition holds. Let $\mathcal{X}$ denote the support of $\mathbf{x}$, $\mathcal{Z}$ the support of $\mathbf{z} = (\mathbf{z}_1, \mathbf{z}_2)$, and $\mathcal{Z}_1$ the support of $\mathbf{z}_1$. Further let $\mathcal{X}_{|z}$ denote the support of $\mathbf{x}$ for a given $\mathbf{z} \in \mathcal{Z}$. To understand what a weak instrument looks like in the nonparametric setting, we need to first delineate between local and global identification. We can think of local identification as being able to point identify $m(\mathbf{x}, \mathbf{z}_1)$ for $\mathbf{x} \in \mathcal{X}_{|z}$, while global identification is the ability to point identify $m(\mathbf{x}, \mathbf{z}_1)$ for $\mathbf{x} \in \mathcal{X}$.

The relevant set for the instruments is defined as

$$\mathcal{Z}_{|z_1}^r = \left\{\mathbf{z} \in \mathcal{Z}_{|z_1} : \operatorname{rank}\left(\frac{\partial g(\mathbf{z})}{\partial \mathbf{z}_2'}\right) = q_x\right\}.$$

This set reveals the region of $\mathcal{Z}$ where the unknown relationship between $\mathbf{x}$ and $\mathbf{z}_2$ has full rank for a given value of $\mathbf{z}_1$. When $\mathbf{x}$ is univariate, $\mathcal{Z}_{|z_1}^r$ is the region where $g(\mathbf{z})$ has a nonzero slope in $\mathbf{z}_2$. Lastly, the relevant set for the endogenous variables is defined as

$$\mathcal{X}_{|z_1}^r = \left\{\mathbf{x} \in \mathcal{X}_{|z} : \mathbf{z} \in \mathcal{Z}_{|z_1}^r\right\}.$$

This relevant set is the support of $\mathbf{x}$ that will allow identification of $m(\mathbf{x}, \mathbf{z})$. Recall that if $\mathbf{z} \in \mathcal{Z}_{|z_1}^r$, then the rank condition holds. Technically, we want an instrument such that $\mathcal{X}_{|z_1}^r \equiv \mathcal{X}$.

With these sets, Han (2013) defines identification of $m(\mathbf{x}, \mathbf{z}_1)$ as being identified over $(\mathcal{X}, \mathcal{Z}_1)$, except for a set with measure zero. Global identification therefore requires that $\mathcal{X}$ and $\mathcal{X}_{|\mathbf{z}_1}^r$ only differ on a set with measure zero. One extreme example of this would be if $g(\mathbf{z}) = z^3$. In this case $g(0) = 0$; however, $\mathcal{X}$ and $\mathcal{X}_{|\mathbf{z}_1}^r$ are effectively identical and so $m(x, \mathbf{z}_1)$ is identified. Given that identification only requires that $\mathcal{X}$ and $\mathcal{X}_{|\mathbf{z}_1}^r$ differ except on a measure zero set, this does not require that $g(\mathbf{z})$ can only be constant on a set of measure zero. The necessary and sufficient condition for identification is

$$\Pr\left\{z \in \mathcal{Z}_{|z_1}^r | z_1\right\} > 0,$$

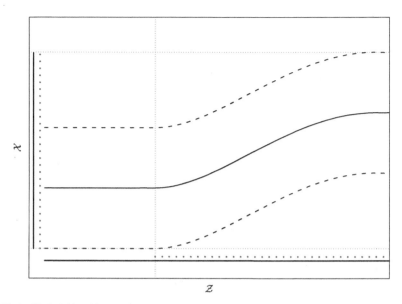

Figure 10.6. Global identification and the relevant set for x

which requires that the instrument(s) takes values where, conditional on z_1, the rank condition is satisfied and so enough variation in x is produced to "reconstruct" the support of x. This is illustrated in Figure 10.6. Here we have the relationship $x = g(z) + \varepsilon$ where $\varepsilon \sim \mathcal{U}[-3/4, 3/4]$ and $g(z) = (15/16)(1 - z^2)1\{|z| \le 1\}$ where $z \sim \mathcal{U}[-1.5, 0.1]$. In this case we have that $\mathcal{Z}^r = [-1, 0.1]$ and $\mathcal{X} = [0.25, 2.6785] \equiv \mathcal{X}^r$. Even though we have a set with positive measure where $g'(z) = 0$, namely, $z \in [-1.5, -1]$, $z \in \mathcal{Z}^r$ produces enough variation in x to effectively mimic $\mathcal{X}$. $\mathcal{X}^r$ and $\mathcal{Z}^r$ are shown as the dotted lines while $\mathcal{X}$ and $\mathcal{Z}$ are shown as the thick lines. The dashed lines are the local support of x, for a fixed value of z.

Next, consider Figure 10.7, which has the same $g(z)$, but $\varepsilon \sim \mathcal{U}[-3/4, 3/4]$ for $z > -1$ and $\varepsilon \sim \mathcal{U}[-0.75z, 0.75z]$ for $z \le -1$. In this case we cannot globally identify $g(z)$ because $\mathcal{X}^r \ne \mathcal{X}$. This specific form of heteroskedasticity has restricted the range over which z can mimic variation in x and impedes full identification of $m(x, z_1)$.

10.4.1 Weak identification

The discussion so far has focused purely on global identification of $m(\mathbf{x}, z_1)$ over $\mathcal{X}$ and $\mathcal{Z}_1$. Han (2013) uses the necessary and sufficient condition for identification to develop the appropriate notion of a weak instrument in the nonparametric context. First, note that identification will not hold if

$$\Pr\left\{\mathrm{rank}\left(\frac{\partial g(z)}{\partial z_2'}\right) < q_x | z_1\right\} = 1$$

for some z_1 in a set with nonzero measure. Alternatively, "non-identification" implies that $\Pr\left\{z \in \mathcal{Z}_{|z_1}^r | z_1\right\} = 0$; no values of the instrument exist that fall with positive

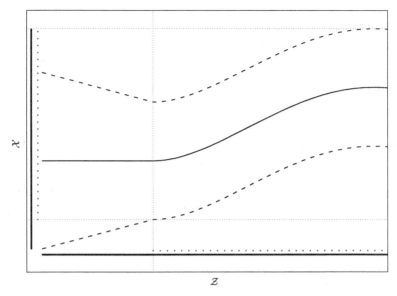

Figure 10.7. Local identification and the relevant set for x

probability into the relevant set. This can happen because there are simply not enough instruments or the excluded instruments are jointly irrelevant for at least one of the endogenous regressors.

Note that having two endogenous regressors (x_1 and x_2) and a single instrument variable (z) does not imply that the number of instruments is a problem. For example, we can use z to instrument for x_1 and $\exp(z)$ to instrument for x_2. In this case, it is still possible to achieve identification. The intuition here is that the nonlinear nature of the problem allows a single instrument to be used as an instrument more than once, depending upon the nature of the relationship between z and the endogenous variables. This is one benefit of the nonparametric setup with respect to tackling endogeneity over linear parametric models.

To formally define weak instruments, we follow Han (2013) and introduce a class of functions from which elements will not allow identification of $m(\mathbf{x}, \mathbf{z}_1)$. This class of functions is

$$\mathcal{G}_{NI}(\mathcal{Z}) = \left\{ g(\cdot) \in \mathcal{G}(\mathcal{Z}) : \Pr\left\{ \operatorname{rank}\left(\frac{\partial g(\mathbf{z})}{\partial \mathbf{z}_2'} \right) < q_x | \mathbf{z}_1 \right\} = 1 \right\}$$

for some $\mathbf{z}_1$ in a set with nonzero measure. Here the set $\mathcal{G}(\mathcal{Z})$ is the set of functions that satisfy several smoothness constraints necessary for Han's (2013) discussion (notably continuous differentiability). The identification region ($\mathcal{G}_I$) is simply the complement of $\mathcal{G}_{NI}$.

Han (2013) defines nonparametric weak instruments as a sequence of functions that are locally equivalent to a function falling in $\mathcal{G}_{NI}$. That is, as the sample size grows, the reduced-form equation becomes closer to the non-identified class of functions. This is similar to the linear parametric setup where the parameters of the reduced-form equation decay to zero at a specific rate. To formalize this notion more clearly, consider

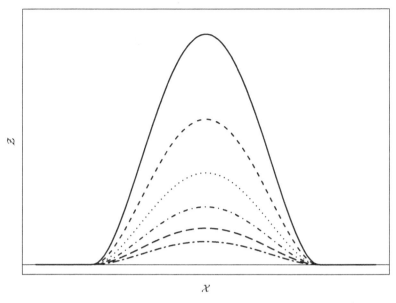

Figure 10.8. Weak identification of $m(x)$

the control function setup, only now our reduced form function $(g(\mathbf{z}))$ is dependent upon the sample size:

$$y = m(\mathbf{x}, \mathbf{z}_1) + u$$
$$x = g_n(\mathbf{z}) + \varepsilon$$

where $g_n(\cdot) \in \mathcal{G}_I$, but steadily moves towards $\mathcal{G}_{NI}$ as the sample size grows. This provides the precise notion of weak instruments in the nonparametric setting. In the linear parametric setup, weak instruments have coefficients that are zero in the limit, whereas in the nonparametric setup, weak instruments are those whose reduced form functional relationship is constant in the limit.

Han's (2013) precise definition of a weak instrument in the current setup is the following: $m(\mathbf{x}, \mathbf{z}_1)$ is weakly identified as $n \rightarrow \infty$ if $g_n(\mathbf{z}) \in \mathcal{G}_I$ for some n and there exists $\bar{g}(\mathbf{z}) \in \mathcal{G}_{NI}$ such that $||g_n(\mathbf{z}) - \bar{g}(\mathbf{z})|| \rightarrow 0$ almost surely as $n \rightarrow \infty$. In the case where no $\mathbf{z}_1$ is in the model and we have a single endogenous variable, this condition simply states that $g(\mathbf{z})$ becomes a constant as the sample size grows. This is illustrated in Figure 10.8. Here our instrument function decays to a constant based on the sample size. In this specific example, our function is $g(z) = (n^{-1/5})(15/16)$ $(1 - z^2) 1\{|z| \leq 1\}$ for $n = 10, 100, 1{,}000, 10{,}000,$ and $100{,}000$, which decays to zero at the univariate nonparametric rate. While the function is never flat for a given sample size, asymptotically, the instrument function behaves as though it is a constant, violating the rank condition and effectively impeding the ability to identify x.

10.4.2 Estimation in the presence of weak instruments

The (estimation) problem with weak instruments is that they represent a form of multicollinearity in the control function. Consider the case where the reduced form relationship is completely flat. In this case $\mathbf{z}$ has no explanatory power and the "resid-uals" from this relationship, up to a constant, are identical to x. Upon placing the residuals as a covariate into the structural function, both covariates, x and $\widehat{\varepsilon}$ have an identical impact on y. Thus, the two functions, $m(x)$ and $r(\widehat{\varepsilon})$ are identical. This prob-lem is termed "concurvity" by Hastie and Tibshirani (1993) and it is the functional equivalent of multicollinearity in the linear in parameters setting.

A solution to regulate the impact of concurvity is local-polynomial ridge regres-sion. Ridge regression solves the same local-polynomial problem, but with an added penalty on the smoothness of the unknown function and its derivatives. For exposi-tion, consider local-polynomial ridge regression in the univariate setting. Our objective function is

$$\min_{a_0,a_1,\ldots,a_p} \sum_{i=1}^{n} \left[y_i - a_0 - a_1 (x_i - x) - a_2 (x_i - x)^2 - \cdots - a_p (x_i - x)^p \right]^2$$
$$k \left(\frac{x_i - x}{h} \right) + \sum_{j=v+1}^{p} \xi_j a_j^2,$$

where the first summand is the traditional objective function from local-polynomial estimation. The second summand is introduced to control how large the fluctuations are of the higher-order derivatives of the unknown function. The ridging of the local-polynomial estimator occurs on the derivatives of the unknown function from order v to p. Here we implicitly assume that $m^{(v)}(x)$ is bounded for all x for $v \le p$.

Progressing to the full matrix setup, recall from Chapter 5 that the local-polynomial least-squares estimator is

$$\widehat{\delta}(x) = \left(\mathbf{X}'K(x)\mathbf{X} \right)^{-1} \mathbf{X}'K(x)\mathbf{y},$$

where $\mathbf{X} \equiv \left[1, (x_i - x), (x_i - x)^2, \ldots, (x_i - x)^p \right]$. Imposing higher-order restric-tions on all derivatives of the function through the matrix $\mathbf{D}$, such that $\delta(x)'\mathbf{D}\delta(x)$ is bounded, the local-polynomial ridge regression estimator is (Seifert and Gasser, 1996, 2000)

$$\widetilde{\delta}(x) = \left(\mathbf{D} + \mathbf{X}'K(x)\mathbf{X} \right)^{-1} \mathbf{X}'K(x)\mathbf{y}.$$

Here $\mathbf{D}$ is a diagonal matrix and the diagonal elements can all be different depending upon the chosen restrictiveness of the ridging (ξ_j). Hall and Marron (1997) and Deng, Chu, and Cheng (2001) suggest setting the first diagonal element of $\mathbf{D}$ to 0, thus only penalizing smoothness of the unknown function, but allowing it to be unbounded.

Given the above discussion, we are now in a position to discuss implementation of the Su and Ullah (2008) estimator in the presence of weak instruments. The first stage local-polynomial regression still proceeds as before. However, the second stage now uses local-polynomial ridge regression instead of local-polynomial regression. After the ridge estimator has been constructed, the counterfactual construction of $m(x, \mathbf{z}_1)$ proceeds as if we are in the strong instrument setting. A data-driven cross-validation procedure can be implemented to simultaneously select the diagonal elements of $\mathbf{D}$ as well as h_1 and h_2.

Han (2013, Theorem 6.1) demonstrates that the impact of weak instruments in the nonparametric setting is a contribution to both bias and variance. In the parametric setting, weak instruments only inflate the variance of the instrumental variables estimator, but do not affect bias. Further, the fact that weak instruments impact *both* the bias and the variance implies that selecting a different bandwidth will not mitigate their presence. That is, we might think to increase the bandwidth of the second-stage local-polynomial estimator to reduce the variance, but because the weak instruments also inflate the bias, their presence is not fully contained. Alternatively, if we were to lower the second-stage bandwidth to lessen the bias, we would still have an unduly inflated variance given the weak instruments. The ridging works to combat the impact of weak instruments in both the bias and the variance independently of the bandwidth.

10.4.3 Importance of nonlinearity in the first stage

A key insight from the work of Han (2013) is that we can amplify the impact of a weak instrument through an erroneous assumption of linearity in the first-stage estimation. The use of a linear first stage may be prudent to avoid issues related to the dimensionality of $\mathbf{z}$. However, this does not come without costs. Specifically, omitted nonlinearities (through the use of a linear function) may produce weak instruments, which would not arise had the first stage been correctly specified.

Recall that Han's (2013) and Newey, Powell, and Vella's (1999) necessary condition for identification implies that (in the univariate case) only a subset of the support of x and z where $g(\cdot)$ is nonlinear may be enough to identify $m(\cdot)$. However, by assuming that $g(\cdot)$ is linear, this can eliminate the identifying region, and potentially exacerbate the "weakness" of the instruments. What this means is that instruments that may be strong when used to model a nonlinear relationship may be weak when modeling a linear relationship.

This insight has important implications for practical work. Namely, since there is little theoretical loss by modeling the reduced form between x and $\mathbf{z}$ in a nonparametric fashion, we should attempt to model nonlinearities in the first stage to assist with identification, unless there is specific economic justification for a linear reduced form. That is, a linear reduced form is prone to misspecification in addition to possibly weak instruments in the linear setting, but not in the nonlinear setting (noting that the converse is not true). Further, if the dimensionality of the reduced form is problematic, we could exploit the methods in Chapter 9 to allow for nonlinearities.

10.5 Discrete endogenous regressor

When the endogenous variable is discrete, a simplification of the model exists that allows for a common two-stage estimation approach without relying on the control function. Further, the "discreteness" of the endogenous variable acts as a type of smoothness restriction, which avoids the ill-posed inverse problem. The following approach was formulated in Das (2005).

Consider the setup described in (10.7), only now x is a single discrete endogenous regressor that takes the values $1, \ldots, J$. Let $d_j = 1\{x = j\}$. We can reformulate the model as

$$
\begin{aligned}
y_i &= m(x_i, \mathbf{z}_{1i}) + u_i \\
&= m_1(\mathbf{z}_{1i})d_1 + m_2(\mathbf{z}_{1i})d_2 + \cdots m_J(\mathbf{z}_{1i})d_J + u_i.
\end{aligned}
$$

Noting that $d_J = 1 - d_1 - d_2 - \cdots d_{J-1}$, we have

$$
y_i = m_J(\mathbf{z}_{1i}) + \sum_{j=1}^{J-1} \left(m_j(\mathbf{z}_{1i}) - m_J(\mathbf{z}_{1i}) \right) d_j + u_i,
$$

where group J acts as the reference group.

Under the common conditional mean assumption of the instruments $\mathbf{z}$ ($E(u|\mathbf{z}) = 0$), we have that for $p_j(\mathbf{z}) = E\left(d_j|\mathbf{z}\right)$ ($j = 1, 2, \ldots, J-1$), the reduced form model is

$$
E(y|\mathbf{z}) = \alpha(\mathbf{z}_{1i}) + \sum_{j=1}^{J-1} \beta(\mathbf{z}_1) p_j(\mathbf{z}),
$$

where $\alpha(\mathbf{z}_{1i}) \equiv m_J(\mathbf{z}_{1i})$ and $\beta(\mathbf{z}_1) \equiv m_j(\mathbf{z}_{1i}) - m_J(\mathbf{z}_{1i})$. For known $p_j(\mathbf{z})$, this implies that when discrete endogenous variables are present, the fully nonparametric setup reduces to that of a semiparametric smooth coefficient model (described in Chapter 9). Note that this is not a restriction that is imposed, but rather one that presents itself given the nature of the discrete variable. Regardless of the presence of endogeneity, this framework holds for a fully nonparametric model in the presence of discrete covariates. Cai, Das, Xiong, and Wu (2006) specifically discuss the large sample theory of the estimator of the control function model when the endogenous covariates are continuous, and this specific semiparametric form is assumed to hold.

Das (2005) gives a series-based estimator for this model; however, as we learned in Chapter 9, this model is estimable in the kernel framework. This estimator consists of two steps. In the first step, nonparametric regression (say, local-constant) is performed to obtain an estimate of $\widehat{p}_j(\mathbf{z}) = \widehat{E}\left(d_j|\mathbf{z}\right)$ for each j ($j = 1, 2, \ldots, J-1$). These $\widehat{p}_j$s are then used as covariates in the parametric component of the smooth coefficient model, which is then estimated. The function levels are then recovered as $\widehat{m}_J(\mathbf{z}_1) = \widehat{\alpha}(\mathbf{z}_1)$ and $\widehat{m}_j(\mathbf{z}_1) = \widehat{\beta}_j(\mathbf{z}_1) + \widehat{\alpha}(\mathbf{z}_1)$. Unlike the Su and Ullah (2008) estimator, no additional counterfactual step is needed. In fact, notice that the residuals from the first stage regression do not enter the second stage and are not required for identification.

10.6 Testing

With the exception of the aforementioned test in Horowitz (2012), to the best of our knowledge there has been little research on specification testing in the control-function setting. There are three main tests that are important for empirical work with the estimators described here, namely, a test for correct specification of both stages, a test for instrument validity, and a test for weak instruments. This area of nonparametric inference is still in its infancy and it is not clear which style of test (e.g., goodness-of-fit or conditional-moment) will become the predominant workhorse for these types of estimators.

Undoubtedly, given the importance of instrumental variable estimation in applied economic work, we expect that tests of these hypotheses will soon be developed. As a crude alternative, we suggest goodness-of-fit tests for both the presence of endogeneity (for instance, an LLLS estimator ignoring potential endogeneity versus the Su and Ullah, 2008, model) and correct parametric specification (by comparing the residual sum of squares across parametric IV and nonparametric IV models). In both cases valid bootstrap procedures would be required to ensure that the specific null hypothesis was enforced.

10.7 Application

Our illustration of the Su and Ullah (2008) estimator follows our discussion in Chapter 5. We focus on cross-country output (Y) as a function of physical capital (K) and human-capital-augmented labor (HL) in country i at time t. In this example we treat K as endogenous and use lagged capital stock as an instrument. This provides us with 1,127 observations. This is smaller than the 1,244 observations used when we ignored endogeneity in Chapter 5, but given that viable instruments in cross-country growth/output studies are of dubious validity (Bazzi and Clemens, 2013), lagged values will suffice to illustrate Su and Ullah's estimator.

Our cross-country production function model can be written as

$$Y_{it} = m(K_{it}, HL_{it}) + u_{it} \tag{10.12}$$
$$K_{it} = g(K_{i,t-1}, HL_{it}) + \varepsilon_{it}, \tag{10.13}$$

noting that our lag is for the previous observation (five years past). We use a local-cubic estimator in the first stage ($p_1 = 3$) and a local-linear estimator in the second stage ($p_2 = 1$). Bandwidths are obtained using the LSCV routine outlined in (10.10). We also use a random subsample of 25% of the first stage residuals to construct our counterfactual estimates, and the bandwidths were found using 10 different sets of random starting values. The bandwidths for our first stage are 0.113 for HL_{it} and 0.111 for $K_{i,t-1}$ (the standard deviations of HL_{it} and $K_{i,t-1}$ are 4.153 and 3.184, respectively). Additionally, the second-stage bandwidths for HL_{it} and K_{it} are 0.151 for HL_{it} and 0.150 for K_{it} with associated standard deviations of 4.153 and 3.971, respectively.[1]

For comparison purposes, we also estimated $m(\cdot)$ in (10.12) using local-linear least-squares, ignoring potential endogeneity in K_{it} using the same second-stage bandwidths from the Su and Ullah (2008) estimator, as well as a linearized Cobb–Douglas model using standard linear instrumental variables (LIV). We used the same second-stage bandwidths from the Su and Ullah estimator as our bandwidths for the LLLS estimator, which ignores endogeneity.

---

[1] For the bandwidth on the control variate, which is integrated out, we use the same bandwidth as that of the endogenous regression, K_{it}.

Table 10.3. *Estimated gradients of the cross-country production function*

	K			HL			
	Q_1	Q_2	Q_3	Q_1	Q_2	Q_3	R^2
Su–Ullah	0.734	0.753	0.793	0.227	0.247	0.323	0.893
	(0.029)	(0.038)	(0.023)	(0.053)	(0.026)	(0.053)	
LLLS	0.800	0.827	0.878	0.184	0.203	0.331	0.994
	(0.019)	(0.042)	(0.019)	(0.167)	(0.028)	(0.097)	
LIV		0.921			0.013		0.948
		(0.008)			(0.007)		

Table 10.3 presents the gradient estimates (and corresponding pairs bootstrap standard errors) for our three models. Beginning with our parametric estimates, the LIV estimator suggests that the impact of physical capital on output is an order of magnitude higher than the impact of human-capital-augmented labor. In both nonparametric models, the impact of human-capital-augmented labor is substantially higher across the distribution of gradients than for the LIV estimator. This suggests that the linear model is missing important nonlinearities. Comparing our two sets of nonparametric estimates, we see that the impact of physical capital is higher by approximately 8-9% while the impact of human-capital-augmented labor is lower by approximately 22-23% at the first quartile and median, and is roughly 2.5% higher at the third quartile for the local-linear estimator, which ignores endogeneity.

The fact that the LLLS estimator fits the data better represents that we are using the optimal bandwidths for the control function estimator, which were found using LSCV. Thus, two features are at play here. First, as we have continually expounded, LSCV tends to estimate bandwidths that are smaller than the optimal levels, leading to overfitting. Second, it could also be the case that our bandwidths for the control function estimator are smaller than the optimal LLLS bandwidths in general. Both of these issues could then explain why the LLLS estimator has a fit of nearly unity.

Figures 10.9 and 10.10 present the 45° plots for the gradient estimates of physical capital and human-capital-augmented labor across the two nonparametric methods. Further, the vertical and horizontal dashed lines represent the LIV estimate for each variable. There appears to be nonlinearity in both variables, which suggests misspecification of the LIV estimator. Additionally, both nonparametric models suggest that human-capital-augmented labor has a positive and significant effect on output, whereas our LIV model, while finding a positive estimate, is statistically insignificant.

Both the 45° plots and the tabulated quartiles of the gradient estimates suggest that there is not much difference between the model that accounts for endogeneity and the one that ignores it. However, a key area where the two models provided differing results is in estimated returns to scale. Figure 10.11 plots the estimate cumulative distribution functions for estimated RTS for both models. Visually, a first-order stochastic

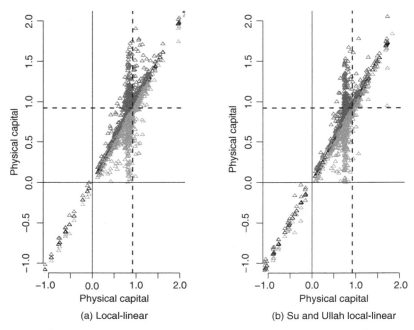

Figure 10.9. 45° plots for local-linear and instrumental-variable local-linear estimators for physical capital

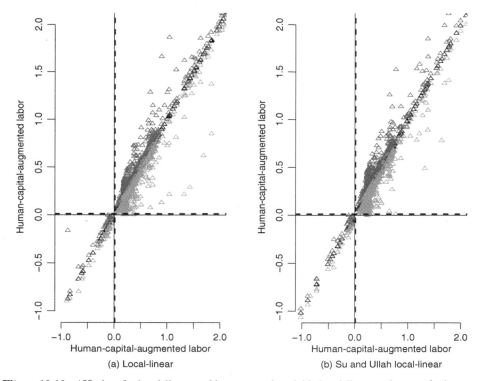

Figure 10.10. 45° plots for local-linear and instrumental-variable local-linear estimators for human-capital-augmented labor

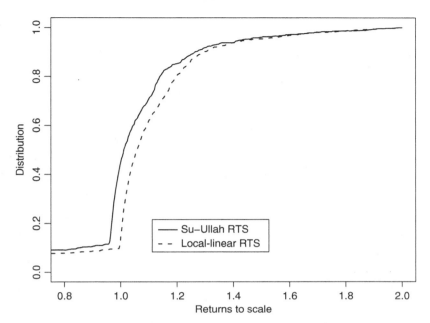

Figure 10.11. Cumulative distribution functions for estimated RTS from the LLLS model and the Su and Ullah model

dominance relationship emerges. Following Henderson and Maasoumi (2013), we formally test for this dominance within our estimates. A Kolmogorov-Smirnov test fails to reject the null of first-order stochastic dominance of the distributions of the estimated RTS, suggesting that the LLLS estimates first-order stochastically dominate the RTS estimates from the Su and Ullah model. This implies that failure to control for endogeneity leads to uniformly higher RTS in the sample.

11

Panel data

Nonparametric estimation of panel-data models are becoming increasingly popular in the literature. Most of the earlier methods were developed by statisticians and focused on random-effects-type estimators (e.g., Lin and Carroll, 2001). These methods are valid when the individual specific effects are uncorrelated with the regressors. This assumption is generally violated with economic data. More recent work allows for correlation between the individual specific effects and the regressors (e.g., Henderson, Carroll, and Li, 2008; Qian and Wang, 2012). These fixed-effects estimators are more difficult to implement, as is the case with parametric nonlinear panel-data models, as taking a simple first difference or averaging over time and differencing does not lead to a parsimonious model.

In this chapter, we outline several existing fixed and random effects nonparametric estimators. We pay special attention here to the rate of convergence of the estimators as well as how incorporating the variance–covariance structure affects estimation. An unexpected result of the current crop of these estimators is that incorporation of the variance–covariance matrix often leads to no asymptotic improvement. This result often occurs because, as we have explained previously, as the sample size increases, the bandwidth decrease towards zero. Therefore as we have larger samples, we end up using a smaller neighborhood of data around the point, mitigating the ability of the exploitation of the variance–covariance structure to improve estimation efficiency. Recent research has successfully overcome this issue (e.g., Yang, 2013; Yao and Li, 2013).

As with each estimator in our book, we discuss bandwidth selection. Here we discuss cross-validation methods which are unique to panel data. The same holds true for bootstrap methods in order to calculate standard errors and perform tests. We consider tests for poolability, correct functional form specification, and a nonparametric Hausman test.

In most of this chapter we discuss one-way error component models, primarily focusing our discussion on controlling for individual effects. It is possible to also estimate models, controlling for both individual and time effects. These are generally referred to as two-way error-component models. The extension from one-way to two-way models is relatively trivial in several circumstances. In the random-effects framework, this just requires specifying a different variance–covariance matrix of the random disturbances. However, for nonparametric fixed-effects estimators, this is often more complicated due to the multiple rounds of differencing which need to occur to eliminate the various effects. This is relatively untouched in both the applied and theoretical literature and so we choose to mostly ignore it at this point. That being said, we do discuss one method that will handle both types of effects in a fixed-effects framework.

In our empirical example, we estimate the worldwide production function with several of the nonparametric panel-data estimators discussed within. We find interesting results in bandwidth selection. Specifically, a leave-one-cross-section-out bandwidth selector typically brings about larger bandwidths than a leave-one-observation-out bandwidth selector. Although we initially hoped for big differences in the estimated relative elasticities, these results are similar to those in previous chapters.

11.1 Pooled models

Consider the nonparametric panel-data model

$$y_{it} = m(\mathbf{x}_{it}) + u_{it}, i = 1, 2, \ldots, n, t = 1, 2, \ldots, T_i \tag{11.1}$$

where y_{it} is the endogenous variable, $\mathbf{x}_{it}$ is a vector of q exogenous variables, and $m(\cdot)$ is an unknown smooth function.[1] Here we define the total number of observations as $nT \equiv \sum_{i=1}^{n} T_i$. Unless otherwise stated, we will allow for our panels to be unbalanced. It is common in economic research to have unbalanced panels and unfortunately most theoretical nonparametric panel data papers only consider the balanced-data case. Therefore, here we show how to estimate each of these models when your panel is unbalanced. Sometimes this only involves minor notational change in the summations, while other times it is more difficult. However, it is much easier to go from the unbalanced to the balanced case than the opposite. Balanced versions of each of the estimators and tests discussed in this chapter can be found in the corresponding references. Further, given the curse of dimensionality, we often need to exploit all the data we can obtain. That being said, you need to question why some of your observations are missing in practice, as this may be a sign of sample selection bias.[2]

We consider the case that the error u_{it} follows a one-way error component specification

$$u_{it} = \mu_i + v_{it}, \tag{11.2}$$

where μ_i is iid $(0, \sigma_u^2)$, v_{it} is iid $(0, \sigma_v^2)$, and μ_i and v_{jt} are uncorrelated for all i and j, $j = 1, 2, \ldots, n$. For now we assume that μ_i and v_{jt} are uncorrelated with $\mathbf{x}_{it}$ for all i, j and t, but we will relax the assumption that μ_i and $\mathbf{x}_{it}$ are uncorrelated later. We are interested in estimating the unknown function $m(\mathbf{x})$ at a point $\mathbf{x}$ and perhaps the slope of $m(\mathbf{x})$, $\beta(\mathbf{x}) = \partial m(\mathbf{x})/\partial \mathbf{x}$. We consider the usual panel-data situation of large n and finite T_i.

The simplest consistent method to estimate the parameters of the model is simply to ignore the correlation structure in the errors. Nonparametric kernel estimation of the unknown function and its gradient can be obtained, for example, by using LCLS estimation. This is identical to the estimation found in Chapter 5, except that we sum over both the cross-sectional unit i ($= 1, 2, \ldots, n$) and time dimension t ($= 1, 2, \ldots, T_i$).

---

[1] Our notation suggests that all cross-sectional units start at period 1, but this can be relaxed.

[2] For a treatment of estimation in unbalanced parametric models, see chapter 9 of Baltagi (2008).

The pooled LCLS estimator is obtained by minimizing

$$\sum_{i=1}^{n} \sum_{t=1}^{T_i} \left[y_{it} - m\left(\mathbf{x}\right) \right]^2 K_h\left(\mathbf{x}_{it}, \mathbf{x}\right)$$

with respect to $m\left(\mathbf{x}\right)$, where $K_h\left(\mathbf{x}_{it}, \mathbf{x}\right)$ is our product-kernel function. Taking the first-order condition and setting it equal to zero gives the pooled LCLS estimator as

$$\widehat{m}\left(\mathbf{x}\right) = \frac{\sum_{i=1}^{n} \sum_{t=1}^{T_i} y_{it} K_h\left(\mathbf{x}_{it}, \mathbf{x}\right)}{\sum_{i=1}^{n} \sum_{t=1}^{T_i} K_h\left(\mathbf{x}_{it}, \mathbf{x}\right)}.$$

The pooled LLLS estimator is based on a similar minimization problem. The goal here is to minimize

$$\sum_{i=1}^{n} \sum_{t=1}^{T_i} y_{it} - \widehat{m}\left(\mathbf{x}\right) - \left(\mathbf{x}_{it} - \mathbf{x}\right) \widehat{\beta}(\mathbf{x})^2 K_h\left(\mathbf{x}_{it}, \mathbf{x}\right), \tag{11.3}$$

with respect to both $\widehat{m}(\mathbf{x})$ and $\widehat{\beta}(\mathbf{x})$. It is perhaps easier to view this problem in matrix notation. Defining y as a $nT \times 1$ vector, $\mathbf{X}$ as a $nT \times (q+1)$ matrix whose itth row is $\mathbf{X}_{it} = [1, (\mathbf{x}_{it} - \mathbf{x})]$, $\delta(\mathbf{x}) = \left[m(\mathbf{x}), \beta(\mathbf{x})'\right]'$ as a $(q+1) \times 1$ vector of parameters, and $K(\mathbf{x})$ as a $nT \times nT$ diagonal matrix of kernel functions $K_h\left(\mathbf{x}_{it}, \mathbf{x}\right)$, Equation (11.3) can be written as

$$y - \mathbf{X}\delta(\mathbf{x})' K(\mathbf{x})y - \mathbf{X}\delta(\mathbf{x}).$$

Similar to before, taking the partial derivative with respect to $\delta(\mathbf{x})$ and solving for $\delta(\mathbf{x})$ leads to the pooled LLLS estimator as

$$\widehat{\delta}(\mathbf{x}) = [\mathbf{X}' K(\mathbf{x})\mathbf{X}]^{-1}\mathbf{X}' K(\mathbf{x})y. \tag{11.4}$$

We note that this looks identical to the estimator in Chapter 5, except now the time dimension is added. Given that we have elected to ignore the structure of the error, we simply have the standard cross-sectional local-constant or linear least-squares estimator, albeit with a larger sample – nT as opposed to n. This estimator is simple and consistent when the individual effect is uncorrelated with the regressors, but it is inefficient. We now consider estimators which take the panel structure into account.

11.2 Random effects

As previously noted, random-effects estimators make the assumption that the individual effect and the regressors are uncorrelated. Nonparametric estimators of this type are common in the statistics and econometrics literatures. In statistics, these fall under the general umbrella of repeated measures problems. The research in this area includes, but is not limited to, Henderson and Ullah (2005); Lin and Carroll (2000, 2001, 2006); Lin and Ying (2001); Ruckstuhl, Welch, and Carroll (2000); Wang (2003); and Wu and Zhang (2002). Here we choose to focus on the estimators presented in Lin and Carroll (2000) and Wang (2003). The former focuses on the issue that often arises of no asymptotic gain when incorporating the error structure, and the latter finds a way to exploit the error structure in order to achieve asymptotic gains.

We begin our discussion with some of the basics of the error structure. In the random-effects case, we make assumptions about the variance–covariance matrix of the errors. For the specification considered in (11.2), if $\mathbf{u}_i = [u_{i1}, u_{i2}, \ldots, u_{iT_i}]'$ is a $T_i \times 1$ vector, then $V_i \equiv E(\mathbf{u}_i \mathbf{u}_i')$ takes the form

$$V_i = \sigma_v^2 \mathbf{I}_{T_i} + \sigma_u^2 \mathbf{i}_{T_i} \mathbf{i}_{T_i}',$$

where $\mathbf{I}_{T_i}$ is an identity matrix of dimension T_i and $\mathbf{i}_{T_i}$ is a $T_i \times 1$ column vector of ones. Since the observations are independent over i and j, the covariance matrix for the full $nT \times 1$ disturbance vector $\mathbf{u}$, $\Omega = E(\mathbf{uu}')$ is a $nT \times nT$ block diagonal matrix where the blocks are equal to V_i, $i = 1, 2, \ldots, n$. Note that this specification assumes a homoskedastic variance for all i and t. Here we allow for serial correlation over time, but only between the disturbances for the same individuals. In other words,

$$
\begin{aligned}
\mathrm{cov}\left(u_{it}, u_{js}\right) &= \mathrm{cov}\left(\mu_i + v_{it}, \mu_j + v_{js}\right) \\
&= E\left[\left(\mu_i + v_{it}\right)\left(\mu_j + v_{js}\right)\right] \\
&= E\left(\mu_i \mu_j + \mu_i v_{js} + v_{it}\mu_j + v_{it}v_{js}\right) \\
&= E\left(\mu_i \mu_j\right) + E\left(v_{it}v_{js}\right).
\end{aligned}
$$

Hence, the covariance equals $\sigma_\mu^2 + \sigma_v^2$ when $i = j$ and $t = s$, σ_μ^2 when $i = j$ and $t \neq s$, and zero when $i \neq j$. It is feasible to reconstruct Ω, which is block diagonal, from here as well. A key feature of Ω is that its structure is independent of $m(\mathbf{x}_{it})$. Thus, modeling the unknown conditional mean as either parametric or nonparametric does not influence how we need to account for the variance structure.

Random-effects estimators typically require the use of Ω^{-1} or $\Omega^{-1/2}$. Inverting a $nT \times nT$ matrix is computationally expensive. This problem is only compounded with nonparametric regression methods. Baltagi (1985, 135) gives a simple approach to constructing these types of matrices when we have a one-way error component model with unbalanced panel. One of the major benefits of his presentation is that it is straightforward to program these matrices. He defines the ith block of Ω^r as

$$\Omega_i^r = \left(T_i \sigma_\mu^2 + \sigma_v^2\right) \overline{J}_{T_i} + \sigma_v^2 E_{T_i},$$

where $\overline{J}_{T_i}$ is a $T_i \times T_i$ dimensional matrix where each element is equal to $1/T_i$ and $E_{T_i} = \left(I_{T_i} - \overline{J}_{T_i}\right)$. Using this notation, we can construct the ith block of Ω^{-1} and $\Omega^{-1/2}$ similarly, for $i = 1, 2, \ldots, n$. In practice, we do not know σ_u^2 or σ_v^2 and we must estimate these parameters. This will be discussed in more detail later.

Interest may also lie in controlling for time-specific effects. The simplest way to control for time effects would be to include a regressor that represents the time period. However, a more formal approach is to consider a two-way error component model. The only difference from the one-way error component model is that an additional term is added into the error which changes over time, but is constant over the cross-sectional units: $u_{it} = \mu_i + \lambda_t + v_{it}$. In the random-effects case, this just requires the user to reconstruct the Ω matrix such that it contains the time effect. We omit this here to save space, but note that for unbalanced panels this variance–covariance structure can be found in Wansbeek and Kapteyn (1989) or Baltagi (2008).

11.2.1 Local-linear weighted least-squares

Lin and Carroll (2000) attempt to model the information contained in the disturbance vector covariance matrix. They introduce an estimator, which Henderson and Ullah (2005) call Local-Linear Weighted Least-Squares (LLWLS), by minimizing

$$y - \mathbf{X}\delta(\mathbf{x})' W(\mathbf{x})y - \mathbf{X}\delta(\mathbf{x}) \tag{11.5}$$

with respect to $\delta(\mathbf{x})$, where $W(\mathbf{x})$ is a kernel-based weight matrix. The key departure from the LLWLS estimator from the LLLS estimator is that $W(\mathbf{x})$ is not a diagonal matrix. The structure of Ω is exploited when constructing $W(\mathbf{x})$ and this will produce a different kernel estimator than the LLLS estimator. This provides the kernel-estimating equations for $\delta(\mathbf{x})$ as $0 = \mathbf{X}' W(\mathbf{x})y - \mathbf{X}\delta(\mathbf{x})$, which gives

$$\widehat{\delta}(\mathbf{x}) = [\mathbf{X}' W(\mathbf{x})\mathbf{X}]^{-1}\mathbf{X}' W(\mathbf{x})y. \tag{11.6}$$

Several weighting schemes for $W(\mathbf{x})$ have been considered, but the most popular is

$$\widehat{\delta}(\mathbf{x}) = \left(\mathbf{X}'\sqrt{K(\mathbf{x})}\Omega^{-1}\sqrt{K(\mathbf{x})}\mathbf{X}\right)^{-1}\mathbf{X}'\sqrt{K(\mathbf{x})}\Omega^{-1}\sqrt{K(\mathbf{x})}y.$$

Henderson and Ullah (2005) give the rate of convergence of $\widehat{\delta}(\mathbf{x})$ for any number of regressors. More importantly, Lin and Carroll (2000) note that the asymptotic variance of (11.6) is actually larger than that of (11.4).

This result was initially unexpected, but Wang (2003) explains that this is natural when T_i is finite. She shows that as the bandwidth goes to zero, the kernel will only have a single nonzero element. In other words, as the bandwidth tends towards zero, we are effectively estimating on a single point, so the correlation structure is unnecessary. Given that we assume independence across cross-sections, the most efficient estimation will occur where $W(\mathbf{x})$ is diagonal (i.e., the LLLS estimator).

A more general approach to LLWLS estimators can be found in Martins-Filho and Yao (2009). In their paper, they consider a much more general case for Ω. Specifically, they provide a set of conditions for which the asymptotic normality of the LLWLS estimator can be established when Ω has a general parametric structure. These results are important because they eliminate the need to repeatedly establish asymptotic normality under specific structures for Ω.

Feasible estimation of (11.6) depends upon the unknown parameters σ_u^2 and σ_v^2. In the balanced-data case, Henderson and Ullah (2005, 406) use the spectral decomposition of Ω to obtain consistent estimators of the variance components as

$$\widehat{\sigma}_1^2 = \frac{1}{n}\sum_{i=1}^{n} T_i \bar{\bar{u}}_i^2, \tag{11.7}$$

$$\widehat{\sigma}_v^2 = \frac{1}{nT - n}\sum_{i=1}^{n}\sum_{t=1}^{T_i} \left(\widehat{u}_{it} - \bar{\bar{u}}_i\right)^2, \tag{11.8}$$

where $\bar{\bar{u}}_i = T_i^{-1}\sum_{t=1}^{T_i}\widehat{u}_{it}$ is the cross-sectional average of the residuals for cross-section i and $\widehat{u}_{it} = y_{it} - \widehat{m}(x_{it})$ is the LLLS residual based on the first stage estimator of $\widehat{\delta}(x)$ in (11.4). In the balanced-data case, the estimator of σ_μ^2 is

$\widehat{\sigma}_\mu^2 = T^{-1} (\widehat{\sigma}_1^2 - \widehat{\sigma}_v^2)$. In the unbalanced case, we require an additional step to estimate σ_μ^2. Specifically, the estimator σ_μ^2 is the off-diagonal element of the estimate of V_i. Baltagi (2008, 183–185) offers several estimators of the variance components (in the unbalanced case) which can be made functional for the nonparametric case by replacing the parametric residuals with their nonparametric counterparts (e.g., the working independence method).

11.2.2 Wang's iterative estimator

In response to the result found in Lin and Carroll (2000), Wang (2003) developed an iterative procedure which eliminates the bias while simultaneously reducing the variation of the nonparametric random-effects estimator. The construction of the Wang (2003) estimator hinges on two key contributions: a direct contribution from the regressand, and a secondary contribution from the residuals from a preliminary estimator that ignores the error structure. The basic intuition is that once a data point belongs in the local neighborhood of $\mathbf{x}$ defined by the bandwidth, all additional data points that belong to that cluster are used as well to estimate the unknown function. For data points that lie outside the local neighborhood, the contribution to the estimate of the unknown function for the remaining observations takes place only through their residuals. The residuals are calculated by subtracting the fitted values from a preliminary step from the true left-hand-side variable. That is, for points near the evaluation point, all points from the cluster are smoothed over directly and for points not nearby and not in an associate cluster, there is indirect smoothing of the residuals. This additional indirect smoothing is what allows for asymptotic reduction in the variance.

We would like to note here that our presentation does not match that shown in Wang (2003), but the resulting estimator is identical. Wang (2003) uses indicator vectors to construct her estimating equation. We follow the discussion of appendix A.7 in Lin and Carroll (2006). In this appendix they show how the Wang (2003) estimator can be written as a profile-kernel estimator.

Profile-kernel methods are often used when maximum-likelihood methods fail. This is common in nonparametric and semiparametric models where the nonparametric function is often referred to as an infinite dimensional parameter. For a deeper discussion of profile estimators, see Murphy and van der Vaart (2000). These methods require specifying a criterion function (typically Gaussian). With this criterion function for individual i, we have

$$\mathcal{L}_i (\cdot) = \mathcal{L} \mathbf{y}_i, m (\mathbf{x}_i) = -\frac{1}{2} \left[\mathbf{y}_i - m (\mathbf{x}_i) \right]' V_i^{-1} \left[\mathbf{y}_i - m (\mathbf{x}_i) \right],$$

where $\mathbf{y}_i = \left(y_{i1}, y_{i2}, \ldots, y_{iT_i} \right)'$ and $m (\mathbf{x}_i) = m (\mathbf{x}_{i1}), m (\mathbf{x}_{i2}), \ldots, m \left(\mathbf{x}_{iT_i} \right)'$. The partial derivative of the criterion function with respect to the unknown function is

$$\mathcal{L}_{i,tm} = \frac{\partial \mathcal{L}_i}{\partial m (\mathbf{x}_{it})} = c_{t_i}' V_i^{-1} \left[\mathbf{y}_i - m (\mathbf{x}_i) \right] = \sum_{s=1}^{T_i} \sigma^{ts} \left[y_{is} - m (\mathbf{x}_{is}) \right],$$

where c_{t_i} is a T_i dimensional vector whose tth element is unity and all other elements are zero and where σ^{ts} is the the (t, s)th element of V_i^{-1}. Note that σ^{tt} and σ^{ts} differ across cross-sectional units when the number of time dimensions (T_i) differ across i.

Lin and Carroll (2006) show that you can estimate $m(\mathbf{x})$ by $\widehat{m}(\mathbf{x})$, where $\widehat{m}(\mathbf{x})$ and $\widehat{\beta}(\mathbf{x})$ solve the first-order condition. Define $(\mathbf{x}_{it} - \mathbf{x})/h = \{(x_{1it} - x_1)/h_1, \ldots, (x_{qit} - x_q)/h_q)\}'$ $\widehat{\beta}(\mathbf{x}) = \partial m(\mathbf{x})/\partial \mathbf{x}$ as the first-order derivative of $m(\cdot)$ with respect to $\mathbf{x}$.

$$0 = \sum_{i=1}^{n} \sum_{t=1}^{T_i} K_h(\mathbf{x}_{it}, \mathbf{x}) \begin{pmatrix} 1 \\ \frac{\mathbf{x}_{it}-\mathbf{x}}{h} \end{pmatrix} \mathcal{L}_{i,tm} \begin{pmatrix} y_i, \widehat{m}(\mathbf{x}_{i1}), \ldots, \widehat{m}(\mathbf{x}) \\ + \left(\frac{\mathbf{x}_{it}-\mathbf{x}}{h}\right) \widehat{\beta}(\mathbf{x}), \ldots, \widehat{m}(\mathbf{x}_{iT_i}) \end{pmatrix}.$$

Note that the argument for $\mathcal{L}_{i,tm}$ is $\widehat{m}(\mathbf{x}_{it})$ for $s \neq t$ and $\widehat{m}(\mathbf{x}) + \left(\frac{\mathbf{x}_{it}-\mathbf{x}}{h}\right) \widehat{\beta}(\mathbf{x})$ for $s = t$. With this information, following the steps for the partial of the criterion function above, we have

$$\mathcal{L}_{i,tm} \begin{pmatrix} y_i, \widehat{m}(\mathbf{x}_{i1}), \ldots, \widehat{m}(\mathbf{x}) \\ + \left(\frac{\mathbf{x}_{it}-\mathbf{x}}{h}\right) \widehat{\beta}(\mathbf{x}), \ldots, \widehat{m}(\mathbf{x}_{iT_i}) \end{pmatrix} = \sigma^{tt} \left[y_{it} - \widehat{m}(\mathbf{x}) - \left(\frac{\mathbf{x}_{it} - \mathbf{x}}{h}\right) \widehat{\beta}(\mathbf{x}) \right]$$

$$+ \sum_{\substack{s=1 \\ s \neq t}}^{T_i} \sigma^{ts} \left[y_{is} - \widehat{m}(\mathbf{x}_{is}) \right].$$

Formally, the first-stage estimation is conducted by using a consistent estimator of the conditional mean. Perhaps the simplest, consistent first-step estimator would be to use the pooled LLLS estimator. Let's call this estimator $\widehat{m}_{[1]}(\mathbf{x})$ and the residuals from this model $\widehat{u}_{it} = y_{it} - \widehat{m}_{[1]}(\mathbf{x}_{it})$. The subscript [1] represents that we are at the step $l = 1$. In the lth step, we determine the estimate of the conditional mean, $\widehat{m}_{[l]}(\mathbf{x})$, and gradient, $\widehat{\beta}_{[l]}(\mathbf{x})$, by solving the kernel-weighted estimating equation

$$0 = \sum_{i=1}^{n} \sum_{t=1}^{T_i} K_h(\mathbf{x}_{it}, \mathbf{x}) \begin{pmatrix} 1 \\ \frac{\mathbf{x}_{it}-\mathbf{x}}{h} \end{pmatrix} \left\{ \begin{matrix} \sigma^{tt} \left[y_{it} - \widehat{m}_{[l]}(\mathbf{x}) - \left(\frac{\mathbf{x}_{it}-\mathbf{x}}{h}\right) \widehat{\beta}_{[l]}(\mathbf{x}) \right] \\ + \sum_{\substack{s=1 \\ s \neq t}}^{T_i} \sigma^{st} \left[y_{is} - \widehat{m}_{[l-1]}(\mathbf{x}_{is}) \right] \end{matrix} \right\}. \quad (11.9)$$

Technical Appendix 11.1 shows that the lth step estimator is equal to

$$\begin{pmatrix} \widehat{m}_{[l]}(\mathbf{x}) \\ \widehat{\beta}_{[l]}(\mathbf{x}) \end{pmatrix} = J_1^{-1}(J_2 + J_3), \quad (11.10)$$

where

$$J_1 = \sum_{i=1}^{n} \sum_{t=1}^{T_i} K_h(\mathbf{x}_{it}, \mathbf{x}) \sigma^{tt} \begin{pmatrix} 1 \\ \frac{\mathbf{x}_{it}-\mathbf{x}}{h} \end{pmatrix} \begin{pmatrix} 1 & \frac{\mathbf{x}_{it}-\mathbf{x}}{h} \end{pmatrix},$$

$$J_2 = \sum_{i=1}^{n} \sum_{t=1}^{T_i} K_h(\mathbf{x}_{it}, \mathbf{x}) \begin{pmatrix} 1 \\ \frac{\mathbf{x}_{it}-\mathbf{x}}{h} \end{pmatrix} \sigma^{tt} y_{it},$$

$$J_3 = \sum_{i=1}^{n} \sum_{t=1}^{T_i} \sum_{\substack{s=1 \\ s \neq t}}^{T_i} K_h(\mathbf{x}_{it}, \mathbf{x}) \begin{pmatrix} 1 \\ \frac{\mathbf{x}_{it}-\mathbf{x}}{h} \end{pmatrix} \sigma^{st} \left(y_{is} - \widehat{m}_{[l-1]}(\mathbf{x}_{is}) \right).$$

Notice that if we ignore J_3, then the only difference with the Wang (2003) estimator and the pooled LLLS estimator is the presence of σ^{tt}. Effectively we rescale all observations within a given cluster by σ^{tt}. In a balanced panel, this effectively drops out and we are left with the LLLS estimator. The contribution of J_3 is what sets the Wang (2003) estimator apart from the pooled LLLS estimator and provides asymptotic gains in efficiency. J_3 effectively contributes the covariance among the within-cluster residuals to the overall smoothing.

To further expound on this point, consider the LLWLS estimator. There, even though the within-cluster covariance is included via W, asymptotically this effect does not materialize since it appears in both the numerator and denominator with the same force. However, for the Wang (2003) estimator, the effect does materialize because the within-cluster covariance only accrues in the numerator (through J_3).

To further provide intuition for the Wang (2003) estimator, consider the balanced-panel case ($T_i = T \; \forall i$). In this setting, σ^{tt} is identical for all individuals. Thus, σ^{tt} can be removed from J_1 and J_2, leaving only $\sigma^{stt} \equiv \sigma^{st}/\sigma^{tt}$ in J_3. Our estimator can now be written as

$$\widehat{\delta}(\mathbf{x}) = \begin{pmatrix} \widehat{m}_{[l]}(\mathbf{x}) \\ \widehat{\beta}_{[l]}(\mathbf{x}) \end{pmatrix} = \check{J}_1^{-1}\left(\check{J}_2 + \check{J}_3\right), \tag{11.11}$$

where

$$\check{J}_1 = \sum_{i=1}^{n}\sum_{t=1}^{T} K_h(\mathbf{x}_{it}, \mathbf{x}) \begin{pmatrix} 1 \\ \frac{\mathbf{x}_{it}-\mathbf{x}}{h} \end{pmatrix} \left(1 \quad \frac{\mathbf{x}_{it}-\mathbf{x}}{h}\right),$$

$$\check{J}_2 = \sum_{i=1}^{n}\sum_{t=1}^{T} K_h(\mathbf{x}_{it}, \mathbf{x}) \begin{pmatrix} 1 \\ \frac{\mathbf{x}_{it}-\mathbf{x}}{h} \end{pmatrix} y_{it},$$

$$\check{J}_3 = \sum_{i=1}^{n}\sum_{t=1}^{T}\sum_{\substack{s=1 \\ s\neq t}}^{T} K_h(\mathbf{x}_{it}, \mathbf{x}) \begin{pmatrix} 1 \\ \frac{\mathbf{x}_{it}-\mathbf{x}}{h} \end{pmatrix} \sigma^{stt} y_{is} - \widehat{m}_{[l-1]}(\mathbf{x}_{is}).$$

$\check{J}_1^{-1}\check{J}_2$ is simply local-linear estimation of y_{it} on $\mathbf{x}_{it}$, our pooled estimator from (11.4). This only needs to be estimated once (and the result stored in your program). $\check{J}_1^{-1}\check{J}_3$ is a local-linear estimation of the averaged transformed residuals from the $(\ell -1)$th iteration on $\mathbf{x}_{it}$. That is, we regress

$$\check{y}_{it}^{[\ell]} = \sum_{\substack{s=1 \\ s\neq t}}^{T} \sigma^{stt} u_{is}^{[\ell-1]}$$

on $\mathbf{x}_{it}$ using local-linear estimation, where $u_{is}^{[\ell-1]} = y_{is} - \widehat{m}_{[\ell-1]}(\mathbf{x}_{is})$. This approach makes implementing this seemingly difficult estimator relatively easy. Iteration is only necessary on $\check{J}_1^{-1}\check{J}_3$.

The Wang (2003) estimator is iterated until you reach convergence. The definition of convergence is somewhat arbitrary. The basic idea is that we want to see that the estimate of the conditional mean is not changing much between iterations. A particular convergence criterion could be $\sum_{i=1}^{n} \sum_{t=1}^{T_i} \{\widehat{m}_{[\ell]}(\mathbf{x}_{it}) - \widehat{m}_{[\ell-1]}$ $(\mathbf{x}_{it})\}^2 / \sum_{i=1}^{n} \sum_{t=1}^{T_i} \widehat{m}_{[\ell-1]}(\mathbf{x}_{it})^2 < \omega$, where ω is some small number, say 0.000001. This may require some amount of finesse for each particular data set. It is probably best for you to start out with a large number, say 0.01, to obtain an initial estimate and see if your results make sense. You can then decrease this number to obtain greater precision. Also, we mention here that the iterations are conducted in a manner that minimizes changes in the estimated function, rather than increasing the fit of the estimated function. Thus, it is conceivable that the once-iterated function may actually fit the data better than the fully iterated function.

It should be noted that Wang (2003) argues that the once-iterated estimator has the same asymptotic behavior as the fully iterated estimator. Her Monte Carlo exercise shows that it performs well for the case of a single regressor, but there is no discussion for the multiple regression case. Therefore it may be feasible to reduce computation time by using a one-step iteration. That being said, in the applications we have encountered, we do not find full iteration to be that computationally expensive for relatively small data sets. Most of our applications only require four to twelve iterations, depending upon the tolerance. In this case, it may just be best to let the estimator converge.

For a feasible estimator, the estimates for σ^{ts} can be obtained by using the residuals from the pooled estimator. The (t, s)th element is

$$\sigma^{ts} = \frac{\sigma_v^2 - \sigma_1^2}{\sigma_1^2 \sigma_v^2 T_i},$$

and the (t, t)th element is

$$\sigma^{tt} = \frac{\sigma_v^2 + (T_i - 1)\,\sigma_1^2}{\sigma_1^2 \sigma_v^2 T_i}.$$

Note that these values depend upon the number of observed time periods for a given cross-section. Further note that this set-up does not include σ_u^2, which as stated previously, requires an additional step to estimate in the unbalanced case.

In practice we do not know the variance components. Several procedures can be used to estimate each of these and most use the pooled LLLS estimator to obtain consistent estimates of the residuals in order to estimate each of the components. For the sake of brevity, we refer you to Section 11.2.1, as well as the references of the papers discussed in the current section.

11.3 Fixed effects

A growing literature in econometrics has recognized the importance of nonparametric methods in the presence of fixed effects (e.g., Evdokimov, 2012; Hoderlein, Mammen, and Yu, 2011; Qian and Wang, 2012). Here we consider two estimators. The first assumes that the individual effects are additive and separable, but allow them to be correlated with the regressors. The second incorporates the individual effects into the unknown function. Each has its merits and downfalls, as we discuss shortly.

11.3.1 Additive individual effects

Henderson, Carroll, and Li (2008) consider the following nonparametric panel-data regression model with fixed effects

$$y_{it} = m(\mathbf{x}_{it}) + \mu_i + v_{it}, \qquad\qquad (i = 1, \ldots, n; \ \ t = 1, \ldots, T_i), \qquad (11.12)$$

where the functional form of $m(\cdot)$ is not specified. The covariate $\mathbf{x}_{it} = (x_{1it}, x_{2it}, \ldots, x_{qit})$ is of dimension q, and all other variables are scalars. The random errors v_{it} are assumed to be *iid* with a zero mean, finite variance, and uncorrelated with $\mathbf{x}_{it}$ for all i and t. Further, μ_i has a zero mean and finite variance. μ_i is allowed to be correlated with $\mathbf{x}_{it}$ with an unknown correlation structure. Hence, (11.12) is a "fixed effects" model.

To remove the fixed effects, you can take a first difference

$$\widetilde{y}_{it} \equiv y_{it} - y_{i1} = m(\mathbf{x}_{it}) - m(\mathbf{x}_{i1}) + v_{it} - v_{i1}. \qquad (11.13)$$

Note that the above difference is to subtract observation $t = 1$ from t. You can also use alternative transformations such as $y_{it} - y_{i,t-1} = m(\mathbf{x}_{it}) - m(\mathbf{x}_{i,t-1}) + v_{it} - v_{i,t-1}$ to remove the fixed effects.[3] Here we will focus on the transformation given in (11.13).

From (11.12) we know that $E[m(\mathbf{x}_{it})] = E(y_{it})$. Under this condition, $m(\cdot)$ defined in (11.13) is identified. This condition implies that we cannot identify an intercept term here, as differencing $m(\mathbf{x}_{it})$ from $m(\mathbf{x}_{i1})$ will remove any constants.

Henderson, Carroll, and Li (2008) derive an estimator that exploits the variance structure. Start by defining $\widetilde{v}_{it} = v_{it} - v_{i1}$ and $\widetilde{\mathbf{v}}_i = (\widetilde{v}_{i2}, \ldots, \widetilde{v}_{iT_i})'$. The variance–covariance matrix of $\widetilde{\mathbf{v}}_i$, defined as $V_i = \mathrm{cov}(\widetilde{\mathbf{v}}_i | \mathbf{x}_{i1}, \ldots, \mathbf{x}_{iT_i}) = \mathrm{cov}(\widetilde{v}_i)$, is given by

$$V_i = \sigma_v^2 (I_{T_i-1} + \mathbf{i}_{T_i-1} \mathbf{i}'_{T_i-1}),$$

where I_{T_i-1} is an identity matrix of dimension $(T_i - 1)$, and $\mathbf{i}_{T_i-1}$ is a $(T_i - 1) \times 1$ vector of ones (note that in the random effects case it was of dimension T_i). It can be shown that $V_i^{-1} = \sigma_v^{-2}(I_{T_i-1} - \mathbf{i}_{T_i-1} \mathbf{i}'_{T_i-1}/T_i)$. Following Wang (2003) and Lin and Carroll (2006), a profile-likelihood approach can be used to estimate $m(\cdot)$. The criterion function for individual i is given by ($y_i = (y_{i1}, \ldots, y_{iT_i})$):

$$\mathcal{L}_i(\cdot) = \mathcal{L}(y_i, m(\mathbf{x}_i))$$
$$= -\frac{1}{2}(\widetilde{y}_i - m(\mathbf{x}_i) + m(\mathbf{x}_{i1})\mathbf{i}_{T_i-1})' V_i^{-1}(\widetilde{y}_i - m(\mathbf{x}_i) + m(\mathbf{x}_{i1})\mathbf{i}_{T_i-1}), \quad (11.14)$$

where $\widetilde{y}_i = (\widetilde{y}_{i2}, \ldots, \widetilde{y}_{iT_i})'$ and $m(\mathbf{x}_i) = (m(\mathbf{x}_{i2}), m(\mathbf{x}_{i3}), \ldots, m(\mathbf{x}_{iT_i}))'$.

Defining $\mathcal{L}_{i,tm} = \partial \mathcal{L}_i(\cdot) / \partial m(\mathbf{x}_{it})$, and $\mathcal{L}_{i,tsm} = \partial^2 \mathcal{L}_i(\cdot) / (\partial m(\mathbf{x}_{it}) \partial m(\mathbf{x}_{is}))$, from (11.14) we obtain

$$\mathcal{L}_{i,1m} = -\mathbf{i}'_{T_i-1} V_i^{-1}(\widetilde{y}_i - m(\mathbf{x}_i) + m(\mathbf{x}_{i1})\mathbf{i}_{T_i-1});$$
$$\mathcal{L}_{i,tm} = c'_{t_i-1} V_i^{-1}(\widetilde{y}_i - m(\mathbf{x}_i) + m(\mathbf{x}_{i1})\mathbf{i}_{T_i-1}) \qquad \text{for } T_i \geq 2,$$

---

[3] Lee and Mukherjee (2008) consider estimation of marginal effects under this scenario, but their estimator will only work with a single covariate.

where c_{t_i-1} is a vector of dimension $(T_i - 1) \times 1$ with the $(t - 1)$ element being 1 and all other elements being 0.

Here we can maximize a kernel-weighted objective function. Define $(\mathbf{x}_{it} - \mathbf{x})/h = \{(x_{1it} - x_1)/h_1, \ldots, (x_{qit} - x_q)/h_q)\}'$ $\widehat{\beta}(\mathbf{x}) = \partial m(\mathbf{x})/\partial \mathbf{x}$ as the first-order derivative of $m(\cdot)$ with respect to $\mathbf{x}$. We estimate the unknown function $m(\mathbf{x})$ by solving the first-order condition

$$0 = \sum_{i=1}^{n} \sum_{t=1}^{T_i} K_h(\mathbf{x}_{it}, \mathbf{x}) \begin{pmatrix} 1 \\ \frac{\mathbf{x}_{it}-\mathbf{x}}{h} \end{pmatrix}$$
$$\times \mathcal{L}_{i,tm}[y_i, \widehat{m}(\mathbf{x}_{i1}), \ldots, \widehat{m}(\mathbf{x}) + \{(\mathbf{x}_{it} - \mathbf{x})/h\}\widehat{\beta}(\mathbf{x}), \ldots, \widehat{m}(\mathbf{x}_{iT_i})], \qquad (11.15)$$

where the argument $\mathcal{L}_{i,tm}$ is $\widehat{m}(\mathbf{x}_{is})$ for $s \neq t$ and $\widehat{m}(\mathbf{x}) + \{(\mathbf{x}_{it} - \mathbf{x})/h\}\widehat{\beta}(\mathbf{x})$ when $s = t$.

Equation (11.15) suggests the following iterative procedure. Suppose the current estimate of $m(\mathbf{x})$ at the $[\ell - 1]$th step is $\widehat{m}_{[\ell-1]}(\mathbf{x})$. Then the next step estimate of $m(\mathbf{x})$ is $\widehat{m}_{[\ell]}(\mathbf{x}) = \widehat{\alpha}_0(\mathbf{x})$, where $(\widehat{\alpha}_0, \widehat{\alpha}_1)$ solve the following equation:

$$0 = \sum_{i=1}^{n} \sum_{t=1}^{T_i} K_h(\mathbf{x}_{it}, \mathbf{x}) \begin{pmatrix} 1 \\ \frac{\mathbf{x}_{it}-\mathbf{x}}{h} \end{pmatrix} \qquad (11.16)$$
$$\times \mathcal{L}_{i,tm}[y_i, \widehat{m}_{[\ell-1]}(\mathbf{x}_{i1}), \ldots, \widehat{\alpha}_0 + \{(\mathbf{x}_{it} - \mathbf{x})/h\}'\widehat{\alpha}_1, \ldots, \widehat{m}_{[\ell-1]}(\mathbf{x}_{iT_i})].$$

Below we give an algorithm for estimating $m(\cdot)$. We note here that we need to use the restriction that $\sum_{i=1}^{n} \sum_{t=1}^{T_i}\{y_{it} - \widehat{m}(\mathbf{x}_{it})\} = 0$ in order for $m(\cdot)$ to be uniquely defined based on (11.13), since $E(y_{it}) = E[m(\mathbf{x}_{it})]$.

Technical appendix 11.2 shows that the next step estimator is

$$\{\widehat{\alpha}_0(\mathbf{x}), \widehat{\alpha}_1(\mathbf{x})\}' = D_1^{-1}(D_2 + D_3),$$

where

$$D_1 = \frac{1}{\sigma_v^2} \sum_{i=1}^{n} \sum_{t=1}^{T_i} \frac{(T_i - 1)}{T_i} K_h(\mathbf{x}_{it}, \mathbf{x}) \begin{pmatrix} 1 \\ \frac{\mathbf{x}_{it}-\mathbf{x}}{h} \end{pmatrix} \begin{pmatrix} 1 & \frac{\mathbf{x}_{it}-\mathbf{x}}{h} \end{pmatrix}$$

$$D_2 = \frac{1}{\sigma_v^2} \sum_{i=1}^{n} \sum_{t=1}^{T_i} \frac{(T_i - 1)}{T_i} K_h(\mathbf{x}_{it}, \mathbf{x}) \begin{pmatrix} 1 \\ \frac{\mathbf{x}_{it}-\mathbf{x}}{h} \end{pmatrix} \widehat{m}_{[\ell-1]}(\mathbf{x}_{it});$$

$$D_3 = \sum_{i=1}^{n} \left\{ \begin{array}{c} \sum_{t=2}^{T_i} K_h(\mathbf{x}_{it}, \mathbf{x}) \left(\frac{1}{\frac{\mathbf{x}_{it}-\mathbf{x}}{h}}\right)c'_{t_i-1}V_i^{-1}H_{i,[\ell-1]} \\ -K_h(\mathbf{x}_{i1}, \mathbf{x}) \left(\frac{1}{\frac{\mathbf{x}_{i1}-\mathbf{x}}{h}}\right)\mathbf{i}'_{T_i-1}V_i^{-1}H_{i,[\ell-1]} \end{array} \right\}, \qquad (11.17)$$

and where

$$H_{i,[\ell-1]} = \begin{pmatrix} y_{i2} - \widehat{m}_{[\ell-1]}(\mathbf{x}_{i2}) \\ \vdots \\ y_{iT_i} - \widehat{m}_{[\ell-1]}(\mathbf{x}_{iT_i}) \end{pmatrix} - \{y_{i1} - \widehat{m}_{[\ell-1]}(\mathbf{x}_{i1})\}\mathbf{i}_{T_i-1}$$

are the differenced residuals. The next step estimate of $m(\mathbf{x})$ is given by $\widehat{m}_{[\ell]}(\mathbf{x}) = \widehat{\alpha}_0(\mathbf{x})$. Henderson, Carroll, and Li (2008, 260) state that $\widehat{\alpha}_1(\mathbf{x})$ gives the next-step derivative estimator of $m(\mathbf{x})$. However, the actual derivative of $m(\mathbf{x})$ for a particular regressor requires you to divide $\widehat{\alpha}_1(\mathbf{x})$ by the bandwidth for that particular regressor.[4] For example, for the dth regressor, $\beta(x_d) \equiv \partial m(\mathbf{x})/\partial x_d = \widehat{\alpha}_1(x_d)/h_d$, where h_d is the dth element of h. We note here that while Henderson, Carroll, and Li (2008) provide a sketch of the proof, Li and Liang (2013) rigorously establish asymptotic normality of the estimator.

Intuitively, if we ignore D_3, this estimator $\{\widehat{\alpha}_0(\mathbf{x}), \widehat{\alpha}_1(\mathbf{x})\}' = D_1^{-1}(D_2 + D_3)$ looks much like the LLLS estimator with y replaced by its prediction in the previous iteration $\widehat{m}_{[l-1]}(\mathbf{x}_{it})$. Instead of smoothing the regressand we are smoothing an initial consistent estimate of it. What D_3 adds here are the residuals from the previous iteration, similar to the iterative random effects estimator of Wang (2003), and this is what leads to the asymptotic improvement. In this case, instead of exploiting the covariance structure among the within-cluster residuals, we are instead exploiting the within-cluster covariance between the covariates and the fixed effects. This can be seen directly by noting that the Wang (2003) estimator includes the residuals, whereas here the differenced residuals are included. This differencing removes the fixed effect and so we are in essence including a pure random error (subject to estimation error) to mimic what appears in J_3 of the Wang (2003) estimator.

Recall that Wang (2003) considered the random-effects case. In her model, a consistent initial estimator can be obtained by replacing V_i by an identity matrix. If we replace V_i by an identity matrix, (11.13) is an additive model with the restriction that the two additive functions have the same functional form. For example, you can use a fourth-order polynomial (or a more sophisticated nonparametric series method) to obtain an initial estimator of $m(\cdot)$.

The variance parameter σ_v^2 can be consistently estimated by

$$\widehat{\sigma}_v^2 = \frac{1}{(2nT - 2n)} \sum_{i=1}^{n} \sum_{t=2}^{T_i} \{y_{it} - y_{i1} - [\widehat{m}(\mathbf{x}_{it}) - \widehat{m}(\mathbf{x}_{i1})]\}^2.$$

However, note that $\widehat{\sigma}_v^2$ is only necessary in order to estimate the covariance matrix. It is not necessary for the estimates of the unknown function and its derivative, because given our specification, $\widehat{\sigma}_v^2$ simply drops out. It is not obvious from first glance of (11.17) how this term drops out because σ_v^2 is hidden in D_3. Technical Appendix 11.2 gives the result.

Henderson, Carroll, and Li (2008) show that under certain assumptions (for example, homoskedasticity and a balanced panel), the relative asymptotic variance of this model, which incorporates the error structure, and the other, which replaces V_i with an identity matrix, leads to an improvement in asymptotic variance as $(2 + T)/4$. When $T > 2$, this ratio is larger than one. That being said, even though the estimator that ignores the variance structure V_i has a larger asymptotic variance (when $T > 2$), it has the advantage that it is robust to possible misspecification in V_i. For example, if v_{it} is serially correlated but you ignore the serial correlation, then the form of V_i will be misspecified.

---

[4] Henderson wishes to thank Yoonseok Lee for pointing this out.

Building on the work of Henderson, Carroll, and Li (2008), Li and Liang (2012) prove asymptotic normality of the profile-likelihood local-linear fixed effects estimator using the theory of backfitting kernel estimators (see Mammen, Støve, and Tjøstheim, 2009).

11.3.2 Discrete individual effects

Perhaps the simplest way to introduce fixed effects would be to use discrete regressors. This is analogous to a least-squares dummy-variable approach in parametric panel data models, except that we need to only introduce one variable to define all cross-sectional units. In other words, we have a single variable of length nT that takes n different values $(1, 2, \ldots, n)$. Note that we do not need to remove one of the cross-sectional units for fear of perfect collinearity (i.e., the dummy variable trap in parametric models). We simply need a single unordered categorical variable for the cross-sectional unit that takes a specific value whenever the data for that firm/country/individual are present. That is, no ordering is required since all we need are distinct cross-sectional units to be represented with distinct integer values.

The specific procedure follows directly from Chapter 8. Consider the nonparametric regression model

$$y_i = m\left(\mathbf{x}_i\right) + u_i, i = 1, 2, n, \ldots, nT.$$

Notice that the data are now listed as $i = 1, 2, \ldots, nT$ as opposed to $i = 1, 2, \ldots, n$ and $t = 1, 2, \ldots, T_i$. Recall that we have three types of data in Chapter 8: continuous, unordered, and ordered. The presence of the fixed effect simply adds an additional unordered variable to our covariates that captures the presence of the individual cross-sectional units. For example, suppose we have a sample of n firms/countries/individuals. An unordered discrete variable (of dimension $nT \times 1$) may look like

$$x^u = (1, 1, \ldots, 1, 2, 2, \ldots, 2, \ldots n, n, \ldots, n)'.$$

Then this variable is treated more or less like any other discrete regressor. It uses the kernel function for discrete unordered data. The rules of bandwidth selection are the same here as well. This includes the upper and lower bounds of the regressor, which can provide important information. To preview later discussion, a bandwidth of zero would imply that each cross-section can be treated separately. In essence, a bandwidth of zero implies that you are only regressing T_i observations to obtain the estimates for the ith cross-section (i.e., sample splitting on the cross-sectional units). On the other hand, a bandwidth equal to the upper bound of unity implies that the variable is irrelevant and is smoothed out. In this case we move back to the pooled model.[5]

Time effects can be incorporated into the model in a similar manner. The only distinction is that time effects need to be treated as an ordered categorical variable. Similar

---

[5] This presents an interesting set-up for examining the poolability of the model in both the cross-sectional and the time dimension.

to the unordered discrete variable for cross-sections above, the discrete ordered time variable would be given as

$$x^o = (1, 2, \ldots, T_1, 1, 2, \ldots, T_2, \ldots, 1, 2, \ldots, T_n)'.$$

Here the distance between the points matters, but the magnitude of the data does not. For example, suppose we have data from 1985 to 2000. We could create an ordered categorical variable that takes the values $1985, 1986, \ldots, 2000$ or equivalently, we could create an ordered categorical variable that takes the values $1, 2, \ldots, 16$. In other words, all that matters is the distance between the points.

Little is known about the asymptotic performance of panel-data estimators in this sense, but it is assumed that the conditional mean is consistent in the presence of discrete regressors for cross-section and/or time. The down side is that it is difficult to think of obtaining consistent estimates of the individual effects. This occurs because the individual effects can vary over time and the time effects can vary over firm. In this sense, you have nT "effect" estimates with nT data points. However, if your concern is simply fitting the data or obtaining consistent gradient estimates from the remaining covariates, then this point may be rendered irrelevant. On the other hand, if your interest is to obtain consistent estimates of the individual effects for a second-stage estimation procedure (e.g., efficiency analysis), then you likely would want to switch to the more restrictive additive time-invariant individual effects, assuming that you believe the additively separable, time-invariant assumptions that these models impose. Provided these assumptions are true, consistent estimates of the individual effects are possible as the time dimension gets large. This is the same result that occurs in the parametric case.

11.4 Dynamic panel estimation

Su and Lu (2013) propose a fully nonparametric dynamic panel-data estimator, allowing for unobserved effects that are correlated with the regressors. The model under study is

$$y_{it} = m(y_{i,t-1}, \mathbf{x}_{it}) + \mu_i + v_{it}.$$

To construct a kernel estimator for this dynamic model we first difference to eliminate the fixed effect, obtaining

$$\Delta y_{it} = m(y_{i,t-1}, \mathbf{x}_{it}) - m(y_{i,t-2}, \mathbf{x}_{i,t-1}) + \Delta v_{it}, \tag{11.18}$$

where $\Delta y_{it} = y_{it} - y_{i,t-1}$ and $\Delta v_{it} = v_{it} - v_{i,t-1}$. At first glance it would seem that this model could be estimated using additive methods as discussed in Chapter 9; however, there is an issue with this line of thinking. The two additive functions are identical, but are evaluated at different points. This issue is identical to the nondynamic fixed-effects case of Henderson, Carroll, and Li (2008) and Qian and Wang (2012). Henderson, Carroll, and Li's (2008) approach was to use profile likelihood, obtaining a solution iteratively, while Qian and Wang's (2012) was to estimate the model, ignoring the additive structure, including $\mathbf{x}_{it}$ and $\mathbf{x}_{i,t-1}$ as regressors (thus doubling the number of regressors), and then using marginal integration to recover $m(\cdot)$.

Su and Lu's (2013) estimator is a simplification of the profile-likelihood estimator proposed by Henderson, Carroll, and Li (2008) and is computationally easier to implement. Here we detail the construction of this dynamic nonparametric panel-data estimator. To begin, define $\mathbf{z}_{i,t-1} = (y_{i,t-1}, \mathbf{x}_{it})$. Assuming that $E\left(\Delta v_{it}|\mathbf{z}_{i,t-2}\right) = 0$, we have

$$E\left(\Delta y_{it}|\mathbf{z}_{i,t-2}\right) = E\left[m(\mathbf{z}_{i,t-1})|\mathbf{z}_{i,t-2}\right] - m(\mathbf{z}_{i,t-2}),$$

which can be expressed as

$$m(\mathbf{z}) = -E\left(\Delta y_{it}|\mathbf{z}_{i,t-2} = \mathbf{z}\right) + E\left[m(\mathbf{z}_{i,t-1})|\mathbf{z}_{i,t-2} = \mathbf{z}\right].$$

If we write out the conditional expectation of $m(\mathbf{z}_{i,t-1})$, formally this yields

$$m(\mathbf{z}) = -E\left(\Delta y_{it}|\mathbf{z}_{i,t-2} = \mathbf{z}\right) + \int m(\mathbf{v}) f(\mathbf{v}|\mathbf{z}_{i,t-2} = \mathbf{z}) d\mathbf{v}, \qquad (11.19)$$

which is known as a Freholm integral equation of the second kind (Kress, 1999). There are a variety of means to solve integral equations of this sort. The simplest means is through iteration and that is the approach we will describe here.

Assuming $m(\mathbf{z})$ was known, the integral in (11.19) could be obtained by setting $\mathbf{v} = \mathbf{z}_{i,t-1}$ and performing local-polynomial estimation with $\mathbf{z}_{i,t-2}$ as the covariate vector and $m(\mathbf{z}_{i,t-1})$ as the regressand. Unfortunately, $m(\mathbf{z})$ is unknown and so we must make an initial guess. Su and Lu (2013) propose a two-stage least-squares sieve estimator. This estimator is initially consistent and so provides a good starting point. However, in simulations we have run, it seems that consistency of the initial estimator is not needed to obtain impressive finite sample results. Thus, it may be possible to use the mean of y.

The iterative estimation routine would then be implemented as follows:

1. For a given bandwidth, run the local-polynomial regression of $-\Delta y_{it}$ on $\mathbf{z}_{i,t-2}$, evaluating this conditional mean at $\mathbf{z}_{i,t-1}$. Call these estimates $\hat{r}$.

2. Let $\widehat{m}_{[0]} = (nT_2)^{-1} \sum_{i=1}^{n} \sum_{t=1}^{T_i} y_{it}$. Here $nT_j \equiv \sum_{i=1}^{n}(T_i - j)$. Using the same bandwidth, regress $\widehat{m}_{[0]}$ on $\mathbf{z}_{i,t-2}$, evaluating this conditional mean at $\mathbf{z}_{i,t-1}$. Given that the model in (11.18) is only identified up to location, a further restriction is needed to ensure full identification. Note that $E\left(y_{it}\right) = E\left[m(\mathbf{z}_{i,t-1})\right]$, thus re-centering our estimate of $\widehat{m}_{[0]}$ by $(nT_1)^{-1} \sum_{i=1}^{n} \sum_{t=1}^{T_i} y_{it} - \widehat{m}_{[0]}(\mathbf{z}_{i,t-1})$ produces our initial estimator of the unknown conditional mean

$$\widetilde{m}_{[0]} = \widehat{m}_{[0]} + (nT_1)^{-1} \sum_{i=1}^{n} \sum_{t=1}^{T_i} y_{it} - \widehat{m}_{[0]}(\mathbf{z}_{i,t-1}).$$

3. Our next step estimator of $m(\mathbf{z}_{i,t-1})$ is

$$\widehat{m}_{[1]}(\mathbf{z}_{i,t-1}) = \widetilde{m}_{[1]}(\mathbf{z}_{i,t-1}) + \hat{r}.$$

Re-center $\widehat{m}_{[1]}(\mathbf{z}_{i,t-1})$ by $(nT_1)^{-1}\sum_{i=1}^{n}\sum_{t=1}^{T_i} y_{it} - \widehat{m}_{[1]}(\mathbf{z}_{i,t-1})$ to produce $\widetilde{m}_{[1]}(\mathbf{z}_{i,t-1})$.

4. Repeat step 3, which at the ℓth step produces

$$\widehat{m}_{[\ell]}(\mathbf{z}_{i,t-1}) = \widetilde{m}_{[\ell-1]}(\mathbf{z}_{i,t-1}) + \hat{r}.$$

Re-center $\widehat{m}_{[\ell]}(\mathbf{z}_{i,t-1})$ to obtain the ℓth step estimator of the unknown conditional mean, $\widetilde{m}_{[\ell]}(\mathbf{z}_{i,t-1})$.

The estimator should be iterated until the difference between successive estimates of the unknown conditional mean is beneath some pre-specified tolerance. We can use the criterion used in both Wang (2003) and Henderson, Carroll, and Li (2008). One additional computational trick that can be used to lessen the computing burden is to save the kernel weights from the local-polynomial estimator used in step 1. Given that the evaluation of the unknown conditional mean does not change, there is no need to recalculate the kernel weights across iterations. For large panels this can result in a dramatic improvement in the computation of the estimator. In our own experience with this estimator, for simple data generating processes (DGPs) convergence occurs within five iterations.

Assessing the gradient of $\widetilde{m}(\mathbf{z})$ is relatively simple. Given that our re-centering is a location shift, we can use the gradients provided from the last iteration of our unknown conditional mean. Lastly, nothing prevents us from using this estimator if dynamics are not present. Thus, this same setup can be used to estimate a simple, fixed-effects nonparametric panel-data model. In comparison to Henderson, Carroll, and Li (2008), it is less computationally expensive because it only requires successive local-polynomial estimation of an updated quantity. This estimator also avoids performing marginal integration as required by Qian and Wang (2012) for their fixed-effects nonparametric panel-data estimator. Su and Lu (2013) prove that the limiting distribution of this estimator is normal.

11.5 Semiparametric estimators

As was the case in Chapter 9, you must have full confidence that the parametric assumptions you are making hold true; otherwise, estimation will likely lead to biased estimators, not only of the parametric component, but also the nonparametric component of your model.

For pooled models, we again resort back to the Robinson (1988) estimator outlined in Chapter 9. There is no difference here, as the data is treated as a cross-section of size nT. One estimator which may be of interest is the additive semiparametric panel-data estimator of Fan and Li (2003). Again, this type of approach circumvents the curse of dimensionality, but at the cost of assuming that the regressors are separable. Li and Stengos (1996) allow for parametric endogenous regressors via an IV approach in a partially linear panel-data model. Other interesting references include, but are not limited to, Baltagi and Li (2002); Berg, Li, and Ullah (2000); and Kniesner and Li (2002).

For the fixed-effects case, Henderson, Carroll, and Li (2008) have a partially linear version of their estimator. Su and Ullah (2006) consider a partially linear fixed-effects model with exogenous regressors. Mammen, Støve, and Tjøstheim (2009) use backfitting to estimate an additive nonparametric model, which allows for correlated individual effects. Finally, Lee (2014) considers nonparametric estimation of autoregressive panel models with fixed effects. The research here is growing quickly and likely will include far more references to come.

There are also several references for panel-data versions of the semiparametric smooth coefficient models discussed in Chapter 9. One of the earlier references is Fan and Li (2004), who allow the coefficients to be a function of time. Cai and Li (2008) study a dynamic nonparametric panel-data model with unknown varying coefficients, but assume the random effects specification. In contrast, Sun, Carroll, and Li (2009) consider a semiparametric smooth-coefficient model for fixed-effects panel-data models. A benefit of the Cai and Li (2008) estimator is that it allows for endogenous regressors.

11.6 Bandwidth selection

Standard methods for bandwidth selection apply in the panel-data setting, but it is possible to speed up the process by looking to predict cross-sectional units as opposed to observations (e.g., Kneip and Simar, 1996). In other words, we are going to use leave-one-cross-section-out estimators as opposed to leave-one-observation-out estimators. In addition to a decrease in computing time, we may also minimize the impact of an outlier firm/country/individual. What we mean here is that if one cross-section is an outlier for any particular reason (measurement error, for example), simply leaving one observation out will still leave $T_i - 1$ potential outliers. Outliers can lead to bandwidths that are much too small. Hence, it would be preferable to leave out the entire set of values for that particular cross-section. Note that our design will not eliminate the problem if more than one outlier firm exists in the data.

Here we show the case of LSCV for panel data. Specifically, consider the LSCV function for a panel data set as

$$
\text{CV}(h) = \sum_{i=1}^{n} \sum_{t=1}^{T_i} \left[y_{it} - \widehat{m}_{-i}(\mathbf{x}_{it}) \right]^2,
$$

where $\widehat{m}_{-i}(\cdot)$ is computed by leaving out all T_i observations of the ith cross-section (i.e., the leave-one-cross-section-out estimator of $m(\cdot)$). Once we have an estimate of $\widehat{m}_{-i}(\cdot)$ for a particular cross-section, we plug in all T_i observations for cross-section i and then compare the estimated fitted values to the true left-hand-side variables.

11.7 Standard errors

The type of bootstrap you choose to estimate standard errors for panel-data estimation will depend on two issues: (1) whether or not your panel is balanced and (2) whether or not your data are homoskedastic. If your data are balanced and homoskedastic, then either the pairs bootstrap or the residual bootstrap should work. However, if either one of these do not hold, then you will likely have to resort to the wild bootstrap. The wild bootstrap for panel data is no different from that discussed in Chapter 5 and hence we omit it for brevity. The pairs and residual bootstrap resemble what we discussed with respect to bandwidth selection in panel-data models and it should follow smoothly.

11.7.1 Pairs bootstrap

One popular method to obtain standard errors in a balanced panel with homoskedastic errors is to use a pairs bootstrap. The basic idea here is similar to the pairs bootstrap in cross-sectional regression, except instead of randomly sampling pairs with replacement for a particular observation $\{y, \mathbf{x}\}$, you randomly sample all the observations for a particular cross-sectional unit with replacement $\{y, \mathbf{x}\}_{t=1}^T$. In other words, instead of making nT random samples, you make n random samples of size T. This still results in nT bootstrapped values of both the left-hand- and right-hand-side variables and hence the number of observations does not change.

The steps for the pairs bootstrap to obtain standard errors is as follows:

1. For each $i = 1, 2, \ldots, n$ randomly sample, with replacement, all T observations $\{y_i, \mathbf{x}_i\}_{t=1}^T$ for a particular cross-sectional unit and call the resulting sample $\{y_{it}^*, \mathbf{x}_{it}^*\}_{i=1,t=1}^{n,T_i}$ the bootstrap sample.
2. Using the bootstrap sample, estimate the unknown function $\widehat{m}^*(\mathbf{x})$ and/or derivative $\widehat{\beta}^*(\mathbf{x})$ via the initial estimator where y_{it} and $\mathbf{x}_{it}$ are replaced by y_{it}^* and $\mathbf{x}_{it}^*$, respectively. Remember to evaluate each estimator at the same values of $\mathbf{x}$.
3. Repeat steps 1 and 2 a large number (B) of times and then construct the sampling distribution of the bootstrapped estimates. Standard errors can be obtained by taking the standard deviation of the sampling distribution for each particular estimate.

11.7.2 Residual bootstrap

The steps for the residual bootstrap are very similar, except that we resample all T residuals with replacement in order to construct our bootstrap sample. The steps to construct a residual bootstrap in order to obtain standard errors is as follows:

1. For $i = 1, 2, \ldots, n$, randomly sample, with replacement, all T centered residuals $\{u_i^* = \widehat{u}_i - \overline{\widehat{u}}\}_{t=1}^T$ for a particular cross-sectional unit. Construct the bootstrap left-hand-side variable $y_i^* = \widehat{m}(\mathbf{x}_i) + u_i^*$ for $i = 1, 2, \ldots, n$. The resulting sample $\{y_{it}^*, \mathbf{x}_{it}\}$ is the bootstrap sample.
2. Using the bootstrap sample, estimate the unknown function $\widehat{m}^*(\mathbf{x})$ and/or derivative $\widehat{\beta}^*(\mathbf{x})$ via the initial estimator, where y_{it} is replaced by y_{it}^* wherever it occurs. Remember that we use the data $\mathbf{x}_{it}$ and evaluate at the same values of $\mathbf{x}$.

3. Repeat steps 1 and 2 a large number (B) of times and then construct the sampling distribution of the bootstrapped estimates. Standard errors can be obtained by taking the standard deviation of the sampling distribution for each particular estimate.

11.8 Testing

In this section we consider three types of specification tests. The first type is to test for poolability of a panel-data set. The second test addresses the functional form assumptions. Specifically, we present tests to test a parametric model versus a nonparametric alternative. Finally, we consider a test that will determine whether a random or fixed-effect estimator is appropriate for a given data set.

11.8.1 Poolability

One of the first questions in any panel-data study is whether or not the data can be pooled. Pooling is appropriate if the parameters of the model are constant over time. We can also think of cases where the parameters are constant across time, but different for specific countries or regions. For example, we could check for poolability of countries and/or regions. The former is more common in economics (partially due to the more common presence of wide panels, i.e. typically, $n > T$) and hence we will focus on constancy over time, but note that similar methods can be constructed to check over the cross-sectional units (e.g., see Jin and Su, 2009). If the data can be pooled, many of the specific panel estimators discussed above can be eschewed for more standard estimators.

Baltagi, Hidalgo, and Li (1996)
One of the first tests for poolability in nonparametric models was proposed by Baltagi, Hidalgo, and Li (1996). They argue that nonparametric tests are necessary for poolability because a parametric test, for example, the Chow test, may falsely reject (fail to reject) the null of poolability when the data are truly poolable because the functional form is misspecified. In its place they propose a method that is robust to functional-form misspecification. Specifically, they consider the following nonparametric model

$$y_{it} = m_t(\mathbf{x}_{it}) + u_{it}, \quad i = 1, 2, \ldots, n, \, t = 1, 2, \ldots, T_i,$$

where $m_t(\mathbf{x}_{it})$ is the unknown functional form that may vary over time, $\mathbf{x}_{it}$ is a $1 \times q$ vector of regressors and u_{it} is the error term. For the data to be poolable we would have $m_t(\mathbf{x}) = m(\mathbf{x})$ almost everywhere for all t, where $m(\mathbf{x})$ is defined as the pooled model. In other words, we want to test the null that

$$H_0 : m_t(\mathbf{x}) = m(\mathbf{x})$$

almost everywhere for all t versus the alternative that

$$H_1 : m_t(\mathbf{x}) \neq m(\mathbf{x})$$

for some t with positive probability.

Under the null $E(u_{it}|\mathbf{x}_{it}) = 0$ almost everywhere, where $u_{it} = y_{it} - m(\mathbf{x}_{it})$. Under the alternative, the residuals from the pooled model will not converge to the true errors and hence the conditional mean of the errors given the regressors will not be equal to zero almost everywhere. Hence, we can construct a consistent test for poolability based on $E[uE(u|\mathbf{x})]$ much in the same way we did in Chapter 6.

Technical Appendix 11.3 shows the derivation of the test statistic of Baltagi, Hidalgo, and Li (1996) as

$$\widehat{J}_{nT} = n |\mathbf{h}|^2 \frac{\widehat{I}_{nT}}{\widehat{\sigma}_{nT}},$$

where (we use J_{nT} instead of T_{nT} to avoid confusion)

$$\widehat{I}_{nT} = \frac{1}{nT(n-1)|\mathbf{h}|} \sum_{i=1}^{n} \sum_{t=1}^{T_i} \sum_{\substack{j=1 \\ j \neq i}}^{n} \widehat{u}_{it} \widehat{f}(\mathbf{x}_{it}) \widehat{u}_{jt} \widehat{f}(\mathbf{x}_{jt}) K_h(\mathbf{x}_{js}, \mathbf{x}_{it}),$$

and

$$\widehat{\sigma}_{nT}^2 = \frac{2}{nT(n-1)|\mathbf{h}|} \sum_{i=1}^{n} \sum_{t=1}^{T_i} \sum_{\substack{j=1 \\ j \neq i}}^{n} \widehat{u}_{it}^2 \widehat{f}(\mathbf{x}_{it})^2 \widehat{u}_{jt}^2 \widehat{f}(\mathbf{x}_{jt})^2 K_h^2(\mathbf{x}_{js}, \mathbf{x}_{it}).$$

The authors prove that the estimator $\widehat{J}_{nT}$ has a standard normal distribution under the null. In their empirical examples they use the asymptotic distribution for testing. We prefer a bootstrap-based test in practice. Here we propose a bootstrap algorithm for this test. The steps used to construct the wild-bootstrap test statistic are as follows:

1. For $i = 1, 2, \ldots, n$ and $t = 1, 2, \ldots, T_i$ generate the two-point wild-bootstrap error $u_{it}^* = \frac{(1-\sqrt{5})}{2}(\widehat{u}_{it} - \overline{\widehat{u}})$ with probability $p = \frac{(1+\sqrt{5})}{2\sqrt{5}}$ and $u_{it}^* = \frac{(1+\sqrt{5})}{2}(\widehat{u}_{it} - \overline{\widehat{u}})$ with probability $1 - p$ where $\widehat{u}_{it} = y_{it} - \widehat{m}(\mathbf{x}_{it})$ is the residual from the pooled estimator.

2. Construct the bootstrap left-hand-side variable $y_{it}^* = \widehat{m}(\mathbf{x}_{it}) + u_{it}^*$ for $i = 1, 2, \ldots, n$ and $t = 1, 2, \ldots, T_i$. The resulting sample $\{y_{it}^*, \mathbf{x}_{it}\}$ is the bootstrap sample. Note that this data is generated under the null of a pooled sample. Using the bootstrap sample, estimate $\widehat{m}^*(\mathbf{x}_{it})$ via pooled LCLS where y_{it} is replaced by y_{it}^*.

3. Use the bootstrap residuals $\widehat{u}_{it}^*$ to construct the bootstrap test statistic $\widehat{J}_{nT}^*$.

4. Repeat steps 1–3 a large number (B) of times and then construct the sampling distribution of the bootstrapped test statistics. We reject the null of poolability if the estimated test statistic $\widehat{J}_{nT}$ is greater than the upper α-percentile of the bootstrapped test statistics.

We should note that Lavergne (2001) is critical of this test partially because the smoothing parameter used in the pooled model is the same in each period. Further, he disagrees that the density of the regressors, $\widehat{f}(\cdot)$, should remain the same across time. He argues that this could lead to problems, which he shows in his simulation exercises. We agree that it may be inappropriate to make these assumptions, and if so, authors should consider the alternative test (Lavergne, 2001).

Irrelevant discrete individual/time effects

An informal way to determine whether or not the data is poolable in either the individual or time dimension would simply be to look at the bandwidths corresponding to these effects. We know from Chapter 8 that when the bandwidth on a discrete regressor hits its upper bound, that the variable is considered irrelevant in the prediction of y. Hence, if you include a discrete regressor for cross-section and/or time and their bandwidths hit their upper bounds, then the individual and/or time variable is irrelevant and hence we are back to the pooled estimator.

We again note that this is informal, but it will hold whether or not the data is estimated via LCLS, or any local-polynomial method. Further, there is no need to construct a test statistic or use a bootstrap. The problem will occur when the bandwidth is close, but not equal to its upper bound. In that case, formal test statistics will need to be constructed. These methods were also laid out in Chapter 8 and hence we refer you back to that chapter for this scenario.

11.8.2 Functional form specification

Here we consider tests for parametric models versus nonparametric alternatives. Specifically, we consider the following possible specifications:

$$y_{it} = \mathbf{x}_{it}\beta + u_{it}, \tag{11.20}$$

$$y_{it} = m(\mathbf{x}_{it}) + u_{it}, \tag{11.21}$$

where we assume a linear specification for simplicity and $u_{it} = \mu_i + v_{it}$. If you believe that μ_i is correlated with $\mathbf{x}_{it}$ in an unspecified manner, then you should employ both parametric and nonparametric fixed-effects estimators. If you are sure there is no correlation, then you may consider parametric and nonparametric random-effects estimators. The basic test will work for either case, but the bootstrap will differ, as we discuss below.

We let $\widehat{\beta}$ denote a consistent estimator of β based on model (11.20), and let $\widehat{m}(\cdot)$ denote the consistent estimator of $m(\cdot)$ based on (11.21). We use H_0 to denote the null hypothesis that model (11.20) is the correct specification, and we use H_1 to denote that (11.21) is the correct model. For testing H_0 we use the test statistic

$$\widehat{I}_{nT} = \frac{1}{nT} \sum_{i=1}^{n} \sum_{t=1}^{T_i} [\mathbf{x}_{it}\widehat{\beta} - \widehat{m}(\mathbf{x}_{it})]^2, \tag{11.22}$$

which is a discrete approximation of integrated squared error.

Under H_0, I_{nT} converges to zero in probability, and I_{nT} converges to a positive constant under H_1. Therefore, I_{nT} can be used to detect whether H_0 is true or not.

We conjecture that I_{nT}, after proper normalization and centering, is asymptotically normally distributed. However, the derivation of such a result is quite complicated in the fixed-effects case, due to the iterative procedure involved in computing $\widehat{m}(\cdot)$. Even if we knew the asymptotic distribution of I_{nT}, it is well known that asymptotic theory does not provide good approximations for nonparametric kernel-based tests in finite sample applications.

Henderson, Carroll, and Li (2008) consider the case where the data are homoskedastic and the panel is balanced. We generalize their bootstrap and also consider the case where the data are unbalanced or heteroskedastic.

In the case of a random effects estimator where the panel is balanced and the error is homoskedastic, the bootstrap is as follows:

1. Randomly sample, with replacement, from the re-centered parametric random-effects residuals $u_{it}^* = \widehat{u}_{it} - (nT)^{-1} \sum_{j=1}^{n} \sum_{s=1}^{T} \widehat{u}_{js}$. Note here that we are resampling the entire set of random-effect vector residuals for a particular cross-sectional unit ($t = 1, \ldots, T$).
2. Generate $y_{it}^* = \mathbf{x}_{it}\widehat{\beta} + u_{it}^*$. Call $\{\mathbf{x}_{it}, y_{it}^*\}$ the bootstrap sample. Use the bootstrap sample to estimate β based on model (11.20), say $\widehat{\beta}^*$, and estimate $m(\cdot)$ based on model (11.21), say $\widehat{m}^*(\cdot)$.
3. Compute I_{nT}^*, where I_{nT}^* is obtained from I_{nT} with $\widehat{\beta}$, and $\widehat{m}(\cdot)$ replaced by $\widehat{\beta}^*$, and $\widehat{m}^*(\cdot)$, respectively.
4. Repeat steps 1–3 a large number (B) of times and reject if the estimated test statistic $\widehat{I}_{nT}$ is greater than the upper α-percentile of the bootstrapped test statistics.

For the fixed-effects homoskedastic balanced panel-data bootstrap, Henderson, Carroll, and Li (2008) replace step 2 in the random-effects resampling plan with

2a. Generate $\widehat{y}_{it}^* \equiv y_{it}^* - y_{i1}^* = (\mathbf{x}_{it} - \mathbf{x}_{i1})\widehat{\beta} + u_{it}^*$. Call $\{\mathbf{x}_{it}, \widehat{y}_{it}^*\}$ the bootstrap sample. Use the bootstrap sample to estimate β based on model (11.20), say $\widehat{\beta}^*$, and estimate $m(\cdot)$ based on model (11.21), say $\widehat{m}^*(\cdot)$.

As noted previously, the above bootstrap procedures will not work if the data are unbalanced or heteroskedastic. The most natural way to think about performing this test in absence of either one of these assumptions is to use a wild bootstrap. This approach works well when using a random-effects estimator. Unfortunately, the wild bootstrap with the standard weights does not always produce the correct size for this particular test when using the Henderson, Carroll, and Li (2008) estimator. This is not an uncommon result. Davidson and Flachaire (2008) note that many tests do not perform well with these weights and suggest using Rademacher weights for some tests. The primary difference is that we don't use the $(1 - \sqrt{5})/2$ weight with probability $p = (1 + \sqrt{5})/(2\sqrt{5})$ and $(1 + \sqrt{5})/2$ weight with probability $1 - p$. Instead, we use a weight of 1 with probability 0.5 and weight of -1 with probability 0.5. Employing these weights produces a functional form test with better size in the limited simulations we have performed for the Henderson, Carroll, and Li (2008) test. This bootstrap will also work for the random-effects estimator but we do not suggest it, as this version of the bootstrap does not have the skewness correction property, which is present with the more popular weighting scheme.

Lin, Li, and Sun (2014) consider an alternative test for correct specification in fixed-effects panel-data models. The benefit of their test is that they are able to establish the asymptotic distribution of the test statistic given their avoidance of an iterative estimator, though the theoretical work of Li and Liang (2013) could be followed to establish the limiting distribution of the test statistic in (11.22). Moreover, Lin, Li, and Sun (2014) show consistency of the bootstrap and advocate on behalf of resampling methods in practice. Their simulations demonstrate that the size and power of their bootstrap-based test are good, lending further credence to the sampling methods outlined above, though more research in this area is warranted.

11.8.3 Nonparametric Hausman test

The question of whether to use random or fixed effects has important modeling consequences in applied work. We know that when the individual effect is correlated with any of the regressors, the random effects estimator becomes inconsistent. The fixed effect estimator wipes out these individual effects and leads to consistent estimates. On the other hand, if the individual effects are uncorrelated with the regressors, both estimators are consistent. In this case the random effects estimator is more efficient. This trade-off is common in econometrics and is often resolved using a testing procedure. Henderson, Carroll, and Li (2008) develop a Hausman-style test for the presence of fixed versus random effects. They suggest a separate bootstrap procedure for the implementation of this test in practice. The model remains as (11.12) with $u_{it} = \mu_i + v_{it}$.

We are interested in testing the null hypothesis that μ_i is a random effect versus the alternative hypothesis that μ_i is a fixed effect. The null hypothesis can be written as

$$H_0 : E(\mu_i | \mathbf{x}_{it}) = 0$$

almost everywhere. The alternative hypothesis is the negation of the null, i.e., H_1: $E(\mu_i | \mathbf{x}_i) \neq 0$ on a set with positive measure. We maintain the assumption that $E(v_{it} | \mathbf{x}_i) = 0$ under either H_0 or H_1. The null and the alternative hypotheses can then be equivalently written as

$$H_0 : E(u_{it} | \mathbf{x}_{it}) = 0$$

almost everywhere versus

$$H_1 : E(u_{it} | \mathbf{x}_{it}) \neq 0$$

on a set with positive measure.

Similar to the conditional-moment tests in Chapter 6, our proposed test is based on the sample analogue of $J = E \left[u_{it} E(u_{it} | \mathbf{x}_{it}) f(\mathbf{x}_{it}) \right]$. Note that $J = 0$ under H_0 and is positive null the alternative. Hence, J serves as a proper candidate for testing H_0.

Let $\widehat{m}(\mathbf{x})$ denote a consistent estimator of $m(\mathbf{x})$ under the fixed-effects assumption. Then a consistent estimator of u_{it} is given by $\widehat{u}_{it} = y_{it} - \widehat{m}(\mathbf{x}_{it})$. Our feasible test statistic is given by

$$\widehat{J}_{nT} = \frac{1}{nT(nT-1)} \sum_{i=1}^{n} \sum_{t=1}^{T_i} \sum_{\substack{j=1 \\ \{j,s\} \neq \{i,t\}}}^{n} \sum_{s=1}^{T_i} \widehat{u}_{it} \widehat{u}_{js} K_h(\mathbf{x}_{it}, \mathbf{x}_{js}).$$

It can be shown that $\widehat{J}$ is a consistent estimator of J. Hence, $\widehat{J} \overset{p}{\to} 0$ under the null, and $\widehat{J} \overset{p}{\to} C$ if H_0 is false, where $C > 0$ is a positive constant. Therefore, we reject H_0 when $\widehat{J}$ takes large positive values. We slightly modify the bootstrap procedure outlined in Henderson, Carroll, and Li (2008) to approximate the finite sample null distribution of $\widehat{J}$. The steps are as follows:

1. Let $\widetilde{u}_i = (\widetilde{u}_{i1}, \ldots, \widetilde{u}_{iT_i})'$, where $\widetilde{u}_{it} = y_{it} - \widetilde{m}(\mathbf{x}_{it})$ is the residual from a random effects model, and $\widetilde{m}(\mathbf{x})$ is a random effects estimator of $m(\mathbf{x})$. Compute the two-point wild-bootstrap errors by $u_i^* = \{(1-\sqrt{5})/2\}\widetilde{u}_i$ with probability $p = (1+\sqrt{5})/(2\sqrt{5})$ and $u_i^* = \{(1+\sqrt{5})/2\}\widetilde{u}_i$ with probability $1-p$. Generate y_{it}^* via $y_{it}^* = \widetilde{m}(\mathbf{x}_{it}) + u_{it}^*$. Call $\{\mathbf{x}_{it}, y_{it}^*\}_{i=1,t=1}^{n,T_i}$ the bootstrap sample. Note here that all residuals within a cluster are scaled by the same point of the two-point wild bootstrap.
2. Use the bootstrap sample to estimate $m(\mathbf{x})$ via the fixed-effects method, denote the estimate by $\widehat{m}^*(\mathbf{x})$, and then obtain the bootstrap residual by $\widehat{u}_{it}^* = y_{it}^* - \widehat{m}^*(\mathbf{x}_{it})$.
3. The bootstrap test statistic $\widehat{J}^*$ is obtained as in $\widehat{J}$ except that $\widehat{u}_{it}$ ($\widehat{u}_{js}$) is replaced by $\widehat{u}_{it}^*$ ($\widehat{u}_{js}^*$) wherever it occurs.
4. Repeat steps 1–3 a large number (B) of times and reject if the estimated test statistic $\widehat{J}$ is greater than the upper α-percentile of the bootstrapped test statistics.

Note that the bootstrap procedure in 1 is somewhat different from other conditional-moment-based tests. Here we construct the test statistic with the fixed-effects residuals (consistent under the null and alternative), but bootstrap with the residuals from the random effects model (consistent only under the null). Henderson, Carroll, and Li (2008) suggest using a random-effects estimator. However, as pointed out in Amini, Delgado, Henderson, and Parmeter (2012), asymptotically the performance of the test is irrelevant to which estimator is used within the bootstrap, but in finite samples the use of the fixed-effects estimator leads to better size performance.

11.9 Application

We have been naïve in past chapters as we have been pooling cross-sections to obtain larger sample sizes, but mostly ignoring that these data are measured repeatedly. Here we finally exploit the data structure by employing estimators designed specifically for panel data. We will start with pooled estimators, which will be very similar to what we saw in past chapters except that we now use leave-one-country-out estimators when calculating bandwidths. We then will move to random- and fixed-effects estimators. We will conclude with several tests designed specifically for the panel-data setting as discussed above.

11.9.1 Bandwidths

The bandwidths from each model here can be interesting, but we are going to focus on two separate sets of bandwidths. First, we are going to look at the difference between the pooled models here and those in Chapter 5. Specifically, what we want to analyze is the difference between the bandwidths from the leave-one-observation-out strategy to the leave-one-country-out approach. We are unaware of anything like this in the literature. Second, we want to examine the bandwidths for country and time from the regression with discrete regressors. These will allow us to check for relevance (albeit informally) of the country and time effects.

Leave-one-out
Table 11.1 shows the bandwidths from both the LCLS and LLLS estimators in both cases. The basic interpretation of the bandwidths remain the same. Each approach shows in the LCLS case that the inputs are relevant. This is expected. In the LLLS case, each approach shows that the regressors enter nonlinearly. This is also expected. The primary difference we see is that the LCLS leave-one-observation-out bandwidths are smaller than those of the LCLS leave-one-country-out bandwidths. As we mentioned before, leaving an entire cross-sectional unit out reduces the impact of a problematic firm/country/individual. In fact, it is our expectation that the bandwidths would rise with a leave-one-country-out bandwidth procedure. We believe that in this situation, and many other potential situations, (in finite samples) the leave-one-observation-out approach will lead to undersmoothing relative to the leave-one-cross-section-out approach. It is also true that the leave-one-cross-section-out approach runs faster given that we only need to evaluate the cross-validation function n times (albeit for T_i points for each i). We therefore advocate for a leave-one-cross-section-out approach when

Table 11.1. *Bandwidths estimated via a leave-one-observation-out and leave-one-country-out approach – LCLS and LLLS estimation with bandwidths estimated via LSCV*

	Leave-one-observation	Leave-one-country	UB	Interpretation
LCLS				
K	1.1255	1.4855	7.5850	Relevant
HL	0.9538	1.0409	7.9586	Relevant
LLLS				
K	2.6311	2.5585	7.5850	Nonlinear
HL	1.8536	1.8381	7.9586	Nonlinear

Table 11.2. *Bandwidths for the regression of output on physical capital, human-capital-augmented labor with discrete regressors for country and time – LLLS estimation with bandwidths estimated via LSCV*

	Bandwidth	UB	Interpretation
K	1.4765	7.5850	Nonlinear
HL	1.2940	7.9586	Nonlinear
Country	0.1041	1.0000	Relevant
Time	0.8340	1.0000	Relevant

applicable. That being said, we are unaware of any package that does this other than the R code that is available on this manuscript's website.

Discrete regressors

Table 11.2 gives the bandwidths for the regression where we use discrete regressors to control for time and country. The bandwidths for the continuous regressors for the LLLS case are similar to what we found in Table 11.1 for the leave-one-country-out bandwidth selector. This makes sense because we also use a leave-one-country-out estimator here. Again, both continuous regressors enter linearly (and if we were to show the LCLS results, they would be deemed relevant).

Our primary focus in this section is on the discrete bandwidths. If you recall from Chapter 8, if the bandwidth on a discrete regressor hits unity, it is smoothed out of the regression. In other words, it is as if it didn't enter the function in the first place. Given that each of our bandwidths are below one, this suggests that both country and time effects are relevant. This result is expected.

11.9.2 Estimation

To avoid being repetitive, we will look solely at median elasticities and returns to scale for each of the LLLS-type estimators. Table 11.3 gives the median estimate from each estimator, along with the corresponding standard error. The results are actually quite similar across estimators.

11.9.3 Testing

The elasticities and returns to scale can give us some indication of which estimator is preferable, but we also like to confirm such suspicions with formal statistical tests. We first focus on poolability of the data using the test of Baltagi, Hidalgo, and Li (1996). Given the criticism of Lavergne (2001), we tried several different sets of bandwidths (noting that the objection is with respect to using the same bandwidth for the pooled and separate models). We found that the p-value bounced around, but was generally

Table 11.3. *Median elasticities for several panel-data estimators – bandwidths estimated via LSCV*

	Elasticity (K)	Elasticity (HL)	RTS
LLLS	0.7442	0.3268	1.0416
	0.1462	0.1377	0.0398
LLWLS	0.7866	0.3134	1.0671
	0.0876	0.0650	0.0632
Wang	0.6636	0.2859	0.9776
	0.0102	0.0069	0.0953
HCL	0.7369	0.3085	1.0110
	0.1179	0.0482	0.0179
Li–Racine	0.8281	0.2552	1.0652
	0.0369	0.0220	0.0241

less than 0.10. In other words, there is evidence to suggest that we should reject the null of poolability.

Noting this rejection, we turn our attention to functional form tests. Given the performance of the generalized quadratic model from Chapter 5, we decided to create a fixed-effects version of that estimator to compare with a nonparametric alternative. To keep consistency between the parametric and nonparametric model in Henderson, Carroll, and Li (2008), we used a long first difference, $Y_{it} - Y_{i1}$, to eliminate the individual effect in the parametric model as well. Note that we are not controlling for time effects. Here we find evidence in favor of the parametric model. Our test statistic is 0.2218 and the bootstrapped p-value is 0.7525. This suggests that the generalized quadratic model may be sufficient to explain output across countries. The unreported elasticities from the GQ model are similar to the other nonparametric models.

Finally, we consider the question of fixed versus random effects. Given that Henderson, Carroll, and Li (2008) do not recommend a particular bandwidth selector, we consider both cross-validated bandwidths from their estimator along with those from the Wang (2003) estimator. Fortunately, the conclusion of the test is the same with either set of bandwidths. Using the fixed-effect (LSCV) bandwidths, our p-value is 0.0375 and with the Wang (2003) (LSCV) bandwidths, our p-value is zero to four decimal places. In other words, we reject the null of random effects. That being said, these test results depend upon the additive separability assumption between the conditional mean and the time-invariant individual effects. A relaxation of this assumption could lead to an alternative conclusion.

12

Constrained estimation and inference

While the nonparametric regression methods we have discussed are flexible, a side effect of this flexibility is that the estimated function may not satisfy certain prior information (exact or assumed), such as monotonicity or positivity. A generic example of this is estimating a conditional mean model where the left-hand-side variable lies between zero and one. It is well known that a local-linear estimator is not guaranteed to produce a smooth function that always lies between these bounds. Thus, it is useful to discuss a set of tools that can be used to ensure that nonparametric estimates satisfy specific smoothness constraints.

An additional benefit of imposing constraints in a nonparametric framework is that it may provide nonparametric identification (see Matzkin, 1994). Also, Mammen, Marron, Turlach, and Wand (2001) show that when we impose constraints on derivatives higher than the first order, the rate of convergence is faster than it would be had the constraints not been imposed.

A rich and diverse literature on constrained estimation has emerged and a multitude of potential estimators have been proposed for various constrained problems. We do not attempt to survey all existing constrained estimation methods. Rather, we refer the interested reader to Henderson and Parmeter (2009) for a detailed survey. Instead, we focus our discussion on three flexible and widely used methods: rearrangement, data sharpening, and constraint-weighted bootstrapping. Each of these methods has its costs and benefits, but all three are sufficiently flexible to warrant further investigation.

Perhaps the most general of the methods, constraint-weighted bootstrapping can be used to impose a wide range of smoothness constraints, from positivity and monotonicity, to constant returns to scale and additive separability. Further, this method is sufficiently flexible that it can be implemented with any of the local-polynomial estimators described in Chapter 5. We detail the implementation of this estimator and conduct inference for general hypotheses regarding the smoothness of the unknown conditional mean.

We end our discussion of constrained methods by imposing various economic constraints on our production function of cross-country output. Namely, we enforce both monotonicity in inputs and constant returns to scale. Not surprisingly, we see that our baseline estimates do not always produce positive effects nor are constant returns to scale prevalent across all observations. Thus, these constrained methods shed light into violations of general production theory, which we expect to hold in the cross-country context.

12.1 Rearrangement

Rearrangement is a technique originally developed to impose monotonicity (increasing or decreasing) on a regression function. Recall that for a univariate random variable x with pdf $f(x)$, if $z = g(x)$ is a monotonic transformation of x, then the pdf of z is

$$r(z) = f[g^{-1}(z)] \left| \frac{dg^{-1}(z)}{dz} \right|.$$

Now, briefly assume that $x \sim \mathcal{U}[0, 1]$ and $g(x)$ is monotonically increasing. Then our monotonic transformation has density

$$r(z) = I_{[g(0),g(1)]}(z) \left(\frac{dg^{-1}(z)}{dz} \right),$$

where $I_{[g(0),g(1)]}(z) = 1$ if $g(0) \le z \le g(1)$ and 0 otherwise. Integrating this, we have

$$\int_{-\infty}^{t} I_{[g(0),g(1)]}(z) \left(\frac{dg^{-1}(z)}{dz} \right) dz = \int_{g(0)}^{t} \left(\frac{dg^{-1}(z)}{dz} \right) dz$$

$$= g^{-1}(t) - g^{-1}(g(0)) = g^{-1}(t).$$

Integration of $r(z)$ yields a CDF, which is always monotonic. This is the key insight of the rearranged estimator. To make the rearranged estimator operational we replace unknowns with estimates.

Rearrangement is detailed in Dette, Neumeyer, and Pilz (2006) and Chernozhukov, Fernández-Val, and Galichon (2009). The estimator of Dette, Neumeyer, and Pilz (2006) combines density and regression techniques to construct a monotonic estimator. The appeal of "rearrangement" is that no constrained optimization is required to obtain a monotonically constrained estimator, making it computationally efficient. Their estimator actually estimates the inverse of a monotonic function, which can then be inverted to obtain an estimate of the function of interest.

To derive this estimator, let $\mathcal{G}$ denote a natural number that dictates the number of equispaced grid points to evaluate the unknown function. Then, the rearranged estimator is defined as

$$\widehat{m}^{-1}(x) = \int_{-\infty}^{x} \frac{1}{\mathcal{G}h_d} \sum_{j=1}^{\mathcal{G}} k^d \left(\frac{\widehat{m}(j/\mathcal{G}) - \psi}{h_d} \right) \psi, \tag{12.1}$$

where $\widehat{m}(x)$ is a preliminary estimator of the unknown function, $k^d(\cdot)$ is our kernel used to construct the density, and h_d stands for "density" bandwidth. For example, if we elected to use a local-constant estimator, then we have

$$\widehat{m}(j/\mathcal{G}) = \sum_{i=1}^{n} A_i(j/\mathcal{G}) y_i$$

from Chapter 5, where

$$A_i(j/\mathcal{G}) = \frac{k^r(\frac{x_i - j/\mathcal{G}}{h_r})}{\sum\limits_{j=1}^{n} k^r(\frac{x_j - j/\mathcal{G}}{h_r})},$$

h_r is the "regression" bandwidth, and we use kernel $k^r(\cdot)$. Note that it is unlikely that x_i is going to be uniformly distributed in practice. This does not matter, however, as we are evaluating $\widehat{m}(\cdot)$, as opposed to x_i, at grid points in (12.1), so the density estimator acts as though the data are uniformly distributed. This is the rationale for setting the upper limit of integration in (12.1) equal to x, a point of interest to evaluate the function. Moreover, if the original data had support beyond [0, 1], it is a simple matter to transform the data to have support on [0, 1], construct the rearranged estimator, and then scale back to the original support. Integration is not even necessary, as we have

$$\widehat{m}^{-1}(x) = \frac{1}{\mathcal{G}h_d} \sum_{j=1}^{\mathcal{G}} \int_{-\infty}^{x} k^d \left(\frac{\widehat{m}(j/\mathcal{G}) - \psi}{h_d} \right) d\psi = \frac{1}{\mathcal{G}} \sum_{j=1}^{\mathcal{G}} \tilde{k}^d \left(\frac{\widehat{m}(j/\mathcal{G}) - x}{h_d} \right),$$

and $\tilde{k}^d(\cdot)$ is the integral of the kernel used for the density, which for the s-class of kernels discussed in this book are available in closed-form solution. For the main kernels we have discussed, they are

$$\tilde{k}_0(\psi) = \frac{1}{2}(1 + \psi)\mathbf{1}\{|\psi| \le 1\},$$

$$\tilde{k}_1(\psi) = \frac{1}{4}\left(2 + 3\psi - \psi^3\right)\mathbf{1}\{|\psi| \le 1\},$$

$$\tilde{k}_2(\psi) = \frac{1}{16}\left(8 + 15\psi - 10\psi^3 + 3\psi^5\right)\mathbf{1}\{|\psi| \le 1\},$$

$$\tilde{k}_3(\psi) = \frac{1}{32}\left(16 + 35\psi - 35\psi^3 + 21\psi^5 - 5\psi^7\right)\mathbf{1}\{|\psi| \le 1\},$$

$$\tilde{k}_\phi(\psi) = \Phi(\psi).$$

The name "rearrangement" comes from the fact that the point estimates are rearranged so that they are in increasing order (monotonic). This happens because the kernel-density estimate of the first-stage regression estimates sorts the data from low to high to construct the density, which is then integrated. This sorting, or rearranging, is how the monotonic estimate is produced. It works because monotonicity as a property is nothing more than a special ordering and the kernel density estimator is "unaware" that the points it is smoothing over to construct a density are from an estimate of a regression function, as opposed to raw data.

One issue with this estimator is that while it is intuitive, computationally simple, and easy to implement with existing software, it requires the selection of two "bandwidths." We use the word "bandwidth" loosely here, as the first stage does not have to involve kernel regression. We could use series estimators, in which case the selection would be over the number of terms. Or, if you use splines, then the number of knots would have to be selected in the first stage. In fact, a parametric estimate could be used in the first stage as well.

Dette, Neumeyer, and Pilz (2006) discuss the optimal bandwidth for the rearranged estimator. The key assumption is that $\lim_{h_d \to 0, h_r \to 0} \frac{h_d}{h_r} = c \in (0, \infty)$. In other words, they require that the smoothing of the density estimator of the function estimates has a bandwidth that decays to zero at (potentially) the same rate as the bandwidth used to construct the function estimates. The importance of this ratio stems from the form of the asymptotic variance of the rearranged estimator. When $c = \infty$, the monotonically restricted estimator is asymptotically equivalent to the unconstrained estimator. Thus, in the limit, the two estimators are the same.

Dette, Neumeyer, and Pilz (2006) suggest that h_r can be chosen using standard methods such as LSCV or an optimal plug-in. To select h_d, however, they rely on asymptotic arguments. First, Dette, Neumeyer, and Pilz (2006) show that the asymptotic bias of the rearranged estimator depends on both h_r and h_d. Given the assumption that h_r and h_d are of the same order, they solve for h_d through the form of this asymptotic bias, resulting in $h_d = \gamma h_r$ for $\gamma > 0$. From the point of view of asymptotic equivalence between the unrestricted and rearranged estimators, this implies $\gamma = 0$. In practice, we would not actually set $h_d = 0$, but rather, would construct h_d at a rate smaller than h_r. For example, in simulations in Dette and Pilz (2006), they set $h_d = h_r^3$, which ensures that asymptotically $\gamma = 0$.

Another issue with the empirical implementation of the rearranged estimator is the choice of k^r and k^d. To determine the appropriate choice of kernel, Dette, Neumeyer, and Pilz (2006) analyze asymptotically the ratio of mean-squared errors for the rearranged estimator (as a function of γ) and the unrestricted estimator ($\gamma = 0$) using a local optimal bandwidth. This ratio depends on γ, k^d, and k^r. By fixing k^r, they can determine the optimal k^d for each γ (or the optimal γ for a given k^d). For the Epanechnikov kernel ($s = 1$), for all $\gamma > 0$ the MSE ratio is greater than one, indicating that we should use $\gamma = 0$ if $k^d = k^r$. Only for the case that $k^d = k^r$ is the uniform kernel ($s = 0$) is γ found to be larger than zero (in this case $\gamma \approx 0.3$ is optimal).

The simplest approach is to implement the rearranged estimator with $k^d = k^r$ and the optimal bandwidth in the regression stage can be selected with your preferred method (LSCV or plug-in) and then the "optimal" bandwidth for the density stage, h_d can be constructed as $h_d = \widehat{h}_r^\alpha$, where $\alpha > 1$. We recommend following Dette and Pilz (2006) and setting $\alpha = 3$.

12.1.1 Imposing convexity

Birke and Dette (2007) use the insights from the univariate rearranged estimator to develop a method to impose convexity on a regression surface. The basic idea is to integrate over the derivative of the unknown function, which has itself been properly monotonized. Thus, Birke and Dette (2007) apply rearrangement to a univariate estimator of the derivative as

$$[\widehat{m}'(x)]^{-1} = \frac{1}{\mathcal{G}h_d} \sum_{j=1}^{\mathcal{G}} \int_{-\infty}^{x} k^d \left(\frac{\widehat{m}'(j/\mathcal{G}) - u}{h_d} \right) du = \frac{1}{\mathcal{G}} \sum_{j=1}^{\mathcal{G}} \tilde{k}^d \left(\frac{\widehat{m}'(j/\mathcal{G}) - x}{h_d} \right),$$

where $\widehat{m}'(x)$ is the first derivative of the unknown function and $\tilde{k}^d()$ is the integral of the kernel. A convex estimator is then constructed as

$$\widehat{m}_C(x, \psi) = \widehat{m}(\psi) + \int_{\psi}^{x} \widehat{m}'(z)dz.$$

Beyond proper selection of the bandwidths, the issue of selecting ψ is also at play. It is easy to see that this estimator will be convex, because as x increases, we are integrating a monotonic function, which by definition gives us a convex function.

An appropriate bandwidth for estimating the preliminary, possibly nonconvex function is $h_r \sim n^{-1/7}$. Birke and Dette (2007) require $\lim_{h_d \to 0, h_r \to 0} \frac{h_d}{h_r^{3/2}} = 0$. This implies that $h_d = \gamma h_r^{\alpha}$, where $3/2 < \alpha < 2$. The rates on the bandwidth for h_d follow from similar arguments for the monotonically restricted regression estimator. For the appropriate choice of u, Birke and Dette (2007) use a minimum-norm approach based on the following logic: the appropriate ψ should be selected such that the distance between the convexified function is as close as possible to the unknown true function. For this setup, distance is chosen as the L^2-norm yielding

$$\psi^* = \min_{\psi} \int_{0}^{1} [\widehat{m}(x) - \widehat{m}_C(x, \psi)]^2 \, dx. \tag{12.2}$$

Birke and Dette (2007, Theorem 2) show that for any u^* obtained from (12.2)

$$\widehat{m}_C(x, \psi^*) = \int_{0}^{1} \widehat{m}_C(x, \psi)d\psi,$$

meaning that we do not actually have to solve the optimization problem. This follows, since $\widehat{m}_C(x) = \widehat{m}_C(x, \psi^*)$, so it is enough to simply take the integral of the convex rearranged estimator over the domain of ψ. The calculation of the convex estimator can be simplified by noting that $\widehat{m}_C(x, \psi) = \widehat{m}(\psi) + \widehat{m}(x) - \widehat{m}_C(\psi, x)$, so the integral only needs to be taken over $\widehat{m}(\psi) - \widehat{m}_C(\psi, x)$,

$$\widehat{m}_C(x, \psi^*) = \widehat{m}(x) + \int_{0}^{1} [\widehat{m}(\psi) - \widehat{m}_C(\psi, x)] \, d\psi.$$

12.1.2 Existing literature

The literature on rearrangement has seen substantial interest in statistics in the past decade. For example, Dette and Pilz (2006) conduct an extensive simulation to compare alternative monotonicity-constrained estimators to the rearrangement estimator; Dette and Scheder (2006) extend the rearrangement estimator to a bivariate setting; Birke and Dette (2007) develop a test of monotonicity using the rearranged estimator; Neumeyer (2007) considers the uniform consistency of the rearrangement estimator; Birke and Dette (2008) consider asymptotic analysis of the rearrangement estimator when the underlying function is only once continuously differentiable (recall that most analysis assumes two smooth derivatives); Birke and Pilz (2009) apply the rearranged estimator to a nonparametric option pricing model; while Dette and Pilz (2009) use the rearranged estimator to estimate a monotone conditional variance of the nonparametric regression estimator.

12.2 Motivating alternative shape-constrained estimators

While rearrangement is becoming an increasingly popular tool for imposing mono-tonicity on a univariate nonparametric regression estimator,[1] it has several several aspects that limit its general applicability. Notably, rearrangement is difficult to extend to more general constraints. Second, rearrangement is not readily extended to settings beyond two or three variables. Given these empirical limitations, we now discuss the intuition behind several alternative shape-constrained tools that are readily adaptable to multivariate settings for general (and numerous) shape constraints.

The goal of general constrained estimation is to estimate the unknown smooth function $m(\mathbf{x})$ subject to constraints on $m^{(\mathbf{r})}(\mathbf{x})$ where $\mathbf{r}$ is a q-vector corresponding to the dimension of $\mathbf{x}$. In what follows, the elements of $\mathbf{r}$ represent the order of the partial derivative corresponding to each element of $\mathbf{x}$. Thus $\mathbf{r} = (0, 0, \dots, 0)$ represents the function itself, while $\mathbf{r} = (1, 0, \dots, 0)$ represents $\partial m(\mathbf{x})/\partial x_1$. In general, for $\mathbf{r} = (r_1, r_2, \dots, r_q)$ we have $m^{(\mathbf{r})}(\mathbf{x}) = \frac{\partial^{r_1} m(\mathbf{x})}{\partial x_1^{r_1}} \cdots \frac{\partial^{r_q} m(\mathbf{x})}{\partial x_q^{r_q}}$.

Given an estimate $\widehat{m}(\mathbf{x})$, we will impose constraints on $\widehat{m}(\mathbf{x})$ of the form

$$L(\mathbf{x}) \leq \widehat{m}^{(\mathbf{r})}(\mathbf{x}) \leq U(\mathbf{x}) \tag{12.3}$$

for arbitrary $L(\cdot)$, $U(\cdot)$, and $\mathbf{r}$, where $L(\cdot)$ and $U(\cdot)$ represent (local) lower and upper bounds, respectively. For some applications, $\mathbf{r} = (0, \dots, 0, 1, 0, \dots, 0)$ would be of particular interest, say for example when the partial derivative represents an elasticity and therefore must lie in $[0, 1]$ (i.e., $L(\mathbf{x}) = 0 \; \forall \mathbf{x}$ and $U(\mathbf{x}) = 1 \; \forall \mathbf{x}$). Or, $\mathbf{r} = (0, 0, \dots, 0)$ might be of interest when an outcome must be bounded (i.e., $\widehat{m}(\mathbf{x})$ could represent a probability and hence must lie in $[0, 1]$, but could be violated with a local-linear smoother). Additional types of constraints that could be imposed in this framework are (log-)supermodularity, (log-)convexity, and quasiconvexity, all of which focus on second-order or cross-partials derivatives. Or, $L(\cdot) = U(\cdot)$ might be required (i.e., equality constraints) such as imposing the sum of elasticities must equal one.

The two-sided constraint (12.3) can be considered a special case of multiple simul-taneous one-sided constraints. Hence for general purposes, we consider restrictions of the form

$$\sum_{\mathbf{r} \in \mathbf{R}_j} \alpha_{\mathbf{r}, j} \widehat{m}^{(\mathbf{r})}(\mathbf{x}) - c_j(\mathbf{x}) \geq 0, \quad j = 1, \dots, S, \tag{12.4}$$

---

[1] It has also proven useful as a technique to ensure that estimated quantile functions do not cross. See Chernozhukov, Fernández-Val, and Galichon (2010) and Flores, Flores-Lagunes, and Kapetanakis (2014).

where S is the number of restrictions, and in each restriction the sum is taken over all vectors in $\mathbf{R}_j$ that correspond to our constraints and $\alpha_{\mathbf{r},j}$ is a set of various constraints. Note that (12.4) could be further generalized to contain more sophisticated constraints such as global concavity/convexity or homogeneity of a given degree (Euler's theorem) by allowing $\alpha_{\mathbf{r},j}$ to be a function of the covariates. In what follows we shall presume, without loss of generality, that for all $\mathbf{r}$, $\alpha_{\mathbf{r},j} \geq 0$ and $c_j(\mathbf{x}) \equiv 0$, since $c_j(\mathbf{x})$'s are known functions of $L(\mathbf{x})$ and $U(\mathbf{x})$. The approaches we describe are quite general and firmly embedded in a conventional multivariate kernel framework, and admit arbitrary combinations of constraints (i.e., for any $\mathbf{r}$ or combination thereof) subject to the obvious caveat that the constraints must be internally consistent (i.e., we could not impose that $\widehat{m}(\mathbf{x})$ is both positive and negative everywhere).

To begin, consider the following general form of the kernel-density and regression estimators for univariate data:

$$\widehat{f}(\mathbf{x}) = n^{-1} \sum_{i=1}^{n} A_i(\mathbf{x})$$

$$\widehat{m}(\mathbf{x}) = n^{-1} \sum_{i=1}^{n} A_i(\mathbf{x}) y_i,$$

where $A_i(\mathbf{x}) = |\mathbf{h}|^{-1} K_h(\mathbf{x}_i, \mathbf{x})$ for the kernel density estimator and $A_i(\mathbf{x}) = \frac{n K_h(\mathbf{x}_i, \mathbf{x})}{\sum_{j=1}^{n} K_h(\mathbf{x}_j, \mathbf{x})}$ for the local-constant regression estimator. Notice first that the presence of n^{-1} is redundant in the kernel-regression estimator. What these estimators suggest is that there is actually two types of weighting occurring in the construction of the estimator. First, there is the common local weighting, captured by the $A_i(\mathbf{x})$ component. Second, and more subtly, there is a global weighting, captured by the n^{-1}, also known as uniform weighting. It is this second weighting that underlies the essence of the constrained methods we are about to discuss. In short, this uniform weighting can be manipulated so that the estimator is forced to satisfy economic smoothness constraints by converting the global weighting scheme, n^{-1} for each observation, to a second local weighting scheme (p_i) for each observation. That is, instead of thinking of the weights as being independent of the observations, we make them observation dependent. This results in

$$\widehat{f}(\mathbf{x}) = \sum_{i=1}^{n} p_i A_i(\mathbf{x})$$

$$\widehat{m}(\mathbf{x}) = \sum_{i=1}^{n} p_i A_i(\mathbf{x}) y_i.$$

The key is how to best select these secondary local weights. The two general methods we describe go about selecting the weights in different fashions, but the intuition is identical: by changing the local weighting of the overall estimator, a nonparametrically estimated surface can be forced to satisfy a range of smoothness constraints.

To provide more intuition behind this discussion, we provide a simple graphical illustration on the mechanics of this nonuniform weighting scheme. Suppose our goal is to impose monotonicity on a conditional mean. For this example we will closely follow the discussion in Parmeter, Sun, Henderson, and Kumbhakar (2014). Our covariate, x_1, is distributed as $\mathcal{U}[-2, 2]$ while our regressand is related to x_1 via $y = x_1^3 + u$, which is monotonic on the domain of interest, and $u \sim N(0, 1)$. Drawing 100 observations from this data generating process (DGP), the local-constant estimator produces a conditional mean that is nonmonotonic. The bandwidth for the local-constant estimator is selected via AIC_c (Hurvich, Simonoff, and Tsai, 1998) and is used for both the unrestricted and restricted conditional-mean estimates. The restricted and unrestricted function estimates are displayed in Figure 12.1. We see that the noise induced from this particular sample has obscured the monotonic relationship. The reweighting successfully mimics the monotonic behavior of the DGP.

To appreciate how the averaging is re-weighted in order to constrain the estimator, Figure 12.2 plots the original points against the weighted points (via constraint-weighted bootstrapping – to be discussed later) for each estimator, while Figure 12.3 plots the actual constraint weights (p_i) against the uniform weights ($1/n$). This shifting of the unconstrained datum allows the fit of the function to preserve monotonicity. The idea is that the data is moved as little as possible to uphold the constraint(s) imposed.

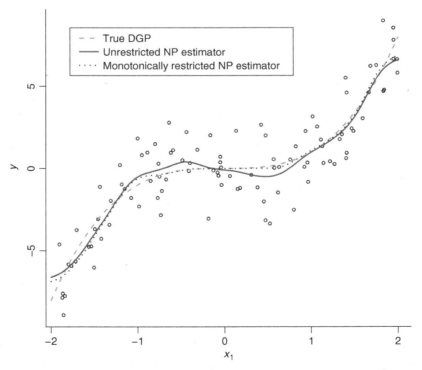

Figure 12.1. Restricted and unrestricted conditional mean estimates of $y = x_1^3 + u$ where monotonicity is imposed, i.e., $j = 1, \widehat{m}_1(x_1|p) \geq 0, n = 100$

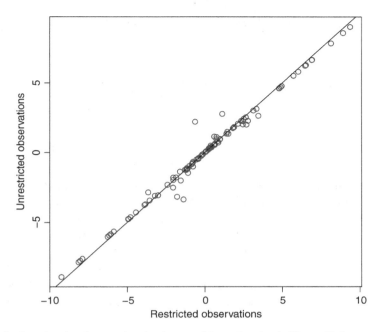

Figure 12.2. Restricted and unrestricted points used for estimation in Figure 12.1

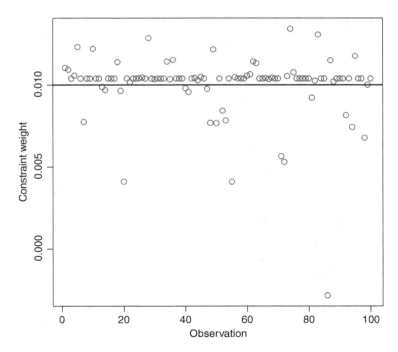

Figure 12.3. Restricted and unrestricted weights used for estimation in Figure 12.1

The determination of how little to move the weights from their uniform counterparts is dictated by the choice of distance metric.

12.3 Implementation methods via reweighting

12.3.1 Constraint-weighted bootstrapping

Hall and Huang (2001) initially proposed constraint-weighted bootstrapping to impose monotonicity on a univariate nonparametric regression surface. Du, Parmeter, and Racine (2013) generalized the method to handle multiple constraints in the multivariate setting while Parmeter and Racine (2012) and Parmeter, Sun, Henderson, and Kumbhakar (2014) applied the method in a production economics setting. The setup of the constraint-weighted bootstrapping estimator is to select the weights (p_i) that satisfy the constraints, such that they deviate minimally from the unconstrained, uniform weights.

In the unconstrained setting we have $\mathbf{p} = (p_1, \ldots, p_n) = (1/n, \ldots, 1/n)$, which represents weights drawn from a uniform distribution. If the bandwidth chosen produces an estimate that *is already* monotonic, the weights should be set equal to the uniform weights. However, if the function itself is not monotonic, then the weights are diverted away from the uniform case to create a monotonic estimate.

12.3.2 Data sharpening

Data sharpening derives from the work of Friedman, Tukey, and Tukey (1980) and was later employed in Choi and Hall (1999). These methods are designed to admit a wide range of constraints and are closely linked to the biased-bootstrap methods of Hall and Presnell (1999). We discuss the method of Braun and Hall (2001) in what follows.

Consider the local-constant kernel-regression estimator with the constraint weights introduced, but place the weights in front of the dependent variable, leaving

$$\widehat{m}(\mathbf{x}) = \sum_{i=1}^{n} A_i(\mathbf{x}) p_i y_i = \sum_{i=1}^{n} A_i(\mathbf{x}) \breve{y}_i.$$

The key difference difference (vs. constraint-weighted bootstrapping) is to select $\breve{y}_i$ so that it deviates minimally from y_i, the original data.

A natural question to ask is why we elect to sharpen the ys as opposed to the $\mathbf{x}$s. There is nothing that disallows sharpening on the $\mathbf{x}$s. However, this is unnecessary for two reasons. First, and simply, given the nonlinearity of the kernel weighting function ($A_i(\mathbf{x})$), any smoothness constraint where sharpening is on the covariate(s) will be nonlinear. Therefore, simple quadratic programming is unavailable, making the problem more computationally demanding. Second, given that the $\mathbf{x}$s are already smoothed (via the bandwidth), it is awkward to think of how smoothing is occurring on the actual data when they are replaced with sharpened data.

It may seem that the discussion of data sharpening does not fall in line with our discussion of secondary weighting; however, this can be shown with the following logic. The general optimization problem for data sharpening with a quadratic distance function is

$$\min_{q_i} \sum_{i=1}^{n} (q_i - y_i)^2 = \min_{p_i} \sum_{i=1}^{n} (p_i y_i - y_i/n)^2 = \min_{p_i} \sum_{i=1}^{n} y_i^2 (p_i - n^{-1})^2.$$

By writing our sharpened dependent data as $q_i = p_i y_i$, we can think of the similarity between the two methods. We will not get identical values of p_i, because even with the same distance metric, the values of the metric for a given vector of ps will be different, given the presence of y_i^2 inside the metric for the data-sharpened estimator.

Note the subtle difference between the data-sharpening methods discussed here and the constraint-weighted bootstrapping methods discussed previously. When we choose to sharpen the data, the actual data values are being transformed while the weighting is held constant. With constraint-weighted bootstrapping, the opposite occurs, the data is held fixed while the weights are changed. However, the two estimators can be viewed as "visually" equivalent. That is, both estimators can be looked at as

$$\widehat{m}(\mathbf{x}) = \sum_{j=1}^{n} A_i(\mathbf{x}) y_i^*, \tag{12.5}$$

where y_i^* corresponds to either the sharpened (q_i) or constraint weighted ($p_i y_i$) values. The difference between the methods is how to arrive at y_i^*. Also, note that both constraint-weighted bootstrapping and data sharpening are *vertically* moving the data, whereas rearrangement *horizontally* moves the data.

12.4 Practical issues

12.4.1 Selecting the distance metric

We now consider how to impose particular restrictions on the estimator $\widehat{m}(\mathbf{x}|\mathbf{p})$. Let p_u be the n-vector of uniform weights $1/n$ and let $\mathbf{p}$ be the n-vector of weights to be selected. In order to impose our constraints, we choose $\mathbf{p}$ to minimize some distance measure from $\mathbf{p}$ to the uniform weights $p_i = 1/n \ \forall i$. This is appealing intuitively since the unconstrained estimator is that for which $p_i = 1/n \ \forall i$, as noted above. In the methods we describe below, a common choice of distance metric is the power divergence metric in Cressie and Read (1984):

$$D_\rho(\mathbf{p}) = \frac{1}{\rho(1 - \rho)} \left[n - \sum_{i=1}^{n} (np_i)^\rho \right], \quad -\infty < \rho < \infty, \tag{12.6}$$

where $\rho \neq 0, 1$. We need to take limits for $\rho = 0$ or 1. They are given as

$$D_0(\mathbf{p}) = -\sum_{i=1}^{n} \log(np_i); \quad D_1(\mathbf{p}) = \sum_{i=1}^{n} p_i \log(np_i).$$

This distance metric is quite general. If we use $\rho = 1/2$, then this corresponds to Hellinger distance, whereas $nD_0(\mathbf{p}) + n^2 \log(n)$ is equivalent to Kullback–Leibler divergence $\left(-\sum_{i=1}^{n} n \log(p_i/n) \right)$.

An unfortunate side-effect of using the power divergence to select the optimal weights is that for nearly all values of ρ, $D_\rho(\mathbf{p})$ is nonlinear in p_i, even if the constraints themselves are linear in p_i. A simpler alternative is to use the L^2-norm, or quadratic distance

$$D(\mathbf{p}) = \sum_{i=1}^{n} (p_i - 1/n)^2. \qquad (12.7)$$

When quadratic distance is deployed, coupled with linear in p_i constraints, the constrained estimation problem can be solved as a simple quadratic program. It is also common to impose an adding-up constraint on the weights themselves, $\sum_{i=1}^{n} p_i = 1$, so that they mimic the behavior of the uniform weights. If this constraint is imposed, we see that

$$D(\mathbf{p}) = \frac{2}{n^2} D_2(\mathbf{p}) + \frac{2}{n} \sum_{i=1}^{n} (n^{-1} - p_i) = \frac{2}{n^2} D_2(\mathbf{p}),$$

since $\sum_{i=1}^{n} (n^{-1} - p_i) = 0$ when the constraint weights add up to one. Thus, for $\rho = 2$, the power-divergence metric will yield a quadratic function of the constraint weights, which can be solved without resorting to nonlinear optimization. This also has consequences for implementation and theory since the L^2-norm is easier to work with (Du, Parmeter, and Racine, 2013) and we do not have to deal with appropriate selection of ρ. Both Hall and Huang (2001) and Henderson and Parmeter (2009) argue that for the most part, the choice of distance metric has relatively little influence on the weights and the resulting estimates. Given this, we recommend the L^2-norm metric studied in Du, Parmeter, and Racine (2013), as it makes implementation easier given the quadratic objective function.

12.4.2 Choice of smoothing parameter

As with all nonparametric estimation methods, the choice of smoothing parameter plays a crucial role in both practice and theory. No mention was given to the appropriate level of smoothing in the aforementioned constrained methods. Few results exist suggesting how the optimal level of smoothing should be imposed. For many of the methods described previously, we could engage in cross-validation simultaneously with the constraint imposition. This may actually help in determination of the optimal smoothing parameter. The simulations of Delecroix and Thomas-Agnan (2000) show that the mean-integrated square error (typically used in cross-validation) as a function of the smoothing parameter typically has a wider zone of stability around the optimal level of the smoothing parameter, suggesting it may be easier to determine the optimal level.

However, engaging in cross-validation and constraint imposition simultaneously is unnecessary in particular methods. For example, the constraint-weighted bootstrapping methods of Hall and Huang (2001) and Du, Parmeter, and Racine (2013) show that the constrained kernel estimator should use a bandwidth of the standard unconstrained optimal order. In this setting both the restricted and unrestricted estimates will have the same level of smoothing. Further tuning could be performed by cross-validation after the constraint weights have been found, and simple checks to determine if the constraints are still satisfied (similar to that described above).

12.4.3 Linear in p implementation issues

Our linear in p implementation discussion is couched in the constraint-weighted bootstrapping framework, but it is easily adapted to the data-sharpening context. Consider two common constraints that you may desire to implement: monotonicity and concavity. The constrained estimator is

$$\widehat{m}(x|\mathbf{p}) = \sum_{i=1}^{n} p_i A_i(\mathbf{x}) y_i. \tag{12.8}$$

We can impose monotonicity and/or (the necessary conditions for) concavity for each observation, $\mathbf{x}_i \in \mathbb{R}^q$, with the following constraints:

$$\sum_{j=1}^{n} p_j A_j^{(\mathbf{r})}(\mathbf{x}_i) y_j \geq 0, \text{ for } \mathbf{r} \in \mathbf{R}_1 \tag{12.9}$$

$$\sum_{j=1}^{n} p_j A_j^{(\mathbf{r})}(\mathbf{x}_i) y_j \leq 0, \text{ for } \mathbf{r} \in \mathbf{R}_2 \tag{12.10}$$

where $\mathbf{R}_1$ is

$$\left[\ (1, 0, \ldots, 0) \quad (0, 1, \ldots, 0) \quad \cdots \quad (0, 0, \ldots, 1) \ \right],$$

while $\mathbf{R}_2$ is

$$\left[\ (2, 0, \ldots, 0) \quad (0, 2, \ldots, 0) \quad \cdots \quad (0, 0, \ldots, 2) \ \right].$$

Note that both $\mathbf{R}_1$ and $\mathbf{R}_2$ are collections of q vectors each of length q. These conditions are enough to guarantee that the estimated function is monotonic and satisfies the *necessary* conditions for concavity. We do not explicitly write out the analytical form for $A_j^{(\mathbf{r})}(\mathbf{x}_i)$, since this will vary depending upon the nonparametric method deployed. We note here that with q covariates and n observations, if we impose monotonicity in each dimension and the necessary conditions for concavity in each dimension, we have $2q \cdot n$ restrictions. Even with 5,000–10,000 observations, these constraints are relatively easy to construct and place on a quadratic programming problem.

To impose concavity using sufficient conditions, we can deploy the Afriat conditions (Afriat, 1967), which do not require estimation of second derivatives and checking semi-definiteness. The Afriat conditions state that a function is (globally) concave if and only if

$$m(\mathbf{z}) - m(\mathbf{x}) \leq \frac{\partial m}{\partial x_1}(\mathbf{x})(z_1 - x_1) + \cdots + \frac{\partial m}{\partial x_k}(\mathbf{x})(z_k - x_k), \quad \forall \mathbf{z}, \mathbf{x}. \tag{12.11}$$

These conditions could be imposed for each point by checking the conditions over the remaining points. Our constraint set would be

$$\sum_{j=1}^{n}\sum_{\ell \neq j}^{n} p_j \left[\sum_{\mathbf{r} \in \mathbf{R}_1} A_j^{(\mathbf{r})}(\mathbf{x}_i)\,(x_{s\ell} - x_{si}) \right] y_j - \sum_{j=1}^{n} p_j \left[A_j\,(x_{s\ell}) - A_j\,(x_{si}) \right] y_j \geq 0,$$

where $\mathbf{R}_1$ is $[(1, 0, \ldots, 0)(0, 1, \ldots, 0)\cdots(0, 0, \ldots, 1)]$, and x_{si} is the sth element of $\mathbf{x}_i$. What this suggests is that to impose concavity at every point, we would have $n(n-1)$ constraints, which clearly becomes computationally intractable for even a reasonable number of observations. However, an interesting aspect is that as we add more covariates (increase q), this does not add more constraints. The difficulty hinges on the sample size and not the dimensionality of the model.

To address this computational issue, as well as similar issues that may arise with other types of linear-in-p constraints that you may wish to impose, we can resort to a constraint-generation approach, which was initially proposed by Dantzig, Fulkerson, and Johnson (1954, 1959) to solve the traveling salesman problem. The idea is simple. Rather than imposing concavity at the outset on every data point, we impose concavity on some (manageable) subset of observations. After the constraints have been imposed, we then check which observations do not satisfy global concavity. We then take observations from this subset and add them to our original set of observations where concavity is enforced and resolve the quadratic program. Again, we check to see which observations still do not satisfy concavity and repeat the analysis until we have a subset of observations large enough that imposing concavity on these points is sufficient to ensure concavity at all points. While there are a variety of ways to select the initial point(s) to impose concavity and to sample from the subset across iterations, this approach to tackling hard programming problems is widespread. An excellent recent example of this approach is Lee, Johnson, Moreno-Centeno, and Kuosmanen (2013), who implement these ideas and discuss a variety of alternative schemes to make it operational. Moreover, Ryan and Wales (2000) use an even simpler idea to enforce concavity. They restrict their estimated (parametric) function to satisfy concavity at a single point. For the data set they use, concavity is satisfied at all points even though the constraints were only enforced on a single observation. We feel that this setup may successfully allow numerous constraints to be imposed using our proposed methodology while alleviating computational burdens, which may be an impediment with a straightforward brute-force approach.

The clear issue at hand with imposing hard constraints is where to start the process, and whether performance of the process is contingent upon which point is selected to start the process. Here we describe several alternative implementation strategies following Lee, Johnson, Moreno-Centeno, and Kuosmanen (2013). In their paper they describe two main ways to select the points to generate the initial set of constraints to then use for the quadratic program. Here we refer to these two approaches as the ordered approach and the distance approach. We describe each in detail.

The ordered approach

The ordered approach proceeds by ordering the observations $\{1, 2, \ldots, n\}$ based on the values of the dth component of the covariates. For example, if we have three covariates, we could order our n observations based on the values of the third covariate. Once we have the ordering, we construct concavity constraints based on the following $n - 1$ comparisons for the constraints defined in (12.12):

$$\{(1, 2), (2, 3), \ldots, (i - 1, i), (i, i + 1), \ldots, (n - 1, n)\}.$$

Instead of constructing constraints for observation i for each of the remaining observations, we only construct the constraint for the next observation, as defined by our ordering across a given covariate. Again, it is arbitrary which covariate to order over, but regardless of the selected ordering, there will be only $n - 1$ constraints to enforce in order to start the constrained estimation procedure as opposed to $n(n - 1)$. For $i = 1, 2, \ldots, (n - 1)$ our constraints are

$$\sum_{j=1}^{n} p_j \left[\sum_{r \in \mathbf{R}_1} A_j^{(\mathbf{r})}(\mathbf{x}_i) \left(x_{s(i+1)} - x_{si}\right) \right] y_j - \sum_{j=1}^{n} p_j \left[A_j \left(x_{s(i+1)}\right) - A_j \left(x_{si}\right) \right] y_j \geq 0.$$

$$(12.12)$$

The distance approach

The distance approach has a more natural feel, but is more computationally intensive. For each observation i, calculate the concavity condition for the unrestricted estimator for those observations within a certain distance of observation i. Here distance can be taken as Euclidean distance, but other forms of distance would suffice. This distance is denoted $\gamma(i)$, the γth percentile of all distances for each observation from observation i. Lee, Johnson, Moreno-Centeno, and Kuosmanen (2013) refer to this distance as the "sweet spot" and recommend using the 3rd percentile of distances for each observation. This is a flexible approach as different observations will have different sweet spots. Moreover, given the difficulty in general for enforcing concavity, this approach attempts to use points nearby when constructing the relevant concavity constraints. Naturally, the distance approach will have more constraints at the onset when enforcing concavity as opposed to the ordered approach, but it may require fewer iterations to satisfy concavity at all points.

Other approaches

Other approaches could be constructed as well. For example, we could employ a random approach whereby pairs of observations are drawn at random to be used for the concavity conditions. We could also consider that all the concavity conditions could be constructed and only the top 5% in terms of being the most violate could be used to set up the conditions. Regardless of the approach, there exist a variety of methods that practitioners have at their disposal to reduce the initial size of the constraint set to begin construction of the constrained nonparametric estimator.

Once an initial constraint-set-generation mechanism has been selected, a method for adding to the set needs to be chosen. It is not guaranteed that the reduced set of constraints will ensure that concavity will be satisfied everywhere. Thus, after the initial programming problem is solved, violated constraints will need to be added into the constraint set. Lee, Johnson, Moreno-Centeno, and Kuosmanen (2013) propose three alternative strategies. First, they suggest adding in the most violated constraint. This is simple in concept, but it may take a large number of iterations to achieve full satisfaction of the constraints. Second, they suggest adding in the most violated constraint for each observation. This routine will add in at most $n - 1$ constraints since it is possible that some observations will satisfy concavity everywhere. This approach is expected to converge more quickly than adding in a single constraint, since more constraints are added to the constraint set at each iteration. The third approach described is to add in all of the violated constraints. The problem with this approach is that it could turn out that we would add in $(n - 1)^2$ constraints, which is not desirable if n is large. We refer to these three alternatives as the "one approach" (a single constraint is added), the "one-for-all approach" (one constraint for each observation is added) and the "all-for-one approach" (all constraints for all observations are added). Lee, Johnson, Moreno-Centeno, and Kuosmanen's (2013) simulations suggest that in terms of run time, the distance approach using the one-for-all setup results in the quickest time to solve the problem.

12.4.4 Imposing additive separability

Recall from Chapter 9 the numerous steps and implementation issues when estimating the additive nonparametric regression function. Here we describe how constrained methods can be used to estimate an additively separable regression model. Note that additive separability implies that for

$$\mathbf{r} = (0, \ldots, \underbrace{1}_{\text{I position}}, 0, \ldots, \underbrace{1}_{\ell \text{ position}}, \ldots, 0),$$

$m^{(\mathbf{r})}(\mathbf{x}) = 0 \ \forall \mathrm{I} \neq \ell$ (i.e., the cross-partial derivative is equal to zero). Thus, enforcing additive separability can be formulated as a linear-in-p smoothness constraint on the unknown function. There are two distinct approaches that we see enforcing this constraint. First, we can use the appropriate cross-partial derivative of $A_i(\mathbf{x})$ for the local-constant estimator, or we could explicitly enforce the constraints on the cross-partial derivatives from the LPLS estimator (assuming the polynomial order is greater than one). For polynomial order of at least 2, the LPLS estimator will provide cross-partial derivative estimators.

Technical Appendix 12.1 demonstrates that the cross-partial derivative of $A_i(\mathbf{x})$ with respect to the ℓth and Ith components of $\mathbf{x}$, for the LCLS estimator is

$$\frac{\partial^2 A_i(\mathbf{x})}{\partial x_\ell \partial x_\mathrm{I}} = \frac{\frac{\partial^2 K_h(\mathbf{x}_i, \mathbf{x})}{\partial x_\ell \partial x_\mathrm{I}} \sum_{j=1}^{n} K_h(\mathbf{x}_j, \mathbf{x}) + \frac{\partial K_h(\mathbf{x}_i, \mathbf{x})}{\partial x_\ell} \sum_{j=1}^{n} \frac{\partial K_h(\mathbf{x}_j, \mathbf{x})}{\partial x_\mathrm{I}}}{\left[\sum_{j=1}^{n} K_h(\mathbf{x}_j, \mathbf{x}) \right]^2}$$

$$- \frac{K_h(\mathbf{x}_i, \mathbf{x}) \sum_{j=1}^{n} \frac{\partial^2 K_h(\mathbf{x}_j, \mathbf{x})}{\partial x_\ell \partial x_\iota} + \frac{\partial K_h(\mathbf{x}_i, \mathbf{x})}{\partial x_\iota} \sum_{j=1}^{n} \frac{\partial K_h(\mathbf{x}_j, \mathbf{x})}{\partial x_\ell}}{\left[\sum_{j=1}^{n} K_h(\mathbf{x}_j, \mathbf{x}) \right]^2}$$

$$- \frac{2 \left(\frac{\partial K_h(\mathbf{x}_i, \mathbf{x})}{\partial x_\ell} \sum_{j=1}^{n} K_h(\mathbf{x}_j, \mathbf{x}) - K_h(\mathbf{x}_i, \mathbf{x}) \sum_{j=1}^{n} \frac{\partial K_h(\mathbf{x}_j, \mathbf{x})}{\partial x_\ell} \right) \sum_{j=1}^{n} \frac{\partial K_h(\mathbf{x}_j, \mathbf{x})}{\partial x_\iota}}{\left[\sum_{j=1}^{n} K_h(\mathbf{x}_j, \mathbf{x}) \right]^3}.$$

Imposing this constraint allows us to impose full additive separability over all covariates, or we could isolate a given covariate. For example, suppose that $q = 3$ and we wish to impose additive separability between x_1 and (x_2, x_3). Regardless of the specific form of the constraints, they are similar to positivity and monotonicity constraints in that the number of constraints is linear in the number of covariates. This makes implementation straightforward. Note that here our discussion focuses on constraining the local-constant estimator. If interest hinged on the local-polynomial estimator, then as pointed out by Parmeter and Racine (2012), we need to be cognizant of the fact that imposing constraints on the derivatives of the local-polynomial estimator will produce a different result than if the constraints are imposed on the $A_i(\mathbf{x})$ that are consistent with the local-polynomial estimator. Deriving the derivatives of the $A_i(\mathbf{x})$ for the local-polynomial estimator is notationally burdensome, while directly constraining the estimated derivatives produced by the local-polynomial estimator may be easier computationally. A potentially interesting research topic would be to compare an additively separably restricted kernel regression estimator to the backfitting and marginal integration estimators in Chapter 9.

12.5 Hypothesis testing on shape constraints

In this section, we describe a test for the validity of arbitrary shape constraints using $D(\widehat{\mathbf{p}})$ as the test statistic. It is a bootstrap testing procedure that is simple to implement and stems from the initial procedure developed in Hall, Huang, Gifford, and Gijbels (2001) and generalized to the multiple-shape-constraint setting by Du, Parmeter, and Racine (2013). The asymptotic properties of the test and the validity of the bootstrap were considered by both Carroll, Delaigle, and Hall (2010) and Du, Parmeter, and Racine (2013).

This bootstrap approach involves estimating the constrained regression function $\widehat{m}(\mathbf{x}|\mathbf{p})$ based on the sample realizations $\{y_i, \mathbf{x}_i\}$ and then rejecting H_0 if the observed value of $D(\widehat{\mathbf{p}})$ is too large. Formally, our bootstrap proceeds as follows:

1. Compute the estimated value of the distance metric $(D(\widehat{\mathbf{p}}))$ for the original sample of data $\{y_i, \mathbf{x}_i\}$.
2. Compute the two-point wild-bootstrap errors from the re-centered residuals (from the constrained model $m(\mathbf{x}|\mathbf{p})$) by $u_i^* = \{(1 - \sqrt{5})/2\} (\widehat{u}_i - \overline{\widehat{u}})$ with

probability $(1 + \sqrt{5})/(2\sqrt{5})$ and $u_i^* = \{(1 + \sqrt{5})/2\} \left(\widehat{u}_i - \overline{\widehat{u}} \right)$ with probability $1 - (1 + \sqrt{5})/(2\sqrt{5})$. Generate y_i^* via $y_i^* = \widehat{m} \left(\mathbf{x}_i | p_i \right) + u_i^*$. Call $\{y_i^*, \mathbf{x}_i\}_{i=1}^n$ the bootstrap sample.

3. Using the bootstrap sample, estimate the distance metric $D \left(\widehat{p}^* \right)$ where y_i is replaced by y_i^* wherever it occurs.

4. Repeat steps 2 and 3 a large number (B) of times and then construct the sampling distribution of the bootstrapped distance metrics. We reject the null (i.e., constraints) if the estimated value of $D \left(\widehat{\mathbf{p}} \right)$ is greater than the upper α-percentile of the bootstrapped distance metrics.

Given this testing procedure, we would like to note that there exist three situations that can occur in practice:

   (i) Impose nonbinding constraints
  (ii) Impose binding constraints that are correct
 (iii) Impose binding constraints that are incorrect

If you encounter 12.5 in practice (i.e., $D(\widehat{\mathbf{p}}) = 0$), Hall, Huang, Gifford, and Gijbels (2001, 609) state, "For those datasets with $D(\widehat{\mathbf{p}}) = 0$, no further bootstrapping is necessary [...] and so the conclusion (for that dataset) must be to not reject H_0."

12.6 Further extensions

We believe that future research should determine the relevant merits of each of the methods described here to narrow the set to a few which can be easily and successfully used in applied nonparametric settings. Given the dearth of detailed simulation studies comparing the available methods highlighted here (notwithstanding Dette and Pilz, 2006), an interesting topic would be to compare the varying methods (kernel, spline, series) across various constraints to discover which methods perform best under which settings. Additionally, we feel that our description of the available methods should help in extending these ideas to additional nonparametric settings, most notably in the estimation of quantile functions (Li and Racine, 2008), conditional densities, treatment effects (Li, Racine, and Wooldridge, 2008), and structural estimators (Henderson, List, Millimet, Parmeter, and Price, 2008).

The methods discussed above range from simple computation (rearrangement) to involving quadratic or nonlinear program solvers. These numerical methods may dissuade you from adopting a specific approach, but we note that with the drastic reductions in computation time and the availability of solvers in most econometric software packages, issues will lessen over time. Given the ease with which a quadratic program can be solved with linear constraints, the method of Du, Parmeter, and Racine (2013) addresses the critique of Dette and Pilz (2006, 56) who note "[rearrangement offers] substantial computational advantages, because it does not rely on constrained optimization methods." We mention here that rearrangement requires slightly more sophistication when we migrate from a univariate to multivariate setting and this clearly becomes a concern in applied work.

12.7 Application

Using the constraint-weighted bootstrapping methods from this chapter (with the L^2-norm distance metric), we impose positive marginal products for both physical capital and human-capital-augmented labor on cross-country output. We also test whether constant returns to scale is satisfied in the data. Unless otherwise stated, we use local-linear regression with bandwidths determined via AIC_c. In the process of conducting this application, in several cases we were forced to adopt the log versions of the variables and hence we did this for the entire application.

12.7.1 Imposing positive marginal product

A standard assumption from production theory is that inputs have positive marginal product. This is an intuitive assumption, as adding in costly inputs would not be rational if output decreased. Here we impose positive marginal product for both physical capital and human capital simultaneously. Table 12.1 presents the quartiles and extreme deciles of the estimated gradients for both per capita physical and human capital for both the unconstrained and constrained regression estimators.

Of the 1244 observations, we have 31 violations of monotonicity for physical capital and 391 violations for human capital. These violations could be due to the natural aggregation that comes with measuring these stocks at a country level and not necessarily a pure violation of microeconomic theory.

When we restrict our gradient estimates, we see that the median and quartile estimates do not change much for physical capital, but dramatically so for the lower decile and quartile in the case of human capital. This is expected since these estimates were negative in the unrestricted setting. Notice that across the extreme deciles and the quartiles that the gradient estimates for physical capital are uniformly smaller than the unrestricted estimates. The constraint weights have shrunk all of the estimates (even those that did not violate the constraint). Interestingly, the opposite is true with human capital. Here, the gradient estimates are uniformly higher across the deciles/quartiles. The constraint weights have expanded all of the estimates (even those that did not violate the constraint). This exercise illustrates the difficulty in directly interpreting how the constraint weights work when multiple constraints are imposed simultaneously.

Figure 12.4 presents the estimated 45° plots (without standard errors) for both the unrestricted and restricted gradient estimates for physical and human-capital-augmented labor. As with our discussion of how the method worked, we saw that many

Table 12.1. *Restricted and unrestricted gradient estimates*

	Physical capital		Human capital	
	Unrestricted	Restricted	Unrestricted	Restricted
D_{10}	0.271	0.257	− 0.392	0.051
Q_{25}	0.505	0.488	− 0.097	0.159
Q_{50}	0.702	0.689	0.243	0.277
Q_{75}	0.817	0.798	0.392	0.400
D_{90}	0.851	0.843	0.577	0.561

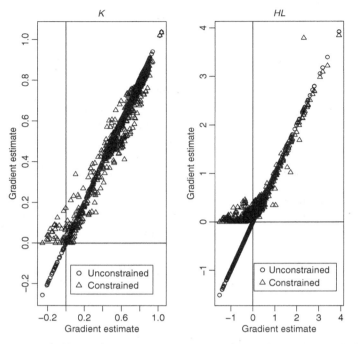

Figure 12.4. Monotonically restricted and unrestricted gradient estimates for physical capital and human-capital-augmented labor

of the corrected gradients appear naturally where the violations occur with less difference between the unrestricted and restricted estimates further from the boundary of the restriction, in this case zero. However, the deviations appear more "random" for physical capital than for human capital. Note the close relationship between unrestricted and restricted gradient estimates that are larger than zero for human capital.

12.7.2 Imposing constant returns to scale

An interesting hypothesis that we can investigate is whether constant returns to scale (CRS) holds for our cross-country production function. Here CRS would imply that $\frac{\partial \ln y}{\partial \ln K} + \frac{\partial \ln y}{\partial \ln H} = 1$. In our estimation, we use the same bandwidths and local-linear estimates, but we add in this constraint an observation-by-observation level. Figure 12.5 plots out the unrestricted returns to scale (RTS) estimates from our data.

CRS is not indicative visually from the data and we have many observations for which there are actually negative returns to scale. However, a majority of the RTS estimates are within fair proximity of one. Our D_p metric is 0.0008 while our bootstrapped p-value is 0.001 using 999 replications. We reject the null hypothesis of CRS in the data. This is intuitive given the varying levels of development possessed by the countries in the data. For less-developed countries, we would expect increasing RTS. We see clearly (that aside from the negative or overtly large estimates of RTS) that our data contain many RTS estimates that are suggestive of both decreasing and increasing RTS.

One concern with imposing CRS given the overall behavior of estimated RTS in the data is that this may overly influence our marginal products. Figure 12.6 presents the

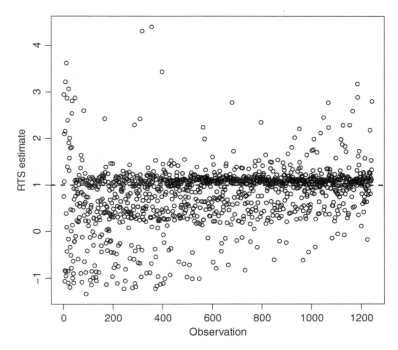

Figure 12.5. Unrestricted gradient estimates for constant returns to scale

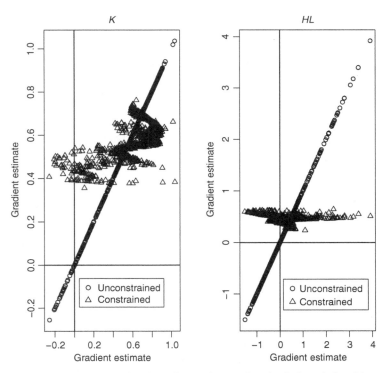

Figure 12.6. Restricted and unrestricted gradient estimates for physical capital and human-capital-augmented labor when CRS is imposed

estimated 45° plots (without standard errors) for both the unrestricted and restricted gradient estimates for physical and human-capital-augmented labor when both monotonicity of the inputs and CRS are imposed. As expected, we see that the estimated returns to both physical and human-capital-augmented labor are greatly distorted by the imposition of CRS, further suggesting that this constraint is likely not supported by the data.

The bizarre relationship between the unrestricted and restricted gradient estimates is actually quite intuitive. Requiring the marginal products to be positive, coupled with the CRS constraints, requires each gradient estimate to be between zero and one. The weird "S" pattern is merely reflective of the fact that when one gradient estimate goes up, the other one must go down to ensure that their sum is one. Had we lessened the restriction to requiring positive RTS or decreasing RTS, these relationships would be much less perverse.

Bibliography

Abadir, K. M., and S. Lawford, 2004. "Optimal Asymmetric Kernel," *Economics Letters*, **83**, 61–8.

Afriat, S. N., 1967. "The Construction of Utility Functions from Expenditure Data," *International Economic Review*, **8**, 67–77.

Ahmad, I. A., and P. B. Cerrito, 1994. "Nonparametric Estimation of Joint Discrete-Continuous Probability Densities with Applications," *Journal of Statistical Planning and Inference*, **41**, 349–64.

Ahmad, I. A., S. Leelahanon, and Q. Li, 2005. "Efficient Estimation of a Semiparametric Partially Linear Varying Coefficient Model," *Annals of Statistics*, **33**, 258–83.

Ahmad, I. A., and Q. Li, 1997a. "Testing Independence by Nonparametric Kernel Method," *Statistics and Probability Letters*, **34**, 201–10.

Ahmad, I. A., and Q. Li, 1997b. "Testing Symmetry of an Unknown Density Function by Kernel Method," *Journal of Nonparametric Statistics*, **7**, 279–93.

Ahmad, I. A., and A. R. Mugdadi, 2006. "Weighted Hellinger Distance as an Error Criterion for Bandwidth Selection in Kernel Estimation," *Journal of Nonparametric Statistics*, **18**, 215–26.

Aitchison, J., and C. G. G. Aitken, 1976. "Multivariate Binary Discrimination by the Kernel Method," *Biometrika*, **63**, 413–20.

Amemiya, T., 1971. "The Estimation of the Variances in a Variance-Components Model," *International Economic Review*, **12**, 1–13.

Amini, S., M. S. Delgado, D. J. Henderson, and C. F. Parmeter, 2012. "Fixed vs. Random: The Hausman Test Four Decades Later," *Essays in Honor of Jerry Hausman (Advances in Econometrics)*, B. H. Baltagi, R. C. Hill, W. K. Newey, and H. L. White (Eds.), **29**, 479–513.

Anderson, G., 2001. "The Power and Size of Nonparametric Tests for Common Distributional Characteristics," *Econometric Reviews*, **20**, 1–30.

Anglin, P. M., and R. Gençay, 1996. "Semiparametric Estimation of a Hedonic Price Function," *Journal of Applied Econometrics*, **11**, 633–48.

Asaftei, G., and C. F. Parmeter, 2010. "Market Power, EU Integration and Privatization: The Case of Romania," *Journal of Comparative Economics*, **38**, 340–56.

Baltagi, B. H., 1985. "Pooling Cross-Sections with Unequal Time-Series Lengths," *Economics Letters*, **18**, 133–36.

Baltagi, B. H., 2008. *Econometric Analysis of Panel Data*, fourth edition, West Sussex, UK, Wiley.

Baltagi, B. H., J. Hidalgo, and Q. Li, 1996. "A Nonparametric Test for Poolability Using Panel Data," *Journal of Econometrics*, **75**, 345–67.

Baltagi, B. H., and D. Li, 2002. "Series Estimation of Parially Linear Panel Data Models with Fixed Effects," *Annals of Economics and Finance*, **3**, 103–16.

Barro, R., and J.-W. Lee, 2013. "A New Data Set of Educational Attainment in the World, 1950-2010," *Journal of Development Economics*, **104**, 184–98.

Battisti, M., and C. F. Parmeter, 2013. "Clustering and Polarization in the Distribution of Output: A Multivariate Perspective," *Journal of Macroeconomics*, **35**, 144–62.

Bazzi, S., and M. Clemens, 2013. "Blunt Instruments: On Establishing the Causes of Economic Growth," *American Economic Journal: Macroeconomics*, **5**, 152–86.

Beran, R., and G. R. Ducharme, 1991. *Asymptotic Theory for Bootstrap Methods in Statistics*, Québec, Centre De Recherches Mathématiques.

Berg, M. D., Q. Li, and A. Ullah, 2000. "Instrumental Variable Estimation of Semiparametric Dynamic Panel Data Models: Monte Carlo Results on Several New and Existing Estimators," *Advances in Econometrics*, **15**, 297–315.

Bianchi, M., 1997. "Testing for Convergence: Evidence from Non-Parametric Multimodality Tests," *Journal of Applied Econometrics*, **12**, 393–409.

Bickel, P. J., and M. Rosenblatt, 1973. "On Some Global Measures of the Deviations of Density Function Estimates," *Annals of Statistics*, **1**, 1071–95.

Bierens, H. J., 1982. "Consistent Model Specification Tests," *Journal of Econometrics*, **20**, 105–34.

Bierens, H. J., 1983. "Uniform Consistency of Kernel Estimators of a Regression Function under Generalized Conditions," *Journal of the American Statistical Association*, **78**, 699–707.

Bierens, H. J., 1987. "Kernel Estimators of Regression Functions," *Advances in Econometrics: Fifth World Congress, Volume I*, T. F. Bewley (Ed.), Cambridge, NY: Cambridge University Press, 99–144.

Bierens, H. J., 1990. "A Consistent Conditional Moment Test of Functional Form," *Econometrica*, **58**, 1443–58.

Birke, M., and H. Dette, 2007. "Estimating a Convex Function in Nonparametric Regression," *Scandinavian Journal of Statistics*, **34**, 384–404.

Birke, M., and H. Dette, 2008. "A Note on Estimating a Monotone Regression Function by Combining Kernel and Density Estimates," *Journal of Nonparametric Statistics*, **20**, 679–91.

Birke, M., and K. F. Pilz, 2009. "Nonparametric Option Pricing with No-Arbitrage Constraints," *Journal of Financial Econometrics*, **7**, 53–76.

Blundell, R. W., X. Chen, and D. Kristensen, 2007. "Semi-Nonparametric IV Estimation of Shape-Invariant Engel Curves," *Econometrica*, **75**, 1613–69.

Blundell, R. W., and J. L. Powell, 2004. "Endogeneity in Semiparametric Binary Response Models," *Review of Economic Studies*, **71**, 655–79.

Boden T. A., G. Marland, and R. J. Andres, 2011. *Global, Regional, and National Fossil-Fuel CO_2 Emissions*, Carbon Dioxide Information Analysis Center, Oak Ridge National Laboratory, U.S. Deparment of Energy, Oak Ridge, TN, doi:10.3334/CDIAC/00001_V2011.

Bowman, A. W., 1984. "An Alternative Method of Cross-Validation for the Smoothing of Density Estimates," *Biometrika*, **71**, 353–60.

Braun, W. J., and P. Hall, 2001. "Data Sharpening for Nonparametric Inference Subject to Constraints," *Journal of Computational and Graphical Statistics*, **10**, 786–806.

Buja, A., T. Hastie, and R. Tibshirani, 1989. "Linear Smoothers and Additive Models," *Annals of Statistics*, **17**, 453–555.

Cai, Z., 2002. "Regression Quantiles for Time Series," *Econometric Theory*, **18**, 169–92.

Cai, Z., M. Das, H. Xiong, and X. Wu, 2006. "Functional Coefficient Instrumental Variables Models," *Journal of Econometrics*, **133**, 207–41.

Cai, Z., J. Fan, and R. Li, 2000. "Efficient Estimation and Inferences for Varying Coefficient Models," *Journal of the American Statistical Association*, **95**, 888–902.

Cai, Z., J. Fan, and Q. Yao, 2000. "Functional-Coefficient Regression Models for Nonlinear Time Series," *Journal of the American Statistical Association*, **95**, 941–56.

Cai, Z., and Q. Li, 2008. "Nonparametric Estimation of Varying Coefficient Dynamic Panel Data Models," *Econometric Theory*, **24**, 1321–42.

Cameron, A. C., and P. K. Trivedi, 2005. *Microeconometrics: Methods and Applications*, Cambridge, NY: Cambridge University Press.

Carroll, R., A. Delaigle, and P. Hall, 2010. "Testing and Estimating Shape-Constrained Nonparametric Density and Regression in the Presence of Measurement Error," *Journal of the American Statistical Association*, **106**, 191–202.

Caselli, F., and J. Feyrer, 2007. "The Marginal Product of Capital," *Quarterly Journal of Economics*, **122**, 535–68.

Chai, A., and A. Moneta, 2012. "Back to Engel? Some Evidence for the Hierarchy of Needs," *Journal of Evolutionary Economics*, **22**, 649–76.

Chen, H., 1988. "Convergence Rates for Parametric Components in a Partially Linear Model," *Annals of Statistics*, **16**, 136–46.

Chen, R., and R. S. Tsay, 1993. "Functional Coefficient Autoregressive Models," *Journal of the American Statistical Association*, **88**, 298–308.

Cheng, M.-Y., and P. Hall, 1998. "Calibrating the Excess Mass and Dip Tests of Modality," *Journal of the Royal Statistical Society, Series B*, **60**, 579–89.

Chernozhukov, V., I. Fernández-Val, and A. Galichon, 2009. "Improving Point and Interval Estimates of Monotone Functions by Rearrangement," *Biometrika*, **96**, 559–75.

Chernozhukov, V., I. Fernández-Val, and A. Galichon, 2010. "Quantile and probability curves without crossing," *Econometrica*, **78**, 1093–1125.

Chevalier, J. A., and G. Ellison, 1997. "Risk-Taking by Mutual Funds as a Response to Incentives," *Journal of Political Economy*, **105**, 1167–1200.

Choi, E., and P. Hall, 1999. "Data Sharpening as a Prelude to Density Estimation," *Biometrika*, **86**, 941–47.

Chow, Y.-S., S. Geman, and L.-D. Wu, 1983. "Consistent Cross-Validated Density Estimation," *Annals of Statistics*, **11**, 25–38.

Christofides, L. N., and T. Stengos, 2001. "A Non-Parametric Test of the Symmetry of the PSID Wage-Change Distribution," *Economics Letters*, **71**, 363–68.

Cleveland, W. S., E. Grosse, and W. M. Shyu, 1991. "Local Regression Models," *Statistical Models in S*, J. M. Chambers and T. Hastie (Eds.), New York: Chapman & Hall.

Cosslett, S. R., 1983. "Distribution-Free Maximum Likelihood Estimator of the Binary Choice Model," *Econometrica*, **51**, 765–82.

Cosslett, S. R., 1991. "Distribution-Free Estimator of a Regression Model with Sample Selectivity," *Nonparametric and Semiparametric Methods in Econometrics and Statistics*, W. A. Barnett, J. L. Powell, and G. Tauchen (Eds.), New York: Cambridge University Press, 175–97.

Cressie, N. A. C., and T. R. C. Read, 1984. "Multinomial Goodness-of-Fit Tests," *Journal of the Royal Statistical Society, Series B*, **46**, 440–64.

Dantzig, G., R. Fulkerson, and S. Johnson, 1954. "Solution of a Large-Scale Traveling-Salesman Problem," *Journal of the Operations Research Society of America*, **2**, 393–410.

Dantzig, G., R. Fulkerson, and S. Johnson, 1959. "On a Linear Programming Combinatorial Approach to the Traveling Salesman Problem," *Journal of the Operations Research Society of America*, **7**, 58–66.

Darolles, S., Y. Fan, J. P. Florens, and E. Renault, 2011. "Nonparametric Instrumental Regression," *Econometrica*, **79**, 1541–65.

Das, M., 2005. "Instrumental Variable Estimators of Nonparametric Models with Discrete Endogenous Regressors," *Journal of Econometrics*, **124**, 335–61.

Davidson, R., and E. Flachaire, 2008. "The Wild Bootstrap, Tamed at Last," *Journal of Econometrics*, **146**, 162–69.

Davidson, R., and J. G. MacKinnon, 2000. "Improving the Reliability of Bootstrap Tests with the Fast Double Bootstrap," *Computational Statistics and Data Analysis*, **51**, 3259–81.

Deheuvels, P., 1977. "Estimation non paramétrique de la densité par histogrammes généralisés," *Revue de Statistique Appliquée*, **25**, 5–42.

Delecroix, M., and C. Thomas-Agnan, 2000. "Spline and Kernel Regression under Shape Restrictions," *Smoothing and Regression: Approaches, Computation, and Application*, M. G. Schimek (Ed.), Wiley Series of Probability and Statistics, New York: Wiley, 109–34.

Delgado, M. A., and W. González-Manteiga, 2001. "Significance Testing in Nonparametric Regression Based on the Bootstrap," *Annals of Statistics*, **29**, 1469–1507.

Delgado, M. A., and T. Stengos, 1994. "Semiparametric Specification Testing of Nonnested Econometric Models," *Review of Economic Studies*, **61**, 291–303.

Delgado, M. S., and C. F. Parmeter, 2013. "Embarrassingly Easy Embarrassingly Parallel Processing in R," *Journal of Applied Econometrics*, **28**, 1224–30.

Delgado, M. S., D. J. Henderson, and C. F. Parmeter, 2014. "Does Education Matter for Economic Growth?," *Oxford Bulletin of Economics and Statistics*, **76**, 334–59.

Deng, W. S., C. K. Chu, and M.-Y. Cheng, 2001. "A Study of Local Linear Ridge Regression Estimators," *Journal of Statistical Planning and Inference*, **93**, 225–38.

Dette, H., 2002. "A Consistent Test for Heteroscedasticity in Nonparametric Regression Based on the Kernel Method," *Journal of Statistical Planning and Inference*, **103**, 311–29.

Dette, H., and M. Marchlewski, 2010. "A Robust Test for Homoscedasticity in Nonparametric Regression," *Journal of Nonparametric Statistics*, **22**, 723–36.

Dette, H., and A. Munk, 1998. "Testing Heteroscedasticity in Nonparametric Regression," *Journal of the Royal Statistical Society, Series B*, **60**, 693–708.

Dette, H., N. Neumeyer, and K. F. Pilz, 2006. "A Simple Nonparametric Estimator of a Strictly Monotone Regression Function," *Bernoulli*, **12**, 469–90.

Dette, H., and K. F. Pilz, 2006. "A Comparative Study of Monotone Nonparametric Kernel Estimates," *Journal of Statistical Computation and Simulation*, **76**, 41–56.

Dette, H., and K. F. Pilz, 2009. "On the Estimation of a Monotone Conditional Variance in Nonparametric Regression," *Annals of the Institute of Statistical Mathematics*, **61**, 111–41.

Dette, H. and R. Scheder, 2006. "Strictly Monotone and Smooth Nonparametric Regression for Two or More Variables," *Canadian Journal of Statistcs*, **34**, 535–61.

Diewert, W. E., 1971. "An Application of the Shepard Duality Theorem: A Generalized Leontief Production Function," *Journal of Political Economy*, **79**, 461–507.

Du, P., C. F. Parmeter, and J. S. Racine, 2013. "Nonparametric Kernel Regression with Multiple Predictors and Multiple Shape Constraints," *Statistica Sinica*, **23**, 1347–71.

Duffy, J., and C. Papageorgiou, 2000. "A Cross-Country Empirical Investigation of the Aggregate Production Specification," *Journal of Economic Growth*, **5**, 87–120.

Duin, R. P. W., 1976. "On the Choice of Smoothing Parameters for Parzen Estimators of Probability Density Function," *IEEE Transactions on Computers*, **25**, 1175–79.

Efron, B., 1979. "Bootstrap Methods: Another Look at the Jackknife," *Annals of Statistics*, **7**, 1–26.

Engle, R. F., C. W. J. Granger, J. Rice, and A. Weiss, 1986. "Semiparametrics Estimates of the Relation between Weather and Electricity Sales," *Journal of the American Statistical Association*, **81**, 310–20.

Epanechnikov, V. A., 1969. "Nonparametric Estimation of a Multidimensional Probability Density," *Teoriya Veroyatnostei i ee Primeneniya*, **14**, 156–61.

Eubank, R. L., and W. Thomas, 1993. "Detecting Heteroscedasticity in Nonparametric Regression," *Journal of the Royal Statistical Society, Series B*, **55**, 145–55.

Fan, J., 1992. "Design-Adaptive Nonparametric Regression," *Journal of the American Statistical Association*, **87**, 998–1004.

Fan, J., 1993. "Local Linear Regression Smoothers and Their Minimax Efficiency," *Annals of Statistics*, **21**, 196–216.

Fan, J., and I. Gijbels, 1996. *Local Polynomial Modelling and Its Applications*, London: Chapman & Hall.

Fan, J., and T. Huang, 2005. "Profile Likelihood Inferences on Semiparametric Varying-Coefficient Partially Linear Models," *Bernoulli*, **11**, 1031–57.

Fan, J., and J. Jiang, 2005. "Nonparametric Inference for Additive Models," *Journal of the American Statistical Association*, **100**, 781–813.

Fan, J., and J. Jiang, 2007. "Nonparametric Inference with Generalized Likelihood Ratio Tests," *Test*, **16**, 409–44.

Fan, J., and R. Li, 2001. "Variable Selection via Non-concave Penalized Likelihood and its Oracle Properties," *Journal of the American Statistical Association*, **96**, 1348–60.

Fan, J., and R. Li, 2004. "New Estimation and Model Selection Procedures for Semi-Parametric Modeling in Longitudinal Data Analysis," *Journal of the American Statistical Association*, **99**, 710–23.

Fan, J., and J. S. Marron, 1994. "Fast Implementations of Nonparametric Curve Estimators," *Journal of Computational and Graphical Statistics*, **3**, 119–27.

Fan, J., and W. Zhang, 1999. "Statistical Estimation in Varying Coefficient Models," *Annals of Statistics*, **27**, 1491–1518.

Fan, J., C. Zhang, and J. Zhang, 2001. "Generalized Likelihood Ratio Statistics and Wilks Phenomenon," *Annals of Statistics*, **29**, 153–93.

Fan, Y., 1994. "Testing the Goodness of Fit of a Parametric Density Function by Kernel Method," *Econometric Theory*, **10**, 316–56.

Fan, Y., and Q. Li, 1996. "Consistent Model Specification Test: Omitted Variables and Semiparametric Forms," *Econometrica*, **64**, 865–90.

Fan, Y., and Q. Li, 2003. "A Kernel-Based Method for Estimating Additive Partially Linear Models," *Statistica Sinica*, **13**, 739–62.

Fan, Y., Q. Li, and I. Min, 2006. "A Nonparametric Bootstrap Test of Conditional Distributions," *Econometric Theory*, **22**, 587–613.

Fan, Y., and Z. Liu, 1997. "A Simple Test for a Parametric Single Index Model," *Journal of Quantitative Economics*, **13**, 95–103.

Fan, Y., and A. Ullah, 1999. "Asymptotic Normality and a Combined Regression Estimator," *Journal of Multivariate Analysis*, **85**, 191–240.

Feyrer, J. D., 2008. "Convergence by Parts," *B. E. Journal of Macroeconomics*, **8**, 1–35.

Flores, C., A. Flores-Lagunes, and D. Kapetanakis, 2014. "Lessons from Quantile Panel Estimation of the Environmental Kuznets Curve," *Econometric Reviews*, **33**, 815–53.

Friedman, J., J. W. Tukey, and P. A. Tukey, 1980. "Approaches to Analysis of Data that Concentrate near Intermediate-Dimensional Manifolds," *Data Analysis and Informatics*, E. Diday, L. Lebart, J. T. Pages, and R. Tomassone (Eds.), Amsterdam, the Netherlands: North-Holland, **13**, 289–305.

Gallant, A. R., and D. W. Nychka, 1987. "Semi-Nonparametric Maximum Likelihood Estimation," *Econometrica*, **55**, 363–90.

Gao, J., and I. Gijbels, 2008. "Bandwidth Selection in Nonparametric Kernel Testing," *Journal of the American Statistical Association*, **103**, 1584–94.

Gao, X., 2007. "A Nonparametric Procedure for the Two-Factor Mixed Model with Missing Data," *Biometrical Journal*, **49**, 774–8.

Gasser, T., A. Kniep, and W. Köhler, 1991. "A Flexible and Fast Method for Automatic Smoothing," *Journal of the American Statistical Association*, **86**, 643–52.

Gibbons, J. D., and S. Chakraborti, 2010. *Nonparametric Statistical Inference*, fifth edition, Boca Raton, FL: CRC Press.

González-Manteiga, W., and R. Cao, 1993. "Testing hypothesis of general linear model using nonparametric regression estimation," *Test*, **2**, 161–88.

Gozalo, P. L., 1993. "A Consistent Model Specification Test for Nonparametric Estimation of Regression Function Models," *Econometric Theory*, **9**, 451–77.

Gozalo, P. L., 1995. "Nonparametric Specification Testing with $\sqrt{n}$–Local Power and Bootstrap Critical Values," *Working Paper No. 95-21 R*, Brown University.

Gozalo, P. L., 1997. "Nonparametric Bootstrap Analysis with Application to Demographic Effects in Demand Function," *Journal of Econometrics*, **81**, 387–93.

Greene, W. H., 2011. *Econometric Analysis*, seventh edition, Upper Saddle River, NJ: Prentice Hall.

Gu, J., D. Li, and D. Liu, 2007. "Bootstrap Non-parametric Significance Test," *Journal of Nonparametric Statistics*, **19**, 215–30.

Guerre, E., I. Perrigne, and Q. Vuong, 2000. "Optimal Nonparametric Estimation of First-Price Auctions," *Econometrica*, **68**, 525–74.

Habbema, J. D. F., J. Hermans, and K. van den Broek, 1974. "A Stepwise Discriminant Analysis Program Using Density Estimation," *Compstat*, G. Bruckmann (Ed.), Vienna, Austria: Physica-Verlag, 101–10.

Hall, P., 1983. "Fast Rates of Convergence in the Central Limit Theorem," *Zeitschrift für Wahrscheinlichkeitstheorie und Verwandte Gebiete*, **62**, 491–507.

Hall, P., 1984. "Central Limit Theorem for Integrated Square Error of Multivariate Nonparametric Density Estimators," *Journal of Multivariate Analysis*, **14**, 1–16.

Hall, P., 1987a. "On Kullback-Leibler Loss and Density Estimation," *Annuals of Statistics*, **15**, 1491–1519.

Hall, P., 1987b. "On the Use of Campactly Supported Density Estimates in Problems of Discrimination," *Journal of Multivariate Analysis*, **23**, 131–58.

Hall, P., 1992. "On Bootstrap Confidence Intervals in Nonparametric Regression," *Annals of Statistics*, **20**, 695–711.

Hall, P., 1995. "Methodology and Theory for the Bootstrap," *Handbook of Econometrics*, volume 4, R. F. Engle and D. L. McFadden (Eds.), Amsterdam, the Netherlands: North-Holland, **39**, 2341–81.

Hall, P., and H. Huang, 2001. "Nonparametric Kernel Regression Subject to Monotonicity Constraints," *Annals of Statistics*, **29**, 624–47.

Hall, P., H. Huang, J. Gifford, and I. Gijbels, 2001. "Nonparametric Estimation of Hazard Rate under the Constraint of Monotonicity," *Journal of Computational and Graphical Statistics*, **10**, 592–614.

Hall, P., Q. Li, and J. S. Racine, 2007. "Nonparametric Estimation of Regression Functions in the Presence of Irrelevant Regressors," *Review of Economics and Statistics*, **89**, 784–9.

Hall, P., and J. S. Marron, 1987. "Extent to which Least Squares Cross Validation Minimizes Integrated Squared Error in Nonparametric Density Estimation," *Probability Theory and Related Fields*, **74**, 567–81.

Hall, P., and J. S. Marron, 1991. "Local Minima in Cross-Validation Functions," *Journal of the Royal Statistical Society, Series B*, **53**, 245–52.

Hall, P., and J. S. Marron, 1997. "On the Role of the Ridge Parameter in Local Linear Smoothing," *Probability Theory and Related Fields*, **108**, 495–516.

Hall, P., and B. Presnell, 1999. "Intentionally Biased Bootstrap Methods," *Journal of the Royal Statistical Society, Series B*, **61**, 143–58.

Hall, P., J. S. Racine, and Q. Li, 2004. "Cross-Validation and the Estimation of Conditional Probability Densities," *Journal of the American Statistical Association*, **99**, 1015–26.

Hall, P., S. J. Sheather, M. C. Jones, and J. S. Marron, 1991. "On Optimal Data-Based Bandwidth Selection in Kernel Density Estimation," *Biometrika*, **78**, 263–9.

Hall, P., and L. Simar, 2002. "Estimating a Changepoint, Boundary, or Frontier in the Presence of Observation Error," *Journal of the American Statistical Association*, **97**, 523–34.

Hall, P., and M. York, 2001. "On the Calibration of Silverman's Test for Multimodality," *Statistica Sinica*, **11**, 515–36.

Hall, R. E., and C. I. Jones, 1999. "Why do Some Countries Produce So Much More Output Per Worker than Others?," *Quarterly Journal of Economics*, **114**, 83–116.

Han, S., 2013. "Nonparametric Triangular Simultaneous Equations Models with Weak Instruments," Working Paper, University of Texas at Austin.

Härdle, W., 1990. *Applied Nonparametric Regression*, Cambridge, UK: Cambridge University Press.

Härdle, W., P. Hall, and H. Ichimura, 1993. "Optimal Smoothing in Single Index Models," *Annals of Statistics*, **21**, 157–78.

Härdle, W., J. Hart, J. S. Marron, and A. B. Tsybakov, 1992. "Bandwidth Choice for Average Derivative Estimation," *Journal of the American Statistical Association*, **87**, 218–26.

Härdle, W., and E. Mammen, 1993. "Comparing Nonparametric Versus Parametric Regression Fits," *Annals of Statistics*, **21**, 1926–47.

Härdle, W., E. Mammen, and M. Müller, 1998. "Testing Parametric versus Semiparametric Modeling in Generalized Linear Models," *Journal of the American Statistical Association*, **93**, 1461–74.

Härdle, W., and T. M. Stoker, 1989. "Investigating Smooth Multiple Regression by the Method of Average Derivatives," *Journal of the American Statistical Association*, **84**, 986–95.

Hastie, T., and C. Loader, 1993. "Local Regression: Automatic Kernel Carpentry," *Statistical Science*, **8**, 120–9.

Hastie, T., and R. J. Tibshirani, 1993. "Varying-Coefficient Models (with discussion)," *Journal of the Royal Statistical Society, Series B*, **55**, 757–96.

Hayfield, T., and J. S. Racine, 2008. "Nonparametric Econometrics: The np Package," *Journal of Statistical Software*, **27**, 1–32.

Heckman, J., and S. Polachek, 1974. "The Functional Form of the Income-Schooling Relation," *Journal of the American Statistical Association*, **69**, 350–4.

Heckman, N. E., 1986. "Spline Smoothing in Partly Linear Models," *Journal of the Royal Statistical Society, Series B*, **48**, 244–8.

Henderson, D. J., 2010. "A Test for Multimodality of Regression Derivatives with an Application to Nonparametric Growth Regressions," *Journal of Applied Econometrics*, **25**, 458–80.

Henderson, D. J., R. J. Carroll, and Q. Li, 2008. "Nonparametric Estimation and Testing of Fixed Effects Panel Data Models," *Journal of Econometrics*, **144**, 257–75.

Henderson, D. J., and S. C. Kumbhakar, 2006. "Public and Private Capital Productivity Puzzle: A Nonparametric Approach," *Southern Economic Journal*, **73**, 219–32.

Henderson, D. J., S. C. Kumbhakar, and C. F. Parmeter, 2012. "A Simple Method to Visualize Results in Nonlinear Regression Models," *Economics Letters*, **117**, 578–81.

Henderson, D. J., Q. Li, C. F. Parmeter, and S. Yao, 2014. "Gradient Based Smoothing Parameter Selection for Nonparametric Regression Estimation," *Journal of Econometrics*, forthcoming.

Henderson, D. J., J. List, D. L. Millimet, C. F. Parmeter, and M. K. Price, 2012. "Imposing Monotonicity Nonparametrically in First Price Auctions," *Journal of Econometrics*, **168**, 17–29.

Henderson, D. J., and E. Maasoumi, 2013. "Searching for Rehabilitation in Nonparametric Regression Models with Exogenous Treatment Assignment," Oxford *Handbook of Applied Nonparametric and Semiparametric Econometrics and Statistics*, A. Ullah, J. S. Racine, and L. Su (Eds.), New York: Oxford University Press, **16**, 501–20.

Henderson, D. J., and D. L. Millimet, 2008. "Is Gravity Linear?," *Journal of Applied Econometrics*, **23**, 137–72.

Henderson, D. J., C. Papageorgiou, and C. F. Parmeter, 2012. "Growth Empirics without Parameters," *Economic Journal*, **122**, 125–54.

Henderson, D. J., C. Papageorgiou, and C. F. Parmeter, 2013. "Who Benefits from Financial Development? New Methods, New Evidence," *European Economic Review*, **63**, 47–67.

Henderson, D. J., and C. F. Parmeter, 2009. "Imposing Economic Constraints on Nonparametric Regression: Survey, Implementation and Extensions," *Advances in Econometrics: Nonparametric Methods*, Q. Li and J. S. Racine (Eds.), **25**, Bingley, UK: Emerald, 433–69.

Henderson, D. J., and C. F. Parmeter, 2013. "A Consistent Bootstrap Procedure for Nonparametric Tests of Symmetry," Working Paper, University of Alabama, Tuscaloosa, AL.

Henderson D. J., C. F. Parmeter, and R. R. Russell, 2008. "Modes, Weighted Modes, and Calibrated Modes: Evidence of Clustering Using Modality Test," *Journal of Applied Econometrics*, **23**, 607–38.

Henderson, D. J., and R. R. Russell, 2005. "Human Capital and Convergence: A Production-Frontier Approach," *International Economic Review*, **46**, 1167–1205.

Henderson, D. J., and A. Ullah, 2005. "A Nonparametric Random Effects Estimator," *Economics Letters*, **88**, 403–7.

Henningsen, A., and G. Henningsen, 2011. "Econometric Estimation of the 'Constant Elasticity of Substitution' Function in R: Package micEconCES," FOI Working Paper No 2011/9, Institute of Food and Resource Economics, University of Copenhagen, Denmark.

Heston, A., R. Summers, and B. Aten, 2011. *Penn World Table Version 7.0*, Center for International Comparisons of Production, Income and Prices at the University of Pennsylvania, June 2011.

Hoderlein, S., E. Mammen, and K. Yu, 2011. "Non-Parametric Models in Binary Choice Fixed Effects Panel Data," *Econometrics Journal*, **14**, 351–67.

Hong, Y., and Y.-J. Lee, 2013. "A Loss Function Approach to Model Specification Testing and its Relative Efficiency," *Annals of Statistics*, **41**, 1166–1203.

Hong, Y., and H. White, 2005. "Asymptotic Distribution Theory for Nonparametric Entropy Measures of Serial Dependence," *Econometrica*, **73**, 837–901.

Horowitz, J. L., 1992. "A Smoothed Maximum Score Estimator for the Binary Response Model," *Econometrica*, **60**, 505–31.

Horowitz, J. L., 2001. "The Bootstrap," *Handbook of Econometrics*, volume 5, J. J. Heckman and E. Leamer (Eds.), Amsterdam, the Netherlands: North-Holland, **52**, 3159–228.

Horowitz, J. L., 2009. *Semiparametric and Nonparametric Methods in Econometrics*, New York: Springer-Verlag.

Horowitz, J. L., 2012. "Specification Testing in Nonparametric Instrumental Variable Estimation," *Journal of Econometrics*, **167**, 383–96.

Horowitz, J. L., and W. Härdle, 1994. "Testing a Parametric Model against a Semiparametric Alternative," *Econometric Theory*, **10**, 821–48.

Horowitz, J. L., and W. Härdle, 1996. "Direct Semiparametric Estimation of Single-Index Models with Discrete Covariates," *Journal of the American Statistical Association*, **91**, 1632–40.

Hsiao, C., Q. Li, and J. S. Racine, 2007. "A Consistent Model Specification Test with Mixed Categorical and Continuous Data," *Journal of Econometrics*, **140**, 802–26.

Hurvich, C. M., J. S. Simonoff, and C.-L. Tsai, 1998. "Smoothing Parameter Selection in Nonparametric Regression Using an Improved Akaike Information Criterion," *Journal of the Royal Statistical Society, Series B*, **60**, 271–93.

Ichimura, H., 1993. "Semiparametric Least Squares (SLS) and Weighted SLS Estimation of Single-Index Models," *Journal of Econometrics*, **58**, 71–120.

Ichimura, H., and L. F. Lee, 1991. "Semiparametric Least Squares Single Equation Estimation of Multiple Index Models," *Nonparametric and Semiparametric Methods in Econometrics and Statistics*, W. A. Barnett, J. L. Powell, and G. Tauchen (Eds.), New York: Cambridge University Press, 3–49.

Ivanov, V. K., V. V. Vasin, and V. P. Tanana, 2002. *Theory of Linear Ill-Posed Problems and its Applications*, Utrecht, the Netherlands: VSP.

Jin, S., and L. Su, 2013. "Nonparametric Tests for Poolability in Panel Data Models with Cross Section Dependence," *Econometric Reviews*, **32**, 469–512.

Jones, M. C., J. S. Marron, and S. J. Sheather, 1996. "A Brief Survey of Bandwidth Selection," *Journal of the American Statistical Association*, **91**, 401–7.

Jones, M. C., and S. J. Sheather, 1991. "Using Non-Stochastic Terms to Advantage in Kernel-Based Estimation of Integrated Squared Density Derivatives," *Statistics and Probability Letters*, **11**, 511–14.

Kaldor, N., 1957. "A Model of Economic Growth," *Economic Journal*, **67**, 591–624.

Kaul, S., K. J. Boyle, N. V. Kuminoff, C. F. Parmeter, and J. C. Pope, 2013. "What Can We Learn From Benefit Transfer Errors? Evidence From 20 Years of Research on Convergent Validity," *Journal of Environmental Economics and Management*, **66**, 90–104.

Kiefer, N. M., and J. S. Racine, 2009. "The Smooth Colonel Meets the Reverend," *Journal of Nonparametric Statistics*, **21**, 521–33.

Kim, W., O. B. Linton, and N. W. Hengartner, 1999. "A Computationally Efficient Oracle Estimator for Additive Nonparametric Regression with Bootstrap Confidence Intervals," *Journal of Computational and Graphical Statistics*, **8**, 278–97.

Klein, R. W., and R. H. Spady, 1993. "An Efficient Semiparametric Estimator for Binary Choice Response Models," *Econometrica*, **61**, 387–421.

Kniesner, T. J., and Q. Li, 2002. "Nonlinearity in Dynamic Adjustment: Semiparametric Estimation of Panel Labor Supply," *Empirical Economics*, **27**, 131–48.

Kress, R., 1999. *Linear Integral Equations*, second edition, New York: Springer-Verlag.

Lavergne, P., 2001. "An Equality Test across Nonparametric Regressions," *Journal of Econometrics*, **103**, 307–44.

Lavergne, P., and Q. Vuong, 1996. "Nonparametric Selection of Regressors: The Nonnested Case," *Econometrica*, **64**, 207–19.

Lavergne, P., and Q. Vuong, 2000. "Nonparametric Significance Testing," *Econometric Theory*, **16**, 576–601.

Lee, C.-Y., A. L. Johnson, E. Moreno-Centeno, and T. Kuosmanen, 2013. "A More Efficient Algorithm for Convex Nonparametric Least Squares," *European Journal of Operational Research*, **227**, 391–400.

Lee, L. F., 1994. "Semiparametric Two-Stage Estimation of Sample Selection Models Subject to Tobit-Type Selection Rules," *Journal of Econometrics*, **61**, 305–44.

Lee, L. F., 1995. "Semiparametric Maximum Likelihood Estimation of Polychotomous and Sequential Choice Models," *Journal of Econometrics*, **65**, 381–428.

Lee, T.-H., and A. Ullah, 2001. "Nonparametric Bootstrap Tests for Neglected Nonlinearity in Time Series Regression Models," *Journal of Nonparametric Statistics*, **13**, 425–51.

Lee, Y., 2014. "Nonparametric Estimation of Dynamic Panel Models with Fixed Effects," *Econometric Theory*, forthcoming.

Lee, Y., and D. Mukherjee, 2008. "New Nonparametric Estimation of the Marginal Effects in Fixed-Effects Panel Models: An Application on the Environmental Kuznets Curve," Working Paper.

Lewbel, A., 2000. "Semiparametric Qualitative Response Model Estimation with Unknown Heteroskedasticity or Instrumental Variables," *Journal of Nonparametric Econometrics*, **97**, 145–77.

Li, C., and Z. Liang, 2013. "Asymptotics for Nonparametric and Semiparametric Fixed Effects," Working Paper, State University of New York at Albany.

Li, Q., 1996. "Nonparametric Testing of Closeness between Two Unknown Distributions," *Econometric Reviews*, **15**, 261–74.

Li, Q., 1999, "Nonparametric Testing of Closeness between Two Unknown Distributions: Local Power and Bootstrap Analysis," *Journal of Nonparametric Statistics*, **11**, 189–213.

Li, Q., C. J. Huang, D. Li, and T. T. Fu, 2002. "Semiparametric Smooth Coefficient Models," *Journal of Business and Economics Statistics*, **20**, 412–22.

Li, Q., X. Lu, and A. Ullah, 2003. "Multivariate Local Polynomial Regression for Estimating Average Derivatives," *Journal of Nonparametric Statistics*, **15**, 607–24.

Li, Q., E. Maasoumi, and J. S. Racine, 2009. "A Nonparametric Test for Equality of Distributions with Mixed Categorical and Continuous Data," *Journal of Econometrics*, **148**, 186–200.

Li, Q., D. Ouyang, and J. S. Racine, 2006. "Cross-Validation and the Estimation of Probability Distribution with Categorical Data," *Journal of Nonparametric Statistics*, **18**, 69–100.

Li, Q., and J. S. Racine, 2003. "Nonparametric Estimation of Distributions with Categorical and Continuous Data," *Journal of Multivariate Analysis*, **86**, 266–92.

Li, Q., and J. S. Racine, 2004a. "Predictor Relevance and Extramarital Affairs," *Journal of Applied Econometrics*, **19**, 533–5.

Li, Q., and J. S. Racine, 2004b. "Cross-Validated Local Linear Nonparametric Regression," *Statistica Sinica*, **14**, 485–512.

Li, Q., and J. S. Racine, 2007. *Nonparametric Econometrics: Theory and Practice*, Princeton, NJ: Princeton University Press.

Li, Q., and J. S. Racine, 2008. "Nonparametric Estimation of Conditional CDF and Quantile Functions with Mixed Categorical and Continuous Data," *Journal of Business and Economic Statistics*, **26**, 423–34.

Li, Q., and J. S. Racine, 2010. "Smooth Varying-Coefficient Estimation and Inference for Qualitative and Quantitative Data," *Econometric Theory*, **26**, 1607–37.

Li, Q., J. S. Racine, and J. Wooldridge, 2008. "Estimating Average Treatment Effects with Continuous and Discrete Covariates: The Case of Swan-Ganz Catherization," *American Economic Review*, **98**, 357–62.

Li, Q., and T. Stengos, 1996. "Semiparametric Estimation of Partially Linear Panel Data Models," *Journal of Econometrics*, **71**, 389–97.

Li, Q., and S. Wang, 1998. "A Simple Consistent Bootstrap Test for a Parametric Regression Function," *Journal of Econometrics*, **87**, 145–65.

Liero, H., 2003. "Testing Homoscedasticity in Nonparametric Regression," *Journal of Nonparametric Statistics*, **15**, 31–51.

Lin, D. Y., and Z. Ying, 2001. "Nonparametric Tests for the Gap Time Distributions of Serial Events Based on Censored Data," *Biometrics*, **57**, 369–75.

Lin, X., and R. J. Carroll, 2000. "Nonparametric Function Estimation for Clustered Data when the Predictor is Measured without/with Error," *Journal of the American Statistical Association*, **95**, 520–34.

Lin, X., and R. J. Carroll, 2001. "Semiparametric Regression for Clustered Data," *Biometrika*, **88**, 1179–85.

Lin, X., and R. J. Carroll, 2006. "Semiparametric Estimation in General Repeated Measures Problems," *Journal of the Royal Statistical Society, Series B*, **68**, 69–88.

Lin, Z., Q. Li, and Y. Sun, 2014. "A Consistent Nonparametric Test of Parametric Regression Functional Form in Fixed Effects Panel Data Models," *Journal of Econometrics*, 178, 167–79.

Linton, O. B., 1997. "Efficient Estimation of Additive Nonparametric Regression Models," *Biometrika*, **84**, 469–73.

Linton, O. B., 2000. "Efficient Estimation of Generalized Additive Nonparametric Regression Models," *Econometric Theory*, **16**, 502–23.

Linton, O. B., and E. Mammen, 2008. "Nonparametric Transformation to White Noise," *Journal of Econometrics*, **142**, 241–64.

Linton, O. B., and J. P. Nielsen, 2005. "A Kernel Method of Estimating Structured Nonparametric Regression Based on Marginal Integration," *Biometrika*, **82**, 93–100.

Liu, Z., and T. Stengos, 1999. "Non-Linearities in Cross-Country Growth Regressions: A Semiparametric Approach," *Journal of Applied Econometrics*, **14**, 527–38.

Loader, C., 1999. "Bandwidth Selection: Classical or Plug-In?" *Annals of Statistics*, **27**, 415–38.

Lukacs, E., 1975. *Stochastic Convergence*, New York: Academic Press.

Lütkepohl, H., and M. Krätzig, 2004. *Applied Time Series Econometrics*, Cambridge, NY: Cambridge University Press.

Mammen, E., 1992. *When Does Bootstrap Work?* New York: Springer-Verlag.

Mammen, E., J. S. Marron, and N. I. Fisher, 1992. "Some Asymptotics for Multimodality Tests Based on Kernel Density Estimates," *Probability Theory Related Fields*, **91**, 115–32.

Mammen, E., J. S. Marron, B. A. Turlach, and M. P. Wand, 2001, "A General Projection Framework for Constrained Smoothing," *Statistical Science*, **16**, 232–48.

Mammen, E., B. U. Park, and M. Schienle, 2013. "Additive Models: Extension and Related Models," Oxford *Handbook of Applied Nonparametric and Semiparametric Econometrics and Statistics*, J. S. Racine, L. Su, and A. Ullah (Eds.), Oxford: Oxford University Press.

Mammen, E., B. Støve, and D. Tjøstheim, 2009. "Nonparametric Additive Models for Panels of Times Series," *Econometric Theory*, **25**, 442–81.

Mankiw, N. G., D. Romer, and D. Weil, 1992. "A Contribution to the Empirics of Economic Growth," *Quarterly Journal of Economics*, **107**, 407–37.

Manski, C. F., 1975. "Maximum Score Estimation of the Stochastic Utility Model of Choice," *Journal of Econometrics*, **3**, 205–28.

Manzan, S., and D. Zerom, 2005. "Kernel Estimation of a Partially Linear Additive Model," *Statistics and Probability Letters*, **72**, 313–27.

Marron, J. S., 1987. "A Comparison of Cross-Validation Techniques in Density Estimation," *Annals of Statistics*, **15**, 152–62.

Martins-Filho, C., and K. Yang, 2007. "Finite Sample Performance of Kernel-Based Regression Methods for Non-Parametric Additive Models under Common Bandwidth Selection Criterion," *Journal of Nonparametric Statistics*, **19**, 23–62.

Martins-Filho, C., and F. Yao, 2009. "Nonparametric Regression Estimation with General Parametric Error Covariance," *Journal of Multivariate Analysis*, **100**, 309–33.

Martins-Filho, C., and F. Yao, 2012. "Kernel-Based Estimation of Semiparametric Regression in Triangle Systems," *Economic Letters*, **115**, 24–7.

Masry, E., 1996a. "Multivariate Regression Estimation Local Polynomial Fitting for Time Series," *Stochastic Processes and their Applications*, **65**, 81–101.

Masry, E., 1996b. "Multivariate Local Polynomial Regression for Time Series: Uniform Strong Consistency and Rates," *Journal of Time Series Analysis*, **17**, 571–99.

Matzkin, R. L., 1994. "Restrictions of Economic Theory in Nonparametric Methods," *Handbook of Econometrics*, volume 4, D. L. McFadden and R. F. Engle (Eds.), Amsterdam, the Netherlands: North-Holland, **42**, 2524–58.

Millimet, D. L., J. A. List, and T. Stengos, 2003. "The Environmental Kuznets Curve: Real Progress or Misspecified Models?," *Review of Economics and Statistics*, **85**, 1038–47.

Morozov, V. A., 1984. *Methods for Solving Incorrectly Posed Problems*, New York: Springer-Verlag.

Muller, H., 1984. "Smooth Optimum Kernel Estimators of Densities, Regression Curves and Modes," *Annals of Statistics*, **12**, 766–74.

Murphy, S. A., and A. W. van der Vaart, 2000. "On Profile Likelihood," *Journal of the American Statistical Association*, **95**, 449–65.

Nadaraya, E. A., 1964. "On Estimating Regression," *Teoriya Veroyatnostei i ee Primeneniya*, **9**, 157–9.

Nadaraya, E. A., 1965. "On Non-Parametric Estimates of Density Functions and Regression Curves," *Teoriya Veroyatnostei i ee Primeneniya*, **10**, 199–203.

Neumeyer, N., 2007. "A Note on Uniform Consistency of Monotone Function Estimators," *Statistics and Probability Letters*, **77**, 693–703.

Newey, W. K., 1985. "Generalized Methods of Moments Specification Testing," *Journal of Econometrics*, **29**, 229–56.

Newey, W. K., 1990. "Semiparametric Efficiency Bounds," *Econometrica*, **58**, 809–37.

Newey, W. K., 1994. "Kernel Estimation of Partial Means and a General Variance Estimator," *Econometric Theory*, **10**, 233–53.

Newey, W. K., and J. L. Powell, 2003. "Instrumental Variable Estimation of Nonparametric Models," *Econometrica*, **71**, 1565–78.

Newey, W. K., J. L. Powell, and F. Vella, 1999. "Nonparametric Estimation of Triangular Simultaneous Equation Models," *Econometrica*, **67**, 565–603.

Newey, W. K., and T. M. Stoker, 1993. "Efficiency of Weighted Average Derivative Estimators and Index Models," *Econometrica*, **61**, 1199–1223.

Ouyang, D., Q. Li, and J. S. Racine, 2006. "Cross-Validation and the Estimation of Probability Distributions with Categorical Data," *Journal of Nonparametric Statistics*, **18**, 69–100.

Ouyang, D., Q. Li, and J. S. Racine, 2009. "Nonparametric Estimation of Regression Functions with Discrete Regressors," *Economic Theory*, **25**, 1–42.

Ozabaci, D., and D. J. Henderson, 2014. "Additive Kernel Estimates of Returns to Schooling," *Empirical Economics*, forthcoming.

Ozabaci, D., D. J. Henderson, and L. Su, 2014. "Additive Nonparametric Regression in the Presence of Endogenous Regressors," *Journal of Business and Economic Statistics*, forthcoming.

Pagan, A. R., and A. Ullah, 1999. *Nonparametric Econometrics*, Cambridge, UK: Cambridge University Press.

Park, B. U., and J. S. Marron, 1990. "Comparison of Data-Driven Bandwidth Selectors," *Journal of the American Statistical Association*, **85**, 66–72.

Park, B. U., and B. A. Turlach, 1992. "Practical Performance of Several Data Driven Bandwidth Selectors (with discussion)," *Computational Statistics*, **7**, 251–70.

Parmeter, C. F., 2008. "The Effect of Measurement Error on the Shape of the World Distribution of Income," *Economics Letters*, **100**, 373–6.

Parmeter, C. F., D. J. Henderson, and S. C. Kumbhakar, 2007. "Nonparametric Estimation of a Hedonic Price Function," *Journal of Applied Econometrics*, **22**, 695–99.

Parmeter, C. F., and J. S. Racine, 2012. "Smooth Constrained Frontier Analysis," *Recent Advances and Future Directions in Causality, Prediction, and Specification Analysis: Essays in Honor of Halbert L. White Jr.*, X. Chen and N.E. Swanson (Eds.), New York: Springer-Verlag, 463–89.

Parmeter, C. F., K. Sun, D. J. Henderson, and S. C. Kumbhakar, 2014. "Regression and Inference Under Smoothness Restrictions," *Journal of Productivity Analysis*, 41, 111–29.

Parsopoulos, K. E., and M. N. Vrahatis, 2002. "Recent Approaches to Global Optimization Problems Through Particle Swarm Optimization," *Natural Computing*, **1**, 235–306.

Parmeter, C. F., Z. Zheng, and P. McCann, 2009. "Imposing Economic Constraints on Nonparametric Regression: Survey, Implementation and Extensions," *Advances in Econometrics: Nonparametric Methods*, Q. Li and J. S. Racine (Eds.), Elsevier Science, **25**, 433–69.

Parzen, E., 1962. "On Estimation of a Probability Density Function and Mode," *Annals of Mathematical Statistics*, **33**, 1065–176.

Pinske, J., 2000. "Nonparametric Two-Step Regression Estimation when Regressors and Error are Dependent," *Canadian Journal of Statistics*, **28**, 289–300.

Polonik, W., and Q. Yao, 2000. "Conditional Minimum Volume Predictive Regions for Stochastic Processes," *Journal of the American Statistical Association*, **95**, 509–19.

Powell, J. L., 1984. "Least Absolute Deviations Estimation for the Censored Regression Model," *Journal of Econometrics*, **25**, 303–25.

Powell, J. L., J. H. Stock, and T. M. Stoker, 1989. "Semiparametric Estimation of Index Coefficients," *Econometrica*, **57**, 1403–30.

Proença, I., 1993. "On the Performance of the H-H Test," CORE Discussion Paper 9305, Center for Operations Research & Econometrics, Universite Catholique De Louvain.

Psacharopoulos, G., 1994. "Returns to Investment in Education: A Global Update," *World Development*, **22**, 1325–43.

Qian, J., and L. Wang, 2012. "Estimating Semiparametric Panel Data Models by Marginal Integration," *Journal of Econometrics*, **167**, 483–93.

Quah, D., 1993a. "Galton's Fallacy and Tests of the Convergence Hypothesis," *Scandinavian Journal of Economics*, **95**, 427–43.

Quah, D., 1993b. "Empirical Cross-Section Dynamics in Economic Growth," *European Economics Review*, **37**, 426–34.

Quah, D., 1996. "Twin Peaks: Growth and Convergence in Models of Distribution Dynamics," *Economic Journal*, **106**, 1045–55.

Quah, D., 1997. "Empirics for Growth and Distribution: Stratification, Polarization, and Convergence Clubs," *Journal of Economic Growth*, **2**, 27–59.

Racine, J. S., 1993. "An Efficient Cross-Validation Algorithm for Window Width Selection for Nonparametric Kernel Regression," *Communications in Statistics*, **22**, 1107–14.

Racine, J. S., J. D. Hart, and Q. Li, 2006. "Testing the Significance of Categorical Predictor Variables in Nonparametric Regression Models," *Econometric Reviews*, **25**, 523–44.

Racine, J. S., and Q. Li, 2004. "Nonparametric Estimation of Regression Functions with both Categorical and Continuous Data," *Journal of Econometrics*, **119**, 99–130.

Racine, J. S., and E. Maasoumi, 2007. "Asymptotic Distribution Theory for Nonparametric Entropy Measures of Serial Dependence," *Journal of Econometrics*, **138**, 547–67.

Racine, J. S., and C. F. Parmeter, 2013. "Data-Driven Model Evaluation: A Test for Revealed Performance," *Handbook of Applied Nonparametric and Semiparametric Econometrics and Statistics*, A. Ullah, J. S. Racine, and L. Su (Eds.), New York: Oxford University Press, 308–45.

Ramm, A. G., 2005. *Inverse Problems*, New York: Springer-Verlag.

Ramsey, J. B., 1969. "Test for Specification Error in Classical Linear Least Squares Regression Analysis," *Journal of the Royal Statistical Society, Series B*, **31**, 350–71.

Rice, J. A., 1986. "Convergence Rates for Partially Splined Models," *Statistics and Probability Letters*, **4**, 203–8.

Robinson, P. M., 1988. "Root-n Consistent Semiparametric Regression," *Econometrica*, **56**, 931–54.

Robinson, P. M., 1989. "Nonparametric Estimation of Time-Varying Parameters," *Statistical Analysis and Forecasting of Economic Structural Change*, P. Hackl (Ed.), Amsterdam, the Netherlands: North Holland, 253–64.

Rodriguez, D., and T. M. Stoker, 1993. "Regression Test of Semiparametric Index Model Specification," Working Paper, Massachusetts Institute of Technology, Cambridge, MA.

Rosen, S., 1974 "Hedonic Prices and Implicit Markets: Product Differentiation in Pure Competition," *Journal of Political Economy*, **82**, 34–55.

Rosenblatt, M., 1956. "Remarks on Some Nonparametric Estimates of a Density Function," *Annals of Mathematical Statistics*, **27**, 832–7.

Rosenblatt, M., 1975. "A Quadratic Measure of Deviation of Two-Dimensional Density Estimates and a Test of Independence," *Annals of Statistics*, **3**, 1–14.

Rosenblatt, M., and B. E. Wahlen, 1992. "A Nonparametric Measure of Independence under a Hypothesis of Independent Components," *Statistics and Probability Letters*, **15**, 245–52.

Ruckstuhl, A. F., A. H. Welch, and R. J. Carroll, 2000. "Nonparametric Function Estimation of the Relationship between Two Repeatedly Measured Variables," *Statistica Sinica*, **10**, 51–71.

Rudemo, M., 1982. "Empirical Choice of Histogram and Kernel Density Estimators," *Scandinavian Journal of Statistics*, **9**, 65–78.

Ruppert, D., S. J. Sheather, and M. P. Wand, 1995. "An Effective Bandwidth Selector for Local Least Squares Regression," *Journal of the American Statistical Association*, **90**, 1257–70.

Ruppert, D., M. P. Wand, and R. J. Carroll, 2003. *Semiparametric Regression*, Cambridge, UK: Cambridge University Press.

Ryan, D. L., and T. J. Wales, 2000. "Imposing Local Concavity in theTranslog and Generalized Leontief Cost Functions," *Economics Letters*, **67**, 253–360.

Schick, A.,1986. "On Asymptotically Efficient Estimation in Semiparametric Models," *Annals of Statistics*, **14**, 1139–51.

Schick, A. 1996. "Root-n-Consistent and Efficient Estimation in Semiparametric Additive Regression Models," *Statistics and Probability Letters*, **30**, 45–51.

Schuster, E. F., and G. G. Gregory, 1981. "On the Nonconsistency of Maximum Likelihood Nonparametric Density Estimators," *Computer Science and Statistics: Proceedings of the 13th Symposium on the Interface*, W. F. Eddy (Ed.), New York: Springer-Verlag, 295–8.

Scott, D. W., R. A. Tapia, and J. R. Thompson, 1977. "Kernel Density Estimation Revisited," *Nonlinear Analysis, Theory, Methods, and Applications*, **1**, 339–72.

Scott, D. W., and G. R. Terrell, 1987. "Biased and Unbiased Cross-Validation in Density Estimation," *Journal of the American Statistical Association*, **82**, 1131–46.

Seifert, B., and T. Gasser, 1996. "Finite-Sample Variance of Local Polunomials: Analysis and Solutions," *Journal of the American Statistical Association*, **91**, 267–75.

Seifert, B., and T. Gasser, 2000. "Data Adaptive Ridging in Local Polynomial Regression," *Journal of Computational and Graphical Statistics*, **9**, 338–60.

Serfling, R. J., 1980. *Approximation Theorems of Mathematical Statistics*, New York: Wiley.

Sheather, S. J., and M. C. Jones, 1991. "A Reliable Data-Based Bandwidth Selection Method for Kernel Density Estimation," *Journal of the Royal Statistical Society, Series B*, **53**, 683–90.

Shen, X., and J. Ye, 2002. "Adaptive Model Selection," *Journal of the American Statistical Association*, **97**, 210–21.

Shiller, R. J., 1984. "Smoothness Priors and Nonlinear Regression," *Journal of the American Statistical Association*, **79**, 609–15.

Santos Silva, J. M. C., and S. Tenreyro, 2006. "The Log of Gravity," *Review of Economics and Statistics*, **88**, 641–58.

Silverman, B. W., 1978. "Weak and Strong Uniform Consistency of the Kernel Estimate of a Density and its Derivatives," *Annals of Statistics*, **6**, 177–84.

Silverman, B. W., 1982. "On the Estimation of a Probability Density Function by the Maximum Penalized Likelihood Method," *Annals of Statistics*, **10**, 795–810.

Silverman, B. W., 1986. *Density Estimation for Statistics and Analysis*, London: Chapman & Hall.

Solow, R. M., 1956. "A Contribution to the Theory of Economic Growth," *Quarterly Journal of Economics*, **70**, 65–94.

Speckman, P., 1988. "Kernel Smoothing in Partial Linear Models," *Journal of the Royal Statistical Society, Series B*, **50**, 413–36.

Staniswalis, J. G., and T. A. Severini, 1991. "Diagnostics for Assessing Regression Models," *Journal of the American Statistical Association*, **84**, 276–83.

Stock, J. H., 1989. "Nonparametric Policy Analysis," *Journal of the American Statistical Association*, **84**, 567–75.

Stone, C. J., 1984. "An Asymptotically Optimal Window Selection Rule for Kernel Density Estimates," *Annals of Statistics*, **12**, 1285–97.

Stone, C. J., 1985. "Additive Regression and Other Nonparametric Models," *Annals of Statistics*, **13**, 689–705.

Storn, R., and K. Price, 1997. "Differential Evolution – A Simple and Efficient Heuristic for Global Optimization over Continuous Spaces," *Journal of Global Optimization*, **11**, 341–59.

Su, L., 2006. "A Simple Test for Multivariate Conditional Symmetry," *Economics Letters*, **93**, 374–8.

Su, L., Y. Chen, and A. Ullah, 2009. "Functional Coefficient Estimation with Both Categorical and Continuous Data," *Advances in Econometrics*, **25**, 131–67.

Su, L., and X. Lu, 2013. "Nonparametric Dynamic Panel Data Models: Kernel Estimation and Specification Testing," *Journal of Econometrics*, **176**, 112–33.

Su, L., and A. Ullah, 2006. "Profile Likelihood Estimation of Partially Linear Data Models with Fixed Effects," *Economics Letters*, **92**, 75–81.

Su, L., and A. Ullah, 2008. "Local Polynomial Estimation of Nonparametric Simultaneous Equations Models, " *Journal of Econometrics*, **144**, 193–218.

Su, L., and A. Ullah, 2009. "Testing Conditional Uncorrelatedness," *Journal of Business and Economic Statistics*, **28**, 256–74.

Su, L., and A. Ullah, 2013. "A Nonparametric Goodness-of-Fit-Based Test for Conditional Heteroskedasticity," *Econometric Theory*, **29**, 187–212.

Su, L., and H. White, 2008. "A Nonparametric Hellinger Metric Test for Conditional Independence," *Econometric Theory*, **24**, 829–64.

Sun, K., D. J. Henderson, and S. C. Kumbhakar, 2011. "Biases in Approximating Log Production," *Journal of Applied Econometrics*, **26**, 708–14.

Sun, Y., R. J. Carroll, and D. Li, 2009. "Semiparametric Estimation of Fixed Effects Panel Data Varying Coefficient Models," *Advances in Econometrics*, **25**, 101–30.

Temple, J. R. W., 1998. "Robustness Tests of the Augmented Solow Model," *Journal of Applied Econometrics*, **13**, 361–75.

Terrell, G. R., 1990. "The Maximal Smoothing Principle in Density Estimation," *Journal of the American Statistical Association*, **85**, 470–7.

Terrell, G. R., and D. W. Scott, 1985. "Oversmoothed Nonparametric Density Estimates," *Journal of the American Statistical Association*, **80**, 209–14.

Tjøstheim, D., and B. Auestad, 1994. "Non-Parametric Identification of Non-Linear Time Series: Projections," *Journal of the American Statistical Association*, **89**, 1398–1409.

Ullah, A., 1985. "Specification Analysis and Econometric Models," *Journal of Quantitative Economics*, **2**, 187–209.

Ullah, A., 1996. "Entropy, Divergence and Distance Measures with Econometric Applications," *Journal of Statistical Planning and Inference*, **49**, 137–62.

Wand, M. P., and M. C. Jones, 1994. "Multivariate Plug-in Bandwidth Selection," *Computational Statistics*, **9**, 97–116.

Wand, M. P., and M. C. Jones, 1995. *Kernel Smoothing*: London: Chapman & Hall.

Wang, M.-C., and J. van Ryzin, 1981. "A Class of Smooth Estimatiors for Discrete Distributions," *Biometrika*, **68**, 301–9.

Wang, N., 2003. "Marginal Nonparametric Kernel Regression Accounting for within-Subject Correlation," *Biometrika*, **90**, 43–52.

Wansbeek, T., and A. Kapteyn, 1989. "Estimation of the Error-Components Model with Incomplete Panels," *Journal of Econometrics*, **41**, 341–61.

Watson, G. S., 1964. "Smooth Regression Analysis," *Sankhya*, **26**, 175–84.

Whang, Y.-J., 2000. "Consistent Bootstrap Tests of Parametric Regression Functions," *Journal of Econometrics*, **98**, 27–46.

Whang, Y.-J., and D. W. K. Andrews, 1993. "Tests of Specification for Parametric and Semiparametric Models," *Journal of Econometrics*, **57**, 277–318.

Wilson, P. W., 2003. "Testing Independence in Models of Productive Efficiency," *Journal of Productivity Analysis*, **20**, 361–90.

Wooldridge, J., 1992. "A Test for Functional Form against Nonparametric Alternatives," *Econometric Theory*, **8**, 452–75.

Wu, H. L., and J. T. Zhang, 2002. "Local Polynomial Mixed-Effects Models for Longitudinal Data," *Journal of the American Statistical Association*, **97**, 883–97.

Yang, K., 2013. "An Improved Local-Linear Estimator for Nonparametric Regression with Autoregressive Errors," *Economics Bulletin*, **33**, 19–27.

Yao, W., and R. Li, 2013. "New Local Estimation Procedure for a Non-Parametric Regression Function for Longitudinal Data," *Journal of the Royal Statistical Society, Series B*, **75**, 123–38.

Yatchew, A. J., 1992. "Nonparametric Regression Tests Based on an Infinite Dimensional Least Squares Procedure," *Econometric Theory*, **8**, 435–51.

Ye, J., 1998. "On Measuring and Correcting the Effects of Data Mining and Model Selection," *Journal of the American Statistical Association*, **93**, 120–31.

You, J., and G. Chen, 2005. "Testing Heteroscedasticity in Partially Linear Regression Models," *Statistics and Probabilities Letters*, **73**, 61–70.

Yu, P., 2012. "Likelihood Estimation and Inference in Threshold Regression," *Journal of Econometrics*, **167**, 274–94.

Zelli, R., and M. G. Pittau, 2006. "Emipirical Evidence of Income Dynamics across EU Regions," *Journal of Applied Econometrics*, **21**, 605–28.

Zhang, W., S. Y. Lee, and X. Song, 2002. "Local Polynomial Fitting in Semivarying Coefficient Model," *Journal of Multivariate Analysis*, **82**, 166–88.

Zheng, J. X. 1996. "A Consistent Test of Functional Form via Nonparametric Estimation Techniques," *Journal of Econometrics*, **75**, 263–89.

Zheng, J. X., 2000. "A Consistent Test of Conditional Parametric Distributions," *Econometric Theory*, **16**, 667–91.

Zheng, X., 2009. "Testing Heteroscedasticity in Nonlinear and Nonparametric Regressions," *Canadian Journal of Statistics*, **37**, 282–300.

Index